# THE WORLD OF
# TIME INC.

ALSO BY ROBERT T. ELSON

# TIME INC.

*The Intimate History of a Publishing*
*Enterprise 1923–1941*

(1968)

# THE WORLD OF

# TIME INC.

*The Intimate History of a*
*Publishing Enterprise*
*Volume Two: 1941–1960*

## BY ROBERT T. ELSON

*Edited by Duncan Norton-Taylor*

*New York* ATHENEUM *1973*

Copyright © 1973 by Time Inc.
All rights reserved
Library of Congress catalog card number 72–94242
ISBN 0-689-10555-X
Published simultaneously in Canada by McClelland and Stewart Ltd.
Manufactured in the United States of America by
Kingsport Press, Inc., Kingsport, Tennessee
Designed by Harry Ford
First Edition

# Acknowledgments

HENRY R. LUCE had a strong sense of history and he began making preparations for this history as early as 1954 when he assigned Alex Groner and the late Celia Sugarman to collect material for this and the earlier volume, *Time Inc.: The Intimate History of a Publishing Enterprise, 1923–1941* (Atheneum, 1968). In the course of their research they interviewed 271 former Time Incers. Meanwhile under the direction of Dorothy Seiler and Lillian Owens there was assembled an archive, which has been steadily expanded, embracing the company's records from its earliest beginnings. On these records, to which no one else has ever had full access, the compilers of this history have drawn freely.

The immediate staff working on the present volume has consisted of the writer and three researchers, Margaret Quimby, Elsa Wardell and Marie McCrum, who also researched the first volume. They continued to interview former Time Incers and persons with the company. The research for the chapter on *Sports Illustrated* was provided by Miss Owens, the company's archivist, assisted by Elaine Felsher. As the time of publication drew near, the staff was again joined by the editor of the previous volume, Duncan Norton-Taylor, a former managing editor of *Fortune*. The manuscript was typed by Barbara White and Diana Franklin and copyread by Mary Newman.

Many people have helped in the preparation of this book; we thank them all. For permission to quote the letters of Dwight D. Eisenhower and John F. Kennedy that appear herein, we are grateful respectively to John S. D. Eisenhower and the John F. Kennedy Library.

R.T.E.

# Contents

Contents

# Illustrations

(FOLLOW PAGE 210)

Shelley and Carl Mydans    Jerome Zerbe–U.S. Navy

Melville and Annalee Jacoby    Carl Mydans, *Life*

Will Lang in Tunisia    Eliot Elisofon, *Life*

Robert Sherrod    Dmitri Kessel, *Life*

William Chickering, Bougainville    William C. Shrout, *Life*

W. Eugene Smith, Okinawa    W. Eugene Smith, *Life*

*Time* and *Life* correspondents,
   photographers and artists    David E. Scherman, *Life*

*Time*'s managing editor with writers, 1948    Herbert Gehr, *Life*

*Time* researchers, 1948    Ralph Crane, Black Star

Whittaker Chambers    Alfred Eisenstaedt

Max Ways

Thomas Griffith    Carl Mydans, *Life*

Dana Tasker    © Roy Stevens

Otto Fuerbringer    David Gahr, *Time*

Roy Alexander

At *Fortune* in 1948    Bob Smallman

Leo Lionni    Holly Whyte

Mary Grace    Vince Loscalzo

Max Gschwind    Walter Daran

Lawrence Lessing    Walter Daran

Robert Sheehan    Holly Whyte

Holly Whyte    Bernard Newman

Richard Smith    Walter Daran

William Harris    Martin Iger

# *Prologue*

THIS VOLUME carries the history of Time Incorporated from December 1941 to December 1960. *Time Inc.: The Intimate History of a Publishing Enterprise, 1923–1941,* published in 1968, told of the founding of *Time,* The Weekly Newsmagazine, by the twenty-four-year-old Yale graduates, Briton Hadden and Henry Robinson Luce, and the bringing out after Hadden's death of *Fortune* and *Life.*

There have been many assessments of Luce. Inevitably he has been compared with the "press lords" of the past—Pulitzer, Northcliffe, Hearst. But "lord" was not quite accurate; as *Time*'s rival, *Newsweek,* pointed out on Luce's death, it connoted "imperious flamboyances" and Luce was "a singularly unflamboyant man."

He is clearly revealed through his relations with his staff. In a complex process he acted upon, and was acted upon by, persons who entertained convictions as strong as his. These relationships are a major theme of this book.

A brief word here about his attitudes and methods. In formulating editorial policies, he sometimes sought to arrive at a consensus in such an elaborate fashion that he exasperated his editors. Manfred Gottfried, longtime managing editor of *Time,* once protested: "Harry, I wish you wouldn't give us so much argument. Why don't you just give us a few orders?" But this went against his grain; orders received without assent meant that persuasion had failed.

It was his habit to ask his managing editors to stand aside for a week or two while he edited their magazines. These visitations were likened by T. S. Matthews, another of the managing editors, to "a strong wind that blew fresh air through the offices but also scattered papers into hopeless confusion. There were usually two noticeable results: the staff got less sleep but the morale went up, and the fin-

ished issue might be uneven but it had some high spots in it." *
Charles Wertenbaker, onetime Foreign News editor of *Time,* left this
account of Luce at work on one of these occasions: "When a finished
piece of work is well written and sound, he edits it very little, and
when it is not, he is always able to give good reasons for not liking it.
Seldom does he tear into a piece of copy and rewrite it from stem
to stern. . . . Many times he lets himself be overruled, and often
lets *Time* print things with which he disagrees, simply because he
feels the arguments against him are better than his own."

As editor-in-chief, his regular role, Luce held himself once removed from operations, leaving the managing editor to be, in a real
sense, the master of his own bridge. One of the most important of
his functions was that of critic after the fact. He pored over copies
fresh from the press. Sometimes his comments were conveyed to the
managing editor in the form of a marked copy with Luce's marginal
notes dispensing cold criticism or enthusiastic praise.

He was a constant commentator on all aspects of Time Inc. operations, not to say all matters in the public realm. Memoranda—slangy,
measured, pithy, enigmatic—flowed or erupted in an unceasing
stream from his desk, and they provide some of the most useful in-
sights into the history of Time Inc. Some have remained, until now,
in Luce's private files, marked, for reasons of his own, "Not sent."
He was an unpredictable suggester of stories and felt frustrated when
managing editors did not act upon his ideas. Edward K. Thompson,
a managing editor of *Life,* recalled: "Harry's complaint, as I once
heard it, was that the only way he could keep a story out of the magazine was for him to express an interest in an idea. And the only way
to get someone fired was for word to get around that he thought
highly of him." The comment was only somewhat exaggerated.

Perhaps Luce's favorite way of bringing his influence to bear was
talking things over—in his office, over coffee in the morning at a
drug store near the Time & Life Building in Rockefeller Center, at
luncheons and dinners at one of his clubs. Old hands received invita-
tions to these affairs with both anticipation and apprehension because
they knew they were to be tested against a probing, always challenging mind. To the newcomer, a first confrontation with Luce was a
tense experience. His was a commanding presence, tall, erect, with
ice-blue eyes under shaggy eyebrows; impatient with the formalities,
brusquely eager to get to the heart of the matter. He respected most

* *Name and Address* (Simon and Schuster, 1960), p. 250.

men who could match his arguments, which issued forth in staccato bursts once likened to those of "a jammed machine gun"; speech was a barrier to swift-flowing rivers of thought, so that he always talked in a kind of verbal shorthand that required the utmost attention in order to fill in gaps between titles, chapter headings and discursive footnotes. Even more disconcerting were his sudden silences when the torrent of words would come to a halt as he thought out his next point. Woe to the listener who accepted this as an invitation to comment or rebut; he might intrude a sentence or two only to have Luce resume his argument as if no word had been spoken. When he chose to listen, he was attentive, quick to pick up the pertinent point but equally quick to dismiss the fatuous or merely time-serving comment; he had little patience with words bereft of ideas.

As the company's chief roving reporter Luce was at his best. At age fourteen he had made his way alone from China where he was born to England—and he remained forever an inveterate traveler. He wrote or cabled reports to his editors on the great and near great whom he interviewed and the sights and even the smells of the countries he visited. He had an intuitive, often prophetic, sense of news and went about fairly bursting with questions. These were frequently startling and unpredictable, as when he asked the emperor of Japan in 1946 how it felt no longer to be considered a god. He never received an answer because the Japanese interpreter's English conveniently failed at that moment.

If Luce as editor-in-chief occupies more space in this volume than Luce the proprietor, publisher, businessman, risk-taker, it is because a successful, expanding and always profitable company presented fewer problems than did the troubled turbulent world reflected in the magazines' editorial pages. However, in addition to being an editor Luce was indeed a publisher and a businessman. The reason that he was able to devote more time to being an editor was that he was so well served by his corporate executives.

Among these corporate executives the one closest to him was Roy E. Larsen. When *Time* was only an idea in the minds of Luce and Hadden, Larsen, a Harvard graduate, resigned from his job with the New York Trust Company to throw in his lot with the two men from Yale. On Hadden's death he became Luce's chief collaborator. From 1939 to 1960 he served as president of Time Inc.—a congenial, soft-spoken, somewhat self-effacing man who was nevertheless a critical force in the development of the company. He launched *The March of Time* on radio and in motion pictures and played an important role in shaping *Life*. His partnership with Luce was never an easy one for him but it was bonded in steel.

At the end of 1941 Time Inc. was nineteen years old and, as Luce described it, "a small Big Business." It was a company informal in structure and managed at the top by a circle of intimates who worked in a free division of labor not always clearly defined. A striking characteristic of the staff was its youth, because the outer limits of seniority were, in effect, set by the ages of its two principal officers, Luce, forty-three, and Larsen, forty-two. Youth generated a certain exuberance and kept alive the spirit of amateurism that marked the company's earliest days.

The Time Inc. publications had acquired a dominant position in magazine publishing. *Time,* The Weekly Newsmagazine, had a circulation in 1941 approaching the million mark; *Life,* with a weekly sale of 3,290,000 and a readership many times that, was asserting its leadership in the mass magazine field. Magazines with much smaller circulations nevertheless exercised wide influence. *Fortune,* with 160,-000 circulation, was read by the top executives of American industry; *Architectural Forum* (with a mere 39,000) stood in the top rank of professional journals. Extending the magazines' audience was *The March of Time,* which once a month was shown in thousands of motion picture theaters. Some 2,500 men and women were employed in the organization's various offices.

By 1960, when this account ends, there were 5,500 people on the payroll of the company and its subsidiaries—a large and by no means anonymous cast. It was impossible in this book to give every person his due.

A significant part of Luce's genius—and that of Larsen—was the ability to hold the cast together. Luce himself was ever mindful of the part that all played in the success of Time Inc. He once told a group of his senior associates: "I am proud to be with you, and I am proud that you are with me. And there is only this self-flattery in that statement: if a man is known by the company he keeps, then this is the company which in my life I have managed to keep, and this is the company by which I would like to be known."

# THE WORLD OF
# TIME INC.

# Journalism at War

I N THE LAST few days of December 1941 Shelley Mydans, a *Life* reporter trapped in Manila by the invading Japanese army, received a terse cable from her editors in New York requesting "another first-person eyewitness story but this week we prefer Americans on the offensive." Just before communications failed, Shelley was able to reply: "Bitterly regret your request unavailable here."

Because of the military censorship in the Philippines, *Life*'s editors could not know how swiftly the situation in the Far East had deteriorated; their cable reflected the almost universal belief at home that somehow, in some way, the genius of General Douglas MacArthur and the bravery of American fighting men would retrieve the disaster set off at Pearl Harbor. By New Year's Day, before the overwhelming rush of Japanese along the Pacific littoral, MacArthur had withdrawn his forces to the Bataan peninsula and the island fortress of Corregidor, abandoning Manila, which he declared an open city. On January 2 Shelley and her husband, Carl, a *Life* photographer, together with some two thousand bewildered and frightened civilians were interned by the Japanese in Santo Tomas University as prisoners of war.

Time Inc.'s editors were only, if only, a little better prepared than most Americans for the conflict that suddenly engulfed them after

Pearl Harbor. Time Inc.'s correspondents and photographers for the past two years had been reporting wars from Finnish forests to the caves of Chungking. The Mydanses had been dispatched to Europe two weeks after the German attack on Poland in 1939; Carl Mydans had photographed the winter war in Finland and had witnessed the fall of France, while Shelley reported from London and Stockholm. They had been based in Chungking, covering the Far East, for nearly a year. After completing a story on Singapore, they had arrived in Manila in mid-October.

With them there were *Time* and *Life* reporter Melville Jacoby and his bride of a month, Annalee. Jacoby had also been in Chungking, where Henry Luce, on a trip there early in 1941, had hired him because of his knowledge of China. An honors graduate of Stanford, he had spent his junior year as an exchange student at Lingnan University near Canton and later had written a master's thesis analyzing the reporting by U.S. newspapers on Far Eastern affairs. In Chungking he had worked for the Chinese Ministry of Information. It was there that he fell in love with Annalee Whitmore, a fellow student from Stanford, who was working for United China Relief; they were married in Manila.

The Jacobys, so far, were luckier than the Mydanses. Just ahead of the advancing Japanese, they and Clark Lee, an Associated Press correspondent, managed to hitch a lift to Bataan on a small freighter, one of the last ships to make the passage through the minefields in Manila Bay. From there Jacoby filed a series of vivid eyewitness dispatches. In mid-February General MacArthur learned that there was no help coming for the men on Bataan; a presidential directive would soon order him to abandon them and establish a new headquarters in Australia. The Jacobys and Lee determined to make their escape, and with the blessings of MacArthur and a letter from him directing the military to aid them—if they were lucky enough to encounter any—they made their way south through the islands on a small ship. They moved only at night while keeping a sharp lookout for Japanese destroyers; finally they found a Filipino vessel that looked seaworthy enough to take them on the last stage of their escape to Australia. "Land looked good," Jacoby rejoiced in a cable when they landed. "Everything in Australia looked good, from the first Allied plane to the green trees and lawns. The engineer had [a] smile on his face when we said good-bye. I found out why. Just as we pulled alongside the docks, a piston cracked and the motors wouldn't

4

have turned another time." MacArthur had already made his famous getaway by motor torpedo boat and B-17 bomber and had established headquarters in Melbourne, where the Jacobys rejoined him.

The Mydanses remained prisoners in Santo Tomas University. There, some months later, Carl heard the end of Mel Jacoby's story.[1] A fellow prisoner who knew Mydans only by sight stopped him one day and said, "You heard the news? That *Time* and *Life* photographer Mydans was killed in Australia. . . . Killed in a plane crash. . . . Got away from the Japs and made it to Australia and then went and got himself killed there." The truth dawned on Mydans: in the long time that the news had taken to filter through to Santo Tomas, his and Jacoby's identities had become confused. Jacoby had indeed been killed on April 29; he was standing beside Brigadier General Harold H. George near the runway of a secret U.S. base in Australia when a plane ran out of control at takeoff, smashed into them and killed them both.

Jacoby was the first Time Inc. man to be killed in the war. His widow continued to file dispatches from Down Under. When New York recalled her to the home office, she asked the editors for "an eighteen-hour-a-day job—right in the middle of the war." The company was willing to assign her to Chungking, but it was not until late in 1944 that her credentials were approved by the War Department and she was permitted to resume work in China.

The Mydanses spent eight months in Santo Tomas and another year in an internment camp in Shanghai. They were finally repatriated on the Swedish exchange ship *Gripsholm,* arriving in New York December 1, 1943. Four months later Carl was off to the Italian front.

The editors of *Time* had closed out the fateful year of 1941 with a patriotic gesture. Before Pearl Harbor they had selected Henry Ford as the subject of the traditional Man of the Year cover story, because the aging automaker had "turned the processes of mass production . . . to the service of the nation." *Time* scratched Ford and substituted the U.S. President because "the use of the strength of the U.S. had become the key to the future of the war, and Franklin Roosevelt was the key to the forces of the U.S."

*Time*'s editor-in-chief Henry Luce disagreed politically with the President, and Roosevelt made no secret of his dislike of *Time.* Most

[1] Told in Mydans' autobiography, *More Than Meets the Eye* (Harper & Brothers, 1959), pp. 79–80.

recently the President had publicly accused *Time* of making "a notable contribution to Nazi propaganda" by printing "a disgusting lie"—the "lie" a fact well known to Roosevelt: that the president of Chile was frequently and notoriously in his cups.[2] Now Luce wrote a note to Roosevelt that concluded: "The drubbing you handed out to *Time* —before Dec. 7—was as tough a wallop as I ever had to take. If it will help you any to win the war, I can take worse ones. Go to it! And God bless you." To which the President responded: "I like your letter . . . because it combines honest patriotism with genuine sportsmanship. . . . The waters of Pearl Harbor have closed over many differences which formerly bulked big."

And so they had over a lot of differences, but an amiable and uncritical attitude toward the government could not characterize a free press for long. Soon, as "censored," anathema to U.S. journalists, began making tracks across stories filed at home and abroad, the press found itself in conflict with Washington. Time Inc. editors had accustomed themselves to a kind of voluntary censorship prior to Pearl Harbor, but an announcement by the administration on December 19 of the establishment of the Office of Censorship aroused fears and suspicions of administration motives beyond protecting the national security. This was reflected in a box which *Time* published on its first news page:

> In wartime to disclose secret military information which might be of value to the enemy is not only illegal but unpatriotic. . . . But *Time* does pledge itself 1) to report, as soon as its disclosure will do no harm, any military information that may be temporarily withheld, 2) to have the courage to send its editors to jail rather than connive at the concealment of any significant facts of a non-military nature.

On the very day after Pearl Harbor *Fortune* was a victim of censorship; throughout the war, because so many industrial processes were classified as important military information, *Fortune* had more censorship problems than did either *Time* or *Life*. On December 8, the deadline for its February issue, an article on the American Locomotive Company, which had been voluntarily submitted to the War Department because it dealt with tank production, was returned with so many deletions that there was no time for revision and it was

[2] *Time Inc. 1923–1941*, pp. 480–81; publication of the story was particularly inopportune because the Chilean president died ten days after it.

sent to press as censored, with an editorial note that most of the deleted material was readily available in standard reference sources. The article began:

> At CENSORED on the shores of Lake Erie in western New York stood an abandoned foundry. Its great steel rafters were gabled by six inches of dust; its floor was pocked with gaping holes where the core ovens once stood . . . That was eighteen months ago . . .
>
> Today that same foundry, swept, painted, and whole of body, throbs with the clangor of industrial creation. Within, 550 workmen at hammers and honers, wrenches and reamers, make the steel framework on which giant field guns will roll into battle. It is the CENSORED arsenal of American Locomotive . . .
>
> What happened to the CENSORED foundry is roughly symbolic of what has happened to the entire locomotive industry in two years of wartime expansion.

Some days later Luce was called on the White House carpet: the president of Brazil protested to Roosevelt that *Life* had violated censorship by publishing in its December 15 issue a picture story on Brazilian air bases, operated by Pan American Airways, from which U.S.-built bombers were being ferried to Europe; that in captioning one picture "a U.S. field" *Life* implied that Brazil had ceded territory to the United States. Luce explained to presidential press secretary Stephen Early that the pictures had been cleared with both Brazilian and U.S. military authorities and had gone to press before war broke out. Early, in exonerating *Life,* wrote the President, "Mr. Luce expressed an eagerness to cooperate—to assist the Government in its efforts to win the war—to serve his Country 'on all fronts.' "

The censor's office under Byron Price, onetime Associated Press editor, proved to be the least restrictive of any among the nations at war, far less constraining than direct military censorship. To fend off as much trouble as possible in a wholly unnatural situation, Luce appointed Eric Hodgins, publisher of *Fortune,* to a new job: editorial vice president, to act as internal censor and represent the magazines in dealing with the Washington agencies.[3] "His judgment may be

---

[3] Hodgins had been a writer, then managing editor of *Fortune* before becoming publisher. He had also been doubling in brass as general manager of *Time;* this had made him, in effect, second in command to his fellow publisher, vice president Pierrepont I. Prentice.

reversed—after the event," said Luce. "But at the point of going to press, his veto power is complete."

*Time* had special problems with Latin American stories, partly as a result of the success of its Air Express edition. Founded early in 1941, the edition had quickly acquired a wide readership, was often quoted in the Latin American press, and the attitudes and opinions expressed in its pages were sometimes confused with official U.S. policy. In the thirties the Southern Hemisphere had been a propaganda battleground in which the Nazis seized an early initiative; to offset this the administration was assiduously promoting the Good Neighbor policy and working hard for the unity of the Americas. Much of the enormous U.S. diplomatic effort stemmed from fear of a Nazi threat to European possessions in the Caribbean, and, after the U.S. entry into the war, to Brazil. This explained Roosevelt's extreme sensitivity to diplomatic protests from South America as manifested in his vehement attack on *Time* for its story on Chile's president.

Almost immediately after Hodgins' appointment as resident censor, Early passed on to Felix Belair, Jr., Washington bureau chief, another note from the President. *Time,* in commenting on the forthcoming inter-American conference in Rio de Janeiro, had described it as a "big roundup" aimed at "corralling the 21 American republics into a homogenous herd." The sensitive Chileans again protested, and the President wrote to Early:

> Honestly I think that something has got to be done about Luce and his papers. . . . It would seem obvious that independent Republics anywhere in the world very properly object to being "corralled into a herd." . . . What to do about this attitude, which is definitely unpatriotic in that it is harmful to the U.S. to a very great degree?

Hodgins sent the President's note to Manfred Gottfried, the managing editor of *Time,* with the comment that *Time* was going to have to report its South American news in more sedate language to stay out of hot water with the White House, and the fact that our South American neighbors must seem to the editors "ridiculously thin-skinned" was beside the point. *"Time* cannot afford by a choice of words to continue kicking up such a pother. . . . I earnestly urge [you] to close the main color-and-vividness valve on South American stories at least 50 percent."

Luce, not Gottfried, was responsible for the offending comment:

Luce had edited the magazine that week. But Gottfried was an independent spirit, in politics a mugwump and in journalism an icono-
clast.[4] He wrote to Hodgins: "I do not see that we have any choice—
difficult as that choice may be in wartime—other than to tell F.D.R.
to go jump in the Potomac. . . . To hell with sedate language!"

Luce agreed that *Time* should not go out of its way to avoid presidential criticism: "It may be *Time*'s duty to evoke from dear Franklin
considerable more fireworks than a peevish blowoff to his confidential secretary." But Luce also felt that the editors could not overlook
the fact that the President, "with our consent and encouragement
. . . is vested with life & death powers over most Americans, and is
in large part responsible for the fate of our country. What then have
we to do? We have to find out, imagine or guess what it is he (or
our government) wants us to do—and cooperate to the utmost consistently with our basic principles—not our mere whims—which we
must defend." A 50 percent reduction in the "color fountain," as
Hodgins suggested, would, he said, get "our lines in good order for
the big battle of principle, when it comes, as it certainly will."

The problem was not just turning down the "color fountain"; the
trouble lay in the news itself. There was little or no good news, and
*Time*'s editors were criticizing the administration for not being frank
with the people. Arguing that a war of attrition seemed in prospect,
*Time* said:

> That meant that bad news would predominate for a long time,
> that good news would remain scarce. Could the people take it?
> Washington did not seem to think the people could. Army and
> Navy communiqués stressed good news, toned down bad. The
> President, in a testy mood, appeared to feel that the people did
> not yet understand the war. . . . But the nation seemed to
> think it could take it. Up & down the country editorial writers,
> living close to the people of their own communities, worried
> more about apathy than the collapse of morale. They wrote with
> bold strokes: AMERICA CAN LOSE; THE WAR CAN BE
> LOST; THIS SHOULD AWAKEN US. The cry was for more
> bad news, for the truth. Washington had coddled the nation too
> long.

U.S. readers could understand the message, but U.S. diplomats worried that such gloomy reporting aided and abetted the enemy propa-

[4] Gottfried, who was hired by Luce as *Time*'s first writer months before the
incorporation of Time Inc., had been managing editor of *Time* since 1937.

gandists in Latin America—or so said a War Department spokesman. *Time*'s own correspondent in Buenos Aires, in fact, wrote the home office that the magazine's pessimistic reports on "the state of the nation" were "bringing confusion to our friends, joy to our enemies."

What to do? The editors were certainly not willing to gut their domestic reports for the sake of a comparatively small foreign circulation. Management, not unsympathetic to the diplomatic problem, was willing to consider suspending sending the Air Express edition to Latin America unless—as a contemporary document put it—"we begin to win the war." [5] Luckily the news began to get better.

It was journalistic instinct to criticize the administration's conduct of the war when the facts seemed to warrant it; e.g., the administration's censorship of the alarming losses inflicted by German U-boats on Allied shipping off the East Coast—a stricture, Time Inc. editors believed, that concealed the navy's failure to anticipate the offensive and to cope with it. Luce felt that, had the people known how serious the situation was, instead of griping about gasoline rationing they would have been ready to accept greater sacrifices. Yet the government hesitated even to black out coast resorts where, against the blazing lights of luxury hotels, the silhouetted tankers were easy targets for the submarines. In April Luce prodded his editors to investigate the situation:

> This week we should turn the heat on in Washington to find out where the U.S. stands, and where we stand. I also hear (perhaps quite incorrectly) that the Navy is slow in mobilizing the correct defense. Correct or incorrect? Haven't we got a hell of a lot of destroyers? I hear that relatively few are on convoy—that the convoy explanation has been overworked.

*Time*'s subsequent reporting on this sensitive subject, as in its coverage of the early confusion in organizing war production, price con-

---

[5] The company's efforts to cooperate in Latin America won it no special favor with the White House. In November 1942, when *Fortune* published an article entitled "Brazil: The New Ally" which made some passing references to the prevailing political instability in Chile, that country protested again. Roosevelt dashed off a note to Under Secretary of State Sumner Welles directing him to file a formal protest with Luce personally over any articles in *Time, Life* or *Fortune* "which in any way hurt the Good Neighbor policy . . . or tend to promote disunity among any of the United Nations. . . . In other words, it is time to build up a complete case."

trol, rationing and the mobilization of manpower, was often very critical in tone. Luce felt obliged to defend such reporting on the grounds that it "stimulated needed thinking on these subjects." But he added: "Much of our task has necessarily been a Cassandra's role. We have not enjoyed it. We have been thankful for every opportunity to report the gallantry of fighting men and the 'courage of the commonplace' displayed by men and women of every race. While we have previewed practically all the failures of policy or management, and while no reader could accuse us of calculating an 'easy' war, we have clearly conveyed our own belief that victory can without doubt be ours."

But victory was still a long way off, that dolorous winter of 1941–42, when Luce and his wife, Clare Boothe Luce, took off to opposite corners of the world—Luce to England, Mrs. Luce to the Far East as a correspondent for *Life*—to see how bad things were. The editor-in-chief's report appeared in the April 13 issue of *Time*. The unsigned piece was entitled "As England Feels . . .":

At this moment one fact is more prominent in [Britons'] minds than any other. That fact is Soviet Russia. Soviet Russia has saved them. If Russia has not saved them from defeat—no Englishman understands defeat, in any case—at the very least Soviet Russia has removed from above their heads . . . the awful scourge of fire from the sky. . . . In a word, Soviet Russia is immensely popular. By comparison, their cousin country of America is scarcely noticed; at best, America is taken for granted; at worst, they think a good deal less highly of America than of themselves, which is not very highly. . . . The mood of England appears to be uncertain and unclear. Meanwhile, whatever England is or is not thinking about the larger issues of her destiny, there is no doubt about what she is doing. England is working hard—very hard. . . . And great though the effort is in field and factory and in the offices, it is secondary to the energy with which England's Army is training itself and straining itself toward wherever opportunity may offer. English soldiers are praying—and wishing—for a fight. And every hour of day or night England's fighters in the air and on the sea are in fact fighting, inviting for themselves every possible death that might be profitable for King and Country.

11

In many groups, and particularly among the younger men, there is, above all, the determination that England shall become terribly practical and terribly competent. Some say: "We must be and become rough and tough." Some say: "We want bad men," adding, deceptively: "We have been too decent. . . ." Rough for what purpose? For the purpose of being worse and more terrible gangsters than have yet appeared on the world's scene? Obviously not—but they have not yet articulated an answer. Willing and eager to die—but for what? Their answer is still not formulated, but you encounter it especially among the serious young men of England—including nine out of ten who have come from the schools that have the ties. They have a certainty that a man must have something greater than himself to live for.

There was no commercial air transport across the Pacific, so Mrs. Luce had to take the long route from Miami to Brazil, across Africa, the Middle East and India. She hoped to go on to Australia. On the first leg of the journey she found herself on the same plane with Lieutenant General Joseph W. Stilwell, en route to his new assignment as chief of staff to Generalissimo Chiang Kai-shek and commander of U.S. forces in the China-Burma-India area. By the time she reached India, the flood tide of Japanese victory blocked her way to Australia, and Stilwell was commanding Chinese troops fighting in the battle for Burma. She flew to Lashio, Burma, where by great good luck she landed only minutes after Generalissimo and Madame Chiang Kai-shek arrived for a council of war with Stilwell and the British commanding officer, General Sir Harold Alexander. Her profile of Stilwell in *Life* was the first major article to introduce this extraordinary soldier to the American people—a commander, Mrs. Luce wrote, who "spends more than half his time smack-bang at the front, wearing an old campaign hat, sleeping and eating with Chinese troops nearer fire than any commander since MacArthur." Stilwell was surprised to find her in Lashio:

"Hullo, hullo," he said brusquely. "Burma is no place for a woman." I started to give him an argument but he was already halfway down the stairs. At the bottom he turned. "Tomorrow morning at dawn I'm driving to Maymyo. If you can get up that early you can join me," he said with half a snort, half a laugh, "on the Road to Mandalay."

On her arrival at Maymyo, headquarters of both Stilwell and Alexander, she found two other members of the Time Inc. staff, *Life* photographer George Rodger and Jack Belden, correspondent for *Time* and *Life*. Rodger, an Englishman, had photographed the Battle of Britain and covered the Free French in Equatorial Africa and the desert war in Libya before making his way to Burma. There he had done the first picture story on the American Volunteer Group, the Flying Tigers, the remarkable band of American pilots working for the Chinese. Rodger took Mrs. Luce in his jeep to see Mandalay; it was smashed and burning after bombing by the Japanese:

> As we whirled through the streets [Mrs. Luce wrote], all creation stank of rotting flesh. . . .
>
> Now and again we saw something still standing: a great blackened pair of temple elephants or giant sacred marble cats. And the mile-long 26-foot-high red-brick walls of Fort Dufferin that enclosed Government House and Thebaw's wondrous Palace were still intact. But in the long green moat that surrounded the fort, where lazy lotus pads drifted on the hot green scum, there floated many strange and hideous blossoms culled by the hand of death. The green little bottoms of babies, bobbing about like unripe apples. The gray, naked breasts of women, like lily buds, and the bellies of men—all with their limbs trailing like green stems beneath the stagnant water. Neither Rodger nor I pointed a camera at these fearful indecencies.

Burma was already lost; Mrs. Luce was lucky to hitch a ride out of Lashio to Kunming. She went on to Chungking, then flew back to India and eventually home. Her "Burma Mission," illustrated by Rodger's photographs, appeared in *Life* in June. It was a critical analysis of the military and political defeat that the Allies suffered there. To an American officer who asked her if she had got her story, she replied that she had—"in three words, '*Veni, Vidi, Evacui*' —which means, we came, we saw, we got the hell out."

Belden stayed with Stilwell in the harrowing retreat from Burma. He was thirty-two, durable and resilient, and he took a certain pride in sharing the dangers and the hardships of the troops. A Colgate graduate, he had shipped to China as a deckhand, picked up a job as a teacher of English at Peking University and then joined the United Press in the field. Time Inc.'s New York editors had hired

13

him sight unseen to cover the Burma campaign on the recommendation of the Chungking bureau. He had the satisfaction of reporting Stilwell's and his own safe arrival in India:

> Marching at a dogged, fixed pace of 105 steps per minute, which became known to us as the "Stilwell Stride," the iron-haired, grim, skeleton-thin General walked into India with tommygun on shoulder at the head of a polyglot party of weary, hungry, sick American, British and Chinese Army officers, enlisted men, Burmese women nurses, Naga, Chin and Shan tribesmen and a devil's brew of Indian and Malayan mechanics, railwaymen, cooks, refugees, cipher clerks and mixed breeds of southern Asia. . . .
>
> For three exhausting weeks Stilwell led our undisciplined, untrained party through a maze of crisscrossing paths, alternately coaxing, urging, commanding them to hurry as we sought to escape the jaws of the gigantic Japanese encircling movement. . . .
>
> Our inadequate rations were augmented by Burmese girl nurses, who, under the direction of Major Gordon Seagrave, Burma-born mission doctor, picked berries and vegetables, made stews complementing the small rice diet. Our ofttimes drooping morale was also kept alive by these girls, all of whom were between the ages of 17 and 22, singing Christian hymns, ancient American jazz, as they marched barefoot downstream through heat-scorched thickets and over rocky trails toward India, always in higher spirits and better health than the male members of the party, to whom at the end of each day they gave medical treatment—piercing blisters, bandaging infections, soothing bruised spirits in as romantic a setting as Hollywood ever conceived.

In May, in the same week that Corregidor surrendered, "very excellent news" (as the navy communiqué issued in Washington put it) came from the Southwest Pacific of a great naval and air battle in the Coral Sea. MacArthur's Australian headquarters announced that Japan's attempt to extend its conquest "south and southeast"—in order, it was implied, to invade Australia—had been repulsed, and that compared to Japanese losses, Allied losses had been "relatively light." The Battle of the Coral Sea was the first naval battle in which

no ship sighted an enemy vessel; the fighting was carried on wholly
by carrier-based planes. But the implication of MacArthur's communiqués was that land-based bombers from his command had played
a large part in the action, and *Time*'s editors therefore divided credit
for the victory between the two services.

The navy in Washington was irked by *Time*'s report. Felix Belair
was called in by "an official governmental source working hand-in-
glove with the Navy Department" and told that "the big victory her-
alded to the world by MacArthur was nothing like as big as it
seemed"; losses had been heavy, including "90 carrier-based planes," [6]
and the Japanese force had not been intending anything like "the
invasion attempt the U.S. public was led to believe." The navy, the
source reported, was anxious about how it could "crawl back off the
limb" of MacArthur's creation and recommended "closer scrutiny or
investigation of Southwest Pacific communiqués."

Luce thought there was more than met the eye in Belair's report;
he scented not only interservice rivalry but friction between Washington and MacArthur. He ascribed this to Washington's preoccupation
with Europe and neglect of the Pacific theater, and he sounded off in
this memorandum to his editors:

> For some time it has seemed obvious that high-ranking people
> in Washington are thoroughly irked by MacArthur. It may be
> mostly MacArthur's fault. But whoever's fault it is, it is a very
> great shame. . . .
>
> Now the real basic trouble in this whole thing, I suspect, is
> that goddamn argument about Hitler being the No. 1 enemy.
> You know my position on that. I'm perfectly willing to accept
> the strategy of my betters but I don't have to be a military expert
> to know that Washington's failure to take the Far East really
> seriously is a) dangerous and b) unfair to the American people.

Luce launched then into a subject that bothered him even more than
Washington's neglect of the Far East:

> There's another thing: what's all this optimism in high Washing-
> ton circles? Hitler sure to be beaten within a year if not before?
> Why keep the good news from the American people? Maybe
> they'd use too much gas celebrating. Well, what's our national

[6] On June 12 the navy acknowledged that the carrier *Lexington,* a destroyer
and a tanker had been lost in the action as well.

15

policy in the great land of the free and the brave: keep on fooling the people or play it straight?

Luce was shooting from the hip, sharing his thoughts with the editors; the memorandum was in no sense a policy directive, although *Life* two weeks later had a scornful editorial paragraph on what it called "the Hollywood war":

> We are fighting two wars—a real war and a kind of Hollywood war . . . a war of props and scenery. In the Hollywood war a hit-and-run crack at the Japs in the Coral Sea is allowed to pass as a major victory. In the Hollywood war each sinking of a Jap ship rates a boastful paragraph in a communiqué, but our casualties are concealed. . . . We are told in the Hollywood war that U.S. war production is now "over the hump," without being warned that U.S. military technology has not yet caught up with the Axis.

Luce himself was fearful that *Life* was becoming an accessory in "the Hollywood war," and he cautioned his editors:

> Most of your war coverage (at home) is propaganda for the Powers That Be—the best propaganda in the country. . . . Up to a point this policy of chief recruiter and ballyhooist for the Army and Navy and WPB and the Shipping Board, etc. & etc. is necessary and okay. But all the more must we be concerned as to just where that point is and at what point we call our minds and souls our own.

In June there was a victory to report about which there could be no doubt whatever: the Battle of Midway, the turning of the tide in the Pacific. *Time* made no mistake on this occasion in its assessment: "The second six months of war last week began for the U.S. at the point where the first six months should have started. . . . In three days of concentrated destruction off Midway, the U.S. had restored the balance of Pacific naval power. Thus for the U.S. began Phase II of the war." A more optimistic tone began to pervade the pages of *Time, Life* and *Fortune*.

16

---

# A Lack of Precision in
# Oracular Writing

A FEW AMERICANS were giving some thought, based on the assumption of a victory, to the shape of the postwar world. In May 1942 *Fortune* published the first of a series of pamphlets on the subject. It was the product of a special department which Luce had begun organizing even before Pearl Harbor, believing that "Americans had a special duty to themselves and to the world to formulate their war aims and to announce them." Roosevelt's Four Freedoms speech and the Atlantic Charter, both praiseworthy statements, were something less than definitive.

The new department was called the "Q department," after the Q ships of World War I (secretly armed merchantmen used to trap U-boats), because, Luce said, "while there is nothing 'secret' about it, we do not wish any publicity." Its purpose was to stimulate thinking about the postwar world by formulating proposals for discussion and supplying information needed to discuss them intelligently.

Luce had long since established to his own satisfaction a philosophical justification for U.S. entry into World War II and the nation's postwar role: it was set forth in "The American Century," [1] his

[1] In May 1940, some months before he wrote his *Life* article, Luce had read a book, *Isolated America* (Alfred A. Knopf, 1940), that so impressed him he distributed a number of copies to Time Incers. Its author, Raymond Leslie

17

most quoted article, published in *Life,* February 17, 1941, in which he summoned the United States to lead the world to a better age of freedom and justice. He continued to pursue the theme. "Because America alone among the nations of the earth was founded on ideas and ideals which transcend class and caste and racial and occupational differences, America alone can provide the pattern for the future," he wrote again in *Life* (February 16, 1942) in his article "America's War and America's Peace." Speaking in Chicago, the citadel of prewar isolationism, he said: "America must be the elder brother of the nations in the brotherhood of man." And to the editors of the Yale *Daily News,* of which he was once managing editor, he predicted that after victory "within the lifetime of most of you . . . we will make out of ourselves, and out of our American Constitution, a more excellent and a more interesting human society than has ever before existed." The *Daily News* reported that when the speaker concluded with the traditional university toast—"For God, for Country and for Yale"—his audience rose cheering.

Luce's attitude toward his country was, as he once acknowledged, "an idealistic, but a . . . profoundly false romantic view. . . . I was never disillusioned with or by America, but I was, from my earliest manhood, dissatisfied with America. America was not being as great and as good as I knew she could be, as I believed with every nerve and fiber God Himself had intended her to be."

Though Luce's patriotic appeals struck a responsive note in a time of great emotion, the chauvinistic overtones disturbed some people. "A whole year of this world's mortal pain, ending in several weeks of crashing defeat for American arms," wrote Freda Kirchwey in the *Nation,* "has served only to tighten the seams and chromium-plate the surface of Mr. Luce's armor of self-righteousness." The *Christian Century,* of which Luce was an attentive reader, had an unkinder cut: "Henry Luce's 'American Century' ideal is ruthlessly plainspoken and entirely devoid of a single Christian in-

---

Buell, had been with the Foreign Policy Association for twelve years, its president for six, before joining *Fortune* in 1939 to head its Round Table. Buell's thesis: "No moral idea, such as that upon which American unity rests, can retain its vitality if its exponents remain passive, neutral, defensive. America will preserve its heritage and realize its hopes only if the sense of frustration and timidity embodied in the phrase 'Isolated America' gives way to a conception of Positive America. If we want to, America can replace Britain as the world's dominant power. We should utilize our strength, not on behalf of imperialism or power politics, but in support of a new concept of world organization, which has become absolutely essential to the maintenance of democracy in the present age."

sight into the nature of a Christian society." The Yale *Literary Magazine,* on whose board Luce had once served, commented: "It was insulting of an old Yaleman, *News*man, Bonesman to preach such jingoistic jargon to undergraduate colleagues." Vice President Henry Wallace joined the chorus: "Some have spoken of the 'American Century.' I say that the century on which we are entering—the century which will come out of this war—can be and must be the century of the common man." Luce wrote Wallace asking what he found in "The American Century" to be inconsistent with his own views. Wallace replied that he did not disapprove of what Luce had written but that "the phrase 'American Century' did rub the citizens of a number of our sister United Nations the wrong way."

The criticism continued to trouble Luce; while he personally could deny any imperialistic motives, he came to regret the words "American Century." "In giving further expression to my views I would like to avoid unnecessary objections," he wrote to Senator Robert Taft in 1943. "I hope that whatever I can do will help toward fundamental unity rather than excessively bitter disputation." Later, in 1946, when Robin Cruikshank, editor of the *News Chronicle* of London, challenged him to "hearten the whole world by giving a more self-confident announcement of what America stands for," Luce hesitated. "When at last I had to say something," he confessed, "I mumbled . . . about some of us having been burnt, long ago, at that fire." Not long after that he picked up a small book by Reinhold Niebuhr, *Discerning the Signs of the Times,* in which the author wrote of the American Century: "Just as nationalistic and universalistic elements were present in the Messianic expectations of even the greatest prophets, so also now each nation mixes a certain degree of egoistic corruption with its more generous hope not only for a reign of peace but also for an 'American Century,' while Russians hope for the realization of a communist world society."

Luce noted: "Having absorbed Niebuhr, I now know about the pitfalls and heresies involved in the American Century. I think I am no longer afraid to 'redefine' the American Century." He never did so specifically, but he did shift his thinking about the postwar world, a shift which was later to surface in his espousal of the concept of world peace through the world rule of law.

To give Luce his due, his was an earnest effort to impart some meaning to a hideous war, to provide a purpose beyond mere survival. He bearded Winston Churchill on the subject. On his trip to Britain early in 1942 he was invited to have dinner with the prime

19

minister at Ditchley.[2] Years later he wrote an account of the confrontation, which occurred

> one night, actually one 2 A.M. in the middle of the war. . . .
> Earlier we had seen a movie, *Custer's Last Stand,* which put the
> old man in a good mood, and I got him to treat me to a personal
> account of the Battle of Omdurman. When Omdurman was
> done, I veered to the question of "postwar planning." The next
> thing I felt was a hearty slap on the back, and Churchill was
> saying: "Never mind about all that, Luce. Just win the war—
> and then all will be well. . . ." Churchill had a profound sense
> of what is meant by a government of free men and after his
> overthrow he took the lead in proclaiming the relevant prin-
> ciples in terms of a United Europe. Had he been in power, he
> would undoubtedly have been a force for the realization of these
> principles. But during the war he was absorbed in one goal—
> victory.[3]

Luce and his editors, undiscouraged, continued to study the subject of postwar planning. Under the direction of Raymond Leslie Buell, the Postwar Department (as it was renamed) produced a number of papers on specific subjects. The first was entitled "The U.S. in a New World: Relations with Britain" and proposed the postwar establishment of an American-British free trade area that would eventually be widened to include other nations, establishment of an Anglo-American committee to plan for demobilization and the setting up of a reconstruction fund. Subsequent studies continued to be published as supplements to *Fortune.*

Not all the studies of the Postwar Department were for publication. One of the most important was purely for the internal enlightenment of Time Inc.'s management and editors. It was written by the company's vice president and treasurer, Charles L. Stillman,[4] who undertook an analysis of the new economics of John Maynard Keynes

[2] The eighteenth century mansion near Oxford, which Ronald Tree, its owner, had lent to Churchill as a wartime weekend retreat.

[3] The account comes from an unfinished draft of a book on which Luce was working at the time of his death. It is quoted at several points in this history.

[4] Stillman, with Time Inc. since 1928, was described by Eric Hodgins as "the only Poetic Treasurer a corporation ever had." "What I meant," explained Hodgins, "was that most treasurers are ultra-competent with balance sheets and budgets and singularly dumb as to the nature of the corporation whose records they are keeping. But Charlie, hired to be a figure-man, understood a much wider world than figures."

and his American disciple, Alvin Hansen. At a time when most businessmen were suspicious of the Keynesian economics as a new form of Socialism, Stillman became convinced that compensatory fiscal policies were not only compatible with the free enterprise system but essential to full employment and an expanding economy. Luce, who was never an economist and who never pretended to have special knowledge in the field, did have a puritan's prejudice in favor of a balanced budget. But Stillman's fifty-page memorandum convinced him that Keynes's doctrine was not inconsistent with fiscal morality and brought about a considerable change in the editorial attitudes of Time Inc. publications.

The editor-in-chief's concern over war aims, which was shared by more than one of his senior editors, got *Life* in trouble with the public and governments in October 1942. At a time when real and disturbing dissensions in Anglo-American relations were coming to the surface, *Life* made an ill-timed contribution by publishing "An Open Letter from the Editors of *Life* to the People of England," blaming British imperialist preoccupations for the failure to open a second front in Europe.

The root of the dissension was Stalin's embitterment over Roosevelt's and Churchill's decision to shelve General George C. Marshall's plan for a direct cross-Channel assault on the continent of Europe in 1942 in favor of a landing on the coast of North Africa, which Churchill had long advocated. The cross-Channel plan actually became impractical when, after the fall of Tobruk, the United States had to divert tanks and bombers to the desert front to save the Middle East. Stalin, hard pressed on all fronts, especially at Stalingrad where the German armies were closing in, furiously kept after the British and Americans to rescue him by a diversion in Europe.

One unwitting spokesman for Stalin was Wendell Willkie, who had been the President's opponent in the 1940 elections. In late August Willkie had embarked on a round-the-world flight to demonstrate American unity, traveling in a government plane; his status as the President's personal representative caused much confusion.[5] The heads of state and government assumed him to be on official business; Willkie considered himself a free agent. Moreover, Roosevelt had not briefed Willkie on the strategic decisions taken by Churchill and

[5] On his return he wrote his phenomenally successful book *One World* (Simon and Schuster, 1943).

21

himself. In Moscow, after a long talk with Stalin, Willkie told reporters: "Personally, I am now convinced that we can best help Russia by establishing a real second front in Europe with Britain at the earliest possible moment our military leaders will approve. And perhaps some of them will need some public prodding."

*Life* not only echoed Willkie's plea but also undertook to do some of the public prodding. The writer of the Open Letter was Russell Davenport, a close friend of Willkie; he had resigned as managing editor of *Fortune* to be Willkie's speech writer and principal strategist in the 1940 presidential campaign.[6] Davenport, who returned to Time Inc. after the campaign, had only recently been assigned to write a page entitled *"Life* on the Newsfronts of the World." This had been a one-page summary of the week's news; Luce envisioned it under Davenport as becoming a page of interpretation and opinion. Davenport's own ambition was to make it "the most important editorial page in America," and eventually it did become *Life's* editorial page. The Open Letter, typical of Davenport's exhortatory style, began:

> Doubtless it is presumptuous for a single periodical to attempt to speak for the American people. Nevertheless, the editors of *Life,* in writing you this open letter, make no apology for their presumption. We assure you that we do speak, in this instance, for a large portion of our 134,000,000 fellow citizens.
>
> We are writing you in a crisis of civilization that mortally concerns us both. No two peoples on this earth are as close as we, whether in their institutions, or their language, or by ties of blood. It is important for us in a most selfish sense that England stand. We therefore take the liberty of addressing you as members of our own family.

The words that followed produced a first-class family row. The author apologized for America's late entry into the war and for this country's past mistakes, such as not canceling World War I debts, but went on to say that though the debt was never paid, "we went ahead with lease-lend just the same." Britain, the letter continued, had suffered grievous losses since the United States entered the war—Hong Kong, Singapore and in the East Indies—but it had gained an ally, and that ally wanted now to know

[6] *Time Inc. 1923–1941,* pp. 416 ff.

what you are prepared to do to help *us*. . . . What we need is something that we have never in all our history—with but few exceptions—received from the English people, namely, concessions in policy.

We Americans may have some disagreements among ourselves as to what we are fighting for, but one thing we are sure we are *not* fighting for is to hold the British Empire together. . . . If your strategists are planning a war to hold the British Empire together they will sooner or later find themselves strategizing all alone. Take this unhappy matter of the "second" front. In a war to hold the Empire together a second front might not be so important at this time. But in a war to assure victory for the United Nations . . . it does seem to be most dreadfully urgent. . . .

Quit fighting a war to hold the Empire together and join with us and Russia and your other allies to fight a war to win by whatever strategy is best for all of us. . . . If you cling to the Empire at the expense of a United Nations victory you will lose the war. Because you will lose us. . . .

And so we say it to you straight, people of England. If you want to keep us on Your Side you must move part way over to Our Side. If you will do so, then you will find that Our Side is plenty big . . . much bigger than the British Raj . . . much bigger than the British Empire . . . as big as all outdoors.

Britons were outraged. The editorial was interpreted as an American threat to make a separate peace if Britain did not bend to the American will. Davenport was quite taken aback by the resonance of his words. In an interview with a London reporter in New York he denied that in writing "you will lose us" he had meant to suggest a separate peace; the editorial was merely a plea for a common strategy.[7] "I hope the tone of my letter was not impolite," he said, rather naïvely. "It was not meant to be." The correspondent's report, which appeared in the London *Daily Mail,* noted that Luce had refused to give either an interview or a statement. The London *Daily Mirror* speculated that "political ambitions of Henry Luce, an American newspaper editor [*sic*] . . . [who] hopes to become a presidential

---

[7] "You know, Eric," said Davenport to Hodgins some weeks later, "the goddamn hell of the whole thing is that I only put those words in for the rhythm."

candidate at the 1944 election . . . are believed to be behind [this] bitter attack."

From London Edward R. Murrow told his listeners on CBS that the article was "an example of loose talk, calculated to give aid and comfort to our enemies. . . . Most people here would probably prefer to consider [it] an irresponsible outburst permitted by democracy" and by no means an expression of prevailing sentiment in the United States. *The New Yorker* found the editorial "patronizing and presumptuous" and reminded *Life*'s editors that no magazine should claim to speak "for the American people. . . . For a long while we have suffered rather patiently under the strain of *Life*'s possessive attitude about this country—its trick of taking a couple of snapshots of somebody somewhere and announcing that 'This is America.' We have never thought it was America and do not think so now."

The White House said nothing—publicly.[8] Privately, "a high administration man" told the radio commentator Raymond Gram Swing[9] that the editorial was "just one piece of activity on the part of a new 'Unholy Alliance' . . . [consisting of] Wendell Willkie, with Davenport as his man Friday, the extreme Left-Wingers, the Bertie McCormick gang,[10] a group of Army officers, and Harry Luce and his publications . . . working toward a coup d'état." Vice president C. D. Jackson, who reported this conversation to Time Inc. headquarters, added this comment: "The sinister part of this rumor is that such an airtight case can be made for it. We have been on the verge of going overboard for the new Willkie lately—and pile his Chungking speech on top of the Open Letter and it certainly documents the case;[11] we know from letters and telegrams received that the extreme Left section of the Liberals was all for the editorial, and

---

[8] The White House was unpleasantly and forcefully reminded of the *Life* editorial some weeks later. When Madame Chiang Kai-shek arrived in New York in November for a visit to the United States, she flourished the editorial at Harry Hopkins, the President's special representative, and asked him to read it because, she said, it represented exactly her point of view.

[9] Swing, a commentator for the American Broadcasting Company, also reported on American affairs for the British Broadcasting Corporation, so was well known in Britain.

[10] Colonel Robert R. McCormick was editor and publisher of the isolationist and anti-British Chicago *Tribune*.

[11] In Chungking Willkie had said, "This war must mean an end to the empire of nations over other nations."

practically every Army officer we talked to since the letter appeared has cheered for it."

The repercussions became so loud that Luce decided to speak up. He denied that there had been any "conscious connection" between what Willkie said and the *Life* Open Letter and issued a statement for distribution to British newsmen in New York:

> Ever since the magazine *Life* was launched . . . its editors have believed that Hitlerite Germany is the enemy of mankind. . . . The Editors . . . are amazed to find that one editorial . . . has been the cause of much misunderstanding in Great Britain. Speaking for the Editors, I am deeply sorry. . . . The fault is partly ours for not having said what we meant as clearly as we should have. The fault lies also perhaps with others who chose to read into the editorial things we did not say. . . . We meant that the war aims . . . ought to be made much plainer. . . . We furthermore believed . . . that there is not yet enough agreement between the governments and peoples of America and Britain.

He met with the British newsmen. It was an unhappy, at times farcical, confrontation. One correspondent drew himself up to full height and told Luce, "May God forgive you, I can't."

Luce also sent the full text of the editorial to Time Inc.'s London office. T. S. Matthews, *Time*'s executive editor who was on a three-months temporary assignment in London, reported back that while the full text was vastly different in sum from the cabled excerpts, it was completely misunderstood: "The British press distrusts, dislikes, and would like to disbelieve the 'Luce publications.' Ditto Henry Luce." Would Matthews make a personal effort to explain Luce's position by calling on Luce's friend Brendan Bracken,[12] then minister of information and perhaps closest of all Churchill's aides to the prime minister himself? His disagreement with the British, Luce said, was on "the necessity for war aims."

The interview did not turn out well. Bracken contemptuously dismissed the *Life* editorial as "woolly" and instead attacked *Time,* which, he said, was "hostile to Churchill, anti-British, misinformed on Britain [and] very badly informed about the situation in India." One article—"Salt in the Sores of India"—was cited as being par-

---

[12] Bracken had once been a part-time correspondent for *Fortune* when he was chairman of the *Financial News*.

ticularly offensive; in it *Time* had come out strongly on the side of Gandhi and Nehru and Indian independence. Matthews reported that he had informed Bracken that Henry Luce would be "amazed to hear *Time* considered hostile toward Churchill and campaigning for India."

"For Pete's sake, get us straight," Luce cabled Matthews. "Of course *Time* has been hostile to Churchill in the sense of being critical. Of course *Time* has been campaigning for a different attitude for India. . . . I am amazed that you should think I am amazed. As for *Life*'s editorial, I thoroughly agree with Bracken. . . . If it had not been woolly we could not have been attacked. . . . Tell Brendan I am devoted to him personally and enormously admire Churchill for all the reasons he knows. And remind him that I disagree with them both as profoundly as ever on several points. I disagreed with them both about China and I disagree with them both about war aims. And I pray God that no amount of disagreement may ever separate our two countries in our march to the future."

Matthews' return visit with Bracken was no more successful than the first; he found Bracken "unwilling to believe that [Luce's] intentions were anything but sinister." He had also interviewed Randolph Churchill, the prime minister's son, and concluded that the Raymond Gram Swing interpretation of the Open Letter was the generally accepted one—"that you, for domestic political reasons, have been and are willing to play fast and loose (to say the least) with Anglo-American solidarity." The most violent version of this had come from Randolph Churchill, Matthews reported: "I have never been treated, by an Englishman and supposedly a gentleman, to such a Hitlerian outburst of abuse, preposterous charges, and vilification. . . . His view of you in a nutshell: 'Harry is a complete opportunist and a hypocrite who wants to be President or something, and for purposes of his own masqueraded for a time as England's sympathetic friend; but about a year ago dropped the mask and is now trying to drive a wedge between the U.S. and England, and attempting to rally isolationist sentiment in the U.S. to his support . . . with the unscrupulous sensationalism that only a completely irresponsible press autocrat can use.' "

Luce then decided to address a not-for-publication letter "to some of my friends in Great Britain." His reason for doing so, he said, was that he would like to avoid at least the criticism "that I do not give my friends in Britain 'much chance' to remain my friends. . . .

The baker's dozen of offending words—which, incidentally, I did not write, did not cause to be written and have forgotten—these few words provided an excuse for letting fly whole dictionaries of abuse and innuendo." He had never advocated anything other than "total and complete victory over our enemies." He wished Britain and its empire well, concluding: "We want no part of any responsibility for its postwar evolution—except as there may arise in America and Britain a common will to create a better world order." He invited his friends to tell Americans what kind of postwar world, in fact, they wanted.

There was a surprising response. Foreign Secretary Anthony Eden reminded Luce that there was intragovernmental discussion of postwar objectives, but the British Cabinet system prevented its members from speaking out as individuals as their American counterparts were free to do. Lord Beaverbrook wrote forgivingly: "If you hit us a blow this time, I know it was intended to fall lightly." The London book publisher Hamish Hamilton, who had been Luce's official Ministry of Information guide on his trip through Britain the previous winter, said he did not question Luce's sincerity but doubted the wisdom of raising the issue in such terms at that time. Bracken cabled: "I think you will not disagree with me if I venture the criticism that there was a lack of precision in that oracular piece of writing. Had it ever occurred to you that because you have been so long our friend we should feel rather raw when the Axis propagandists made use of your name to hit us?" Ronald Tree, Luce's host at Ditchley the night he dined with Churchill, wrote to say that the episode was over and done with. To Tree, Luce replied, "I believe a higher priority must be given to 'war aims'. . . . It has been a little on my conscience that I did not say this to the Prime Minister. But I knew that others had said it to him. And during the memorable day at Ditchley, I did not feel it appropriate to provoke an argument when there was no lack of more agreeable conversation." [13]

Luce's letter to his British friends was one of the few occasions on which, while accepting overall editorial responsibility for what *Life* said, he privately disavowed the writer. The episode left the writer of the Open Letter unhappy and disturbed; unhappy because he was fearful—so he wrote John Shaw Billings, managing editor of *Life*—that "Harry's confidence in me has collapsed." Hitherto Davenport

---

[13] He did, in fact, bring up the point (see p. 20) but didn't press it.

had enjoyed a fairly free hand in selecting subjects and writing his page, but his copy was now subjected to much more careful scrutiny. He wrote Luce, ostensibly offering his resignation but in fact asking for a clearer definition of his own responsibility. He was willing, he said, to remain responsible to Luce and to Billings—but with important reservations: "This means that practically all the suggestions that the two of you make will be carried out—but not necessarily all. If I am to produce a page of stature, there must be a real delegation on your part and on his . . . and I will be developing objectives, sometimes difficult to define, of which neither of you may be aware."

In the light of what had happened, this astounding proposal left Billings "flabbergasted." He told Luce that he could not accept the proposal that there should be an important page in *Life* "over which I (or you) surrendered editorial veto power." It is a measure of Luce's and Billings' extraordinary patience and their admiration of Davenport's writing ability, that, instead of accepting Davenport's resignation, they smoothed his feathers and he continued to write the page for another year.

The Open Letter controversy once more brought Luce unwanted and unsought personal publicity, of which he had more than his share in 1942, much of it unfavorable and a matter of rising concern to his fellow executives. They were made acutely aware of the problem by a survey of press comment following the Chilean incident in which 70 percent of the editorials cheered the President and scolded *Time;* the same survey showed that the increasing attention paid to Time Inc.'s editor-in-chief was on the whole uncomplimentary both to him and his magazines. On studying this report president Roy E. Larsen wrote that "increasing publicity about Harry in one connection or another is increasing the spread of the general impression that Time Inc. is a one-man editorial show. . . . The inevitable end of this will be the easily promoted idea that Harry runs a stable of anonymous, unknown writers and editors."

Larsen proposed immediate remedial measures, including an institutional advertising campaign aimed at making as many people as possible aware of "one hundred or two hundred or three hundred Time Incers." The hoped-for result would be to impress on readers the fact that Time Inc. consisted of "men who obviously are not slaves, but personages in their own right, who therefore must have a voice in the direction of our magazines. Then it will be impossible to pin the Hearst label on Harry."

Larsen's recommendations were followed; there was a change in the traditional policy of anonymity. More credits and by-lines were henceforth given to staff photographers and writers on *Life,* both in the magazine and in the company's promotion. More slowly the same policy was followed on *Time;* war correspondents' eyewitness accounts appeared with increasing frequency under by-lines. The now familiar Publisher's Letter, which P. I. Prentice introduced, contributed to the policy by giving readers a greater insight into how the magazine was edited and produced; it also was a vehicle for introducing editors, writers, correspondents and researchers to *Time*'s readers. The company also encouraged *The March of Time* to make more use of *Time* and *Life* personnel in their radio reporting. In the long term the policy was successful in dispelling the illusion of a faceless, monolithic organization, yet it in no way lessened Luce's responsibility as editor-in-chief or deflected the lightning from him when storms arose.

Storms, or at the least, small squalls, continued to play around Time Inc. Luce and *Time* were attacked by the Chicago *Tribune*'s Colonel McCormick, and by his cousin Eleanor Patterson, editor-publisher of the Washington *Times-Herald,* and by her brother Captain Joseph Patterson of the New York *Daily News,* whom *Time* had once labeled "The Three Furies" of isolationism.[14] The *Times-Herald* identified Luce as one of the "Having a Wonderful Time Boys"—men and women in the public eye who were "having a wonderful time" because of the war. Congressman Martin Dies's Un-American Activities Committee, which was investigating press criticism of Congress, issued a report declaring that "the spearhead of the attack upon Congress as an institution comes from a group of men who have had long training and experience in the ideology of Karl Marx" and listed *Time* as one of the offending publications, along with the *New Republic,* the *New Masses* and the *Daily Worker. Time,* the committee said, had been "drawn sucker-fashion into this movement to alter our form of government."

C. D. Jackson [15] undertook to sum up for the editor-in-chief the whole state of the company's public relations at this juncture. "The Administration doesn't like us and is secretly pleased at the Chicago

[14] *Time Inc. 1923–1941,* p. 479.
[15] Charles Douglas ("C. D.") Jackson, whose business ability was combined with a fine sense of humor, had been with Time Inc. since 1931 as assistant to Luce and since 1937 had been general manager of *Life.*

29

*Tribune*–Dies attack," he wrote Luce. "The old-line Republicans don't like us for obvious reasons. Many of the Willkie Republicans don't like us [because] we withdrew our all-out 'right-or-wrong' support. The higher-ups in the Army and Navy don't like us because we have pricked the seat of their pants too often. Congress doesn't like us because we indict them as a whole while protesting loudly against indictments of the press as a whole. . . . The English think we are a fountain of anti-British propaganda. . . .

"I know that our purpose in life is to inform, not to be loved. But when so many different kinds of people go all the way from puzzlement to rage . . . there must be some reason. . . . One high-placed editor member of the family put it as follows: 'We are in all these different kinds of doghouses because we have been living dangerously; *but* we haven't been living dangerously with a purpose—we just happened to be on that streetcorner.' "

Jackson felt that much of the trouble would be solved if Luce took a firmer editorial hold on the magazines: "When necessary . . . throw your weight around and see to it that something is published in the way you want it published simply because you want it published that way. I think there are a lot of people around here who would be more than happy to have your editorial judgment reflected uniformly throughout the pages of our publications. And when we make an enemy, let's make him because we are agin' him and not because he doesn't know what we are for or against."

This was the kind of advice that Luce, who asserted his right to direct policy but was unwilling to curtail the day-to-day freedom of his editors and writers, almost invariably rejected. He replied that the problem was less one of editorial attitudes than of public relations. In the past the promotion departments had run interference for the editors; they must do so again. Jackson was then assigned to take over full responsibility for public relations. But his services were lost when the State Department requested that he be given leave of absence for an urgent diplomatic mission to neutral Turkey (following which he was enlisted by the Office of War Information and assigned to General Eisenhower's headquarters in North Africa). Editorial vice president Eric Hodgins was thereupon given full responsibility for the company's public relations.

CHAPTER

# 3

*"Globaloney"*

I**N THE CONGRESSIONAL ELECTIONS** of November 1942 the Republicans in a surprising comeback gained forty-two seats in the House and nine seats in the Senate, and among the new Republicans elected was Clare Boothe Luce as the representative from the Fourth Congressional District in Connecticut. Mrs. Luce, in winning, regained for her party the seat held by her stepfather, Dr. Albert E. Austin, from 1938 to 1940.

Her husband had evidenced far more interest in her candidacy than she had at first. She was still trying to make up her mind about running when he called a meeting at their Connecticut home of some *Time* editors and Washington bureau chief Felix Belair, who observed, "It is going to be very difficult for *Time* if Clare runs, because it will be almost impossible for the magazine to be objective." Luce replied angrily, "It will be interesting to see if you fellows can be as objective as I can be about this matter." Mrs. Luce then announced that she would not run. "You certainly messed things up," Luce told his Washington chief the next morning. Mrs. Luce, however, was persuaded, and she won handily.

*Time*'s contribution to her campaign was a favorable three-column story (a lot for a congressional candidate), which referred to her as Miss Boothe, noted her marriage to the editor-in-chief, dwelt largely

31

on her career as a playwright, editor and correspondent and on her commitment to a harder war effort. The story did not mention her opponent. Her husband helped her with some speeches during the campaign and temporarily assigned one of his aides, Wesley Bailey, to be in charge of her publicity and advertising.

Belair's fears were borne out, but in a way that he did not anticipate. A succession of Time Inc. editors, trying too self-consciously to be detached, either treated Mrs. Luce with a distinct lack of gallantry or ignored her when she was making news, in a way that became a source of frustration and embarrassment to both husband and wife. Mrs. Luce from the first was aware of the special problem. After the heat of the 1942 election campaign she wrote Allen Grover, vice president and assistant to Luce: "I couldn't tell you, to save my life, if I'm functioning, or being of any use to anyone just now. All I know is I'm embarrassing Time Inc. plenty, and that may be good for their souls, but it makes me feel like a wifely heel!"

*Time* did report her maiden speech in Congress, which was on the then highly controversial subject of postwar airways:

Democrats had expected a plea for aid to China; Republican Clare Luce picked a topic of perhaps greater importance: Who will rule the postwar airways? In this new sphere, air-minded Clare Luce sprung an old American phobia: that a shrewd and calculating John Bull is going to hornswoggle a naive and idealistic Uncle Sam unless somebody watches out.

Said she: "On the very day the shooting stops, the British naturally desire to be in a position to put muscles and flesh on their international airways system. And perhaps even fat in some places—with Lend-Lease planes." . . .

House members pricked up their ears. But Playwright Luce was just warming up. She sailed into the as-yet-vague concept of "freedom of the air," and its chief proponent, Vice President Henry Wallace. Said she: "Mr. Wallace . . . has a wholly disarming way of being intermittently inspiring and spasmodically sound. . . . He does a great deal of global thinking. But much of what Mr. Wallace calls his global thinking is, no matter how you slice it, still 'globaloney.' . . ." Republicans chuckled.

In noting the comment on the speech, much of it biting, *Time* said that while a section of "the old Isolationist press" had been delighted,

"the stoutly international, Anglophile New York *Herald Tribune"*
could find in it no taint of isolationism. But then *Time* added:

> Anything but delighted were British newsmen in Washington.
> . . . Shooting at the speech's most vulnerable spot, the London
> *Times*man wrote: "Not by a single word did she show any
> awareness that the rights of innocent passage and free land-
> ing . . . must and would be reciprocally agreed as between
> sovereign nations." . . .
> British reactions at week's end: that the U.S., far from being
> impotent, was likely to be an all-too-formidable commercial air
> adversary for Britain when the fighting stops. It had not been a
> good week for the Brotherhood of Man. Perhaps Clare Luce
> had started a much-needed process of clearing the atmosphere.
> Her subject was more important than the speech or its rever-
> berations: it is the key to the whole postwar world. This was
> just the start of the debate.

Eric Hodgins who, in addition to his other duties, was at that time
editing the National Affairs department (now renamed U.S. at War),
recalled that when the writer turned in the first version of the story
he sent it back saying, "Make it tougher." A second and third version was required before Hodgins was satisfied. It was then marked
by the managing editor, "Show Luce," and came back with the
comment, "Good story."

Mrs. Luce did not agree, feeling that it did not do justice to her
argument and made her appear both naïve and an Anglophobe. She
had even more reason to object to an offhand comment which subsequently appeared in *Fortune* referring to "ill-mannered cracks like
'globaloney.' "

Luce was extraordinarily diffident in approaching his editors on
behalf of his wife. He wrote a note to the managing editor of *Time:*
"I come as suppliant to ask for something which, if I were not me, I
might be able to suggest as a plain matter of journalistic truth and
relevancy. I want to ask you to print a *fact*—if it is a fact. And, *if*
it is a fact, it is a hell of a news-worthy fact . . . that the first
prominent person in 'public life,' certainly the first person in elective
office, to propose flatly an alliance with Great Britain was Representative Clare Boothe Luce of the 4th District of Connecticut. . . .
I am asking only for the publication—in three or four lines—of a

fact, if it is a fact. . . . It seems to me that common justice will support the petition of Y'r humble s'v't."

*Time's* response was minimal. Soon afterward, in a story reporting a speech that Churchill had given at Harvard, it said that the British prime minister had asked that Britain and the United States continue their military alliance after the war and from the item dropped this footnote: "A military alliance with Great Britain has already been urged by two leading Republican spokesmen: Representative Clare Boothe Luce and Governor Thomas E. Dewey."

Luce once said to Gottfried, "I don't know what's the matter. If Clare were anybody else's wife, *Time* would just love to write about her." Gottfried found it curious that Luce could not understand the discomfort inherent in a situation in which his editors were writing about his wife. Clare Luce once complained to Gottfried that she felt the tone of *Time's* critical coverage suggested to other congressmen that she and her husband were quarreling, adding, "It's not that I care what *Time* says about me, but it's embarrassing in Washington."

A *modus vivendi* was found for the problem that was hardly satisfactory, so far as news coverage was concerned: it was agreed that henceforward none of the Time Inc. magazines was to mention Mrs. Luce's name, and she disappeared, for a time, from their pages. Years later, at *Time's* fortieth anniversary dinner, attended by hundreds of public personages who had appeared on the magazine's cover, Luce introduced his wife in these words: "There are quite a few people in this room who ought to have been on the cover of *Time* and haven't been for various reasons. I should now like to pay my respects to all of them by saluting one of them, one who has not been on the cover for a unique but very poor reason: she married the editor-in-chief."

# A Corporation at War

A S IN ANY OTHER BUSINESS, management had to cope with problems arising from the dislocations and distortions of a wartime economy. Fortunately the company was in excellent
shape; Charles Stillman reported on December 27, 1941:

> There is no more desirable account in the country than Time
> Inc. Its credit is tops and its earning power is tops. It is on a
> sound basis of profitable relationships with its suppliers. The
> success . . . in lowering costs is not due to reduced margins of
> profit. It is due to cooperation with suppliers in working out im-
> provements in equipment and methods and by a willingness to
> accept specifications and changes therein which are in accord
> with the best production methods available. This has led to
> harmonious relationships.

An early wartime problem was that of manpower. "You could count
the Time Inc. people too old for Selective Service on the fingers of
one hand," said Andrew Heiskell, the twenty-seven-year-old general manager of *Life*.[1] At one point the armed services and the
Washington agencies appeared so likely to strip the company of key

[1] Heiskell had joined the infant *Life* in 1937 and had worked briefly on the
editorial side, then as assistant general manager before succeeding Jackson.

35

personnel that Luce became alarmed and told Hodgins, "Please, for God's sake, go down to Washington and ask some pointed questions —say, for example: is the patriotic thing for Time Inc. to do to go out of business?" The Selective Service averted this fear, common to many corporations, by setting up a system of deferments that permitted essential industries (Time Inc.'s rating by the War Manpower Commission) to retain a cadre of key personnel sufficient to carry on the business. By September 1942, however, 167 Time Inc. employees had left for the armed forces and government service. The call of duty even depleted the board of directors. William Hale Harkness, whose family's investment had helped to make possible the publication of *Time,* resigned to take an army commission; Artemus L. Gates, the president of the New York Trust Company, had resigned from the board two months before Pearl Harbor to become assistant secretary of the navy for air.

Their resignations reduced the number of directors from eight to six, but more important, in the eyes of Luce and Larsen, reduced the number of outside directors from six to four. The two men had always placed a high value on the advice of the outside directors, to whom they looked for a check and balance on their own management decisions. Furthermore, Luce wanted to be relieved of his duties as board chairman in order to devote more time to the editorial direction of the company. Although the number of directors was not increased, Luce proposed that his brother-in-law, Maurice T. ("Tex") Moore, a board member since 1939, take Luce's place as chairman, thereby strengthening Moore's role while allowing Luce the extra time he required.

Moore, whose nickname derived from his birth in Deport, Texas, was a partner in the Wall Street firm of Cravath, de Gersdorff, Swaine & Wood, which had represented Time Inc. in legal matters since 1928, when Luce had somewhat diffidently asked Moore whether his firm would be interested in representing so small a corporate client; Moore had assured him that Cravath's blue-chip practice flourished by helping small companies grow into bigger ones.[2]

[2] Moore attended Trinity University, then located in Waxahachie, Texas, entered Columbia Law School and upon graduation in 1920 joined the Cravath firm. In 1926 he married Luce's second sister, Elisabeth; later the couple lived abroad for a year where Mrs. Moore was a sometime correspondent for *Fortune.* Moore also became Luce's personal counsel. Though the family ties were close, they played only a minor part in Luce's choice of his brother-in-law as corporation counsel.

At the time Luce had originally asked Moore to join the board, his brother-in-law had issued a caveat: he wrote to Luce that he thought the position of director was "not an enviable one. . . . One of the vices in the system is that the officers and other important employees . . . look upon directors only as necessary evils. A director's relative popularity with the management depends on how few questions he asks and how fast he says yes. Harmony seems to require unanimity, and this often requires just playing along. . . . I do not wish to imply that as a director I would be any more outspoken than I have often been as counsel. The only difference is that unless I were shown, or unless I felt it reasonable to take the judgment of the other directors in the circumstances, I might have to vote no, whereas just as general counsel I can be cheerfully overruled." Notwithstanding this declaration of independence, or because of it, Moore had been elected to the board.

In considering the proposal that Moore become chairman, neither Luce nor Moore envisioned the chairmanship as a full-time executive position. "What we really want," Luce wrote, "is responsibility that all policies which *should be* determined are determined and (as checker-upper) that policies determined are in fact executed with reasonable thoroughness." Larsen recalled: "At the time when Moore agreed to become chairman, legal complications were piling up in every direction—tax problems, wartime labor problems and just plain company law—and neither Harry nor I were knowledgeable in this field, and so we turned to Tex."

One month after Moore was elected chairman his law firm was successful in having dismissed in the New York Supreme Court a worrisome suit that had been hanging fire since 1939. Francis L. Corcoran and two photographers, Anton Bruehl and Ira W. Martin, had filed a suit claiming $250,000 on the ground 1) that in the summer of 1932 they had submitted a prospectus and a dummy for a picture magazine pursuant to an agreement with Time Inc. that if their idea were accepted they would be compensated, and 2) that they had performed services in developing the idea of a picture magazine. The implications of the case were that the company had stolen their idea for the publication of *Life*. Luce and Larsen had indeed discussed the idea with them. But Corcoran et al.'s dummy was only one of a number of experimental ideas that were considered and then dropped in favor of establishing *The March of Time* in motion pictures.[3] In

[3] *Time Inc. 1923–1941,* p. 225.

any case, the idea for a picture magazine had been current ever since the *Illustrated London News* was established in 1842 and had spread to many other countries including the United States, where *Frank Leslie's Illustrated Newspaper* had once flourished.

Time Inc.'s record of long experimentation with the use of pictures was also cited. One piece of conclusive evidence that helped destroy the Corcoran suit came from Mrs. Luce, who testified that in 1931 she had presented to her then employer, *Vanity Fair* publisher Condé Nast, a memorandum proposing that he buy the humor magazine *Life* and turn it into a picture magazine. Justice Ferdinand Pecora, after hearing voluminous testimony, dismissed the case, finding that there had been no use or adoption of an original idea.

The company records for September 1942 provide an interesting example of how Moore's influence was brought to bear as guide and counselor. Stillman, as treasurer, was one of the businessmen who early foresaw that the industrial expansion expedited by war would bring about a postwar age of light metals, plastics, electronic communication and worldwide air transport. He was eager that the management of the company engage in "a degree more of experimentation to enable Time Inc. to take advantage of new developments from which it could profit both operationally and financially." He proposed, therefore, "a coordinated research-development-investment policy" for which he envisaged raising the authorization for long-term investment of the company's surplus funds from $2,000,000 to $5,000,000. His argument concluded:

> Instead of integration toward ownership of facilities [i.e., paper mills and printing plants] we have chosen to become the most expert and adept in buying in a competitive market in such a way as to expedite the application of new technology to our particular problems. . . . It is time to consider whether an expansion of this type of activity, involving more men and more money, is or is not timely, expedient, and wise. . . . This is a favorable time to extend rather than contract long-term commitments in good American equities. In less mealymouthed phrases, if we should have $5,000,000 of good stocks on hand today we stand a good chance to see them worth $10,000,000 or more within a year or two following a victory.

It was a bold forecast when nearly everyone else was predicting a postwar depression. The company was following in a limited way such a policy, which Stillman described as "conservatism mixed with

38

experimentation." One such experiment had been the purchase of 1,000 preferred shares in Interstate Broadcasting Company, the operators of New York radio station WQXR; the purchase had been made, Stillman said, "so we can watch the insides go around without any responsibility for the outcome . . . to pick their brains." Moore was by no means against this course but he was concerned lest it divert management from its main job, and he cautioned Luce:

> Our business is journalism. It is not just the making of money. . . . Undue, untimely ants in the pants expansion has wrecked all kinds of enterprises. If we have that kind of expansion, Time Inc. will not be an exception. . . . The protection of our surplus funds for [the reasonable needs of our business] requires in my judgment that they be kept liquid. . . . It is a source of strength to be able to buy printing and paper plants. The very fact that we can, may mean that we will not have to. It is a source of strength to be able to buy a radio chain . . . and the same is true if for some reason it becomes necessary or desirable to buy or start a daily. . . . I think that there is a danger of spreading our top management too thin. It has its hands full now, and there will in all likelihood be further drafts on management for war jobs. . . . I think we should concentrate on our main show and not get a lot of sideshows that the top management cannot keep up with adequately.

The board compromised; it adopted Stillman's policy to the extent of a blanket authorization for raising the investment ceiling to $5,000,000, but investments specifically authorized remained for the time being in the range of $2,000,000. One of the first new investments Stillman made was the purchase of 25,000 shares of General Precision Equipment Corporation, one of the principal companies then interested in the development of television equipment.

Moore's reminder that there would be further drafts on manpower was timely because of the rapid expansion of the company's War Task Division. This was an outgrowth of a committee appointed in March 1942 to coordinate and be a central clearinghouse for the various projects that the company had undertaken on behalf of the government. Long before Pearl Harbor *The March of Time* had set up for the armed services a school for cinema photographers, which by July 1942 had graduated fifty-five and had another twenty-three in training; this had been followed by the formation of *Life*'s Photography School for still photographers. The projects mushroomed. The armed services were soon utilizing Time Inc.'s publishing skills for the production of recognition journals, photographic manuals, gunnery guides, target identification folders and combat-morale presentations. Before the end of the war more than two hundred employees were working on these projects, most of them classified. The work was done at cost and without profit to the company.

The most rapid and dramatic expansion in publishing was in the circulation of both *Time* and *Life* outside the United States. Time Inc. correspondents were reporting how eager the troops were for news. From Australia Robert Sherrod cabled that American soldiers were "the news-hungriest mob in history." Walter Graebner, after a long roundabout flight from New York to Moscow by way of Brazil and Africa, reported that "in Gold Coast messes copies of *Time* are torn into single sheets so many can read at once." The experience gained in printing and distributing the first airmail edition, *Time* Air Express, for Latin America proved invaluable in helping to meet the overseas demands. By November 1942 *Time* was preparing to print a special edition for the U.S. troops in Australia, using page-size negatives made in Chicago and flown across the Pacific. A miniature "Pony" edition—without advertising and at first lacking a cover —was developed originally for the troops in Britain. By the end of 1943 *Time* editions were being printed in Mexico City, Bogotá and Buenos Aires (for Latin America); and in Sydney, Calcutta and Teheran. In October 1943, at the request of the army's Special Services Division, a *Life Overseas* edition was launched, printed on lightweight paper and carrying no advertising. It was distributed by surface transport to the armed forces in all theaters.

It had become apparent by late 1942 that some form of paper rationing was inevitable (it was formally imposed in 1943), so the company decided to limit advertising in advance of the government action. The war boom had brought a heavy influx of advertising to the Time Inc. magazines, enough to make management uneasy; Andrew Heiskell pointed out that "the present bulk of advertising . . . is not in line with a) a hard war, b) our editorial preachings of economy and c) the good reputation of advertising." Vice president Howard Black,[4] who was in charge of advertising sales, then an-

---

[4] Since he joined the company in 1924, Black's outstanding sales ability had taken him from the early staffs of both *Time* and *Life* to overall responsibility for advertising in the Time Inc. magazines.

nounced a decision to limit *Time* to 104 pages of editorial and advertising matter, and *Life* to 132. A page limitation was not set for *Fortune* because that magazine, with its smaller circulation, was not a major consumer of paper and also for the very sound business reason that *Fortune* was sold at a bigger markup per pound on the paper allocated to it than either of the other magazines; however, its page size was trimmed.

*Time* and *Life* salesmen found themselves in the very unusual position, for salesmen, of persuading good customers to reduce their orders. An enviable job? The salesmen did not think so; one recalled, "We were like ducks ordered to fly backward. Our feathers weren't put on that way."

The conflict between patriotism and journalism also had its repercussions on the business side. The salesmen not only had to "unsell" advertising but explain why the critical and sometimes caustic tone of *Time* and *Life* reporting was not unpatriotic but in the public interest. Early in 1942 publisher Larsen had warned the *Life* salesmen: [5] "If things get bad and people get hysterical and think the Press shouldn't criticize, will Time Inc. have the guts to fight it out? If you fellows hold the fort, we can lose 10,000 subscriptions and not worry, but if six advertisers get off the boat, you know what it means to get them back. Time Inc.'s publications must speak bluntly and you must be the soft-spoken diplomats who explain to our influential friends why it must be so." In August *Life* published a lead story headlined "Detroit Is Dynamite," the first paragraph of which set the tone for what followed:

> The news from Detroit is bad this summer. Few people across the country realize how bad it is. Wildcat strikes and sit-downs, material shortages and poor planning at the top have cut into Detroit's production of war weapons. Detroit's workers . . . seem to hate and suspect their bosses more than ever. Detroit's manufacturers, who are the world's best producers, have made a failure of their labor relations.

The editors stated their reason for running the article succinctly: "This country has been fed to the teeth with undocumented optimism," said an office memo. The fact that the criticism would rile some of the most important advertisers was fully recognized. The

[5] Roy Larsen had been publisher of *Life* since its founding, a position he continued to hold after becoming president of the company in 1939.

magazine's relations with Detroit were particularly sensitive; it had been a hard job, not yet successful, to persuade the automakers to give *Life* advertising parity with the *Saturday Evening Post*. The *Post* had long been their favorite medium, and they preferred its editorial stance to Time Inc.'s. "Detroit Is Dynamite" hit them hard. They had converted to war production with considerable skill; now they were being rapped on a particularly tender spot. *Life's* general manager warned the salesmen that the article "won't make you any friends." It was an understatement.

It fell to the lot of such men as W. Dickinson Wilson, *Life's* associate advertising manager and its principal contact with Detroit, to repair the damage. Wilson was a Yale man who had sold space in theater programs before joining *Life's* original sales staff. He had the bearing, and something of the courage, of a British Guards officer, and had established good contacts with the advertising executives in the automotive industry. Now he faced the job of selling them all over again.

It was a long campaign, finally successful. Such crises were unsettling to Wilson and his colleagues. "At one time or another," Wilson recalled, "General Motors was mad at us, Chrysler was mad at us, Ford was mad at us—fortunately, never all three at the same time." The salesmen accepted the state of things bravely and philosophically, even took a special pride in the division of editorial and advertising (church and state) that made their job so difficult and uncertain. "The advertisers," Wilson said, "didn't like us; but when they cooled down they respected us the more for our candor—until we riled them the next time."

# From Tarawa to "Easy Red"

THE CORRESPONDENTS representing Time Inc. in World War II filed millions of words (not counting thousands censored in the field) before the surrender of Japan. No one attempted even to guess the number of photographs taken on behalf of *Life;* for the photographers, covering the war represented an unparalleled opportunity to expose mankind at its worst—and best.

At the time of Pearl Harbor a number of *Life*'s photographers were technically enemy aliens; born in foreign countries now at war with the United States, all had taken out first papers, but they were for a time forced to surrender their cameras. Though this restriction was soon modified and they were permitted to resume photography, they were not allowed overseas. Indirectly, this proved to *Life*'s advantage, reserving for coverage of the home front some fine talent. Thus German-born Alfred Eisenstaedt in his essay, "Penn Station" (April 19, 1943), depicting the heartbreak of wartime parting, produced a set of pictures as memorable as any from the battlefronts. German-born Fritz Goro employed his photographic skill in explaining science in terms of photography. Walter Sanders, also German born, recaptured the spirit of early America in his photographs of representative homes, "How America Lived."

Also, worthy of mention among the home front pictures were

43

those made by Andreas Feininger, an American born in Paris, brilliant son of a distinguished artist, who focused on the U.S. heartland. His essay on American place-names was wonderfully evocative of the nation's past.

Even before Pearl Harbor *Life* had problems in getting permission for photographers to go to military installations or out with the fleet. Executive editor Wilson Hicks, who was responsible for assigning photographers to stories,[1] had seen in operation the British pool system, by which the correspondents took turns in covering events. He realized that if *Life* were accepted as a member of a news photo pool, it would get transportation priorities not available to other magazines. The army and navy accepted the idea, and a pool consisting of the three major news-picture agencies and *Life* was set up; all pictures by pool members were available to all media, but newspapers had not yet acquired the knack of using picture sequences; only *Life* presented a coherent panorama of the war.

Pre-eminent among *Life* war photographers—and not only because she was the first woman war photographer—was the unflappable, dauntless Margaret Bourke-White. She was accredited to the Army Air Forces, which, with *Life,* had first use of her pictures. She was a seasoned war photographer before Pearl Harbor, having photographed Nazi air raids on Moscow and having been the first non-Russian photographer to visit the Soviet front. Because she traveled on air force orders, she had special access to transport and was the first photographer with the U.S. Eighth Air Force in Britain, although she was not permitted to go on bombing missions. She was already a familiar figure around the bases there when King George VI arrived at one of them for an inspection. As always she was in army slacks, but on this occasion—the victim of a hairdresser whose rinse had gone wrong—she was flaunting a mop of bright blue hair. The king exclaimed, "Who is that extraordinary woman with the extraordinary hair?"

On her way from Britain to North Africa after that invasion, Maggie's ship was torpedoed. She managed to save two of her six cameras and thus to record the ordeal of her rescue from the sea. Safe ashore, she promptly wangled permission to take off on a bombing run over Tunis. Her "luck" often exasperated other *Life* photographers, among whom there was a tremendous rivalry for space.

[1] Managing editor John Billings once said, "I trust in God and Wilson Hicks for pictures."

Eliot Elisofon, who had landed at Casablanca and joined Eisenhower's invasion troops, complained to New York—only half jokingly: "I come here in the original operation. Have sense enough to get off and wait for a chance, and then have her scoot in under my nose and she is lucky enough to be torpedoed on the way. I wonder if she'll get out a book on 'Torpedoed in the Med' or 'Afloat in a Negligee.' . . . Oh I've got the Bourke-White Blues."

Elisofon, who joined the staff in 1942 after five years of freelancing for *Life,* had his share of "luck"; he was the first photographer to produce pictures of battle action in Tunisia. There he joined up with Major General George S. Patton, who nicknamed him "Hellzapoppin." Elisofon had his own narrow escape when a transport plane on which he was a passenger crashed on takeoff and burned; like Bourke-White, he managed to save one of his cameras and photograph the wreckage. Early in the fighting in Tunisia, before he became battle hardened, Elisofon wrote this account to Wilson Hicks:

> I have just finished my second attempt to photo a battle. It certainly is about the most difficult thing in the world. The most important thing I have found is to see only through the camera. . . . The big thing to think about besides safety is pictures. Sometimes this is more difficult than a distant observer can realize. Two days ago we were bombed too damn close at Sened. Usually I am pretty careful and stay away from heavy concentrations of half-tracks as the Germans love them as targets, but you can't do it all the time. A point was reached where we had to be right with them for certain pictures. Of course that was the time about thirty Ju-88s came over. We had no foxholes and no time to run so Will [Lang] [2] and I flopped. Sure enough an element of three decided to bomb our area. I was on my back ready to photo hits near us, but when I saw the bombs come out and start right for us, I must admit I turned over, put my entire body under my helmet and said "Maybe this is it. . . ." Of course I missed a great picture of bombs coming to the camera and a magic eye sequence or even three quick Contax pix would have been terrific but I am not ready yet for that. . . . Of course my picture quality is going to stink. One of my Contaxes now is half jammed. I was changing lenses in a foxhole as some

[2] *Life's* correspondent.

45

planes approached and a soldier slid into the hole throwing a
bucket of sand into the open camera. . . . I have tried desperately to avoid pretty pix. . . . I don't know what the censors will do with some of my pix of American casualties but
they are enough to make any American fighting mad. . . .
Plenty of blood, believe me. Too damn much. . . . I have not
been able to photo from a tank. They will not allow one into
battle with the window open, for which I cannot blame them.
I should have made one on the road to battle of a long line of
tanks framed from the bow gunner's window but I just got the
idea now. You get all sorts of ideas afterwards. But I expect to
use them. This war is not ending in any great hurry.

Elisofon was right. There was still plenty of time for good pictures.
In June 1943 the Museum of Modern Art in New York gave a one-
man show of his North African photographs.

No photographer was closer to the slogging infantry than Robert
Capa, nor is any other so well remembered for his photography
under fire; even among his fellow photographers he became a legend
because he survived so many battles, starting with his front-line
coverage of the Spanish Civil War. A wiry, sardonic Hungarian,
Capa, beneath his wise-cracking façade, was a deeply compassionate
human being who hated war.

The independent Capa had twice been fired by *Life* and had quit
once. An enemy alien, he had somehow managed after Pearl Harbor
to wangle his way to London working for *Collier's,* and for that
magazine moved on with the American forces in North Africa.
There, in the summer of 1943, Capa applied once again to *Life* and
was hired by cable. He found a place with the 82d Airborne Division, which was about to parachute into Sicily from central Tunisia
as the spearhead of the invasion force. "As long as you're willing
to jump and take pictures of my division in combat," said Major
General Matthew B. Ridgway, the 82d's commander, "I don't care
whether you're Hungarian, Chinese or anything else. Have you ever
jumped before?"

"No, sir," replied Capa.

"Well, it isn't natural," said Ridgway, "but there's nothing to it."

On D day Capa was with the first wave of troops that went ashore
on the "Easy Red" section of Omaha Beach. There his camera recorded the gray dawn landing under heavy fire, pictures that showed

men plunging through the surf amid anti-invasion obstacles, sinking landing craft and the bodies of dead comrades. Capa brought back 106 pictures from "Easy Red," but of these only eight survived. In developing the film the excited London technician let the dryer overheat, ruining the emulsion. The remaining handful of pictures, which *Life* published, were so vivid and dramatic that to this day they are definitive of the terror and confusion of D day.

To say that *Life* photographers were ubiquitous is almost an understatement. On D day David Scherman went over on an LST and later came back to Britain with it. As the ship prepared to land, he focused his camera on the bow doors to record "the immediate mad activity that I was sure would attend our arrival"; in the lens was Capa, also ready to shoot. Scherman's pictures taken on D day ended up in the overheated dryer with Capa's films.

In covering the surrender of Cherbourg, Capa's flashbulbs annoyed defeated Lieutenant General Karl Wilhelm Dietrich von Schlieben, who complained to the American officers. They explained that they could not interfere with the working of a free press. "I am bored with the whole idea of a free press," snapped Schlieben. Capa retorted in German, "And I am bored with photographing defeated German generals." Capa had a great many narrow escapes but none closer than when he was captured by three G.I.'s during the Battle of the Bulge; they were sure, because of his accent, that he was a German infiltrator and were about to shoot him on the spot. It was Capa who provided the editors of *Life* with their cover picture for V-E Day: an American G.I. giving a mock Nazi salute before a great wreath-encircled swastika in a stadium in Nuremberg, the scene of Hitler's huge mass rallies.

He commanded the respect and affection of his fellow photographers. J. R. Eyerman, who, while accredited to the Atlantic Fleet, covered the invasions of North Africa and Sicily and the battle in the Gulf of Salerno and later joined Vice Admiral Marc Mitscher's Task Force 58 in the Pacific, once said: "Very often you see so many wounded that you tighten up inside, get sort of numb. But that isn't good for pictures. You have to let yourself feel—that's why Capa is so respected as a war photographer; he's got a heart way out to here. That picture of his in last week's *Life* (the mothers of Naples lament their dead sons) is one of the greatest pictures of the war. Capa knew how they felt; he got the candid shot before they knew he was around. Being a good war photographer is not a matter of

47

being on hand, clicking a shutter and putting in a plate—that's just getting a record; it's seeing through the eyes of the people at home and controlling yourself so you can be receptive."

A tremendous pride of craftsmanship combined with a willingness, indeed a compulsion, to take risks characterized *Life*'s photographers. Bernard Hoffman, who had been with *Life* from pre-publication days and who photographed the jungle war of Merrill's Marauders in Burma and flew with the first B-29s to bomb Japan, described a *Life* photographer as "a strange sort of guy who gives excess value because he is really working for himself even though he is working for *Life*." A good example was W. Eugene Smith, who spent three years in the Pacific, covered thirteen island invasions including Tarawa, Saipan, Guam, Leyte and Iwo Jima and flew on raids over Tokyo and Eniwetok. He was finally wounded in Okinawa and at last invalided home, to the great relief of his editors who had tried in vain to persuade him not to take so many personal risks. William Shrout, who worked in the Southwest Pacific and the China-Burma-India theater, severely injured his leg in the landing at Rendova in the Solomons.

Dmitri Kessel, disappointed because in his first assignment, to the invasion of Attu in the Aleutians, he did not hear a shot fired, made up for it when he was parachuted into Nazi-occupied Greece. There he joined the Greek partisans. He was in Athens when civil war broke out and photographed the first conference between the Greek leaders and Churchill, who had come to "straighten things out." Kessel recalled that they met in a room "dimly lit with kerosene lanterns. . . . I had to shoot without using a flash . . . and at a very slow speed. I tried to move close to the table and lean on it, supporting myself on my elbows, but . . . I couldn't squeeze myself in. I had to shoot from the Greek side because I was primarily interested in pictures of Churchill and Archbishop Damaskinos, who sat alongside [him]. Finally I got behind one of the Greek leaders . . . and whispered into his ear not to move . . . then I rested my camera on his bald spot and began to shoot. Suddenly Churchill noticed me and after posing for a moment he ordered me to take pictures of the other side. . . . But I continued to take pictures of him, and he almost shouted at me to take the other side. . . . I moved to Churchill's side to take pictures of [the Greeks]. I did not lean my camera on Churchill's bald spot."

The war photographers were extraordinarily mobile, switching battlefronts from the Pacific to Europe, and in some cases back again. Robert Landry, who was aboard a cruiser in the Pacific when the Japanese attacked Pearl Harbor, managed to cover the desert fighting in Libya, the capture of Cherbourg in Normandy, and the postwar trial of Quisling in Norway. Frank Scherschel covered Arctic convoys, flew with navy flyers in the Pacific and photographed the liberation of Paris. Ralph Morse was torpedoed off Savo Island in the Pacific, where he was in the water for six hours supporting a wounded officer, and ended the war as the pool photographer covering the German surrender at Rheims. William Vandivert was in Burma and China, and finished the war in Belgium, France and Germany. John Phillips' photographs spanned the whole political history of the war; he covered the fall of Austria and Czechoslovakia, the conferences at Cairo and Teheran, and three times went through the enemy lines on assignment to Tito's partisans.

John Florea flew from carriers, photographing the assault on Tarawa by the marines; in the last days of the war in Europe he was on hand when the U.S. and Red armies met at the Elbe. Peter Stackpole covered the fighting in Funafuti and Tarawa and barely escaped the last futile Japanese banzai attack on Saipan. George Strock, assigned to MacArthur's headquarters, took one of the first pictures of American dead that the U.S. censors permitted to be printed: three soldiers lying in the surf on the beach at Buna in New Guinea. "Strock had a way of disappearing for days at a time," Wilson Hicks said, "but finally he came through with the picture of the dead soldiers. You send a man into nowhere and he gets the one picture that stirs the whole country."

Some photographers joined *Life* literally on the field of battle. George Rodger, the Englishman who had been with Jack Belden in Burma (p. 13), traveled 150,000 miles on various war assignments before he met *Life*'s editors in New York. George Silk, a pugnacious young New Zealander, had fought at Tobruk, where he was captured; he escaped and later joined *Life* in Australia, going on to cover the fighting in Italy, southern France and the Ardennes.

Inevitably, this account of *Life*'s photographers at war must slight the meritorious work of many other photographers whose pictures were used by *Life*.

*Life* artists added another dimension to the visual record. Their employment was consistent with *Life*'s original prospectus, which

49

promised that it would "send staff artists to make drawings of stories which cannot be satisfactorily photographed." The artist had one advantage over the photographer of thirty years ago: he could use color at will, as the photographer could not because fast color film was not yet available. The artists who painted and sketched the war for *Life* were men who were already known, not as illustrators or commercial artists but for their work in museum collections.

Daniel Longwell, executive editor of *Life,* who was himself a collector and in later years president of the American Federation of Arts, kept a close supervisory eye on *Life*'s war-art project. The undertaking had its start, and the nucleus of war artists was assembled, when seven leading painters were commissioned to depict U.S. military scenes for the July 7, 1941, Defense issue of *Life.* The subject of the Close-Up for the issue was a veteran top sergeant whose portrait was painted by Tom Lea. Soon after that Longwell had Lea at sea with the Atlantic Patrol and then switched him to the Pacific; Lea was on the aircraft carrier *Hornet* when he saw the carrier *Wasp* blown up in the waters southeast of the Solomon Islands. After Pearl Harbor, Longwell had added to the corps of war artists such names at Peter Hurd, Barse Miller, Paul Sample, Ogden Pleissner, Fletcher Martin, Floyd Davis and Henry Billings,[3] many of whom had originally contributed to the Defense issue. In late 1942 Lieutenant General Brehon Somervell, head of the Army Services of Supply, directed the chief of engineers to launch an army art project. Congress, however, decided it was a boondoggle and eliminated the appropriation. Longwell then stepped in and offered, on behalf of *Life,* to fulfill the army contracts with the artists, some of whom were already overseas.

The artists were no less enterprising than the photographers in getting up to the front lines. Aaron Bohrod, who had first been in the South Pacific, and Byron Thomas got to the beachhead in Normandy without having formal accreditation. They simply went to the coast of the English Channel and persuaded a British merchant ship to ferry them across and got a Coast Guard cutter to land them on the beach. They spent three days wandering and sketching at will before they were rounded up and shipped back to Britain by Time Inc.'s accredited correspondents, who feared that the artists' disregard for regulations would get them all in trouble. A couple of

[3] Brother of *Life's* John Billings.

days later Thomas, reading news of the invasion's progress, observed to Bohrod, "You know that village you were at? We've only just captured it."

One of the war artists, Lucien Labaudt, was killed in an airplane accident in India, and Edward Laning was seriously wounded in Italy.

In June 1943 *Life* assembled 146 of the war canvases it had commissioned for a show at the National Gallery in Washington; the collection was later exhibited at the Metropolitan Museum of Art and other museums from coast to coast. An *Art News* jury of experts described the exhibition as "a great show of War Art, not only as an historical record but as an entirely new departure in both magazine and reporting technique." Thirty-eight paintings were selected for color reproduction in a thirty-seven-page portfolio which appeared in *Life*'s last issue of 1943 under the title "Experience by Battle."

Longwell's persistence, despite pressure to disperse these valuable paintings by way of gifts to individual museums, resulted in the *Life* collection of war art being preserved intact. On December 7, 1960, it was presented by Time Inc. to the Department of Defense on the understanding that it would be maintained in perpetuity as a collection. Some of the paintings now hang in the corridors of the Pentagon in Washington.

As artists added distinction to *Life*'s reporting from the battlefronts, so *Fortune*'s and *Time*'s map-makers, on the home front, were exploiting old techniques and inventing new ones to keep readers abreast of the action. On *Fortune* Richard Edes Harrison had introduced perspective maps with his "Vulture's View" of Ethiopia during the Italian-Ethiopian conflict in 1935. By 1942 the bird's-eye view had become that of the air age. His fold-in map supplement, "One World, One War," was soon tacked up on the walls of countless government offices.[4]

Harrison's skill had been so much in demand not only on *Fortune* but throughout the rest of Time Inc. that in 1938 more help was needed, and *Time* hired Robert M. Chapin, Jr., formerly of *Newsweek*. With the coming of the war Chapin evolved a technique for illustrating battle actions on his unique air-brushed topographical maps using overlying symbols and other devices to focus the reader's attention. "I try to dramatize the news of the week, not just produce

[4] In 1944 a book of Harrison's *Fortune* maps, *Look at the World* ("drawn from the point of view of the air age"), was published by Alfred A. Knopf.

a reference map like those in an atlas," he said. His work appeared in almost every issue of *Time* during the war years and frequently thereafter.

One of the most interesting of all the maps ever produced by Time Inc. was the joint creation of Harrison and R. Buckminster Fuller, whose many-faceted talent and enthusiasm Luce greatly admired though Fuller was not yet well known. The concept behind the map was Fuller's, the cartography Harrison's. It appeared in *Life* as a fifteen-page spread, including, on cover stock, a removable insert which the reader could cut out and glue together, thus creating his own "Dymaxion World." Had he successfully accomplished this, and had he then sliced his effort in half, the exhausted reader would have found himself the possessor of two rough prototypes of Fuller's revolutionary geodesic dome.

By V-J Day some eighty Time Inc. war correspondents had filed dispatches with David Hulburd, chief of the news bureau.[5] Much of this material was purely for the background guidance of the editors, but included in it were some outstanding eyewitness accounts of battle.

One of the most prolific and gifted of the war correspondents was John Hersey, who, in addition to a steady file of dispatches, wrote and published three books during the war: *Men on Bataan,* in which he drew heavily on the dispatches of his colleague Mel Jacoby; *Into the Valley,* a personal account of a marine company in action against the Japanese on Guadalcanal (Hersey received a special commendation from Frank Knox, Secretary of the Navy, for his heroism in aiding the wounded); and *A Bell for Adano,* a Pulitzer Prize-winning novel, later made into a play and a movie, based on an article Hersey wrote for *Life* which described the experiences of a young Italian-American major who was the senior civil affairs officer of an occupied town in Sicily.[6] Before going to Guadalcanal Hersey spent six weeks aboard the *Hornet* and with Tom Lea witnessed the sinking of the *Wasp.* He arrived in Sicily three days after the invasion, where he survived his third and fourth plane crashes of the war. His overseas service as a Time Inc. correspondent ended with an eight-months stint in Moscow.

[5] David Hulburd, hired in 1929, was Time Inc.'s first full-time correspondent, working in Chicago. Later he moved to San Francisco to open an office there. In 1937 he was brought to New York to head the news bureau.

[6] *Men on Bataan* (1942), *Into the Valley* (1943), *A Bell for Adano* (1944) —all published by Alfred A. Knopf.

Robert Sherrod was another name with which wartime readers of both *Time* and *Life* became increasingly familiar. On the outbreak of war he left the Washington bureau to become a correspondent with the American forces in Australia. Later he was in the Aleutians. He landed with the marines at Tarawa in November 1943 and from then on stayed with the corps. The marines came to look on Sherrod as one of their own. He wrote two books about their war in the Pacific, *Tarawa* and *On to Westward,* and after the war the corps asked him to write the *History of Marine Corps Aviation in World War II.*[7] "The toughest battles make the best stories," he wrote. "My job was writing stories, so I followed the Leathernecks." A painstaking, courageous reporter with no literary pretensions or ambitions, he took a modest view of the correspondent's job: "[It] is not to write complete stories. He cannot write with the perspective which time alone can furnish. Leave that to the historians and their mountains of official records. At best, the war correspondent can write what he sees and hears and feels; he can perhaps reflect the mood of men in battle, as those men appear and talk and fight"[8]—as in the terror he described when he went ashore with the marines on Tarawa:

> "Oh God, I'm scared," said [one marine]. . . . I gritted my teeth and tried to force a smile that would not come and tried to stop quivering all over (now I was shaking from fear). I said, in an effort to be reassuring, "I'm scared too." I never made a more truthful statement in all my life. I was not petrified yet, but my joints seemed to be stiffening. . . . I do not know when it was that I realized I wasn't frightened any longer. I suppose it was when I looked around and saw the amphtrack scooting back for more Marines. Perhaps it was when I noticed that the bullets were hitting six inches to the left or six inches to the right. I could have sworn that I could have reached out and touched a hundred bullets. I remember chuckling inside and saying aloud, "You bastards, you certainly are lousy shots." That, as I told Colonel [Evans F.] Carlson next day, was what I later described as my hysteria period. Colonel Carlson, who has been shot at in a number of wars, said he understood.[9]

[7] *Tarawa* (1944) and *On to Westward* (1945), published by Duell, Sloan and Pearce; *History of Marine Corps Aviation in World War II,* published by Combat Forces Press, 1952.
[8] *On to Westward,* Preface.
[9] *Tarawa,* pp. 66–67.

Will Lang stayed with the infantry.[10] After the North African campaign, he covered the invasion of Italy where, on the second day of
the Salerno campaign, he found himself the only correspondent with
an American regiment that was completely surrounded and cut off
from the coast by a superior German force. Three weeks later, in
Naples, Lang was the first American correspondent to enter the city
right behind the advance British reconnaissance cars. Subsequently
Lang reported on American troop landings from the Nettuno beachhead just below Rome, having spent long weeks with the Fifth Army
fighters scrabbling their way foot by foot through the mountains to
Cassino. "By his cheerful sharing of all dangers and hardships he has
come to be considered a member of the 'All-American Division,'"
General Ridgway wrote to *Life*. He was again with the infantry in
the invasion of southern France, advancing with the Third Division
up the Rhone valley.

Sherrod and Lang went through their invasions unscathed, but
other *Time* and *Life* correspondents were not so fortunate. Jack
Belden, who came back from the tough Burma campaign with a
very bad case of jungle fever, transferred to the Italian front and
volunteered to go ashore with the first wave at Salerno. There he
was severely wounded on the beachhead, in spite of which he managed to dictate an eyewitness account. In January 1945 twenty-eight-
year-old William Chickering, who had been covering MacArthur's
campaigns from New Guinea to Leyte, became the first and only
Time Inc. correspondent to be killed in battle during World War II.
He was standing on the bridge of the *New Mexico* watching the
bombardment that preceded the landing on Luzon when his ship was
hit by a kamikaze attack.

To cover the high point of the war in Europe—the cross-Channel
invasion—Time Inc. had assembled in Great Britain an invasion task force of correspondents and photographers that was
second only to that of the United Press and Associated Press in size.
Headed by Charles Wertenbaker, former *Time* Foreign News and
World Battlefronts editor, who had been sent to London from the
job of cable editor of *Life* to be chief military correspondent, it consisted of eleven reporters and nine photographers. Among the reporters was Mary Welsh,[11] who would cross the Channel in the wake

[10] Lang left the Chicago *Daily News* to join Time Inc. as Chicago correspondent in 1937. Later he worked in Washington and was a *Life* correspondent in London at the time of the North African invasion.

[11] In 1946 she married Ernest Hemingway, a fellow war correspondent
whom she had met in London.

54

of the invasion. William Walton jumped with the 82d Airborne and landed in a pear tree:

> I dangled about three feet above ground [he cabled] unable to swing far enough to touch anything. . . . I was helpless, a perfect target for snipers and I could hear some of them not far away. In a hoarse, frightened voice I kept whispering the password, hoping someone would hear and help. From a nearby hedge I heard voices. . . . Never has a Middle Western accent sounded better. I called a little louder. Quietly Sergeant Auge, a fellow I knew, crept out of the hedge, tugged at the branches and with his pig-sticker cut my suspension cords. I dropped like an overripe pear.

For the next two days Walton was under constant fire, never had his boots off, got three hours sleep in seventy-two, but somehow managed to hang onto his typewriter. From then on he was almost continuously in the thick of the fighting with one or another of the American armies and ended by reporting Rundstedt's counterattack in the Ardennes.

The *Life* that appeared on the newsstands three days after the invasion was a demonstration of editorial improvisation. No pictures were on hand—there was no time to get them from Europe. But *Life* substituted twenty-two pages of new copy after the original issue had gone to press, including a panoramic map, spread over two pages, showing the Allied fleets and planes moving toward the Normandy coast. The map had been drawn and engraved several months before and laid away at the printers to await the flash from England. *Life*'s editors had had no inside tip on the invasion; its military affairs expert, John G. ("Garry") Underhill, Jr., had merely chosen the most likely spot for such an assault and the map was drawn on the long chance that his hunch would pay off. Also in this issue was a two-page spread of what appeared to be an aerial photograph of an invasion fleet. This had been created from models prepared by the noted designer, Norman Bel Geddes, who deployed his miniature ships plowing through seas whitecapped with powdered sugar on tables in his Rockefeller Center studio. *Life*'s improvisation dramatized the magnitude of the military operation.

By December 1944 John Billings was telling *Life* publisher Larsen of an editorial dilemma: the public can have too much of any subject, and war pictures were beginning to pall. "War pictures per se are at a high discount in the magazine," he wrote. "It is the old problem of pattern, of pictures, any kind, quickly growing to look all alike. The good war pictures today are flukes, the chance shots of drama rather than the monotonous reportage of what is, after all, a dirty business."

One dramatic picture that came to his desk Longwell rejected as not chance at all but a "phony [i.e., posed]," he said. It was the raising of the U.S. flag by the marines on Mount Suribachi on Iwo Jima, taken by the Associated Press's Joe Rosenthal. Longwell cabled correspondent Sherrod on Iwo asking about the circumstances under which it had been taken. According to Sherrod, Rosenthal's picture was not of the first flag-raising (this he never claimed); that one had been staged for the marines' own magazine, *Leatherneck*. What Rosenthal had done was to collect a bigger flag and restage the event. *Time* used it, with the comment that "Iwo would be a place-name in U.S. history to rank with Valley Forge, Gettysburg and Tarawa. Few in this generation would ever forget Iwo's shifting black sands, or the mind's images of charging marines, or the sculptured picture of Old Glory rising atop Mount Suribachi."

Three weeks later *Life* finally published the picture. In so doing, it acknowledged that, whatever the circumstances under which it was taken, it had become to the nation, and to the marines, a symbol of their heroism. Longwell commented: "The great thing was that the country believed in that picture, and I just had to pipe down." *Life* ran with it another picture famous in U.S. history, Leutze's painting of Washington crossing the Delaware. The caption duly noted that, years after it had been established as a classic, it became generally known that "the artist . . . had painted it from German models in a boat on the Rhine."

In its September 17, 1945, issue *Life* carried pictures of the surrender ceremonies on the battleship *Missouri*. On November 5 twenty-two Japanese emerged from the jungles on Guam and surrendered to a passing G.I. truck driver. They did so by handing him a copy of the September 17 *Life* which they had picked up from a rubbish pile. Attached was a note: "We had been lived in this jangle from last year, but now we known by this book that the War end."

In 1944 Time Inc. commissioned Gordon Carroll to select from its war dispatches some examples of the writing of its foreign correspondents for publication as a book, which was entitled *History in the Writing."* [12] A gratifying comment came from *The New Yorker,* whose editors were more often prone to criticize than to praise Time Inc.: "Whether one likes or dislikes the publications these correspondents work for, the fact is evident, as this collection of their dispatches from 1941 to D Day demonstrates, that a more able group of journalists has rarely been gathered together."

A view of how the war correspondents themselves felt about their work for *Time* and *Life* was provided by Fillmore Calhoun, who had covered the war in North Africa and Italy and later became *Life's* Foreign News editor. On resigning from the company in 1955 he wrote to Luce:

> During the war one of our correspondents once sent a cable explaining that he would have to delay covering an assignment because the airplane he was riding in had just crashed and burned on takeoff. . . . He tagged onto his dispatch: "Quote the things we do for Harry Luce exclapoint unquote." . . . He had merely put into cablese what we all said from time to time. It was a sort of secret password among us. No other correspondents, for instance, were ever heard to say, "The things we do for Hugh Baillie!" Or for Kent Cooper, or Roy Howard, or Col. McCormick or anyone else with the possible exception of Helen Reid who was also considered a person and a friend as well as a boss. With pride we put this phrase like a chip on shoulders to confront critics and belittlers and we went to great lengths to cover up any sentimentality in what we said by applying the phrase to everything from taking on an extra bomber flight to sacking up with a Red Cross girl. We may have been unruly but we knew this: We were treated as the elite, and we thought we were of course; we were not cramped by junky directives from the home office; we did not have to spend our time and energy rewriting official handouts; we were urged to get stories that had meat on them and—unique then as it still is—we were urged to trim that meat into decent, printable English. If we "blamed" all this on you, it was also a way of saying "Thank you," as well.

[12] Duell, Sloan and Pearce, 1945.

# The M.E. Is Boss—Or Is He?

Tᴵᴹᴱ, anticipating a great Russian victory in the Battle of Stalingrad, chose Joseph Stalin as Man of the Year for 1942.[1] By January 1943, in fact, the tide of the war had turned: German troops stumbled in the wastes of Russia and Allied forces had seized the initiative in North Africa and the Pacific. With all that this portended for the future, Luce emphasized once more to his colleagues the need to think about the question of winning the peace, which was the problem, he wrote, of "whether or not we Americans as a nation, the leaders and the led, can develop a good Foreign Policy. There is no Foreign Policy which the American people can vote for at the present time. The American people are a people in search of a policy."

If there was no foreign policy that deserved the votes of the American people, Luce was sure he knew why. On reading a story in *Time* that was laudatory of the venerable Secretary of State, Cordell Hull, he had written: "The Hull story is the most brilliant defense of his policy I've ever read. It's always a pleasure to see the

---

[1] A reader twitted *Time:* "I quite agree with your selection. . . . However, it is interesting to compare the Christlike expression given to his portrait today with the satanic mien he bore on your cover as Man of the Year for 1939 [the year of the Nazi-Communist Pact]."

old Judge thus revered. History, however, will think different. For in the cruel condensation of History, the answer will be: Failure." Early in December 1942, riled anew by the American collaboration with Vichy's Admiral Jean-François Darlan in North Africa, he had addressed another memo to *Time*'s editors:

> The [State] Department's policy is all nakedly clear now—i.e., completely unprincipled expediency. Necessity knows no principles. . . . We were appeasers in Europe and, until the late fall of 1941, we were appeasers in the Pacific—on the grounds of expediency. . . . Nothing has changed. The important thing now is to explain to Americans that all our policy is mere (or super) expediency. . . . There is a detail which makes the whole subject so difficult—our picture of Judge Hull as a noble man. He is a noble man. How then can his policy have been the most unprincipled in our history? That's a long story—going back to 1933 if not further. It is easier to say now simply that he is old. He is too old to handle a revolutionary and counter-revolutionary world. He ought to have departed in peace when Chamberlain cried "peace in our time."

In January 1943 the State Department published a White Book which included an account of its dealings with Japan from the invasion of Manchuria in 1931 until Pearl Harbor.[2] In reporting the document, *Time* said that "the cumulative effect of its pages was to make the efforts of U.S. diplomacy seem much more real and wise in retrospect than they had often seemed in prospect." The story concluded with a quotation from a New York *Times* editorial: "It is hard to see how our government could have done more, in honor, than it did to stave off the worldwide war." The editor who had approved this story was vice president Eric Hodgins. Luce, on reading it late at night, reached for the telephone. The call remained engraved for years on Hodgins' mind. "I caught the most blistering hell ever in my Time Inc. experience," he remembered. "When I say Luce was furious, I mean bursting furious." The next morning he found on his desk a Luce memorandum recalling his previous dicta on Hull and the State Department and laying down the law as Luce seldom laid it:

[2] *Peace and War: United States Foreign Policy, 1931–1941.*

In cases where news is to be interpreted . . . it is the responsibility of the Managing Editor, the Senior Editors and the Ass't Managing Editor to know what views relevant thereto have been expressed by the Editor-in-chief. . . . In cases where it is intended to render an interpretation at variance with the views of the Editor-in-chief, it is the responsibility of the above to advise the Editor-in-chief prior to publication. Opportunity to become acquainted with the views of the Editor-in-chief has never been lacking and will not be lacking for those interested. Continued failure to exhibit interest in this matter will henceforth be regarded as incompatible with the efficient conduct of *Time*.

Hodgins, outraged, indited his own memo: "I may not have made very much sense over the telephone last night for I had been in bed and had to be roused to take your 11:45 call. Now, your memorandum of this morning is so harsh that I do not know how to reply to it. . . . I never intended that this little story should [do more] than indicate that the Department, unlike the Army & Navy, was not caught by total surprise on December 7. . . . In my own mind, I was saying something much less inclusive than the effect I caused in yours. Since this is prima facie evidence of bad journalism, I apologize— but I am smarting under the tone of your today's memorandum which appears to address itself to disaffected and contumacious employees who have to be '—or elsed.' It isn't so."

Luce's anger, as it so often did, subsided quickly enough, but there was a lingering frustration. "Yes, my memo was too harsh," he wrote. "And perhaps you will listen sympathetically and privately to the why. *Time* (and the other mags) is evidently a huge responsibility for *all* of us—to myself, no less than to others. And so, even though our collective wisdom is far, far better than my personal wisdom, I can't get away from my own responsibility. . . . But too often I'm overwhelmed with a sense of futility when *Time* seems to speak in a sense, not merely different, but diametrically opposite to what I would have said if I had been personally on the job! . . . In the past two years I've said twenty times to *Time*'s M.E.s that I was available for consultation any hour day or night on this continent— and I have almost *never* been consulted! Perhaps M.E.s haven't wanted to bother me or be bothered. Well, now I guess I'm in for plenty of bother."

What Luce would have said about the White Book was said in a

*Life* editorial the following week: "Under all the moralizing of *Peace and War* there is an absence of real moral judgment which is utterly shocking. Almost everywhere the State Department has turned, its basic doctrine has been expedience: not what was good or what was evil, not which side was right or which wrong; but rather, how can we avoid it and what can we get away with."

Part of the problem was Luce's own fault. Often he was not consulted because he put his senior editors under no compulsion to do so. "Harry just plain disliked giving orders," Hodgins once said. "He would prefer to discuss, to soliloquize, debate and do everything else imaginable in preference."

It was ironic that at this juncture Luce's eyes had fixed on a man who held a number of views totally at variance with his own, and that after some months of sidling around him, he appointed him to succeed Gottfried as *Time*'s managing editor.

Gottfried himself had suggested in August 1941, on his fourth anniversary as managing editor, that Luce begin to think about a successor. He was in no hurry to give up the job; in fact he anticipated another four years at it. The job, while exhausting, was—as he later wrote Luce—"the only wholly fascinating job that I have ever known." He had been the operating head of the editorial department through four years of stupendous and fast-breaking news. He had accommodated himself to two difficult publishers: the egocentric, tempestuous Ralph McAllister Ingersoll [3] and the critical and impatient Pierrepont Isham Prentice, [4] both of whom were journalists and reluctant to be restricted to a purely management role. Gottfried was self-assured and self-effacing, with no outward trace of temperament. His whole journalistic career having been encompassed by *Time* itself, he was never dismayed at the difficult art of effective summary. He was well liked personally, though his editing often

[3] Ingersoll left his job as managing editor of *The New Yorker* to become associate editor of the new *Fortune* in 1930. He was *Fortune*'s managing editor from 1931–35, then was named general manager of Time Inc. and vice president. When management was decentralized in 1937, he was named publisher of *Time* as well. In early 1939 he resigned to start the New York newspaper *PM*.

[4] Prentice came to Time Inc. at the same time as Ingersoll, to be business manager of *Fortune*. From 1934–41 he was circulation director of all the magazines. In March 1941 he became publisher of *Time*. He had been a vice president since 1939.

61

depressed writers; he had a heavy hand with a pencil, tending to rewrite a great deal of copy. A researcher recalled that one Monday night, when the final checked, edited version of a cover story was about to be sent via Teletypesetter to Chicago, Gottfried appeared with a copy of the story. Striking out line after line, he completely rewrote it.

The choice of a managing editor was always a long process with Luce—intuitive and visceral, involving ambiguous and sometimes devious approaches to the man to be superseded and to his successor. Luce once popped the question to a group of associates: "Who would you pick for managing editor of *Time* if you had to bet a million dollars on the right man?" "This was no theoretical question," Gottfried once observed. "It was exactly the kind of bet that Luce had to make every time he picked a new one."

Luce looked at first for a compromise. He thought he might retain Gottfried's experience and administrative ability while transferring a greater part of the actual editing to the man who in most ways was the obvious candidate to succeed him. This was Thomas Stanley Matthews, who was then editing U.S. at War. Matthews had come to *Time* from the *New Republic* in 1929; he had written book reviews for the most part until 1937, when he was made an assistant managing editor in charge of the critical departments. In 1939 he was appointed editor of the National Affairs section and the same year was named associate executive editor. He was a skilled word handler and a man committed to high standards in style and taste. His "nose for news" was not of a conventional sort; he had almost no interest at all in the business world, except to disdain it. But he had what could be described as a poet's sense of human events. He was an exacting editor: his penciled notes on indifferent copy—"Choctaw! Try it again in English"; or on the end of a dull story, "Why do I have to read this?" or the ultimate rejection of shoddy work, "!!!"— were a goad to some, an insult to others, Gottfried felt, "which neither told the writer what was specifically wrong with his copy nor how to fix it." John Knox Jessup, who wrote in *Time*'s Business section for a while, said, "We used to think of Tom as the headmaster manqué of St. Paul's or Groton." Yet many writers found working under him an education; his editing, said Duncan Norton-Taylor, who was writing on *Time* in 1942, was "a lifting up; he respected the writer's judgment, but deplored lack of grace, which he often supplied with great skill and wit."

Luce thought that his editing was something *Time* needed; more sober and responsible in its approach to the news than ever before, the magazine lacked literary finish. It had not completely shaken off the stylistic bad habits of its early years or achieved an acceptable new tone.

Luce's first proposal was that Matthews would become executive editor under Gottfried, who would retain his full authority, be in every sense "captain in charge of the ship" but would delegate to Matthews the editing of all copy and the responsibility for getting out the issue—except for some special features such as the cover story, which would be reserved to Gottfried.

The compromise did not work. Gottfried found it difficult to change his working habits, and in July 1942, after only three or four months of the arrangement, a thoroughly exasperated and frustrated Matthews wrote a memorandum to Luce:

Under the terms of the latest new setup, Gott was supposed to do no copy-editing at all (well hardly any . . .). Actually, he is now reading at least two-thirds of the copy . . . and, often, rewriting the lead stories for U.S. at War, World Battle-fronts and Foreign News. I am sure he would admit, if pressed, that he is rewriting (he might think of it as "editing" but I don't) too much. But I think he might also assert that he had to. Why? Because the writers *and* editors of those stories are so far off the beam that, as sole keeper of *Time*'s conscience, he has to write the stories himself because no one else can or will? You see where that leaves the writers and editors who suffer under Gott's rewriting. The more it goes on, the more they tend to feel, "What the hell's the use?" Their stories, no matter how carefully researched, written and edited, become simply raw material for Gott. . . . The effect on their own sense of re-sponsibility (not to mention other forms of morale) is obvious. And the more Gott rewrites, the more he finds to rewrite. The more he "edits," the more he "edits." I have never told Gott that I thought I was a better editor than he was. I have some-times told you that Gott is a better editor than I am—in an invaluable, backstopping, braking way. But I'm now about ready to tell anybody that when it comes to working with a pen-cil on a piece of copy, I'm not only a better editor than Gott— his "editing" isn't editing at all, and mine is. My gripe is that

63

Gott is not only keeping much of the responsibility of my job away from me, but is doing part of my job that I could do much better than he can.

Because of the wartime shortage on the writing staff, another problem intruded itself. At Luce's suggestion, Prentice, the publisher, was pressed into editing the Business section. Matthews took a dim view of this:

> When Prentice started as editor of Business, I told him that I was going to deal with the editor of Business as editor of Business, and not as publisher—and he was quite hurt and shocked. Nevertheless, I am under no illusions: I know that the editor of Business is also the publisher, and that the more he edits, the more inevitable it will be for him to become editor of *Time*. And I still think the publisher of *Time* (unless he is also to be the editor of *Time*—which perhaps he should be although I certainly don't think so) should have nothing whatever to do with the editorial side of *Time*—except as a perennial critic after the fact, a perennial proposer well before the fact; in short, hands off the current issue, and no fooling. . . . Last Monday [*Time*'s press night], for the first time since 1937, I disliked my job—I mean the actual job, not the one I'm supposed to have. I am 41 years old and my hair is turning gray. If assistant managing editor is the best job *Time* thinks I can do for it, I'd like to know.

Shortly after writing this complaint, Matthews went off on a scheduled vacation. In his absence Luce took over as managing editor, relegating Gottfried to an interim assignment as senior editor of two of the front-of-the-book departments. After several weeks of this, Luce wired Matthews to come back and discuss a new proposition: that Matthews, instead of returning to his job as executive editor, would go on special assignment for three months as temporary head of the London office, then take over as managing editor. The idea was to broaden his outlook and give Luce a chance to discuss his intentions with Gottfried and Prentice. The discussion with Gottfried turned mainly on what he would do thereafter.

"I suggested that I be dropped from the masthead," he recalled, "but Luce would have none of that. He decided to put my name under his as Editor. This was typical of Harry's generosity and loyalty. There was no question of my having equal authority; he was making me the gift of status—the handsomest gift he knew how to make."

Meanwhile, in England, Matthews had developed "reservations," he wrote Luce on his return, "that may seem serious enough to you to make you reconsider your offer." He had conceived the idea of a British edition of *Time,* which would be a very different magazine from the one published in the United States; *Time* as it was would not do at all in bridging the Atlantic, and in telling Luce why, Matthews disclosed some ideas as to what *Time* should be that portended trouble between them.

He questioned *Time*'s tone and its pattern, and "its surreptitious opinion." He thought *Time* had to make up its mind whether or not it was going to be "purely a *news* magazine or follow a definite political line. The present compromise, in which it often appears to be a newsmagazine with tendentious hints inserted between the lines, is not, it seems to me, a permanently possible compromise." The *Time* he imagined could be a journal of opinion, "but of the absolutely unimpugnably best available comment, interpretation and opinion." He mentioned the London *Economist* as "a pale likeness of what I have in mind—an *Economist* staffed and written by the best and clearest journalistic writers on both sides of the Atlantic," published simultaneously in London and New York. "*That* is the magazine which I now dream of editing. To get the chance of editing it, I would do my damndest—if you still want to try me—as managing editor of *Time* for an indefinite period. That is, of course, if the job and I get along all right. Also, of course, if you still feel that you want to try me, knowing that I have set my eyes on still higher things."

Luce still wanted him, and in January 1943 he made the announcement of the appointment, at which Matthews, for all his reservations, exhibited a natural elation. He wrote again to Luce: "The milestone in *Time*'s history is a Washington Monument in my own." He quoted the words of a friend who had told him that his job would have "more responsibilities for good and evil, more need for courage and clarity than any other editorial post in the U.S.—maybe in the world." But on receiving the substantial increase in salary that went with the new job, he felt impelled once again to assert both his satisfaction in his appointment and the reservations he still held about it:

First of all, to plagiarize Holy Writ [Matthews was the son of an Episcopal bishop], I feel that it is good for me to be here.

65

In other words, I'm damn glad to be here. . . . But what bothers me at present is the feeling that *Time* and I may not be in agreement about who I am. Perhaps my case can best be put in a series of negatives:

1) I am married, and *Time* is not the name of my wife.
2) I am not yet completely licked as a writer.
3) I hate the Republican Party.
4) As a reader and as a writer, I consider *Time* badly written—which means, in *Time*'s language, misinformative.

*Time*'s business is information. Information is different from *news,* in the accepted newspaper sense of that word. . . . Information is facts in perspective.

The function of *Time* is twofold: 1) to *take in* all the facts; 2) to *give out* information (i.e., relevant facts set in their proper perspective).

What is the "proper perspective?" It is the perspective . . . of the writer and of the editor. It will vary according to their intelligence, knowledge, emotional background. . . . No editor can help reflecting, to some extent, the point of view of his age and class.

When the new managing editor took over, he let the staff know that a new order was in prospect; he set forth his prejudices in a speech that evidently made a strong impression on Luce for he had it distributed to the top executives of the company. "Some of you already know some of my own prejudices," Matthews said. "For the benefit of those who don't, I might state a few of them now: 1) A prejudice in favor of getting to work early, and a prejudice in favor of those who feel the same way. 2) A prejudice in favor of the facts; an equal prejudice against the notion that the facts will always speak for themselves. 3) A prejudice in favor of knowing the tools of your trade and how to use them—which for a journalist means knowing the meanings and spellings of the words he uses; knowing the rules of grammar and punctuation and when to break them; knowing how to construct a sentence and how to build a paragraph. 4) A prejudice against those who think you can write well without thinking well, or make an original phrase without original thought. 5) A belief that good writing makes good sense, that bad writing muddles the sense. 6) A prejudice against writing between the lines."

He made thereafter a declaration of editorial sovereignty; he told

Prentice that henceforth he was not to speak to any writer or editor without first consulting him. Prentice was taken aback, and relations between managing editor and publisher did not improve thereafter; Prentice was heard to complain, "Harry has me locked up with the nastiest cobra in the latitude."

Prentice believed the managing editor to be responsible to him for producing a magazine that could be sold readily to the reader and the advertiser; Matthews recognized no such responsibility. While Gottfried was managing editor, Prentice had been on close terms with the editors. By Matthews' edict he was now restricted to writing memoranda about the editorial product and organization. But his critiques were often so blunt and undiplomatic that they were a source of serious friction. Even his good friend Eric Hodgins once had to remind him that "you are speaking about the most notable magazine publishing success of the modern world, and not a poor broken-down jalopy of a magazine produced with such appalling incompetence that any issue may be, and might well deserve to be, its last."

Among the bones of contention between Prentice and Matthews was the publisher's insistence that *Time* should give readers the news that interested them, not what the editors thought they should be interested in; and that what mattered was content, never mind literary style. Prentice complained that the writers looked upon themselves as "writers" and not "journalists" and believed that *Time* should hire journalists of established reputation rather than aspiring young "amateurs." Prentice pressed his argument to the point where Luce, in a fit of annoyance, issued the following proclamation:

Whereas, in memos and otherwise, Prentice keeps harping on the idea that the Editors of *Time* regard themselves as "writers" rather than as "journalists" and

Whereas Prentice was formerly a journalist practicing in the purlieus of Boston and Philadelphia and

Whereas Matthews was formerly a writer practicing under the elms (or whatever) of Princeton

Now therefore I, by the authority invested in me by a thorough-going fed-up-ed-ness with a stale argument, do hereby proclaim and decree that from this day forth Matthews recognizes that he, Matthews, is a struggling journalist trying to make good and that Prentice recognizes that he, Prentice, has the

honor to be publisher of the best damn written magazine in the
. . . business . . . *Time,* The Weekly News-magazine.

In witness whereof I hereby put my sign and seal as the Old
Bolshevik demanding that noses for news lie betwixt ears for
music.

Despite Matthews' earlier exasperated criticisms of Gottfried as a
managing editor, their relations were cordial enough. The new managing editor had told his staff that he was going to miss the old
managing editor "very much," and in fact he appealed to him for
help soon after taking over. "He came to me very worried," Gottfried recalled, "because he thought too many writers were becoming
time-servers, not writing out of their own conviction, but writing to
please the boss and to collect the salary check." Matthews asked him
to write a memo "telling each writer in so many words that he was
not expected to write anything unless he thoroughly believed it himself." Luce concurred in the project. "You have that most ancient of
philosophical dilemmas," he wrote Gottfried, "How to achieve (in
our staff) that freedom which without unity is a delusion and that
unity which without freedom is a snare."

Gottfried produced a writer's charter of freedom and self-respect.
Some excerpts:

> *Time* never did and does not now demand servility, intellectual
> or otherwise, from the members of its staff. On the contrary
> *Time* does demand from every staff member the most forthright
> intellectual honesty and frankness in dealing with its editors and
> readers. . . . If anything is in danger of going into the maga-
> zine which you believe is incorrect, naturally your first appeal
> is to your senior editor. . . . If it is still not settled in the way
> you believe correct, it is your duty to carry your appeal to Patty
> Divver [research chief], to Tom Matthews, to myself, or to
> Harry Luce. . . . Of course if you exercise your right of appeal
> the editors may overrule you . . . but you are not alone in that
> periodical frustration. The price of the degree of intellectual
> democracy that we try to practice is that virtually no one can
> ever have any story exactly as he wants it. . . . The magazine
> has to have a generally consistent point of view. . . . You can-
> not expect to be *Time*'s theater reviewer, for example, unless
> your general approach to the theater is in reasonable conformity
> to that of the editors. But if you are *Time*'s theater reviewer, the

presumption is that you were hired and continue to hold that job because that reasonable conformity exists. And that being the case it is your job to say in your reviews not what you think the senior editor or the managing editor would like you to say but what you believe is the truth. . . . *Time*'s success rests not only on being interesting but on the fact that its readers believe what it says. . . . It is not only your right but your duty to stand up for the facts as you see them and to exercise your squawking rights. In the days to come when you yourself are in a position of authority . . . it will be up to you to encourage others to do the same. For all of us, the freedom and the responsibility of the press begins at home.[5]

Despite Matthews' determinedly independent attitude, he was not without some inward qualms. Like all new managing editors, he was subjected to considerable back-seat driving—a recipient of the usual flow of memoranda from Luce and the target of a weekly critique of the magazine by his predecessor. It was with evident relief that a month or so after taking over his desk he received a note from Luce saying: "This issue gives me the definite impression that you are *on top of the job*. . . . Someone said last week that he couldn't notice any change since you took over. That's fine—the audience shouldn't be aware of 'how' a show is directed. But the style of direction is inescapable to those who have eyes to see this sort of thing." Matthews replied, "Whew! What a relief. I haven't heard a word from anybody, so far. . . . I'm having more than an occasional twinge now of liking the job, which I take to be a *very good sign*. And I still hope for miracles—but please don't expect any."

[5] At *Time*'s twentieth anniversary dinner on March 11, 1943, Hodgins made the same point: "An early custom grew up, which has now hardened into a constitutional right and a high privilege—the right and privilege of telling the boss that he is crazy. The boss even *wants* to be told he is crazy. He suspects it himself, but an independent, confirming opinion is usually a tremendous help. I am not suggesting mass insubordination. If the boss persists in his actions after you have told him that he is crazy, you in your turn must take that in good part."

# A Question of Republican Partisanship

I N U.S. POLITICS the thing which mainly concerned Luce as 1943 began was to get his friend Wendell Willkie, his party's strongest candidate, he thought, back into the good graces of the Republicans. Willkie, *Time* reported, was "in a fair way to being consigned to the role of Elder Statesman unless he could . . . do a better job of playing politics according to the time-honored rules." Even the success of his spectacular round-the-world flight in 1942 was "dimmed by his failure to command the firm support of his party."

Luce sought him out. Luce described the encounter some years later:

The advice I had to offer was that Willkie should devote a considerable part of his time and attention to meeting and talking with the leaders and other members of the Republican Party. . . . While supporting every other cause in the world, Willkie did not seem to be charting a clear course for the Republican Party. . . .

The bitter anti-Willkieites in the party, such as Publishers McCormick and Patterson, were already pounding Willkie for having "sold out" to Roosevelt—they were savagely making him out to be Tweedledum to Roosevelt's Tweedledee. Willkie did not seem to be meeting this charge. And in the November 1942 elections he had missed a great chance to establish his party leadership by his failure to go on the radio a week or two before election day. . . .

How much of all this we talked of that very evening in January, I have forgotten. But . . . the point I wanted to emphasize at that time was that Wendell should get out and "meet the folks." . . .

In the next few months Willkie did an amazing job. . . . A few months later he said to me with boyish gusto, "Harry, from being the Republican who knew the fewest party leaders I am going to become the man who knows more of them than anybody else—and I'm going to do this in one year!" . . . He did it—and like any game it had its thrill. Indeed this was the greatest game of all. One night in June in a taxi going down Park Avenue he was urging me to go all the way into politics. The cab arrived at my hotel just as he reached a climax of enthusiasm. Journalism, he said, is fine but "this is the Sport of Kings!"

But he continued to disappoint Luce with the vagueness of his views. Willkie had launched a new "crusade"—a favorite word with him— for "internationalism." When *Time*'s congressional correspondent, Frank McNaughton, after a dinner with Willkie, wrote Luce that Willkie would do better if he got down to the hard realities of politics and talked in less idealistic terms, the editor-in-chief's reply revealed his own growing doubts about his friend: "The fault is not that [Willkie] is too 'idealistic,' but, rather, that his idealism is not quite on the right beam. . . . His crusade is not correctly lined up with the historical realities. . . . What is Willkie's crusade—he calls it internationalism? But what the hell is that? Does he mean a real Super-State? There isn't going to be any Super-State."

It is not clear whether or not Luce sensed then that Willkie was burned out. He was still partial to him but he was looking over other Republican possibilities. The favorable coverage given, first in a profile in *Fortune* and then in a cover article in *Time*, to Ohio Governor John W. Bricker worried some members of the staff. Walter Graebner, who had recently returned from assignment in Moscow to serve as *Life*'s cable editor for a few months and was touring the country to become reacquainted with the American scene, sent a dispatch from Cleveland:

> Nearly all the people I talked with felt that *Time*'s story gave Bricker a much bigger boost than he deserved. . . . He would be simply hopeless as a President. He is just too small a man for the White House. . . . Fritchey thinks that if *Life* published an equally favorable story, Bricker might very well get the nomination.[1]

But Luce was not prepared to dismiss any possibility. When *Time* published a mildly derisive story about the candidacy of General Douglas MacArthur, which was being urged by Senator Arthur Vandenberg, Luce rebuked his editors: "We have undertaken to bring against this MacArthur candidacy the cruelest journalistic weapon, namely, ridicule. It may be that my sense of humor, such as it is, needs repairing. . . . But, meanwhile, I feel very strongly that Douglas MacArthur should be treated with respect and that any attempt to ridicule his supporters should be abandoned if it spatters disrespect or ridicule on him." He also thought that *Time* on another occasion had dealt too flippantly with New York Governor Thomas E. Dewey: "Your two-inches on Dewey are really laughable. Either that, or you are playing a terrific gamble that you will be able to laugh off Dewey."

The momentary reconciliation between President Roosevelt and Luce, after Pearl Harbor, had not long survived. The President detested both Luce and his wife, and the feeling was reciprocated. The Luce magazines were among the President's severest critics, and now Mrs. Luce sat among his political opponents in Congress. The President took great delight in a derisive verse entitled "Au Clare de la Luce" by librettist Howard Dietz, published in the newspaper *PM,* and asked majority leader John McCormack to get a "freshman Congressman on our side" to quote it in the House: "I think it is wholly parliamentary."[2]

---

[1] Clayton Fritchey was then a special writer on the Cleveland *Press* and *Time* and *Life* correspondent in that city.

[2] Excerpts:

> "O Lovely Luce—O Comely Clare!
> Do you remember—way back there—
> Holding your lacquered nails aloft,
> 'The war we fight,' you said, 'is soft.'

Luce, on his part, worked up a fine head of steam when the Office of War Information's picture magazine, *Victory,* eulogized the President. It made Luce "m–a–d, M A D. . . . Nothing is doing more to create misunderstanding between the U.S. and other peoples than the exported adulation of F.D.R. The notion that F.D.R. is adored by all Americans (except a few evil millionaires) is not only a dangerous lie; it is also just a plain lie." The editors evidently took a different view: some weeks later *Time*'s cover story on OWI Director Elmer Davis said that Davis' explanation for sending pro-Roosevelt propaganda abroad was "common-sensible [because] the President 'symbolizes the United States, both as a powerful nation and as a land of liberty and democracy. This fact is a national asset. . . . A Government information agency would be stupid not to capitalize on it.' "

Luce's attitude toward the President was further embittered by one of the major disappointments of his life. Late in 1942 he applied for war correspondent credentials because he wanted to visit Chungking. The papers were not forthcoming; he was told that they were in process; in March he was told that they were available at Ninety Church Street, an Army facility in New York; two days later they were canceled: "On account of the extreme stringency of transportation, credentials at present are not being issued . . . to publishers, editors and executives who wish to make visits to combat areas." *Time*'s editor-in-chief appealed in vain, first to General George C. Marshall, army chief of staff, who appeared evasive and rather embarrassed, then to Secretary of War Henry L. Stimson and finally, in a personal interview, to Roosevelt himself, who was responsible for the edict in the first place. The President promised to look into the matter, but the credentials were never issued while Roosevelt lived. Luce was convinced that the order was directed at him personally and was an act of spite.

\* \* \*

"But ere you pack your Vuitton grip
To take the Washingtonian trip,
While still responding to the toasts,
Remember this: that words are ghosts.

"And when it's mealtime, never stoop
To see the letters in the soup.
The ghosts may form like homing birds
'My God,' you'll cry, 'I ate my words!' "

73

The question of editorial policy on *Time* continued to weigh on Luce as 1943 wore on. The attitude of *Time*'s editors often exasperated him. The editor-in-chief was indignant when a colleague dismissed a Postwar Department paper on U.S. relations with Europe as having no bearing on what was said in *Time*. Foreign News editor Charles Wertenbaker, Gottfried and Matthews promptly heard about it:

> I recently had occasion to remark that [the Postwar paper] ought to help straighten out some of *Time*'s wobbly ideology about Europe. And our associate said, somewhat kiddingly, that of course the Postwar Memo was not regarded by *Time* editors as any "gospel." Well, maybe we don't have any gospel around here. But if there is any gospel around here it is the Postwar Memos. To which I should add this—that if any "gospels" contrary to or inconsistent with the Postwar Memos are to be uttered or implied in *Time*—then the Editor of *Time* has a right to be given notice of same and to consider said contrary-gospel before publication. Is this a reasonable proposition—or has all my yammer to Senior Editors for four years been so much crap? And how much longer do I have to say what in order to be understood?

On another occasion Luce, impatient with staff members who objected to a partisan approach in *Time,* complained to Allen Grover about "our everlasting goddamn neutrality." "I think your words are harsh," said Grover. "It [nonpartisanship] served *Time* well for many years. . . . Now, perhaps, *Time* can serve the nation better with open avowal of those principles we deem vital to the nation. We have, in fact, decided that it can. But these questions will not down in my mind: Do *Time readers* know this? Do they understand *why* we have abandoned a kind of 'neutrality' for a kind of advocacy?"

Typically, Luce approached the problem by way of a committee, a "Sanhedrin," as he called it. He set himself a deadline to produce some "clear-cut formulations of Time Inc. editorial attitudes and convictions" and came up with a two-part, "tentative and confidential" paper entitled "The Practice of Freedom," which he sent to Larsen, Hodgins, Gottfried, Prentice, Matthews and Black. The whole of Time Inc.'s editorial attitudes and principles, Luce wrote, could be summed up in one word: "Freedom." A devotion to freedom involved the acceptance of certain "Articles of Faith" that included a belief in the Bill of Rights, in the republican form of government and in the free competitive enterprise system "as the only system compatible with political and human freedom." In the second part of his paper Luce explained how he would interpret the credo in terms of practical politics and immediately aroused the suspicion that the "Articles of Faith" were, in the words of Eric Hodgins, "nothing but a Republican smoke screen." The first question was: "Shall we take sides in the forthcoming Presidential elections?" Luce's answer:

> If I were to answer "No"—that would be the answer that most of us would probably like to arrive at. The answer I have arrived at is "Yes and No—Maybe-yes and maybe-no." And that, someone may reasonably say, is to have arrived exactly nowhere. My attempt here is to show that my answer is an arrival and a precise one. . . .
>
> 1) First, we cannot very well take sides in the Presidential election until we see what the sides consist of. And we cannot predict with accuracy now.
>
> 2) However, as knowledgeable people, we cannot pretend that we have no idea as to how things are tending, and if we want the "better side" to win in November 1944, what we do now may be no less important than what we do (or don't do) on election eve. We cannot evade the responsibility of foresight. Therefore it seems to me that we may as well agree that our disposition is definitely in favor of the Republican Party.

In this document Luce was laying out a course of policy which he felt fully justified, given his own convictions. His associates rejected its very premise. His co-editor Gottfried took on himself the job of telling Luce that "the feeling that *Time* must not be a partisan, from motives however high, is strong in our ranks from bottom up." Gottfried predicted that *Time*'s U.S. at War editor "will have torture of soul trying to reconcile this feeling with what is asked of him. . . . Between your conscience, his conscience, and the writers' consciences —and the compromises in execution which are made out of mutual esteem—there is every prospect that the reporting of the campaign will be thoroughly bitched up—worse than last time. . . . I believe that the only way to get the editorial results that you want would be for you to edit USAW yourself. . . . Perhaps it would also be necessary for you to write as well as edit the section." Gottfried said that

75

*Time*'s partisanship had injured its reputation in 1940 and might destroy "the basis of *Time* as an institution" if continued.

However much taken aback, Luce dutifully circulated Gottfried's memo among the same group to whom he had sent his own memo, with a singularly mild comment and the suggestion that Gottfried tell them "just what our attitude should be."

What Gottfried said in essence was that the Articles of Faith should include the assertion that *"Time* is non-partisan, . . . seeks to serve no interest which is not wholly consistent with the interests of the nation and of humanity. Thus *Time* does not think of its function as being to get things done—that is the prerogative of the sovereign people. Our function is to assist in getting things understood."

No final policy paper was ever agreed upon. One thing the exercise did accomplish was to reveal (so Eric Hodgins thought) "a degree of suspicion, distrust and misunderstanding" between the editor-in-chief and the senior editors of *Time,* and so he wrote Luce:

You are facing the major problem that every Head Man of every successful enterprise always faces as he and his organization grow and mature. You are growing remote.[3] . . . You are a great figure in your company, in your profession, in the U.S., and the world. As Luce, The Reputation, grows, Luce the guy whose handwriting is hard to read, who has a habit of starting his lunch with prune juice and was an Alpha Delta Phi in college, becomes more and more unknown, even to such people as represented in the Senior Group. And the unknown gives rise to fear, of which the symptoms can be mistrust and suspicion: "What's Harry up to *now?"*

[3] This situation had not been helped by the move into Rockefeller Center in 1938, where the elevator starter had taken it upon himself to provide an extra unofficial service already being given other top executives. He would walk with Luce to an elevator and instruct the operator to take him directly to his floor. Luce's solitary rides became legend, and the psychological effects on the staff were more damaging than he could have realized. There was endless speculation: that Luce was too impatient to wait for the elevator to fill, that he feared he would not recognize members of the rapidly expanding staff, that he wanted the time for prayer. If he prayed on these rides, the elevator operators never knew it. According to one old-timer, now a starter in Rockefeller Center, Luce always chatted with him. Another, who wanted to become a film editor, got a beginning job with *The March of Time* as a result of his elevator conversations with Luce. After the company's offices were moved to the new Time & Life Building in 1960, Luce took the self-service elevators along with everybody else.

I really don't know anybody in the company who doesn't exhibit a certain amount of moral cowardice in dealing with you. . . . You . . . feel frustrated that so often "the Luce Publications" don't follow the lines that you, the author of their beings, would like to see them follow. Nevertheless, the fact remains: people are afraid of you. It is an anomaly, but there it is.

And here's another anomaly. . . . I have seen you abandon, without the slightest trace of a hurt ego, some pet idea that you have had because somebody punctured it. . . . And yet . . . you are acquiring a reputation for being dictatorial. At various staff meetings everyone, of course, looks to you and defers to you, as they should. You have more ideas per minute on all sorts of subjects than anybody else in the company and very often these spill out too volubly. And on more than one occasion somebody who can't get a word in edgewise comes to the mistaken conclusion: "Harry doesn't want to *listen* anymore." [4]

So your remoteness works two ways: it makes people afraid of you and it makes some people who are not particularly afraid of you reluctant to get involved with you because they wonder if you really understand their minute day-by-day or hour-by-hour or deadline emergencies; the *understanding* which used to exist so universally between you and the staff of ten or fifteen years ago is now blurred by the fact that you and they are living in different worlds.

Hodgins suggested then that all through the coming politically turbulent year Luce make every effort to remain as close to the editors of *Time* as he could. He added that he wished Luce "were not so *committedly* a Republican" because

I know that throughout the company the doctrine of "my party, right or wrong," is almost impossible to cram down anybody's throat. I often ask myself this question: If the Republicans in

[4] This was not the first time Luce had been criticized for his conversational habits. Earlier Grover had written him this memo: "Subject: Banging on the Table. Your conversation is usually *very* good—sometimes lengthy, but really very good. Anyway, I enjoy it. In fact, it is good enough so that you don't have to emphasize it by banging on the table with all the cutlery at hand, knives, forks, spoons, etc., not to mention that ring which you use to great advantage if there isn't a fork handy. I mention this because several people recently have remarked that your conversation is getting noisier than a Tommy-gun drill."

1944 nominate a man like John W. Bricker, "the honest Harding," what will Harry do? If you were to become a Bricker man because he was the party's nominee, an awful lot of people around here will be appalled and will think, "Well, now we've finally lost forever the Harry that we used to know."

Luce replied:

There are a few scattered points I ought to make. . . . It is, of course, very difficult to generalize about the question of how to be a successful "Head Man." . . . On the one hand, there is the ideal picture of the friendly, familiar boss; on the other, the aloof but correct, protocol, "through channels" chief executive. Perhaps I have exhibited the faults of both and the merits of neither. Certainly, to judge from results, my attempts at "familiarity" are discouraging. . . . For four years I have been "closer" to the "personnel" of *Time* than of any other publication. My relations with *Life* and *Fortune* have been handled in much more "executive" manner through Managing or Executive Editors. The ultimate logic of this would be that the further away I get the better for all concerned. . . . As to my talking too much and not listening. You are quite right. I have been worried about this and will try to correct. (Aside from sheer garrulity, it's been partly the result of a desire to disclose my whole mind without reservation.)

Shortly after this exchange, a Time Inc. correspondent answered a question posed to him by Soviet Ambassador Andrei Gromyko as to who was the *Time* policy maker on Russia by explaining that a number of people handled the Russian stories and that there was no single policy maker. The answer was thoroughly discouraging to Luce, and he complained about it to Grover:

Don't you think that Time Inc. staffers and Public Relations men might be made a little less hesitant about acknowledging that there is such a character as the Editor-in-chief and that he is not quite as innocuous as President Whosis of Russia? Of course the main trouble is Time Incers' horror of recognizing any such monstrosity as Policy at all. . . . God knows I am plenty and regularly embarrassed by seeming (to myself at least) to be somehow responsible for everything in *Time, Life,* etc. But to combine this embarrassment with the embarrassment of continually

78

finding myself to be the little man who wasn't there—is an embarrassment of the riches of embarrassment.

At Luce's request Hodgins drafted a statement in which he tried to get over the point that "Policy and having one was not an awful and shameful thing." But when it was distributed to the staff, another row was kicked up, and Gottfried said he feared that "it will undo all my efforts to get writers to realize that they are responsible journalists and not merely guys who are hired to 'write for the boss.' "

The policy debate had one important by-product: Time Inc., with President Robert Hutchins of the University of Chicago, launched a commission under the auspices of the university to ponder freedom of the press. "What was uppermost in my mind," Luce said, "were my own troubles as Editor or Editor-Publisher. I thought I knew enough about the nature of things to know that the troubles of my occupation were related to philosophy and morals—even more directly and immediately than is the case with most occupations. Furthermore I was aware . . . that the contemporary world of thought and moral philosophy was in a somewhat acute state of confusion—and that therefore 'correct' answers to philosophical and moral questions of the day were not readily available but could be supplied, if at all, only by the very best philosophical talent and effort." A panel of distinguished scholars began a three-year investigation.[5]

On February 11, 1944, Luce made still another effort to persuade his colleagues to align the Time Inc. magazines behind the Republican Party. He invited fourteen of his senior editors and corporate executives to a meeting and dinner at the Pillement Suite of the Waldorf-Astoria; each of the invitees received in advance a nine-and-

[5] Luce was disappointed in the Freedom of the Press Commission's General Report, finally published in 1947, which he believed was "philosophically uninteresting." *Fortune* published the full text as a supplement in its April 1947 issue with an accompanying editorial expressing disappointment in the report's superficiality. The commission felt that the primary threat to freedom of the press came from bigness and a lack of quality in the mass media and went on to suggest a doctrine of accountability. In the matter of bigness Luce believed that the commission had overlooked the proliferation of small newspapers and other periodicals as well as avenues of expression opened by the dominant electronic medium of radio. On quality he felt that the press was doing a fairly good job with news but needed to give more thought to culture. On accountability the commission was not sufficiently explicit for Luce who wanted to know who was accountable to whom for what.

a-half-page memorandum which began: "The topic for discussion at the meeting Friday at 4:59 p.m. is Time Inc.'s stand in the 1944 elections. It is to be hoped that we can arrive at some well-defined and soundly based conclusions within a few weeks, if not at this meeting." The meeting began on schedule, broke for dinner (breast of native guinea hen with juniper berries, salad and cheese) and then went on to break up finally after midnight.

The memo deposed that the issue between Roosevelt and the Republicans had not yet been drawn clearly, and until it was, the importance or non-importance of the election could not be clear in the editors' minds. The memo then proceeded to the question of Willkie. "Willkie is, at this date, my personal preference for the Republican nomination. But the political position with which I have less sympathy than any other is the one which says: 'If the Republicans don't nominate Willkie, I'll vote for Roosevelt.' . . . The Willkie-or-else position must be based on one of two grounds. One, that he is the only Republican who is individually capable of properly discharging the office of President." He thought that was nonsense. "The other ground for the Willkie-or-else position is that he and he alone represents enlightenment or liberalism in the Republican Party." He thought this a somewhat better argument, but he would ask the Willkie-or-else people: "Are you in fact New Dealers? Why do you want a *Republican* New Dealer?" He answered the question for them: "You'd like to have a change—without change." Which brought him back to the question of issue: "Is there a fundamental issue trying to get itself expressed between the Republican Party and Roosevelt? If there isn't—let's relax. If there is such an issue, then there is no warrant for saying that it cannot be represented except by one certain man."

The "Willkie-or-else" position had its effect on Time Inc. Russell Davenport resigned as chief editorial writer for *Life,* because of his health, it was announced. His colleagues knew that the real reason was that he had given up hope of Willkie's candidacy and had decided in that case to vote for Roosevelt. He did not want to write editorials supporting any other Republican candidate. John Knox Jessup, who had been an editor both of *Fortune* and *Time* and had succeeded Raymond Buell as chairman of Time Inc.'s Postwar Department, was chosen to replace him.

Grover kept rough notes on the Waldorf discussion; they conclude with the comment: "Discussion of *Time* objectivity—it's been going

80

on for at least 12 years—and went on until 12:30. No general conclusion on this point but vaguely general agreement." The notes pretty
clearly indicate that those present, Luce excepted, showed no great
enthusiasm for espousing the Republican cause.

Three days after the dinner Willkie formally announced his candidacy. He risked everything on the Wisconsin primary. He was the
only declared candidate on the slate, but he was opposed by delegates
pledged to Minnesota Governor Harold Stassen, MacArthur, and
those supporting the man whom *Time* called "the glistening dark
horse who pretends to be invisible"—New York Governor Thomas
E. Dewey. Willkie for the moment seemed his old fighting self, making forty speeches in thirteen days, flaying the New Deal domestic
policies and Old Guard Republicans for their isolationism. He suffered a humiliating defeat: Dewey won seventeen delegates, Stassen
four, MacArthur three and Willkie none.

Luce was editing *Time* that week, and the story on Willkie's defeat
reflected his own feelings:

> Wisconsin had clearly voted no confidence in global good will
> and a foreign policy of generalities. They had voted against the
> "crusade" kind of internationalism—against a crusade which
> had never been clearly defined, which was hopelessly confused
> with New Dealism, and which neither Mr. Roosevelt nor Mr.
> Hull seemed yet to have joined. To say nothing of Messrs.
> Churchill and Stalin. No one could doubt the Wisconsin voters'
> willingness to "participate" internationally, but they want to do
> it on a "realistic" basis—and as Republicans. . . . Wisconsin,
> it seemed, had voted out of the way a massive road-block on the
> way to realistic internationalism.

*Time*'s story shocked some of Luce's associates. Matthews, who considered the Wisconsin primary "a political tragedy," wrote him: "The
story gave me the impression that after all, it was a pretty good
thing—now the Republican Party can proceed unimpeded on its way
toward that old realistic internationalism. . . . Well, *maybe*. Personally, I doubt every word of it." Gottfried objected to running the
story under the heading of "The Nation"; he argued that "anyone
who regards himself as a Democrat—as presumably about half the
nation does—can hardly help feeling that only partisans could regard
the fortunes of one party's candidates as the working of a nation as
a whole."

81

"I am by no means entirely happy with the 'Wisconsin' story," Luce admitted. "However, I would have been even less happy with a story which Friend Willkie would wholly have approved of. Essentially there was one important paragraph missing . . . which should have said, yes, this *was* a defeat for 'internationalism' and a victory for 'isolationism.'. . . Yes BUT—In effect we jumped too fast to the 'But,' omitting the 'Yes.'. . . Just a word as to what has been happening in the last few months. . . . The 'United Nations' concept has become almost meaningless. The Smuts speech rallying Empire,[6] the almost blatant lone-handedness of Russia, the strident announcement of de Gaulle that nobody was going to give orders to France . . . point to the relative meaninglessness of United Nations compared to the meaningfulness of what we may call 'nationalism.' The mistake of the Willkie internationalists is a failure to revise their projection of internationalism in order to fit the facts. . . . An American consciousness of American national interest is an essential stage of development of internationalism."

On his return from Wisconsin Willkie met Luce over the dinner table at the home of Luce's sister, Mrs. Maurice T. Moore. Luce later recorded what happened: "It was clear that he was angry, but conversation remained polite until, at dessert, something touched him off. His face became a bowl of fury. He half rose and I really thought this giant of a man was going to reach across my sister and sock me. He restrained himself except for saying: 'Harry, you may be the world's best editor, but you are certainly the world's worst politician.' An odd thing to say since it was the *Time* story that had made him so angry." Some days later Willkie wrote Luce, not to apologize but to explain:

I thought the article misstated the facts . . . and therefore drew erroneous conclusions. Naturally, being human and in view of your many expressions of friendship for me, I thought it appropriate to call your attention to what I, at least, thought an undeserved blow at a time when the blows were coming rather thick. . . . But forget it. I am the first to recognize your complete right to express any opinion you have in publications which

[6] South Africa's prime minister, Field Marshal Jan Christiaan Smuts, in a speech in London in November 1943 had proposed that the self-governing dominions share with the mother country the administrative burdens of the colonies. It was essentially a plea for the tightening of the bonds of commonwealth and empire.

you own. . . . I do hope you have more luck in shaping the Republican Party than I have had. Perhaps after some experience in your new endeavor you will decide that your field is journalism where I, and all others who can recognize obvious merit, know you as the number one.

A cable that Luce sent to C. D. Jackson, who was by then with the Psychological Warfare Division of SHAEF in London, left no doubt that he actually welcomed Willkie's defeat notwithstanding his personal respect and friendship. He said he felt "a certain sense of relief from a long and painful situation. Republicans are now, as it were, on their own to develop as Republicans. If any voter doesn't like what they do, he can vote for the Democrats. So why should anybody get psychotic? Incidentally, people regarded by me as shrewdest believe Roosevelt's re-election unlikely."

In June 1944, just before the Republican convention, Luce announced another important change in editorial management: John Shaw Billings, the managing editor of *Life* since its first issue, became editorial director of Time Inc., and executive editor Daniel Longwell, a founding father of the picture magazine, succeeded him as managing editor. The change was not made because of any dissatisfaction with *Life;* under Billings *Life* was a smooth-flowing operation and during the war reached its peak in performance.

Luce's desire to have Billings associated directly with him as editorial director stemmed, so he explained, from a certain dissatisfaction with his own performance. "I have never been able to run the job of Editor-in-chief really efficiently," he told his senior colleagues. "There is a job for a sort of Inspector-General who *systematically* inspects and systematically does something about what his inspection reveals." Billings was a natural choice because Luce and he had worked together harmoniously ever since the days when Billings took over the managing editorship of *Time* in November 1933.[7] In his views on life and politics Billings was more conservative than Luce, but he was not a man to impose his political convictions on others and in such matters was content to follow Luce's lead.

Billings had been a superb administrator. He was firm, decisive and methodical. He had delegated much of the creative side of *Life* to Dan Longwell and had left the procurement of pictures and the

[7] *Time Inc. 1923–1941*, pp. 201–3.

handling of the photographers to the other executive editor, Wilson Hicks. In his large cork-lined office, over the long layout tables, Billings chose what went into the magazine and made the layouts. While the staff was a little in awe of this big, quiet-spoken man and addressed him as "Mr. Billings," he was well liked—a true father figure in the midst of a lively company of young people. Though Billings never evidenced strain or stress, the work had impaired his health, and there was no doubt that he welcomed the proposal for a change. When Luce outlined the new job, he had only one reservation: "You know my point—my only point, really—i.e., I don't want to lose my identity as a practicing journalist and editor in the Olympian mists of corporate responsibilities."

In announcing the change to the staff, Luce made, at least on paper, a grant of direct editorial authority second only to his own. In the past, he wrote, the managing editors had been responsible to the editor-in-chief: "Hereafter as heretofore, the Editor-in-chief will consult with Managing Editors and others. But all decisions directly affecting editorial operations will be made by the Editorial Director. The authority of the Editor-in-chief will be exercised by the Editorial Director. The authority of Managing Editors will be subject to the Editorial Director—and to no one else."

Billings passed into the "Olympian mists" in spite of himself. He functioned very efficiently as Luce's deputy, a role he understood, intervening as little as possible, using his authority with the managing editors with great restraint, on occasion fulfilling the role of mediator between them and the editor-in-chief. Inevitably, because of the very nature of the job, Billings' own worst fears were realized: he became less and less the practicing journalist, more and more the staff officer, and thus his new eminence brought him few of the satisfactions that had been his as managing editor.

The candidate for the Republican nomination whom *Time*'s editor-in-chief liked least was the man who appeared to be the likeliest to win the nomination—Thomas E. Dewey. Nevertheless, Luce was personally embarrassed and displeased because he felt that *Time* and *Life* had treated the New York governor too roughly. The March 20 issue of *Life* had carried a full-page picture of Dewey at his rarely used desk in the executive chamber of the Capitol with the caption: "The desk in this room is so large, the chair so deep, that Tom Dewey sits on two telephone books when being photographed here."

84

Both *Time* and *Life* had carried pictures of Dewey dwarfed by his pet Great Dane, pictures that gave rise to a quip for the opposition, "I think I'll vote for the big man with the little dog." [8] Dewey's stiff, humorless and overbearing manner made him a target for writers, cartoonists and photographers; they resented the slick professionalism of this young man of forty-two who, long before the convention assembled, seemed to have the Republican nomination in his pocket.

Luce himself was reluctant to accept Dewey's nomination as a *fait accompli.* In an editorial *Life* advised the Republicans that before "stampeding to Dewey" they consider the claims of midwestern candidates, naming as possible alternatives Stassen of Minnesota, Ohio Governor Bricker or either of the Ohio senators, Harold H. Burton or Robert A. Taft. In its issue of June 26, published shortly before the convention assembled, the magazine carried a profile of Stassen by associate editor Robert Coughlan. Luce told his managing editors, "This article will dramatically speak up for all those who are not 'satisfied' with either Dewey or Roosevelt." The message was clearly spelled out by Coughlan, who predicted that the election would probably be fought between Roosevelt and Dewey but "to a considerable number of voters . . . it will all seem a little tiresome. . . . It is not exciting to be forced to choose between two inadequacies. . . . It is . . . plain to a lot of people that Stassen is the Perfect Republican Candidate for the election of 1944."

Willkie was also making a last-minute effort to stop Dewey, whom he thoroughly disliked, and he enlisted Luce's help. Willkie would have none of Stassen who he said had welshed on a promise to support his candidacy, but he would be happy to support Governor Leverett Saltonstall of Massachusetts. Luce recalled, "Naturally, Willkie's hope could be—it was his only hope—that if the convention got deadlocked, he might have a chance." As the Chicago convention got under way, a small group met and agreed to put forward the Massachusetts governor.

"Within an hour or two, Saltonstall came in," Luce reported. "A couple of people took him into a bedroom. Fifteen minutes later they came out—obviously, Saltonstall wasn't having any." Luce found that as he "roamed around the Convention Hall . . . it was clear that the Dewey organization had everything well in hand. But there was plenty of anti-Dewey talk. What I remember of the convention

[8] Roosevelt was often pictured with his Scottish terrier, Fala.

itself were speeches by ex-President Hoover and by Clare Boothe Luce. The hall was gaily decorated; the speeches, in the atmosphere of wartime intensity, were wildly applauded. But the man who really had the affection of the convention was Senator Bricker [who was nominated for the vice presidency]. There must have been a lot of cheering and roaring for Dewey when his time came but it has faded from my memory. All I remember is that Dewey had it from start to finish, but not *con amore.*"

Mrs. Luce's speech was, indeed, a sensation of that convention and an occasion for *Time* editors to break the rule that she was not to be mentioned in the Time Inc. magazines. The speech was an attack on Roosevelt, cheered by ardent Republicans, attacked by Democrats as "cheap demagoguery." Mrs. Luce undertook to tell the story of "G.I. Jim," the dead buddy of G.I. Joe—"the heroic heir of the unheroic Roosevelt decade." She asked whether Jim's death was "historically inevitable" and concluded: "Might not skillful and determined American statesmanship have helped to unmake [the war] all through the thirties? . . . These are bitter questions. . . . But it was not a Republican President who dealt with the visibly rising menaces of Hitler and Mussolini and Hirohito."

*Time,* which went to press on the same night the convention opened, made a brief mention of the speech, written from an advance text; it accompanied this with a picture, taken from the rear, showing Mrs. Luce getting into a car. *Life,* which closed the following Saturday, like *Time* made no editorial comment on the speech but it did have a more flattering picture, together with a caption which gave a slightly fuller summary of what she said. Luce was disappointed that *Time* failed to report the convention's reaction to the speech in the issue of the following week, and he complained to Gottfried. The fact was that Mrs. Luce, angered by *Time*'s picture, had insisted to Gottfried that the editors revert to their previous rule and make no further mention of her. Gottfried explained this to Luce, who was apparently unaware of his wife's intervention, and declared furthermore that a follow-up story on the speech would have been an embarrassment: "You naturally heard from the people who liked it but it was a speech that had its partisans and anti-partisans even among Republicans. That being the case we should have had to report both reactions. . . . I can only assure you that there was not one bit of prejudice that entered into that decision—nor was there any principle. . . . This was a case where expedience would serve *Time* and the public better than valor." Luce replied:

I quite understand the reasonableness of your decision. Nevertheless I regret it—for I disagree as to one point. I believe that *Time* did have every justification for saying something to the effect that to millions of listeners Clare's speech was tremendously moving. The justification for saying this essentially is the fact that the overwhelming majority of non-Rooseveltians thought it was a wow. . . . The point is that here was a chance to say that the wife of the Editor of *Time* had done good—at least on *her* team. And I think the point in popular psychology which you miss is that people think it is not "noble" but just strangely inhuman that the editors of *Time* should never, by any fluke, find a good word for the boss's wife. . . .

A little later in the summer, in a "private and confidential" memorandum to the senior editors of the magazines, Luce wrote:

The matter of Clare Boothe Luce seems to be recognized as a definite "Time Inc." problem. . . . I take this opportunity to make the point in order that you may be sure to understand one of the human aspects of the situation. Anyone who goes into politics must expect to take plenty of attacks and even smears. At the same time, practically all politicians can expect to get a lot of puffing and praising from their own side. And Clare has had more than her full share of attacks. But she has so far got relatively little puffing and praising . . . from her own side. . . . *One* of the reasons is that other publications—both newspapers and magazines—are not over eager to give strong favorable publicity to the wife of Publisher Luce. Meanwhile, for many years one of the main smears against her has been the thousand-time repeated allegation that she owes practically everything to the enormous press buildup she has received in the enormously powerful Luce press. It is, I think you will agree, a bit tough on her.[9]

---

[9] Commenting on the manuscript of this book to the author, Mrs. Luce wrote: "I was greatly touched by the memoranda Harry sent his editors on the score of *Time*'s handling of his wife. What a rough thing it all was on him, too. Vis-à-vis me, he always defended the editors. When I wasn't around, he defended me to his editors. You know, I never knew this before."

Mrs. Luce became a prime Democratic target in the 1944 campaign; several Cabinet officers and the President himself elected to speak for her opponent and against her in her congressional district. Listening to the President on the radio on election night, Mrs. Luce heard Roosevelt announce that the returns indicated that she would be defeated, adding, "I think [that] would be a very good thing for the country and that is a rough thing to say about a lady." A little later her husband came into the room, and when she told him what Roosevelt had said a grin spread across his face. "Well," said Luce, "the President is certainly wrong about this one." The returns by this time showed that Mrs. Luce's re-election was assured: she won by a margin of 2,000 votes. *Time* on this occasion did have a "good word for the boss's wife"; it saluted her victory thus: "A freshman Congresswoman had passed over to the old campaigners' ranks."

Notwithstanding his lack of enthusiasm for Dewey, Luce personally supported the party ticket even to the extent of trying to win Willkie's endorsement for the candidate. Willkie was undecided as to whether or not he would support the Republican ticket; he was known to be disaffected and to be receiving tentative feelers from the White House to align himself with Roosevelt. Luce invited Willkie to dinner at his apartment with the chairman of the Republican National Committee, Herbert Brownell, and wrote this account of the occasion:

> We had a basic document for discussion: Dewey's opening campaign speech on foreign policy. . . . Willkie came in, looking more than ever like a huge woolly bear—but a bear in a bad, dangerous mood. . . . He nit-picked here and there but, sure enough, he had to say that it met his (Willkie's) test of being "right" on postwar foreign policy. Willkie shifted his attack to the character of Dewey. . . .
>
> Dinner came in. It was a painful hour. Willkie behaved atrociously—grumbling, growling and saying everything he could think of against Dewey. . . . Dinner was taken away. Whiskey came. The animal force of Willkie mounted as he lashed out in all directions. Finally, around midnight, Willkie got up and lumbered off. Brownell went over to the couch and flopped. I sank into my big chair. . . . Neither of us said a word for minutes and minutes. When we finally aroused ourselves, we agreed that maybe the important job had been done—Willkie had a chance to get everything off his sour belly and had seen how much

88

Dewey, with my full accord, wanted his support. A week or so later I was going to England to have a look at the buzz-bombs and I felt I had to have a serious talk with Wendell before I left. Wendell talked very dispassionately and reasonably. . . . However, it was going to be tough for him to come out strongly for Dewey. Our long talk ended with Willkie saying he would do nothing until I got back and that we would talk again. . . . Either before or very soon after I got back from England, Willkie collapsed of a heart attack. . . . He lingered on for a [month] at the hospital. I wrote him one or two notes of friendship. But I did not ask to see him because to see him was to talk politics—it was the main bond between us and it was, of course, his absorbing interest.

The funeral service was held in the spacious Fifth Avenue Presbyterian Church. The poem "God Give Us Men!" was read. It was extraordinarily appropriate: Wendell Willkie was a mighty man.

Luce was depressed at the outlook for the 1944 presidential race. "It may be impossible to interest anybody (even ourselves) in anything much in this campaign," he wrote. He did his best in the weeks to come by flooding his editors with suggestions for political stories and arguments as to why this was no Tweedledum and Tweedledee affair. But all issues paled beside the war which Roosevelt was at that point waging victoriously. Dewey had great difficulty in coming to grips with his opponent; the attacks on the failure of the New Deal and the worn-out old men in Washington seemed irrelevant to the obviously successful conduct of a global war. And *Time*'s editors could not be inspired to any enthusiasm for the Republican candidate. Early in October Luce wrote to managing editor Matthews:

I asked Publisher Prentice what he thought about *Time*'s handling of election news. . . . He said that the question needed two answers. "Journalistically," he thought *Time* was doing just fine—spilling beans, revealing card tricks, etc. But, he said, if you want to know whether *Time* has given any slightest hint that Luce is for Dewey—the answer is No. He didn't think any recent story had done Dewey any good. I'm sure his verdict will be a real comfort to those who think the political convictions of *Time*'s Editor should be completely obscured in *Time*.

Luce tried logic, cajolery and, as in this case, sarcasm, to bring his staff to see things his way, but that was as far as he would go. When a reader wrote him saying that he owed it to America to "state unequivocally the position" of *Time, Life* and *Fortune* in respect to the election, Luce wrote a letter so frank that, on second thought, he never mailed it:

> *Life* has an editorial page, clearly so labeled. So has *Fortune*. Every week or month the opinions of their editors—the reflections of what you call "prejudices and interests"—are there displayed for all who wish to read, agree with, consign to hell-fire or otherwise react to. But, you say, *Time* has no such editorial page. True enough. There is more than one reason why, but one very potent reason is that the staff of *Time* has in the past disagreed with my feeling that it should have one. . . .
>
> I am a Republican. There have been occasions when I have voted against a candidate or a program espoused by the party to which, most of the time, I consider I belong. And I hope my convictions are not so unalterable that such a time might never come again.
>
> A magazine like *Time* . . . is in its nature much more concerned with the political scene than *Life* or *Fortune* will ever be. For all you know, I might personally very much like to commit *Time* to a down-the-line espousal of *all* the political doctrines that appeal to me as an individual. But the satisfaction I would be likely to get from that might turn out to be a very short-range satisfaction indeed compared to the satisfaction of continuing to see on *Time* a staff that continues to think for itself: influenced, perhaps, in ways by no means always known to me, by what *it* thinks *I* think, but still making evident every week that it reserves to itself its own opinions.
>
> Does this pragmatic attitude have its drawbacks? Indeed it does. Sometimes I cannot for the life of me understand why a *Time* writer or editor saw a set of facts as he did, when I see them so differently. Sometimes *Time* is accused of an inconsistency and I must agree with the accusation. Sometimes *Time*— and I along with it—gets stigmatized as a hopeless old stick-in-the-mud; sometimes both of us appear as Dangerous Radicals— all depending upon who is doing the criticizing.
>
> When the day comes that I consider my political opinions as

final, unchangeable, and the last word, then I shall have no recourse but to lock the steering gear on *Time* and proceed in a
straight line thenceforth forever, to whatever terminal my intellectual journeys take me. But I still fall short of such ultimate
certainties.

But, as Luce said, *Life was* different, and in 1944, for the first time,
the magazine came out unequivocally for a candidate; in the 1940
campaign Luce had almost but not quite declared for Willkie, settling in the end for an article, signed by himself, emphasizing the
importance of the election. Jack Jessup, who wrote the sequence of
three editorials declaring for Dewey, remembered that Luce told
him he had written and stashed away in his desk drawer his own
editorials just in case Jessup's contribution did not measure up.

A *Time* cover story on Dewey, published in the October 23 issue,
did present the case for the Republican candidate and reported a
gain in Republican prospects and hopes: "State by state, there was a
Republican surge of strength. GOP chairman Herb Brownell joked
about hiring a few pessimists, to keep him from getting too happy.
He said he couldn't believe all the glowing good news that flooded in;
for if the reports were true, or even close to the truth, Tom Dewey
was not only elected, but by a landslide." In the next issue *Time*
said: "By all counts this was one of the queerest, bitterest—and
closest—of all the Presidential races in U.S. history. . . . The polls
were indecisive—if they showed anything it was that Dewey had
drawn nearly level since midsummer. (Only the gamblers saw it as
3–to–1 for Roosevelt, and not much money was being bet.)"

An important issue of the campaign was one that—as *Time* said
—"Tom Dewey could not make, with any taste, although others were
making it for him. That was the issue of the President's age and
health, which are respectively 62 and pretty good." The magazine
quoted the White House physician, Vice Admiral Ross T. McIntire,
that there was "nothing wrong organically with him at all. He's perfectly O.K. . . . The stories that he is in bad health are understand-
able enough around election time, but they are not true." To meet
the issue head on, Roosevelt elected to show himself in New York,
Philadelphia and Chicago; the New York trip was made in the cold
drizzle of a chill Saturday afternoon in October. *Time* reported:
"Most of the time the President was smiling, and the chill and the
rain brought a pink glow to his face. At times he relaxed, and when

91

he did so, the sallowness in his cheeks showed, and the heavy lines on his face; then he looked tired. Pictures of him smiling or tired were taken by all newspapers, and they made their selections according to their political sympathies. Some thought the performance bravura, others brave."

"The big irresponsibility—or the big failure of the American press," Luce recalled some years later, "came in 1944 when we did not indicate, especially in *Life*'s pictures, that Roosevelt was a dying man." Managing editor Longwell called Luce in to see the pictures of the Roosevelt tour. Luce remembered: "He showed me, oh, a hundred pictures of Roosevelt—two hundred. In about half of them he was a dead man! But we just decided 'No, let's print the ones that are the least bad.' And thereby—by trying to lean over being fair or something—or kind—we infringed our contract with readers to tell them the truth. Actually, that truth *was* in the pictures."

In reporting the election result, *Time* concluded:

It was Franklin Roosevelt in a walk-away. His popular percentage was a shade lower than in 1940, his Electoral College vote a smashing victory. Once the returns began piling in, there was never any doubt.

The people did more than reject a tradition against extra Presidential terms. They reversed a historic decision of 25 years ago, when the U.S. embraced isolationism after World War I. In the 1944 election no isolationist could find comfort. . . .

Probably the biggest if least exciting factor in the election was a widespread feeling that the U.S. could not risk changing Presidents in wartime.[10]

Luce was disappointed, but in a letter to Republican Representative John M. Vorys of Ohio, whom he had known at Yale, he confessed, "I am not feeling too badly about the outcome." However, he did feel "an exhaustion of frustration [after] five or six years of pretty intense effort," as he described it to an associate. Willkie's failure rankled more than Dewey's defeat, for, Luce said, "I believe that the

[10] In covering the President at the polling booth on election day, *Time* described his irritation when the lever of the voting machine did not work and quoted him as saying, "The goddamned thing won't work." This brought a flood of mail and a Roosevelt denial that he had taken the Lord's name in vain. But *Time* stood behind its reporter who, it said, was about five feet away when the incident occurred.

Republican Party of 1944 was . . . a good risk for America. And I could see no other half-good risk. That is why I felt it was so tragic that Willkie was making an ideological camel's-eye test for the party—especially, and, yes, I say it with some bitterness, especially as it was so easy to construct an ideological camel's-eye through which by no possibility could Willkie have passed. God rest his soul."

The battle and Luce's partisanship had been hard on *Time*'s staff. One casualty of the 1944 campaign was the U.S. at War editor, Sidney Olson. Olson was a young man who played an important part in the education of a generation of Time Inc. editors in practical politics. Utah born and educated, Olson, after a stint in Salt Lake City journalism, came east to try his hand in Washington, landing a reportorial berth on the Washington *Post*'s city desk. His advancement on the *Post* was rapid and he became the youngest city editor that the paper had ever had; in 1939 he received an offer from *Time*. He had a lot to learn about *Time* writing, but *Time* editors, notably the editor in charge of National Affairs, T. S. Matthews, learned a lot about practical politics from Olson. Olson knew the ways of Washington and a lot about grass roots electioneering, subjects which up to that point were largely a closed book to graduates of Eastern universities. In the 1940 campaign he wrote the controversial story in which *Time* sought to explain the crowds that gathered around Willkie despite his faltering campaign: "as one sad Old Guardsman pontificated to another: dead whales on flat cars also attract crowds." In 1942, when Matthews was in Britain, Olson served temporarily as assistant managing editor; shortly after Matthews became managing editor in his own right, Olson was appointed senior editor in charge of the U.S. at War section to relieve Eric Hodgins.

Because he shared Luce's absorbing interest in politics, Olson gained Luce's confidence and friendship, an association that also worked to his disadvantage: it brought him under suspicion by Matthews and other staff members of being as partisan a Republican as Luce and of writing and editing to please the boss. Though Matthews and Olson did not come to an open break, the tension during the 1944 campaign was such that shortly before the election Olson asked Luce to relieve him of the U.S. at War post once it was over. Besides everything else, he was bored with politics after five years in the department. "I've had it," he wrote Luce. Olson thus took himself out of the line for promotion on *Time*, where he had often been spoken

93

of as a future managing editor. He asked for a roving commission as a war correspondent, and following the election went overseas, turned in some distinguished reporting and later returned to become a staff writer for both *Life* and *Fortune*. But the executive ranks never again opened up to him. An ambitious and proud man, Olson resigned in 1950 to leave journalism and enter public relations and advertising. He had a successful career as a vice president of the J. Walter Thompson agency.

# "The Ghosts on the Roof" and Other Spectres

U NTIL LATE in the war, a majority of Americans looked upon their Soviet ally with cordial feelings of friendship and admiration, and thought benevolently of Stalin as Uncle Joe; and looking westward, they cheered on the Chinese under Chiang Kai-shek who were suffering under the Japanese invaders. But as the Soviet ascendancy in Eastern Europe took shape and flaws in Chiang's government became plain, Americans began slowly to divide, both on the possibilities of a peaceful postwar world with a powerful Communist dictatorship and of a united, democratic China under the regime of Chiang Kai-shek.

In the critical campaigns of the winter of 1942–43 and summer of 1943, at a terrible cost to themselves the Russians tore the heart out of the invading Nazi armies. Their colossal sacrifice wiped clean for a time Americans' past suspicions of Communism and the memory of their consternation at the Nazi-Soviet Pact of 1939. The Russians were the heroes of the hour. Typical of the mood during the period was a special issue of *Life* in March 1943, the first issue ever devoted to a single country. It was a journalistic *tour de force*, brought off in the face of initial, and characteristic, Soviet hostility to the foreign press. As the *Life* editorial explained:

Putting this issue together was quite an adventure. *Life* Correspondent Walter Graebner was in charge of the field work in Moscow, and he had a tough job. At that time the Russians were angry at *Life* because of some captions that they claimed were "unfriendly to the U.S.S.R." But even if they had loved us, they had almost no photographers available, and there was a desperate shortage of film, flashbulbs and photographic paper. The problem was partly solved with captured German film; and at the last minute photographic paper was flown in from—of all places—Leningrad, which was tightly locked in siege but which happened to have a small supply. Various official agencies came to our aid. . . . And we finally got four photographers.

The principal article in the issue was by Joseph E. Davies, a former U.S. ambassador to the Soviet Union. A capitalist of impeccable credentials, which included marriage to the multimillionaire heiress Marjorie Post Hutton, Davies believed that postwar unity depended on the cooperation given by Great Britain and the United States to the peace-loving Soviet Union. His view of Russia was so uncritical that it provoked at least one caveat from within the organization. *Life*'s general manager Andrew Heiskell wrote to the editors: "A quick reading . . . gives you the impression that Joe and his pals are St. Peter and the archangels and that Americans are right at present in purgatory with an option on Heaven if they will behave themselves." There were a few outside critics: the Chicago *Journal of Commerce* thought the editors were so carried away by good will toward the Russian people that they seemed "to have nothing but resounding praise for the Communist Party."

But the Writers' War Board, a semiofficial group of authors organized to mobilize patriotic sentiment, applauded *Life,* and the St. Louis *Post-Dispatch* declared the issue to be "a contribution to international understanding that can scarcely be over-estimated." The Russians' reaction was reserved: the Soviet ambassador to the United States, Maxim Litvinov, said that "in general [the issue] was fair." [1]

In an editorial some weeks after the issue *Life* reported that four-fifths of the letters received expressed general approbation and one-

---

[1] The editors prepared a specially bound copy for presentation to Stalin and asked the Soviet embassy to translate the cover inscription, "To Generalissimo Stalin from the Editors of *Life,*" into Russian. Too late, a Russian expert pointed out that the translation read, "To Comrade Stalin from the workers of *Life* Magazine."

fifth were critical, the criticism ranging from "modulated complaint to apoplectic abuse." The editorial concluded, therefore, that ". . . there exists an instinctive basis for understanding between the two peoples. This does not mean that we should overlook or laugh off the political differences which separate the U.S. from the U.S.S.R. Indeed it is all the more important to establish some basis of mutual admiration and trust because the unresolved issues between the two nations are so great. . . . We think the American people and their government are willing and eager to break down these impalpable barriers of the mind and assure the Russian people of our sympathy and good will. . . . So we hope that someday soon the Soviet Union will shed the shell of secrecy within which it now dwells, candidly state its aims and aspirations . . . and thereby make it possible for the two great Federal Republics to cooperate on a basis of mutual respect." Such were the roseate hopes of 1943.

In March 1944 *Time* noted a change in the diplomatic climate; an article entitled "Cause for Alarm" reported the evident deterioration in relations among the Big Three—the United States, Great Britain and Russia—since the Teheran Conference of November 1943. The article reported a new note of unease and suspicion about Soviet intentions: leading American columnists were disposed to place at least some of the blame on the Roosevelt Administration for its failure to clarify U.S. objectives; Arthur Krock of the New York *Times* predicted, "Because of the fog that masks our policy and has produced diplomatic inaction . . . Soviet Russia will dominate the postwar structure."

*Life* then ran probably the first article in a major U.S. magazine to sound a loud alarm on the aggressive postwar objectives of the Soviet Union. It appeared in the issue of September 4, 1944. Though the headline was innocuous—"The World from Rome"—the subtitle signaled the explosive message: "The Eternal City Fears a Struggle between Christianity and Communism."

The author was William C. Bullitt. Scion of a wealthy Philadelphia family, Bullitt as a young diplomat had been a member of the American delegation at the Versailles Peace Conference. He had headed a secret mission to Lenin's Soviet government in 1919 and returned with arrangements for a peace settlement and recommendations for recognition of the revolutionary regime. When his diplomatic efforts were rejected, Bullitt resigned, and, after gaining widespread notoriety with revelations about the Versailles negotiations that were

97

damaging to the Wilson Administration, he retired to private life. After a divorce from his first wife, he married the widow of John Reed, the American writer and a hero of the Communist revolution, who is buried under the Kremlin walls. In 1933 Roosevelt brought Bullitt out of retirement and appointed him the first U.S. ambassador to the Soviet Union. Though Bullitt's relations with Stalin were at first good, the ambassador returned from his tour in the Soviet Union in 1936 disillusioned with the Soviet dictatorship. Shortly thereafter he was made U.S. ambassador to France. After that country's capitulation to Hitler he returned to Washington and resigned his post. In 1944, just before he accepted a commission as a commandant in de Gaulle's Free French forces, John Billings signed him up to write some articles on the state of Europe.

In "The World from Rome" the former ambassador took what *Time,* for its part, described as "a flesh-creeping look at postwar Europe":

Today, when the moral unity of Western civilization has been shattered by the crimes of the Germans . . . Rome sees again approaching from the East a wave of conquerors. And dominating the hearts and minds and, indeed, the talk of all men throughout Italy is the question: "Will the result of this war be the subjugation of Europe by Moscow instead of by Berlin?" . . . They know that it was necessary for the U.S. to send supplies . . . to the Soviet Union when Hitler broke with Stalin and attacked Russia in 1941. But they believe that when future historians draw up the major mistakes in this war, a high place among the errors will be given to the decision of the American government in the summer of 1941, when Mr. [Harry] Hopkins [the President's personal representative] was sent to Moscow, to ask no promise of the Soviet government respecting the independence of the states of Europe.

Bullitt then went on to say that the Italians predicted that Finland, the Baltic States, Poland, Rumania, Bulgaria, Hungary and Czechoslovakia would be dominated by the Soviet Union after the war and that they feared that Austria, Yugoslavia and Italy itself were also in danger of falling under the control of Moscow.

Seldom has any article in *Life* provoked such a reader reaction. A contemporary Letters report said that of the first 285 letters and telegrams received only thirty-four were favorable and 251 were "nauseated, enraged, disappointed, or perplexed in varying degrees of intensity." Shock and outrage were expressed to the point of hysteria. An Open Letter to Luce from the National Council of American-Soviet Friendship, Inc., and signed by such celebrities as Albert Einstein, the writers Louis Adamic and William Rose Benét, Serge Koussevitzky, conductor of the Boston Symphony, and Harvard professor Ralph Barton Perry asked:

> Does *Life* magazine really wish to split up the United Nations coalition just as complete victory over the Axis is approaching? And do you, Mr. Luce, as one of the most powerful and influential editors in the United States, honestly want to line up your publications on the side of anti-Soviet slanders and the evil cause of war against Soviet Russia after the present conflict is over?

The New York *Times* published lengthy cabled excerpts from a savage personal attack by *Pravda* on Bullitt; he was described as "a liar" who "exposes himself as a spy who has assimilated the instructions of German Fascist propaganda." Max Lerner, then editorial director of the newspaper *PM,* fulminated: "This is the first time, outside of the pages of the lunatic fascist press or the Hearst press, or the McCormick-Patterson axis, that the slimy whispered agitation for a split between America and its Russian partner in the war has found articulate expression."

Within the staff tempers also boiled over. John Osborne, *Time*'s Foreign News editor, who had recently elected to interrupt his desk routine by going to Europe for a few months as a war correspondent, cabled from Rome: [2] "I seriously request that you inform Mr. Luce . . . that I consider [the Bullitt article] a travesty on journalism and a disgrace to Time Inc. . . . an offense against our world and our poor chances of making it livable for the next half century." Vice president Eric Hodgins delivered a scorching memorandum to Luce: "Twenty years of a Fascist tyranny scarcely make Rome the vantage point for any reporter, let alone Bill Bullitt, seeking out the multifaceted truth. . . . I wish that a tendentious reporter had not forced us along a path of controversy where neither truth nor untruth can be

[2] John Osborne came to *Time* in 1938 as a National Affairs writer after reporting for the Associated Press and newspapers in Washington and the South. After the war began he wrote in the National Defense section; late in 1941 he went to Europe as a war correspondent. In 1943 he became the editor both of World Battlefronts and Foreign News.

discovered but only mischief-making on a vast, international scale." Under the guise of a report to Roy Larsen on the company's public relations, Hodgins later renewed his attack:

> The article, the reaction to it in the press and from readers, plus Mrs. Luce's commentary thereon in the *Daily Mirror* . . . make evident the futility of trying to consider "public relations" as in any way divorced from editorial policy. . . .[3] The article produced encomiums from Captain Patterson's *Daily News* . . . sotto voce from Archbishop Spellman, representing the Church—all more or less strange bedfellows for Time Inc. . . . A situation in which our publications can even be thought of as marching directly counter-current to the direction of contemporaneous history is not something to be viewed with equanimity.

The top editorial management stood behind the Bullitt article. Writing to Larsen, editorial director Billings said: "Publication was thoroughly justified. It well may be that the reaction to this article foreshadows a great split in U.S. opinion on Russia . . . and that journalistically its publication is about the smartest thing *Life* ever did." Luce fully concurred. In replying to Osborne's protest from Rome, he cabled: "Your stern rebuke . . . has been considered with great seriousness. Whether or not it would change your opinion, I can assure you on my own direct information that Bullitt correctly represented a highly important point of view." He more directly challenged the Open Letter from the National Council of American-Soviet Friendship, writing to its executive director asking for "objective information" as to the past or present Communist affiliations of the letter's signers. In his reply he noted, too, that the New York *Times,* in a recent dispatch from its Rome correspondent, reported widespread fear that Italy might succumb to Communist influence, and that the correspondent had added that it would be "impolitic" to publish the full truth. Asked Luce: "Did Mr. Bullitt write and did *Life* publish too much of the truth?" The editor-in-chief never wavered in his belief that the Bullitt article was a journalistic milestone; two years later, in 1946, with the Iron Curtain drawn across

---

[3] In a column she was then writing in the *Daily Mirror,* Mrs. Luce had said: "Biggest journalistic bombshell on Roosevelt diplomacy to date will be Bill Bullitt's article . . . out Friday in *Life."* Winchell picked the item up: "Clare Luce, the legislator, gleefully colyumed recently that Bill Bullitt's article . . . would give F.D.R. the hot foot."

the European continent, Luce wrote Bullitt: "I am very proud of the part which our journals have played in orienting American opinion toward the truth about Russia. Your *Life* article opened the battle for truth when it took great courage (as well as insight) to do so."

When Foreign News editor Osborne went to Europe in the summer of 1944, Matthews appointed as his substitute David Whittaker Chambers, one of two senior editors in charge of the back-of-the-book critical departments. To all but an intimate circle of close friends (and some implacable enemies) Chambers appeared to be just a reticent, plump man of middle height, who invariably dressed in dark, rumpled suits and seemed the man least likely to disturb the tenor of an editorial office.

He was, in fact, a man consumed by the passionate conviction that the greatest foe of the United States was Communism. He had waited impatiently five years for an opportunity to edit the Foreign News section. "I had once told the managing editor of *Time* [i.e., Matthews], who was also my friend," he wrote in his autobiography, *Witness,* "that the one section of *Time* I really felt equipped to edit was Foreign News." [4] He entered into it as a man with a mission:

I held certain facts to be self-evident on the basis of almost every scrap of significant foreign news: 1) the Soviet Union was not a "great ally"—it was a calculating enemy making use of World War II to prepare for World War III; 2) the Soviet Union was not a democracy; it was a monstrous dictatorship; 3) the Communist International had been dissolved in name only; in effect, it still functioned; 4) the Soviet Union was not a thin-skinned, under-privileged waif that must at any cost be wheedled into the family of free nations, but a toughly realistic world power whose primary purpose at that moment of history was conquest of the free world; 5) the indispensable first step in that conquest was the control of Central Europe and China; 6) the Chinese Communists were not "agrarian liberals," but Chinese Communists, after the Russian Communist Party, the Number One section of the Communist International. [5]

Chambers' convictions derived from a Communist past. The child of a miserable marriage between a commercial artist and a one-

[4] Random House, 1952; p. 497.     [5] *Witness,* p. 497.

101

time actress, he had been raised in Lynbrook, Long Island. He was a promising, brilliant and melancholy student at Columbia University; he returned from a European vacation trip in 1923 convinced that "World War II was predictably certain and that it was extremely improbable that civilization could survive it." [6] He read Marx and Lenin and turned then to Communism; as he testified under oath to the House Committee on Un-American Activities in 1948:

> I . . . joined the Communist Party in 1924.[7] No one recruited me. I had become convinced that the society in which we live, Western civilization, had reached a crisis, of which the First World War was the military expression, and that it was doomed to collapse or revert to barbarism. . . . In the writings of Karl Marx, I thought that I had found the explanation of the histor- ical and economic causes. . . . In the writings of Lenin, I thought I had found the answer to the question: what to do?

He had gone to work for the Communist *Daily Worker.* The wages were small—when they were paid at all—and he supplemented his earnings by translating books. One of them, *Bambi,* by the Austrian author Felix Salten, turned out to be a best seller. Caught in fac- tional struggles in 1929, he broke with the party and the *Worker* but remained a dedicated Communist. During this period he wrote a number of stories for the *New Masses,* a Communist-controlled literary monthly, and the praise which these elicited from Moscow convinced American Communists that they must lure him back into the party; in the early spring of 1932 they made him the editor of the *New Masses.* He edited only a few issues when suddenly he dis- appeared from the magazine and the party circles. Under party orders he entered the underground organization, becoming a courier in the United States for the Soviet Military Intelligence. Then in 1937 he repudiated Marx's doctrines and Lenin's tactics. He testified to the Un-American Activities Committee: "Experience and the record had convinced me that Communism is a form of totalitarianism, that its triumph means slavery to men wherever they fall under its sway and spiritual night to the human mind and soul. I resolved to break with the Communist Party at whatever risk to my life or other tragedy to myself or my family. Yet . . . I could still say to someone at

[6] Ibid., p. 194.

[7] A lapse of memory that Chambers later acknowledged; he joined the party in 1925.

that time: I know that I am leaving the winning side for the losing side." He broke with the Communist Party the following year and for a year after that he lived in fear of his own life and the lives of his wife and two children and in direst poverty.

> One night, in the spring of 1939, my wife opened her purse and showed me that it contained less than fifty cents. It was all the money that we had. . . . The morning mail brought a letter from my friend, Robert Cantwell, the author of *Laugh and Lie Down,* and later, the biographer of Hawthorne. Cantwell was then one of the editors of *Time* magazine. Some time before, Cantwell had asked me whether he should take the job that *Time* had offered him. I had urged him to. . . . He was one of the people who urged me to break away from the Communist Party. He helped me with money and part-time work after I broke. . . . His letter, on that rather desperate morning, urged me to go to New York.[8]

T. S. Matthews was then editor in charge of the back-of-the-book departments. Cantwell told Matthews that his friend was a gifted writer, a practiced journalist and former member of the Communist Party; nothing was said about Chambers once having been a courier for Soviet Intelligence. On the basis of some trial book reviews Matthews hired him at $100 a week in April 1939. "I have always insisted," wrote Chambers, "that I was hired because I began a review of a war book with the line: 'One bomby day in June. . . .' "[9]

Matthews remembered that he found him "unprepossessing but impressive, and at first took him with a large grain of salt. There was an air of suppressed melodrama about him, as if he were being followed or in danger of his life. He was taciturn, suspicious and seemed to have a fixation about Communism."[10] Like most new writers Chambers had his difficulties in meeting *Time*'s demand for succinct but lively writing. At first he was depressed, fearing failure greatly because *Time* not only offered him, at age thirty-eight, a better livelihood than he was likely to find again, but a kind of sanctuary. His depression was accentuated by loneliness; Chambers was aware that among his new associates he was an odd man out.

---

[8] *Witness,* pp. 85–86.     [9] Ibid., p. 86.
[10] T. S. Matthews' book review of *Cold Friday;* New York *Herald Tribune,* November 15, 1964.

"He came to us from a world we knew nothing about," said Duncan Norton-Taylor, who became one of Chambers' closest friends and the editor of his posthumous book, *Cold Friday*,[11] "and found himself in a world that was completely new and strange to him. He yearned for companionship." But he was not a man who gave his trust or made friends easily.

He made a place for himself because he was an able writer. At first he was inclined to downrate the job of book reviewing and persisted, in spite of the advice of his friend Cantwell, in trying to be transferred to the Foreign News department. But when he was given a trial in that department, his polemical approach did not please Frank Norris, the editor then in charge of the section. Norris complained to managing editor Gottfried, "I wish you would speak to that boy. He evidently thinks that having changed sides, he has to play capitalist and denounce Communists." When Gottfried took Chambers to lunch to try to explain that because he was now working for the capitalist press, he need not feel he had to attack the enemies of capitalism, Gottfried recalled that "Chambers turned his head away in an effort to conceal a smile. It was obvious to me that he thought capitalists were innocents, not aware of the conspirators who were about to overthrow them." Chambers was tried in other departments but repeatedly found himself back in Books.

Book reviewing was a job in which he excelled. He was widely read in several languages, both in literature and history; he had a broad range of cultural interests and a knack for analyzing and simplifying complicated subjects. He began to explain to his friends that the Books section was really the editorial page of *Time*. "No one could comment on books without at the same time commenting on the whole range of views and news," he wrote. "The Communists understood this just as well as I did, and, throughout my Books assignment, I wrote under a barrage from them and their unwitting friends. But it was no longer a massacre; it had become an artillery duel. 'Every week,' said one of my amused friends, 'that mortar goes off in the last five pages of *Time*.'"[12]

His work brought him to Luce's attention. In 1941 Luce asked him to undertake the job of commissioning and editing a series by leading philosophers which was being scheduled for *Fortune*. In the summer of 1942 he promoted Chambers to senior editor and put

---

[11] Random House, 1964.     [12] *Witness*, p. 493.

him in charge of all *Time*'s back-of-the-book departments except Business.

Chambers had installed his family on a farm northwest of Baltimore where he felt they were safe from Communist reprisal. He saw them only on weekends, commuting by rail and bus from New York. He was an almost demonic worker; as the deadlines neared he often worked thirty-six hours at a stretch, catnapping in his office. In November 1942 he suffered intense chest pains that were diagnosed as angina pectoris, and he was forced to take an eight-months leave of absence; when he returned in the summer of 1943, the work that he had shouldered alone was divided between himself and another senior editor. It was a year later, with Osborne in Europe, that he got his chance to edit Foreign News. He was elated with his new job, writing to Luce:

> I should like to edit Foreign News for a long time to come. . . . It is my first choice, my second and my third. . . . I have spent some 15 years of my life actively preparing for FN. Some of those years were spent close to the central dynamo that powers the politics of our time. In fact, I can say: I was there, I saw it, at least in a small way, I did it. . . . In dealing with international affairs, I feel like a man in a dark but familiar room: I may bump against the furniture, but I'm usually sure where the door and windows are. . . . I want to sit here and figure out history.

The Foreign News section began immediately to reflect his anti-Communist opinions; this strongly controversial approach to the news generated internal criticism. He was acutely aware of it. "My assignment sent a shiver through most of *Time*'s staff, where my views were well known and detested with a ferocity that I did not believe possible until I was at grips with it," he wrote. "With my first few Foreign News sections, the shiver turned into a shudder." [13] The hostility that surrounded him was, in fact, real enough. But by this time he was a senior editor of proven competence. He turned out to be a superb technician, particularly skilled at the mosaic art of putting a *Time* section together. He enjoyed not only the confidence of his managing editor and editor-in-chief but had as well some loyal friends among his peers. They remember him with deep

[13] Ibid., p. 497.

affection. "Once Whit accepted you as a friend, the bars were down," his colleague Sam Welles recalled. "There never has been a better talker or conversationalist or a wittier or more delightful man, when he cared to be." Henry Grunwald, who was a novice writer under Chambers, remembered him as a humane and considerate editor who helped him overcome cover-story nerves by taking him to the movies.

To others Chambers was an enigma. He never lost his conspiratorial manner, developed in his years in the underground, and remained inordinately suspicious of those who did not enjoy his confidence. Louis Kronenberger wrote in his memoirs: "He had a disquieting way of peering at people, even of 'going at' people, a way of making them confused or of undermining their sense of security; which around the office came to seem now a deliberate conspiratorial tactic, now a form of self-dramatization." [14] He infuriated one of the chief researchers assigned to his section by giving her deliberately inaccurate lists of scheduled stories so that she wouldn't know what he was up to. He alienated the senior editor in charge of the U.S. at War section by failing to pass along copies of Foreign News stories so that coverage could be coordinated. He often rewrote stories without explanation to his writers and rode roughshod over the objections of researchers.

His chief adversaries were among the foreign correspondents. The relationship between the Foreign News editor of *Time* and the correspondents at the time was ambiguous. The editor, subject only to the veto of the managing editor, had the last word on what appeared in his department. He was expected to be, and usually was, guided by the correspondents' dispatches, but if he believed them to be wrong he was free to disregard them. The correspondents in turn were not responsible to the Foreign News editor but to the chief of the news service. Chambers made no attempt to make the system work, if indeed it could have been made to work. He regarded most of the correspondents, because of the prevailing liberal attitudes, as hopelessly naïve in respect to Communism. The senior correspondents serving *Time* overseas regarded themselves as his peers or betters. Charles Wertenbaker in Paris and John Osborne had edited Foreign News before him; John Hersey in Moscow, by then an editor of *Life* reporting for all the magazines, had been a senior writer in Foreign News and World Battlefronts; Walter Graebner, in charge

[14] *No Whippings, No Gold Watches* (Little, Brown and Company, 1965, 1970), pp. 132–33.

of the London office, had served the company in a number of editorial posts before Chambers joined the staff. They openly rebelled when Chambers persisted in ignoring their cables.

Graebner sent heated objections to the new line taken by the magazine. "Is it a coincidence that in two successive issues strong implications should be made that there is a yawning gap between the United States and the Soviet Union?" he inquired of vice president Allen Grover, who among his other assignments kept an overall eye on the news service. "The subject is treated subtly, Allen, but in my opinion there's no mistaking the treatment." In his answer Grover, who also disagreed with Chambers' editing, went out of his way to point out that the new approach had the full approval of the editor-in-chief: "No, it's not a coincidence. . . . [Luce] is the person who's responsible for the treatment, and he likes it this way. Needless to say, there is a lot of discussion of it here in New York."

The fact that Luce supported Chambers by no means stemmed the rising tide of protest. Hersey was so frustrated because his work was not being used that he told the New York office that he might as well come home.[15] The cable editor in *Life*'s news bureau, Fillmore Calhoun, who had recently returned from an overseas tour, wrote a furious memorandum: "Hell, I read the incoming cables and week after week I am amazed to see how they are either misinterpreted, left unprinted or weaseled around to one man's way of thinking. I like Whit and I admire his slickness, but I wouldn't trust him with any set of facts concerning Russia anymore than I would trust John L. Lewis to ask for less wages for his coal miners." Even C. D. Jackson, on leave and attached to Eisenhower's headquarters outside Paris, intervened on behalf of the correspondents, writing Luce at the end of September: "I have read a lot of their stuff as filed and I have also read their stuff as it appeared in *Time*. . . . There is off-the-record wonderment and discouragement over why *Time* does what it has been doing lately."

---

[15] In July 1945 Hersey resigned from Time Inc. to free-lance. His resignation was a great disappointment to Luce, who entertained the thought that Hersey might one day become *Time*'s managing editor. Luce had a deep paternal feeling for him, who, like himself, was born in China, the son of a YMCA official; like Luce, Hersey had gone to Hotchkiss on a scholarship and then on to Yale, where he became a fellow member of Skull and Bones. Like Luce, he had taken postgraduate work in England (though at Cambridge, not Oxford). Hersey, a committed Democrat, could not accommodate himself to Luce's political views.

Billings wrote Wertenbaker that "by late November, Harry became so disturbed by the quantity (if not the quality) of complaints against Whit's editing that he asked me to look into it." In January 1945, after Billings had made his report, Luce delivered his own judgment in a memorandum addressed to Billings, who relayed it to the senior correspondents and the New York editors:

> It is my opinion that the correspondents did a fine job. . . . It is also my opinion that the Foreign News Department under Chambers did a fine job. How can these two opinions be held in view of very strong complaints by the Senior Correspondents . . . ? In general . . . the Senior Correspondents wished to convey the information that the rulers of the world, each in their respective capitals, are well meaning people who are trying to do their best for their own countries and the world. In general . . . the Foreign News Department wished to convey the information that even in that part of the world misnamed the United Nations, things were not going very well. The posture of events in January 1945 seems to have confirmed Editor Chambers about as fully as a news-editor is ever confirmed. The whole of the inquiry reveals only one really serious question and that, as everyone knows, has to do with the "attitude" toward Soviet Russia. . . . F.N. has given a disproportionate amount of space and emphasis to the problem of Russia. Overemphasis may rightly be criticized but there were good reasons for erring in this direction. For example: 1) During this period a great part of the news was the Soviet liberation of Eastern Europe and the Balkans; 2) Concurrently, the "Communist" problem came crashing to the fore in China—aided by a worldwide leftist attack on the Chinese Government; 3) Prior to this period—and also for justifiable reasons—there had been much too little frank and intelligent presentation of the "problem" of Russia; 4) There was in this period a strong propaganda which attempted to smother honest reporting of Russian policy —or to try to smear it as Hearstian, etc. In view of the situation thus indicated, F.N., in my opinion, did a brilliant job of presenting, in terms of current events, the course of Russian (and/or Communist) policy.
>
> Two more points. . . . First, if Chambers' editing has suggested that he doubts Russia's desire for peace, then he has

been guilty, as perhaps indeed he has, of unclarity. For far from disbelieving in Russia's desire for peace, our view is that Russia is, if anything, over-exploiting her own and the world's desire for peace. . . . Secondly . . . Chambers has to some degree failed to distinguish between, on the one hand, the general revolutionary, leftist, or simply chaotic trends and, on the other hand, the specifically Communist politics in various countries. Chambers fully agrees that this distinction should be sharply made and if this distinction is sharply made, that in itself will, I think, go far to bring FN and the Correspondents in line.

There remains only one real question . . . and that is the relation between the Kremlin and Communist trends or activities throughout the world. I have just been told, in a highly confidential manner, that Stalin is, after all, a Communist. I am also somewhat less confidentially informed that the Pope is a Christian. Some will say: what does it matter . . . and what does it matter that Hersey advises me that he, John Hersey, is a Democrat? . . . A good Foreign News Editor, while guarding against the prejudices arising from his own convictions, will not ignore the circumstance that the Pope is a Christian and Stalin a Communist and Hersey, God bless him, a Democrat.

While Luce stoutly upheld Chambers, the editor-in-chief evidently felt that the tone of Foreign News had become too controversial. However strong Luce's own opinions, however dogmatic his memoranda, he was not a crusading editor in the sense of wanting to be too far out of the mainstream of current thinking, and whenever he felt that the magazines had gone too far or too fast in any direction, he applied the brakes. He applied them to Chambers, characteristically, in an oblique fashion. The Luce memorandum stated that the Foreign News department's disproportionate emphasis on the Soviet Union had taken too little into account the fact that "much (perhaps much the most) of the fault for the tragic and wholly unnecessary deterioration of world politics has been the fault of the U.S.—partly the fault of the U.S. as a whole, specifically the fault of the State Department, and beyond all the fault of the President. Owing to departmentalization, F.N. had to tell its story without sufficient reference to the . . . U.S."

In fact, at the time, so preoccupied was Chambers with Communism that he took little interest in U.S. affairs. Luce proposed to overcome over-departmentalization of the news by the creation of a new department called International, which would have as its scope diplomacy on a world scale and be free to take over all stories on international relations from both the U.S. at War and the Foreign News sections. Billings assured Wertenbaker that the new department would take over from Foreign News many of the stories that had given cause for complaint. John Osborne returned from his stint in Europe to head the new department and Chambers was made the permanent Foreign News editor. Chambers certainly felt that he had been undercut; some time after the new section appeared, Billings reported to Luce: "Chambers is eating his heart out in FN which he feels International has emasculated."

Yet it was not the new International section but Chambers who produced the most brilliant and prophetic assessment of the Big Three meeting at Yalta in February 1945. The communiqué from the last meeting of Roosevelt, Churchill and Stalin was not particularly informative, and the first U.S. press reaction was that the meeting had ushered in a new era of international understanding; second thoughts and misgivings were reflected by *Time* in the second week after the meeting, but it remained for Chambers to produce a political satire in *Time*'s issue of March 5, 1945, entitled "The Ghosts on the Roof" that was uncannily accurate in forecasting the course of postwar Soviet policy. His preface:

"The Big Three Conferees dispersed under cover of an all but newsless fog of military security. But here & there was vouchsafed a glimpse—such as Franklin Roosevelt's afterdeck chats with Near Eastern potentates; here & there a sound, like the short snort from Socialism's old warhorse, George Bernard Shaw. Snorted Shaw: '[The Yalta Conference is] an impudently incredible fairy tale. . . . I for one should like to know what really passed at Yalta. . . .'

"Taking Mr. Shaw's lead, one of TIME's editors has written the following political fairy tale. . . ."

*With the softness of bats, seven ghosts settled down on the flat roof of the Livadia Palace at Yalta. They found someone else already there: a statuesque female figure, crouching, with her eye glued to one of the holes in the roof. . . .*

*"Madam," said the foremost ghost, an imperious woman with a bullet hole in her head, "what are you doing on our roof?"*

*Clio, the Muse of History (for it was she), looked up, her finger on her lips. "Shh!" she said, "the Big Three Conference is just ending down there. What with security regulations, censorship and personal secretiveness, the only way I can find out anything these days is by peeping. And who are you?" she asked, squinting slightly (history is sometimes a little shortsighted). "I've seen you somewhere before."*

*"Madam," said a male ghost, rising on tiptoe to speak over his wife's shoulder (he also had a bullet hole in his forehead), "I am Nicholas II, Emperor and Autocrat of All the Russias. . . ."*

*"Nicholas—how nice to see you again!" cried History. "Wherever have you been? And the Tsarina Alix! Your four charming daughters, I presume—gracious, but those bullet holes are disfiguring. And the little hemophiliac—Tsarevich Alexei! . . . Why, I've scarcely given you a thought since that time when the Communists threw your bodies down the mine shaft in Ekaterinburg [now Sverdlovsk]. Whatever brings you here?"*

*"This, Madam," said the imperial ghost, "is no strange place to me. It is our former estate of Livadia." [He cited its spectacular features until the Tsarina cut him short.]*

*"Don't hedge, Nicky," she cried. . . . "He's trying to cover up the fact that he wanted to eavesdrop on the Big Three Conference. He doesn't like to admit it in front of the Tsarevich," she added in a stage whisper, "but His Imperial Majesty is simply fascinated by Stalin—"*

*"Stalin! You?" gasped the Muse of History.*

*"Yes, yes, oh yes," said the Tsar eagerly. . . . "What statesmanship! What vision! What power! . . . Stalin has made Russia great again!"*

*"It all began," said the Tsarina wearily, "with the German-Russian partition of Poland. . . . But after [that] Nicky insisted on returning to Russia. He began to attend the meetings of the Politburo. The Politburo! Oh, those interminable speeches . . . Ah,* Katorga! *  . . . And then," the Tsarina added, "Stalin overran Estonia, Latvia, Lithuania."*

*"Bessarabia," cried the Tsar, "was recovered from Rumania."*

*"And Northern Bukovina," cried the Tsarina, "which had never been Russian before."*

---

* *Meaning: Hard labor!—an expletive used by Old Bolsheviks instead of Oh, Hell!*

*"Foreign Minister Saracoglu of Turkey was summoned to Moscow," said the Tsar, "and taken over the jumps. For a moment I thought we had the Straits."*

*"Constantinople," breathed the Tsarina, "the goal of 200 years of Russian diplomacy."*

*"After that," said the Tsar, "it could not be put off any longer."*

*"What?" asked the Muse of History.*

*"Why, my conversion," said the Tsar. "I—I became a Marxist."*

*"He means a Leninist-Stalinist," said the Tsarina. . . .*

*"Stalinists!" cried the Muse of History. . . .*

*"Of course, we could not formally enter the Party," the Tsar explained. "There was the question of our former status as exploiters in Russia. Even worse was our present status as ghosts. It violates a basic tenet of Marxism which, of course, does not recognize the supernatural."*

*"One might suppose, though," said the Tsarina, "that since the Party was, so to speak, responsible for making us what we are, the Central Control Commission would stretch a point in our case."*

*"And now," said the Tsar, peering through the chink in the roof, "the greatest statesmen in the world have come to Stalin. Who but he would have had the sense of historical fitness to entertain them in my expropriated palace! There he sits, so small, so sure. He is magnificent. Greater than Rurik, greater than Peter! For Peter conquered only in the name of a limited class. But Stalin embodies the international social revolution. That is the mighty, new device of power politics which he has developed for blowing up other countries from within."*

*"With it he is conquering Rumania and Bulgaria!" cried the Tsarina.*

*"Yugoslavia and Hungary!" cried the Tsar.*

*"Poland and Finland," cried the Tsarina.*

*"His party comrades are high in the Governments of Italy and France."*

*"A fortnight ago they re-entered the Government of Belgium."*

*"Soon they will control most of Germany."*

*"They already control a vast region of China."*

*"When Russia enters the war against Japan, we shall take Manchuria, Inner Mongolia, Korea, and settle the old score with Chiang Kai-shek. . . . When the proper time comes, we shall sweep through Iran and reach the soft underbelly of Turkey from the south. . . ."*

112

*" 'You have a world to win,' "* cried the Tsarina. *" 'You have nothing to lose but your chains.' "*

*"I must ask you, Madam,"* said the Muse of History, *"to stop dancing up & down on this roof. These old palaces are scarcely more substantial than you ghosts. . . . Your notions about Russia and Stalin are highly abnormal. All right-thinking people now agree that Russia is a mighty friend of democracy. Stalin has become a conservative. In a few hours the whole civilized world will hail the historic decisions just reached beneath your feet as proof that the Soviet Union is prepared to collaborate with her allies in making the world safe for democracy and capitalism. The revolution is over."*

*"Grazhdanka! [Citizeness!]"* cried the Tsarina, *"you have been reading banned books. Those are the views of the renegade Leon Trotsky."*

*"The Muse cannot help being an intellectual,"* said the Tsar generously, *"but I do not think that we should charge her with Trotskyism. I must say, though, that for a Muse of History, you seem to have a very slight grasp of the historical dialectic. . . . History, Madam, is not a suburban trolley line which stops to accommodate every housewife with bundles in her arms."*

*"I think I liked you better, Nicholas,"* said the Muse of History, *"when you were only a weakling Tsar. You are becoming a realist."*

*"Death,"* said the Tsarina, *"is a somewhat maturing experience. What Nicky means is that between two systems of society, which embody diametrically opposed moral and political principles, even peace may be only a tactic of struggle."*

*"But have not the gentlemen downstairs,"* asked History, *"just agreed to solve the Polish and Yugoslav questions in a friendly fashion?"*

*"What makes Stalin great,"* said the Tsar, *"is that he understands how to adapt revolutionary tactics to the whirling spirals of history as it emerges onto new planes. . . . We Marxists believe that in the years of peace Britain and the U.S. will fall apart, due, as we Marxists say, to the inability of capitalism to solve its basic contradiction— that is, its inability to provide continuous work for the masses so that they can buy the goods whose production would provide continuous work for the masses. Britain and America can solve this problem only by becoming Communist states."*

*"If that were true, Stalin would be wrong,"* said History, *"because America and Britain, though they may undergo great changes, will*

113

*not become Communist states. More is at stake than economic and political systems. Two faiths are at issue. It is just that problem which these gentlemen below are trying to work out in practical terms. But if they fail, I foresee more wars, more revolutions, greater proscriptions, bloodshed and human misery."*

*"Well," said the Tsarina, "if you can foresee all that, why don't you do something to prevent it?"*

*The Muse of History drew the Tsarevich to her, for he had become restless. "Poor little bleeder," she said, stroking his hair, "different only in the organic nature of your disease from so many others who have bled and died. In answer to your question, Madam," she said, glancing at the Tsarina, "I never permit my fore-knowledge to interfere with human folly, if only because I never expect human folly to learn much from history. Besides, I must leave something for my sister, Melpomene, to work on." \**

\* *In the Greek Pantheon, Melpomene was the Muse of Tragedy.*

No one assigned Chambers to write "The Ghosts on the Roof"; he conceived and carried the idea through and submitted a draft to Matthews, who somewhat apprehensively decided to run it. Chambers described the reaction to its publication in melodramatic terms. "To most of my colleagues, 'The Ghosts on the Roof' was a culminating shocker. Feeling ran so high against it, the general malevolence swelled into my office so fiercely, that again I closed my door, this time to edit in a semblance of peace. One of the writers who dropped in described the hubbub outside my closed door . . . as 'like the night of a lynching bee.' It took courage in those day for *Time* to run a piece like 'The Ghosts on the Roof.' " [16]

The reader reaction as measured by the letters to the editor was almost wholly adverse. Readers wrote that the article did "a grievous disservice" to peace and argued that it was "reckless sabotage to suggest that the Russians are not honest on their side, and that the attempt [to work together] is doomed to failure." In an editorial comment accompanying the letters, the editors pointed out that the magazine

> neither said nor thinks that Soviet–U.S. collaboration is "doomed to failure." . . . Capitalistic, democratic *Time* expects and welcomes the prospect of competition between Communist Russia

[16] *Witness*, p. 501.

114

and Capitalist U.S. *Time* believes, with the late, great Wendell Willkie: "Russia is neither going to eat us nor seduce us. . . . I have never understood why it should be assumed that in any possible contact between communism and democracy, democracy should go down."

Chambers' editorship of the Foreign News section ended abruptly six months after publication of "Ghosts." In the autumn, returning one weekend from Baltimore, he blacked out on the train; in his initial discouragement, he told Matthews that he was leaving the office for good and would write book reviews from his farm. When he recovered, he changed his mind and asked for his job back, but Matthews, who had seen Chambers work himself into two physical collapses, was determined to put him on a less exacting schedule, and by that time he had assigned the section to another editor.

The news that he could not return to Foreign News was a bitter blow to Chambers. He suspected Matthews of ulterior motives and only later did he understand that the decision was indeed dictated by management's concern for his health. At first he felt that he had fallen down "the whole flight of editorial steps"; [17] in fact he was reduced in neither salary nor rank but, after a brief return to book reviewing, was assigned as an editor-at-large on Special Projects and given a substantial increase in salary. He wrote some of the magazine's most distinguished cover stories—on Marian Anderson, Albert Einstein, Arnold Toynbee, Reinhold Niebuhr. From time to time, when he was not working on Special Projects, he was asked to edit various departments while the regular editor was on another assignment or on vacation. In July 1946, when Chambers was scheduled to substitute for his successor in the Foreign News section, Matthews, mindful of past tensions, wrote him a memorandum:

> The news of your grey imminence has not been well received by TLI [this was the name for the newly formed *Time-Life* International division under which the foreign correspondents operated]. I tell you this, not as a piece of amusing office gossip nor as a merely friendly warning from the sidelines. The situation affects both me and you. I expect that there may be difficulties between you and TLI—but I also expect to take a hand in them, if they occur. If there is any dragging of the feet or

[17] Ibid., p. 504.

throwing sand in the gears on TLI's part, I want to know about it right away. And I shall expect you to do as you would be done by. I neither ask nor look for friendliness between you, but I do insist on good behavior, on both sides. . . . To the best of my knowledge and belief, the morale of [the writing] staff is good; and their performance has been better than adequate. I have no fears on the score of performance, when you take over. Neither have I any real fears for their morale—if you will only exercise those Christian virtues of charity and patience which I (and perhaps not many others here) know you possess.

However much he enjoyed Special Projects, Chambers regarded the work as something of an anticlimax; certainly his heart was not in it as it was when he was waging his weekly personal crusade against Communism. It would be two years before he would again step out on that crusade, this time in his spectacular duel with Alger Hiss, who was then enjoying a respected place high in government circles.

While great enthusiasm had been inspired by Russia's heroic defense of her land, Americans' emotions were more deeply engaged in China, which had been fighting the Japanese for many years before the attack on Pearl Harbor. With the Chinese, moreover, Americans had ties through commerce, art, literature, and the great Christian missionary effort, in which the Luce family had played a notable part. Until 1943 the U.S. press was overwhelmingly sympathetic to the Chinese and pro-Chiang Kai-shek, but the Time Inc. magazines had striven especially hard to keep their readers constantly aware of China's tribulations.

Luce had come back in 1941 from his visit to Chungking, where Chiang's government had retreated before the invading Japanese, and had thrown himself with new vigor into the cause of getting aid for China, while Washington was giving priority to the war in Europe. He had brought home with him Theodore H. White, whose dispatches from China had helped dramatize and personalize the plight of the Chinese people under Japanese attack. A cocky young man of twenty-six, he was a colorful and courageous reporter and a skillful writer. In the summer of 1941 he wrote a series of articles for the September issue of *Fortune* that was probably the most extensive journalistic account of China at war published up to that time by any American magazine. In January 1942, after Pearl Harbor, he re-

116

turned to Chungking by way of India. His profile of Chiang Kai-shek, which appeared in *Life* in March, hailed the generalissimo as the leader of "the restless masses of Asia," who might some day attain "greater influence than any other single being of our age."

In the article White expressed the same tremendous admiration for the Chinese leader that Luce had long felt. Luce once confessed himself "hopelessly sentimental" about China; he wanted to see the land of his birth emerge from the war "a stronger, more excellent nation, linked to the U.S. in an honorable partnership." In this hope Luce was perhaps no more sentimental than Roosevelt, at whose insistence a cynical Stalin and a reluctant Churchill would be forced to admit Chiang and China to their exalted fellowship as one of the Great Powers. It was American official policy to accept Chiang as the key to China's resistance to the Japanese and to pin on him the hope for China's postwar unity.

Conditions within China were rapidly deteriorating, however, under the blockade imposed with the closing of the Burma Road in the spring of 1942. Despite Roosevelt's moral support, the country was at the end of the milk run for lend-lease, and the promises of supplies to be flown in over the Hump were frequently more honored in the breach. There were dissensions between Great Britain and the United States as to China's value as a partner in war, and among the military as to whether those supplies which could be spared could best forward the war against Japan by being allocated to Stilwell's Chinese ground troops or to General Claire Chennault's air force.

In an effort to stir Americans to greater efforts on behalf of China, the generalissimo's wife, American-educated Mayling Soong, undertook a visit to the United States. Madame Chiang's formal tour of the country began in February 1943 with appearances in the House and the Senate; of her address to the House *Time* said: "She knew that what she said might not have great effect on strategies already determined. But it could have—and in her first appearance it certainly did have—more effect than anything which has yet happened, in giving one great people the kind of understanding of another great people that is the first need of a shrinking, hopeful world." Her triumph before Congress was capped by her appearance at a jammed Madison Square Garden rally which was organized by Luce and John D. Rockefeller, Jr. "The potency of the charm and mind of the Madame," reported *Time*, "had already made her mission a tremendous personal success."

117

There appeared about that time, in *Time*'s issue of March 22, 1943, a disturbing dispatch from White which was both a heart-rending account of human suffering and a damning indictment of Madame Chiang's husband's regime. In harrowing detail White told of a famine in Honan Province, of "dogs eating human bodies by the roads, peasants seeking dead human flesh under the cover of darkness, endless deserted villages, beggars swarming at every city gate, babies abandoned to cry and die on every highway. . . . Of Honan's 34 millions we estimated that there have been three million refugees. In addition, five million will have died by the time the new harvest is gathered." The appalling tragedy, said White, was caused by the army's insistence on collecting a grain tax from farmers in the face of known crop failures and compounded by the government's "tremendous miscalculation" in not sending grain into the province in time. *Time* did not tell the whole tragic story because it did not have it at press time: the first three takes of White's cable had been sent straight to New York by a remiss telegraph clerk in Honan Province; the fourth was sent through Chungking where, as White later reported, the censors "butchered the guts out of [it]."

White had gotten word of the famine in *Ta Kung Pao,* Chungking's biggest newspaper, which thereupon was suspended for mentioning it. In a private, and uncensored, letter to the home office, White reported that after his return from Honan to Chungking

> I saw everybody I knew there and yelled to high heavens. . . . The thing wound up with my seeing the Generalissimo himself. . . . First he didn't believe my story about the dogs digging bodies out of the sand. Then I made Harrison Forman [of the London *Times,* who had accompanied White on his Honan trip] show him the actual pictures. . . . Then I told him about the army taking the people's grain and the old boy said it was impossible. . . . Then he started to believe me. . . . All this meant hell for the men who had been handling relief. . . . The Generalissimo has one simple remedy for that sort of graft when it can be gotten to his attention—stand them against the wall.

Honan, White continued, left him mentally sick, depressed and filled with dire forebodings:

> This country is dying almost before my eyes. The blockade is killing it, and the currency is blowing up. Everything rotten in

118

the country now stems from the blockade and the inflation. . . . Until the United Nations plunge through and rescue her, China can be counted out.

Two months later, White reported again:

*Time*'s story actually did result in getting action up there in Honan. The reaction cabled back from the States was so sulphurous that it galvanized even the army into disgorging. . . . I received this letter from Bishop Megan in Loyang: . . . "The grain came rushing in from Shensi by trainloads. . . . The provincial government got busy and opened up soup kitchens. . . . The military shelled out some of their much surplus grain. . . . Cash really poured into Honan."

The contrast between the reality of China—blockaded, bled by runaway inflation—and the illusion of China as a heroic, powerful ally needing only an infusion of American aid (as pictured by Madame Chiang) worried some friends of China in this country. The novelist Pearl Buck, whose Pulitzer Prize-winning book, *The Good Earth,* had given thousands of Americans an intimate look at Chinese life and culture, believed that the glittering tour of Madame Chiang had carried pro-Chinese feelings to a point from which Americans needed to be brought back lest, in disillusionment, they turn against their ally. She asked Luce to publish an article by her in *Life*.

In it she argued for greater military aid to China but also for a clearer understanding of what was happening in that country. As China became more isolated, she wrote, the great liberal voices of China were being silenced and the bureaucracy was becoming more and more oppressive; free speech was being suppressed, official corruption was increasing. The Chinese continued to regard the generalissimo as a great man, she conceded, but his greatness in the future would be measured by how effective he could be "in dealing with these evils on the negative side, and in providing the people with the technique of democracy on the positive side." She concluded: "We are in the process of throwing away a nation of people who could and would save democracy with us but who if we do not help them will be compelled to lose it because they are being lost themselves."

The decision to publish Pearl Buck's article was a difficult one for Luce. He wrote down his thoughts as he pondered the pros and cons

119

of publication: "Being considerably, if not fully, aware of the faults or evils in Chinese administration, I would naturally welcome anything that can be done to improve the actual situation." But at the same time he did not wish to do anything to undermine the confidence of the American people in their Asian ally:

> An appreciation of China is about the only thing the American people are united on. . . . Even the men-of-ill-will, even Col. McCormick, go along on this. Now, let the general approval of China be open to widely conflicting views, involving the basic integrity of the leaders of China—and I hate to think of the hash that can be made out of the situation from both left and right. President Roosevelt can take the Buck analysis as an excuse for his insufficient aid. Col. McCormick can make equally good use of it . . . crying a pox on all international friendships. Labor and left-wingers . . . will smear good-will to the Chiang-Soongs as a capitalistic racket. The alleged "capitalists" . . . will start to sell China short as rapidly as possible. The religious groups will lack "reason for the faith that is in them." . . . I doubt whether any purely propagandistic problem since 1939 has been so genuinely important. But we believe in truth. Yes, however deeply our nation has suffered propagandistically both from Moscow and Berlin, we believe in the strategy of truth. What is the truth that ought to be told to the American people that has not been told? . . . The plain fact is that China has been struggling into modernity—her own modernity, but modernity nevertheless—and that for 16 years the Generalissimo and the Madame have led that struggle. Could there have been better leaders—or worse? Could they, being the leaders, have done substantially better—or substantially worse? Surely, these are not easy questions.

Luce decided in the end to publish the Buck article because he did not want to be "found guilty of having misled the American people."

He wrote to White to explain his thinking about the Buck article and to say: "In Chungking, you are, of course, daily confronted with all the things that are not being done as well as they should be. But just think, Teddy—the great fact is that Chungking is still there! That's the fact you have to be concerned about explaining. . . . You have always had immense faith in China and in the Generalissimo. . . . Perhaps you felt that you had communicated too much faith—or a too easy faith. I simply write to say you need have no such fears. It is still the faith—and not the defects of the faith—which it is most of all important to communicate."

The Honan famine story was not the only dispatch critical of the Chungking regime which White had filed and *Time* had printed, and Chinese diplomats in New York had complained. White learned of this and expressed his "sincere gratification to the home office for backing me in my policy of reporting as I see it." The tensions and problems of reporting from Chungking were obviously getting on his nerves, however—he was petulant about New York's treatment of other news from China for which he had no direct responsibility—and early in 1944 he was recalled from Chungking for rest and recuperation, and to write, free from Chinese censorship, an article for *Life*. It had to be submitted to the American military censors in the Pentagon; in asking that his report be released for publication, White wrote: "The true situation in China, today, is appalling. . . . I know that I reflect the views of the staff of the American Army in Asia. I have been chided many times personally by Lt. General [Joseph W.] Stilwell for the lush and unrealistic tone of all American public writing on China and its war effort." Meanwhile, Luce, in a memorandum to Billings, Gottfried and Matthews, had summed up Time Inc.'s policy:

> As a result of what he [White] writes and of our further delibera-
> tions with him, our attitude on certain Chinese questions may
> undergo a change. However, for your guidance, our Chinese
> policy on the following points is as follows:
>     1) *Communists*. We regret the existence of this gash in
> China's body politic but we in no way offer any implied advice
> to Chiang Kai-shek as to how he ought to handle the problem.
>     2) *Unity*. We are *for* liberal progressive democracy in China
> . . . but we should realize that China's top priority is the need
> for Unity. Remember the priority that Lincoln gave to the
> Union. . . .
>     3) *Soongs*.[18] The most difficult problem in Sino-American
> publicity concerns the Soong family. They are or have been the
> head and front of a pro-American policy. It ill befits us there-

[18] The eldest of the three Soong sisters was married to H. H. Kung, minister of finance until November 1944; the second was the widow of Sun Yat-sen, founder of the Chinese Republic; the youngest was Madame Chiang Kai-shek. Their brother, T. V. Soong, was minister of foreign affairs during the war.

121

fore, to go sour on them. On the other hand, they are probably increasingly less popular in China. . . . Restraint is indicated.

White's " *'Life'* Looks at China," published in the May 1 issue, by implication indicted Chiang for "the flat, black deadlock of politics in Chungking" and his wife for falsely representing China to the American people. It accused the Chinese government of being controlled by "a corrupt political clique that combines some of the worst features of Tammany Hall and the Spanish Inquisition. Two silent and mysterious brothers, Ch'en Li-fu and Ch'en Kuo-fu, known to all the foreigners of Chungking as the 'CC clique' . . . practically control the thought of the nation through a combination of patronage, secret police, espionage and administrative authority." White estimated that ten divisions of Chiang's best troops who might have been fighting Japan were in the province of Shensi to seal off the Communist armies: "Even medical supplies destined for the Communist armies have been seized by the central government cordon." He felt that after the defeat of the Japanese, a Chinese civil war was "almost inevitable." The article also told of the repeated U.S. failure to make good on promised delivery of supplies and excused inaction by the Chinese armies because their munitions were "so pitifully small that no sane Western staff could conceive of sending troops into battle with so small a national reserve." White, like Pearl Buck, concluded with a plea for greater military support for China.

On reading the draft, Luce had told White, "You have written undoubtedly the most important article about China in many years —perhaps ever." While he offered "some points for discussion," he did not impose his views on the article. White was delighted. "When I came back to New York, I was told that you would never let anyone publish anything like the things I wanted to say," he wrote Luce. "I was scared as Hell, Harry, at what I thought would be an inevitable clash between my convictions and your policy."

The Chinese reaction was curious. White returned to Chungking in June 1944, somewhat apprehensive as to his reception in official quarters. To his surprise he was greeted cordially by the Kuomintang bureaucrats and coolly by his friends among U.S. government officials and correspondents who had become disenchanted with Chiang, and who criticized White for applying "too much whitewash."

The reaction could be explained by the fact that the situation had deteriorated steadily during White's absence in the United States—

so much so that the article was outdated by the time it was published.

Economic conditions had brought the country to a state of near paralysis. In north Burma, beset by frustrations, General Stilwell was struggling against almost impossible odds to open the Ledo Road. In a new offensive Japanese forces had routed and disgraced some of Chiang's best divisions in Honan, and were driving south toward the U.S. Fourteenth Air Force bases in east China. Chiang's chief concern appeared to be to contain the Communists inside the areas around Yenan, where they had set up an autonomous government.

In the latter half of June Roosevelt sent Vice President Henry Wallace to Chungking to try to persuade the Nationalists to make their peace with the Communists and join forces against the Japanese. Wallace was unsuccessful. By July the Joint Chiefs of Staff were so alarmed over the imminent collapse of China that, at their suggestion, Roosevelt proposed to Chiang that Stilwell be put in command of all the armed forces in China, including the Communist. Humiliating as it would have been for the generalissimo to have a foreigner in such a position, the loss of face was compounded by the suggestion of Stilwell for the job. Relations between the two men had become increasingly bitter. Stilwell referred to Chiang as "the Peanut" and believed him to be the "main obstacle to the unification of China and her cooperation in a real effort against Japan." The generalissimo had long been pressing for Stilwell's removal from the theater. Above all, Chiang believed that putting an American in charge of the Communist armies would bring them aid and support that they would use against him.

When, in September, Roosevelt cabled a peremptory message, delivered to Chiang by Stilwell, virtually ordering him to place "General Stilwell in unrestricted command of all your forces," the generalissimo was enraged and demanded Stilwell's recall. Major General Patrick Hurley, Secretary of War under Hoover, who had arrived in Chungking that month as the President's personal mediator between the general and the generalissimo, finally advised Washington in October that "if you sustain Stilwell in this controversy, you will lose Chiang Kai-shek and possibly you will lose China with him." Roosevelt then recalled Stilwell. In trying to minimize a painful situation, he told his press conference that the quarrel with the generalissimo was "just one of them things."

To most members of Chungking's American colony, a tightly knit group of military staff officers, diplomats, and correspondents, Stil-

123

well's dismissal seemed an outright betrayal of the American and Chinese interests. To White, a longtime admirer of Stilwell, it was a tragic and catastrophic failure of American policy in China.

He poured out his bitterness and anger in a thirteen-page letter to Luce which the Chungking censor left virtually untouched: "Stilwell was relieved because of Chiang's embittered opposition to him; Chiang's opposition sprang from the fact that he could no longer tolerate . . . a group of men whose standards of honesty, efficiency and responsibility were so strikingly at variance with his own apparatus. . . .

"I have never tried so hard as I have in the past few months to come to an appreciation of [the generalissimo]. . . . Chiang has outlived his historical usefulness. . . . [He] is a man of almost appalling ignorance. He is not only ignorant, he is unaware of his ignorance. . . . He brooks no opposition, he requires a sort of smirching reverence. . . . He buzzes now from task to task with a lack of concentration that bespeaks a complete lack of confidence and trust in the very apparatus he creates. . . . There has come a turning against the Generalissimo such as I had never believed possible."

Turning from present to future, White offered his suggestions for a sound U.S. policy. These included no more "meddling" in Chinese internal affairs, by which he meant abandoning support for Chiang except as it is "coldly conceived as being a purely military expedient. . . . We must prepare ourselves psychologically for the shock of civil war that will come in China as soon as Japan is defeated. We must disassociate ourselves from the Kuomintang and Chiang Kai-shek. I do not know the nature of the Chinese Communist Party, and do not know whether we can ever supersede Russia as foreign patron in their estimation. I think there is such a possibility and I think we should investigate all angles. We should be keenly alert for the development of any group in China who will give this people decency in administration."

*Time,* in a cover story on Stilwell in its issue of November 13, 1944, totally rejected the view of its Chungking correspondent. The article was written by Fred Gruin (and edited by Whittaker Chambers).[19] It did praise Stilwell as a friend of China, and placed the

[19] Graduate of Columbia University ('33, Phi Beta Kappa) and the Columbia School of Journalism, Frederick Gruin, a native of New York City, had done a brief reporting stint on the *Hudson Dispatch* (Union City, N.J.) and spent eight years as a senior editor and writer on the New York *Times* "News of the Week in Review" before joining *Time* as a writer in 1943.

blame for his recall on Washington: "As usual Chungking, not the U.S. or Yenan, was criticized for the Stilwell incident." The story cited a dispatch from the New York *Times* correspondent Brooks Atkinson which, in sentiment akin to White's reaction, interpreted Stilwell's dismissal as "the political triumph of a moribund, antidemocratic regime that is more concerned with political supremacy than in driving the Japanese out of China." *Time* observed that Chinese Communists and their sympathizers "have never reported Yenan's rigorous press censorship (much stricter than Chungking's), its iron party discipline, 'traitors' (concentration) camps,' secret police, other totalitarian features." *Time* also said:

"General Stilwell's recall clumsily terminated an embarrassing episode—but not the basic situation from which it resulted. Stripped to the bare facts, that situation was that Chungking, a dictatorship ruling high-handedly in order to safeguard the last vestiges of democratic principles in China, was engaged in an undeclared civil war with Yenan, a dictatorship whose purpose was the spread of totalitarian Communism in China. At the same time Chungking was locked in a life & death struggle with Japan." Justifying Chiang's reluctance to come to terms with the Communists, *Time* concluded: "If Chiang Kai-shek were compelled to collaborate with Yenan on Yenan's terms, or if he were forced to lift his military blockade of the Chinese Communist area, a Communist China might soon replace Chungking. And unlike Chungking, a Communist China (with its 450 million people) would turn to Russia (with its 200 million people) rather than to the U.S. (with its 130 million) as an international collaborator."

White, meanwhile, had taken off for Yenan with the second group of foreign correspondents to visit Communist-held areas since 1939. Most of them were deeply impressed by the absence of censorship at that time, the apparent support of the peasantry, the energy, enthusiasm and dedication of the Communists, which they contrasted to the inefficiency, rigidity and corruption in Chungking. They echoed the Communists' best-known apologist, Edgar Snow, who had made a similar report as long ago as 1937 in his book, *Red Star Over China*.[20] White himself left Yenan with a "profoundly sympathetic attitude" toward the Communists and returned to Chungking to be confronted by, and to react furiously to, the Stilwell cover story, a report of which he had seen in a Domei agency bulletin.

[20] Victor Gollancz, London; Random House, 1938.

125

"We have indulged in an all-out attack on the Yenan Communists and have whitewashed Chungking. I can't believe it." He threatened to resign, "as I have no other way of preserving my integrity." At which Luce, for the first time in his correspondence with White, evidenced some irritation. "Keep your shirt on until you have full text. . . ." he replied. "Your views have always been respected here but I do not think it becomes you to get angry if for once your editor does not instantly follow your instructions."

White then wrote a piece on the Communists in North China "to make the Americans realize that there are reservoirs of strength, courage and honesty in the Chinese people that can still be mobilized." Although censored in Chungking, the article conveyed White's enthusiasm for the Yenan regime and urged United States cooperation with the Communists against the Japanese: ". . . the Party is willing to go to any lengths to be friends with the U.S. . . . If their friendship is reciprocated it can become a lasting thing." It was printed over White's by-line in the December 18, 1944, issue of *Life*.

White was presumably pleased that *Life* would publish his story, but he continued to brood over *Time*'s Stilwell cover and to send Luce morose advice of his intention to resign if *Time* "willfully fails to tell the [China] story." Luce was not unsympathetic. "Your letter seems to assume that I am a supporter of Kuomintang," he cabled. "Nothing could be further from the truth. We have consistently distinguished between the good and the bad in Kuomintang and you will recall that in April 1941 I told Generalissimo his Kuomintang was thoroughly unpopular and for ample reasons. . . . I deeply regret the pain and embarrassment you have endured in past few weeks and we hope that 1945 will be the best year ever for you and for *Time* in our Asiatic assignment."

Neither outcome appeared likely.

# The Present Becomes
# "The Unthinkable Future"

THE DEATH OF Franklin D. Roosevelt on April 12, 1945, said *Time,* "everywhere, to almost everyone . . . came with the force of a personal shock." To his successor the editors were friendly but a little patronizing. "With almost complete unanimity, Harry Truman's friends—in Washington and across the land—agreed last week that he 'would not be a great President,'" *Time* reported. "By this they did not mean that he would not be a good President. But he would not be a bold, imaginative, daring leader, carrying the U.S. people through reforms and upheavals and crises and flights of idealism as Franklin Roosevelt did. . . . The future would be entered in slower tempo."

*Life* observed: "This modest, perhaps too modest, man obviously did not want the job that Roosevelt so obviously loved. There was something finally elusive about Roosevelt's character, the elusiveness that suggests magic and breeds myths. Truman's character is anything but elusive and invites no more and no less confidence than your next-door neighbor's. The people therefore turn to Truman as to a neighbor, tendering a readiness to help. They know they will have to take a little more political responsibility on themselves from now on. Nobody can do their thinking for them any more."

Luce was inclined to take a more favorable view of the new

President. Five days after F.D.R.'s death, he wrote to him encouragingly, saying he had just come from a meeting

> where, as in nearly all meetings these days, the principal topic was the new President. Three or four of those present had known you more or less and they were called upon to give their opinions. Unanimously they expressed their complete faith in your ability to discharge successfully the great duties of your office in your own way. And this sense of confidence in you found ready response among all the others present.
>
> I know of no better way to communicate to you my profound good wishes for your Presidency than to tell you of the confidence which, among themselves, a great number of your fellow citizens already feel in your character and ability.

Truman, who took office twenty-five days before the final fall of Germany, had almost no preparation for his awesome responsibilities. He had been a reluctant candidate for the vice presidential nomination, and after his election he had not been admitted to the inner circle of Roosevelt's advisors. He had not been briefed on the staggering problems he was called upon to deal with; Truman did not even know then of the research his government had been doing on the atomic bomb.

The San Francisco Conference called to organize the United Nations was about to assemble as he took office. Its charter had been drafted by the United States, Great Britain, the Soviet Union and China at a series of meetings in 1944 held at Dumbarton Oaks, Washington, D.C., and made public during Franklin Roosevelt's election campaign as his "Great Blueprint" for peace. ("A revelation from Mount Sinai . . . something sacred, not to be disputed," Luce said.) Luce had forthwith assigned the Time Inc. Foreign Policy Advisory Committee (a successor to the Postwar Department) to do some research into the Dumbarton Oaks proposals. Raymond Leslie Buell was chairman of the project, with Luce, Billings, John Davenport of *Fortune*,[1] Jack Jessup of *Life* and John Osborne of *Time* collaborating.

On the eve of the United Nations conference, in May 1945, *Fortune*

---

[1] Davenport, Yale 1926, was Russell Davenport's younger brother. He joined *Fortune*'s writing staff in 1937 and became a member of the board of editors in 1941.

published the Buell paper ("Dumbarton Oaks and San Francisco") as a special supplement. The report declared: "Dumbarton Oaks is not good enough and never was; San Francisco can and should do better." The Soviet assumption was that the Yalta agreement settled everything. Secretary of State Edward Stettinius told Luce after the Yalta Conference that when Roosevelt proposed the San Francisco Conference, Stalin asked, "For what?" When the President explained that it was "to discuss the Dumbarton Oaks proposals," Stalin asked, "What is there to discuss?" The supplement quoted the anecdote. The gist of what *Fortune* had to say was:

The American people are in favor of joining a world organization to keep the peace. So are we.

The American people are also in favor of maintaining, for many years, a naval and military establishment at least as powerful as that of any other nation. Only if these two propositions are put together is it possible to talk sensibly and honestly about the Dumbarton Oaks proposals. . . .

The plan has three considerable merits. The first is that any great power—particularly the U.S.—can join it without sacrificing freedom of action or jeopardizing such security as it may create for itself. The second is that it sets up machinery for continuous international consultation. A third is that the Assembly and the world court are provided with great opportunities, though little power.

But the proposals have many serious flaws and they all add up to this: the plan's reliance on Big-Power agreement is so desperate that no peaceful alternative is envisioned.

Among the amendments *Fortune* proposed were:

The charter should genuinely recognize the principles of justice and law.

In order to give significance to the rule of law a definition of "aggression" should be included in the charter.

The Assembly should have the right to make recommendations on any matter relating to peace and security if the Security Council has not acted on the question, say, within three months.

The Assembly should have the power to propose amendments to the charter by a two-thirds vote, and the amendments should become effective when ratified by a majority of the members

129

including three of the five (instead of all) permanent members of the Security Council.

The Conference should consider the principle of "weighted representation" in the Assembly, which would be more effective and influential if the great powers were more adequately represented there.

The Security Council's role should be modified by broadening the obligation of the Council to investigate all disputes that threaten world peace. Specifically, the right of any one of the Big Five to veto an investigation should be abolished. The charter should encourage regional arrangements for the maintenance of peace.

The charter should contain a convincing declaration of principles with regard to colonial and non-self-governing peoples.

The charter should include an "international bill of rights."

In the preparation of the *Fortune* supplement the Time Inc. committee had the benefit of consultation with two influential men associated with the U.S. delegation at San Francisco who were prime movers in the effort to amend the proposals. The first was Senator Arthur Vandenberg, the ranking Republican member of the Senate Foreign Relations Committee. Before the war Vandenberg had been an isolationist; he supported the war once the United States was attacked, but was still chary of making postwar commitments for America in international affairs. In 1943, in a letter addressed "Dear Mr. Luce," the senator had complained that *Time* misrepresented his position in a story; when amends were made by publishing his letter, a friendly relationship developed between the editor-in-chief and the senator who thereafter were on a "Dear Harry"–"Dear Arthur" basis. After her election to Congress Mrs. Luce became a friend of the senator and brought the two men into a still closer relationship. In January 1945 Vandenberg made a notable speech in the Senate in which he renounced his previous isolationism, declaring that "no nation hereafter can immunize itself by its own exclusive action." Thereafter until his death in 1951 he was a central force in the shaping of American foreign policy. Luce had persuaded him to take a close look at the Dumbarton Oaks proposals and called his attention to their failure to give more than passing reference to "justice."

"Senator Vandenberg was enough of a political philosopher to be

130

outraged," Luce recalled. "He made a speech in the Senate—perhaps his greatest—on the need for concepts of justice and law in the quest for peace."

The other man with whom the Time Inc. editors consulted was John Foster Dulles, chief advisor to the U.S. delegation, who had been foreign policy advisor to Governor Dewey in the 1944 presidential campaign. Vandenberg and Dulles were able at least to get verbal recognition, at San Francisco, of the concepts of justice and law in international relations. Some, but by no means all, of the suggestions made in the *Fortune* study were adopted at the conference.

Luce left for Guam while the San Francisco Conference was still in session, to see the still unfinished Pacific side of World War II at first hand. With Roosevelt's death the ban on publishers visiting the war zones was rescinded, and Luce's friend, Secretary of the Navy James Forrestal, had invited *Time*'s editor-in-chief to visit the fleet.[2] He was joined in Honolulu by senior editor Roy Alexander and together they traveled 30,000 miles in thirty days. One pleasant surprise for Luce occurred as he was leaving Guam to join the aircraft carrier *Yorktown* for two weeks at sea; he asked the whereabouts of the destroyer escort *McGinty* on which his son Henry ("Hank") Luce III was serving as an ensign. It was at anchor in the harbor and father and son had five minutes together.

By the time Luce arrived the naval war in the Pacific was all but over; the *Yorktown*'s planes swept up and down the Japanese coast bombing Kyushu at will, meeting little opposition. A page of Luce's notes, "A Quiet Cruise of a Task Group," survives among his papers:

1) On a dawn patrol, one airplane and pilot go straight in the drink from the catapult. Destroyers picked up the body.

2) A jeep falls down the shaft of the airplane elevator, hits an 'Airedale' [sailor slang for pilot], miraculously does not kill him.

3) On the flight deck, an airplane propeller starts whirling by mistake, hits a man in the backside, cuts off a leg, nearly throws him overboard, but not quite; man survives.

[2] Under Truman's policy editors and publishers were allowed to travel in the Pacific area, but only in groups or "suitably paired" so that their reports could be checked against each other in case one should "give a biased picture of what he had seen." Luce was "paired" with Frank Schroth, publisher of the Brooklyn *Daily Eagle*.

4) One of our airmen on patrol knocks down a Jap airplane as it is about to kamikaze one of our destroyers; another of our men just fails to connect with another Jap plane and it succeeds in crashing on destroyer which sinks in two minutes.

His companion aboard the *Yorktown,* Alexander, recalled how Luce adjusted to the naval routine:

> Luce was always to be found in the Petty Officers Mess playing acey-deucey, which he did hour after hour. . . . He finally had a well-regulated day. . . . At noon he sat in the wardroom with the chaplain, Father [Joseph] Moody, who was a history buff, and they discussed history for an hour after chow was over, eating untold quantities of ice cream. And then he used to disappear. Where he was in the afternoon, as I quickly found out, was visiting a gunner's mate in the overhang of the flight deck. The gunner's mate was known all over the ship as a man of no words at all and he and Luce would just be sitting on ammunition cases drinking coffee.

Luce returned with the conviction that "almost nobody in the Navy from high Admirals to Seamen Second Class seems to have any clear idea about how the war with Japan is to be brought to a victorious close. Metaphorically as well as literally, nobody knows where we go from here or why."

He was convinced, however, that Japan was already beaten and that the war could be ended and much bloodshed avoided by some modification of the "unconditional surrender" formula laid down by Roosevelt at the Casablanca Conference in January 1943. In recollections of the Pacific trip, he wrote:

> I spent a morning at Cavite in the Philippines with Admiral Frank Wagner in front of huge maps. . . . He showed me that in all those millions of square miles [of East Asian seas] there was literally not a single target worth the powder to blow it up; there were only junks and mostly small ones at that.
>
> Similarly, I dined one night with Admiral [Arthur W.] Radford on the carrier *Yorktown.* . . . Radford had invited me to be alone with him in a tiny room far up the superstructure of the *Yorktown,* where not a sound could be heard. Even so, it was in a whisper that he turned to me and said: "Luce, don't you think the war is over?" My reply, of course, was that he

132

should know better than I. For his part, all he could say was that the few little revetments and rural bridges that he might find to bomb in Kyushu wouldn't begin to pay for the fuel he was burning on his task force.

When I got back home, I went straight to my friend Jim Forrestal. I had hardly completed a sentence before Forrestal picked up the telephone and called Secretary of War [Henry L.] Stimson. Stimson having gone to Long Island for the week-end, Forrestal sent me to Under Secretary of State [Joseph C.] Grew. Both Forrestal and Grew and others understood—or strongly hunched—that Japanese surrender could be obtained almost immediately—on one condition, which was that Japan should be allowed to retain the Emperor.

Grew had long been urging Truman to issue a declaration to Japan, as an inducement to surrender, that the emperor could remain as head of state. Forrestal shared his views (as did Stimson). Luce's first-hand report from the Pacific reinforced their feeling that "unconditional surrender" should be modified. But only a week before Luce went to Washington, the President had approved plans of the Joint Chiefs of Staff for an invasion of the Japanese home islands. The President and the JCS also thought it was necessary to encourage the Soviet Union's entry into the Pacific War, so that Russian troops could cope with Japanese forces in Manchuria and thus make victory complete. And Truman wished to wait for the Potsdam Conference in mid-July before issuing any ukase to Japan, feeling that then the declaration would demonstrate Allied unity of action and purpose. The atomic bomb, at this point still untested, remained an unknown military factor in the equation. Luce obtained an interview with Truman but the President, thinking *Time*'s editor-in-chief was merely making a courtesy call, cut short the interview before Luce could make his case.

The atomic bomb was dropped on Hiroshima on August 6, a Monday, the day *Time* went to press, so that issue covered only the stupendous news, with whatever background information on how the bomb had been achieved was immediately released.

Two days after the White House announcement Francis Cardinal Spellman recorded in his diary: "Russia declares war on Japan. Harry Luce and Joe Kennedy came to see me to ask if I would ask President

133

Truman for five or six days' truce to give Japan a chance to surrender." [3] The next day the second atomic bomb fell, on Nagasaki,
and five days later Japan surrendered unconditionally with the status
of the emperor still in doubt.

That week *Time* carried on its cover an orange sun crossed out in
black; inside, a three-page section entitled "Victory" led off with an
article entitled simply "The Bomb":

*The greatest and most terrible of wars ended, this week, in the echoes
of an enormous event—an event so much more enormous that, relative to it, the war itself shrank to minor significance. The knowledge
of victory was as charged with sorrow and doubt as with joy and
gratitude. More fearful responsibilities, more crucial liabilities rested
on the victors even than on the vanquished.*

*In what they said and did, men were still, as in the aftershock of a
great wound, bemused and only semi-articulate, whether they were
soldiers or scientists, or great statesmen, or the simplest of men. But
in the dark depths of their minds and hearts, huge forms moved and
silently arrayed themselves: Titans, arranging out of the chaos an age
in which victory was already only the shout of a child in the street.*

*With the controlled splitting of the atom, humanity, already pro-
foundly perplexed and disunified, was brought inescapably into a new
age in which all thoughts and things were split—and far from controlled. As most men realized, the first atomic bomb was a merely
pregnant threat, a merely infinitesimal promise.*

*All thoughts and things were split. The sudden achievement of
victory was a mercy, to the Japanese no less than to the United
Nations; but mercy born of a ruthless force beyond anything in
human chronicle. The race had been won, the weapon had been
used by those on whom civilization could best hope to depend; but
the demonstration of power against living creatures instead of dead
matter created a bottomless wound in the living conscience of the
race. The rational mind had won the most Promethean of its con-
quests over nature, and had put into the hands of common man the
fire and force of the sun itself.*

*Was man equal to the challenge? In an instant, without warning,
the present had become the unthinkable future. Was there hope in
that future, and if so, where did hope lie?*

*Even as men saluted the greatest and most grimly Pyrrhic of*

[3] Robert I. Gannon, S.J., *The Cardinal Spellman Story* (Doubleday & Company, Inc., 1962), p. 359.

134

*victories in all the gratitude and good spirit they could muster, they recognized that the discovery which had done most to end the worst of wars might also, quite conceivably, end all wars—if only man could learn its control and use.*

*The promise of good and of evil bordered alike on the infinite— with this further, terrible split in the fact: that upon a people already so nearly drowned in materialism even in peacetime, the good uses of this power might easily bring disaster as prodigious as the evil. The bomb rendered all decisions made so far, at Yalta and at Potsdam, mere trivial dams across tributary rivulets. When the bomb split open the universe and revealed the prospect of the infinitely extraordinary, it also revealed the oldest, simplest, commonest, most neglected and most important of facts: that each man is eternally and above all else responsible for his own soul, and, in the terrible words of the Psalmist, that no man may deliver his brother, nor make agreement unto God for him.*

*Man's fate has forever been shaped between the hands of reason and spirit, now in collaboration, again in conflict. Now reason and spirit meet on final ground. If either or anything is to survive, they must find a way to create an indissoluble partnership.*

The article was written by James Agee, one of *Time*'s most gifted writers.[4] Managing editor T. S. Matthews, who had been on vacation, had returned to the office on the news of the Japanese surrender. He

[4] Agee's sixteen-year career in Time Inc. is an example of how the organization somehow managed to accommodate the gifted nonconformist. Agee came to *Fortune* from Harvard in 1932 and was hired by Ralph Ingersoll, then managing editor, in accord with Luce's dictum that it was easier to transform poets into business journalists than bookkeepers into writers. Agee's well-recognized literary talents were not easily harnessed to the task of business analysis, but he survived. Out of one *Fortune* assignment—with the talented photographer Walker Evans—to look at sharecroppers in the South came Agee's and Evans' book *Let Us Now Praise Famous Men*, which was first published in 1941 (by Houghton Mifflin Company) and then republished in 1960, five years after Agee's death. Matthews, when editing *Time*'s back-of-the-book sections, brought Agee from *Fortune* to *Time*, where he worked on many sections from Books to Cinema. At the same time he wrote a signed column for the *Nation* which helped make him known. He finished his career with the company, like Whittaker Chambers, as a writer on Special Projects. The brilliance of Agee's film criticism transcended the anonymity that cloaked most *Time* writers and won for him a reputation that led him to a full-time career in Hollywood motion pictures where, among other achievements, he is remembered for his brilliant scenario for John Huston's *The African Queen*. His posthumously published autobiographical novel *A Death in the Family* (McDowell, Obolensky, Inc.) won a Pulitzer Prize for 1957.

found that acting managing editor Dana Tasker had the issue well in hand, but in the many stories scheduled that week there was no single article on the overall implications of Hiroshima. With the kind of editorial inspiration that Matthews often displayed, he turned to Agee and let Agee's own inspiration do its work.

There were those, including some on the Time Inc. staff, who felt that it would be a mistake to spare the emperor. Robert Sherrod, who had seen more of the Japanese in battle than any other Time Inc. correspondent, wrote to Luce urging that the magazines take a strong line against retention of the emperor, who, he said, was the source of Japan's "great spiritual strength." Luce did not agree. "If we killed every single Japanese, that wouldn't prove [the U.S.] 'spiritually' stronger," he replied to Sherrod. "One of the sure signs of spiritual weakness is the desire to settle an argument on purely physical terms. . . . My willingness to let the Japs have their Emperor at this point is based mainly on the practical consideration that as a result of the catastrophic nature of the war, the one thing which is absolutely certain about Japan is that Japan will go through a period of very profound economic and social change. The corollary of this certainty is the near-certainty that the Emperor of ten years from now, if he exists at all, will bear no resemblance to the Emperor-image with which we and the Japanese have been recently and un-happily familiar. . . . I am not *for* the Emperor (God forbid); but I am not for prolonging the war simply in order to hang him— because I think he's very nearly a dead bunny anyway."

When the arrangements for formal surrender dragged on, *Time* and *Life* both expressed a certain impatience, summed up in this *Life* editorial: "Have we beaten Japan? . . . Certainly the Japanese government's behavior since surrender has not been reassuring. . . . Obviously the Japs show no psychological acceptance of defeat. The Emperor has, in effect, merely called off the war in order to prevent 'irreparable harm to the human race'·from further use of the atomic bomb. Thus he is not only still Emperor but a world savior to boot." Luce disagreed and chided his editors for being

a little naive . . . in taking as seriously as [you] did the gripes against the ending of the war. . . . This is not to say that the procurement of Jap surrender was handled in the way I think it ought to have been. For example, I don't think the atomic bomb

136

was handled right; if the Japs have any good "alibi," it's the bomb. The Japs were beaten without the bomb and I believe surrender could have been procured without the bomb. I don't know whether we will handle the Japs intelligently or not. But there is nothing in the surrender terms to prevent our doing so.

Luce always remained convinced that Japan could have been induced to surrender and without use of the atomic bomb; in 1948, in a speech at Milwaukee, he said, "If, instead of our doctrine of 'unconditional surrender,' we had all along made our conditions clear, I have little doubt that the war with Japan would have ended no later than it did—without the bomb explosion which so jarred the Christian conscience. . . . The United States must never again fight a war for 'unconditional surrender.' "

The President, on August 9, 1945, declared that the United States, Great Britain and Canada, who had the secret of atomic bomb production, "do not intend to reveal that secret until means have been found to control the bomb so as to protect ourselves and the rest of the world from the danger of total destruction." Then, two days later, in what Atomic Energy Commission Chairman David Lilienthal later described as "the principal breach of security since the beginning of the atomic energy project," [5] the Smyth report was released; [6] it narrated the history of American development of atomic energy and revealed that the secret of the bomb lay in the technology of its production, in engineering know-how. This made it evident that other countries could, and probably would, produce atomic bombs in time.

In the fall and winter of 1945–46 the administration and Congress worked out a transfer of control over American atomic energy installations from military to civilian agencies. Meanwhile there ensued a vehement, sometimes near hysterical debate in which the atomic scientists took a leading part. Proposals to save the world from destruction ranged from the immediate establishment of a world government to appeals for mass conversions of mankind. Scientists were concerned lest officially imposed secrecy stifle scientific progress and inquiry.

Time Inc. publications devoted a great deal of space to this debate

[5] Hearings before the Senate Section of the Joint Committee on Atomic Energy, January–February 1947, p. 32.

[6] Henry DeWolf Smyth, *Atomic Energy for Military Purposes* (Princeton University Press, 1945).

without indicating an editorial position. When *Fortune*'s managing editor Ralph Delahaye ("Del") Paine, Jr., proposed to publish, in the November 1945 issue, an article by Dr. Louis N. Ridenour, a physicist not involved in the development of the bomb, Luce was disturbed by Ridenour's argument that U.S. security lay not in secrecy but in what he called "the security of achievement," by which he meant keeping the United States ahead of the world in scientific progress. Luce was wary of the scientist's argument that secrecy was unimportant. He wrote to Paine urging that he postpone publication: "To 'wait' is, generally speaking, not a good rule in journalism. But in the case of the atomic bomb, I think the chances of being wrong are so great that, even journalistically, it could be smart to wait." His counsel of caution was overridden; the article appeared as scheduled.

Luce tended to reject the more extreme arguments of the atomic scientists because, as he told his editors:

A) They feel a sudden profound evangelical and wholly un-natural concern of conscience about their business. (For 100 years the scientists have been excused from all moral responsi-bility and have excused themselves, while looking disdainfully down at the moral muddle of the race, which they regarded as irrelevant and unnecessary as it was pathetic, tragic and ridiculous.)

B) They want desperately to do something but *they don't know what to do nor how to do it.* e.g. They are inclined to plump for world government and then find that they are dis-tressingly incompetent to answer any of the relevant questions about World Government which, to date, only Clarence Streit has solved to his own satisfaction.[7]

e.g. They are finally inclined to plump for something vaguely in the form of a spiritual reformation—and then they are really completely up a tree.

C) All of which I regard as very optimistic—but we must not confuse the scientists' evangelical concern with any hope that they know what to do about it. Because they don't.

Up to this point, beyond stating that it was "crazy" even to think of sharing the atomic secret with the Russians, Luce had remained

[7] Streit was the author of *Union Now* (Harper & Brothers, 1939), founder of the "Federal Union" movement for a federation of the Atlantic powers.

silent in the atomic argument; he was determined, he said, "to keep my seat in the peanut gallery of this Atomic Hippodrome." But he spoke up from his seat when Truman, Britain's Clement Attlee and Canada's Mackenzie King in November 1945 proposed that the United Nations create a special commission which would provide for free exchange of scientific information and for controls to see that atomic energy was used only for peaceful purposes, and proposed a convention for the elimination of all weapons of mass destruction. Luce wrote his editors: "The obvious, it seems to me, has now been well stated."

# The Ordeal of China

V ICTORY IN THE PACIFIC brought forward again the problem of China. Stilwell's recall (he was replaced by Major General Albert C. Wedemeyer as Chiang's chief of staff) restored some harmony to official Sino-American relations. But with the defeat of their common enemy, civil war between the Nationalists and the Communists became imminent. From Chungking Theodore White ominously warned *Time* that China faced almost insurmountable problems and that Japan in her death throes still had the power to convulse all Asia; in his opinion the only way to assure stability and peace in the Orient was "to establish within the next few weeks mechanisms and principles for the surrender of Japanese garrisons such as shall satisfy all portions of Chinese society—Kuomintang and Communist alike."

When Luce read White's gloomy cable, he lost his temper, warning the editors of *Time* that it was that of "an ardent sympathizer with the Chinese Communists. There may be some good reporting in it but it is entirely from one point of view. . . . From White's dispatch one would gain the impression that nobody in all China is happy that Victory (and Peace of a sort) have been won. . . . Though I do not have White's advantage of being on the scene, I would lay a small bet that quite a few millions of Chinese will receive the news of Victory (or Jap defeat anyway) with at least a moderate degree of pleasure. And I would think that among them might be a guy named Chiang Kai-shek—even though he must be almost as aware as White of the terrible costs which China has paid and of the vast problems with which he and his fellow Chinese will be confronted."

*Time* was scheduling a cover on Chiang, and White filed a second cable that further irritated his editor-in-chief:

> China this week [is] entering the gravest crisis. . . . It is true, indeed, that Chiang Kai-shek is the key personality. . . . But if Time Inc. adopts the policy of unquestioningly, unconditionally supporting his hand we will be doing a monstrous disservice to millions of American readers and to the Chinese whose personal concern this is. . . . We hope that you will select facts in an impartial, judicious manner warranted by the enormous dimensions of this tragedy. For Jacoby and myself this piece is a testing stone. . . . We feel our policy should be non-partisan, directed to middle-road, democratic peaceful solution. If this is determined otherwise we shall consider this a repudiation of ourselves as reporters and will want to be relieved of the current assignment and return home at least to put the case directly before the editor-in-chief for final settlement of our status and China policy.

Luce replied:

> We desired nothing except non-partisan reporting. We realized this might be an unreasonable request in view of your avowed partisanship . . . *Time*'s policy regarding China is exactly what you describe as non-partisan directed to middle-road democratic peaceful solution. Such a policy obviously doesn't include efforts to overthrow the duly recognized President of China. . . . If in view of your convictions you cannot do a professional objective job, I will thoroughly understand and we may be obliged to cancel Chiang cover. In any case, after witnessing armistice ceremonies, it's obvious that you must come home immediately to come to an understanding with your editors on what's meant by a non-partisan policy directed to middle-road democratic peaceful solution.

This acrimonious exchange had crossed a message from the chief of the news service granting White's request to attend the surrender

141

ceremonies and then to return home. White hotly resented Luce's charge of partisanship and said so in a return cable, adding: "In past year every major treatment of China problem displayed divergence our views and [that cable] was attempt [to] alert you to that fact and underscore it."

In order to evade the Chungking censorship, White filed from Manila en route to the Japanese surrender ceremonies a personality sketch of Chiang which likened the generalissimo to Stalin and in which he blamed Chiang alone for the coming civil war. The generalissimo, he wrote,

> permitted his government to impose upon the people one of the most merciless and brutal of totalitarian systems. The misery and bitterness thus engendered was capitalized by the Communist party to create a system and army of their own. . . . By the policy of no compromise [Chiang] has forced [the Communists] into what may become total, abject subservience to the Soviet Union. Unless their party can be brought away to stand independent in participation in Chinese affairs, China's independence and integrity are a myth. Unless [the Communists] can be convinced that Chiang's promises and concessions offer an adequate guarantee for laying down their arms, there can be no peace.

This assessment was countered by one prepared by Luce and Billings for the guidance of the editors:

> The difference between the "dictatorship" of Yenan and the so-called "dictatorship" of Chungking is . . . a difference of fundamental political theory. Chiang Kai-shek, to keep his group in power, must constantly work to maintain a balance between factions supporting him—political manipulation, concession and compromise in our sense. The Chinese Communists indulge in no such political balance or manipulation. No opposition factions are tolerated. . . . The Chinese Communists are a part of international Communism and not a local agrarian growth . . . their leaders regard themselves as Marxists first and Chinese second. Chiang has consistently urged the Communists to join a National Assembly for a really *united* Chinese government. Under such a system the Communists would be just one of several parties in the government. The Communists . . .

142

reject the idea of a united government and demand a "coalition government." . . . If Chiang should accept coalition government, this is no guarantee that the Communists would stick to their assigned areas and not infiltrate the non-Communist areas. . . . The U.S. Government backs a united China. If Soviet Russia, whose aims and actions in China are darkly obscure, should get behind a divided China with coalition government and if both the U.S. and Russia began to push hard, there would be a head-on collision.

In *Time*'s view, set forth in the resulting cover story, the generalissimo's government had a firm, popular support and, given peace, could establish an effective administration.

The *Time* story coincided with the publication of the terms of the thirty-year Sino-Soviet Treaty of Friendship and Alliance, signed in Moscow on the day Japan surrendered. A by-product of the Yalta Conference, the treaty recognized the Chiang regime as the legitimate government of China and affirmed Chinese sovereignty over Manchuria; Russian aid would go only to the Nationalist government. The treaty, *Time* said, "for the present kicked the props out from under the Chinese Communists." Luce felt the treaty could be "one of the most fruitful ever made"—a judgment he was later to admit was fleeting.

Luce had been wanting to revisit China ever since his trip there with Mrs. Luce in the spring of 1941. In October 1945, with a personal invitation from Chiang, he landed in Chungking—at a tense and critical time. Mao Tse-tung and Chou En-lai were in Chungking negotiating with the Kuomintang for a political settlement. Ambassador Patrick Hurley, who had been acting as mediator, had returned to Washington for consultation. Meanwhile, troops of both sides were jockeying for military advantage. Communist guerrillas were harassing Nationalist-held cities and blocking and destroying the railroads by which the Nationalists were attempting to move supplies and extend their control.

Luce met Mao at a party given in the Communist's honor at which Mao delivered a speech. "His face is heavier and more peasant-like than that of most national officers," Luce reported. "His sloppy blue-denim garment contrasted sharply with his host's snappy beribboned uniform. [Mao] started slowly with a slight clearing of

143

the throat after nearly every phrase, but he built up gradually to a full-voiced shout at the end. He said . . . that the thirty percent of the problem [of reaching agreement between Nationalists and Communists] which remained to be settled 'will be settled by discussion and *by no other means*' (great applause) and that China must find 'unity under Chiang Kai-shek.' " Mao, Luce reported, "was surprised to see me there and gazed at me with an intense but not unfriendly curiosity. His remarks: polite grunts." Luce's meeting with Chou was more relaxed. "We had a nice talk—and completely frank from the moment we sat down. He said we hadn't been very nice to them recently. I said that was too bad because we had a worldwide battle on our hands with worldwide left-wing propaganda—and it was just as nasty as skunk. At my request, he said he would put me in touch with the Communists . . . in Shantung."

The reference to Shantung was in anticipation of Luce's visit to North China. There he visited Tsingtao, where he and his family had spent happy vacations,[1] and then went on to Peiping, where he was able to visit Yenching University, which his father had helped to found and where a building was named in his father's honor. Luce's energy and curiosity during the tour made a great impression on his hosts; a staff correspondent of the Central News Agency provided the Chinese press with this *Time*-like account of Luce's visit to the North:

> Rarely did he [Luce] hesitate to hammer home his point whenever he sensed the ambiguity or evasiveness of the information he was given. His directness and knack of ferreting out facts sometimes embarrassed the men he interviewed. . . . He has an inbred flair for news . . . which few of his contemporaries could hope to excel.
>
> The 47-year-old publisher whose strength of will rarely is challenged has a particular taste for Oriental delicacies. . . . Once during a dinner in Peiping, a specially prepared fried duck so thoroughly pampered his palate that he immediately called in the cook . . . to shake hands . . . and even toasted the excellence of his cuisine. . . . On another occasion at a Chinese banquet, Mr. Luce underestimated the strength of Chinese yellow wine. He emptied his cup so many times that an extra cup might have put him under the mahogany.

[1] *Time Inc. 1923–1941*, p. 26.

At Tientsin in North China Luce visited U.S. Marine headquarters; there his life was threatened by an enraged marine, but Luce was not aware of this bizarre episode until many years later. In 1953 Willard R. Hasbrook of San Bernardino, California, who had been stationed in Tientsin at that time, wrote Luce: "One of my buddies decided that Henry Luce was the prime mover in the campaign to keep North China occupied by the marines and felt obliged to put a round in the chamber of his M–1, aim the rifle very coolly at the small of the back of the man who was keeping him from going home. Needless to say, the man was very bitter and more than slightly neurotic and it took some talking, a great deal of persuasion and force to wrest the M–1 from him and quiet him down. Believe me, I watched your departure . . . with a great deal of relief." [2]

In Peiping, nearing the end of his trip, Luce told a group of Chinese newsmen: "In coming to China I had one question in mind and that was whether it would be reasonable to be optimistic about the future of China. So far it seems to me that the answer is definitely in the affirmative."

Just before leaving, he wrote to Madame Chiang Kai-shek:

The biggest surprise, and the happiest, was to find that the spirit of the people in North and East China is so strong and healthy. [They] do not seem to have been either cowed or corrupted by eight years of life under enemy and puppet control. . . . If the people can be given a chance to translate such eager spirit into hard, rewarding work, then the salvation of China will be close to fulfillment.

At the same time he ventured some suggestions and criticisms:

There is an immediate need for understanding between the West and the East of China. . . .

It is the desire of all that the economy of China should be restored with utmost speed by every lawful means. One danger is that government bureaucrats . . . may inhibit the recovery of Chinese economy. . . . Every form of lawful economic activity should be encouraged. . . . Small-time Government bureaucrats can do more harm than good. . . .

[2] Luce replied to Hasbrook: "Certainly never before have I received a letter from a stranger which held such personal interest for me . . . It's a curious feeling to learn years later that your number was almost up. And how can I thank you enough for your interference in changing the signals?"

145

As to the Communist problem . . . A) the overwhelming desire of the people is for peace. B) The onus for disturbing the peace falls more and more on the Communists even in territories in which they were strong; C) There are undoubtedly many bands which are nothing but bandits. . . . D) Therefore it seems to me that the government while being generous to the true Communists in all that concerns peaceful political activity would have a popular mandate to proceed vigorously, though soberly, against lawless military activity of every sort. . . .

Sometime in the next few weeks it would be most opportune for the Generalissimo to express his interest in the development in China of a vigorous and intelligent press . . . what we want is a Chinese press which will do a tremendous job of education in China and which will command the respect of the world.

Luce's optimistic view on China's future, later reflected in various interviews and reported in the press, alarmed some of his Chinese friends, who feared it would have an adverse effect on U.S. aid. Premier T. V. Soong reminded him: "The rehabilitation of China is no less difficult than that of Europe." Yet Luce was by no means as overoptimistic as might have appeared; his own observations supported the view (later put forth by the State Department White Book of 1949) [3] that China's economy had survived war and occupation in better shape than anticipated and there was no reason why, as Luce argued, a resilient and energetic people, given political stability, should not manage a rapid recovery.

But political stability was denied them. One stabilizing force had been the U.S. military presence. Ever since the Japanese surrender the United States had provided logistical support to enable Chiang's forces to take over garrisons occupied by the Japanese; in some cases U.S. Marines had held the garrisons pending the arrival of Nationalist forces. The prospect of clashes between Americans and Communists increased. At home, to an outcry that the United States was intervening in a civil conflict abroad was added the familiar and impatient demand, "Bring the boys home." In a two-page editorial in *Life*, Luce pleaded for continued American aid and intervention, at least to the extent of letting U.S. troops guard rail lines that were being attacked by Communist guerrillas.

[3] *United States Relations with China*, pp. 127 ff.

A new development suddenly exploded in the bitter and wavering situation. In November Patrick Hurley resigned, charging that "a considerable section" of the State Department was "endeavoring to support Communism generally as well as specifically in China." Hurley, who had gone to China in September 1944 as Roosevelt's personal emissary to Chiang, later becoming ambassador, was attempting to carry out U.S. policy which was to mediate between the Kuomintang and the Communists. Like so many others, Hurley had bought the Moscow line that the Chinese Communists were "margarine" Reds, not the genuine article. Frustrated and angered by his failure to bring the two factions together, he had first turned on his advisors in the Chungking embassy; now he exploded these blanket charges. Truman moved swiftly to defuse the controversy. He summoned out of retirement General George C. Marshall, whom he regarded as "the greatest living American," to become his special envoy to China. Americans joined together in praising his initiative.

White, who had come home from China just before Luce left on his trip, was temporarily without assignment and on leave; he and Annalee Jacoby began a book based on their experiences there.[4] There was no question of White's going back to China for *Time*. The headquarters for Time Inc. operations in China—business as well as editorial—was shifted from Chungking to Shanghai and there William Gray now presided as chief correspondent. When the government was relocated in Nanking in 1946, Fred Gruin was assigned to the capital.

White discussed future assignments with Luce. He was not interested in writing in the head office; the one foreign assignment he wanted was one that Luce would not give him: that of Moscow correspondent. Luce put the situation in this way to a small group of his senior associates in a "strictly confidential" memo:

Teddy has, as he says, a great affection and respect for *Time*. So his general loyalty to *Time* is in no sense in question. Still, the question I opened with was and is *the* relevant question in his case—and Teddy answered it, in its various phases, with an honesty for which I like and respect him. At one point, pursuing the question, I said to him: "Are you willing to take any job I assign to you from copy boy to managing editor?" His answer: "No." Then a little later: "Will you take any post in the Foreign

---

[4] At the end of her leave, in May, Mrs. Jacoby resigned.

field that I assign you?" Answer: "No." . . . A very rugged
character is Teddy. That's fine. . . . While I regret that he
feels unable . . . to sign on for general service to Time Inc.,
he is probably doing the right thing for himself. What he offers
to us is a highly specialized service. I am not buying it at this
time.

Their parting, however, was friendlier than most of their associates
had reason to believe at the time.

The White and Jacoby book, *Thunder Out of China*,[5] appeared
in October 1946 and was a Book-of-the-Month Club selection. *Time*
gave it a four-column review, crediting the authors with "an obviously sincere and not wholly unsuccessful effort to be fair. Yet the
same inner flame which made them such tireless reporters of the
war gradually heats their indignation till it boils over in angry judgments of Chiang himself as well as of corrupt men in his administration. They are not blind to the dangers of Communism, but as their
condemnation of Chiang grew, they came to prefer the Communists
by comparison."

The ordeal of China profoundly affected not only Luce and White but
also other editors who were caught up in the China story. Luce had
sent Charles J. V. Murphy[6] of *Fortune* to Chungking just before
White left there, to report what was to be Chiang's triumphant return to Peiping, Nanking and Shanghai—a return that was delayed
because of the widening civil war. But Murphy came back eager
anyhow to write an article on Chiang, the background of the civil
war, and his assessment of what was needed to salvage the Nationalist cause; one of his convictions was the vital need for the Nationalists
to control Manchuria. He was occupied that winter and well into the
summer of 1946 writing what turned out to be a four-part piece
intended for *Life*, which John Billings edited down to two parts.

The article was pro-Chiang. "I may err in not dwelling more on
certain shortcomings which are not alone the result of his intellectual
deficiencies," Murphy wrote Luce, "but also those of all China. . . .
Needless to say, I regard him as a truly great man." The piece pre-

---

[5] William Sloane Associates.
[6] Charles Joseph Vincent Murphy, Harvard 1926, joined Time Inc. in 1936
as a writer on *Fortune,* after newspaper and free-lance experience. Later he
was a staff writer on *Life,* then rejoined *Fortune*'s board of editors in 1952.

dicted that the coalition which George Marshall was trying to effect must by the nature of things fail, nor was it in the U.S. interests to press it.

Yet Luce hoped that some good might come of Marshall's efforts, because of the tremendous prestige of the man himself and the public support that the mission had engendered. At George Marshall's own request, Luce had given leave to James R. Shepley of the Washington bureau to go to China in advance of the mission to set up arrangements and handle preliminary negotiations.[7] Later, again at Marshall's request, Luce granted leave to John R. Beal of the Washington bureau to become political advisor to Chiang, under contract to the Chinese government.[8] Marshall felt Chiang needed a counselor who understood Washington thinking and American public opinion to keep his government from taking extreme measures that would have an adverse effect on American opinion, such as suppressing opposition newspapers and banning critical books.

Murphy had his piece ready for publication at last in September, when one day Billings came into his office and dropped the manuscript on his desk. "It's not running," he said simply. The decision had been Luce's, who still clung to hope for the Marshall mission and had been told, moreover, by some of his senior associates that they felt Time Inc. was injuring its reputation by its continuing commitment to Chiang. Luce told a bitterly disappointed Murphy, "Never mind, it's time to get off the hook with Chiang." "We've never been on the hook," Murphy retorted. "Now is the time to get on." It was some time before the two men spoke to each other again. Some ten years later, Murphy recalled, Luce remarked at a lunch

[7] Shepley joined *Time*'s Washington bureau in 1942 after an apprenticeship on his father's newspaper, the Harrisburg *Patriot,* and the United Press, where he had covered Congress. He served as a war correspondent in the India-Burma theater. In 1944 he was commissioned as a captain and assigned to the office of Army Chief of Staff General Marshall; he helped to write and edit the chief of staff's final report on the war. Returning to *Time,* he covered the Pentagon; after the Marshall mission he rejoined the Washington bureau, which he headed for nine years.

[8] John R. Beal was born of missionary parents in India and educated in the United States. On graduation from Ohio Wesleyan University and after working on several small papers in Ohio and New Jersey, he, like Shepley, had joined the United Press and had covered Congress. In 1944 he was hired by *Time* to cover the Senate. He went to China early in 1946 and served on the generalissimo's personal staff for fifteen months, then returned to *Time*'s Washington bureau. In 1970 he published his account of the Marshall mission, *Marshall in China* (Doubleday & Company, Inc.).

149

with some of his editors, "My worst mistake was in not printing Charlie's article."

In October 1946 Luce decided that he himself should fly out again to China. He was received in Nanking, where the government had moved in May, by all those concerned in the mediation efforts: the generalissimo and his wife; Chou En-lai, still acting as chief negotiator for the Communists while the Communist forces, despite the cease-fire arranged by Marshall, were actively battling the Nationalists; General Marshall; and U.S. Ambassador J. Leighton Stuart, who had been appointed in July 1946. The ambassador was an old friend and colleague of Luce's father, like him a missionary; he had long been president of Yenching University in Peiping. Frequently Stuart was Luce's host at dinner in Nanking. Luce recalled one particular conversation with the ambassador when "he was especially disturbed. He had been conferring with Chou En-lai and he said to me, in evident astonishment: 'You know, Harry, these Communists don't *think* like Chinese.' The significance of this remark was that Leighton Stuart was known, both favorably and critically, as one of the few Westerners who knew China so well that 'he thinks like a Chinese.'" Stuart had come to an opposite conclusion from Marshall: he believed that the only way out was American support of Chiang, including use of American troops if necessary. "So we had the ironic situation of the man of God favoring military action," Luce recalled, "and the soldier unwilling to use the sword."

Some twenty years later Luce wrote of his own meeting with Chou En-lai:

> I must record the utter confidence as well as the good humor with which Chou En-lai spoke to me. While he didn't say so in so many words, I had the chilling feeling that he expected soon to be in control of all China. At the end of my stay, I figured he was right. . . . History says that the Communists took over mainland China in 1949. I have trouble remembering that date, because as far as I am concerned, the Communists had won in 1946, when the Marshall mission ended.

Chou tried to persuade Luce that the Communists genuinely wanted a cease-fire. He did indeed want a cease-fire—but at a price (as Luce learned when Stuart produced for him the latest Communist demand): the wholesale withdrawal by the Nationalists from key front-line positions.

After his return Luce warned *Time*'s editors against taking a "pox-on-both-your-houses" position, which characterized so much of the then current reporting from China. At the same time he recognized that until the Kuomintang improved the economic situation and stopped the inflation Chiang's government was in for trouble. "What is to be hoped for," Luce concluded, "is that within the next few years a new era of Chinese politics opens up—probably involving splits in the Kuomintang as well as the development of fresh political movements."

He cabled Ambassador Stuart that he and Marshall should not underestimate the willingness of American public opinion to support "a program of vigorous assistance to China through [a] constitutional national government." The cable also warned that if the negative and defeatist view reflected in the Jacoby-White book and certain State Department circles was to prevail, "then we better abandon everything except the simplest Christian missionary effort."

But the Marshall mission was coming to an end and the general was preparing to return home. From Nanking Gruin wrote that Marshall, as a military man, had warned Chiang that he was overextended and could not sustain a long war, which would cause complete economic collapse, and that therefore he should make one more attempt at a political settlement. Chiang, while professing willingness to co-operate, rejected Marshall's military judgment, still arguing that given the arms he could defeat the Communists. Shortly after, Gruin wrote:

> Marshall, who has been severely criticized by the Communists as a two-faced reactionary villain, may turn out to be their chief, if inadvertent comfort. Presumably, if he returns home a failure in his mission . . . he will blame it mostly on the Gimo . . . advocate a policy of no military supplies and a niggardly hand otherwise. . . . This will encourage the Communists, if they need any encouragement.

On leaving China, Marshall placed the blame for his failure on Kuomintang "reactionaries" on the one hand and "irreconcilable Communists" on the other, and urged China's liberals to unite under Chiang's leadership to produce good government. *Time* interpreted the statement to mean that American policy in the future would continue to be "geared to the legal Government of China."

151

But Gruin's guess was not far off. As Marshall left China to return to Washington, he was named Secretary of State to succeed James F. Byrnes. At an off-the-record press conference in Washington a few weeks later (*Time*'s Washington bureau reported), the new Secretary condemned the corruption in Nanking and said that "the U.S. could not afford to be dragged through the mud by all-out, unreserved support of such a government." The withdrawal of Marshall from China was followed by a sudden aggravation of the monetary crisis there; in desperation, Premier T. V. Soong urgently appealed to Luce and warned of the imminent collapse of Chiang's government. But Marshall was now in the driver's seat. *Time* commented bitterly:

> Mediator George C. Marshall had whisked U.S. policy out of China. In its wake was a vacuum which threw the Chinese Government into crisis. . . . Secretary of State George C. Marshall watched the crisis develop without taking or preparing any action. . . . There was no question but that China's Communists viewed the plight of [Chiang's] government with relish. They liked U.S. no-policy even better than U.S. mediation.

The stage was set for the final act in the tragedy of Chiang's regime.

# The "Gruntling" of
# Winston Churchill

I N 1946, as the U.S. position in China was so rapidly deteriorating, the Soviet Union was tightening the grip of Communism on Eastern Europe. The warnings of former Ambassador Bullitt in *Life* and Chambers' "The Ghosts on the Roof" in *Time* were now being echoed by many men in high places. The most memorable of the warnings was delivered by Winston Churchill, in March, at Westminster College, Fulton, Missouri. "A shadow has fallen upon the scenes so lately lighted by the Allied victory," he said. "Nobody knows what Soviet Russia and its Communist international organization intends to do in the immediate future. . . . From Stettin in the Baltic to Trieste in the Adriatic, an iron curtain has descended across the Continent."

The initial reaction of the liberal and leftist press was generally hostile. In New York, when he spoke at a dinner at the Waldorf-Astoria, from which Under Secretary of State Dean Acheson had pointedly excused himself, Churchill was picketed by Communist sympathizers. Moscow waited eight days, then labeled Churchill a warmonger, and Stalin in a calculated insult compared him to Hitler.

In an editorial *Life* came to Churchill's defense:

He never hides the articles of his own faith. In his own words, he never ceases "to proclaim in fearless tones the great princi-

ples of freedom and the rights of man, which are the joint in-
heritance of the English-speaking world. . . ." For some time
this crusading note, this faith in human freedom, has been
curiously lacking in American statements of policy and even
more in American policy itself. . . .

There is a very good chance that peace, as well as progress,
may be the by-product of balanced tension and creative rivalry
between the U.S. and Russia. . . . But if it is to be a true and
mutually fructifying balance, American foreign policy needs
something more than "toughness" and a will to peace. It needs,
to balance the Communist idea, what Hamilton called an "active
principle" on our side.

In the same issue *Life* published articles by Joseph P. Kennedy (who
had served from 1937 to 1941 as ambassador to Great Britain) and
John Foster Dulles. The editors did not altogether agree with
Kennedy, who was for keeping the United States militarily and
economically strong and for taking a firmer line toward Russia, but
warned against "minding other people's business on a global scale"
by attempting to spread liberal democracy throughout the world.
"Mr. Kennedy does not give sufficient weight to the practical need
for American idealism in American foreign policy," said the editors.
"The conflicts in the modern world concern ideas and ideals no less
than bases and bread." The Dulles piece was more to *Life*'s liking.
It was a summary of a report made by the Federal Council of
Churches, which Dulles had drafted. The United Nations Charter,
said the statement, needed a "spiritual drive" to galvanize it into a
"positive force for human welfare." On a second point, the article
urged that the United States hasten progress toward self-government
among the dependent peoples of the world.

*Life*'s editorial concluded:

These liberation movements are more our business than
Russia's; their slogans are those of Jefferson, Lincoln and Wilson, not Karl Marx. Men have not changed; they still seek
liberty and justice above all things.

Coincident with the publication of the editorial, Churchill was guest
of honor at a private dinner given by Luce at the Union Club of
New York with a dozen of his senior associates.

*Life* had been fishing for some time for the rights to Churchill's memoirs, which the old ex-journalist was sooner or later bound to write. A first hook had been baited—the editors suspected they would never catch him on just one—immediately after he lost the election in July 1945. New York cabled London bureau chief Walter Graebner to offer him $25,000 an article for four articles on any subject he cared to write about. Churchill's office replied that he did not contemplate writing for the moment but that when he did *Life's* offer would be kept in mind.

A few months later Graebner received a telephone call from Churchill's son, Randolph. Over a drink at the Ritz, Randolph told Graebner, "Father, you know, has just come back from a holiday [at Lake Como]. He painted all the time he was there, and some of the things he's done are quite good. I think you might be able to get him to let you print them in *Life*. I know you want him to write articles, but the old man isn't interested now."

Churchill was living temporarily at Claridge's in London. Graebner went to see the paintings next morning. They were laid out on chairs, sofas and tables, a whole roomful of pictures, and Churchill arrived in about five minutes, wearing his Royal Air Force blue siren suit and with the inevitable cigar.

"You made me a very good offer," Graebner recalled his saying. "I was greatly touched by it because it's the best offer that I've ever had—five dollars a word. Hmm. Hmm. I would like to write for you but I don't feel that I can at present. I am now in retirement from journalism—a retirement which I was obliged to enter when I joined the government. If I came out of retirement and wrote I would have to pay 19/6 to the pound in income taxes. But I have done these paintings while on holiday in Italy and I thought perhaps they might take the place of one article.[1] Some of them I think are pretty good." He eyed his paintings with obvious pride. "Talent, you know, has many outlets!"

Graebner cabled New York the suggestion that buying first reproduction rights on the paintings might "give us the inside track to his memoirs." The editors agreed, and a deal was made: sixteen pictures for $20,000.

Shortly after, Graebner was in New York when he received a tantalizing message from Churchill: "When are you coming back? I have something to discuss with you." Graebner was received this

[1] The payment for the paintings would be subject to capital gains tax.

time at Churchill's new London home, 28 Hyde Park Gate. The great man was in bed wearing a Chinese dressing gown; on his stomach was a bed table and placed neatly in the center was a stack of manuscripts. He peered over his spectacles and said, "I will read to you for a while, but all this must be in confidence for the time being." Then, in his House of Commons style and with appropriate gestures, he read part of one of three speeches he had made before Parliament in secret sessions during the war. From time to time he stopped and asked Graebner what he thought; finally he said, "When I sent you the telegram in America, I thought that it might be possible to let you have these speeches for *Life* if your people were interested." The asking price was $75,000.

Luce's reaction, scribbled on Graebner's cable, was: "In my opinion $75,000 is Churchillian highbinding. I would offer $50,000 —and mean it." Churchill held out for $60,000, offering some additional material; *Life* finally got the three secret speeches for $50,000.

"We just about concluded the deal on New Year's Day 1946," Graebner wrote, "when Churchill asked me to Chartwell for lunch. It was a good lunch, with champagne and quite a lot of brandy. After lunch we went for a long walk around his estate to see how the workmen were getting along with the repair of his complicated watering system. I fell into one of the reservoirs, causing Churchill to remark: 'I knew this would happen. You are too precipitous. Now you must come in and warm yourself in front of the fire with a glass of whisky.' It was a cold snowy day and I warmed myself for several hours while Churchill talked about the war, described his admiration for Lawrence of Arabia ('What a commander he would have made in this war with me behind him!'), recited *Locksley Hall* to prove that Tennyson was a prophet, etc., etc. For a time the final talks on the Secret Speeches became stuck at one point when Churchill said he felt that he'd have to cut several critical passages on de Gaulle. I expressed a fear that [deletions] would materially lessen the value of the speeches. Churchill then said that perhaps it might be better to delay the entire publication. Obviously I couldn't hide my disappointment, for Churchill said: 'I can see that you are unhappy. Your face tells me just what you feel.' I cabled the difficulty about de Gaulle [to the editors in New York] who agreed at once to the deletions, which were, actually, quite small."

In the January 7, 1946, issue of *Life* there appeared eight pages

156

in color of the Churchill paintings; in the January 28 issue the magazine ran the first of the secret speeches, the second on February 4. "Technically Churchill's painting is not equal to his statesmanship, but it is pervaded by the same spirit of dogged realism," said *Life*. "Like Eleanor Roosevelt's prose, it is earnest, straightforward and innocent of professional polish." Churchill was quoted as saying, "I must say I like bright colors. I rejoice with the brilliant ones, and am genuinely sorry for the poor browns." Churchill was delighted with the reproductions, writing Luce, "I have not felt nearly as shy about letting them be seen by an immense audience as I thought I should be."

Only two of the three secret speeches were published.[2] The one omitted concerned British shipping in 1941 before the United States entered the war and was considered of only minor interest to American readers. Luce thought that the two which were printed were a bore. One was on the fall of Singapore, the loss of H.M.S. *Repulse* and *Prince of Wales* off Malaya, the escape of the *Scharnhorst* and *Gneisenau* and mounting losses in the North Atlantic; the other dealt with the Allies' deal with Admiral Darlan—it was from this one that Churchill had requested deletion of some comments on de Gaulle (his "heaviest cross"). "It was, of course, a pig in a poke," Luce wrote Longwell. "And I believe that *Life* has got to buy some such pigs in order to keep a position in the meat market. Also, the prestigious flamflam *may* make it worth while. Also, it can be worth the space plus the money if, in some sense, Churchill becomes 'our author.'"

It was certainly Longwell's conviction that it was worth the money and the effort, and when Churchill paid his first postwar visit to the United States, to make his Iron Curtain speech at Fulton, Longwell spared no pains to—as he put it—"gruntle" him.[3] He showed him many small courtesies, kept him informed of every detail in connection with the publication of the speeches. *Life* also tempted him with a $50,000 fee to make a radio broadcast on a national hookup which he finally declined, deciding that he should not make a U.S. broadcast under commercial auspices. It was just before he sailed for

[2] Churchill was pleased to be paid for all three.

[3] Christopher Morley, the author and editor, had once praised Longwell, then a book publisher, in an article in the *Saturday Review of Literature* as a man who knew how to "gruntle" authors; Longwell just assumed that all writers were "disgruntled," Morley wrote, and that the only way to handle them was to see that they were "gruntled"—coddled and cared for.

Britain after the Fulton speech that Luce entertained him at dinner at the Union Club.

As Luce made clear in a confidential note to his associates, the dinner was intended to be "primarily a social rather than a working affair. Our eminent guest is doing heavy work in the world. Like good workingmen, he loves his work, no doubt. Nevertheless it is work, and tonight we don't want to overtire him with overtime work. . . . So let every Time Incer, as a joint host, try to contribute to Churchill's enjoyment. [The evening] will be a success if we get our guest well and happily in the groove of discussion—with him, of course, doing 80% or 90% of the talking."

In Time Inc.'s archives is an account of the dinner written by Charles J. V. Murphy. Cocktails were served in a reception room, during which ritual, according to Murphy,

Mr. Churchill's eyes lighted upon an imposing portrait on the wall. Striding across the room, he halted before the solemn, haughty countenance of what appeared to be an eighteenth century personage. He squinted at it fiercely, then asked bluntly: "Who is that blighter?" The question caught the host between wind and water. . . . For a moment the painfully contrived structure of Mr. Churchill's beloved Anglo-American community based upon a common cultural heritage hung in the balance; then Harry, after a hasty glance at the little brass nameplate on the frame, announced with something less than his customary aplomb that it was William IV. "William IV?" answered Mr. Churchill in obvious surprise. "Hrumph. . . . Looks more like Lord Rosebery to me. . . . Same heavy jowls. . . ." "Ah," Harry said, waving gaily at the brooding portrait, "but there the resemblance ends." This learned sally into the characters of England's inept and blundering monarch and the erudite and devoted biographer of our guest's father, Lord Randolph Churchill, caught the rest of the company off guard. However, the conversation was almost immediately restored to a less demanding altitude as Harry took the guest by the arm and wheeled him around to view a monumental creation of the Union Club's hors d'oeuvres department.

As a centerpiece the club chefs had prepared a huge American eagle carved from ice, holding mounds of caviar. The eagle was slowly melting, and as Churchill accepted a martini he eyed the sculptured bird and remarked, "The eagle seems to have a cold." He then asked if he might be seated, and, according to Murphy,

Harry himself brought up a chair and the old man sat down in front of the dissolving ice eagle and contemplated the caviar with satisfaction. On seeing a *Time* editor spread the caviar on dry toast, the gourmet was galvanized into registering a sharp warning: "This stuff needs no reinforcement." To set the example, he spooned himself a whopping helping which he transferred with scant interruption from his plate to his mouth, occasionally emitting an appreciative belch. "I hope, gentlemen," he announced, "you don't find me too explosive an animal." Thinking that Churchill was referring to the controversial Fulton speech, Harry at once started to protest, saying that on the contrary Mr. Churchill had only put into words what was gravely in the minds of many Americans. But the guest . . . cut off the compliment, saying, "I am happy to hear that, sir, but the explosions I had in mind were those given off by my internal pleasure." As he downed another spoonful, he added reflectively, "You know, Uncle Joe used to send me a lot of this, but I don't suppose I'll ever be getting any more."

The Soviet onslaught had certainly shaken him. One moment the situation was "a crisis of the most urgent nature, holding real danger for my country." But on second thought he was inclined to regard the Russian reaction as an ill-tempered, crude and typical Communist trick. He pointed out how Moscow, before uttering a word, had waited eight days to judge world reaction and prepare its line; how then the whole apparatus of propaganda had opened up on him, with Stalin himself joining the historians and editorial writers in an orchestra of abuse and vilification. "This in itself," he concluded, "is flattering." He could not resist making fun of the clumsiness of the process and even at Stalin's heavy-handed attack on him personally. "You know," he suggested half seriously, "if *I* had been turned loose on Winston Churchill, I would have done a much better job of denunciation." The thought gave him pleasure. Brightening perceptibly, he went on to tell how Hitler had attacked him in almost identical terms: "Warmonger, inciter of wars, imperialist, reactionary, has-been—why, it is beginning to sound almost like old times." . . . It nettled him to be told that many Americans

159

could not fathom his hostility toward Russia and a suggestion
that his attacks were taken by some earnest citizens as Red-
baiting brought the almost fierce retort: "I won't change on that
account."

Among those present, Murphy recalled, were some who felt that
Churchill had indeed been Red-baiting. But on the whole Luce's
associates, obeying their host's pre-dinner injunction, were happy to
keep the honored guest in his "groove of discussion." One moment of
tension occurred when *Fortune*'s John Davenport asked: [4]

"How did it happen, Mr. Churchill, that you and Mr. Roosevelt were so misled at Yalta as to offer such a high price to
the Russians in order to lure them into the Pacific war—a war
that was already won?"

The host sat up as if stabbed. Waggling an ecclesiastical fore-
finger at Editor Davenport, he said sternly: "Mr. Churchill, it
is hardly necessary to answer that question. Foremost among the
subjects on which Mr. Davenport certainly is not an expert is
the Far East and the Japanese war." It is doubtful that Mr.
Churchill even fully appreciated the submerged differences that
accounted for the flurry which, as seen from his chair, whirled
up out of nothing. How could he have known of the schism inside Time Inc. which during the war had divided its editors
among those who subscribed to the doctrine that the Pacific
war was *the really tough war* [Murphy's emphasis], the consequences of which would have the most decisive effect on the
American destiny, and others who held, with Editor Davenport,
that Europe was *the* important war. . . . Mr. Churchill, having fought out this very question with the American Chiefs of
Staff and indirectly with the American public, must have been
surprised by the intensity of feeling lingering among Time Inc.
editors. On the other hand, his political judgment had been
challenged and, refusing to be sheltered by Harry's intervention,
he gallantly seized the nettle.

Churchill's answer was the predictable and stock answer: the prospect of long and bloody conflict if the Japanese islands had to be in-

---

[4] Davenport was co-author, with Murphy, of *The Lives of Winston Churchill*, which appeared in *Life* in 1945 and later that year as a book (Charles
Scribner's Sons).

vaded; and then he lapsed into his own version of Yalta. The "flurry" did not mar a "famous" evening.[5] Gruntled but still not hooked to a contract, Churchill departed for England, where *Life* would continue to pursue him.

During the spring there were two important contributions to the shaping of American attitudes toward Russia. One was a report made from Moscow to the State Department by a then little known Foreign Service officer, George F. Kennan. The second was an analysis of Soviet policy written for *Life* by John Foster Dulles.

Kennan's analysis was "leaked" discreetly to a few journalists, among whom was Sam Welles,[6] a wartime reserve Foreign Service officer, who was then writing in *Time*'s International section. Welles summarized it in a memorandum that became the basis for a *Time* story in April 1946. Kennan's name was not mentioned.[7]

Russia wants power [the *Time* story said]. Russia wants prestige. Russia wants security. Russia regards the peace as an opportunity better than any the Czars ever had, better than the Bolsheviks are likely to have even in a decade or two. . . .

By the ideological nature of the disease, Communism feels safe only when it is the doctor. In search of such safety, Russia has annexed 273,947 square miles since 1939—an area bigger than Texas. She has placed behind the quarantine of "friendly" (*i.e.,* docile) governments the nations on her borders, and now has the two chief exceptions, Iran and Turkey, under deep-sea pressure. . . .

Russia's economic power is expanding into the vacuums left by the shattered industries and trading spheres of Germany and Japan. Her social system, while it challenges centuries of Western progress, has an undoubted appeal for millions. Her political

[5] In his account Murphy reported that vice president Grover, "a precisionist in such matters," noted that the honored guest during the evening drank "one martini, two sherries, four or five glasses of champagne, and one formidable *ballon* of brandy."

[6] Princeton 1935, Rhodes Scholar at Oxford, Welles became a *Fortune* writer in 1938, transferred to *Time* in 1939. During the war he was assistant to John Winant, U.S. ambassador to Great Britain. He returned to *Time* late in 1945.

[7] A year later his name became well known when he was identified as author of the article, "The Sources of Soviet Conduct," signed simply "X," in *Foreign Affairs,* in which "containment" was proposed as a method of dealing with Soviet Russia.

techniques are self-confident, ruthless and capable of infinite variety, from military terror to humanitarian tracts. Directly and indirectly, she uses any number of organizations, in any number of ways, to run her errands.

She joins international bodies only when it suits her interests. . . .

But despite her fears and ambitions, Russia does not want war. Though eager to grab, she is highly sensitive to firm and unified opposition. Russia is still weaker than the U.S. alone and much weaker than the West as a whole. If the rest of the world lives up to the UNO Charter, Russian desires are not likely to overstep the bounds.

The Dulles analysis appeared in *Life* in June. It was inspired by Stalin's *Problems of Leninism,* which Dulles regarded as a blueprint for Soviet policy. He argued that Russia sought nothing less than a worldwide Pax Sovietica and that the only way the United States could effectively combat Communism was by Americans showing that they cherished and were willing to fight for the freedoms which the Soviet policy would destroy. The American system, Dulles wrote, must "demonstrate" its capacity to cure social ills. America must maintain a strong military establishment since the Russians believed that a lack of force showed that the "man who does not put a lock on the door of his house has nothing in it that he greatly values." America must give economic aid. America must "adhere steadfastly to principle."

The Dulles article (in two parts) drew some static from the left but provoked no such storm as had the Bullitt article of 1944. The climate had changed. The reason was Russian intransigence, which was building up fear and resistance not only in the United States but in Europe. Luce, who made a quick trip to occupied Germany and Austria with a group of U.S. publishers under War Department auspices, came back "somewhat more optimistic than when I went," he told his associates. He found in Europe a will to resist Communism and more vitality in the anti-Communist and non-Communist parties than he had anticipated. In London Prime Minister Clement Attlee told him: "I want to assure you that British Socialism owes a great deal more to Christ than to Marx." [8]

[8] Two years later Attlee amended his words: "Luce, I assure you that British Socialism owes everything to Christ and nothing to Marx."

In Germany Luce ran into a minor functionary:

[In Frankfurt] one morning, I was standing outside the house of our correspondent waiting to motor to Munich, when along came a very stout, very blue-eyed, very cheerful man enjoying a cigar. He asked if he could get a ride with us to Munich. He was, I gathered, an economist. Our conversation en route was rather general, but I found him more than averagely interesting. So I made a date with Herr Professor Ludwig Erhard to walk through the city of Munich the next day. We walked for about two hours through the weirdly vacant and silent streets. . . . In every street the rubble had been neatly piled on either side— so we walked down the middle, the sidewalks being unsafe. As we walked along, the Professor kept repeating . . . with growing insistence and enthusiasm, "Free enterprise! Free enterprise! Free enterprise!—that is the only hope." [9]

While the U.S. publishers were traveling around Europe, the Council of Foreign Ministers, in session in Paris to prepare draft peace treaties, was approaching deadlock after failure to reach agreement on any of them. Byrnes presented the draft of a four-power, twenty-five-year treaty for complete disarmament of Germany after the occupation ended, but he got nowhere with the Russians. When the conference finally broke down, press comment on Byrnes was reserved. Hesitating to proclaim a breach with Russia or indict Molotov, most papers continued to speculate on ways to gain Russian cooperation. The French, *Time*'s Paris correspondent reported to Luce, felt that Byrnes had wrecked the conference by pretending to be cooperative but in reality having been unreasonably stubborn. Luce came to his defense. He wired Senator Vandenberg, who had been a member of Byrnes's delegation: "As you know, and as indicated in *Time* and *Life,* I believe that Byrnes and his advisors at Paris displayed statesmanship of a high order." Vandenberg replied that in his judgment, too, the Secretary of State had done "a magnificently courageous and constructive job"; the United States had had to "demonstrate that the 'appeasement' days are over. . . . I do *not* believe

[9] In June 1965, at a dinner in New York after Columbia University had conferred a doctorate on him, Erhard, chancellor of West Germany since 1963, said that it had been this talk with Luce that encouraged him to press for acceptance of his idea of a market economy, which was not very popular with the military government at the time, and gave him hope for Germany's and Europe's future.

that Russia wants war—at least not yet. I do *not* believe we are in danger of war by *reasonably* standing our ground with *firmness* but with *patience*. . . . If Russia *is* bent upon ruthless expansionism, then it is only a question of time before we face a showdown in defense of our own democracy."

*Life* ran an editorial in May 1946 which was to be remembered by its author, Jack Jessup, as one that "helped to start the cold war." Jessup recalled Luce tearing out a cartoon from the New York *Times* which "showed the Western foreign ministers standing around in a huge cloud of smoke labeled 'misunderstanding.' This sappy cartoon became our theme for that week's editorial. There was no misunderstanding, we pointed out; there was a *world-wide conflict*. Why kid around? Byrnes probably already knew this, but neither he nor Truman felt like telling it to the American people. So we did, and by the end of that year the American people were giving their informed support to Byrnes's policy of 'patience and firmness.' We also helped clear the opinion track for rearmament, for NATO, for the rebuilding of Germany and for other essential measures of those years when peace-loving Americans gradually faced the fact that peace must be waged as well as loved."

The relationship between Luce and Jessup was a very special one based on both trust and friendship. While Jessup was adept at distilling Luce's thoughts into an editorial, it was by no means a one-way street. The chief editorial writer usually initiated ideas and editorial positions and sometimes challenged Luce's. And when they disagreed, as happened on occasion, there would ensue "some extended and gargling incoherence between the two friends," as *Time* and *Fortune* writer Wilder Hobson once described it, "that would find Jessup paused in bafflement." Although Luce, on rare occasions, then wrote his own editorial, the usual upshot of a disagreement was a strong Luce editing of a Jessup draft.

In the November 1946 congressional elections domestic issues, not foreign, were more on the voters' minds; inflation, strikes, the black market, postwar shortages of every kind from meat to housing weighed against the administration. Campaigning under the slogan "Had enough?," the Republicans won control of the Eightieth Congress. The election was described by *Time* as "quiet and unemotional" and one in which "the majority of Americans had cast a protest vote [against] too much Government in too many things."

Luce had no personal interest in the election. Mrs. Luce had announced that she would retire from politics at the end of her term as representative for "good and sufficient reasons." Her conversion to Roman Catholicism, she explained, had decided her against running lest "a few cynical people" be tempted to inject the issue of religion into a campaign for her re-election.[10] Two years before, she had suffered a shattering personal tragedy: her only child, a student at Stanford University, was killed in an automobile accident.[11] Though prostrate from grief for a time, Mrs. Luce had gone on to win her seat in the 1944 election and, in her second term, was if anything even more active politically. But the death of her daughter continued to depress her (and was one of the reasons for her seeking consolation in religion). Also, life in Congress had begun to pall; she had no desire to make a career of it.

The Republican leadership kept pressing her to reconsider; her name was prominently mentioned for the Connecticut senatorial nomination. In August, *Time* reported her final "No," ran an appreciative review of her congressional record and dropped a footnote:

The story of Clare Luce, though told in nearly every other publication in the land, has been told hardly at all in the pages of *Time* or its sister publications. *Time* editors, beginning with Editor-in-Chief Henry R. Luce (husband), fumbled the story, because they were too fearful of being damned if they told it or damned if they didn't. Despite the reticence of Time Inc. publications, Clare Luce's enemies were continually yawping about the vast publicity support she got from the "Luce publications."

---

[10] The publicity given to Mrs. Luce's conversion led one Midwestern Presbyterian minister (himself a convert from Catholicism) to write to Luce's pastor, the Reverend Dr. George A. Buttrick, protesting that Time Inc. magazines gave too much publicity to Catholicism. The inference was that Luce, influenced by his wife, might forswear his Presbyterian faith. Luce often showed a remarkable patience with such intrusions into his private life. He wrote Dr. Buttrick's correspondent: "I realize that the concern which you and others have expressed may seem to be confirmed by the news of my wife's conversion to Catholicism. I am happy for her, that she has found a Christian faith. But as for the Editor-in-Chief of Time Inc. publications, an ample road to salvation was marked out for him in childhood and it will be obvious to you that he must take that road or none."

[11] On Ann Brokaw's death *Time* in its obituary notice reflected the editor-in-chief's affection for his stepdaughter; she was described as the "daughter of Connecticut Representative Clare Boothe Luce and Henry R. Luce."

The Republican victory in the 1946 elections was less significant than an extraordinary new phenomenon in the United States. In 1946 isolationism was for the time being laid to rest; the recriminations about Yalta would linger on, but Secretary of State Byrnes, working closely with Senator Vandenberg, had neutralized foreign policy as an issue in politics. This was reflected in *Time*'s choice of Byrnes as Man of the Year for 1946 at a moment when he was about to be succeeded by George Marshall. In a "convalescent" year, *Time* commented, Byrnes's "patience" and Vandenberg's "firmness" had converged into a bipartisan policy that became "the most important new factor in world politics." This proved to be true, with the exception of a still vacillating U.S. policy on China.

# Converting from
# War to Peace

IN A MEMORANDUM written during the war, Charles Stillman had discussed the postwar opportunities that would open up for the company, and also observed: "We are fighting for long life and not, as we once were, for the next breath." Prior to the war management had little time to make long-range plans. It had dealt serially with the problems of growth, which had culminated in the crisis raised by the unanticipated public demand for *Life*—success that had almost broken the corporation's back. No sooner had *Life* become profitable than war intervened. The resulting surge in business more than doubled Time Inc.'s revenues in the six years from 1939 through 1945, but with no increase in profits: in 1939 on revenues of $29,311,000 net income was $3,207,000; in 1945, the year the war ended, on revenues of $74,157,000 net income was $3,041,000. The reason, of course, was that wartime excess profits taxes were calculated on a calendar base that included two years when the start-up costs of *Life* were at their peak. "As successful as *Life* became during the war," Stillman said, "it was just a tax collecting agency for the government." The company was later to recover $7,745,000 of these wartime earnings but not until twelve years after the end of the war. However, the experience gained from this tremendous new volume of business was profitable in another

167

way: the skill and ingenuity of management were tested in coping with material shortages and wartime restrictions, and in expanding from a domestic publishing house to a corporation operating around the world.

Spurred on by Stillman, the company set up a new-projects committee to examine half-a-dozen ventures that might be launched once the war ended. Stillman, chairman of the committee, was convinced that the company should look beyond magazines even though the magazines could expect a "brilliant postwar business future." He felt that "the opportunities [in other fields] are so obvious and compelling that no progressive American company . . . could ignore all of them. It would have to try one . . . just to be in the swing. . . . We are big enough so that we can afford the losses involved in experimentation." He urged the selection of one major project that could be tackled on what he called an "all-hands-to-bail-her" basis. Among the projects considered appropriate were a national newspaper, book publishing and ventures in radio and television.

President Roy Larsen—notwithstanding his own past success with *The March of Time* broadcasts—was against expansion into radio; he had already told the directors that he had

> grave doubts about extending Time Inc.'s activities into the creating and developing of radio programs. . . ´. Everything I feel about radio goes for television. . . . It is primarily show business. . . . I hope that first emphasis in any postwar expansion plans for Time Inc. will be in the field of the printed word. . . . One reason I hate to see us getting into another field is for fear that we will not give enough attention to the investments we have in the magazine field, and become easy prey for some new group of youngsters with a big idea and nothing else to think about.

But the temptation to enter radio was still strong. The company did acquire a 12.5 percent interest in the American Broadcasting Company, but when a reorganization took place there in 1945, Time Inc. sold its holdings. While Larsen had gone along with the ABC deal as an investment, he still remained adamant on the point that "whether business is good or bad, our first consideration and first call for all the brains and talent we have here must be made by our present products." Larsen, age forty-four, wrote to Stillman, age thirty-nine: "Sometimes, in the face of your enthusiasm for going into new proj-

168

ects—whether on an investment or management basis—I get the feeling that I am surely getting old and too damned conservative. But I would be less than honest not to express the thoughts and concerns which I have, even though the obvious reason for them is my old age." For a while, at least, Time Inc. would stick to the business it knew best.

An important by-product of the postwar planning was the introduction of an annual forecast, which became known to a generation of the company's business managers as "the fix." Once a year management, with the help of consulting economists, made an estimate of forthcoming economic conditions to establish guidelines for decisions on budgeting and production.

The first of these "fixes," in 1943, looked ahead to postwar requirements in paper and printing. The study indicated that wartime paper controls had interrupted a growth trend in magazine circulation and that at the conclusion of hostilities Time Inc. must be prepared to increase its advertising and circulation capacity. On these assumptions, orders were placed, in collaboration with printers, for postwar delivery of new equipment and for increased paper supplies.

Like every other publisher, Time Inc. was acutely short of paper during the war years; witness to the steady deterioration in quality and weight of the paper was an April Fools' Day memorandum circulated in 1945 by the production department:

> Although *Time* stock is now so thin it is possible to read an advertisement from either side of the sheet with equal clarity, it has been decided not to increase advertising rates on this account. It is felt that the goodwill value will offset the fact that the advertiser is getting something for nothing.

Nevertheless, reduction in paper weight and other measures taken to stretch out the available supplies did enable Pierrie Prentice, publisher of *Time,* to boast with justifiable pride that, with no reduction in editorial content, "We have still been able to carry more circulation for our domestic edition [and] are now printing a total of some 750,000 copies a week of our other editions. In other words, the total circulation of *Time* under paper rationing has gone up from about 1,250,000 to just under 2,000,000. As far as I am concerned, what this all adds up to is another miracle of the loaves and fishes."

The company had rigorously held to a policy of not owning real

169

estate, paper mills, or printing presses; by avoiding direct involvement in the manufacturing process, Time Inc.'s managers were thus able to concentrate on the special problems of publishing. In 1945, however, a departure from previous practice took place; during the year three paper mills were acquired in a crash program to assure an adequate paper supply for the future, and, because of the acute shortage of office space in Chicago, the directors approved the purchase of the eight-story Michigan Square Building at 540 North Michigan Avenue for $2,250,000.[1]

An aggregate of $9,663,000 was invested in the three paper mills: the Bryant Paper Company of Kalamazoo, Michigan; the Maine Seaboard Paper Company of Bucksport, Maine; and the Hennepin Paper Company of Little Falls, Minnesota. Even as these acquisitions were made, Time Inc. further increased commitments to its old suppliers to take more paper from them as soon as they could enlarge their production. In addition to its initial investment in the mills, the company allocated $2,253,000 to finance improvements and began construction of a new $3,000,000 coating mill at the Bryant Paper Company.

While Stillman played the decisive role in initiating this program, David W. Brumbaugh, elected a vice president in 1945, was taking over more and more operations; his was the total responsibility for procurement and for the production and distribution of the magazines. When he became chairman of a committee to integrate the production of the new mills, he and Stillman warned their fellow executives that "other persons not members of this committee, up to and including Stillman, should not attempt to meddle in this area. This program, involving the expenditure of millions of dollars in these several mills and schedules of delivery of equipment as well as paper flow far more complex than anything heretofore attempted, will tax the patience, ingenuity and teamwork of all concerned."

This was by no means overstating the problem. Although management had considerable knowledge of paper technology and related manufacturing operations, it entered into a contract with the experienced and technically proficient St. Regis Paper Company for consultation and management services. The company was interested in

---

[1] The building, which was to house Time Inc.'s Chicago subscription fulfillment office for the next twenty-four years, was sold for a capital gain of $3,900,000 in 1969, when the fulfillment staff moved to its new Time & Life Building at 541 North Fairbanks Court.

rapidly restoring the prewar quality of the paper used in the magazines—the reason for the additional investment in the coating mill. In a word, increased capacity and better quality were given immediate priority over the usual business objective of reduced costs.

In late 1946, its future paper supply assured, and with a determination to revert to its policy of avoiding direct involvement in manufacturing, Time Inc. sold the paper properties to St. Regis.[2]

In keeping with Larsen's dictum about expanding in the "field of the printed word" was *Time*'s excursion into international publishing. By war's end the magazine was published in twenty separate editions, printed on every continent except Antarctica, and had acquired civilian and military circulation outside the United States of 1,125,-000. Meanwhile, *Life Overseas* at war's end had grown to a circulation of 625,000. By and large, expansion of overseas circulation had been carried out as a service operation with little thought of cost or profit and by 1945 was showing an annual deficit of more than $500,000, money which the management felt was well spent in terms of good will and experience.

The wartime operations of *Time* overseas were largely under the direction of Pierrie Prentice, who originated the idea of the Pony edition, and his assistant, E. C. Kip Finch.[3] By the time hostilities ended, Time Inc. had a staff of over 350 full and part-time publishing operatives in various parts of the world.

This staff not only had been called upon to exercise initiative and ingenuity but had often operated close to the front lines and at great personal risk. In late 1943 Stillman's assistant William B. Harris, working for the publisher's office, flew on a British courier plane from Scotland to Stockholm to set up a Scandinavian edition of *Time*. He watched in the blackness as the bomb bay doors of the Mosquito bomber opened and closed beneath him over enemy-held territory while the pilot tried to cope with icing conditions. The most frightening experience of the overseas publishing representatives was that of Mary Johnson Tweedy, who was based in Calcutta as the liaison agent between the army and the local printer of the China-Burma-

---

[2] Part of the deal involved St. Regis stock, of which more was subsequently acquired. When in 1957 the company liquidated most of these holdings, it made a profit of $7,709,000 after capital gains taxes.

[3] Finch, a graduate of Columbia and Harvard Law School, was hired in 1936 as an office boy and held a variety of jobs in the corporate and publishing areas.

India Pony edition. Mrs. Tweedy, who was then four months pregnant, parachuted from a disabled plane over the Himalayas. She, her husband and the crew were rescued by local tribesmen. When the baby was born, the infant and her parents were awarded the Caterpillar Club insignia of those who had survived a life-saving emergency parachute jump.

In the Philippines, before printing equipment could arrive in Manila, correspondents Carl Mydans and William Gray were pressed into service and cabled that Mydans' friends, the GHQ Engineers, had printed *Time*'s Pony while the battle for the Intramuros district still raged nearby, and that 5,000 copies of the first magazine published in the city were being distributed free to troops of the MacArthur command and an allotment had also been given to the internees of Santo Tomas. Four days after the First Cavalry Division occupied Tokyo, *Time* was being printed on a Japanese press.

Some publishing plans were never realized. In anticipation of the surrender and occupation of Germany, a team was assembled to translate *Time* into German for circulation in the occupied territories. This project, known within the company as *Umlaut,* was finally abandoned at the end of 1944, partly because no agreement could be reached with the U.S. military and OWI and partly because of the difficulty of translating *Time.*[4]

On the other hand, one wartime venture became one of the company's most profitable subsidiaries. In 1943, seeking to conserve paper to increase domestic circulation, Prentice decided to establish a special Canadian edition from which all U.S. advertising except that directly aimed at the Canadian market would be excluded. Though the edition was identical to *Time* in news content, Canadian readers protested the limited advertising and the thinness of their magazine. In order to meet these complaints management incorporated a new two-page editorial section entitled Canada at War, a page

---

[4] While experimentation with *Umlaut* was going on, Grover reported to Luce that the War Department was interested in the idea but insisted on telling *Newsweek* that it could have the same publishing opportunity. Had Luce any objection? Luce: "Yes. Forget it." Grover: "Forget what? *Umlaut?*" Luce: "The whole idea of *Umlaut,* but you wouldn't let me. . . . The introduction of the idea of competition is wholly spurious. For what is more elementary in the whole concept of competition than that somebody should have an idea? But, what the hell, anyway we weren't looking for profit. . . . So far as Time Inc. is concerned, so far as I'm concerned, it's a lot of grief, trouble and distraction. But sure—forget it. Forget what? Forget my grouse. . . . Forward, *Umlaut!*"

of which also ran in the domestic edition. The Canadian edition gained steadily in advertising and circulation and within a year was profitable in its own right. Although the Canadian news section was eventually dropped from the U.S. edition, for Canada it was enlarged from two to three pages, with its own full-time staff of editors, writers, researchers and a news service with bureaus in Ottawa, Toronto, Montreal and Calgary. In addition part-time correspondents were lined up in other Canadian cities.[5]

By midsummer 1945 (but only after much discussion) Luce himself had prepared plans to set up a separate division which would have jurisdiction over all overseas publishing and editorial personnel. It was to be headed by a managing director responsible to the president and the editor-in-chief and assisted by a chief of correspondents. By then, C. D. Jackson had returned from service at SHAEF. His past experience in the company, the fact that he was an accomplished linguist, and his wartime duty overseas made him an obvious choice for managing director of the new division, *Time-Life* International, which was established in September; Charles Wertenbaker, who had headed the Paris bureau since the end of the war, became chief of foreign correspondents.[6]

Time Inc.'s far-flung wartime correspondents corps had now to be reorganized to provide peacetime news and picture coverage from the news centers of the world. The scattered printing operations (Calcutta, Tokyo, Rome, Paris, Stockholm, Cairo, Sydney, Honolulu, Manila, São Paulo, Buenos Aires) had to be evaluated, relocated and staffed to provide civilian circulation, and, not least, the hope was to begin "the grim trek out of the red."

In accepting the new job Jackson appealed to his colleagues for their support and acceptance, writing: "It is essential for the morale and success of this new Division that the whole Company recognize that this represents the first bigtime postwar expansion of the Com-

---

[5] An expanded Canadian edition of *Time* is now edited and printed in Canada and frequently originates its own cover stories.

[6] After a year Wertenbaker resumed his position as head of the Paris bureau by mutual agreement between him and management; Manfred Gottfried became chief of foreign correspondents. Wertenbaker had assembled an outstanding staff, but he had no interest in budgetary or administrative matters and had not worked out a satisfactory liaison with the editors. On his part, Wertenbaker preferred to live in Paris. His indifference to economic realities continued and, as Jackson wrote to him, "It can all be summed up in one word—work! Like God on the subject of sin, you are against it." At the end of 1947 there was an amicable parting of the ways.

pany, in which all should be intellectually and journalistically involved." His friend Andrew Heiskell put it somewhat differently: "Wow! If your hair is not all gray within a year, I'll be surprised. You have managed in one fell swoop to put under your wing 80% of Time Inc.'s headaches. I admire your courage."

One day after Jackson's appointment, Larsen, to the surprise of the staff, announced a new publisher for *Time*. Prentice had served nearly five successful years in that office but his feud with managing editor Matthews over the authority of the publisher had never ceased. Prentice had reminded Luce of the situation when he wrote him that reorienting *Time* to the peacetime world would henceforward be his most absorbing publishing problem and expressed the wish that there was "someone in the Editorial Department with whom I could work on it. For in a sense . . . it is pretty cockeyed to be announcing circulation guarantees and advertising rates for a magazine about whose pattern I am still almost completely in the dark." It was the expression of a situation and a feeling which "we ought not to let continue," Luce told Billings.

He had worried about it and had even prepared a memo to Gottfried and Matthews: "For two years, in order to protect Tom from any needless harassment, I have kept Prentice off the editorial lot. Well, dammit, we have to have a Publisher or General Manager or something. And there ought to be a decent liaison between Publishing and Editing." But he never sent the memo and he shied away from decisive action. Some months later he raised Prentice's hopes by telling him that he would establish his position with the editors, but again failed to act. Prentice told Larsen he would remove himself as publisher if this would ease matters—and was surprised when Luce and Larsen promptly accepted his offer. Larsen explained (Prentice recalled) that "for five years I had been stirring things up on *Time,* and he and Harry thought the time had come to let things settle down. By way of illustration he compared my tenure to the way the Roosevelt Administration kept things stirred up. Now, he said, we think it's time to let things calm down." As Prentice joined fellow vice presidents Black and Stillman on the corporate staff, his disappointment at leaving *Time* was assuaged by Luce's overall assessment of the job he had done: *"Time* was a mess when you took over as publisher," he said, "and you straightened all that out."

The man appointed to succeed him was James A. Linen III, who thus became the first of the younger generation of postwar managers. He had joined the company after graduation from Williams College in 1934. He came to Time Inc. seeking a job because of an old family relationship: his grandparents' financial support had helped Luce's parents enter the China mission field. Luce took him on as an editorial trainee, but Linen, who recognized that he was neither a writer nor an editor, transferred to sales, first for *Time* and then for *Life,* where he became advertising manager. During the war he served with the OWI. On his return he expected to resume his old job, but Luce and Larsen, to Linen's agreeable surprise, offered to make him publisher of *Time.* Luce introduced him to Matthews by saying, "Tom, here is your new partner." Linen's first move was to remove the publisher's office from the editorial floor, a sign of his recognition of the independence of the editorial department.

Luce and Larsen had been giving some thought to redefining the position of publisher. When Luce first created the job in 1937, he declared that the publisher had overall responsibility for his magazine's welfare—in theory, was head of a vertical and semiautonomous division. It had not worked out that way; Prentice described his own problems as publisher: "I had 100 percent responsibility without even 50 percent authority, and that made the job 200 percent more difficult. I had to try to run *Time* with a production department and a business office that worked for Charlie Stillman, an advertising sales department that belonged to Howard Black, and an editorial department that belonged to Harry."

Before Linen's appointment Luce had invited the incumbent publishers Prentice and William D. Geer [7] of *Fortune,* and the general manager of *Life,* Andrew Heiskell, to redefine the publisher's role. Heiskell's memorandum was a realistic analysis of current policy:

> The accepted picture of a publisher is that of the top man on a publication. Time Inc.'s three publications are run by four men, three of whom are not publishers but area chiefs, and the fourth [Larsen] who is a part-time publisher. Since these four men are more competent in their respective fields than anyone else in Time Inc. it is difficult to create full-fledged responsible pub-

[7] Geer joined Time Inc. shortly after graduating from Yale in 1929. He was successively a *Time* writer, assistant circulation manager, editor of *The March of Time* radio and cinema, assistant vice president, general manager of *Fortune* and, since 1943, its publisher.

lishers. . . . Our present organization table is therefore a hydra-headed structure with department heads taking orders from two or three different persons. . . . There are few, if any, persons in Time Inc. who are being taught to think in combined editorial, advertising, production, circulation and public relations terms. . . . One of the end results . . . is that too many decisions concerning more than one department go to Larsen because he alone knows how to measure their effects on the various segments of our organization. The present structure is the result of the meshing of strong, competent personalities, not the result of logic. . . . The system works because among other things we have been operating in boom years. But when we hit hard times the pinning down of responsibility will become more essential for it is as easy to bestow praise for success on many as it is difficult to divide the blame for failure among several persons.

Realistically, Heiskell suggested that the publishers should be held primarily responsible for the departments that created revenues. "It does seem to me that we should work toward this type of structure within the next ten years if we want Time Inc. to outlast its human creators," he wrote.

His memo made its point; in January 1946, age thirty, he was named publisher of *Life,* replacing Larsen. Years later Larsen commented: "For my money, the actual start of the publisher system was when Linen and Heiskell became publishers of *Time* and *Life.* . . . The important thing is that more and more responsibility was put on the publishers . . . and the relationship . . . of the managing editor and publisher was worked out." Howard Black said that the change from horizontal to vertical management, giving the publishers wide authority and autonomy, meant the virtual turning over of the magazines to the publishers "in trust."

Expansion occurred in the field of manpower. During the war years Time Inc. paid those who entered the armed services a portion of their salaries ranging up to 60 percent, determined by the years of service and number of dependents. Lieutenant L. L. Callaway, Jr., [8] with *Time* advertising prior to joining the navy, wrote to Roy Larsen:

[8] Advertising director of *Fortune,* 1954–59, and of *Sports Illustrated,* 1959–63; publisher of *Newsweek,* 1963–69.

176

"Homes have been kept together, insurance has been paid up, and worry about our family finances is almost completely absent." In answer to a questionnaire as to whether they intended to return to the company, Time Inc.'s military absentees indicated overwhelmingly that they wanted to return.

In 1945 Luce ordered "some mighty smart and lusty hiring in the next twelve to eighteen months." Assigning editorial vice president Eric Hodgins to this job, Luce wrote: "There is room, and need, in Time Inc. for almost every kind of journalistic talent. We need both writers and editors and they *are* not the same kind of people—no, certainly not."

As a "fisher of men," Hodgins succeeded well beyond the laws of probability, for in addition to a score of writing and editing talents he netted two future managing editors. In September 1945 Hodgins reported a recent rehiring on *Fortune:* "Hunt, George (Captain USMC). Former office boy; now apprentice writer." Hunt's wartime service with the marines had earned him the Silver Star and the Navy Cross and inspired him to write a book entitled *Coral Comes High* about his experiences as a company commander in the battle of Peleliu.[9] His subsequent career in Time Inc. carried him to the post of managing editor of *Life.*

Within a month there came to Hodgins' office, according to his contemporary account, "a handsome gentleman of thirty-one with a blue eye, a level gaze, a deep voice and a serious manner enlivened by a quick smile." He was a University of Minnesota graduate (magna cum laude) who had spent three years studying history, economics and politics at Hertford College, Oxford, on a Rhodes Scholarship. On his return from Britain he joined the Washington *Post,* covering Congress, the White House and the State Department. He had entered the navy in 1942 and was about to be discharged as lieutenant commander. Hodgins, impressed by his visitor, thought Hedley Donovan to be "a very good gamble indeed." Donovan was hired by *Fortune* on December 3, 1945; *Fortune* thus acquired a future managing editor, and Time Inc., subsequently, an editor-in-chief.

In December 1945 Luce wrote Larsen that he was impressed by the "great amount of problem-solving" that had been accomplished during the year. He listed among the things in which they could take

---

[9] Harper & Brothers, 1946.

satisfaction the purchase of the Chicago building and the paper mills, the establishment of *Time-Life* International, the successful re-employment of the returning veterans, and the fact that the maga-zines were "converting from war to peace, efficiently and without much fanfare, by far the biggest volume of advertising business of any publisher." Meanwhile, despite some concern expressed by Larsen about overtaxing management, the company was contemplat-ing still another major investment: the construction of its own build-ing in New York. To that end it had taken an option on a prime building block between Forty-seventh and Forty-eighth Streets bounded by Park and Madison Avenues, site of the Hotel Marguery.[10] Luce concluded his survey: "The point is partly that we perhaps should slow down on all further activities until we have got every-thing we have started well in hand. . . . We have in recent months done a great deal to enable us to do a bang-up job of editing and publishing. The most obvious is the amassing of 300,000 tons of paper. But under the same head come the various efforts . . . to straighten out our editorial and other *organizations*. My point is that having done all this . . . it might now be well to put a greater per-centage of our efforts on the use we make of the means, both physi-cal and organizational, which we have provided." The emphasis on doing the present job well before tackling anything else was a recur-ring theme with Luce.

Luce never lost his sense of surprise, even wonder, at the rapid growth of the company. When he was presented with the budget for 1946, he was once again struck by "the tremendous difference be-tween the size of the operation that was Time [Inc.] before the war (1939) and the operation that is Time in 1946. . . . All this has a kind of overnight quality since, even though six years is a long time, 1946 is the first peace-year following 1939." Though the budget projected a healthy increase in the company's profits, Luce questioned whether the profit margin was not still "too low for the

---

[10] A 1944 survey conducted by Harrison, Fouilhoux & Abramovitz had emphasized that Time Inc. should stay in midtown New York: "Time In-corporated *could* publish in the country, but the writers and editors we have talked to are almost unanimous in their blind belief that *Time* makes New York and New York makes *Time*. The joys of Middletown don't appeal to the average spellbinders of *Time*. They'd rather live on pâté de foie gras in New York than roast beef in Pelham, Riverdale or Chappaqua. While all seem to like one another, the idea of going to the golf course with the same guys you've worked with all week doesn't seem to appeal."

178

kind of hazardous, speculative enterprise that a lively paper ought to be." He suggested that the economies should come primarily from "the mechanical or semi-mechanical parts of the operation, leaving part of the margin for expenses in the 'intangible' department where there is always a certain amount of lag in getting rid of old ideas and routines and developing fresh and even 'adventurous' journalism." Here Luce the editor was doing a little wishful thinking at the expense of Luce the businessman. But he was adamant on the need for economies; the board minutes in December 1945 read: "Mr. Luce said . . . it should be recorded that not only the directors but the officers and others in management had very much in mind the matter of costs; that, indeed, it is the number one thing in our minds." Unfortunately, a sudden and unforeseen increase in costs in the "mechanical" departments upset the budget and profit projections. For all its postwar planning, Time Inc. management could not insulate the company from the successive shocks attending an economy in transition from war to peace.

In retrospect, the conversion of the U.S. economy was all but miraculous. There was very little unemployment—a work force of 57,000,000 a year after V-J Day had absorbed some 10,000,000 returned veterans—and most American industry had already converted from military to civilian production. But it was often a rough and rocky passage; the wartime controls weakened in the face of a wave of strikes, prices rose under irresistible pressure and a black market flourished. In May 1946 the directors were told that management had seriously underestimated the degree of inflation; by July costs were $7,000,000 higher than had been foreseen. Allen Grover, writing to Luce who was on vacation in New Hampshire, had recently reported: "If you want to suffer a little for the sake of those Puritan ancestors, you can ponder the fact that I believe costs are up another million dollars on the latest budgets. . . . This company is in a fair way to being badly whipsawed. . . . Our production and fulfillment costs have risen fantastically, which I *suppose* we should have anticipated. And the nature of the business does not permit us to raise the price of the product to compensate for these so-called 'uncontrollable' increases. So far as I can see the only thing left to do is to raise sharply the rates per page per thousand. Thank God the magazines have high quality and high popularity, else we would be in a real jam if we raised the rates and our customers refused to buy."

179

Grover was referring to the advertising rates, for which a six-months notice of an increase is customary. Management soon did "the only thing left to do." Increases effective in 1947 were announced for all the magazines. Meanwhile, for the first time since either magazine had been published, the per-copy price was raised from 10 to 15 cents for *Life* and from 15 to 20 cents for *Time*. Larsen recalled that Luce was against the increase for *Time* because "he felt that there should be no more price resistance between *Time* and its readers than there is in the case of a newspaper—that 15 cents was now a normal price, whereas 20 cents or 25 cents was not."

Time Inc.'s difficulties in coping with rising costs were compounded by a critical situation in circulation fulfillment that threatened for a time to reduce operations in the subscription department to near chaos. Throughout the war the fulfillment department had been coping with an increasing shortage of trained clerical labor and a steadily increasing volume of subscriptions and changes of address among an unusually mobile population. This had swamped the Chicago office and led to a rising volume of complaints. The company's postwar plans had included converting costly, repetitive handwork to machines which would eventually handle the subscriptions faster and at less cost. But the machines had to be perfected and the human and mechanical efforts meshed; meanwhile, the volume of complaints had risen from a normal monthly rate of 5.7 per thousand subscriptions to 21 per thousand, and the expense of straightening things out rose accordingly. Subscribers who sent in their money and failed to receive magazines were understandably furious. One letter arrived written on asbestos since the subject was, said the correspondent, too hot for paper; another complaint was attached to a barrel stave with a label attached reading, "Lose this in your files, damn you." Others had recourse to verse. A Mrs. Chalmer C. Taylor of Bloomington, Illinois, wrote:

> I'm not hurt but I am shocked
> For I've been writing you since Oct. . . .
> And I've given time, ink, money—Want my shirt?
> If conversion's making trouble
> Fer gossakes! On the double
> Save my sanity and reason—REconvert!

*Life* replied:

> I can understand your wonders
> At the mystifying blunders. . . .

Almost three years were required to work out the troubles. *Time* tried to pacify the subscribers by publishing a brochure in which caricatures of the machines by *Time* cover artist Boris Artzybasheff illustrated the procedures involved.

Time Inc.'s management did not at first fully appreciate, or at least identify, the fact that it was *Life* which was the main source of the company's budgetary forecasting problem. It was Luce who, in August 1946, pinpointed the problem. Reviewing the failure of the budget estimates for that year, he wrote privately to Larsen:

> I address [these comments] *to you alone* so that I may write freely and frankly without risk of hurting anyone's feelings. . . . Business success is probably built on intuition rather than analysis but analysis, *provided it is correct,* is useful. And I may mix in a certain amount of "business philosophy" so that you and I may compare notes on that score also. . . .
>
> There has been totally insufficient recognition that the cause of our troubles is almost exclusively the magazine *Life.* It is, on the one hand, *Life* which holds forth promise of profits someday of $10,000,000 and over; it is also, at this moment, *Life* which is the almost exclusive cause of our troubles. The troubles not caused by *Life* could be almost instantly cured. That is, e.g., if Time-Life International is a trouble—well, we could liquidate very quickly, with little cost and minimum danger to our prestige. . . . If you hadn't had *Life* to throw Circulation Fulfillment into a hopelessly unmanageable snafu . . . you would never have got into such trouble with only the other publications. But perhaps my point can most fully—and perhaps humorously—be summarized by the statement that if *Life* didn't exist to upset the whole magazine paper market, we would have hardly any paper troubles—worth mentioning. And Charlie Stillman would have practically nothing to do!

Perhaps what he said was obvious, Luce continued, but he had not heard the point made in office conversations or in the budget memoranda. This added up to

> *suppression of correct analysis.* . . . The great fact which I think our suppression failed to remind us of was that *Life,* unlike *Time,* and outstanding among all publications, is a *package proposition.* A manufacturing package proposition. Had we had

181

this clearly in mind, we might have been much quicker to recognize the necessity for a 15 cent price. . . . A clear recognition of that would have caused us to realize that we were much more subject to the trials and hazards of other manufacturers—strikes and all—than we apparently [thought]. That is, I suspect that last January most *manufacturers* (as distinct from admen and department store men) were more bearish about the immediate outlook for their business than we were.

Luce felt especially that labor costs for handling subscription fulfillment were too high:

> It just doesn't make sense to me. . . . I visualize a good, average $40 a week secretary and it just seems to me that she could take care of a year's worth of six Mrs. Lizzie Smiths (four of whom don't cause any trouble at all) in a day—and have plenty of time left for two hours out for lunch and to go to the movies. Well, geewhittaker, says I, if the genius of mass organization can't double a lone secretary's efficiency—what the hell is mass organization for?
>
> So, I say, it just doesn't *seem* right, looked at with a completely ignorant but naked eye.
>
> Now, I make this point because I don't get a sense of a particular goal of sense-making efficiency at which we were aiming. That doesn't mean you (and others) haven't got it. But it is not, as it were, put up on the Bulletin Board.

The year 1946 turned out to be disappointing: although revenues increased by $22,000,000 to $95,955,000—of which *Life* contributed almost $64,000,000—the company's net income increased by less than a million ($4,007,000 versus $3,041,000 in 1945). More significant, the wartime excess profits taxes of 1945 did not apply to 1946, and operating profits before taxes as a percentage of revenues had dropped from the 12 percent level of 1945 to a low figure of 5.5 percent in 1946.

The profit situation improved greatly in 1947 as the nation shook off the vestiges of wartime controls and the economy boomed, although inflation mounted. This prosperity was reflected in the circulation of *Time* and *Life*. By the end of 1947 *Time* was delivering a circulation of 1,600,000, large enough to challenge the old leader of the industry, the *Saturday Evening Post,* in certain categories of

182

consumer advertising. And, while the *Post* boasted again, as it could not in the war years, that it carried more advertising pages than any other weekly magazine, *Life* had far outstripped it in circulation and its advertising revenues of $75,872,000 exceeded the *Post's* by more than $16,000,000. With 5,369,000 copies, *Life* now delivered the largest weekly circulation of any magazine (*Post* circulation in 1947 was 3,958,000), and its dollar volume of national advertising was larger than that of any other magazine or radio network. With television in its infancy and as yet no threat, vice president Howard Black told *Life's* salesmen: "Selling *Life,* from here on, is going to be one of the most challenging jobs you can find. The excitement will be in selling the magazine that . . . is on top of the heap. The challenge will be to keep it there." [11]

However, the burgeoning revenues of *Time* and *Life* were carrying a number of unprofitable divisions. *Fortune* had suffered a precipitate postwar decline in advertising in spite of increased circulation; *Time-Life* International was incurring dual losses in trying to establish abroad both *Time* and the new fortnightly, *Life International.*[12] Also, *Architectural Forum,* while marginally profitable, was not on a consistently sound operating basis, and *The March of Time,* while still producing an edition once a month that was shown in some 12,000 theaters to an estimated audience of over 23,000,000, was slowly being squeezed out of the film business by high production costs and the reluctance of theater owners to show and pay for short subjects.

[11] One category that consistently brought the wrath of readers down on all the magazines was liquor advertising (over 3,000 complaints in 1947). In mid-1948 Luce wrote to his friend Dr. Henry P. Van Dusen, president of Union Theological Seminary: "I am writing to you, just as one might write to a distinguished lawyer or scientist, to ask . . . whether the Presbyterian Church in the U.S.A. has made a duly constitutional and official pronouncement on the subject of the publication of liquor advertisements and whether a person who publishes liquor advertisements can remain a member in good standing. . . . I should be very much obliged if you would give me a strictly professional as distinct from a purely private opinion." There is no record of Dr. Van Dusen's reply.

[12] *Life International*—first issue July 22, 1946—grew out of and replaced the purely military *Life Overseas.* One edition worldwide, it was a specially edited fortnightly, in English, predominantly sold on newsstands, with advertising addressed exclusively to foreign audiences. Edgar R. Baker was manager of *Life International.* Edition editor was Donald Burke, who had edited *Life Overseas;* in 1947 David Kerr succeeded him when Burke left to head the Cairo bureau.

Fortunately, 1947 was the year in which certain postwar planning began to pay off. Though wages and the prices of materials increased, machine efficiencies and better technology were in part able to offset these increases. And in Chicago the new subscription fulfillment system finally began to function properly, with a resulting sharp reduction in the number of complaints and substantial savings. The result was that on an increase of $25,000,000 in revenues to a new high of $120,404,000, the company reported a "notable year" with net income of $7,433,000 as compared with the previous year's $4,007,000, and an operating profit of 10 percent.

Encouraging as was this trend, Luce had come to the reluctant conclusion that the company should abandon the ambitious project to build a major New York skyscraper on the Hotel Marguery site whose square footage would be much more than the company required and would put it to a considerable extent in the real estate business. The board concurred. It was a great disappointment to Pierrie Prentice, who since leaving the job of publisher of *Time* had been planning the new building.[13] The decision was characteristic of Luce's own caution whenever he was faced by a diversion from the main business of publishing magazines. In a memorandum to his colleagues announcing his "strong presumption against the building," Luce noted that current stock quotations valued the company at about $60,000,000 and that "however little may be the 'capital' which we may plan to put in this building, I think a $30,000,000 building is too big an undertaking for a company valued at $60,000,-000." In any case, he said, "our profit and loss situation is not satisfactory. The actual 1947 profit and loss is perhaps satisfactory *but* it will be at least a year before we can say that we have established a real peacetime pattern of profits for our operations." He was also uncertain about the economic outlook, adding, "This is not incon-

---

[13] "It wasn't just that I had spent most of my time on the building plans," he recalled. "The important thing was that for two years I had been heading up the greatest team ever put together to plan a building—a team that included Andy [Andrew J.] Eken, builder of the Empire State Building; Wallace Harrison, who ended up the top architect of Rockfeller Center; as business advisor Joe [Joseph O.] Brown, one of the four men Mr. Rockefeller had paid $100,000 a year apiece to supervise the planning and erection of Rockefeller Center; as real estate and leasing manager Bill Zeckendorf; as air-conditioning engineer the great Charles Leopold; as acoustical consultant Dr. Richard H. Bolt, head of the acoustical laboratory at M.I.T. . . . When we did not go through with the building Wally Harrison used many of the ideas for our Tower plan in the U.N. Building."

184

sistent with the view I share with you that 'there *must* not be a severe depression' in the next year or two. . . . I also think that this country is engaged (by general agreement, so to speak) in an extraordinary effort to achieve a new plateau of standard of living and I believe this *can* be achieved but, somewhat like our own profit and loss account, it ain't been proved yet. (**P.S.** The betting on Time Inc. should be better than the betting on the average of the economy.)" Beyond considerations of profit and loss, he thought, there were "too many other things which have higher claims on our efforts and resources. . . . We have a hell of a big job just to keep on doing what we're supposed to be doing—namely, giving a little 'light and leading' in this profoundly troubled world."

CHAPTER

13

# "Re-thinking" the Magazines

ERIODICALLY, the Time Inc. magazines went through a phenomenon known in company argot as "re-thinking." The process usually—but not always—began with the asking of various unsettling questions on the executive floor, developed into long conferences in editorial offices, and culminated in great and small wrenchings of policy and personnel. For several years, beginning in the summer of 1946, *Time, Life* and *Fortune* experienced the phenomenon.

In the case of *Life* the re-thinking originated with the managing editor. As the magazine approached its tenth anniversary, Dan Longwell wrote to Luce suggesting that the time had come to change command. He had been managing editor since mid-1944 when Luce hoisted John Billings up to the thirty-third (executive) floor to be editorial director of all Time Inc. magazines. Before *Life* was born Longwell had been the man most responsible for working out its format; he was an idea man and an enthusiastic planner, but he had no great gift for administering the staff, which had grown from seventy-five to more than two hundred. He recognized his limitations, and in accepting the job left vacant by Billings he had made it clear to his staff that his was only an interim appointment. "It might as well be an open secret," he told them, "that what the present editorial management of *Life* is looking for and seeking to develop is a new executive team composed of today's younger men."

By mid-1946 he felt he had developed such a team, and the main point of his memorandum to Luce was to announce that the team was ready to go into action: "I have done everything I could for ten years to develop Joe Thorndike into a managing editor." To be assistant managing editor he nominated Edward K. Thompson—a "natural leader." He said he had set a certain time to prove them both. "I think they are proved."

Joseph J. Thorndike, Jr., a somewhat reserved New Englander, had been hired by *Time* as a writer on his graduation from Harvard; later he asked to be assigned to Longwell on the experimental work that led to *Life* and moved with him onto the staff. In the first ten years of *Life* he had written articles, made layouts, headed up several departments and, when Longwell assumed the managing editorship, served as his assistant. Thirty-two years old, he knew the techniques of *Life* as well as anyone. Though he had handled news assignments, Thorndike's main interest was in the feature departments—science, art, education, etc.

Thompson, thirty-eight, Midwestern born, educated at the University of North Dakota (Phi Beta Kappa), served a city editorship on the Fargo, North Dakota, *Forum,* then moved on to become picture editor and assistant news editor of the Milwaukee *Journal.* As *Time's* and one of *Life's* first part-time stringers he did so well that in 1937 he was offered a full-time job in New York as assistant to the picture editor, Wilson Hicks. His competence in picture journalism as well as in news coverage won him rapid promotion and by 1941 he was *Life's* news editor. An army reserve officer, he was assigned to the tank corps in 1942, then transferred to air forces intelligence, serving first in Washington, then on Eisenhower's staff in Europe. He returned to *Life* in September 1945.

Longwell saw a continuing role for himself as a senior advisor, with Hicks still in charge of pictures and photographers. But the main burden of getting out the issues would fall on the younger men. "I am certain we have a good publishing team in Thorndike and Thompson," he assured Luce, adding:

I don't want you to think I'm running out on my job. . . . . It's been strenuous and I've aged, but I love it. I know no greater fun than putting together an issue of *Life* . . . I said it should be a young man's magazine, and I mean it. One of *Life's* troubles is that it is ten years old. That sounds trite, but it isn't. We've reached a high but dead level of competence. We're professionals. We've done everything. The first thing we must do, I think, is to forget all about that and go back and do everything all over again.

Luce penciled a note: "Yes." The Longwell memo continued:

Our first and primary duty as editors is to make the magazine reflect its title. It is a wonderful title. It is a wonderful magazine. *Life* can lash out, but *Life* does like people. It likes America, and is passionately for the democracy of the individual. It believes with great feeling in the dignity of man. *Life* will print the shocking and the horrid, but it loves the beautiful. And above all, *Life* has a sense of humor.

Again Luce penciled a note: "Excellent! Swell. But it is precisely *this* which hasn't recently come *through*." Longwell had thus provoked a "re-think."

To begin with, Thorndike and Thompson were invited to present their views. Thorndike made some suggestions on organization and format of which Luce generally approved. Thorndike also argued that *Life* must express the spirit of the times, adding, "in order to embody a *Zeitgeist,* of course, there must be a *Zeitgeist* to embody, and one which is accepted by the great majority of the people." To this Luce objected, replying, "A *Zeitgeist* is not something 'accepted.' On the contrary. It may be said that History usually moves *upstream.*"

Thompson was more critical. The magazine, he said, tended to overstress "mass culture and charm." Writing as "an unreconstructed newspaperman," he felt *Life's* huge circulation must be attributed to

the kind of sensational reporting that only *Life* produces. We're sensation mongers and have been, perhaps unconsciously, all the time. . . . The old Denver *Post* maxim about a dog fight in Denver being more important than a war in Europe was probably sound news doctrine but we brought the war into dog-fight focus. Other publications didn't take the pains we did to explain the technique of conflict until the Army defined a military secret as 'something known only to the high command, the enemy and *Life* magazine.' . . . [For the future] we know some of the things we want to plug—better homes, movies, books and in general better ways to use leisure. We've pretty well worked out the kind of political system we're going to strive for and we'll have to get going on ways to encourage labor peace. But we must remember that the means *Life* uses to reach its readers are simple, direct and perhaps brassy—our technique has something in common with display advertising. . . . You've heard scores of people say that *Life* outdid the newspapers in reporting the war. I say we have to keep on reporting the news more excitingly than the newspapers. . . . In planning our future let's make plenty of provision for book larnin' and gracious living but let's see that it is wrapped around some good solid sensations.

Luce was generally pleased with both memoranda. "I feel all we have to do is to put [them] in a cocktail shaker, add a bit of lemon or sugar or both from the 33rd floor, shake well, and drink deeply. The concoction might be a little heady but I have the impression that it would all mix quite palatably."

But Luce was still not ready to accept the order of rank that Longwell recommended. During the summer of 1946 Thorndike and Thompson edited *Life* under Longwell's supervision, Thorndike handling the early sections and Thompson closing the issue, with a good deal of sideline coaching from all sides. Inevitably this arrangement sharpened the unacknowledged and perhaps subconscious rivalry between the two men—a kind of situation which Luce, a fierce competitor himself, often encouraged. In September it was Billings who called a halt to the game, writing the editor-in-chief:

*Life* seems to suffer from a jittery uncertainty, hard to define . . . [lacks] a smooth even flow of purpose. . . . Perhaps because too many top people are, directly or indirectly, pulling and hauling at the issue editor—Larsen, Heiskell, Longwell, Billings, Luce. . . . There still seems to be a divergence of views of what *Life* is all about among its managers. . . . If one man were editing straightaway for the next couple of years, there would be less feeling of fuzzy command.

Billings forced Luce to a decision; first, however, Luce wrote his own fourteen-page "pragmatic prescriptions, with only occasional 'philosophic' explanations" to guide the next managing editor.

189

The "pragmatic prescriptions" proposed more emphasis on photography for its own sake, stronger coverage of art,[1] and a new direction for *Life*'s Modern Living department which should be "the nexus between The Editorial and The Advertising":

We speak of wanting a "philosophical unity" for the magazine. The magazine as a physical and dynamic entity includes a powerful amount of advertising. If we really want a "philosophical unity" we have got to get one which does not pretend that the advertising does not exist.

Now what is the main moral problem presented by advertising? It is, of course, that advertising powerfully directs and concentrates the attention of the reader on material satisfactions. It is more and more the style these days, even among businessmen, to denounce Russian Communism as "materialistic." But there is, of course, no greater propaganda of materialism than American advertising. Is it therefore just plain and unqualifiedly wrong in any serious moral philosophy? No—not at any rate in Christian morality, for Christian morality based on Christian theology does not separate matter and spirit into two different worlds of evil and good. . . .

Concretely, it is the first job of Modern Living to show how the multiplicity of goods in an industrial age can be used with relatively better rather than relatively worse taste. A broad latitude is, of course, left to the whims of fashions—in clothes, food, architecture or anything else. Being so deeply involved in the contemporary, *Life* can't, for example, refuse to have anything to do with clothes if it thinks that contemporary fashions, as a whole, stink. But it can, without becoming hopelessly eccentric, choose the less bad among the bad and, with a combination of subtlety and earnestness, try to point the way out of a period of bad taste (in anything) toward good taste.

He also "prescribed" that the magazine should contain in every issue a "serious offering," by which he meant one strong article or continuing series such as the still hoped-for Churchill memoirs. If the new "prescriptions" could be added to what *Life* was then providing,

---

[1] Luce put such a high premium on art in *Life* that in 1946 he proposed that Francis Henry Taylor, director of the Metropolitan Museum of Art, might take charge of the program. Taylor, although tempted by the possibility of "developing the great medium you have at your disposal for . . . popularizing the arts," felt that he was under obligation to the museum's directors to continue with the projects he had initiated there.

190

said Luce, "then, perhaps, the High Command can say to any competent Managing Editor: 'Take it from there—do what you like, have fun, raise hell, promote better babies, or any other hobby, until, for some unpredictable reason you seem in danger of losing your grip on 6,000,000 circulation, in which case you will be promptly retired by a ruthless publisher.' "

In October 1946 Luce announced that Thorndike would succeed Longwell as managing editor; Wilson Hicks would remain in his old capacity of executive editor, and Thompson would become assistant managing editor. For masthead purposes, Longwell was named chairman of a nonexistent board of editors, a title conferring status without authority, and left free to be senior advisor and a free-wheeling idea man.

Luce knew that in choosing Thorndike over Thompson he ran the risk of losing Thompson, who frankly told Luce at the time that he was making the wrong choice but agreed to try to make the new arrangement work. Luce wrote to Longwell: "Ed was disappointed, of course, but is full-out to do his part in making a great new team." On taking over, Thorndike followed Luce's suggestion to delegate responsibility for advance planning and weekly execution to a number of divisional editors who were analogous to the senior editors on *Time;* they were to "handle their stories from start to finish." Thompson was put in charge of the biggest and most important division— that of news. In theory this left the managing editor free to concentrate on the issue going to press.

As the new managing editor, Thorndike edited *Life*'s tenth anniversary issue. *Time* in its Press section described Thorndike as a "dark-haired, sad-visaged Harvardman," who, in his own words, was "regarded by most people as a taciturn New England type, although by Massachusetts standards . . . jovial and loquacious." *Time* took the occasion also to summarize *Life*'s history, notably its circulation growth with "the saturation point . . . still ahead." In its anniversary issue *Life* itself peered back to its beginnings and ahead to a hopeful future. Its editors looked up the newborn baby who had graced its first issue under the headline "Life Begins" and found him a fifth-grader in Portland, Oregon, who "could scarcely be more typical . . . a husky, healthy, inquisitive American kid."

But as the months went by there was widespread agreement that something was still wrong with *Life*. After an initial honeymoon period, Thorndike became subject to an unusual amount of Monday morning quarterbacking. Much of the criticism stemmed from an all too familiar publishing syndrome: "The magazine isn't as good as it used to be." Billings invariably replied to this oft-heard criticism, "It never was." In *Life*'s case this was characterized by a kind of nostalgic longing for what can only be described as the magazine's earlier "amateurism." At its best the early *Life* conveyed a sense of wide-eyed wonder, and, at its worst, an unblushing vulgarity. Longwell felt that the magazine's "essential job [was] first to rediscover America. . . . Certainly we must be guided by the great news events, but using turmoil as a guide is in reality a lazy way to work." Thompson said he was trying "to find an area where the vitality, the amateurism, the frequent bad taste of the first couple of years of *Life* can be recaptured," and Luce felt that it was necessary to give *Life* "a 'lift'; to see how we [can] give to the final printed results of our efforts a new or renewed quality of attractiveness, charm, freshness, excitement—'inspiration.' "

The managing editor was, in part, a victim of Luce's idea of the divisional system. With the planning delegated to them, the divisional editors vied with each other in producing "big acts" and serious journalistic offerings. What had once been a young, ebullient, freewheeling staff seemed bowed down now by responsibility for the education and instruction of its vast audience while too frequently forgetting that *Life* was also supposed to be entertaining. After reading a sheaf of divisional memoranda outlining ideas for future stories, Luce told Thorndike: "My mind is literally overpowered, paralyzed, by the nightmare of a tidal wave of knowledge by which, it seems, *Life* can and will engulf me. In sheer self-protection I have a frenzied desire to get away from it all." He then wrote for *Life*'s executives a parable entitled "The Tawny Pipit":

A year or two ago there appeared in this country a movie called *Tawny Pipit*. It was an English movie—terribly English. For your information, the tawny pipit is a little bird. From what I saw of the bird, it seems to be a very ordinary inoffensive sort of thing. But for some reason or other, in the middle of World War II, a group of English bird-lovers got excited about this creature and presently the excitement spread throughout the land. . . .

If a parable is any good, it needs no expository moralizing. But being a poor parable-sayer, you will have to bear with me while I moralize.

192

The English have always been great nature-lovers. Not so much now perhaps (what with socialism and everything)—but years ago, the subject of Nature in all its forms popped up every day in letters to the *Times* and often flowed over into the more vulgar press. . . .

Besides being nature-lovers the English were also a lot of other things—on the whole very exasperating to non-Britishers. They were, above all, poets and dramatists. The composite moral then is this: as long as the English were on top of the world, their imaginations were on top of themselves. (Cause and effect is the other way around.) Everything they saw, everything they learned, was absorbed into their imaginations. They never let their imaginations be overwhelmed by mere knowledge. Another way of putting it is that they managed to keep life very *personal*. And they repelled all knowledge which could not be subordinated to the imagination. This is the moral of *Tawny Pipit*. Why all this excitement about an absurdly unimportant bird? Because of its scientific oddity? That was only an excuse. It was because through their extraordinary imaginations Englishmen established a profound sentimental relationship between themselves and a bird.

Then there was also the question of Drama—for this is the land of Shakespeare and Noel Coward. That is, something has to *happen* in time and space. So it was in the story of the Tawny Pipit; it did something; confidentially, it had a baby. And so it was years ago with all the letters to the *Times*. The subjects of birds, beetles, bees, ants, foxes, rabbits, horses, dogs, cats came apropos of something—usually something pretty important like birth or death or love.

That is why we speak of the "news-peg." But how deadly many "news-pegs" are. The very phrase has, in our business, come to mean something both phoney and dull. But whatever is observed through the imagination and the heart, never lacks for a news-peg. If you want to make Nature or Science or anything else interesting, it must be loved by the writer and the editor. *Amor omnia vincit.*

The wit and grace of the "Tawny Pipit" memo eased the implied criticism; less easy to take was a following twelve-page memo to Thorndike with copies to Billings, Heiskell, Longwell, Hicks and Thompson in which, among other matters, Luce, provoked by a

*"Life* Goes to a Party" story which he considered "phoney, contrived, vulgar," admonished Thorndike that he should never

> settle a dubious question of taste without concurrence of at least one senior colleague. And what I'm saying is that if two very top editors agree that a given item is *not* in bad taste or is for some reason necessary, I would feel safe, even if my own judgment were contrary. (Unless I came generally to mistrust their judgment.) . . . Another thing on this point of taste, there's a rule of good editing which says it's just as important what you *don't* print as what you do. *Not* to print dull stuff is just as important (and just as difficult) as *to* print interesting stuff. . . . *Life* can always avoid being dull, speciously and for a moment, by being shocking or weird. Just remember that nearly everything in *Life* is conspicuous; therefore when *Life* is vulgar it is conspicuously vulgar. . . . The editorial problem of *Life* is very real. Some things have to be done—or we might really get into trouble in 1949. . . . But . . . we are not too far away from being able to put the elements together so that the whole effort will hit the target instead of being an unfortunate near miss.

Thorndike agreed "with most of the specific points" that Luce had raised, but he wrote to him:

> What does dismay me is the very serious criticism *implied* in your memo—and most especially the proposition that such criticism should be aired among all my principal colleagues. I propose instead that we discuss our differences and that you make your complaints explicit. . . . If it turns out that the faults which make *Life* in your view "an unfortunate near miss" are ones which you think—and I think—I can fix, then I will try to do so. If, on the other hand, they are traceable to a basic difference of viewpoint . . . I will resign.

Luce was genuinely surprised by Thorndike's reaction and assured him, "I shall certainly do my best to make the case against [your resignation]—with full respect for your views and candor as to mine." But he seemed insensitive to Thorndike's point that his criticism of the magazine should be for the managing editor's eyes only. Six weeks later, after new and more critical memoranda—sent as before to his associates—Thorndike did resign, telling Luce, "I do not believe it is right for the boss to indicate his dissatisfaction publicly or to hold round-table discussions of what is wrong with the way the subordinate does his job. To do so undermines the authority requisite to the job."

Luce persuaded Thorndike to withdraw his resignation, but it was only a matter of time before he and *Life* would part. "If Thorndike had not been a competent manager himself, the whole [divisional] system might well have collapsed in disaster," Billings said later. "He lost track of his material as it came in from five different sources and was constantly in trouble trying to give his issues flow and balance and variety and unity. Sometimes the issues were notably rough and jerky as he tried to carpenter together the miscellaneous and uneven lumber he was offered by his divisional editors. Another factor against success was the wide difference among his editors' talents." What might have been his fatal mistake: "More and more Thorndike devoted himself to the back of the book and went off on Fridays, leaving Thompson to close out the front news sections— always a dangerous procedure for an M.E. who wants to keep control over the texture of his magazine. Perhaps this organizational experiment fundamentally failed because Thorndike gradually lost interest in his job." Thorndike was, in fact, tired and growing restless. He had worked since graduation only for Time Inc. and if he was to break out to publish or to write on his own, he felt it was now or never.

When, in August 1949, Luce proposed the formation of an "Editor-in-Chief's Committee [for] a constant and continuous *evaluation* of the development of the magazine," Thorndike quit, this time for good. "My authority has been appreciably diminished over the last eight months," he told Luce, "and the set-up you propose would, in my judgment, destroy it completely." He cleared out his desk and left his office abruptly during the noon hour, although he departed without lasting rancor, for in 1951 he accepted the invitation to co-edit, with Joseph Kastner, *Life's Picture History of Western Man,* a book based on a series on Western culture which had appeared in the magazine under his managing editorship. He went on to become a founder of the American Heritage Publishing Company, Inc.

To replace him, Luce turned to the man who had been waiting in the wings. Ed Thompson understood the weaknesses of the divisional system and made it a primary condition of his acceptance that as managing editor he be allowed to operate in his own way. "No M.E. was ever given a freer hand or less top-side direction," said Billings.

The results were quickly manifest. Thompson organized the staff around his own office, abolished the divisional set-up and named assistants, but every line of editorial authority led directly to him. The magazine seemed to rebound and in fact soon entered its most successful decade.

Early in 1948 Luce wrote to a group of his senior executives:

> We are at the beginning of a process of "re-thinking" *Fortune.* And this time, D.V., we intend to finish the job. . . . We have never done a job such as it is now intended to do for and with *Fortune.* . . . Neither *Time* nor *Life* has ever been so radically revised, in one single effort, as it is now proposed that *Fortune* should be revised. . . .

Actually, it was not the first time *Fortune* had faced a "re-think." Albert L. ("Bill") Furth,[2] a wise and witty man who would spend twenty years on *Fortune,* fourteen of them as its executive editor, once summed up, for a group of advertising salesmen, the history of the magazine:

> I've been at this business a long time, and *Fortune* has undergone great changes in that period. . . . The constant in the equation has been the perpetual "reexamination of *Fortune.*" In retrospect, this process appears to me in the form of intense dinner meetings in private rooms of clubs, each dinner preceded by an agenda on some variation of the theme, "What the hell shall be done about *Fortune?*" I can recall dinners where the topic was to change *Fortune* to a fortnightly; and dinners where the topic was to keep *Fortune* as a monthly and *add* a fortnightly; and times when it became exceedingly difficult to tell whether the proposal was to publish *Fortune* one time *more* each month or one time less. The dinners began back in the '30s, at the Yale Club. They soon were moved to the Cloud Club, and grew a bit rougher. In the middle '40s, Harry Luce

---

[2] Furth was a native of Alameda, California, and graduated from the University of California at Berkeley in 1924. After a stint on the Oakland, California, *Tribune,* he came east, serving as a seaman for six months before joining the New York *Evening Journal.* In 1930 he was hired by *Time* as a writer in the Aeronautics and Press sections and in 1936 he joined the editorial staff of *Fortune.* No man was held in greater affection by his colleagues.

convened us at the Racquet Club, and then at the Union Club. In each step in this rising social scale, the food and drink became more elegant and the after-dinner sessions longer and more unnerving. When I heard that Harry had joined the Links Club, I thought to myself, "Oh, Brother, this is *it!*"; but we never did get into that much trouble.

But in 1948 *Fortune* was clearly in some serious financial trouble. During World War II the flood of industrial advertising had caused the magazine (as onetime publisher Eric Hodgins put it) "to bulge like a lady carrying twins." With the end of hostilities, the advertising dried up. To make matters worse, the publisher, William Geer, while well qualified for his job, was in failing health. *Fortune* had plunged into the red, losing over $600,000 in the first two postwar years; further losses were projected for 1948.

With the re-think there surfaced a flood of criticism on the editorial side. "I wonder what's the matter with this magazine that it doesn't spark me into more interest," wrote Billings, undertaking to interpret the reaction of the average reader. "They're always trying to tell me so much I'm not interested in, in so many words that put me to sleep." Charles Stillman wrote, "I am sick and tired of . . . lugging around the present format. . . . It is a fine look-through magazine but good intentions derived from looking through the magazine simply do not get resolved into reading." Hodgins, who had resigned as editorial vice president to resume writing as a member of *Fortune*'s board of editors in 1946, was even more blunt: during the war, he said, *Fortune* "busted apart. . . . Big ideas were gone, and replaced by fragmentation into columns, departments, signed articles from Men of Distinction and of No Particular Distinction." John Davenport described the magazine as "a stately galleon which is in fact lost on the high seas."

Luce circulated some "Rough Notes on a Radical Revision of *Fortune*" which he said were sent out to his co-workers "in the spirit of: 'Don't shoot the piano player. He's trying to compose a tune; please help him work it out in the key and more or less along the lines he's started. If after a while the tune just won't play . . . then we'll start over again.' " Luce tentatively outlined a new format which he hoped would accomplish the mission he had set for the magazine—to "undertake to be a leading spokesman, and a leading source of light and guidance, for the successful development of

American political-economy." A major premise for the success of this "new" *Fortune* was that it should be written throughout from a clear and consistent point of view in basic sympathy with private enterprise. *Fortune,* he thought, "has failed to establish a sufficient degree of harmony of opinion among editors, to say nothing of researchers. . . . This failure, apart from its moral irresponsibility, has also been just plain bad journalism."

The *Fortune* editorial staff at the time represented a wide spectrum of political and economic opinion—from John Davenport, a dedicated and sophisticated disciple of Adam Smith, to Keynesian John Kenneth Galbraith, who was shortly to join the Harvard faculty, to a number of writers and researchers who were leftists in varying degrees. Presiding over polemicists, economists, sociologists, not to say some very competent journalists, was Del Paine, who had nominated himself for managing editor in 1941 as the man to straighten out the magazine's then tangled administrative affairs. A gracious if taciturn New Englander, Paine never made any concessions to the usefulness of loud, clearly enunciated dialogue, but what emerged, when one caught his words, was a Yankee's skepticism and distrust of all dogmatists. He was unhappy over Luce's proposals:

> Taking your ["Rough Notes"] as the description of a magazine . . . *Fortune* would have lost something of its painstaking integrity and sense of careful workmanship. If you take the "stately galleon" as the proper figure (which obviously I don't), we propose to put radar in the binnacle, four Pratt & Whitneys on the poop, Jet Assistance Take-Off on the royal yardarms, two Fairbanks-Morse Diesels in the bullion room, and, opening everything wide, proceed under bare poles toward—my god, the secret orders were blown overboard when that damned engineer forgot to feather the variable-pitch Hamilton props!

Executive editor Bill Furth also reacted negatively to Luce's notes:

> I'm unhappy because, evidently, you mean what you say; when you speak of the "NEW" *Fortune* you use "new" in a dictionary sense. No hucksterism here; no "new" to connote irradiation with Vitamin Whatzis or the addition of retractable gizmos to the plastic lining. . . . A new magazine. Therefore, not *Fortune.* Therefore too bad.

198

Hodgins was impatient with a Luce suggestion that *Fortune* should carry "short pieces," for he viewed

> with alarm and distaste the incessant modern desire to engrave all knowledge on the head of a pin. . . . I think that you are making your assumptions for the new *Fortune* on the basis that all conventional publishing and advertising pressures decree its circulation must continue to rise. . . . I had hoped that part of your assumptions would contain a bold notion for getting rid of the people who do not have the intellectual capacities for *Fortune* and who damage its prestige by their repeated statements that they get it but don't read it.

In his "Rough Notes" Luce had proposed certain new departments, dealing with subjects of especial interest to the businessman. "To none," said Hodgins, "can I make any *editorial* objection. It is merely that no matter how I wiggle my Ouija board I cannot make it spell out Success for them."

Luce received these blasts with equanimity; he wrote Furth, "Don't think I think I solved anything in that memo. I am convinced only that we do have a problem and one which requires from us some pretty 'decisive decisions.' "

On the basis of further thinking and the suggestions of his colleagues, Luce rewrote the "Rough Notes" into a "Directive for the Editorial Development of *Fortune*." It began by stating that the magazine's mission was to "assist in the successful development of American Business Enterprise at home and abroad," and then described in specific detail how this mission was to be accomplished. The magazine was "1) to report, vividly and coherently, the moving story of American Business Enterprise; 2) to offer 'light and leading' for criticism, appreciation and problem-solving." In its original prospectus *Fortune* was designed to be "the most beautiful magazine" in America and undertook to cover the whole industrial civilization; *Fortune* was now to be redesigned along more functional lines and was to concentrate more exclusively on a review of business and the political economy. The outstanding innovation was the Business Roundup, which would follow, in Luce's words, " 'The March of Business,' up hill and down hill, from month to month." The departments to be added included Law and Labor, the latter to inform management about labor but to be written *"in the interest of*

*Labor."* There was to be more emphasis on science and technology, and there were to be short articles.

Luce's directive contained several proposals that were completely unacceptable to Paine. One was for two advisory councils, a small one to consist mainly of selected company officers and directors, the other of outstanding businessmen. Paine objected that the first contravened the long-standing tradition of "decent separation" between the business and editorial departments, and the second exposed the magazine to "the danger . . . of too great commitments to particular schools or viewpoints." In offering his objections, Paine wrote:

> I wish I could say, "When do we start?" But I'm certainly short of whole-hearted enthusiasm at this moment. Perhaps, again, the reason lies in some skepticism about the amount of "light and leading" that any magazine can provide *if it sets out to do so.* Perhaps I distrust the concept of any magazine with a mission. . . . The acres of half-baked, wrong-headed, soft-headed, trite and repetitious "light and leading" I have cut out of the manuscripts of some of my more distinguished associates! And add in all that got by! . . . I guess I want to know; I guess I don't want to be told. And I suspect the reader doesn't want to be told—except to confirm his prejudices.

Years later Paine remembered his duel with Luce this way: "As Harry never let me forget, his remarkable document was a 'directive.' He was 'directing' me, the then editorial field commander, to carry out written orders. At my truculent worst, I finally refused to accept such detailed orders. I said it would be a lot easier for all concerned if he got himself a new managing editor. To which he replied without hesitation: 'I don't think you are a very good managing editor of the old *Fortune.* I think you will be a very good managing editor of the new *Fortune.'* "

Luce made some concessions. In the final draft of the directive the advisory boards were dropped and a number of other modifications made, but the overall thrust of the original remained intact.

The staff of *Fortune* was no happier about the changes than was its managing editor. They were also upset by the infusion of new editorial executives who threatened the old lines of authority. Jack Jessup, a gentle man not cut out for office revolutions, was transferred from *Life,* where he was chief editorial writer, to *Fortune* as chairman of the board of editors, a job defined by Luce as "primarily responsible for the development and presentation of effective, harmonious editorial policy. By this I emphatically do not mean something called the 'Editor of the Editorial Page.' . . . The Chairman of the Board of Editors will strive to keep the light of clear, liberal policy shining through the pages of *Fortune* at all times." From Washington, where he had been chief of the bureau, came the writer of this history, with the title of assistant managing editor.

The first and immediate effect of the Luce directive, however, was not seen in the magazine itself but in a reawakened interest of businessmen in the magazine; circulated as a promotion piece, the Luce directive was extraordinarily successful; more than nine hundred business executives sent in comments on it in personal terms, offering both praise and criticism.[3]

For the better part of 1948 Luce concentrated on *Fortune*'s problems, working closely with its editors; but it was more than a year before *Fortune* jelled into the shape he had proposed, with Paine, a very stubborn man, still in charge.

In late 1948 Elson departed from *Fortune* for a new assignment, and in 1951 Jessup was recalled to *Life* to take up again the post of chief editorial writer. Thus Paine and Furth were left to run the magazine in pretty much their own way, and with the aid of some key additions to the staff.

Daniel Bell, former managing editor of the *New Leader* and *Common Sense* and assistant professor in the social sciences at the University of Chicago, had been hired to write the new Labor department and for ten years provided *Fortune* with what many considered the most perceptive reporting on the subject then being written. (He left journalism to resume his academic career in August 1958.) In 1950, in the words of Hedley Donovan, who was soon to

---

[3] One was a letter from Richard A. McDonald, executive vice president of Crown Zellerbach Corporation, expressing the hope that "your writing boys get away from the highbrow language like that contained in the prospectus. . . . If they don't, the *Fortune* reader will need a dictionary in one hand and an aspirin bottle in the other. When opinion surveys reveal that only one American out of seven knows what the term 'collective bargaining' means, how in the world can you possibly interpret American business to readers with such words as 'osmosis,' 'verbal abstractions,' 'irrelevant fluff,' 'technocratic heresy,' 'pragmatic success and moral vindication of the vocation' and the 'schizophrenic days of the 2nd or 3rd New Deal?' " McDonald's letter was mimeographed and distributed to the staff.

become associate managing editor, "Bill Harris [4] had the wit to recommend, and Paine the nerve to buy, the remarkable journalistic property known as Sandy Parker.[5] From this followed the conversion of Business Roundup from a good idea into the strongest single feature in *Fortune,* and the appearance in the middle-of-the-book, too, of a highly successful journalism of economic research."

*Fortune* had some of the best practitioners in the field of business journalism, writers accomplished in the techniques of constructing the edificial *Fortune* story. For years they had written in anonymity, the theory being that it was the magazine that spoke, not just the individual. But by 1952 by-lines were becoming quite frequent. One of the most talented and indefatigable of the writers was Gilbert Burck, who came to *Fortune* in 1939 after serving as an editor of the old Frank Munsey publication, *Railroad Magazine.* Among others who, month in, month out, continued to narrate the "March of Business up hill and down hill" were Robert Sheehan, who could write in almost any department or field with grace and wit; John McDonald, who helped Alfred P. Sloan, Jr., to draft and edit his now classic business autobiography, *My Years with General Motors;* [6] Freeman Lincoln, talented son of the novelist Joseph C. Lincoln; Herbert Solow, an intellectual crusader; Lawrence Lessing, who made notable contributions in reporting on the technological and scientific frontiers of business; Richard Austin Smith, who was a skillful analyst of corporate failures.

Under the impetus of the directive to seek ways to be of particular interest to business executives, Paine encouraged Perrin Stryker to launch into the "management problem" field; by 1955, *Fortune* had published some twenty-five of Stryker's stories, gaining a name for the author and doing much good for the magazine. William H. Whyte, Jr., who had come to *Fortune* in 1946 after serving in the U.S. Marine Corps, began a long series on business' efforts to com-

[4] William B. Harris, a member of the board of editors, who had come to *Fortune* from Wall Street in 1937, left to work with Charles Stillman during the war (see p. 171) and returned to *Fortune* in 1945.

[5] Sanford Parker, who received his B.A. from Columbia in 1937 and remained to do graduate work in economics, was the staff economist on *Business Week* and an economist for McGraw-Hill and the National Industrial Conference Board before joining *Fortune.*

[6] Doubleday & Company, Inc., 1964. In his own right McDonald wrote a popular interpretation of the theory of games, *Strategy in Poker, Business and War* (W. W. Norton & Company, 1950).

municate, which was published as *Is Anybody Listening?* [7] He also
wrote a series on the problems of business society out of which grew
the widely read and influential *The Organization Man.*[8]

Paine must also be credited with bringing along and training
Donovan, who would succeed him as managing editor.

While Luce was never satisfied with any of his magazines, he was
much less critical of *Time* than of the others in the postwar forties.
Yet the magazine that came closest to fulfilling his expectations during most of this period was edited by the most restless, dissatisfied
and disgruntled of all the managing editors.[9] The relationship between Luce and T. S. Matthews was complex. The two men had a
high, if grudging, respect for each other, and Luce's journalistic
intuition complemented Matthews' literary skill. Yet their personalities, rubbing against each other like two dry sticks, produced fire.

From 1943, when he became managing editor, Matthews made
notable improvements in *Time,* purging the last vestiges of its eccentric style, giving the magazine a new, mature tone. He reorganized the editorial command, subdividing some of his own authority between two assistant managing editors. One was J. Dana
Tasker, who had charge of covers, graphics, and illustrations of all
kinds. A graduate of Amherst, where he studied English under the
poet Robert Frost, Tasker came to journalism after a stint of teach-
ing at Deerfield Academy; he had written book reviews for the
literary weeklies, worked on the *Reader's Digest* and *Newsweek* before joining *Time* in December 1937. Though he edited in nearly
every department, Tasker's major contribution to *Time* was its
covers; he recruited a number of distinguished artists to paint cover
portraits, among them Boris Chaliapin, the son of the great Russian
bass; Boris Artzybasheff; Guy Rowe (Giro), and Ernest Hamlin
Baker, who did nearly four hundred "news portraits." It was Tasker,
too, who initiated the use of symbolic backgrounds in the portraits,
which were for so long the trademark of *Time* covers.[10]

Matthews' other assistant managing editor was Roy Alexander,
who joined *Time* in 1939. He was a seasoned newspaperman, a

[7] Simon and Schuster, 1952.          [8] Simon and Schuster, 1956.

[9] According to that editor's own account of his years at Time Inc. in *Name
and Address: An Autobiography* (Simon and Schuster, 1960).

[10] Tasker remained with *Time* until 1953, when he resigned as executive
editor to join Cowles Magazines Inc. (*Look, Quick*) as editorial director.

former assistant city editor of the St. Louis *Post-Dispatch,* a major
in the Missouri National Guard and a pilot who during the war
years tested planes for Grumman Aircraft during his weekends. He
first specialized in aviation and military matters, edited Army and
Navy and later World Battlefronts during the war, then, after the
election of 1944, National Affairs until his promotion to assistant
managing editor. He was an easy-going and convivial man with an
earthy vocabulary and a loyal following. His maturity and experience
marked him as Matthews' probable successor.

As at *Life,* the re-thinking of *Time* started with the managing
editor. In February 1946 Matthews sent Luce a "prospectus or whatever you want to call it on the editorial setup of *Time."* It began
with the contention that *"Time* ought to be a good place to work—a
much better place, by a damn sight, than it actually has been." The
trouble with the staff was that instead of feeling like "trusted partners
in our enterprise, individually and collectively [they] feel more like
employees, with an employee's limited stake in the job and narrow
concern with his particular part of it." There were too many editors,
with the writer having his copy "pawed over by at least two . . .
the pat-a-cake possibilities tend to reduce him, in his own mind (and
sometimes performance) to the mere role of leech-gatherer." He
wanted to hire more writers so that the staff could "do the work without putting so much on any one person that he will work himself to
death (and by death I mean, of course, only such way stations as
coronary thrombosis, schizophrenia or premature senility)"—an
obvious reference to the managing editor's own exacting schedule.
Matthews was not greatly exaggerating. A letter to him from Priscilla
Baker, the wife of writer A. T. ("Bob") Baker ("I haven't dared
let Bobby see it") described the suffering that went with writing for
a weekly newsmagazine:

I do want to attack such an ornery system as working until
midnight or two and three o'clock on Saturday, Sunday and
sometimes Monday *nights.* By Monday the writer is so exhausted he has to have two drinks at lunch to get through
the day. By Tuesday he is nearly dead; he sleeps all morning
and the rest of the day he is barely able to hold up a book or
hang onto a drink. That leaves one day, Wednesday, and four
nights out of seven for
> social doings
> cultural activities

contemplating one's navel
fresh air and exercise
reading poetry or prose
talking to one's wife
wondering what it is all about

I can only think of three jobs that are important enough to work such an exhausting amount of hours: an obstetrician in an understaffed hospital or town; the president of any country; a general in time of war. I think it is ridiculous to go at such a killing pace just to get out a weekly news magazine, even though a good one.

About cover stories; I shall use Bobby and the [Robert] Frost cover as a more or less typical example. He worked for ten days and ten nights straight, no weekend, no morning for sleeping, nothing. O.K. It had to be done that way. It was a good story. He was pleased with it. But does he get any time off after he is finished? No. He doesn't even get the two days off that he missed. So what happens? He is so exhausted he gets a cold. A cover story virus. . . .

I refuse to believe that the organization of *Time* can't organize a more sensible schedule. Thursday and Friday they go to the office and do nothing all day except some desultory reading of newspapers. Saturday, Sunday and Monday are spent in feverish activity. Plus the physical strain of working about 52 hours in three days is the mental (writing is difficult) and the emotional—at least once a fortnight the writer has an argument defending his principles (Democratic) with one of the top editors (invariably Republican). Incidentally it is strange that the nearer they get to the top the more Republican the editors get. . . .

I think the reason the writers don't complain is because 1) they are grateful to be so well paid . . . 2) they like the people they work for and with 3) they like to write.

Matthews in his memo predicted that *Time* could achieve 2,000,000 circulation by January 1947 (it was then 1,514,000) but could do so only by raising *Time*'s "quality." He did not use the word "adult," though he may have in conversation; in any case, Luce pounced on it in his reply:

As to being "adult"—well, it is true that in the nature of *Time,* we seem capable of committing some awful gaffes . . . but,

205

good God, overall who is more "adult" than *Time?* By "who"
I mean what national popular publication or what "commentator." . . . My big point is that *Time* has lived through a long
worldwide war and into a baffling peace . . . keeping its mouth
open all the time on practically every subject . . . and having
had every opportunity in the world to make a fool of itself,
*Time* finds itself enjoying the confidence of millions of the more
literate creatures now inhabiting the globe . . . pretty good
prima-facie evidence of "adulthood."

Luce's response was, as a matter of fact, a tribute to Matthews'
editorship. Between the two, for a while, there was an uneasy peace.
In May 1947, with Matthews concurring, Luce announced that Roy
Alexander would assume the title of executive editor, a move that
confirmed the expected line of succession. The immediate occasion
for the announcement was the temporary assignment of Matthews
to an experimental project that had been in the works for several
years and was nearing a point of decision.

The project was the brainchild of William S. ("Willi") Schlamm, a
member of *Fortune*'s board of editors.[11] He had persuaded Luce to
consider seriously a monthly magazine of opinion which would
solicit contributions from the leading intellectuals of Europe and
America, a version of, but superior to (Schlamm explained), the
*Atlantic Monthly* and *Harper's.* It commended itself to management
as a postwar project on a modest scale, and Schlamm was given a
small budget to solicit articles for an experimental dummy. It was
to be called *Measure,* and Schlamm went to work building up a bank
of articles against an undetermined date of publication. In assigning
Matthews to the project, Luce was mindful of Matthews' own expressed ambition to edit a magazine of ideas and opinion. There was
even a tentative understanding that if the magazine was viable,

---

[11] Schlamm, born in Austria, had been a member of the Communist Party
in post–World War I Vienna, and his first journalistic experience was on
Communist publications there. In 1929 he broke with the party. Thereafter
he was associated with such liberal-leftist publications as the Vienna *Weltbühne* and the Berlin *Weltbühne,* where he succeeded as editor the Nobel
Prize–winning pacifist, Carl von Ossietzky, who was arrested and sent to a
concentration camp. In 1934, in Prague, Schlamm founded and published
*Europäische Hefte,* an international affairs weekly widely considered one of
the best in Europe. He came to the United States in 1938 after the Munich
crisis. He had written two anti-fascist books. In this country he was a free lance
and sometime columnist of the socialist *New Leader* before joining *Fortune*
in 1941.

Matthews would become its editor, with Schlamm as his managing editor.

Matthews spent two months working on *Measure;* he reported that *Measure* was feasible, but that he did not believe that Schlamm's insistence that he and Matthews share authority as "partner-editors" would work, and he returned to *Time.* To Schlamm's bitter disappointment, in January 1948 the project was suspended because of Larsen's feeling that it would put too much burden on management and Luce as editor-in-chief could not give it sufficient personal attention.

The editorial team of Matthews and Alexander functioned smoothly and to Luce's satisfaction. In a memorandum written in anticipation of the magazine's twenty-fifth anniversary, the editor-in-chief said, "During the last year or two quite a few issues of *Time* have caused me to say to myself: 'Well, I guess some people would know how to put out a better current events magazine but—*I* wouldn't.' . . . This does not mean that, about every other issue, some line in *Time* is not capable of putting me through the roof, etc. & etc. I just say *Time* is a very good paper. . . . As long as the present editorial Skipper (Matthews) and crew and their Shore-boss and engine crew (Linen & Co.) do as good a job as they're doing, I'm a standby."

But the skipper was far from happy, no matter how smoothly things appeared to be going. In his autobiography, Matthews attributed his despondency to the fact that he could not admit that *Time* was not only Luce's invention but his property; that in his (Matthews') mind the magazine was a public trust not subject "to the whims or dictates of one man." [12] He chafed increasingly at the way Luce exercised his authority. Though Luce might assuage souls and egos with warm overall praise, his day-to-day criticisms could be waspish. This was especially true throughout 1947, when he was fighting attacks of gallstones, a condition finally relieved by an operation in October of that year. In September one memorandum in particular outraged both Matthews and Alexander; Luce wrote about Harry Bridges' threatened general strike in Hawaii:

I understand that Harry Bridges intends to conquer Hawaii once and for all this winter (about February).

He pretty nearly did it in November 1946 and you will recall

---

[12] *Name and Address,* p. 252.

that *Time* endeavored to be of the greatest possible assistance to him.

This is to state as a matter of policy that, for the purposes of this 1947–48 battle, Time Inc. is 100% in favor of the property owners, capitalists and corporations of Hawaii and 100% against Harry Bridges and anyone who is in any way allied with him. (If there are any worse names for property owners and capitalists such as "reactionaries" we are for them, too.)

I hope—but without real hope—that Time Inc. led by *Time* will give some dynamic reflection of the above-stated policy. I realize that is unlikely—if for no other reason than that I have laid it down as categorical policy. Therefore all I can say is that anything in *Time* which can be reasonably construed as contrary to the above policy will be regarded as a serious breach of responsibility.

And don't send the stories to me for advance reading. Read for yourself.

On reading this note, Billings intervened and admonished him:

A memo such as this one, I fear, fails to accomplish its policy purpose, principally because in your displeasure you indulged in wild exaggeration of your position and in bitter sarcasm. Its reception by Matthews and Alexander was bad. They would have agreed in general with your position . . . but the tone in which you stated that position got their backs up. We have all been fighting your battle to get rid of the notion that "press lordism" operates in Time Inc., but such memos as this one make it tough going at times. The editors feel that they are being slapped down like bad little boys and lose their valuable sense of team play with the Editor-in-Chief. . . . I think you would have done better to think twice before you began to swing.

Matthews said that on this occasion he demanded and got an apology, which he later regretted doing.[13]

But if Luce was frequently irritable or impatient, his staff sometimes treated his suggestions in a cavalier manner. Several weeks before the Bridges matter, Luce had sent to *Time*'s editors a suggestion from his friend industrialist Sinclair Weeks that there might

[13] Ibid., pp. 253–54.

be an interesting *Time* story in a case recently decided in the Massachusetts Supreme Court. Whoever followed up the suggestion reported that the case had been decided the preceding week and therefore was not current news. The matter was dropped without notifying Luce. When he arrived at his office on the Monday after the row over Bridges, there was waiting for him a letter from Weeks asking what happened to the suggestion. Luce sent it to Billings with this note:

I have spent most of the weekend feeling ashamed of myself because of the shameful position into which I put Matthews & Co. I came to the office full of resolve not only to reform but to be cheerful, too. And the first letter I take up lands me back in the same old nerve-rack.

Matthews' growing impatience with his job and Luce was apparent to some of his associates. In October 1947 Luce spoke at a staff dinner. John Billings was away on vacation at the time and vice president Grover, reporting on the occasion to him, said that most of the audience liked Luce's speech. An exception was Matthews, who, said Grover, "simply doesn't like anything these days that I can see and certainly not Harry Luce. Tom is acquiring a marvelously holier-than-thou attitude, and if he thinks everything Harry does is so lousy, I wonder that he doesn't take his pot full of Ivory Flakes [14] and write some more bad books and verses."

In August 1948 Matthews sent Luce an eleven-page critique of the magazine in which he prodded Luce for

accepting, or seeming to accept, *Time*'s present performance as, after all, the best that can be expected and probably good enough; an attitude that implies: we'll be doing all right for the present if we just keep her steady as she goes. . . . Well, I think if we keep her steady as she goes, we're in imminent danger of running the ship under or of being ignominiously passed by some strange sail that has not yet even appeared on the horizon. . . . I think it's time to do something about *Time*. . . . As its most dutiful (if not most enthusiastic) reader, I would say that it is generally uninspired and consequently uninspiring. Then why doesn't the Managing Editor damn well inspire it?

[14] Matthews' mother was a daughter of the founding family of Procter & Gamble.

. . . He cannot, under the present set-up and with his present
staff. . . . The staff . . . might be classed as competent; it
could also be called mediocre. . . . I don't say that *Time* has
become as dull as the N.Y. *Times;* but it has become dull in a
way all its own.

The managing editor said he wanted to regain *Time*'s cover-to-cover
readership, to improve the writing staff, and "last and most important," get away from *Time*'s "flinty" tone—"('malicious, but not
altogether insane?')." It was an extraordinary criticism considering
that Matthews was editing the magazine.

At about this juncture Luce threw up his hands. He told Matthews
to take a year off to develop concrete ideas for improving the magazine he found so distasteful.

**World War II Correspondents**

To the left:
Shelley & Carl Mydans
on Guam

To the right:
Melville & Annalee Jacoby

Below left:
Will Lang
in Tunisia

Below right:
Robert Sherrod

Above:
William Chickering
at Bougainville landing

To the left:
W. Eugene Smith
on Okinawa

**Just before D-day 1944**
*Time* and *Life*
correspondents,
photographers
and artists
in London
Front row,
left to right:
Robert Capa
Frank Scherschel
Mary Welsh
David Scherman
Ogden Pleissner
John Morris
Wilmott Ragsdale
Byron Thomas

Second row:
Robert Landry
Ralph Morse
Aaron Bohrod
Walter Graebner
William White
Sherry Mangan
William Walton
Denis Scanlan
George Rodger

**Time 25th anniversary**
in 1948
Writers &
managing editor
Front row, left to right:
Carl Solberg
Walter Stockly
Duncan Norton-Taylor
T. S. Matthews,
(managing editor)
Paul O'Neil

Second row:
Richard Oulahan
George Burns
Harry Lennon
Marshall Smith
Henry Grunwald
John Tibby

Third row:
Robert Hagy
Paul Scalera
Gilbert Cant
Mark Vishniak
Craig Thompson
Alexander Eliot
Max Gissen
Robert McLaughlin

Fourth row:
Chandler Thomas
Jonathan Leonard
William Miller
A. T. Baker
Irving Howe
Willard Rappleye
John Weeks
Hart Preston

Fifth row:
Bruce Barton
Edward Cerf
Herbert Merillat
Gilbert Millstein
Robert Cantwell
Roland Gask
Robert Fitzgerald
Ted Robinson

Sixth row:
Douglas Auchincloss
James Agee
Ben Williamson
Allen Ecker
Richard Williams
Robert Lubar
Thomas Dozier
Henry Bradford Darrach

**Time researchers in 1948**
First row, left to right:
Essie Lee
Shirley Weadock
Margaret Quimby
Content Peckham,
(Sr. editor & research chief)
Constance Lailey
Marylois Purdy
Constance Ways
Dorothea Bourne
Ruth Brine
Jean Sulzberger

Second row:
Terry Drucker
Judith Friedberg
Joan Forsyth
Barbara Beckett
Margaret Thompson
Dorothy Potts
Paula Hoffman
Terry Colman
Rinna Grossman
Solie Tootle

Third row:
Beka Doherty
Joan McAllister

Mary Elizabeth Fremd
Virginia Hobbs
Mary Vanaman
Joan Lailey
Violet Price
Janet Kimball
Fay Degan

Fourth row:
Eleanor Tatum
Marianna Albert
Louise Maynard
Ruth Silva
Carolyn Pfeiffer
Helga Boedtker
Doris Getsinger
Ruth Mehrtens
Manon Gaulin
Ellen Turner

Fifth row:
Eleanor Stoddard
Marjorie Smith
Shirley Truby
Helen Newlin
Lily Lesin
Lucy Thomas
Eva Schwarz
Sally Eaton

**Among Time's editors, 1948**
from left to right:
Whittaker Chambers
Max Ways
Otto Fuerbringer
Dana Tasker

Bottom row:
Thomas Griffith
Roy Alexander

**At Fortune in 1948;**
From left to right:
Herbert Solow
Gilbert Burck
Albert Furth
Luce
Ralph D. Paine
John Davenport
Patricia Divver
John K. Jessup

Above: art director
Leo Lionni took *Fortune*
into new and modern art forms.

Below:
Mary Grace, head of
*Fortune's* proofroom and
monitor of deadlines

Above:
Max Gschwind introduced
a unique technique with
his scientific drawings

**Among Fortune writers:**
Above:
Lawrence Lessing
Robert Sheehan
Holly Whyte

From left to right:
Richard Smith
William Harris

**On Life**
From left to right:
Joseph J. Thorndike,
managing editor 1946-1949
Edward K. Thompson,
managing editor 1949-1961
Charles Tudor,
art director 1945-1961
George Hunt,
managing editor 1961-1969
Ralph Graves,
managing editor 1969-1972

At left:
John Osborne

From left to right:
Sally Kirkland
Mary Leatherbee
Joseph Kastner
John K. Jessup

**Life's photographers in 1960**
Included the four
whose names appeared
on the masthead
of the first issue
(front row, center)
First row, left to right:
James Whitmore
Paul Schutzer
Walter Sanders
Michael Rougier
Nina Leen
Peter Stackpole
Alfred Eisenstaedt
Margaret Bourke-White
Thomas McAvoy
Carl Mydans
Albert Fenn
Ralph Morse
Francis Miller

Second row:
Hank Walker
Dmitri Kessel
N. R. Farbman

Yale Joel
John Dominis
Gordon Parks
James Burke
Andreas Feininger
Fritz Goro
Allan Grant
Eliot Elisofon
Frank J. Scherschel

Third row:
Grey Villet
Edward Clark
Loomis Dean
Joe Scherschel
Stan Wayman
Robert W. Kelley
J. R. Eyerman
Ralph Crane
Leonard McCombe
Howard Sochurek
Wallace Kirkland
Mark Kauffman
George Silk

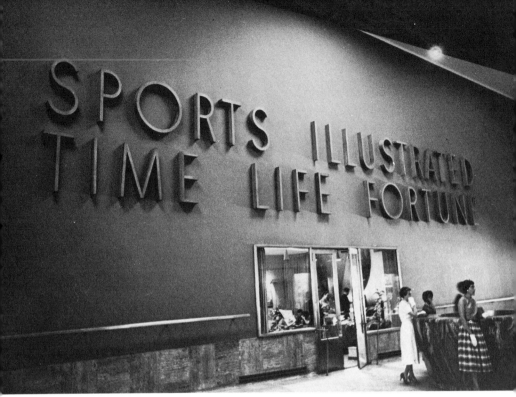

**Sports Illustrated** gets top billing in the lobby of the Time & Life Building.

Above:
Andre Laguerre
managing editor 1960 –

To the left:
Sidney James,
managing editor, until 1960,
then publisher until 1965

Above left to right:
Harry Phillips, Jr.
1st publisher

Richard Neale, on
original staff

William Holman
1st advertising dir.

Second row:
Jerome Snyder,
art director 1954-1960

Richard Gangel
succeeded Snyder

**Original research staff**
Top row, left to right:
Kathleen Shortall
Margaret Jeramaz
Helen Brown
Mary Snow
Pat Murray

Below:
Dorothy Stull
Virginia Kraft

Above left to right:
John Tibby,
asst. managing editor

Roy Terrell,
executive editor 1970-

Richard Johnston
preceded Terrell
as executive editor

James A. Linen,
president of Time Inc.,
1960-1969

**1948 board meeting**
Clockwise from lower left:
Samuel W. Meek
Roy Larsen
Paul Hoffman
Luce
Maurice T. Moore
William V. Griffin
Robert A. Chambers
David Brumbaugh
Charles Stillman
Howard Black
Absent:
Artemus L. Gates

**The Time & Life Building** on
New York's Avenue of the Americas

Above left:
James R. Shepley,
president, 1969-

Above right:
Andrew Heiskell,
chairman of the board
since 1960

**Group vice presidents**
appointed in 1972
Top row left to right:
Arthur Keylor
Rhett Austell

Second row:
Charles Bear

Bernhard Auer
became assistant to
the chairman in 1972

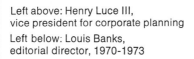

Left above: Henry Luce III,
vice president for corporate planning

Left below: Louis Banks,
editorial director, 1970-1973

Above:
Roy E. Larsen
Below:
Henry R. Luce
with
Hedley Donovan

# The Churchill Memoirs
# Are Landed

O NE DAY in the spring of 1946 Luce visited Winston Churchill
at his country home at Chartwell. The guest admired his
host's paintings and Churchill asked him to choose one for
himself. Luce was delighted with a landscape of the grounds but
offered a mild suggestion—wouldn't it be enlivened by the introduction of a few more sheep in the foreground? The artist, far from
being offended, said he would be happy to oblige.

Some months elapsed, however, before the landscape followed
Luce back home across the Atlantic. A letter from Walter Graebner
explained the delay: "Churchill asked me to tell you that your
painting will be ready very soon. He said you would have had it
long ago if he had not been dissatisfied with his attempts up to date.
He is now painting it for the fourth time. . . . Churchill said, 'I
managed to get some sheep to pose for me.' " At last the landscape
arrived, and with it a note from its creator: "I hope you will admire
the sheep. They are certainly a great improvement upon the two
miserable quadrupeds which first figured in the landscape." Luce was
delighted with the painting he had edited:

Your painting arrived safely and I am not only tremendously
pleased but also relieved. . . . Events in the realm of world

politics have moved so much more swiftly than in the world of art that I wondered whether the world might not disintegrate before those sheep had successfully crossed the Atlantic waving their tails behind them.

Such pessimism is once again rebuked. The sheep have done it—they are a huge success . . . the picture delights me. It hangs on my office walls and is the first and only picture there. I look forward to living pleasantly with it for many a year and expect my son to treasure it and carry it safely into the 21st century. How brightly then will burn the fame of its author, when civilization will have known that it was saved by his efforts and by his eager love of all that is not barbarous.

*Life* had continued to press for Churchill's memoirs with the greatest patience and determination. Whenever the editors had raised the subject, Churchill became a little vague—yes, he had a number of papers and he might leave them to his children to do something about. . . . He was not yet ready to do business. . . . Meanwhile, in Britain his friend Lord Camrose, editor-in-chief and principal proprietor of the *Daily Telegraph,* had signed Churchill for his publishing concern under the terms of a trust set up for Churchill's heirs, so that in the end it was Camrose, not Churchill, with whom *Life* had to deal: the memoirs, which Churchill had begun to write, were for sale, but to the highest bidder, and when Camrose came to New York in the fall of 1946 to peddle them, he made it clear that the price for the U.S. serial rights, excluding book sales, would have to be more than a million dollars. The New York *Times* was also interested, and General Julius Adler, vice president and general manager, suggested that *Life* and the *Times* make a joint bid for concurrent publication. He worked out the details with president Roy Larsen; the final bid was $1,150,000, of which *Life*'s share was $750,000 and the *Times*'s $400,000, with the understanding that Churchill would produce five volumes of approximately 150,000 to 200,000 words each.

Camrose would have been content to have "a little letter" to seal the agreement, but the American publishers felt that there should be a contract. This took many months of negotiations involving *Life*'s publisher Heiskell and Adler of the *Times* which were so complicated that the quip went around to "forget the memoirs and just read the contract." One sticking point was *Life*'s insistence that Churchill

212

should not write for any other U.S. magazine. Churchill protested that this would take away his "freedom"; he had, in fact, been negotiating in the interim with *Collier's* for the publication of an article; Longwell solved this dilemma by buying it up for $25,000 (with the *Times* paying its share). Churchill finally made a "gentleman's agreement" to publish with Time Inc. only, but he refused to put it in the contract. Another problem was providing for the eventuality of Churchill's death: what if he died before completing the memoirs? Churchill invited Heiskell and Adler to visit him at Chartwell where he put on a great show of health and vitality, jumping up on couches to pull pictures off the walls and leading his guests on a very strenuous walking tour of the grounds. As he saw them to their car, he tapped his chest and said, "The body is sound, the body is sound." Months before the negotiations finally came to a successful conclusion in June 1947, Luce wrote a note to Churchill: "The delays have often put a considerable tax on our mutual patience. . . . Part of the fault may lie in the character of the American nation which Burke found to be contentious and litigious. The British seem to have maintained a happy custom over many years of doing things by gentleman's agreement or by letter."

Luce need not have been so apologetic, as Edward, Duke of Windsor might have told him. Windsor, visiting his mother in London, had a visit from Churchill, who was well launched on his memoirs. He had spent the morning dictating and held the duke spellbound reciting some of his freshly minted paragraphs. "I've been doing a little writing myself," the duke remarked. "As a matter of fact, I am writing three articles about my early life for the same magazine, for *Life,* and the editors are anxious that they should appear ahead of yours. But, of course, that will not bother you, sir. It's a case of the pygmy before the giant."

Churchill looked at the duke suspiciously for a moment and then grinned. "Well, I have nothing to worry about," he replied. "My contract is signed—and a very good one, I might add."

The duke was indeed also writing for *Life,* and incidentally on the basis of a letter agreement. Charles J. V. Murphy had been assigned to help him, a job that was no sinecure even though it was being carried on at Cap d'Antibes on the Riviera. Murphy reported to the home office in some exasperation:

213

The Duke is a man of iron resolve. He refuses to let his social life interfere with his memoirs. In theory we have a schedule— a morning session from 10 to 12:45; an afternoon session from 5:30 to 7:30. The afternoon session, I regret to say, has a bad habit of evaporating. There is a steady procession of guests through La Croe, dinner parties, cocktail parties at Cannes or in local villas, and two evenings a week, I should say, at Monte Carlo. . . . However, he has been most faithful about the morning sessions.

The duke finished the articles in the Ritz in Paris during the late fall of 1947 at a time when two days a week there was no heat and no electricity during the day, working in a sweater from breakfast until nightfall in a bedroom littered with papers and documents. When a *Life* photographer came to take pictures of the author at work, the duchess protested, "But David, you can't be photographed in this scene." The duke replied, "But darling, this is the way any writer's room looks when he is writing."

Murphy sent the manuscript to New York with this comment: "Some of it is quite wonderful—Tom Sawyer and Huckleberry Finn out of DeBrett's Peerage." While he wished there were more "struggle," he argued that it was implicit in the story, "the struggle against the dull, unreal semi-ecclesiastical life of the constitutional monarch; and against the outmoded precepts of his royal education." The three articles were published beginning with the December 8, 1947, issue of *Life* under the title "The Education of a Prince."

The following winter Murphy began working with the duke on the second part of his memoirs, which carried his story up to and through the abdication.[1]

Churchill meanwhile was working at a furious pace. In April 1947 Graebner sent the editors a report on "their author":

Churchill does most of his work in bed either at Chartwell or at 28 Hyde Park Gate. Sometimes he'll work in bed all day up till midnight. If he works out of bed it's always in his siren suit. (I don't think I've seen him out of it more than twice—and one of these times was at his daughter's marriage.) He keeps

[1] This appeared in four sections in *Life,* commencing in May 1950; an expanded version of the *Life* articles was published by G. P. Putnam's Sons under the title *A King's Story* in 1951.

six secretaries busy; they work in shifts so that someone is on hand 16 hours or more a day, seven days a week. One secretary drives with him to and from the country, as Mr. Churchill uses this time to dictate. "I can do about 1,000 words while motoring to Chartwell—never less than 800," says Churchill. One of his secretaries told me it was hell to take down the dictation going around some of the Kentish curves.

The delicate problem of editing Churchill's prodigious output was one which his publishers at first approached very warily. In the summer of 1947 Longwell and a staff went to Britain to begin arrangements for illustrating the memoirs, a major project in itself in which thousands of paintings, photographs and cartoons were studied as suitable illustrations and innumerable new pictures taken, including the first color photographs ever of the interiors of the Admiralty, No. 10 Downing Street and the quarters of the Carlton Club. Longwell was allowed to see the preliminary drafts of the first chapters and he reported to Luce:

I spent a couple of hard days blue-pencilling the mss., highlighting high points, pointing out slow spots. I did it up with a brief typed sentence commenting on each chapter and sent it along with a note tactfully suggesting more original writing and the relegation of some of the documents to appendices. Camrose had told me . . . that no one in England could tell Winston what to do. It was risky, but I think it worked. The chief secretary at Chartwell called Walter [Graebner], said the old man was very pleased.

Mrs. Churchill proved an invaluable ally; at one point Graebner reported to the home office: "I think perhaps Mrs. Churchill has done more to help . . . than all the rest of us combined. Last night at the end of dinner, completely out of the blue, she said, 'Winston, I have now finished Volume III and I hope you will pay some attention to the little notes I have made in the margins. You must make a great many changes. I got so tired of the endless detail about unimportant battles and incidents. So much of the material is pedestrian.' Churchill growled and was annoyed for a few minutes, but then said that he was 'going through it again.' All ended happily with Mrs. Churchill throwing napkins at her husband."

In November 1947 Luce got his first look at a semifinal manuscript of Book I, Volume I, dealing with the events between the wars. He too was worried about the problem of editing, for he wrote to Graebner: "I have dealt with some very brilliant writers in my time but nothing could adequately prepare me to be W. S. C.'s 'editor.' However, I hope he won't mind too much." He had prepared a critique in which he said to Churchill:

> As an editor, there is only one major criticism. . . . It seems to me that the architectural proportions of this book are not as well worked out as they might be. . . . There are many places . . . where the sense of the surge of events is given in a most masterly manner. But the onward movement is not consistently maintained. The principal reason for the slackening of pace is, probably, the inclusion of so many passages from your speeches, articles and memoranda. . . .
>
> As a reader rather than as an editor, I would like to raise the question as to whether your implicit analysis of the course of European history goes deep enough. You interpret the drift to catastrophe mainly in terms of unnecessary folly and unnecessary weakness. . . . I would also like to know more explicitly what you, my chief guide through purgatory, have to say about why the human race in this period was doomed or doomed itself to so much folly.

Churchill accepted the criticism gracefully and said that he was "in much agreement with what you say . . . and I have no doubt the quotations will be greatly reduced, or melded in the narrative." He answered the question about "unnecessary folly" with eloquence:

> The reason is because in those years there happened exactly what is happening today, namely no coherent or persistent policy, even in fundamental matters, among the good peoples, but deadly planning among the bad: . . . The lack of willpower and conscious purpose among the leading states and former allies drew us upon these slippery slopes of weak compromises, seeking the line of least resistance, which led surely to the abyss. The same thing is happening now, only with greater speed, and unless there is some moral revival and conscious guidance of the good forces, while time remains, a prolonged eclipse of our civilization approaches. . . . I shall make this abundantly plain before this part of the work leaves my hands.

216

Luce followed his criticism with a personal letter expressing hope that Churchill would enjoy his forthcoming winter vacation at Marrakesh and regretting that he would not be there "in the honored role of host." The "gruntling" of Churchill continued beyond and above the contract. During the negotiations Churchill had expressed the wish to go to Marrakesh but pointed out that the currency restrictions prevented his drawing upon his own funds. His American publishers, *Life* and the New York *Times*, had thereupon invited him to be their guest. Longwell budgeted $10,000, of which the *Times* paid its share, for what proved to be the first of six vacations which Churchill enjoyed at his publishers' expense. Luce concluded his personal note: "Here's to you, Sir—the modern Joshua, making his strategy and blowing the trumpet against the walls of foreboding. The trumpets *shall* sound, the walls *will* fall. My kindest regards."

Graebner, who had received Luce's note for personal delivery to Churchill at Chartwell, first read it over the phone to him. The old man was pleased; two hours later he called Graebner, asking "to hear that 'lovely letter' again."

Luce had one matter on his mind which up to this point he had only referred to obliquely and he now took Churchill by the horns:

I want to mention . . . a point deeply embedded in my heart —but of which I hesitated to write you the last time. It is about Roosevelt. It is not all about Roosevelt; of that we might never agree. But it is simply about . . . Roosevelt's responsibility for America's failure to do its part in preventing the so-unnecessary war.[2] . . . The serious critics of Roosevelt charge him with two great betrayals of the nation's and the world's vital interests:

1) He, whether out of stupidity or intention, did not permit this country to resume its normal growth in productivity and widely shared prosperity.

2) He played a most two-faced and ineffective part in the efforts to prevent the so-unnecessary war.

Both these betrayals were related. . . .

Your view of Roosevelt is whatever it is—as you saw him in the war and as you look back on him. And I neither expect nor desire to change that view. But I feel that I have some sort of personal obligation (or understanding) to write to you what I have written.

[2] Churchill, who was convinced that Hitler could have been stopped in the Rhineland, called World War II "the unnecessary war."

Churchill did not reply. Later Luce learned that pressure had been brought on Churchill "for political reasons" to delete or paraphrase the Roosevelt-Churchill wartime correspondence. "I am sure it would be best to ignore these political considerations," Luce cabled Churchill. "I respectfully submit that the only wise course to pursue is to tell your story as you saw it and see it. I say this well realizing that you are going to have many kind words for Roosevelt which will be a pain in the neck to me."

*Life* could use only a fraction of the hundreds of thousands of words Churchill wrote. Jay Gold, who had been managing editor of the *Virginia Quarterly Review* and an associate editor of the *American Mercury* and *The New Yorker* before coming to *Life* in 1948, was assigned the job of tailoring the Churchill text to the magazine's special needs, a formidable task in view of the fact that the material edited from the Churchill narrative had again to be approved by the author. Churchill let the sentences march on and on. On hearing that he was thinking of extending the work to six volumes, Longwell asked Gold to write a memorandum making specific suggestions for cuts. Gold thought he was writing for Longwell's eyes only and was brutally frank about Churchill's many windy and dull pages. In a friendly, inconsequential note to Churchill, Longwell concluded: "P.S. You may be interested in the memorandum from Jay Gold." Gold was horrified on learning that Longwell had sent his memorandum to Churchill and tried to get Graebner to intercept it; too late, it was already on Churchill's desk. Gold thought that he might have to resign, but Churchill took the criticism in stride. He wrote to Luce: "I have endeavored to profit by the criticisms of Mr. Jay Gold which Longwell kindly sent me. I should like him to read the final version in order that he may see what excisions I have made, and I shall be glad to know his opinion." A little later Graebner reported: "For the second time . . . Churchill said that he would like to have comments from Jay Gold on the final drafts. . . . He did not mind at all the 'caustic' tone of Jay's comments. . . . He said [they] were very intelligent and correct—'I agreed with all of them.' "

In the spring of 1949 Churchill came to the United States to speak at the Massachusetts Institute of Technology; Gold was summoned into the presence. Churchill, who was staying with Bernard Baruch in New York, received Gold in his bedroom and from the bed proceeded to try out on him some salient passages from his forthcoming speech, watching to see how Gold reacted. He then spoke of the next volume and said, "I hope you will treat it as you would the work of any unknown contributor whose work you are about to reject. I hope you will tell me in complete candor what you think of it." Then, with one arm under his head, he extended the other and, rolling his hand in a slow circular motion, added, "But—you needn't be rude." Some months later Gold learned that he had further passed muster; a letter from Graebner to Longwell informed him that "during his vacation Churchill hopes to 'get on to the Gold standard' and make many of the revisions which Jay suggested."

Churchill had barely accustomed himself to *Life*'s editing when he was confronted with *Life*'s checking system. He resented the idea of having mere researchers challenging the facts supplied by his own documents or experts whom he had consulted, and at first every change suggested elicited "thunderbolts." Many of the errors resulted from Churchill's own system of work: he assembled the documents for a particular period and then would dictate a preliminary draft; since he sometimes did not put in his false teeth, the errors often were those of the secretary, who could not always understand him. Churchill had the provisional drafts set in type and revised many times. (Working from a rough outline called "Minutes," he produced successive drafts designated "Provisional Final," "Almost Final," and sometimes the "Final" would be followed by what Churchill called "Overtake.") Errors were sometimes caught, sometimes perpetuated by these cumbersome procedures. But when enough errors were brought to his attention, Churchill suggested that *Life* not only check the excerpts that were to appear in the magazine but the whole work. The researchers appreciated the compliment; the editors gracefully declined for them.[3]

Publication of Churchill's "War Memoirs" began with the issue of April 19, 1948, with excerpts from six volumes appearing intermittently into 1953. The Conservative Party regained control of the government in 1951, and Churchill was once again prime minister. This created some problems with Volume VI; he had some reservations about releasing it while he was in office. He also felt that his

---

[3] Among the *Life* picture researchers who worked on the Churchill memoirs in New York was Constance Babington Smith, a young Englishwoman who, while working as a photo interpreter in the British WAAF, had discovered the V-1 and experimental rocket installations of the Germans at Peenemünde on the Baltic coast. Churchill called her "Miss Peenemünde."

American publishers should make an additional payment for it. He acknowledged that he had no legal claim; to guard against Churchill's known wordiness and the possibility that the memoirs would run beyond five volumes, the contract had specifically provided that $230,000 would be paid for each of the first four volumes and the same amount for the final one, regardless of how many he wrote between the fourth and the last. But he felt that he had a claim in equity because, as he said, "had I not been able to complete my tale, or had I compressed it into five volumes, you would have had, I suppose, to have paid a large sum of money to someone else to fill the gap." The publishers countered with the suggestion that he be their guest on another of his winter vacations. For the moment Churchill had to decline because of his official position, but in 1955, having resigned, he again availed himself of their hospitality.

In December 1953, at the time the last invitation was extended, Luce wrote Churchill offering him $50,000 a volume for the serial rights to his long-projected *History of the English-Speaking Peoples,* adding that he hoped to talk personally with him about the payment for Volume VI because "I should be very unhappy indeed if any misunderstanding on this question should mar the memory of a working relationship into which we have put so much effort and from which we have obtained so much solid pride and pleasure." (The working relationship continued; *Life* published excerpts from Churchill's *History* at intervals from 1956 through 1958.)

Was all the effort and money lavished on Churchill worthwhile? There were those who doubted it. In the circulation department enthusiasm cooled rapidly when the managers could produce no evidence that the publication of a Churchill article increased sales; indeed, according to Heiskell, "the series had a devastating effect on newsstand sales." Luce and Larsen took a more elevated view. At a time when checkbook journalism was running strong and competition for the now-it-can-be-told memoirs of the war leaders was fierce, *Life* landed the first one and, by all measurements, the finest.

# "The Little Old Voter
Fooled Everybody"

THERE IS NO EXACT agreement as to when the cold war began,
but 1947 is the year in which the West initiated counter-
moves against Stalin's expansionist policies, and events in
1948 left no doubt that the cold war was a fact. That was the year
in which the Communists took over Czechoslovakia and the Soviets
blockaded Berlin. It was also the year when Harry S. Truman hu-
miliated the whole U.S. press, including *Time, Life* and *Fortune,*
whose editors had confidently predicted his defeat, by winning the
presidency in his own right. And it was a year during which the
dramatic accusations were made by *Time*'s senior editor Whittaker
Chambers that launched the trial of Alger Hiss.

In its first issue of the year *Time* republished Chambers' "The
Ghosts on the Roof" because the editors believed that it would "re-
pay a second reading" as the world entered 1948. At the same time
the editors named Secretary of State George C. Marshall as their
Man of the Year for 1947, as a symbol "that the U.S. people, not
quite realizing the full import of their act, perhaps not yet mature
enough to accept all its responsibilities, took upon their shoulders the
leadership of the world." The reference was to the Truman Doctrine,
proclaimed in March 1947, calling for support for "free peoples who

221

are resisting attempted subjugation"[1] and to Marshall's plan for the rehabilitation of Europe, first proposed in June 1947, now awaiting final ratification by Congress.

To most *Time* readers the choice of the Secretary of State must have seemed an obvious one. The wartime chief of staff, in spite of the failure of his China mission, retained the profound respect and admiration of most Americans, irrespective of party. But the choice of Marshall as Man of the Year could only have had Luce's qualified assent. His attitude toward Marshall was conditioned by Marshall's attitude toward China.

For a long time Secretary of State Marshall appeared to be wholly undecided about what policy the United States should follow in China. In July 1947 he did ask Lieutenant General Albert C. Wedemeyer, Chiang's former chief of staff, to go to the Far East and bring back some recommendations. But the Wedemeyer mission was a diplomatic disaster. The general's ideas, which included more aid to Chiang Kai-shek, were not acceptable to the administration,[2] and on leaving China he unwittingly delivered a blow to the regime which he hoped to help. Chiang Kai-shek assembled his aides to hear a farewell speech from Wedemeyer and urged the general to be outspoken about the maladministration and corruption which were undermining his regime. Wedemeyer took him at his word. His audience was hurt and offended, the Communists delighted; Wedemeyer's criticism was quoted by Chiang's opponents in this country as conclusive proof that further aid to China would be money down a rathole.

For a period following the return of Wedemeyer, the Time Inc. magazines reduced their coverage of China; Fred Gruin, in Nanking, protested that the editors were inattentive to his cables. Gruin's was a very difficult assignment: not only did China seem to be the forgotten country but his own life in the capital of China was far from pleasant. He wrote Luce: "The ties between the anti-government people here (in the Embassy, U.S.I.S., press corps, UNRRA, etc.)

---

[1] The Truman Doctrine had been called forth by the President's request for aid to the governments of Greece and Turkey against Communist pressure. *Time*'s approval had been somewhat grudging. Truman "clawed crabwise before the winds of political expedience," *Time* said, asking, "Why is it right for the U.S. to fight Communists' efforts to enter the Greek Government when it had lately been urging Chiang Kai-shek to take Communists into the Chinese Government?"

[2] His report was not made public for two years.

and the anti-government people back home (Teddy White, etc.) are old, tried and true. Personally, this tie-up has given me my most discouraging moments. . . . Many correspondents treat me and my family practically as social pariahs because we don't have their ideological views—in fact, I've discovered that long before I got to China the pressmen . . . had me ticketed as 'Harry Luce's pet' come to do what Teddy White couldn't be forced to do!" Luce was sympathetic and explained that he himself was to blame for playing down the Chinese situation:

> Months ago, I did declare a state of considerable relaxation about China—except that I urged more detailed narrative descriptive *war* reporting. I did this for the simple reason that it is useless to try to get people effectively interested in China when, by every possible means, the U.S. Government, in this case personified by the great and super-noble Marshall, makes it plain that it doesn't give a tooting damn about China.

Nevertheless, Luce was even then making one more journalistic effort on China's behalf. He had persuaded his friend former Ambassador Bullitt to go there and write an article on ways and means of aiding Chiang. He hoped that Bullitt's eminence would carry more weight in Washington than an article by a *Time-Life* correspondent. Bullitt's trip coincided with the Wedemeyer mission, and his article appeared in the October 13, 1947, issue of *Life*. Bullitt recommended both economic and military aid to China—he estimated the need in terms of more than a billion dollars—and proposed that General Douglas MacArthur take over coordinating the program. The Bullitt proposals were no more acceptable to the administration than those of General Wedemeyer, which had been along many of the same lines.

Luce went to Washington to appeal for help from a number of men, including Robert Lovett, another old friend, who had recently succeeded Dean Acheson as Under Secretary of State, and Senator Vandenberg. He wrote Vandenberg after their meeting:

> With Bob, as with you, I had a mission, namely, to do my duty about China. The measure of the degradation of American policy in the Pacific is the fact that a few guys like Judd [3] and

[3] Congressman Walter H. Judd of Minnesota was a tireless advocate of aid to China; he had been a medical missionary in that country before returning home and entering politics.

me have to go about peddling a vital interest of the United States and a historic article of U.S. foreign policy as if it were some sort of bottled chop-suey that we were trying to sneak through the Pure Food laws.

Neither Vandenberg nor Lovett could give him much encouragement. At the moment, as chairman of the Senate Committee on Foreign Relations in the Republican-controlled Eightieth Congress, the senator was trying to push through approval of the European Recovery Program. Aid to China would have to wait, he told Luce, and all he could do would be to press Marshall to release a long-promised China program as soon as possible.

In February 1948 Harry Truman did request an appropriation of $570,000,000 for economic aid to China. Secretary Marshall still excluded military assistance because, as he explained to the House and Senate Committees on Foreign Affairs and Foreign Relations in executive session, this would involve "obligations and responsibilities on the part of this Government which I am convinced the American people would never knowingly accept." *Time* considered the administration's attitude "negative" because both Truman and Marshall "doggedly insisted that Europe must have a priority on U.S. aid, that real recovery could be accomplished only by China itself."

However, when Congress in April approved the Foreign Assistance Act of 1948 (which authorized the European Recovery Program and set up the Economic Cooperation Administration), $338,000,-000 was included for economic aid to China and $125,000,000 in "special grants," a euphemism for military aid. This was viewed by radio commentator Eric Sevareid as a victory for "Republican Representative Judd of Minnesota and publisher Henry Luce. . . . It was inevitable that the great prestige of Secretary Marshall would come a cropper on some issues sometime, but the curious thing is that he has failed to win his case on this issue of China's military needs, a topic on which he has been regarded . . . as the government's number one expert." Luce derived no personal satisfaction from his so-called victory because evidence was accumulating that aid to China was probably too late to save a crumbling regime.

Another Time Incer became deeply involved in the affairs of China when treasurer Charles Stillman took a leave of absence to join the U.S. mission headed by Roger Lapham which was to program and administer the China economic aid appropriation. The eleven-man team which Stillman headed was charged specifically with the investigation of the country's industrial, transportation and power problems. The experience proved both frustrating to Stillman and disappointing to Luce. Stillman on his arrival found an appalling situation in which little could be done to break through the inept and corrupt bureaucracy and effect any meaningful economic reforms. Before the end of the year the ECA decided that it was useless to spend more money in the areas with which Stillman was concerned, and he returned to the United States with the conviction that there was little hope for the Nationalist regime on China's mainland.[4]

Reports from *Time-Life* correspondents provided confirmation. In late October *Life*'s correspondent Roy Rowan and photographer Jack Birns escaped from Mukden just before it fell to the Communists. The fall of that city sealed the Communist takeover of Manchuria and was the beginning of a series of stunning defeats for the Nationalist forces. From Nanking Manfred Gottfried, chief of *Time-Life* foreign correspondents, cabled a report home which *Life* published: "Until I came to Nanking I had not realized how completely the Chinese of the cities have lost confidence in Chiang Kai-shek. . . . They feel toward him as Americans felt toward Herbert Hoover in 1933. . . . China is very nearly lost."

As the Communists continued to gain, there was talk again of trying to bring Nationalists and Communists into some kind of coalition. Luce wrote to John Osborne, who had recently returned to New York after spending two and a half years as head of the London bureau to become Foreign News editor on *Life*, suggesting a line for a *Life* editorial:

> If [coalition] is what the Chinese want—or have to take—with their desire for "peace at any price"—then that's up to them. . . . We are sorry it turned out this way. We think it might have turned out differently . . . if, as it might, the Chiang Government had done a real job of reform in connection with all-out American aid. . . . A strong note of regard for the Chinese people can be struck. . . . Maybe they will find, as they hope, that Communism will be de-fanged in its encounter with the

---

[4] There was talk even then of the Nationalists going to Formosa, and some of the people who worked with Stillman went over and took part in the industrial developments there.

fluidly stubborn character of China. We wish them well. We wait and see.

The subsequent editorial described Nationalist China as "dying" and acknowledged that *Life*'s editors' "interest and belief in China have not been shared by most Americans or by the U.S. Government. We are certain that if it had been otherwise the Communists and their masters in Moscow would at this moment be losing Asia, not winning it. But the present overwhelms the past; what has been done and not done is of no matter now."

In December 1948 Luce made one last approach to Chiang Kai-shek, writing "at the request of a number of friends of China." The message suggested:

First, [you] declare that the Yangtze will be defended under your personal leadership.

Second, give to the ablest man in China, not counting your-self, the task of forming an entirely new government whose primary requisite shall be a capacity to govern.

Third, let this government be representative of all non-Communist elements in China.

Fourth, let there be a mighty demonstration of loyalty to this government by governors of provinces, mayors of cities, leading intellectuals and other representative men.

Fifth, let this government establish itself on the mainland of China in Canton or some other place, at a safe distance from the Yangtze front line so that there could be assurance that it would have at least six months in which to administer govern-ment while the loyal soldiers of China . . . defend the Yangtze.

There is no indication that Chiang seriously considered this pro-posal. In January 1949 Peiping fell to the Communists and its old name, Peking, was restored; in April the Communists crossed the Yangtze and occupied Nanking; in May they occupied Shanghai; in October the Nationalists abandoned Canton; in November Chung-king fell to the Communists and in December the Nationalists fled to Formosa.

The Department of State, anticipating the final debacle, published its still controversial 1,540-page White Book, *United States Rela-tions With China,* which detailed U.S. policy in the years 1944 through 1949 and placed the blame on the Nationalist regime. Angrily, *Time* attacked the White Book and summed up the editors' view of the China tragedy in these words:

> Judging the disaster, the U.S. had to face truths as bitter as they were plain. No one could deny the U.S. diplomats in China had faced fiercely stubborn problems, equally stubborn men. The Chiang regime (like the Greek government, which the U.S. also supported) suffered at one time or another from many of the worst vices known to governments: corruption and disunity, incompetence and indecision. Yet in a world racked by the evil and destruction of first fascist, then Communist aggression, the American job was to work with the world it found and know what world it wanted. In China, it tried and it failed. At no point in the long chronicle of its failure had it displayed a modest fraction of the stamina and decisiveness which had checked Communism in Europe. For its Asia policy, it had filed a petition in bankruptcy, seemed desperately to be seeking solvency in platitudes and recriminations.

On February 25, 1948, the Communists took over Czechoslovakia. Two weeks later Jan Masaryk, the foreign minister, whom the Communists had allowed to stay in office, jumped or was thrown to his death from his third-floor apartment in Czernin Palace in Prague. Masaryk, who had been a speaker at a *Time*-sponsored Council on World Affairs in Cleveland the year before, was known to many Time Incers as a friend.

The Communist coup and Masaryk's death had a profound effect on an already tense international climate. Another war seemed suddenly near. Secretary Marshall called the situation "very, very serious." From Berlin the military governor of the U.S. Zone in Germany, General Lucius D. Clay, cabled Washington: "Within the last few weeks, I have felt a subtle change in Soviet attitude which I cannot define but which now gives me a feeling that [war] may come with dramatic suddenness." The editors of *Time* (and *Life*) laid the blame for the crisis on a weak U.S. foreign policy. Said *Time*: "Except for a few notable exceptions, U.S. leadership in world affairs had been unimaginative and uncertain. . . . The Czech coup might not have been tried if the U.S. had not looked helpless in Greece, helpless in China, and silly—or worse—in Palestine." A special four-page article in *Time* entitled "Struggle for

227

Survival," written by senior editor Max Ways, sounded a Cassandra-like note:

> Ten Years From Now a divided, stunned and defeated U.S. may be trying to adjust itself to a Communist-ruled world.
> Ten Years From Now a weary, mangled and victorious U.S. may be trying to salvage what it can from the radioactive wreckage of the world.
> Ten Years From Now a busy, peaceful U.S. may be helping to push forward the frontiers of freedom everywhere in the world.
>
> The problem for Americans is how to make the second alternative more likely than the first, and the third more likely than the second. Almost certainly, in those ten years, some Americans will die fighting—perhaps a few score, possibly millions. Almost certainly, billions of dollars will be poured out. There will be no safe course—only choices between dangerous courses.

After describing the strategic threat of Soviet Russia and recommending specifics for action, the article concluded:

> To the leaders and the nations who want to commit suicide by yielding to Communist pressure, the U.S. needs to bring not only life and help, but counter-pressure.
> The nations attacked by the Axis in World War II bear a share of the guilt for the slaughter. They could have stopped it—almost bloodlessly—by stopping Hitler in 1933, in 1936, perhaps even in 1938. They could have stopped Japan in 1931.
> The U.S. and its friends have the power to stop World War III. If they don't, they will be guilty, along with the aggressor, ten years from now.

The article had the editor-in-chief's emphatic approval; he wrote to managing editor Matthews, with a copy to Ways: "The best thing on the subject yet—by far. Respectful congratulations."

The American voters were disinclined to take the cataclysmic view of "Struggle for Survival"; in any case, they were heartened by the country's strengthened military posture, the success of the Berlin airlift and the palpable signs of recovery in Europe by the time they went to the polls. Despite all the political predictions, "the little old

228

voter fooled everybody," as *Time* had it, and elected to the presidency the man who, precipitated into the job three and a half years before, had told reporters that he felt as if "the moon, the stars, and all the planets had fallen on me." *Time,* like 90 percent of the press, had flatly predicted the defeat of Harry Truman and the election of New York Governor Thomas E. Dewey. The victor attributed this collective error to the sheer blind partisanship of what he called the "kept press and paid radio." Partisanship played its part but does not explain an error of such magnitude.

Primarily there was the tendency to underrate Truman as a political force and personality. At the time of Roosevelt's death he commanded widespread sympathy, then suffered a sharp decline in popularity that culminated in the Republican victory in the 1946 congressional elections. But in 1947 he came back strongly; the Washington correspondents noted a gain in his own confidence and in his popularity in the opinion polls. As the winter progressed, the President's standing in the polls dropped sharply again. On the left flank, former Vice President Wallace, who had announced in December that he would run on a third party ticket, appeared to be making damaging headway. The Southern wing, flapping at Truman's liberal stance on civil rights, was about to fly off in fury. In late February when Truman addressed the Jefferson-Jackson Day dinner in Washington, *Time* reported that "there was no thunderous applause, no wild enthusiasm, no rebel yells. The attitude of the audience was one of polite, bored tolerance toward the man [the Democrats] are stuck with in 1948." Two weeks later, appraising the "new low point of the Truman stock," the magazine said: "Mr. Truman had often faced his responsibilities with a cheerful, dogged courage. But his performance was almost invariably awkward, uninspired and above all, mediocre. He had declined to assume real leadership. Most of the time, instead of leading, Mr. Truman had been whipped around the curves like the last car of the train. . . . From all over the country came a chorus of tired complaints: 'He means well but he don't do well.' . . . Only a political miracle or extraordinary stupidity on the part of the Republicans could save the Democratic party, after 16 years of power, from a debacle in November."

Republican success in 1946 encouraged some early and lively competition for the GOP nomination. It was assumed that Senator Robert Taft would be a candidate. Early in March 1947 New York attorney Herbert Brownell called on Luce to ask him to serve with an "inner group" working for Governor Dewey's nomination. Luce sidestepped, consenting to serve "only in the sense of being willing to be helpful for the general cause of American action in the world. . . . We must try, so far as possible, to avoid an overheated argument within the Republican Party as to foreign policy." To a friend who asked for his opinion of Dewey, he wrote, "I doubt if he would be a great President but I am sure he would be an able one."

Luce's personal preference for the 1948 nomination was Vandenberg of Michigan, who, however, sent a note offering *Life* an exclusive article on why he would *not* be a candidate. *Life* published the article in March 1947, but it did not have the effect the senator desired. *Time* commented, "Despite his disavowal of any ambition to be President, and his age (he would be 64 on his inauguration), no politician would count him out." None did. His name continued to be high on the list of prospective candidates, while he did all he could to stay off it. And just before the Republicans assembled in convention, *Life* carried a full-page picture of the senator and an editorial describing him as "probably the brightest dark horse that ever champed a political oat. . . . It would hardly be surprising if he turns out to be the Philadelphia 'surprise.' "

It was wishful thinking. When Dewey failed to win the nomination on the first ballot, Luce made a final effort to generate a Vandenberg draft. James Bell, one of Time Inc.'s reporters covering the convention,[5] recalled: "After the second ballot there was an adjournment for dinner. Many observers thought that Tom Dewey had the nomination in the bag and the next ballot would do it. But Harry hadn't given up. He rushed up to his old friend, the Kansas City *Star*'s Roy Roberts, and said intensely, 'Roy, you've got to swing Kansas and Missouri behind Arthur on the next ballot.' Roberts said, 'Harry, I couldn't do it if I wanted to and anyway it wouldn't do any good. Arthur doesn't have a prayer.' Harry was so angry he stomped away. Once the dust of battle had cleared both men apologized."

Dewey had been nominated unanimously on the third ballot. In its first judgment of the candidate *Time* was measured:

---

[5] Bell, a graduate of the University of Kansas, class of 1940, worked as a reporter on the Topeka *Daily Capital* before joining Time Inc.'s Chicago bureau in 1942. After serving in the Signal Corps in the Pacific during World War II, he rejoined the Chicago office in 1945 and in 1948 was transferred to Washington as the White House correspondent.

Tom Dewey had already shown that he could mature and grow in political stature, that he could learn political lessons. Would he now demonstrate to a hopeful nation and a watching world that he could match his efficiency with imagination and his genius for teamwork with bold leadership?

Even before the Republicans had assembled in Philadelphia, sure that they would nominate a winner, Truman had begun to fight back "against the pollsters and the Republican-controlled press," as he put it, in his pursuit of the nomination. He carried his case to the voters on a coast-to-coast trip, delivering seventy-six speeches, seventy-one of them extemporaneous, in two weeks. At first the crowds and their response were disappointing. In Omaha his appearance at the Ak-Sar-Ben Coliseum, with seats for 10,000, had drawn only 2,000 people, and *Life* wrote the whole trip off as a failure; it did not note that Truman gathered momentum as he rolled westward. His target was the Eightieth Congress—"the worst we've had since the first one began"—in which the Republican majorities, while supporting his foreign policy initiatives, had blocked his domestic program, although Truman, just as uncooperative, had used his veto seventy-five times to block Republican-sponsored legislation. Battle lines were drawn on this partisan issue. If Harry Truman was extreme in his criticism, the Time Inc. magazines were too effusive in their defense of Congress. Writing in *Fortune,* the chief of the Time Inc. Washington bureau [6] took temporary leave of his critical faculties and declared: "Not since the First Congress, which implemented the Constitution, has any Congress dispatched more important public business with more thorough thought and care and, on its own unbossed judgment, more rightly than the Eightieth Congress." This judgment, somewhat toned down, was echoed by *Life* and by *Time*.

Truman faced a sullen, dispirited Democratic convention which met after a ragtag coalition of New Dealers, big city bosses and Southern politicians had embarrassed him by trying to draft General Dwight Eisenhower, who had resigned as chief of staff and become the president of Columbia University. A group of diehard Southerners walked out when the newly organized Americans for Democratic Action forced through a strong civil rights plank; some weeks later they nominated South Carolina Governor Strom Thurmond on the

[6] Now the writer of this history, who hopes that it will stand critical scrutiny better than his *Fortune* article.

Dixiecrat ticket. Yet Truman rallied the party and electrified the convention with a slashing acceptance speech: "On the twenty-sixth day of July, which out in Missouri they call Turnip Day, I'm going to call [the Eightieth] Congress back and I'm going to ask them to pass laws . . . which they say they're for in their platform. . . . Now my friends, if there is any reality behind that Republican platform, we ought to get some action." *Time* was at least moved by "his political courage": "Said one delegate: 'You can't stay cold about a man who sticks his chin out and fights.' . . . From being a fading and futile minority President he had suddenly appeared in a new and more popular guise as an effective rabble-rouser."

The 1948 political conventions were the first to be given full-scale television coverage. For what now seems the very modest price of $135,000, *Life* joined the National Broadcasting Company in sponsoring the telecasts; the NBC television commentators and a *Life* team presented interviews and special background material, including films prepared by *The March of Time,* competing with CBS, WPIX and a DuMont team which was working with *Newsweek* editors and reporters. The *Life*-NBC arrangement gave some fifty members of the *Life* staff an exhilarating experience in a new medium. The group was headed by publisher Andrew Heiskell and National Affairs editor Sidney L. James. John Crosby, television and radio critic of the New York *Herald Tribune,* reported:

> *Life* reporters and NBC commentators eyed each other with some coolness at first, grew into bosom buddies toward the end. Mrs. Clare Boothe Luce, wife of *Life* Editor-in-Chief Henry Luce, materialized ethereally in the television pool room, asked many questions about all the gadgets, including one which proved a severe strain on the composure of all within earshot: "But who's paying for all this?"

By present-day standards the coverage was technically awkward and, in the case of the *Life* reporters, often amateurish, which was not surprising considering the state of the art and the complexity of the undertaking. Ernest Havemann, a member of the *Life* team, remembered that, "because somebody threw a wrong switch," one of the best programs produced by the *Life*-NBC team was not seen on the NBC network but on a rival network. The convention-hall studio was a barren closet measuring approximately ten by thirteen feet;

next to it was a workroom only slightly larger into which were packed at least seventeen men and women deemed essential to the telecasts. Even at its dullest moments the workroom was a bedlam.

For all the confusion, the *Life*-NBC show got high marks from the critics. George Rosen of *Variety* said it "copped all the television honors." Crosby agreed. To the amusement of the *Life* staffers, he wrote: "The *Life*-NBC team seemed beautifully organized, knew where—with some exceptions—it was going from minute to minute and succeeded in luring an impressive number of the more important people in front of its cameras."

Unlike the 1940 and 1944 campaigns, when great tension was generated in the Time Inc. editorial rooms, the 1948 election produced little heat. The conviction that Truman would lose was shared even by those Time Incers who were Democrats; it was reinforced by the opinion polls, all of which showed Dewey leading. In September Elmo Roper, whose *Fortune* Survey had been uncannily accurate in previous campaigns, reported that his figures showed "an almost morbid resemblance" to those of the Roosevelt-Landon figures at about the same point in the campaign of 1936. "My whole inclination is to predict the election of Thomas E. Dewey by a heavy margin," he said, "and devote my time and efforts to other things." The October *Fortune* ran the Roper analysis, based on an August polling, with the comment that it was the last pre-election poll it would publish because of the "overwhelming evidence." Roper assured everyone that voters did not change their minds over short periods around election time. He did take another sample of opinion in late October, which showed a decline in Dewey's popularity, but the figures, the pollster decided, were not significant.

During the campaign *Time* reported accurately enough that the crowds turning out for Truman "yelled, whistled, clapped" and showed tremendous enthusiasm. *Time* concluded that the voters "were vastly entertained" by the President—but not "particularly impressed by the import of what they heard." As the crowds gathered "in startling numbers," however, the editors discovered that Truman had developed "his criticism of the 80th Congress into an effectively political issue. . . . He had consistently outdrawn Dewey." Correspondent Windsor Booth, who was traveling with Truman, called National Affairs editor Otto Fuerbringer a week before the election to say that he had a hunch Truman was going to win, but when

Fuerbringer told him to file the story, he demurred. And shortly before the voting Luce said, "Wouldn't it be terrible if Truman were to win," but he was laughed down by his editors. In its last issue before the election *Time* acknowledged that the President "had given the creaking Democratic Party doughtier and more spirited leadership than it deserved," but the editors still predicted that Dewey would be the victor.

*Time*'s reporting of the Dewey campaign also registered the fact that the Republican candidate was not arousing much enthusiasm. "Thomas E. Dewey turned on his smile . . . and promised a new era of strength, unity and integrity. Rain beat down on the train in Erie, Pa. The man who was almost president spoke from an improvised platform, poking his head out from under a tarpaulin to show that he did not mind getting wet." The magazine described the "mildly curious crowds" which "seemed interested but never deeply stirred." His speeches were "not electrifying. 'As never before,' the candidate solemnly declared, 'we need a rudder to our ship of state and we need a firm hand at the tiller.' " When Luce grumbled that *Time* tended to underplay the Republican candidate, *Time* declared: "From the start, Tom Dewey had acted like the winner—unruffled, confident and a trifle self-consciously benign. . . . By the end of the campaign the U.S. voters had bestowed upon Tom Dewey a gradual and grudging measure of respect."

Perhaps *Time*'s reports of the campaign were unconsciously perceptive. The fact was, none of the editors cared for the governor. One writer capped his account of one of Dewey's busy weeks with the comment: "On the seventh day the candidate rested." Wiser heads removed it from the copy. After the election Fuerbringer was a little taken aback when his neighbor in Larchmont, New York, the poet Phyllis McGinley, told him, "It was perfectly evident to me that you were trying all along to tell us that Truman was going to win."

*Life* with unparalleled recklessness captioned a picture of Dewey in an issue published before the election "The Next President." At the time the betting odds on Dewey were eighteen to one, with some bookies quoting as much as thirty to one. *Newsweek,* polling fifty leading Washington correspondents, found fifty of them predicting a Republican victory. Even journalists partial to Truman conceded his probable defeat: Richard Rovere of *The New Yorker* said that the American people seemed willing to give Truman everything but the presidency.

\* \* \*

On the morning of election day Truman predicted that the pollsters "are going to be red-faced tomorrow." On the morning after, the red-faced media set off on an orgy of soul-searching, of "eating crow," or, as *Life* put it, "wearing sackcloth and ashes." *Life*'s editors were sent hundreds of pages torn from the magazine bearing "The Next President" picture scrawled with epithets. *Time* received letters denouncing its comment, "the little old voter fooled everybody"—which had been the inspiration of T. S. Matthews—as patronizing, smug and condescending. Elmo Roper apologized, saying he couldn't have been "more wrong," but *Fortune*'s editors insisted on sharing the blame, telling their readers that a re-examination of the figures showed that "in measuring the more basic attitudes the poll may not have failed so completely as the editors." What had been overlooked were the figures from Roper showing voter dissatisfaction with high prices, the housing shortage and other domestic issues which Truman had exploited in his attack on the Eightieth Congress. *Life*'s John Osborne circulated a memorandum to his colleagues asking if it was "sufficiently realized hereabouts that the national press, and especially *Life* and *Time,* have suffered a major blow?" Matthews said that while he would amend Osborne's comment to *"including Time and Life,"* he agreed with him and thought that "the press has been pretending to much more wisdom (or is it smartness?) than it had any right to claim, and has been getting away with murder." Joe Thorndike, managing editor of *Life* at the time, wrote to Luce:

> I do think that we ourselves were misled by our bias. . . . We were too ready to accept the evidence of pictures like the empty auditorium at Omaha and to ignore the later crowds. We were too eager to report the Truman "bobbles" and to pass over the things that were wrong about the Republican campaign. . . . I myself had many misgivings . . . but thought that what the hell, the election was already decided, we could get after the Republicans later. That was very wrong.

He called for "a very sober rededication to the principles of honest journalism."

Luce felt no less badly about the failure of his magazines. Acknowledging that he had been "the recipient of a number of memoranda" and "verbal instructions" from members of the staff, he wrote to his associates in another one of his memoranda which he decided not to distribute:

235

There is a wide-spread feeling that the spectacular blunder of "the press" was due not only to technical errors or negligence, but had also a deeper cause. . . . I agree. . . . There is at least a strong presumption that such a blunder should reveal errors or inadequacies in editorial policy. . . . We of Time Inc. have a serious task ahead of us—namely, the reconsideration of such basic editorial policies or attitudes as we may have adopted. . . . To what extent the editorial policies of Time Inc. as of November 2nd were ascribable to me is problematical. But at any rate I claim my right and privilege to be credited with the prime responsibility for whatever in those policies was mistaken or inadequate.

He promised to "take the initiative in such re-orientation of our policies as may be required. Practically this means that you should exercise as much restraint as possible during the next few weeks in adopting angles and attitudes. . . . The less Time Inc. publications commit themselves in the next few weeks, the freer we will be to adopt such policies as may be the fruit of reflection."

To the defeated candidate, toward whom he had felt no more than lukewarm, Luce wrote: "I've been thinking about you and wishing like anything that for your sake, as well as for the sake of history, things had turned out differently. And whatever kind of a beating you have taken, something called Journalism [has] taken a worse one. You've probably read about all the red-faced editors, etc."

"You have no reason to have a red face," Dewey replied. "The farm vote switched in the last ten days and you can analyze figures from now to kingdom come and all they will show is that we lost the farm vote which we had in 1944 and that lost the election."

Luce's secretary provided a postscript to the election in a note to the Washington bureau, canceling reservations made for Mr. and Mrs. Luce at the Carlton Hotel in anticipation of their attending the installation of a Republican administration: "I doubt very much if they'll be very interested in seeing Mr. Truman inaugurated!"

On a Sunday evening in August 1948 senior editor Whittaker Chambers received a long-distance call from Washington. A correspondent from the Hearst newspapers asked, "Are you the *Time* editor who has just been subpoenaed by the House Committee on Un-American Activities?" Chambers had expected that sooner or later he would be

236

called but he did not know that he had already been subpoenaed and that the committee had announced the fact to the press.

The committee had heard the testimony of Vassar graduate Elizabeth Bentley, a repentant former Communist courier. She had named thirty-two government officials who she said had supplied her with classified documents to pass on to the Russians. These individuals had thereupon either taken the Fifth Amendment or had categorically denied her charges. The committee, seeking corroborative evidence, seized upon a suggestion of a New York *Sun* reporter that it call Whittaker Chambers. It is not surprising that his name should have come up, for his Communist background was known in Washington; Chambers had unburdened himself in 1939 to Assistant Secretary of State Adolf Berle and later, on a number of occasions, to the FBI. Miss Bentley did not know Chambers, or his name, but she had heard in the underground of "the man who went sour."

The subpoena was served on Chambers the next day. On that morning he had coffee with Luce. By coincidence, the serving of the subpoena had come at a critical point in his relations with Time Inc. He had been lent to *Life* for its series, "The History of Western Culture," a project for which he was particularly qualified and to which he had contributed with distinction. But the first draft of his article on the Reformation provoked, so Chambers wrote Luce, "a head-on clash of historical viewpoint—between the economic interpretation of history and the humane interpretation of history," a quarrel which had brought him, he said, to the verge of breakdown. The *Life* editors in charge of the series and their historical advisor, Jacques Barzun of Columbia University,

> tore out whatever gave life to the piece . . . and left a mess of lath and plaster that I am ashamed to have had anything to do with. For the editors understood the meaning of the piece plainly, hated it explicitly and mangled it with knowing love. . . . My distress is only superficially due to the editorial mangling. . . . The real cause goes much deeper. For it strikes at the heart of my continued usefulness to *Time*. The increasingly agitated theme among the abler men around here is: Has a man who has something to say and the ability to say it any real place at *Time?* Do not hacks do the job better than a man who is struggling to express thought and feeling that is against the average editorial grain and which *Time* formulas and pressures were

237

perhaps never intended to contain? Should not *Time* and the strugglers part company with mutual respect and without rancor? Hitherto I have said: no. Now I face the question in an acutely personal form.

Instead of resigning, however, Chambers made a proposition to enter into a new relationship with the company in which he would no longer be "tied to the office or the hierarchy" but would contract to write a certain number of articles for *Life* and make himself available to the managing editor of *Time* for special cover assignments. It was to discuss this proposal, presumably, that Luce had asked Chambers to have coffee with him on the morning the subpoena was served. Chambers told Luce that he was going to testify: "It seems to me that you will not want me around here any longer." Luce, who, of course, knew of Chambers' former Communist affiliation, replied, "Nonsense, testifying is a simple patriotic duty."

Chambers took the train to Washington. In his first appearance before the committee he read a prepared statement on his Communist past and named the members of the group with whom he had worked. The group's purpose, he said, "was not primarily espionage. Its original purpose was the Communist infiltration of the American Government. But espionage was certainly one of its eventual objectives." It was the name of Alger Hiss that made the headlines. Hiss held the presidency of the Carnegie Endowment for International Peace, a prestigious position which crowned a career in public service. He had been an honors graduate from Harvard Law School and had gone to Washington as secretary to Supreme Court Justice Oliver Wendell Holmes. He climbed rapidly in New Deal circles; in 1936 he joined the State Department where he served as executive secretary of the Dumbarton Oaks Conference, on Roosevelt's staff at Yalta, and as international secretary-general of the San Francisco Conference founding the United Nations. *Time* once called him "one of the State Department's brighter young men," and on another occasion described him as being "in a class by himself." He had been nominated for his Carnegie job by Chairman of the Board John Foster Dulles.

Two days later, at his own insistence, Alger Hiss appeared before the committee to deny under oath the allegations made by Chambers. To one member, Richard Nixon, his appearance was "as brilliant as

238

Chambers' had been lackluster."[7] In a manner which Nixon described as "coldly courteous and, at times, almost condescending," Hiss reviewed his record in government, denied ever having been a Communist and ever having known "a man by the name of Whittaker Chambers."[8] He conveyed the impression that he had been either the victim of mistaken identity or of a malicious slander. At the conclusion of Hiss's testimony Representative John Rankin, who had previously congratulated Chambers, turned bitter and disbelieving of the *Time* editor and drew a laugh from the audience when he said, "After all the smear attacks against this committee and individual members of this committee in *Time* magazine, I am not surprised at anything that comes out of anybody connected with it." When the committee withdrew to executive session, Nixon recalled, "it was in a virtual state of shock. . . . One Republican member lamented, 'We've been had. We're ruined.' "[9] Some members wanted the investigation dropped and the files turned over to the Justice Department. Public opinion was almost wholly on the side of Hiss; even on *Time* many of Chambers' associates were well prepared, even eager, to believe Hiss. Only Nixon on the House Committee had argued for the continuation of the investigation, pointing out that Hiss had not categorically denied knowing Chambers. The committee's chief investigator, Robert Stripling, backed him up, and Nixon was made the chairman of a subcommittee to pursue, if he liked, what Truman denounced as a "red herring" to divert voters' minds from the failures of the Eightieth Congress.

The subcommittee spent many hours interviewing Chambers and Hiss separately; it became apparent that Chambers had a very intimate knowledge of Hiss's private life. Then in a bizarre face-to-face meeting of the two men arranged by the subcommittee, in a New York hotel room, Hiss, after inspecting Chambers' dentures, finally admitted that he had once known him. He had known him as a man with bad teeth named George Crosley, an impecunious free-lance writer. But this still did not prove that Hiss had been a Communist. Hiss himself continued to deny it and maintained an aggressive posture. Once in executive session before the committee and again in an open session, he challenged Chambers to repeat his allegations without benefit of congressional immunity.

[7] *Six Crises* (Doubleday & Company, Inc., 1962), p. 5.
[8] Ibid., p. 6.     [9] Ibid., p. 10.

Chambers accepted the challenge. On radio's "Meet the Press" he answered a direct question categorically: "Alger Hiss was a Communist and may still be one." Now it was Hiss who hesitated. It was only after such newspapers as the Washington *Post,* which had defended him editorially, began asking why he had not brought suit that he filed for libel in the U.S. District Court in Baltimore, asking modest damages of $50,000, later amended to $75,000.

By now *Time* itself was deeply involved. From coast to coast the newspapers were repeatedly referring to Chambers as "the $30,000-a-year senior editor of *Time,*" [10] and the company had a barrage of letters from readers, who, ignoring Chambers' exposure of Communist infiltration in Washington, denounced the magazine for having an ex-Communist on its staff. Of the first 156 letters received on the case, 144 were critical, and the trend continued. Thus it was very much in *Time*'s interest that Chambers win his case. The directors authorized employment of counsel on his behalf; the official resolution was preceded by this explanation by president Larsen to the board: "If Chambers' story is correct, as the management believes it to be, the Company has a substantial interest in making certain that he is represented by able counsel and that the defense of the action is properly conducted."

Neither management nor directors knew the whole story at this point. Chambers had deliberately skirted the question of espionage, and, immediately after Hiss brought his suit, he denied to a grand jury in New York that espionage was involved. He perjured himself, so he later wrote, because he wished to spare both himself and Hiss this final exposure. In fact, the whole story might never have come out if Hiss's counsel in the pretrial examination had not questioned Mrs. Chambers so savagely and been so insistent that Chambers produce documentary evidence that he knew Hiss. Chambers made up his mind to take a final, irrevocable step. He had retrieved a cache of documents, including sixty-five typed pages of copies and summaries of confidential State Department papers, four memoranda in Hiss's own handwriting, two strips of developed microfilm and three cylinders of undeveloped microfilm, that he had given to his wife's nephew for safekeeping ten years before; the nephew had hidden them in an unused dumbwaiter shaft in his mother's house in Brooklyn. The documents and the memoranda Chambers handed over to

[10] In 1947 Chambers' salary was $16,000; with a bonus his earnings totaled $24,100. In January 1948 his salary was raised to $21,000.

240

the attorneys; the microfilm he kept back, hiding it in his farmhouse in Maryland.

The lawyers on both sides took a look at the material that Chambers gave them. They agreed that more than libel was involved and called in the Department of Justice. In taking custody of the papers the chief of the Justice Department's Criminal Division warned that no one was to talk to anyone, even to members of the congressional committee, under the risk of being cited for contempt of court.

But hints of this new development soon leaked to the press. Nixon and Stripling called on Chambers and he confirmed that there had been a new development but that his lips were sealed; at the same time, according to Nixon, he told them that if the Justice Department did not act, "I have another bombshell in case they try to suppress this one." [11] Nixon, who was about to leave on vacation, signed a *subpoena duces tecum* for any and all relevant documents in Chambers' possession. It was in response to this order that Chambers led the committee investigators to a pumpkin on his farm, took the top off and produced the rolls of microfilm. When the story broke, the first reaction was one of unbelief and ridicule. "The guffaw that went up about the pumpkin was nationwide," wrote Chambers. Many newspaper readers assumed that the films had lain in the pumpkin for months; in fact, they had rested there only one day because Chambers, suspecting that investigators working for Hiss were prowling around his farm, had decided to remove them from his house.

With the microfilm in the hands of the committee, the Justice Department, which had so far taken no apparent action on the documents in its possession, now acted with great alacrity and had subpoenas issued to Hiss and Chambers to appear before the grand jury in New York. Testimony before that body, and hearings of the committee, elicited the full gravity of Chambers' charges against Hiss. When Hiss denied that he had turned over any State Department documents to Chambers or to any other unauthorized person and that he had met with Chambers after January 1, 1937, he was indicted by the grand jury for perjury.

Chambers' admission of his espionage had deeply embarrassed Time Inc. Neither Luce nor Larsen understood that he had been a Communist spy when they asked the directors to undertake his defense. Mrs. Luce recalled overhearing a conversation between her

[11] *Six Crises,* p. 47.

husband and Chambers shortly after the revelation of the "pumpkin papers." Luce reproached Chambers for not telling him he had been a spy, to which she remembered hearing Chambers reply: "But you knew I was a Communist and all Communists were working for the Soviet Union. If a man of your sophistication didn't understand the nature of Communists and Communism, God help the country." In any case, Luce and Larsen agreed that Time Inc. would have to withdraw its legal support and that Chambers must be asked for his resignation—a job that Luce delegated to Larsen, who summoned Chambers to his office and heard him say, to Larsen's great relief, "Roy, I think I should resign." "Perhaps you should," Larsen replied. Chambers immediately sat down at a typewriter and wrote out his resignation:

> I have been called upon to expose the darkest and most danger-
> ous side of Communism—espionage. This can be done only if a
> man who knows the facts will stand up and tell them without
> regard to the cost or consequences to himself. I cannot share
> this indispensable ordeal with anyone. Therefore, with a quiet
> and firm mind, I am withdrawing from among the colleagues
> with whom I worked for so many years and whose support has
> been loyal and generous.

The two trials of Alger Hiss for perjury are no part of this history; in the first the jury disagreed, voting eight to four for his conviction; in the second, which ended on January 21, 1950, Hiss was convicted and sentenced to five years imprisonment. (He served three years and eight months with time off for good behavior.) The verdict was seen by Chambers' friends as his vindication, and raised for the management of Time Inc. the question of re-employing him. The idea had some support from outside the company. William L. White, who had once worked for *Fortune* and had taken over his father's post as editor of the Emporia *Gazette,* wrote Luce, "I feel that in the eyes of the public, [Chambers] will not have that complete vindication . . . he now so richly deserves, until he is restored to his old job with you." Pierrie Prentice, then editor and publisher of the *Architectural Forum,* asked Luce if he could offer Chambers a job on that magazine, and Luce told him to "write at once asking if he might be interested." But before Chambers could reply to this invitation, Luce, with Matthews' warm support, had decided to ask him to return to *Time.* In the time it took Chambers to make the trip to New York in order to hear

242

Matthews confirm this news, Luce had changed his mind, under the pressure of strenuous objections raised on the executive floor that the rehiring of such a controversial figure would be injurious to the company's public relations. There was nothing for Prentice to do but withdraw his offer also. Matthews met his friend after he taxied up to the office from Pennsylvania Station and later reported to Luce:

> I've seen Whit and told him it was no go. I did *not* go into the various reasons; it wasn't necessary. It was apparently not much of a surprise to him; he'd been thinking it over too, and was in some doubts about whether he should take such a job at all—let alone come back to *Time.* I also took the liberty of apologizing to him, in both our names, for having broached the matter before we were sure we were willing to go through with it.

A troubled Luce wrote to Chambers a few days later that he was not sure that "the right decision" had been made and suggested another meeting. Chambers declined because he did not believe it would accomplish anything and would only "turn the knife in the wound." At his Maryland farm he settled in to write his autobiography, *Witness* (the story of his witness in turn "to each of the two great faiths of our time," God and Communism), which would be as controversial as almost everything surrounding this mild-looking man. The serial rights to the manuscript were offered to *Life,* but Luce made the unprecedented suggestion that not *Life* but *Time* serialize the book. However, before Time Inc.'s bid was in, Chambers' agent had a bid for the serial rights from the *Saturday Evening Post,* and although Time Inc. offered to raise its bid, the deal was made with the *Post.* Money was not the final consideration. Chambers later wrote Luce that he had decided to take the *Post*'s offer because he feared that in offering the book to Time Inc. he had embarrassed the company. "We wanted [*Witness*] definitely and categorically," Luce replied. "Within three working days after I got the manuscript I consulted six people highly relevant to *Time,* including President Larsen and Publisher Linen. Five out of six concurred with me. . . . Never in my recollection did such a radical idea [running a book serially in *Time*] get such a large measure of instant approval."

When *Witness* came out in book form,[12] *Time* gave it an exceptionally long and favorable review, saying: "Its depth and penetration

---

[12] Random House, 1952.

make *Witness* the best book about Communism ever written on this continent. It ranks with the best books on the subject written anywhere." In 1953 at the time of the congressional investigations of Communism in schools and colleges, Chambers did again contribute to *Life,* which, in its issue of June 22, published his article, "Is Academic Freedom in Danger?" But on Chambers' death in 1961, the ambivalence that had marked his relations with his colleagues throughout his career at Time Inc. was reflected in obituaries in *Time* and *Life. Time* was reserved in its account of Chambers and revised its earlier judgment of *Witness,* noting that it was an autobiography cast "in the classic confessional mold, its fire somewhat dampened by its self-pity—a book that has curiously passed out of conversation." In an editorial written by Chambers' steadfast friend Jack Jessup, *Life* said:

> If America is at all prepared to wage the great struggle with Communism for its own and mankind's soul, it is in part thanks to Chambers' courageous and eloquent struggle with himself. That struggle is fortunately preserved in his monumental book, *Witness.* . . .
>
> For Chambers, politics were apocalyptic, their real question being whether mankind would save its freedom by rediscovering the original source of freedom, namely faith in God. . . . He shook us and warned us . . . as the prophets of old.

# "We Don't Have to Be More 'Socialist'"

THOUGH SHOCKED and chastened by their failure to read the mind of the American electorate, the editors of *Time* in the new year 1949 still did not hesitate to tell their readers the meaning of Truman's election. In the traditional Man of the Year article (Truman, who else?), his victory was attributed to an acceptance of "the new orthodoxy"—orthodox because:

> It was no longer radical—it had been accepted for 16 years . . . a doctrine that held that the Government should be something like a modern, bureaucratic Great White Father to all its peoples . . . not only to protect the helpless, but also to make full employment, regulate business and let labor run on a minimum of regulation . . . a doctrine that meant guaranteed security—for the farmer and the worker, and for the old and the sick. In 1948, the U.S. wanted a man who believed in that doctrine. It rejected the party . . . which it suspected of wanting to change it.

They were words of resignation, even acceptance: the editors read into the election result a permanent shift to the left in American politics. The feeling was reflected in a letter which Luce wrote to Dr. Reinhold Niebuhr on returning a manuscript offered for publication;

245

the editor-in-chief, almost sounding as if he was throwing in his hand, rejected the article because it was addressed

> to an America which, confident and even over-confident in its "rightness," is taking a vigorous initiative in the world. I see, at the moment, no such America. . . . I think this country, far from having a strong George-Washingtonian belief in the rightness of its cause at home and abroad, is actually very uncertain of itself, very divided and confused in its "soul," and almost totally lacking in basic realistic notions as to its "objectives" in the world situation.

The new muted tone of the magazine, along with the announcement that at year's end T. S. Matthews would take a year off as managing editor of *Time* and the resignation of David Hulburd as chief of the domestic news bureau, apparently convinced a number of correspondents that important changes in editorial policy were impending. In order to quiet disturbing speculation, vice president Jackson suggested that Luce explain his thinking, and the editor-in-chief undertook to do so in a letter to Paris bureau chief Andre Laguerre,[1] copies of which were distributed to other editorial executives:

> As to what might be called working journalistic policy (as distinct from policy in public affairs) there is certainly no change. . . . There must only be constant examination of our performance with a view to better understanding of our shortcomings. . . . With regard to our policy on public affairs . . . while we may desire to steer by the stars, nevertheless we have to deal with the particular weather. . . . Thus what it makes sense to advocate in one year is irrelevant the next. . . . Now, to come down to cases, about the Truman election and its effect on our policy. It is my personal view . . . that the election of Truman was a misfortune for the U.S. and the world, and I blame myself that our publications were not more vigorously in the politics of 1947–48, so that we might have done our little

[1] Laguerre joined the Paris office in early 1946. As a private in the French army, he was evacuated from Dunkirk, later served as de Gaulle's liaison man with the English-language press in Algiers and London. The son of a French consul general in San Francisco, he was educated in part in American schools; before the war he had worked on newspapers in London and Paris. Hired by Charles Wertenbaker, then chief of foreign correspondents, Laguerre soon distinguished himself as a shrewd diplomatic reporter and was made head of the Paris bureau in 1948.

bit more effectively to relieve the Democratic Party of the vast responsibilities for which it was ill-fitted.

Matthews had once needled Luce with the observation that *"Time is no longer an exciting, or even a particularly interesting, experiment; Time is an institution—like the Republican Party, the Union Pacific, or the Church of Latter-day Saints."* But Luce did not regard the Time Inc. magazines as "Republican papers." The point he was trying to make was that it was time

> to reconsider as cogently as possible the deepest interests of our country, to recheck and refresh our notions as to the great issues of human destiny before trying to decide once again by what political means these interests and the issues can best be served in future years.

He invited Laguerre to comment specifically on "where and how in American terms . . . shall we draw the issue between Socialism and Progressive Capitalism, between welfare and the Pre-Police State?"

> I was born and bred a Bull Mooser [he wrote]; today I find myself more often than not on the "conservative" side of issues. Why? Because I have grown old and rich? I hope I am not *that* old, and the Democracy has happily seen to it that I am not *that* rich! Then why? Why do I not rejoice that Progressivism has gone gloriously on from triumph to triumph? . . . Between Teddy Roosevelt and F.D.R. there was a big difference. . . . I think there is a real danger that since natural American Bull Moosism has long since been subverted into Tammany Hall maternalism, America will slip and slide into Socialism with . . . a dose of backwoods "fascism" and bigtown gangsterism. . . . What do you think—as you view it from over on your Socialist continent?

Laguerre did not think that even if Truman's election indicated a slide into Socialism, Time Inc. should sit by merely as an observer of the phenomenon:

> I make a very sharp distinction between the responsibility of a politician and a journalist. Dewey today would be entitled to retire from the center of the stage. . . . But Luce is not in the position of Dewey. . . . Surely Luce, the journalist, has a con-

247

tinuing responsibility which does not diminish because the deafness of his listeners might increase? . . . Surely the first thing . . . is to bring the question into the light of day. Paternalism—socialism—whatever you like to call it—is, in your own words, a big danger in the U.S. Let's begin by saying why and where it is a danger. . . . Journalistically, by shouting, "Yah, socialism!," we won't get anywhere. But by reporting what is going on, and why, and where it is taking us, maybe we will. The worst thing is to duck the issue.

On reading Luce's letter to Laguerre, publisher Heiskell of *Life* wrote to Luce, both noting and questioning what he called "a spiritual lassitude in editorial thinking" resulting from the assumption "that we are unavoidably heading into the state insurance society":

> Isn't it true that the surest way to guarantee the gloomy future . . . is to assume that we *are* detached observers, endowed not with spirit but an M.I.T. machine which can scientifically project the course of human events? . . . If only people would remember that even the great and somewhat time-tested theories of physics are nevertheless based in the first place on sensory knowledge, which, any scientist will tell you, is completely misleading and untrue. . . . Sometimes I think we prefer to make a point with a not-quite-true little fact than with a firmly believed opinion. . . . Therein lies our danger and therein lies that gradual, inevitable march to ——*ism*.

Luce was jarred into action. "More than ever, the Editor-in-Chief feels rather culpably on-the-spot for current deficiency of light and leading," he wrote. "Something must be done." He assigned five senior editors to research and write policy papers on current issues— including Socialism in America—and himself set off on an investigation of Socialism in Europe.

He wrote to Gottfried, chief of foreign correspondents, telling him he did not want "red-carpet treatment. I do not want to see the Pope just for the sake of having it said that the Editor of *Time,* etc. saw the Pope. It would be a great privilege to see him if it is felt that he would like to give his views personally to an American Editor." He didn't want the American ambassador to Italy to "throw" him a dinner; "anyway, he wouldn't. Why should he?" Notwithstanding, the red carpet rolled out before him and his companion, Allen Grover, who said of the trip: "We saw everyone of any account politically in six countries, not to mention de Gaulle and the Pope. At the end Harry had gained six pounds and I had lost ten."

At Zurich, when told that his flight to Vienna had been canceled, Luce demanded, "Where have you got a plane to?" Told by a flabbergasted clerk that there was a departure to Amsterdam in twenty minutes, he and Grover climbed aboard. As always, Luce sent back a series of reports, most having to do with his happy discovery that Europe had not yet succumbed. "Le Plan Marshall, as they call it here, came just in time. The complete changeabout has almost the quality of a miracle. . . . Most of Western Europe simply does not want Socialism. Everywhere there is more or less of a crisis of . . . faith in Socialism, that is to say the Socialists do not believe in Socialism." In Rome he found confirmation. "When we went to call on de Gasperi [Alcide de Gasperi, the premier of Italy], almost the first thing he said to me was: 'I am very happy that we are achieving such good results through freedom of enterprise and individual initiative.' The American who comes to Europe with the fixed idea that Europe is basically Socialist . . . would have been surprised . . . if he could have seen the beamingly happy and enthusiastic expression on the Premier's face as he said this."

He did find an obverse side of the coin in Britain: "What is above all to be admired in the Socialist Government is precisely that they have had the courage of their coherent convictions and have been faithful to their beliefs. It is therefore really rather silly for Americans (and some Britishers) to take the view that the British Socialists aren't serious about Socialism."

But his most important conclusion was that

Western Europe has quite clearly rejected Communism . . . [which] now has no appeal to the heart, mind or imagination of Western Europe. But Europe still cannot defend itself from Soviet attack. . . . If America really wants to "participate" in the life of Europe, the key point of participation will be in organizing a defense of Europe effective enough to discourage invasion.

When he returned to New York the policy papers written by his associates were waiting for him, but they no longer seemed so urgent. Somewhat apologetically, he addressed his editors:

249

Last March, I thought it might be necessary for us to re-examine our premises and either a) take a position more to the "left" of where we had been in order not to be hopelessly out of step with the world of Truman, Attlee and Mao Tse-tung or b) if as a matter of conviction we could not do this, then dig ourselves well in (intellectually) for a fight which we would recognize as probably being a cause lost, however noble.

But coming back from Europe and surveying the scene in Congress, I found to my surprise and relief, no such thing. We don't have to be more "Socialist" in order to keep up with realities in Europe and, by golly, the land of "free enterprise" has not, for the moment, decided to bolt down the road to Socialism. Quite on the contrary, the Socialists or near-Socialists here and abroad are losing their nerve (their faith) and the principles of "responsible liberalism" stand out again as the best there are. If all this seems to be a little too easy, and even flippant on my part, let me introduce a solemn note. *The principles of liberalism are the best there are, in the absence of any other coherent set of principles, having clear intellectual formulation and wide understanding and acceptance.*

"The desire to be 'progressive' rather than 'conservative' correctly states our problem," wrote Luce. Pragmatically, the editors should address themselves to specific schemes to advance "human welfare," such as in medical care, industrial relations, agriculture. Philosophically, as journalists, their first task was

> to ask the *right* questions. If the proper study of mankind is man, then one right question is: What is a man? And another right question is: What is a man for? . . . In the pursuit of answers to those two questions, there is the one certain guarantee of "progressivism" and indeed of the profoundest radicalism. . . . The more I examine our "policy" problems, the more it seems to me that they lie mainly in the field of "ideas." This is not entirely good for popular or semi-popular journalism. An "event" is more manageable by journalism and has a wider common denominator of interest than an "idea." And yet the handling of ideas is probably the principal challenge of our journalism now.

There is no record of what Luce's managing editor of *Time* thought of all this; it was certainly within the framework of his own philos-

250

ophy of journalism. But Matthews was taking his sabbatical year to think out a new, more inspiring *Time.* Halfway through it, during the first trial of Alger Hiss, he had gone to Europe and would not return to the office until the ordeal of his friend Chambers was nearing its climax with the conviction of Hiss.

While in Europe Matthews' wife was stricken with a fatal illness; he brought her back to the United States and in order to remain with her took a leave of absence. In his despair he told his deputy, Alexander, that he would "almost certainly" never return to be managing editor, but when Luce, on hearing this from Alexander, wrote Matthews to ask what he wanted to do next, Matthews was furious: "Do you really think that, if I had decided not to come back as M.E. . . . I would have left it to Alex to report my decision? I have no intention of abandoning the bridge from which I am on shore leave."

When Luce and Matthews met, late in 1949, to discuss Matthews' future, Luce told him that he had decided to make Alexander managing editor and that he was thinking of vacating his own title of editor, which he had held since *Time*'s founding, in favor of Matthews. Some weeks elapsed, however, before Luce made his final decision, which was telephoned to Matthews by publisher Linen just before Mrs. Matthews died. Matthews received a copy of the announcement to the staff, with a letter from Luce, on the morning after his wife's funeral. The formal announcement read:

> I am happy to announce the appointment of Thomas S. Matthews to be Editor of *Time,* succeeding me, and the appointment of Roy Alexander to be Managing Editor. . . . The job of Managing Editor which [is] one of the toughest and most exacting jobs in America, will continue to be just that in Alexander's hands. Our advance lies in the fact that the Managing Editor will now have, ranking him, an Editor able to survey in greater perspective what needs to be done for the constant improvement of *Time.*

"Your letter, and the announcement," Matthews wrote Luce, "were as generous and heartening as only you can be. They arrived . . . when the world seemed to need some color—and you supplied it, in just the right place and with a master's hand." But he was to find, so he said later, that the title, no matter how earnestly bestowed, was an empty one.

*     *     *

251

Toward the end of 1949 Luce thought of making a trip to India. "He seems to feel happily useful," Billings wrote to Grover, "only when he is on large tours of inquiry, shooting through the firmament like an inquisitive comet." But by the beginning of 1950 he was thinking of running for the U.S. Senate. An article in the Greenwich, Connecticut, *Time* written by its managing editor, Bernard Yudain (who later joined Time Inc.)—headlined "Henry R. Luce Reported Possible Republican Candidate for Senate"—declared that Republican pressure was being put on Mrs. Luce to run for the Senate, but she "reportedly desires to step aside in favor of her husband." The New York *Times* quoted Luce himself as saying, "I have [the candidacy] under consideration. Several Republican leaders who seemed very much to want me have asked me to think about it, and I am thinking about it." The same article reported that Mrs. Luce, when asked if her decision not to run was final, replied, "If you were to ask me whether I may change my mind, I would say that ladies have been known to do it." The *New Republic* suggested that Mrs. Luce was "keeping her name in the speculation primarily to keep other names out." The state Republican leaders, the magazine said, "would prefer Clare—who has been tested at the polls—to the untried tycoon."

The Connecticut senatorial race in 1950 was of particular interest because two seats were open. The senior senator, Democrat Brien McMahon, was a strong candidate for re-election. Senator William Benton, who had been appointed by his former advertising partner, Governor Chester Bowles, to replace Raymond Baldwin when he resigned to accept a judgeship, was running on the Democratic ticket for the two years left of Baldwin's term. Luce was considering entering the race against Benton, a good friend. It was a pretty unsettling prospect for many of Luce's associates. T. S. Matthews wrote him:

It should be, of course, nobody's business but your own whether you choose to run for office or not. Why should you, or any citizen, be disfranchised to that extent? And wouldn't you be a good man to have in the Senate? From the plain citizen's point of view, these are merely rhetorical questions. But, whether or not you can take the plain citizen's point of view (that's up to you), I can't. From *Time*'s point of view, which is necessarily mine, I say we can't afford to lose any more editorial ability— yours least of all. And . . . what becomes of the balance of power in Time Inc.'s organization, with you out of it? With you

252

here, everyone knows that the editorial department is and will remain the senior partner in Time Inc.'s business; with you gone, nobody can be sure how much or how soon it will be curtailed, frustrated and relegated to a ruinously equal or even subservient position.

In reply Luce expressed regret that the question of politics had entered his life, but "since it has I must do a certain amount of coping with it before it is disposed of one way or the other." As for the matter which Matthews had raised—the future role of the editorial department—Luce wrote:

> Your letter gives me an opportunity to make one commitment and that is that as long as I live the editorial aims and responsibilities of Time Inc. will take precedence over business considerations. (And I hope—and believe—long after.) I would not make this commitment without being morally certain that it could be made good.

One other whose opinion Luce solicited was his son Hank, then a reporter on the Cleveland *Press,* who wrote:

> I am greatly honored by your request for my feelings on the subject. . . . I don't know if the company is ready to get along without you. . . . As for the job of Senator itself . . . aside from the great issues, you'll have to be concerned with many details . . . spend a lot of time talking to a lot of people who are just too dumb for any use. . . . I don't think Congress will get religion by your presence in it a mere two years. Yet your sacrifice in that time may have been big. . . . If you've an eye on a cabinet job in the event of a GOP presidential victory, I suppose that being a Senator would be a good spot from which to apply!

At the end of January Luce announced that he would not be a candidate. He wrote a friend: "The weight of evidence pointed to a very difficult campaign and my end decision was that I could be of greater service as an editor than as a campaigner." How he really felt, perhaps, he disclosed in a note he sent to Frank McNaughton, Time Inc.'s congressional reporter, who had been after him to make the try: "The way I feel today after a bad night on the train, it would be plain silly to take up a new career!"

253

---

# It Was "One Hell of a Fight"

**W**HEN *Time* in its twenty-fifth anniversary issue, March 8, 1948, undertook to tell its own success story, Luce, reading a draft, complained:

The first sentence of Take 3 is wrong as hell. *Time* did *not* rise on a tide of prosperity. Maybe if there hadn't been prosperity, we might have sunk. But it's certain that what we *didn't do* was to rise like something on a tide: we had one hell of a fight for at least five long years. The fight was probably not well conducted —put it down to inexperience or whatever, but it was one hell of a fight. . . . I find myself complaining that you make it all sound too sweetly reasonable and easy. . . . It just sort of makes me wish that when I was a young man I'd been smart enough to pick such a smooth proposition instead of the one I got into!

To be sure, Time Inc. had reported a record net income of $7,433,-000 on revenues of $120,404,000 for the previous year (and would turn up with another record of $9,009,000 on $130,981,000 in revenues in its anniversary year), but these accomplishments were not without risks and anxieties. The rapid growth of the company in the prosperous postwar years was accompanied by ever bigger gambles. *Life* had increased its circulation base to 5,200,000—never before had any company printed and distributed, week in, week out, so many copies of a magazine in such a short span of time. The production and distribution of the increased circulation required the employment of a great deal of capital. Continuing concern over the financing of *Life*'s operations was reflected in a memorandum to the directors from comptroller Arnold Carlson in November 1948, which noted that "the Corporation's working capital (net current assets) has failed to keep pace with the growth in the business." While the company's operating profit margin improved slightly in 1948, it was "still very low for what we consider the needs of this kind of business," and the problem, as always, stemmed from *Life*. While *Life* in 1948 contributed by far the largest net income of any division, its percentage of profit, always lower than *Time*'s, had recently declined. Despite careful planning, costs continued to rise.

Management had already begun a series of stratagems with percentages and nickel-and-dime decisions that could translate into millions of dollars made or lost. Late in 1947 *Life* announced a forthcoming increase in advertising rates of 9 percent (the second one with no increase in the circulation base). This was done in the face of the fact that advertisers still looked on the *Saturday Evening Post* as the old tried-and-true, a prejudice that kept the *Post* ahead of *Life* in the number of advertising pages, although *Life* with its higher rate (by virtue of its bigger circulation) led the *Post* in dollar volume.

*Life*'s problem was always to persuade advertisers that it could do things for them as well as, or better than, the *Post*. In the immediate postwar period Roy Larsen had come up with a brilliant promotional device. He launched a sales-training program for men coming out of the services, offering them one year's employment as a "retail representative," with the promise that at the end of the period they would have first crack at any available advertising salesman's job with Time Inc.[1] The young men were assigned to *Life* offices across the country, not to sell advertising in *Life* but to persuade distributors and retail stores to feature products advertised in *Life;* soon, from coast to coast, in shop windows and on retail counters red labels and posters blossomed on all manner of goods, proclaiming

---

[1] The program started in 1945 with fewer than a hundred men. By 1951, *Advertising Age* reported that thirty men were then operating for *Life* and that 163 had been through *Life*'s Retail Rep course, thirty-eight of whom were still employed in various divisions of Time Inc.

that they were "Advertised in *Life.*" It was not lost on manufacturers that dealers thought it was fine to be in *Life.* In *The Curtis Caper* Joseph C. Goulden told of a *Saturday Evening Post* salesman who, calling on the National Biscuit Company, found that it was not a *Life* salesman but the *Life* sales trainees who had beaten him to the sale. The biscuit company told the *Post* man: *"Life* moves cookies, and I have 150,000 dealers to keep happy." [2]

But the increased rates that became effective in 1948 encountered resistance from some major (non-cookie) advertisers and raised the critical question whether a strategy based on an expanding circulation had been right in the first place. In April Larsen wrote to the board of directors:

> It is hard to understand that advertisers have not yet been sold on the permanency of the new big American market or on *Life's* new big circulation and high cost. . . . This comes down to a question as to whether we are right or the advertisers are right. If we are wrong, it must mean that we should not have 5,200,000 [circulation base] and that we are lucky to have even our reduced profit margin, at the highest volume of advertising we have ever carried. That would really be serious. I personally think the advertisers are wrong, but perhaps it is going to take television, and television's expensive advertising, to coax them into higher advertising appropriations. Can we wait for that?

His own answer was no. He proposed that *Life* set its circulation goal at 6,000,000 in the next two years, and that meanwhile *Life* strengthen its financial position and again increase its per-copy price and raise subscription rates. *Life* and the *Post* were both selling at 15 cents. (In the beginning *Life* had sold at 10 cents to the *Post's* historic 5 cents.) By now setting its per-copy price 5 cents above the *Post's*, the thinking was, *Life* would suggest to the advertiser its superior standing among readers; 20 cents would also increase circulation revenues and reduce the degree of *Life's* dependence on advertising. Subscription prices would also go up slightly. If the circulation base stood up at the new rates, *Life* would then proceed toward 6,000,000.

Larsen also anticipated a challenge from television, to which this new large circulation would offer an important alternative. In 1948

[2] G. P. Putman's Sons, 1965; p. 85.

there were only thirty-nine television stations on the air and less than a million sets in use, but Larsen correctly foresaw that television

> will work startlingly well for many big advertisers. This is going to call for major adjustments in advertising thinking. I am assuming that television in a few years will be as widespread and have as large audiences as radio has now. . . . At the moment *Life,* with its 5,200,000 circulation and 25,000,000 readers, is showing exciting results at retail outlets. But the impact of a network television program on retail sales should be tremendous and, because the medium will be new, it will excite the imagination of dealers and give *Life* really stiff competition at retail outlets.

The directors approved Larsen's pricing strategy. There was a drop in newsstand sales but a substantial increase in subscriptions. "It was quite extraordinary the degree to which the public became aware of the price differential," said publisher Heiskell. An increase in subscribers tended to increase the pass-along readership. Also, said Heiskell, "We foresaw the great trend to suburbia, and it didn't look as if we were going to be able to reach suburbia except through subscriptions." The continuing conversion of newsstand buyers into subscribers offset the rapid decline in the number of newsstands in the central cities and concentrated the magazine's circulation in areas of greater buying power.

The big manufacturers of consumer products, however, were still dubious about increasing their advertising appropriations. Many top executives in 1948 were raised in the Great Depression and still had vivid memories of it; they were not sure that postwar prosperity would last; many still did not understand how a swiftly expanding population and a great new industrial machine had expanded consumer demand.

Trying to dramatize this new economy, Heiskell and his promotion director, George Wever, were making use of a new multiple-camera-projector system, devised by inventor Fred Waller, which permitted the projection of full-color slides on five giant screens simultaneously or in various combinations; it was the precursor of the Cinerama process.[3] To create a presentation called *The New America,* Wever

---

[3] Time Inc. and Laurance S. Rockefeller were the major stockholders in the Cinerama Corporation, which was formed in 1947 to produce motion pictures by a similar technique. The company was liquidated in 1950; its successor, Cinerama Inc., in which Time Inc. held no interest, produced *This Is Cinerama.*

sent a team of photographers from coast to coast. They produced a series of remarkable panoramic pictures that showed not only the natural glories of the United States but how dramatically the country had expanded since the war—the new factories, the prosperous and exploding suburbs with their schools and shopping centers. The message was clear: the country was confident and had money to spend.

Primarily intended for prospective *Life* advertisers, *The New America* struck a responsive chord in many viewers. The presentation toured the country for more than two years and was seen by 100,000 business executives and thousands of community leaders. At the request of the U.S. Army, it was translated, revised and turned over to its Civil Affairs Division for extensive showings in Germany, Japan and Korea.

Confidence was the keynote of *The New America*. But in March 1949 Charles Stillman (who with Howard Black had just been named executive vice president) had to describe an abruptly altered economic situation in his "fix": "We have just finished a year in which production, employment and advertising were at blue sky levels. But now the war-born causes of inflation have about run their course and the downward adjustments in the economy which began to appear last summer and fall have become apparent."

The country was experiencing its first postwar readjustment. Its repercussion, apparent in advertising sales of all the magazines, was felt at *Life* in particular. Shepard Spink, who had built up the sales staff as advertising director, had resigned, to be succeeded by Clay Buckhout, then *Life*'s advertising manager. Buckhout's first-quarter report for 1949 to Howard Black struck a somber note: *Life* had run only 777 pages of advertising, 149 fewer than for the same period a year earlier. "The basic reason for the drop-off," Buckhout wrote, "is that our rate is causing greater seasonal variation and [another reason is] the uncertainty that has existed in the business world."

Management countered with a reduction in advertising rates of 3 percent, effective in July, with no decrease in the circulation base. This was made possible, said Larsen in a letter to the trade, because of the savings in physical costs resulting from the $50,000,000 postwar investment in manufacturing improvements by the company and its suppliers. He said, "We believe that increased selling effort plus price adjustments to a more valuable dollar and a more productive

258

dollar are the two effective steps which can contribute today toward a stable economy tomorrow."

While advertisers welcomed a reduction in rates, the trade received *Life*'s announcement with some skepticism. *Tide,* a magazine about advertising founded by Briton Hadden but long since sold by Time Inc., commented:

> Most advertisers received the news with the hope that it would start a trend toward lower advertising rates generally; but they and everyone else in the industry wondered about the reasons for *Life*'s move. . . . Rumor . . . had it that *Life* was meeting with opposition from several advertisers, had in fact experienced some cancellations because of high rates.

Luce wrote to Black: "1) *Tide* gives us a very bad break—but journalistically justifiable. 2) What most strikes me is that there is no recognition that *Life* is entitled to get a few cents more than the *Post* or *Collier's*. Aren't we entitled to a few cents more for big size, better paper and printing? No. Aren't we entitled to a few cents more for millions and millions of extra readers? No. Rather discouraging."

The *Life* reduction in rates did not start a trend; the recession of 1949 was short-lived and inflationary pressures were renewed. In 1950 *Life* increased its rates once more—this time by 4 percent effective April 1951. But the mid-1949 reduction in the *Life* advertising rates, together with the fall-off in advertising sales, together with the effect that the business setback had on other divisions of the company, resulted that year in a drop of $2,250,000 in the company's net income. Nevertheless, the 1949 net—$6,758,000—was still the third best in the company's history.

To president Larsen "the most striking performance" of the record year 1948 had been that of *Time-Life* International which, for the first time, showed a small profit. When the division was organized, the difficulties of doing business abroad, said managing director C. D. Jackson, "were only dimly foreseen and sometimes wishfully brushed aside." In its first three years TLI reported losses of more than $2,000,000.

The division had done a remarkable job of consolidating the wartime editions of *Time* into four principal editions—Atlantic, Pacific, Latin American and Canadian. New printing technologies and worldwide air service made it possible to deliver *Time* virtually around the globe the same week it appeared in the U.S. Composition for the international editions was done at the central printing plant of R. R. Donnelley & Sons Company in Chicago. Offset film positives of the pages were then flown overseas to printing plants in Paris, Honolulu and Tokyo; from there the magazines were flown to various countries. The Canadian edition, printed in Chicago and distributed from there, was the most successful both from the standpoint of advertising sales and circulation. The Latin American edition was well received; it was printed in Jersey City and shipped by air to each major city in South America. It also carried additional editorial material on Latin America. Success was a relative term, however; the total weekly circulation of the international editions of *Time* in 1948 was not much more than 260,000.

An international edition of *Life* presented more difficult problems. *Life*'s wartime *Overseas* edition had never been as widely distributed as *Time*. Management had considered the possibility of publishing after the war a multilanguage edition of *Life* but this was scrapped in favor of the bi-weekly *Life International* in English, which in 1948 had a circulation of over 250,000. It was printed in Chicago and shipped overseas by surface transport; this meant that the "spot news" content of the domestic edition had to be eliminated to avoid outdating the issue before it arrived. In theory this should not have diminished *Life International*'s appeal, because there was ample fare of lasting interest, but in 1948 the magazine had yet to prove itself as a viable venture.

Early losses had forced some modification of the expansive ideas Luce had once had of several area directors taking up stations abroad and being responsible for all kinds of high-level public relations in addition to business and editorial operations. A letter from Jackson acquainted area director Walter Graebner in London with a new reality in the fall of 1946:

Budgets in the past have been almost academic yardsticks. When they were exceeded the worst that happened was "Oops, sorry!" and when they were beaten it was sort of cute. But a budget . . . within which an operation *must* fit "or else" is something new and foreign to Time Inc. Beginning right now, I am convinced that this is the New Order. . . . Harry Luce has, out of economic sagacity as well as necessity, considerably altered his world-wide, silk-hat, public relations representation ideas [but] he very sensibly has not allowed the pendulum to swing too far from riches to rags. Harry, Roy and Tex Moore are still more than willing to give TLI a run for its money, but beginning right now they want to know at all times what we are doing, where we are going, and how we propose to get out of the red.

The problems in publishing overseas in 1946 and 1947 arose, as successive annual reports explained, from "constantly changing restrictions and limitations imposed by foreign countries in the field of imports and dollar exchange . . . more acute dollar shortages abroad . . . distribution difficulties and multiplying censorship problems." C. D. Jackson was one of the more effective advocates of the industry in persuading the State Department to agree that the circulation of American publications abroad was in the national interest. This was recognized in the passage of the Smith-Mundt Act, which specifically authorized the Secretary of State to encourage the dissemination of information about the United States through the circulation of American media. This found practical expression in a Marshall Plan appropriation under the Foreign Assistance Act of 1948, which authorized the purchase by the U.S. government from U.S. publishers of blocked currency and guaranteed the convertibility of funds to reimburse them for certain physical costs of production and distribution. At the same time the Department of Defense took similar action in respect to occupied Korea and Japan. Fortunately, before these funds were made available, *Time-Life* International had already turned the profit corner. While the profit in 1948 was small, the annual report for the year noted that it was "significant of the opportunity we believe to exist in this field."

At this point Jackson was drafted by Luce for a new assignment: to get *Fortune* back on a paying basis. He was succeeded in TLI by Edgar R. Baker.

After graduation from George Washington University and three years with the Lend-Lease Administration, Baker had been hired in 1944 to work on "Project X"—the proposed multilanguage edition of *Life*—and had transferred to the international division as manager of *Life International*. Following extensive travels around the world to get the edition established, he had become deputy to Jackson. He, too, on assuming his new job, was faced with a new and disturbing challenge, for in 1949 the British pound and some thirty other currencies were devalued, again upsetting the delicate balance of international trade. But by this time the base for international publishing had been soundly established and the division in the 1950s was in a position to expand its operations.

Luce, as recounted, had spent much of his time in 1948 on the editorial reorganization of *Fortune*. Jackson, called in as publisher to follow through on the business side, found the magazine indeed in a bad way financially. It had lost $805,000 in 1948 and the budget projected an even greater loss of $984,000 for 1949.

Since Time Inc. did not publish the profit or loss of individual divisions, the staff had little appreciation of the situation. Jackson decided on shock treatment; he called the whole staff together, from office boy to managing editor, and told them just where *Fortune* stood. Patricia Divver, chief of research and member of the board of editors, remembered him telling the staff, "If you betray me it will be dangerous for the magazine because in publishing a losing proposition snowballs downhill. But I am going to tell you the truth, because it's up to you." He also told the staff that in order to turn the operation around it would be necessary to reduce the staff and that some of those listening to him would have to find new jobs. Nothing of what he said ever leaked. "Nobody tipped the gossip columns," said Miss Divver, "and it wasn't even known in the company."

In his first year at *Fortune,* Jackson commandeered *Time-Life* International's business manager, Charles B. Bear, who knew from experience the hard realities of budgeting in adversity, and cut the magazine's staff drastically—although most of those affected found jobs elsewhere in Time Inc.

*Fortune* at the time was housed in the Empire State Building because there hadn't been room for the staff in the Rockefeller Center quarters. This was one reason for low morale; *Fortune* employees felt separated and forgotten. Jackson made it his first priority to find room for them back at headquarters. "The job was to get the editors to be enthusiastic about the new *Fortune,*" he recalled. "The job was also to get the circulation picture unscrambled and healthy, which had to follow from the editorial improvement; and then to generate excitement about the magazine, so that the salesmen could capitalize on that and sell some advertising. . . . Everybody cooperated a hundred percent after he was asked to cooperate. But you can't expect 150 or 175 people to volunteer spontaneously. The job of the publisher was to get them in the frame of mind where they would be doing the equivalent of volunteering. Nobody dragged his feet."

In 1951 *Fortune* was once more in the black; early that year Jackson took a year's leave of absence to serve, at the request of President Truman, as president of the National Committee for a Free Europe. A committee of three (executive editor Furth, Bear, and assistant to the publisher Brooke Alexander) managed the publishing side until his return; later, in 1953, Del Paine stepped out of the managing editor's office to take on the publisher's role.

*The March of Time,* throughout the war and until 1951, continued to be exhibited monthly in thousands of movie theaters—13,000 in the United States and abroad at its peak. In its sixteen years it won more than forty awards, citations and prizes for excellence including two Oscars from the Academy of Motion Picture Arts and Sciences. It was praised by cinema critics as an outstanding producer of documentaries. But as a business venture it never was profitable except marginally so in 1938 and 1939. In the prewar years management believed that its minimal losses were money well invested because of the prestige and promotion that both *Time* and *Life* derived from it.

With the onset of war in Europe, producer Louis de Rochemont, who with Larsen had originated the movie version of *The March of Time,* had plunged into frantic activity; in addition to producing the monthly release and operating the school for service cameramen, he undertook a series of naval training films; after Pearl Harbor he began production of a full-length feature, *We Are the Marines.* A brilliant producer but no administrator, de Rochemont worked himself into a physical breakdown. He finally left the company—to become a producer of feature pictures for the Twentieth Century-Fox Film Corporation, where he proved himself once again a brilliant producer of documentaries; among his films was *The Fighting Lady,* the saga of the aircraft carrier *Yorktown.*

Louis de Rochemont was succeeded as producer of *MOT* by his younger brother Richard. He had been with *The March of Time* since its earliest days, first as European representative responsible for many of *MOT*'s most important foreign subjects, and then as managing editor. Larsen once commented about him to Luce: "While he is not the genius of production that Louis is . . . I think he can turn out a picture which can be as good. . . . And, most importantly, I would have confidence that it was being done in a businesslike way."

In 1942, in expectation of higher revenues, distribution of *The*

*March of Time* had been shifted from RKO to Twentieth Century-Fox, then headed by the aggressive Spyros Skouras. But this arrangement was not particularly successful, either. The prevalence of double features and the eighteen-minute length of *The March of Time* created problems for the Fox salesmen. After the war, Richard de Rochemont faced a new situation. Features grew even longer and the cost of short films soared. Movie audiences, sated with war and crisis, yearned for entertainment. RKO had had the Walt Disney films in direct competition with *The March of Time* in the short subject market; similarly, Fox had the Terrytoon series. The exhibitors, never at any time too enthusiastic about documentaries, preferred—when they had to buy short subjects—to buy cartoons. *MOT*'s hopes for higher revenues from Fox distribution evaporated as the gross fell below that of the RKO years. *Time* and *Life* movie reviewers did nothing to help relations between *MOT* and the Fox salesmen. After reading *Life*'s review of one of its big box office spectaculars, *Forever Amber,* one salesman sounded off to his boss:

> I have just read the last *Life* magazine . . . and I never had anything make me so mad in my life. . . . To think that the owners of that magazine . . . who expect us to sell . . . *The March of Time* which is the most unpopular two-reel subject on the market . . . would allow such an article as that to be published. . . . If I were in Mr. Skouras' place, I would cancel every contract . . . and refuse to handle any more of their lousy product.

At one point Skouras did consider canceling the contract with Time Inc.; at another, Larsen gave serious thought to discontinuing the distribution of *The March of Time* as a theatrical short subject. In 1950 *The March of Time,* in an economy move, reduced its schedule of releases from thirteen to eight a year—a move which still further reduced its revenues.

De Rochemont and his associates by this time were exploring other sources of revenue; since 1946 *MOT* had been producing commercial films for other organizations on a fairly large scale; another obvious field was producing films for television. In 1948 *The March of Time* contracted with Fox to produce a twenty-six-installment TV documentary based on General Eisenhower's best-selling *Crusade in Europe.* This was assigned to associate producer Arthur Tourtellot, a former newspaperman who had joined *The March of Time* as a script writer. In producing *Crusade,* Tourtellot and his two film edi-

264

tors, Jack Bush and Wolf Matthiessen, previewed some 165,000,000 feet of war film taken by Allied and enemy cameramen, from which they selected the 47,000 feet that comprised the final edited version. General Eisenhower was enthusiastic about the project and appeared on the program with the last installment in an interview with Dick de Rochemont.

Fox sold the series to the American Broadcasting Company, which hoped to sell it to a commercial sponsor; when no sale was forthcoming, *Life* and *Time* sponsored it on a thirty-three-station network beginning in the spring of 1949. It was later rerun by ABC with various commercial sponsors. It was very well received, winning the George Foster Peabody award as the best television educational program, the Alfred I. du Pont plaque for outstanding public service, and one of the first "Emmys" of the Academy of Television Arts and Sciences. But it was not a profitable venture for *The March of Time*.

The division nevertheless continued to demonstrate a certain creative vitality; in 1950 it won its second Oscar for *A Chance to Live,* the story of a group of Italian shoeshine boys who established a self-governing community, and in the same year a one-hour feature, *The Golden Twenties,* enjoyed a moderate success at the box office and was well received by the cinema critics—with the possible exception of *Time*.[4] The company had much to be proud of in *The March of Time*'s record; de Rochemont wrote:

> We have influenced the motion picture. We have added something to the vocabulary, and we have started trends from which we were unable to profit. If *The March of Time* should disappear tomorrow, it still has its place along with Méliès, Griffith, Chaplin, Eisenstein, Flaherty and Disney. We are, and I still speak historically, among the innovators.

But, as de Rochemont himself pointed out to Larsen, the division was in a frustrating situation: its costs were too high to be sustained by the declining rentals from theaters, "and in the television field we

---

[4] *Time* always tended to be critical of *The March of Time,* which irritated Larsen and Luce, although neither would dictate favorable treatment. Luce liked *The Golden Twenties* and on reading *Time*'s review, he wrote to Editor Matthews: *"The New Yorker,* generally reputed to possess a critical faculty, and not famous for its partiality to the works of Time Inc., gives a very good review. . . . Good reviews have been published elsewhere including the New York *Times.* Thus there does not seem to have been any truth-in-journalism necessity for the sour review in *Time.*"

have the high motion picture costs at a time when TV revenues have not risen to a point where they are even comparable with the already inadequate short-subject motion picture revenues."

When the inevitable decision was made to end production of *The March of Time* with the August 1951 release, Bosley Crowther of the New York *Times* wrote with sadness about the "passing of a cinematic friend. . . . *The March of Time* has stood up as a symbol of real accomplishment in the 'pictorial journalism' field." Richard de Rochemont, with the end of the regular releases, resigned to pursue an independent career as a producer of short-subject and industrial films.

The division continued until 1953 under Arthur R. Murphy, Jr., as manager and Arthur Tourtellot as director exploring the possibilities of production for television. Though the television audience continued to expand, *MOT* in its role of journalist was in competition with the networks, and the fact was that the networks were not making any money on news. For *MOT* there were no residual rights on a news program for TV—once created, the show had to make it the first time or it was dead. Since this was a basic problem, it was decided not to continue at that time in television programming.

Although the *Time* division seemed to have few of the problems besetting the others, it was always the object of considerable attention, for in the eyes of top management it was the foundation stone on which the company rested. In 1949 Luce, addressing *Time*'s advertising salesmen, put it this way: "There is a very special thing about [*Time*]. I did not plan it that way although, of course, I am very glad to take all the proceeds; but I can't take the credit. Nobody planned it that way, but it happens that *Time* is a very good economic proposition, so that it is possible in the case of *Time* to run a good business with a perfectly proper margin of profit and, in my opinion, anything in such a speculative business as this needs a big margin of profit."

Howard Black put it to the salesmen in another way: "What do you think is most important to Time Incorporated? . . . Our number one choice is obviously *Time* Magazine. . . . If *Life* Magazine had bad years, it would cost our company a great deal of money because, as Heiskell says, 'Every time you sneeze on *Life* you either make $100,000 or it will cost you $100,000 because it's so big.' We would hate to have anything detrimental happen to any of the other magazines [but] if something serious happened to *Time* Magazine it would pull the props right out from under our company and we cannot afford, above anything else, to have that happen."

There seemed very little danger, at the time, of this happening. The magazine had been consistently profitable, staff morale was high, particularly so in the business and advertising departments, and there was general agreement that *Time* was a success. The circulation, once it passed the 1,500,000 mark in 1946, seemed to have reached a kind of plateau, maintained with less cost for promotion than the other magazines. By 1950 *Time* had almost twice the circulation of its nearest direct competitor, *Newsweek*.

*Time*'s public relations were still a source of worry in some quarters of management. To old complaints of flippancy, bias and partisanship was added a new objection, that it was becoming "too powerful"—an objection which Luce characterized as "both a compliment and a cause of hostility." At the same time, *Time* was voted the most "useful" of American magazines in a poll of newspaper editors. Luce wrote: "I have never seen any account of *Time* which came anywhere near articulating the correct reconciliation between, on the one hand, the esteem which *Time* enjoys and merits and, on the other, the more or less valid objections and allergies to it."

The publisher couldn't do much about the complaints which, fair or not, went back to the editorial department. Linen, as publisher, was at the time concerned about some slowdown in advertising sales. Meanwhile Luce was asking questions as to why *Time*'s circulation seemed to have stopped growing. In fact, the publisher was holding down *Time*'s promotion and maintaining circulation at the current figure in order to enhance the division's profit. Luce was inclined to reject such a bias. He addressed his senior colleagues thus: "I'm afraid I think that we have not sufficiently desired circulation for its own sake and that we have let the question of advertising sales and advertising profits play too big a part in our thinking. . . . I think we ought, beginning right now, to press just as hard as we know how to achieve 2,000,000 circulation just as soon as we can . . . AND PRICE MUST NOT BE A BARRIER." The decision to move forward set the pattern for the fifties.

In May 1950, with revenues rebounding from the brief setback in 1949, Luce addressed a dinner meeting of his senior executives and expressed his gratitude and appreciation of the work they had done:

267

In 1950, for the first time in the history of Time Inc., all our publications, all our activities, are successful. They are successful not only at the box office but . . . in the opinions of a large part of mankind. This is a considerable consolation for our efforts over the years. . . . Some time ago we paid Mr. Churchill $1,000,000 for his memoirs. I was thinking the other day, suppose we could have gotten Dwight Eisenhower as the head of Time Inc. That would have been a much better investment. If ever an opportunity like that could come, I would feel very happy. . . . But probably you are stuck with me for quite a long while; and for my part, I am very glad I am stuck with you.

Luce was indulging in a little poetic license: *The March of Time* and *Life International* were still in the red; so was *Fortune,* although it was rapidly recovering. But the first year of the new decade was again a record one for consolidated revenues and the operating profit margin was 11 percent, although because of the excess profits tax enacted following the outbreak of the Korean war, net income was $8,501,000, a little less than that of the record year 1948.

# CHAPTER 18

# A Confrontation with a
# Well-known Demagogue

U NDER DATE OF October 31, 1951, Senator Joseph R. McCarthy addressed a letter to Luce which began:

As you know, ever since I commenced the public phase of my fight against Communists high in our government, the Communist *Daily Worker* has led a vicious personal smear attack against me, which has been gleefully joined in by a vast number of the camp-following elements of the press and radio. You, of course, are fully aware of the extent to which *Time* Magazine has joined in this campaign.

The senator had been inspired to the attack by *Time*'s issue of October 22, which carried his picture on the cover with the caption: "Demagogue McCarthy: Does he deserve well of the republic?" The article inside described him as "burly, ham-handed . . . a two-fisted drinker" whose self-designated role was that of a "sentry . . . who maliciously cries wolf, shoots up the coconut trees and keeps the camp in a state of alarm and confusion."

From the beginning of what McCarthy called "the public phase" of his fight against Communism, *Time* and *Life* had viewed him with skepticism as to his motives and distaste for his methods. Up until

269

the publication of the cover story the senator had ignored the Time Inc. publications. Now he turned on them furiously.

When McCarthy first came to Washington in December 1946, *Life's* editors chose him as the subject for a picture story on a freshman legislator. He was thirty-eight, young for a senator, and a marine corps veteran; both *Time* and *Life* had reported how in Wisconsin's Republican primary he had surprisingly defeated the incumbent, Senator Robert M. La Follette, Jr. His defeat of Howard MacMurray in the November election had again brought him brief mention in *Time*. The *Life* reporter assigned to McCarthy asked him to tell her his exact words on arriving in the capital, and she quoted him as saying: "Shit! It's raining." The New York editors found neither the senator nor his pictures very interesting and didn't run the story; the quote and pictures were immured in Time Inc.'s library.

*Time* mentioned him off and on after that; it was four years before his name reappeared in *Life*. In those years he got very little publicity anywhere—a few stories in Washington newspapers when he served a bachelor dinner to some women reporters, when he openly lobbied for the Pepsi-Cola Company, when he defended the Nazis charged by the U.S. Army with the Malmédy massacre during the Battle of the Bulge. With so little accomplished, McCarthy cast about for some cause to identify him to Wisconsin voters. He found it in alleged Communist infiltration of the U.S. government, a subject of which he had little direct knowledge and less understanding but his timing was sensationally right.

With Alger Hiss's conviction for perjury at his second trial in January 1950, many Americans were now convinced that, as Whittaker Chambers had charged, there had been treason within the government. Anger and outrage were heightened, not lessened, when Secretary of State Dean Acheson declared, "I do not intend to turn my back on Alger Hiss," citing Chapter 25 of the Gospel according to St. Matthew, beginning with verse 34. The public mood was described by *Time* in the issue of February 13, 1950, which noted that almost as President Truman announced his decision to go ahead with the H-bomb, "the U.S. learned it had been playing the game of survival with the enemy looking over its shoulder at all its top-secret cards. The arrest in London of Communist-Scientist Klaus Fuchs, a spy who had worked at top level atomic jobs in the U.S., led a jittery Washington to wonder whether even the deepest of military or state

270

secrets were safe from the U.S.S.R.'s agents."

This issue of *Time* was still on the stands when McCarthy's name skyrocketed into the headlines with his charges, first made in a speech in Wheeling, West Virginia, that a large number of Communists in the State Department, "known to the Secretary of State," were "still working and shaping policy." He repeated his charges on the floor of the Senate. *Time* reported: "Wisconsin's rash-talking Joseph R. McCarthy rose and swung the tails of not one, but 81 Communists and party liners (or so he said) in a wild attempt to decapitate both Harry Truman and Dean Acheson in one horrendous swing."

A Senate subcommittee under Millard E.Tydings of Maryland began hearings on McCarthy's charges, and after listening for some days *Time* said: "Loud-mouthed Joe McCarthy had been irresponsible all right—and worse. He had made a wretched burlesque of the serious and necessary business of loyalty check-ups. His charges were so completely without evidence to support them that he had probably damaged no reputations permanently except his own."

While Luce did not disagree with this verdict, he was a little irritated that his editors did not fully appreciate the political significance of McCarthy's accusations. He called their attention to a New York *Times* Washington dispatch which had reported that the McCarthy charges were "bad for the Truman Administration and bad for the Democrats in Congress," and wrote to the editors of *Time, Life* and *Fortune:* "This is the kind of factual truth which such people as the enlightened editors of Time Inc. deeply dislike to recognize. And for good reason. It is an affront to the democratic dogma. But every dogma has its painful moments. Or perhaps there's another reason. Enlightened editors are so eager to tell the people that they ought not to approve McCarthy that they forget to tell the people the shocking fact that they [i.e., the people] *do* approve McCarthy."

However, when Senate Republican leader Robert A. Taft condoned McCarthy's reckless course, *Life* wrote in an editorial: "We deplore the wild and irresponsible behavior of Senator Joseph McCarthy. We deplore the aid and comfort which he has received from Senator Taft and some others. . . . It is right to fight Communism; it is wrong, wicked, to smear people indiscriminately, most of whom are good Americans. . . . What you can best do for America and for American principles is not to join in the McCarthy lynching bee."

This editorial (of April 10, 1950) was written when the Time Inc. publications were themselves under fire from perfervid anti-

Communists. Columnist Walter Winchell had kept up a drumfire against *Time* for (he charged) harboring Reds. The radio commentator Fulton Lewis, Jr., was conducting a running attack against Time Inc. because the editors had ridiculed his airing of charges by George Racey Jordan, a wartime major in the U.S. Army Air Forces, that Henry Wallace and Harry Hopkins had forced U.S. officials to give atomic secrets to the Soviet Union. Jordan had first offered his story to *Life,* which turned it down as unfounded. When Lewis broadcast the story, *Life* said in an editorial that the "U.S. public was misled and insulted by a disgraceful abuse of the news. . . . The broadcasters and sponsors who bring [Fulton Lewis] and others of his breed to the millions . . . have a lot to answer for."

Winchell and Lewis were joined by *Counterattack,* an anti-Communist newsletter which in March 1950 ran this item:

> IT PAYS TO SUPPORT COMMUNIST FRONTS. Would you like to have your picture on the cover of Life magazine and be described as an "azure-eyed . . . critic's darling?" Would you like to do the cover design for a special anniversary issue of Fortune? . . . .
>
> Marsha Hunt's picture appeared on front cover of Life magazine last week. Her free publicity exceeded $1,000,000 when you consider Life's circulation of almost 5½ million at 20 cents per copy [Miss Hunt's alleged Communist-front associations were then listed]. . . .
>
> And in Feb. 13 issue, Life magazine gave favorable publicity to Judy Holliday [whose activities on behalf of front organizations were also described]. . . .
>
> A "proud American eagle" adorned the 20th anniversary (Feb. 1950) cover of Fortune magazine . . . but the record of the man who made the cast for this eagle won't (we hope) inspire Fortune readers. They are mostly well-to-do businessmen. If Communists seized power in the U.S. most of them would probably end up in slave labor camps . . . if they lived.
>
> William Zorach, designer of the eagle . . . has carved himself a niche in the Communists' Hall of Front Supporters.

*Counterattack* then asked its readers to write to Luce (and to Gardner Cowles, president of Cowles Magazines Inc., whose offense was publishing an article in *Look* on conductor-composer Leonard Bernstein): "Tell them that by aiding those who support Communist fronts they are helping build power of CP in U.S., and that this is incompatible with the anti-Communist stand both men have taken in their publications."

Luce did not let *Counterattack* go unheeded. In a letter to J. G. Keenan, its president, he challenged the newsletter to match its record of anti-Communism with that of Time Inc., but he went on to say: "We have not yet adopted a policy of suppressing all news of purely artistic achievement by people who are deficient in political understanding. . . . Also, we have not as yet engaged or organized a private F.B.I. to check up on all painters, sculptors or other artists to give them a loyalty clearance before any of our Art Directors may give them any assignments. Do you think we should? . . . In the great Struggle for the World, millions and tens of millions must be leagued together. You and I can't expect that all the tens of millions of anti-Communists at home and abroad will have exactly the same kind and degree of anti-Communism. I suggest to you that, except on the most crucial matters of policy, it would be well to cultivate a considerable tolerance and even friendliness among allies."

The attacks on Time Inc. inspired a steady stream of nagging letters to the editors, and *Time*'s Publisher's Letter of June 5, 1950, wryly took note of the changing mood:

> From the end of the war until last year, [the] largest part of the mail in the angry category belabored the editors for being too anti-Communist. . . . Well, times have changed. . . . The balance of criticism has shifted. Now more of these people seem to think that *Time*'s viewpoint on the news tends to the Communistic side. . . . In the past few years there has been a perceptible move to the right in the U.S. Today few citizens fail to see the menace of Communism. Some, however, both moved and confused by the charges of Senator McCarthy and others, have compounded the hysteria which says that any man is right who cries anti-Communist.

With the Korean war the anti-Communist sentiment grew more intense. McCarthy and McCarthyism battened on it, and in the congressional elections of November 1950 the senator emerged as a very dangerous man politically.[1] He was the key figure in a vindictive,

[1] "McCarthyism" was coined for *Time* by T. S. Matthews in a moment of inspired outrage. The word eventually found its way into *Webster's Third*

and successful, campaign waged against his senatorial foe and in-quisitor, Senator Tydings, whose subcommittee had issued a report calling McCarthy's accusations against the State Department "a fraud and a hoax." "South and west," *Time* reported, "where voters may have discounted a good part of what McCarthy said, they nevertheless decided that where there was so much smoke there must be some fire. (The Democrats had argued that so much smoke only indicated an arsonist.)"

By mid-1951 McCarthyism had become a national obsession. On July 4 reporters of the New York *Post* and the *Capital Times* of Madison, Wisconsin, approached 273 citizens in Madison asking them to sign a petition that incorporated the Preamble to the Decla-ration of Independence and found only twenty willing to do so. This was pointed to as an example of a climate of fear prevalent in America and was so cited by the President in a speech. To *Time*'s editor Matthews also it was evidence that "many U.S. citizens *are* intimidated, and *do* fear the Inquisition." Managing editor Alexander sharply disagreed; to him the incident was merely a newspaper stunt, proving nothing. "What Inquisition? Why should anyone have signed this petition?" he wrote. "To whom was it addressed? What was its purpose—stated purpose? What this story mainly shows is the ignorance of Harry Truman."

Luce replied to the Matthews comment irritably and impatiently. To Luce the Madison incident was "one of the most silly, ridiculous damn things in any silly summer season. *Many* Americans are *not* fearing any inquisition. Some are. Among the some are 'liberals' or ex-liberals. . . . For years & years liberals thought it was their privilege to hound and inquisit others. Practically every businessman was a villain, in their book, until proven innocent. . . . Most poli-ticians, in *your* book, are villains until proved innocent—aren't they? And how about Journalism—it is a villain in your book, isn't it, which barely on occasion shrives itself? . . . Look, Tom, we are all sinners and all have 'fallen short' as St. Paul says. . . . Men judge each other and society from very narrow biases. Both yours and mine are doubtless narrower than they ought to be."

A few weeks later, when Truman resumed his attack on McCarthy-

---

*New International Dictionary:* "a political attitude of the mid-twentieth century closely allied to know-nothingism and characterized chiefly by opposi-tion to elements held to be subversive and by the use of tactics involving personal attacks on individuals by means of widely publicized indiscriminate allegations esp. on the basis of unsubstantiated charges."

274

ism, again without naming the senator, *Time* ran a story that reflected less of Matthews' attitude than that of Luce, Alexander and *Time*'s new National Affairs editor, Max Ways.[2] The liberal press, Ways believed, was inflating McCarthy; his theory was to deflate him by paying him the minimum of attention:

> Truman's statement . . . is certain to inflate "McCarthyism" as a national issue. What is it? . . . The essence of "McCarthyism" is not McCarthy's callous disregard for the truth. It is the thing he stumbled upon: a deep-seated public belief that Communists did infiltrate the U.S. Government, influencing its policies to the detriment of the U.S. national security. This belief is founded on many facts known to the public before Joe McCarthy opened his big mouth at Wheeling. . . .
>
> Throughout the investigation of Communists in Government, Truman, Acheson & Co. gave the impression that they thought the whole thing was nonsense. . . .
>
> The policy of pretending that Communist influence on the Government didn't exist can be called "Trumanism." It is the real father of "McCarthyism."
>
> "McCarthyism" is not going to be stopped by Truman speeches or by the witch-hunting of witch-hunters, or by proving that McCarthy is a slippery character and no gentleman. "McCarthyism" is going to be around until Harry Truman, the President of the U.S., eliminates from U.S. foreign policy the tendency to appease Communism. This tendency is the red afterglow of Communists in & around the Government. It keeps "McCarthyism" bright & shining.

The article was interpreted by some readers as a retreat. The columnist Joe Alsop wrote to Luce protesting what he called "the almost tolerant, almost amiable note that has lately crept into *Time*'s han-

---

[2] Ways entered journalism in 1926 as a reporter on the Baltimore *Sun;* in 1930 he joined the Philadelphia *Record* as reporter and editorial writer on foreign and domestic news. During World War II he was an economic analyst for the Board of Economic Warfare before joining the Foreign Economic Administration as chief of its enemy branch which prepared studies of German and Japanese war production for the Joint Chiefs of Staff. In April 1945 Ways came to *Time* as a writer for the new International department which John Osborne was editing. When Foreign News editor Chambers blacked out on the train in the fall, Osborne was placed in charge of both Foreign News and International. After Osborne was made chief of the London bureau at the end of 1945, Ways became senior editor of these departments. In August 1951 he was appointed editor of National Affairs.

dling of McCarthy." Luce answered in a noncommittal note; however, he then suggested to Jack Jessup, who had just returned from *Fortune* to resume his old role as *Life* editorial writer: "It's about time now to hit [McCarthyism] hard. The general proposition is that 'Communism' has become too much the . . . scapegoat of everything that's wrong with us. The fact is that Communism is no longer a real issue, even indirectly, in America."

The *Life* editorial combined this theme with a lecture to the Republicans, and to "Mr. Republican" himself, Senator Taft. It advised Taft to repudiate McCarthy because "Communism, McCarthy version" would be "a phony issue by 1952; but McCarthyism is not and never will be a phony issue, because truth and decency are at stake. . . . Joe is becoming a liability and a danger, both to the Republicans and the nation." Taft did not appreciate the sermon; he told a member of Time Inc.'s Washington bureau that he could not be and ought not be "held responsible for everything every other Senator says." Moreover, he felt McCarthy's "general position" was correct: the administration's policies had fallen in with Communist policies in the past.

It was about this time that *Time*'s editors were working on the cover story of October 22 on "Demagogue McCarthy." Senator Benton had introduced a resolution calling for McCarthy's expulsion from the Senate and presented to a subcommittee a ten-count bill of particulars of McCarthy's "corruptibility and mendacity." *Time*'s decision to undertake a full-dress review of McCarthy's career was not unanimous; Max Ways opposed it, still feeling it would only serve to inflate McCarthy's already overblown ego. His feeling was confirmed by McCarthy's own reaction: he was delighted to cooperate on the story. He invited Time Inc.'s congressional reporter, James McConaughy, to accompany him on a week's speaking tour, which provided McConaughy with mountains of copy, including substantiation for the story's assertion that the senator was "a two-fisted drinker." But the larger import of McCarthy, as *Time* summed him up, was that: "1) His antics foul up the necessary examination of the past mistakes of the Truman-Acheson foreign policy. 2) His constant imputation of treason distracts attention from the fact that patriotic men can make calamitous mistakes for which they should be held politically accountable. 3) There are never any circumstances which justify the reckless imputation of treason or other

276

moral guilt to individuals in or out of office. 4) McCarthy's success in smearing Tydings and others generates fear of the consequences of dissent. This fear is exaggerated by the 'liberals' who welcome McCarthyism as an issue; but the fear exists—and it is poison in a democracy."

McConaughy courageously took an advance copy of the magazine to McCarthy and reported to New York: "He read it through, carefully, while I waited. He said he had been thinking about doing something about Time Inc. anyway, and this convinced him; but that he would wait until after the magazines were off the stands before denouncing us—he wasn't going to help us sell any copies."

McCarthy claimed that there were a number of false statements in the article, although the only one that he himself ever publicly identified as such was *Time*'s statement on Gustavo Duran. Duran was a Spanish composer who had served in the Spanish Republican army and later worked for the U.S. government in Cuba during World War II. McCarthy labeled him a Communist; *Time* said he was "never a Red, was definitely and clearly anti-Communist." Mc-Carthy said he had evidence to the contrary—and that this evidence was in *Time*'s own confidential files. As it turned out, to *Time*'s embarrassment, it was.[3]

Keeping to his word, McCarthy waited until the following week when copies of the issue had been replaced by a new one to write Luce the letter, released to the press, which began by coupling *Time* with the Communist *Daily Worker* in a "vicious personal smear attack against me." The letter went on:

> I would like to call your attention to statements in that article about the evidence which I gave on Gustavo Duran. As you know, all of the material which I have given about Duran's background came from Army Intelligence files. . . . In this connection, I would like to call your attention to a memorandum

[3] How McCarthy came into possession of a copy of the confidential *Time* file was subsequently explained by Nora de Toledano in an article in the February 1952 issue of the *American Mercury* attacking *Time* and the cover story. Mrs. de Toledano wrote: "When the Duran case first came to light in 1947, *Time* had collected all available material on it. And in *Time*'s Washington Bureau in 1951 somebody remembered the existence of this file. Some honest [*sic*] person in that bureau recognized the necessity of breaking traditional loyalty to his own organization out of a greater loyalty to the welfare of his country. The *Time* file on Duran found its way to Senator McCarthy."

in the files of *Time* Magazine, dated April 25, 1947, written by Jim Shepley, who, I understand, was one of your Washington correspondents at that time. . . . Your own files on Duran, if true, also show that I greatly understated the case against Gustavo Duran. In view of the above, I would like to hear from you as to what, if any, action you intend to take to correct not only false statements in regard to Duran but the many false statements in the story.

The Washington bureau had indeed reported in 1947 that intelligence sources believed Duran was a Communist, but the report had also concluded with this warning: "Remember that counter-intelligence operations do not involve proof of assumptions. They are made on a working basis for the purpose of neutralizing foreign espionage and on occasion for disseminating false information." No one could explain why the 1947 dispatch which remained in *Time*'s files had been overlooked or ignored.

Without waiting for *Time* to reply, McCarthy sent the editors a telegram, also released to the press, reasserting his previous charges against Duran and adding that McConaughy had found the charges convincing. The telegram concluded:

It is quite evident that the purpose of the article published in *Time* . . . was intended solely to discredit McCarthy so that in the future he could no longer be believed regardless of his evidence.

This is one of the most dishonest examples of prostitution of freedom of the press which has ever come to my attention. . . . Unless *Time* corrects the false statements on Duran and the other deliberate distortions of the facts in that story within one week's time, I shall have no choice but to make public your complete file in this matter so that the public may be aware of the sinister dishonesty of your magazine in this typical case.

Although the editors felt that *Time*'s defense of Duran might have been too unqualified, they still did not believe that there was sufficient proof to support McCarthy's charge against him and wanted to know details of the other so-called "false statements in the story" —so Luce wrote the senator. As to whether McConaughy found McCarthy's statements on Duran convincing, McConaughy had a short answer: "Hell, no." McCarthy supplied no further details.

In January 1952 McCarthy sent Luce a registered letter, text again released to the press, telling him that he was advising all *Time*'s advertisers "of the type of publication" they were supporting, doing so, he said, "not because of any personal feeling which I have towards you or any of the staff of *Time* Magazine, but because I feel that I would be derelict in my duty . . . if I failed to expose every cancerous growth which is endangering the health of this country.[4] I am sure you will agree that the policy of *Time* Magazine to throw pebbles at Communism generally but then to parallel the *Daily Worker*'s smear attack upon individuals who start to dig out the dangerous secret Communists, is rendering almost unlimited service to the Communist cause and undermining America."

So far, other editors had been content to let *Time* and McCarthy fight their little battle without comment. Now the press, touched on a sensitive nerve, reacted vigorously. *Editor & Publisher,* the Washington *Post, Business Week* and even McCarthy's New York supporter, the *Daily News,* all rose to *Time*'s defense. Said the *News* of the senator's appeal to advertisers: "That probably wouldn't work, Senator, for the simple reason that most advertisers don't worry overmuch about the editorial policies. . . . They want to sell their products. . . . A difference of opinion is okay. But you're no blushing oratorical violet, Joe, and you've got the whole U.S. Senate as a sounding board. How about settling your squabbles that way, without getting suckered into fouling out."

The senator went ahead undeterred, mailing *Time*'s advertisers a letter attacking the magazine together with Mrs. de Toledano's article in the *American Mercury*. One or two small companies withdrew their advertising. One large chain-store operator did try to bring pressure on *Time* by threatening *Life;* publisher Heiskell recalled, "I finally had to throw him out of my office."

The cover story had one influence on *Time;* it stiffened the de-

---

[4] McCarthy had tried the "hit-the-pocketbook" approach to control the press once before and had had just enough success in it to encourage him in this new effort. In 1950, angered by Drew Pearson's attacks on him, McCarthy, in a speech in the Senate, called on his followers to write protesting letters to the editors of 650 newspapers which carried Pearson's column and to boycott Adam Hat Stores, Inc., which sponsored Pearson's weekly broadcast over the ABC network. With the lame excuse that it was trying a new advertising approach, Adam Hat promptly dropped Pearson's program, but the American Broadcasting Company agreed to continue the program on a sustaining basis until another sponsor was found.

termination of National Affairs editor Ways to give McCarthy no further publicity. Despite the heavy press coverage of Benton's efforts against the Wisconsin senator during the rest of 1951 and 1952, Ways recalled that week after week, when it came to the final editing of National Affairs, he would drop the story on McCarthy. He did so, he remembered, despite the protests of Luce who was always uneasy when news which the rest of the press was featuring was being slighted in *Time*.

CHAPTER

19

---

# "*Was MacArthur Right?—*
# *Of Course He Was*"

L IFE photographer David Douglas Duncan was relaxing on a
beach near Tokyo on a Sunday morning in June 1950 with
nothing much on his mind except some captions for a picture
of a bronze Buddha. He hoped he could interest *Life* in his artistic
effort, undertaken as a respite from the world's troubles that he had
been covering for almost a decade; he had seen action on Bougainville and Okinawa as a marine combat photographer; hired by *Life*
as a roving photographer, he had ranged through the Balkans and
the Middle East, working alone most of the time; in Palestine he had
narrowly escaped death. His reveries were shattered when someone
on the beach gave him the news that the North Koreans had crossed
the thirty-eighth parallel and were driving south. He rushed back to
Tokyo, collected his gear and hitchhiked on army planes as fast as
he could to a new and savage theater of war.

Frank Gibney, *Time-Life* bureau chief in Tokyo, had arrived in
the South Korean capital of Seoul the day before. Gibney, who had
just recently taken over the bureau, was a graduate of the navy's
Japanese language school, had served as an intelligence officer in
the Pacific, later in the American Occupation forces in Japan. Only
a month before the North Korean invasion he had filed a report on

the work the American army had done in equipping and training the South Korean army. He had written, "No one now believes that the Russian-trained North Korean army could pull off a quick, successful invasion of the South without heavy reinforcements."

Gibney was not the only one caught by surprise. When news of the attack came, President Truman was at his home in Independence, Missouri; Secretary of State Dean Acheson was at his Maryland country home. It was not clear at first whether the North Koreans were attacking in force or whether this was another of the raids which had often disrupted the demarcation line between the North and South. But when it was apparent that an all-out offensive was under way, Acheson immediately requested a meeting of the United Nations Security Council, which the Soviet representative was boycotting at the time in protest at the continued presence of the representative from Nationalist China. In the absence of the Soviet representative, who would have vetoed any action, the council passed a resolution calling for an immediate cessation of hostilities and a withdrawal of the North Koreans behind the thirty-eighth parallel. Two days later, in the face of continued fighting, the council passed another resolution requesting all members of the United Nations to aid the South Koreans. Even before the resolution was passed, Truman had ordered the U.S. Air Force and Navy to provide support. He also sent the Seventh Fleet into the Formosa Strait to discourage any outbreak between mainland China and Formosa, took measures to strengthen the defense of the Philippines, and ordered increased aid for Indochina. He justified all this as a "police action." At the end of the week, with the South Korean defenses crumbling, Truman sent in elements of the American Occupation forces from Japan.

The President's first moves to meet the Communist challenge had won virtually unanimous approval in the United States; as *Life* said in an editorial, "The reaction of the plain man seems to have been, 'At last! It was the only thing to do.' Both the President and the plain man are to be congratulated: the President for the courage of decision and the plain man for net good judgment on a very complicated matter." In Korea the remnants of a shattered South Korean army and a contingent of U.S. infantry, most of them young and untried soldiers grown soft on Occupation duty, fought a rearguard action. "A small band of heroic youngsters led by a few remarkable generals was holding off a landslide," Truman wrote later.[1]

---

[1] *Memoirs*, Volume II (Doubleday & Company, Inc., 1956), p. 347.

The week following the invasion, after Seoul had fallen, *Time* carried its first eyewitness report from Frank Gibney. In the retreat from the South Korean capital he and a New York *Times* correspondent, Burton Crane, were driving a jeep over the Han River bridge when it was blown up prematurely by the retreating South Korean army. Though the jeep was hurled fifteen feet in the air, Gibney and Crane suffered only minor injuries. Gibney followed up his eyewitness report with a cabled request for a new pair of eyeglasses. Pictures that Duncan took of the fighting appeared in *Life* barely a week after he landed.

On the eleventh day of the fighting Duncan and Gibney were joined by *Life* photographer Carl Mydans. Mydans, who only weeks before had turned the Tokyo bureau over to Gibney, was in New York when he heard the news of the invasion, five minutes before he was scheduled to be interviewed on television. He called managing editor Thompson and got permission to return to the Far East, finished the broadcast, rushed home, collected his gear and departed. When his first pictures of the Korean war appeared in *Life,* it was like a grim replay in this veteran and heroic photographer's career. Luce cabled Mydans a personal note of congratulations on "your reappearance . . . in an advanced and dangerous position as a recorder of American history in these times. You are a reassuring symbol of the fact that in a decade America has become a veteran in world affairs."

By the end of July six American newsmen had been killed in those "advanced and dangerous" positions. Among them was *Time-Life's* Wilson Fielder. Chief of the Hong Kong bureau, Fielder, thirty-three, was the son of missionary parents, raised in China and fluent in Chinese. He had graduated from Baylor University and cut his teeth in journalism on the Waco, Texas, *News-Tribune.* After wartime service with the marines and a stint as night city editor for the Associated Press in San Francisco, he had been hired by *Time* to return to China as a correspondent and there had covered the last phase of civil war on the Chinese mainland. At the onset of the Korean invasion Fielder took off for Japan, leaving behind his wife and ten-months-old son. He first saw action aboard the U.S.S. *Juneau,* then joined Major General William F. Dean's 24th Division. During the retreat from Taejon Fielder was reported missing. Carl Mydans searched for him among the American units and found a lieutenant colonel whom Fielder had been with from the beginning of the Taejon battle and had stayed with during the retreat into the nearby hills. As Mydans told the story:

283

Then Colonel Ayers, looking down into the city, saw some Americans still trapped there. He took a small group back in to try to lead them out—and Wilson went in with them.

There, where the road turned, in some nameless village short of the town, the North Koreans came upon them. Their group was split and Ayers never saw Wilson after that. He himself made it—after many days—back through the enemy to safety. But Wilson never did show up.

"Perhaps he'll make it too," Ayers told me hopefully, when we still had hope.

He didn't, though. Long afterward, along that yellow road, we found his body.[2]

Fielder's place was taken by James Bell, then chief of *Time*'s New York news bureau. With Fielder's disappearance very much on everyone's mind, Bell went out on his first overseas assignment with instructions to get a thorough briefing in Tokyo before he went into Korea, and then to keep out of the battle zone until he had learned the ropes. He spent two days in Tokyo and went to the front. In August 1950 *Time* and *Life* both carried his eyewitness story of a marine assault force moving against "a barren, useless place" called No Name Ridge:

> Hell burst around the leathernecks as they moved up the barren face of the ridge. Everywhere along the assault line, men dropped. . . . The casualties were unthinkable, but the assault force never turned back. It moved, fell down, got up and moved again. . . .
>
> For more than an hour the assault force stumbled and struggled forward against a solid wall of fire. A Red mortar was knocked out by artillery, but the machine guns and automatic weapons continued without letup. As the marines neared the crest, their line ripped apart; the North Koreans rose from their positions and came forward throwing grenades. . . .
>
> The assault force was ordered to withdraw. Men too exhausted to cry crawled back down the ridge with no name. For all their terrible sacrifice the ridge was still in enemy hands.
>
> The ridge became quiet. . . . I sat there . . . wondering if the stream of litter bearers would ever stop coming up out of that damned valley.

[2] *More Than Meets the Eye* (Harper & Brothers, 1959), p. 301.

John Osborne, who had been made director of *Life*'s editorial page in 1949, was in the Philippines, the first stop on a planned Asiatic tour. Luce cabled him, designating him as senior *Time-Life* correspondent in the Far East. Osborne went to Formosa and from that Nationalist stronghold filed a dispatch that was a portent of bitter controversies to come. It reflected the anger of Chiang's government, which wanted to pursue its own actions against the Chinese Communists, at the restraint put on it by the Seventh Fleet and the continuation of Washington's "old down-the-nose political attitude" toward it. In a second dispatch, derived from an unattributable interview with Chiang Kai-shek, Osborne advised: "The Generalissimo has unlimited confidence in MacArthur and would be happy to place the fate of Formosa and of Nationalist China in his hands. . . . He knows of no other American who is capable of directing an effective U.S. program in Asia."

From Formosa Osborne moved on to the front, from which he filed an account of "The Ugly War" that was prophetic of mistakes later to be repeated in Viet Nam. "War against the Communists of Asia cannot be won—not really won—by military means alone. To attempt to win it so . . . is not only to court final failure but also to force upon our men in the field acts and attitudes of the utmost savagery . . . the blotting out of villages where the enemy *may* be hiding; the shooting and shelling of refugees who *may* include North Koreans in the anonymous white clothing of the Korean countryside, or who *may* be screening an enemy march upon our positions."

In August *Life* sent out a new staff photographer, Hank Walker, who, like Duncan, had been a marine combat photographer in World War II. Thus in September, when MacArthur launched his brilliant amphibious attack on Inchon, outflanking the North Koreans, *Time* and *Life* had coverage from five reporters and photographers. Gibney, Walker and Bell went ashore with the assault troops. Walker's landing craft was struck and he transferred to another; he then teamed up with Bell to join the marines on their twelve-mile march to capture Kimpo airfield. There the two of them spent a night under continuous, suicidal charges by the North Koreans. In the morning, on his way back to Inchon to file his dispatch, Bell was injured in a jeep accident, suffering a broken arm and chest injuries. At the beachhead he dictated his story to Mydans, who at MacArthur's request had made the amphibious landing with the general. Duncan scored something of a scoop by being the first photographer to reach the recaptured capital of Seoul.

Though there was tremendous comradeship among the *Life* photographers, there was also fierce competition for space in *Life*'s pages. Duncan felt that his Seoul pictures did not get sufficient prominence and complained by cable to Thompson: "I certainly overestimated value you placed on having someone first into that town. . . . All pix look same anyway so didn't make any difference where taken or when except to me and own personal satisfaction so really shouldn't give a damn." Thompson usually listened patiently to complaints, but Duncan's cable irritated him. "Guess it is my turn to be a little indignant," he replied. "I used more of the South Korean windup than . . . I thought was justified. . . . In view of your cable I think it was kind of silly to bother. . . . Possibly at some future time a system can be worked out whereby the photographers can take the pictures, shuttle in to edit and lay them out, and then write the text block and captions. I have sadistic moments when I think I might enjoy sitting back and watching photographers have at each other for the available space. Until that happy day, however, I'm afraid there isn't much to do but allow that archaic system of having editors to continue." Duncan sent a cheerful, unchastened reply: "It's wonderful when we're both mad, only you're much more devastating therefore unquestionably still the maestro. As for as Hank and Carl, they're good friends but as photographers I am shooting against them just as much as AP, Acme, SEP or any guy on this earth."

Mr. Truman's "police action" was indubitably a war, though Congress had never declared it and the administration and the country were not prepared to wage it to the limit or to an ultimate conclusion. Luce apparently felt that Korea might be the beginning of a general war. He suggested that *Life* embark on a major editorial series on "War—its theory and practice," explaining that the raison d'être

is that in the next few years Americans will have to live with War as they have not since the days of the settler and the Minute Men. The "moral" of the series is that (a) the theory and practice of War changes and reflects the changing circumstances of human life but nevertheless (b) War always has been, is and always will be part of man's fate until Kingdom come. . . . War is one of the great perennial themes along with Love and Death. . . . Just as politics is inseparable from economics, so

286

both politics and economics are inseparable from War. "I hate war"—is that a valid or invalid attitude? The answer probably is neither or both. In "our time," the complete moral and psychological rejection of War seems to have gained a total validity. . . . After the mud and trenches [of World War I], it was thought that War was so hideous that nothing could possibly justify it. . . . And now what? For one thing the Soviet Union has never for one single moment in all its 28 years of existence given War anything less than top position a) in its national policy b) in the minds of its subjects. . . . In any case *we* are not going to end War without practicing it some more—and living with it.

Ed Thompson diplomatically told Luce that the theme was good but that he had "some question about the timing, lest we be accused of warmongering." After polling his associates he told Luce that the *Life* editors were dead against the idea and gave him their reactions. Assistant editor Robert Wallace wrote, "I shudder to think what would happen if this document should fall into the hands of Yakov Malik [the permanent Soviet representative to the United Nations Security Council]." Foreign News editor Fillmore Calhoun argued against the suggestion because "1) it repeats what we will have to keep on doing to cover the news; 2) it is how to have peace—not how to make war—that interests people." Emmet Hughes, articles editor, also took exception: "I would simply question whether *Life*'s readers would rejoice to find both our fine Korean coverage and our militant exhortation on the editorial page now capped by intensive and lavish treatment of this particular historical theme week after week." Only two staff members, George Hunt and Tom Carmichael, comprising the Military department, saw any merit in the suggestion, and they conceded that the idea was good "only if we don't set about to glorify war."

No more was heard of "War—its theory and practice"; Luce's reaction was recorded in another of his "not sent" memoranda, in which he recorded his thoughts of the moment. This one read:

Bob Wallace shudders to think what would happen if my memorandum on War should fall into the hands of Yakov Malik. I can give him at least this reassurance: it couldn't be worse than what happened to me as a result of its falling into the hands of the Editors of *Life*. Any plea of mitigation I might make against the severely moral condemnation of my colleagues can only be made in a hoarse and feeble whisper. But I should like to urge the rather pitiful extenuations that the document was written in the greatest possible haste and was not intended for an audience of more than two or three. I am sure that the Managing Editor would wish all of you to regard this moral lapse as a family secret.

With the Inchon landing and the MacArthur forces pushing north, the Korean war seemed to be coming to a triumphant end. The editors decided that Gibney and Bell should come home to recuperate and that Duncan and Mydans should be replaced. Hugh Moffett, National Affairs editor of *Life,* took over the Tokyo bureau from Gibney; Dwight Martin, a writer on *Time*'s Foreign News staff, who had been a *Time* correspondent in the Far East and had flown out of Nanking two days before it fell to the Communists, succeeded Bell; Roy Rowan, *Life*'s Rome bureau chief, returned to the Far East where he had covered the Chinese civil war. Walker remained in Korea to be joined by Howard Sochurek. Sochurek was a new man on the *Life* staff but no stranger to war photography; as commander of the 3234th Signal Photo Detachment he had covered operations of the 77th Division in the Pacific during World War II. Curtis Prendergast, a former Foreign Service officer who had been attached to the U.S. consulate in Seoul, was hired as a correspondent.

Walker covered the assault and capture of the North Korean capital of Pyongyang, and a day later Sochurek, who had taken one practice jump, parachuted down with the 187th Airborne Regimental Combat Team north of Pyongyang in an operation that was unsuccessful in one of its most important objectives—the rescue of American prisoners of war; the Reds had already slain most of them. Walker's pictures of the fall of Pyongyang were headlined prematurely "Hard Hitting U.N. Forces Wind Up War," and the accompanying text block read, "The end of the war loomed as plain as the moustache on Stalin's face."

After the fall of Pyongyang, Walker and Hugh Moffett went on a tour of the front; at Onjong, Moffett witnessed the interrogation by Republic of Korea troops of a prisoner they had just captured. He was a Chinese. He gave his name, his outfit and information on other Chinese units which had crossed the Yalu in mid-October. Moffett's report and Walker's pictures of the prisoner reached New York after some delay and appeared in *Life*. Moffett also interviewed a ROK general who warned that there were 40,000 Chinese troops in Korea; "I didn't vouch for this guy's estimate, and *Time* didn't either, not playing it for the tipoff it really might have been," Moffett wrote, but *Time* printed the story in its issue of November 6.

With Roy Rowan, Walker pushed on to the Yalu and took pictures of the frozen river. In the issue carrying the news of the Chinese onslaught, which began in the last week of November, *Life*'s editors ran one of the pictures and in hindsight wrote the caption: "Footprints on the Yalu where it had frozen solid come from Manchurian side to Korea and were a warning to U.N. troops that Chinese Red agents or combat troops on patrol were on the move." But no one had taken the warning at the time.

Chinese intervention in force had been heavily discounted, largely because of the meeting of the President with General MacArthur at Wake Island in mid-October, when the general assured his commander in chief that organized resistance by the North Koreans would end by Thanksgiving Day. He doubted that the Chinese would intervene, and if they did, he told the President, not more than 50,000 or 60,000 Chinese troops could cross the Yalu; if they tried to reach Pyongyang he was confident that there would be "the greatest slaughter."

An experience which Luce had at this juncture tells something of the nation's sudden awareness of a disastrous miscalculation. Believing, like everyone, that the war was all but over, he had started on a leave of absence granted him by the directors. He took off on a trip to the Middle East and was returning from a visit to the northern provinces of Iran at the end of November when he received a cable from the home office telling him that his wife was seriously ill. The cable also informed him that the Chinese had intervened in the Korean war in force. He immediately flew back to New York, where he found his wife recovering from her illness. But he was quite unprepared for the change in the mood of the country:

Despite what I had heard en route it came as a shock that the New York *Times* was publishing eight column headlines with the smell of panic. I had a call from John Foster Dulles, then a very special assistant to Secretary of State Acheson. Dulles said he was at his home in New York and could I come after dinner. When I got there I found Foster and Brother Allen and

289

a foreign service officer. . . . The atmosphere was solemn. Foster Dulles put the situation to me concisely and precisely. He said the American army had been surrounded and a Marine division too. "It is," said Dulles, "the only army we have. And the question is: shall we ask for terms?" I could not believe my ears and that is what I said.

Truman and the U.N. allies abandoned any thought of liberating all of Korea and hoped at the most to restore the status quo ante; war with Red China, with the possibility of war with Russia, was to be avoided at all costs. But MacArthur responded to the shock and surprise of the Chinese attack with characteristic militancy. Proclaiming "an entirely new war," he wanted to carry the fight to Red China, urged the use of the Nationalist forces from Formosa and publicly expressed his outrage at the restrictions placed on him.

Hank Walker was with Lieutenant General Walton H. Walker's Eighth Army covering the chaotic retreat south through Pyongyang. Moffett, who had been severely injured when his stalled jeep was sideswiped by a racing personnel carrier, watched from his hospital bed as the casualties were brought in and dictated a vivid description of "the most disastrous bug-out in America's military history." When Duncan, back in New York, heard that the First Marine Division, with which he had served in World War II, was trapped at the Changjin Reservoir, he took off without waiting for assignment or credentials. On arriving back in Korea he was told that GHQ had put Changjin off limits to correspondents, but he persuaded a marine observation pilot to fly him in. The First's commander, Major General Oliver Smith, greeted him: "You're asking for it, son. You didn't have to come. But after all, it's your division. We're glad to have you aboard." Duncan covered the division's retreat (General Smith called it "just fighting in another direction") along what the marines called "Nightmare Alley" in weather so cold that Duncan's camera shutter froze and he had to warm it by holding the camera against his body. One soldier looked up as he heard Duncan's shutter click; bearded and bleary-eyed, he grinned and said, "Should'a shaved." Duncan's pictures appeared in the 1950 Christmas issue of *Life*.

Carl Mydans, like Duncan, was in New York when news of the Chinese invasion came; he asked for and got reassignment to Korea. His return followed closely upon Lieutenant General Matthew B. Ridgway's taking command of the Eighth Army after General Walker was killed in a jeep accident. Mydans photographed Ridgway's dramatic tour of the battle lines as he laid down the dictum that there would be no more retreats.[3]

Unhappily, there were more retreats, which John Dominis and Carl Mydans photographed; with Joe Scherschel, who had joined *Life* in 1948, Dominis covered the campaign as the allied forces moved north again. When Dominis left Korea, Michael Rougier joined Scherschel in reporting the Reds' spring offensive in 1951.

While *Time* and *Life* had applauded Truman's courage in intervening in Korea, the magazines were critical of the administration's overall Asian policy, of its "strange, vacillating policy on Formosa" and its failure to mobilize an all-out American effort for the war. The magazines' chief target was Secretary of State Dean Acheson who, said *Life,* was "the symbol of appeasement of Communism everywhere in Asia" and of "all the soft-headed unrealistic thinking about world politics which has brought us again under the shadow of catastrophe." MacArthur, on the other hand, commanded the editors' great admiration. In a cover story *Time* quoted his chief of staff, Major General Edward M. Almond, as saying, "He is the greatest man alive." *Life* saluted him: "Never was an American soldier more deeply imbued with the sense of the conduct befitting him under the American Constitution."

When MacArthur called for the widening of the war, his arguments were endorsed by the editors of *Time* and supported in a series of editorials in *Life*. In the first, published in the issue of December 11, 1950, declaring that "the news is of disaster," *Life* said: "World War III moves ever closer. . . . The Chinese Communist armies assaulting our forces . . . are as truly the armies of the Soviet Union as they would be if they wore the Soviet uniform. . . . We do not 'want' war with China. The Communists force war upon us. Until and unless they cease to do so, there will be no possibility of peace with China. These are the facts and the prospect is war." In its issue of January 8 *Life* said: "*Life* sees no choice but to

---

[3] *U.S. Camera Annual, 1951,* paid a tribute to the work of Duncan, Mydans and Walker by devoting almost its entire section on Korea to their war photographs, commenting, "This daring trio of *Life* photographers, individually and as a unit, turned in the best all-around news coverage of the entire Korean campaign [in 1950]." The White House News Photographers Association awarded Walker first place in its War Class.

acknowledge the existence of war with Red China and to set about
its defeat, in full awareness that this course will probably involve
war with the Soviet Union as well." In a following editorial *Life* tore
into Acheson: "It is terrifying, it is wrong, that this proud priest of
'coexistence' with Soviet Communism . . . should still be in a position to shape the President's most vital conceptions and statements
of American foreign policy." It went on to ask: "If 'coexistence'
with the present Soviet Communist system is impossible, is total
war 'inevitable?' Maybe so, maybe not," answered the writer, but
"what no man has a right to say is that we can live peaceably and
happily *with* this prodigious evil. . . . The Soviet Empire . . . will
continue to expand unless it is opposed with all our strength [and]
that includes the steady, calm and constant acceptance of the risk
of all-out war."

The editorials, certainly reflecting Luce's own view, were written
by John Osborne, recently returned from duty in the Far East as
senior correspondent. He was, it will be recalled, one of the correspondents who had objected most strongly to former Ambassador
Bullitt's warning against postwar Soviet expansionism and to the
anti-Communist stance of the Foreign News section when Whittaker
Chambers was editing it. Osborne, always a man of passionate convictions, had come a full, convinced 180 degrees.

The administration sought to counter the *Life* attack. Without
mentioning *Life* by name, Philip Jessup, ambassador-at-large, addressed an audience at Union College: "There has appeared a line
of argument which is no less dangerous because its authors have
been unwilling to be perfectly frank. . . . The . . . idea is that the
United States can save itself only by resorting to preventive war.
This is the inescapable logic of the position even though the conclusion is hedged by saying that maybe war is inevitable and maybe
it is not." George F. Kennan, on leave from his post as counselor of
the State Department, in an article in the *New York Times Magazine,*
accused the administration's critics of using "tricky words."

Osborne went to Washington to discuss the matter in off-the-
record talks with State Department officials and found them more
aroused and indignant than he had anticipated. (Acheson refused
to see him.) Reporting back to New York, he said that Dean Rusk,
assistant secretary of state for Far Eastern affairs, subjected him to
"an angry diatribe"; Paul Nitze, director of the department's policy
planning staff, "flushed very deeply, pounded his right fist on his

desk and said: 'This job is hard enough . . . without having to undergo that kind of thing.' He added: 'What you say on that page has a great effect on us and what we are trying to do here.' "

Osborne was subjected as well to fierce criticism within Time Inc. from his own colleagues, and there was an angry and adverse reaction from the readers. Osborne agreed that his editorials had gone too far. He wrote two editorials in March 1951, entitled "This Way to Peace," in which he explained that *Life* believed that there was a valid hope for peace and that World War III was not inevitable. After listing the policies which might avert all-out war, some of which it said the administration was already following, *Life* conveyed a more hopeful note than hitherto: "Actually there are good reasons for believing—as, for example, General Eisenhower believes —that we have a good chance of winning the struggle without atomic war. . . . A will to win is the key to our best hope of a valid way to peace."

By the time these editorials appeared the situation in Korea had greatly altered. Under Ridgway the U.N. forces had stabilized their lines and were pushing back to the thirty-eighth parallel; presently the war was back virtually to where it had begun. When minority leader Joseph W. Martin read to the House a letter from the imperious MacArthur challenging the concept of a limited war and declaring that "there is no substitute for victory," Truman, who had already decided that MacArthur's "insubordination" had become intolerable, was aroused to a point of fury and relieved him of his command. Luce and most of his senior editors lined up with MacArthur. An editorial in *Life* which Osborne said Luce wrote, "replacing one by me that he thought too tepid," declared: "He [MacArthur] was ousted for no petty reason but because he chose to challenge the whole drift of events and the dominant attitudes of the Government of the United States. . . . In defending his removal of MacArthur, Truman moved on to a calamitous error: he defined the policy of the United States in a way that ties the nation's hands and gives all initiative, all power of choice to the enemy." The *Time* stories on MacArthur left no doubt of where the magazine's sympathies lay; MacArthur was right, the President was wrong.

In Time Inc.'s Tokyo office the sympathies of the correspondents were with the President; many correspondents in the field thought that MacArthur was too old, out of touch with reality and, in his messages home, was playing politics. As bureau chief, Moffett provided a running file on events in Tokyo, and he received a number of queries from New York that, he said, "tipped the pitch the home office was taking. The press reports out of the U.S. indicated that most everybody had gone off his whack; they were going to impeach Truman and issue sainthood to MacArthur in San Francisco. I lunched at the press club and had about three martinis. I vowed right there, 'I'm going to tell them idiots a thing or two.' So back at the office I compiled a two-page cable. . . . The burden of it was that MacArthur had done a lot of things wrong. We had a strong conviction that the removal of MacArthur would make things go a lot better in the war."

New York would not accept Tokyo's version of events. In reporting the reaction of the editors, Manfred Gottfried cabled Moffett, "Realize Tokyo bureau favored Truman on the policy issue but you were not canny in making case." To which Moffett replied, "Sublimely confident that we are right and you guys are wrong, we are now going to have a party celebrating the departure." They submitted the bill for the party to the home office, which paid it without comment.

MacArthur's return was covered by both magazines for what it was: one of the most spectacular demonstrations of emotion since the end of World War II. For the moment, the general was the hero. When *Time* put Truman on its cover, many readers, without reading the accompanying article (which was favorable to MacArthur and critical of the President), ripped off the cover and mailed it to the editors, torn to bits or marked with vituperative comments. *Life*'s headline on the pictures of MacArthur's address to the joint session of Congress was "An Old Soldier Fades Away Into New Glory."

Luce was one of the few visitors to whom the general gave an audience on his arrival in New York, and for his associates the editor-in-chief provided this historical footnote on the general's personal reaction to the news of his dismissal:

MacArthur was completely surprised; he had no idea this was coming. He got really eloquent when he spoke of "insubordination"—complete and utter nonsense. (I am glad I got that word deleted from *Time* and *Life* stories.) It was absolutely instinctive with him to obey orders. (Max Ways made this point well.) He had obeyed orders under Roosevelt. And then came this socker: he said there was just no comparison between the

294

latitude he had under Roosevelt and his almost complete lack of same under Truman and the Pentagon. . . .

MacArthur then proceeded to explain . . . what he was trying to do by his alleged talking-out-of-turn. In the absence of any intelligible objectives, he was trying to propose some. The implication was that if at any time he had been given alternative but precise policy objectives, he would have accepted them. Or, if then he couldn't in conscience agree, he might have quit —but what seems innate in MacArthur is that by God he carries out orders—if he gets them.

Though Luce never wavered in his admiration for MacArthur, he was too good a journalist not to see that, after those first triumphal weeks, Senate hearings on the circumstances surrounding MacArthur's removal were of diminishing interest to the public. Luce suggested to *Time* managing editor Alexander, "Maybe you ought to try to get a change of pace. . . . The Great Debate is in *general* boring; only certain details such as [General] Bradley's professional slurs on MacArthur are interesting."[4] When MacArthur undertook a speaking tour around the country, Thompson suggested to Luce that "maybe we should have an editorial, more in sorrow than in anger, which in a gentle way would disengage *Life* from MacArthur. . . . I checked my impressions with Alexander, who is thinking of saying 'Hey, be careful' to the General in *Time* this week." MacArthur had made a speech in Boston to the effect that the Korean war had been fought without purpose, and *Life*'s editorial found itself disagreeing with the magazine's distinguished friend and supporting an old enemy: "On this question of whether the war in Korea was fought to good effort or to no effect, we think General MacArthur is wrong and Mr. Acheson is right."

As 1951 neared its end Luce, in a memorandum, nominated MacArthur for *Time*'s Man of the Year. But he ran into vigorous dissent from *Time* editor Matthews, whose comments penciled on Luce's memorandum give the flavor of the intraoffice dialogue:

*Luce:* [MacArthur] won the Korean war—as fully as he was allowed to. . . .

*Matthews:* Couldn't and didn't. . . .

---

[4] Omar Bradley, chairman of the Joint Chiefs of Staff, had said, among other things, that MacArthur "would involve us in the wrong war, at the wrong place, at the wrong time, with the wrong enemy."

*Luce:* MacArthur made in 1951 one of the speeches that will "go down" at least in American history. . . .

*Matthews:* But his later speeches! Didn't know when to stop.

*Luce:* The Old Soldier has not "faded away" . . . .

*Matthews:* I think he has faded—from an *effective* position to one of doubtful effectiveness.

*Luce:* . . . In December [1950], *Time,* more or less in accord with the rest of the press, was saying that MacArthur had led the U.S. into the most disastrous defeat in our history. . . . But before January was out, MacArthur's armies were safely undefeated.

*Matthews:* Not quite the same as victory!—which he promised.

Luce lost the argument; the Man of the Year for 1951 was not MacArthur but Mohammed Mossadegh, the tearful premier of Iran, chosen as the symbol of the turbulent anti-Western spirit of the Middle East. In its cover story, explaining its rejection of the man who certainly had dominated the news for most of the year, *Time* said of him:

> Many thought Douglas MacArthur the logical choice. . . . The arguments were impressive: 1) he was winning the Korean war, in so far as he was permitted to win it, when he was fired; 2) his speech before Congress breathed a sense of high public duty long absent from U.S. affairs; 3) the Japanese Treaty was a monument to his bold and generous effort to find a new U.S. relationship with Asian peoples;[5] 4) to millions of Americans, he remained the No. 1 U.S. hero, by no means faded away.
>
> However, by year's end MacArthur had abdicated a position of national leadership to become spokesman for a particular group. Some passages in his later speeches were ambiguous and inconsistent with his own basic line of thought and action. These ambiguities, plus the distortion of MacArthur by his friends of the Hearst and McCormick press, led some to conclude that MacArthur was an isolationist; others, that he was an imperialist. Both tags were absurd, yet the figure of MacArthur in U.S. life was neither as clear nor as large in December [1951] as it had been in April.

In July 1951 the Korean truce talks had begun and continued until July 1953, a long, frustrating stalemate marked by intermittent

[5] The Japanese treaty was signed September 8, 1951.

fighting and continued casualties. The last phase provided none of the swift-moving drama of the war's first stages, but *Time* and *Life* reporters and photographers continued to risk their lives in covering it. Mike Rougier made one of the most memorable picture stories to come out of Korea, "The Little Boy Who Wouldn't Smile" (*Life*, July 23, 1951), the poignant story of a war orphan that touched the hearts of thousands of *Life* readers and brought unsolicited contributions by the hundreds. In the period of the truce talks Margaret Bourke-White also returned as a war correspondent at her own insistence and spent several weeks with the National Police on forays against Communist guerrillas who were waging their own savage war. John Dille, a *Life* correspondent, went to Korea just before the talks began and, after spending two years in the war zone, returned to write a much underestimated book, the title of which was descriptive of the last phase: *Substitute for Victory.*[6] The book took sharp issue with MacArthur.

On MacArthur's return *Life* tried to persuade the general to write his memoirs; MacArthur spurned all offers. In 1954, however, Major General Courtney Whitney, MacArthur's aide and confidant, offered the editors of *Life* his story; as publisher Andrew Heiskell said, it would be "MacArthur who speaks, even though the by-line is Major General Whitney." It would be the authoritative record of MacArthur's World War II career, the occupation of Japan, the Korean war and the period after his recall.

The editors soon discovered, however, that General Whitney was no writer, and they assigned Charles J. V. Murphy, who had worked so successfully with the Duke of Windsor, to collaborate with him. But this collaboration did not work at all. Whitney asked that Murphy be replaced. "Murphy has made up his mind to rewrite me from A to Z and nothing is going to change his decision," Whitney complained to Heiskell, inadvertently revealing that there was still another collaborator at work—"Do you realize that he crossed out some of General MacArthur's *own* words?" To replace Murphy, whose lèse majesté could not be forgiven, A. B. C. Whipple,[7] *Life's* assistant articles editor, was assigned to the project; he worked eight

[6] Doubleday & Company, Inc., 1954.

[7] Addison Beecher Colvin ("Cal") Whipple, Yale '40, joined *Life* in 1941 directly after completing work on his M.A. at Harvard. He was a reporter in the Chicago and Washington bureaus before moving to the *Life* editorial staff in New York. He was a writer in National Affairs and a copy editor before becoming assistant articles editor.

months on the manuscript, successfully, as is attested by this progress report which he wrote for managing editor Thompson:

> I have retaken the Philippines. By the grace of God Almighty, and despite superior enemy forces, I have accomplished the impossible in what without a semblance of a doubt is the greatest rewrite operation in the history of the last 48 hours. I am now preparing to effectuate plans, as audacious as they are daring, to occupy Japan and fight the Communists in Korea with my Army, my Navy and my Air Force while at the same time overcoming the obstacles thrown in my path by Washington with no other resources than those of Courtney Whitney. All that remains of the Philippine Campaign is a minor 'mopping up' operation in an isolated area on the 40th floor of the Waldorf Towers.

Excerpts from the book under the title "MacArthur's Rendezvous With History" appeared in *Life* in the summer of 1955.[8]

The issue of MacArthur's behavior in Korea was revived the following year when *Life* began publication of the second volume of Harry Truman's memoirs.[9] *Life* had begun negotiations for his story as far back as 1952, when Truman was nearing the end of his term. Despite *Life*'s past criticisms of his administration, Truman had been attracted by its offer; Congress had not yet made pension provision for ex-presidents and he had no private means. For $600,000 Time Inc. bought world rights to the memoirs, with right of resale, i.e., book publication, newspaper syndication, etc. Truman applied to the Internal Revenue Service for a tax ruling, and a closing agreement was worked out whereby he was to be paid in installments over five years, easing his tax burden.[10] It was a good proposition for Truman—and for *Life;* after the resale of the rights, the magazine's out-of-pocket cost for the ten installments which appeared in the fall of 1955 and in early 1956 was little more than $100,000.

---

[8] The complete book, *MacArthur: His Rendezvous with History,* was published in January 1956 by Alfred A. Knopf.

[9] *Years of Trial and Hope* (Doubleday & Company, Inc., 1956).

[10] When Eisenhower sold his war memoirs, *Crusade in Europe* (Doubleday & Company, Inc., 1948), he asked for and got a ruling from the Internal Revenue Service that, as he was not a professional author and this was a one-time publication, the proceeds from the sale should be treated as a capital gain. Congress later decided that this had been too generous a break and outlawed such arrangements in the future.

Truman with the help of his friend William Hillman had assembled a staff and gone to work. But in February 1954, when Ed Thompson paid a visit to Kansas City where Truman had set up his office, he found that while about 100,000 words of personal conversations had been transcribed, there were only some thirty-five pages of manuscript. The raw material he found "honest" and "lively," and he quoted Truman as saying, "I don't regret a single decision I made and if I had it to do over again I wouldn't change a thing." Said Thompson, "I'm not really worried that he will be too objective." But Thompson was worried about the lack of progress and tactfully proposed that *Life* send a staff man to advise how to cut and edit the raw material. Truman agreed and *Life* writer Ernest Havemann asked for and got the assignment.

Truman proved to be a difficult collaborator, his staff even more so, and after four months in which he found he could do little in shaping the material, Havemann asked to be relieved. To replace him editor Kenneth D. McCormick of Doubleday, which had bought the book rights from Time Inc., suggested that Hawthorne Daniel become the publisher's representative in Kansas City and work with the former President's personal staff. On July 4, 1955, Truman turned over a 500,000-word manuscript to Heiskell and Thompson with a sigh of relief: "I never really appreciated before what is involved in trying to write a book."

The former President had promised Thompson and his publishers that the narrative would be "straightforward and direct [with] no embellishments to come between me and the facts." It was plain spoken all right but there was some disagreement as to his "facts." After the first few installments of Volume I [11] appeared, former Vice President Henry Wallace, former Secretary of State James F. Byrnes and former Attorney General Francis Biddle, among others, wrote letters to *Life* refuting the Truman version of history. *Life* published the letters with no objection raised by the ex-President.

In Volume II, among other subjects, Truman took up the question of China, and this time Luce raised the question of "whether we should have our own 'go' at Author Truman . . . New York *Post* is outraged that Truman had 'no doubts' whatever about the Hiroshima bomb. My angle is that the one thing Truman must never do is to 'think.' The man of no doubts, no thoughts—that is the strength,

[11] *Year of Decisions* (Doubleday & Company, Inc., 1955).

charm and outrageousness of Harry S. Truman." [12] In the same issue *Life* in an editorial strongly disputed his views, recalling that in 1948 "we called Mr. Truman's China policy one of 'disastrous neglect half-hidden by irrelevant sermonizing.' It still reads that way in his *Memoirs*." From the former President came no comment; he said what he wanted to say and paid no heed to his critics.

As for his comments on MacArthur, they were contained in the installment that *Life* ran in the issue of February 13, 1956. Mac-Arthur, said Truman, had been wrong in his evaluation of Communist intentions and capacities. "I have never been able to make myself believe that MacArthur . . . did not realize that the 'introduction of Chinese Nationalist forces into south China' would be an act of war; or that he . . . did not realize that the Chinese people would react to the bombing of their cities . . . as the people of the United States reacted to . . . Pearl Harbor; or that . . . he could have overlooked the fact that after he had bombed the cities of China there would still be vast flows of materials from Russia so that, if he wanted to be consistent, his next step would have to be the bombardment of Vladivostok and of the Trans-Siberian railroad! But because I was sure that MacArthur could not possibly have overlooked these considerations, I was left with just one simple conclusion: General MacArthur was ready to risk general war. I was not." In the end, Truman said, he had to relieve MacArthur because "if there is one basic element in our Constitution, it is civilian control of the military. Yet time and again General MacArthur had shown that he was unwilling to accept the policies of the Administration. . . . If I allowed him to defy the civil authorities in this manner, I myself would be violating my oath to uphold and defend the Constitution."

In the same issue of *Life* MacArthur was given space to reply. He rebuked Truman for failing "to rise above these petty instincts based upon spite and vindictiveness which have so frequently led him into

---

[12] In later years Luce revised his opinion of Truman; in his unfinished book he wrote: "Harry Truman is a candidate for the rank of one of the great American Presidents. He deserves that estimation. He deserves it because, in world leadership, he so often did what was so courageously right. Some might say that as the President of the United States he could have done no other, as events mounted into crises. And it is true that most of what he did (in world affairs) had the instant backing of the Congress and of the people. Nevertheless, the truth of human affairs is that someone else could have faltered, temporized, fumbled. Harry Truman didn't. Truman's American instincts led him rightly and he had the courage, with growing confidence, to follow them."

violent and vulgar public controversy." Truman's attitude toward Asia had changed since the beginning of the Korean war. "Mr. Truman's decision to meet Communist aggression in its military effort to seize Korea would have been a noble one indeed had it been implemented with unswerving courage and determination. But he proved unequal to the task. After Red China entered the conflict, he yielded to counsels of fear and abandoned pledged commitments to restore to the people of Korea a nation which was unified and free."

Let it be recorded as a postscript that seven years later, in 1963, Major General Courtney Whitney appeared again in the offices of *Life*, this time carrying with him a manuscript in the general's own hand of what MacArthur, in his eighty-fourth year, called his "reminiscences," which "are not a history . . . not an autobiography . . . not a diary . . . but [have] something of all those elements in them." *Life* serialized them in 1964.[13]

Luce predicted that the book would rank "with the greatest historical writings of any age." A few weeks after the general's death, Luce said of him:

> MacArthur was fallible like all mortals. Like all mortals, he was even capable of illusion. But there was a depth in his military strategy, there was a depth in his contemplation of war and peace, there was a depth in his understanding of nationhood. And it is this quality of depth which we should endlessly seek in our statesmen, in all our professions, and in our citizenry.

To the hypothetical question of whether MacArthur was right or wrong about Korea, Luce returned a firm answer shortly before his own death in 1967:

> Was MacArthur right? Of course he was. It was both ridiculous and immoral to allow the murderous Communist bombers to have "sanctuary" beyond the Yalu. Sanctuary! How blasphemous can you get!
>
> An unambiguous defeat should have been handed out to Communist China. If we had punished Communist China for its aggression, it is probable that the Communist regime in China would have fallen, and that we would not now be fighting in Viet Nam.

---

[13] Later that year *Reminiscences* was published by McGraw-Hill Book Company.

# "Of Paramount Importance": To Put a Republican in the White House

ELEVEN MONTHS BEFORE the Republican convention of 1952, in the summer stalemate of the Korean truce talks, *Life* published an article entitled "Taft or Eisenhower: The Choice Narrows." The article described the intense activity of dedicated party workers on behalf of Senator Robert A. Taft and warned that if the supporters of Eisenhower did not bestir themselves, the convention's choice would be decided long before it assembled. At the moment, the Ohio senator's prestige and popularity within Republican ranks were never higher, and there also was widespread resentment against the so-called Eastern kingmakers and liberals, who were blamed for the nomination of two luckless candidates: Willkie in 1940 and Dewey in '44 and '48. "Mr. Republican" or "Fighting Bob," as they called Taft, aroused a partisan spirit.

Even though Taft commanded great respect in the party, many Republicans, mindful of the party's minority status and its five successive defeats in presidential elections, doubted if so confirmed a Republican could win. This doubt, plus the enormous popularity of Eisenhower, kept the general's name alive as a possible candidate in spite of the fact that he had never admitted to being a Republican. "Almost within hours after Truman's defeat of Dewey," the general wrote in his memoirs, "the pleas were that I should seek the Republican nomination in 1952." [1] When Truman recalled him from the presidency of Columbia University to active duty as supreme commander of NATO forces in Europe, Eisenhower meditated over the idea. "I decided to remain silent, not to declare myself out as a potential political factor, and went off to Europe." [2]

At his Paris headquarters throughout the summer and autumn of 1951 Eisenhower received a stream of visitors—senators, representatives and governors—who "invariably . . . wanted to talk about the political outlook." [3] In September he received an old friend from World War II days, Senator Henry Cabot Lodge, Jr., of Massachusetts. When he was at Columbia, Eisenhower had made a number of speeches on the growing centralization of government, irresponsible spending and American responsibilities in the world. In effect, Lodge told him that if he believed what he said, he should let Lodge organize a nationwide campaign for him; the Republicans needed a candidate who would uphold the principles Eisenhower espoused, who would unify the party and attract enough independent votes to win the election and who would erase, through a successful administration, the memories of the Depression that was blamed on the GOP. The general agreed to "think the matter over."

Luce was already for the general: "I felt that it was of paramount importance to the United States that a Republican should be put in the White House—almost any Republican," he recalled later. "It had been 20 years since there had been a Republican Administration. . . . I thought . . . the American people should have the experience of living under a Republican Administration and discovering that they were not thereby reduced to selling apples on street corners." On another occasion Luce reminisced: "There were two questions about Eisenhower. First, was he a Republican or was he a political neuter with, if anything, Democratic leanings? Secondly, did he have the least desire to be President? Both questions showed amazing ignorance of so conspicuous a man. Ike was raised a Kansas 'Republican'; he had learned at his mother's knee faith in God and adherence to such basic Republican principles as sound money and balanced budgets. And however discreet he may have been, however 'non-partisan,' he would certainly not resist a good chance to be President."

Luce found the decision to choose Eisenhower over Taft a pain-

---

[1] *Mandate for Change, 1953–56* (Doubleday & Company, Inc., 1963), p. 10.
[2] Ibid., p. 14.    [3] Ibid., p. 16.

ful one: "I respected Taft—as who did not? I respected him for his profound knowledge of the domestic political agenda—things like housing, education, labor relations. I was largely in agreement with him on these matters; he was a progressive conservative and he was disgusted with many diehards who hailed him as their champion. And what about world affairs? Was he an isolationist? Certainly not. He was an internationalist, though not of the bleeding heart variety. He was not an enthusiast for world leadership. But he fully appreciated its necessity—the necessity both of opposing Communism and, beyond that, of working for a system of world order informed by law. Also, and not so incidentally, I knew him personally as a Yale man. His brother Charlie and his cousin David Ingalls, who was his campaign manager, were two of my closest friends.[4] But I decided I must go for Eisenhower. . . . I was sure that Eisenhower could win. I was not sure that Taft could."

In its first issue of January 1952 *Life* published an editorial, "The Case for Ike." Within a week of its appearance Senator Lodge assured officials in New Hampshire that Eisenhower was a Republican so that his name could be legally entered in the primary; in Paris Eisenhower confirmed it and in a letter to "Dear Harry" wrote that while the editorial had "erred grossly on the side of generosity in your estimate of my capacity," it had been "one of the·factors that helped influence me to break my policy of complete silence."

The Eisenhower statement, *Life* reported, worked like "a starter's gun on the people's imagination." On February 8, 1952, 15,000 people filled Madison Square Garden to shout themselves hoarse chanting, "We like Ike." A film of the rally was flown to Paris and made a greater impression on the general, so he said, "than had all the arguments presented by the individuals who had been plaguing me with political questions for many months."[5] Luce was in Europe at the time because Prime Minister Churchill—during a visit in the United States to see President Truman—had asked Luce to accompany him back to England on the *Queen Mary*. Two days after Eisenhower had seen the film, Luce arrived at Eisenhower's headquarters. He remembered finding the general "in good conversational form [and] it was quite clear to me that he didn't need any persuad-

---

[4] Readers of *Time Inc. 1923–1941* will recall that Ingalls declined to make a pre-publication investment in *Time*, although Mrs. Ingalls bought $5,000 worth of stock.

[5] *Mandate for Change*, p. 20.

ing . . . so we didn't spend much time on politics as such. Instead, we got on such subjects as the gold standard." Luce left the session with the general "happily under the agreeable spell of a great personality and with a sense of confidence that the Republican Party had a winner." As Eisenhower remembered the meeting, Luce spent the time telling him why he was so qualified to be president; their meeting, he said, had helped persuade him to resign as supreme commander and return home as soon as possible.

Luce, after the meeting, had lunch with the *Time-Life* Paris staff at the Berkeley restaurant, and the maître d', in honor of his distinguished guest, capped the menu by presenting a superb soufflé. The editor-in-chief took the first forkful and began: "Now I want to tell you what Ike told me." And tell them he did, with his fork still in the air as the great dish sagged and expired. Finally the maître d' swept up the remains and left silently while Luce continued with his glowing account.

The Eisenhower victory in New Hampshire and his even more impressive showing in Minnesota, where 107,000 wrote his name in on the ballot, inspired *Time* to write that "an Eisenhower boom of tremendous proportions is sweeping across the land." However, Taft, after his April victories in Nebraska and Wisconsin, *Time* reported, left no doubt that he was "still in the race and running hard."

Luce, wishing to challenge the policy of containment which he regarded as negative, turned his efforts toward a project which he hoped would bring agreement on a "positive" foreign policy for the Republicans. He persuaded John Foster Dulles to write for *Life* a précis for a foreign policy to which he hoped all Republicans could subscribe. It was a more troublesome undertaking than the editor-in-chief had anticipated. "It seems damned difficult to define it," he wrote while working with Dulles on the article. "Probably events of one sort and another will overtake us before we can a) get the Positive Policy defined and b) get it to have *meaning* in the minds of Americans and c) get it to achieve ideational power abroad." The article, "A Policy of Boldness," finally finished, advocated that "the free world . . . develop the will and organize the means to retaliate instantly against open aggression by Red armies, so that, if it occurred anywhere, we could and would strike back where it hurts, by means of our own choosing." It also argued for a political offensive aimed at the liberation of the satellite peoples from Soviet domination by peaceful means. Luce was delighted when Taft gave a speech which, according to the editor-in-chief, "was practically built around the Dulles article." He told Thompson that *Life* could boast that it had published what was "the embryo of a united Republican foreign policy."

Eisenhower, while permitting his name to go before the primaries, said he would not campaign for the nomination so long as he was in uniform; he refused to speak out on political issues or to give interviews. The Taft camp taunted his supporters with the obvious question: what did Eisenhower stand for? In an attempt to break through his candidate's silence, Luce sent the author of this history to interview Eisenhower in Paris. Only reluctantly did the general agree to talk and then with the strict proviso that whatever he said must be written "as your opinion." The reporter was armed with questions from his fellow editors; Eisenhower was gracious but proved himself a master of filibuster. He talked and talked, and to the few questions he permitted at the end of an hour the answers were purposefully ambiguous. The resulting cable home added little to what the editors already knew:

> Ike says "No matter what anyone says or does I am determined to be absolutely honest with myself. . . . A lot of people talk to me of issues. Certainly there are issues . . . but the word has become a cliché. People make the most ridiculous requests of me. One man . . . wrote me asking what I thought the rediscount rate should be. . . . Before making public policy statements I would like to have the benefit of the best advice the country has to offer. . . ." All of which is not to say that Ike does not feel deeply on a number of subjects. He feels, for instance, that there is altogether too much of a tendency to think that the emergency has passed. . . . He believes that the job of securing the peace runs far beyond military appropriations and that we must not only meet the threat of Soviet military action but that of political action as well . . . that one of the immediate prime areas of danger is Indochina. . . . He would like to see a start made on a Pacific security pact but recognizes the formidable spiritual and morale factors . . . in rallying oriental resistance to Communism. . . . He is friendly to Chiang and would put no obstacle in way of Chinese undertaking to liberate themselves from Mao's tyranny.

Luce was frankly disappointed, not in Eisenhower but in his reporter. When Eisenhower did come home in June, he continued to speak

306

in generalities, but his personality strengthened his hold on the public. Of his first appearance in his home town of Abilene, Kansas, *Time* reported: "They saw Ike, and they liked what they saw . . . in a way they could scarcely explain. . . . He made them proud of themselves and all the half-forgotten best that was in them and in the nation." Of Taft's pre-convention campaign *Time*, in its issue of June 2, reported: "In the campaign's early stages, the Taft camp generated more emotional fervor than the Eisenhower campaign. . . . Taft's long fight for the nomination has won votes—but it has also lost votes. . . . On TV panel programs, 'Fighting Bob' sometimes gives the unfortunate impression that he wants to fight everybody about everything. In private, personal fact, Taft is not over-aggressive or arrogant. He comes over that way as a result of breaking down his natural reserve. . . . Toward the independent voters . . . Taft takes a rather high and mighty line. Says Taft: 'We cannot afford to modify our principles to secure the support of a limited number of mugwumps.' "

Luce confided to a paper found in his files his discomfiture over Eisenhower's failure to get down to specific issues. He recorded that he found himself more in agreement with Taft than with Eisenhower, because frankly he did not know where Eisenhower stood on the "great issues" of foreign and domestic policy, but in the end he concluded: "I still think Ike has a better chance of winning than Taft. . . . I still think Ike will make a good president. . . . I still think the country will get a 'lift'—not because of Ike but because of the return to power of the Republican Party with all its latent resources of talent, vigor, brains and enterprise. Question is whether there is any validity to my reservations about Ike, and whether, if so, then there is any editorial duty to utter them." He resolved the question in Eisenhower's favor, yet Luce always remained conscious that the general was not the party's man in the strict sense of the word; he wrote of Eisenhower years later: "He reaped where he had not sown."

The Eisenhower-Taft struggle reached a bitter pre-convention climax in a fight over what delegates would be certified to represent Georgia, Louisiana and Texas. In years past the Republican delegates from southern states had by and large been handpicked by party hacks. They wielded voting strength in the national convention that was out of all proportion to the strength their states could contribute to the party's candidate. In 1952 the Eisenhower enthusiasts, political amateurs and some Democrats challenged the old-line party

307

retainers by selecting their own slates of delegates. At Chicago the Republican National Committee, faced with sixty-eight contested Taft delegates from the three southern states, voted to seat fifty for Taft and eighteen for Eisenhower. The Eisenhower supporters declared that they would appeal to the convention itself, and the general, on his way to Chicago, made a series of whistle-stop speeches in which he spoke darkly of "chicanery," "star-chamber methods" and "smoke-filled rooms." To thwart the Taft forces, the convention passed a "fair play" amendment.[6]

In its reporting of this episode *Time* took a lofty tone that turned what was essentially a political power play into an issue of high moral principle; *Time*'s line was echoed in a *Life* editorial. Perhaps even more influential with the delegates was a *Time* story published the week before the convention opened which analyzed the delegate situation, pointing out that the Eisenhower strength was greatest in those states which were most likely to swing the election. Although the credentials committee ruled in favor of a Taft compromise on the delegate conflicts in the southern states, the convention seated the Eisenhower delegates. Senator Lodge, Eisenhower's campaign manager, wrote to Luce after the convention: "You were a veritable tower of strength. . . . In putting the spotlight of publicity on the events in Texas [*Time*] played a tremendous part in laying the basis of public opinion for our 'fair play' amendment. The article in *Time* . . . showing that the Taft delegate strength came largely from areas which would be ineffective at election time, was a brilliant stroke. I had a pile of copies of that issue of *Time* in my office at Chicago and gave one to every person who came in. . . . One of the lasting satisfactions of this adventure has been the fact that you and I have worked so closely for such a great cause."

Lodge's letter gives a somewhat misleading picture of the part that Luce played. The *Time* stories on the delegate fight and the analysis of delegate strength were both inspired by National Affairs editor Max Ways.

Luce saw the nomination of Eisenhower (with Senator Richard Nixon as his running mate) as a triumph of the democratic process; summing up his own impressions he wrote that it was "a truly great convention. . . . The great majority of the 1,206 delegates were not just little politicians subject to the usual manipulations and the

---

[6] The amendment barred sharply contested delegations from voting in the convention until after the contests had been settled.

ordinary calculations of politics; they were for the most part men with strong political convictions . . . deeply sincere about their differences, and remarkably uninclined to trade them out." Three of Luce's associates—Moore, Larsen and Black—telegraphed him: "We salute you on great victory for American people and want to express our profound respect for your effective activities as citizen, statesman and journalist." [7]

In the middle of January 1952 President Truman called Governor Adlai Stevenson of Illinois to Blair House. The meeting set off a spate of speculation. Quite fortuitously *Time* had already scheduled a picture of Stevenson for its cover and a complimentary review of his record as governor. The story was entitled "Sir Galahad & the Pols." Now, with the Truman-Stevenson meeting as a newspeg, the article asked: "Did [Truman] want Stevenson to run as Vice President? That was one rumor. Or had Truman decided not to run at all, and to ask Stevenson to head the Democratic ticket? That was another rumor. Or was the oldest, biggest pol of them all turning to Sir Galahad for advice on how to win? That seemed hardly likely. Whatever the truth behind the rumors, this much was evident: in a cold season for the Democrats, Adlai Stevenson is politically hot, and Harry Truman feels the need of a little warmth."

The cover story was edited by Matthews, a close friend of Stevenson since their classmate days at Princeton. The Illinois governor had other old-time contacts with members of the *Time* staff. John Martin, *Time*'s first managing editor, had been a reporter for the *Daily Princetonian* when Stevenson was its managing editor, and at one point Stevenson had considered quitting the Harvard Law School to go to work for the infant *Time*. Stevenson had met many Time Incers and during the war years when he was working for Secretary of the Navy Frank Knox had been helpful to members of Time Inc.'s Washington bureau.

When Truman, at the traditional Jefferson-Jackson Day dinner in Washington, made the dramatic announcement that he would not

[7] Time Inc.'s arrangements for coverage of the Republican convention of 1952 were elaborate. In addition to working reporters and photographers there were editors, executives and a reporter from the company house organ to report on the reporters. Business managers blanched when they saw the expense accounts. In future years Time Inc. attendance at political conventions was limited to working reporters and photographers, although the ruling, it must be admitted, was sometimes more honored in the breach.

run again, *Time* and *Life* paid somewhat grudging tribute to the man whom they had so frequently criticized. Said *Time:* "[The President] said that he was proud that he had come 'from precinct worker to President.' It was a long way—and Americans can be proud of Harry Truman's journey. . . . It is no shame to Harry Truman that he could not keep pace with the awful responsibilities of his job." *Life,* in an editorial, observed: "There can be no final arbitration of Mr. Truman's place in history in this election year. But in the particular matter of voluntarily deciding to leave the White House . . . he reverted to an old, admirable and wholly democratic American tradition. . . . [He] opened the door to new leadership in his own party and ensured at least some change in Washington, no matter what happens in the election."

While Stevenson refused to declare himself a candidate until after the Democratic convention assembled, *Life* was obviously betting that Stevenson would be nominated. It carried a nine-page spread on the governor in the issue which appeared the week before the convention, describing him as "the Democrats' best foot," "quiet, dignified, patrician . . . a gentleman and scholar . . . an impressive candidate for any party in any year." *Time* in the same week raised the shadow of the Hiss case, commenting: "The Eisenhower-Nixon ticket would give Stevenson the toughest possible political opposition. Nixon is the man who broke the Hiss case, and Nixon could make effective capital out of the fact that Stevenson aided Hiss's defense with a deposition during the first Hiss trial. The Democrats would scarcely relish a campaign that fought the Hiss case again."

But in reporting Stevenson's acceptance speech *Time* acknowledged that it "struck an entirely new, deeply appealing note." Matthews, who was at the convention, was flattered when one of his associates asked if he had written it. Matthews had no hand in the speech but he may have had a small, and inadvertent, part in the naming of the vice presidential candidate. After his nomination Stevenson told Matthews that he didn't know enough about the choices to make an intelligent selection. *Time*'s editor had heard some favorable discussion of Alabama Senator John Sparkman, "who was not even a name to me," [8] and passed the name on to Stevenson. Later in the campaign, in a cover story on Sparkman,

---

[8] "Portrait, with Scratches: Adlai Stevenson," *Vogue,* May 1966.

the magazine said of the vice presidential candidate that he was "so resolute a compromiser that it takes a political micrometer to tell just where he stands."

The campaign of 1952 was an emotional one: Korea, McCarthyism, Communism, corruption were issues generating high tension. Within the company's editorial offices the campaign brought again a personal confrontation between Luce and Matthews. Although Luce had only recently told his associates that he thought Communism in the United States was no longer an issue, he was quick to sense that the Democrats were doing better with McCarthyism than the Republicans were doing with Communism. He wrote a memorandum to his editors: "I think we should seize every opportunity to remind ourselves, our brethren and sistren and our readers that Communism is still infinitely more dangerous than McCarthyism. McCarthyism is offensive. Communism is dangerous." The editor-in-chief was also mindful that Eisenhower's statements on this issue had been vague and he added: "If the result of Eisenhower's nomination is to weaken or obscure the case against the Democratic Party in regard to Communism at home and abroad—then I shall deeply regret that I gave any encouragement to the Eisenhower cause." There followed a *Time* story:

> Joe's irresponsible accusations . . . outrage many fair-minded Republicans. . . . On the other hand, a lot of Republicans are far more concerned about Communist influence in Government than about Joe's methods of getting at it. Joe is offensive. Communism is dangerous. Moreover, Joe is undeniably a Republican, and up for re-election this fall. Wisconsin is a touchy state . . . and its G.O.P. vote is needed both in the presidential election and in the Senate. The McCarthy issue is a wonderful way for the Democrats to pick up votes and, at the same time, fog up the Democrats' own record of denying or ignoring that there are or have been Communist influences in Government.

Luce's memorandum became the basis for a staff discussion, after which Matthews wrote to him sarcastically: "Should we be anti-anti-anti Communist? . . . 2) How do you 'fight' Communism-in-the-U.S. except as McCarthy 'fights' it? 3) How many voting Americans would agree today that the U.S. is now reaping the fruits of a disastrous policy? 4) If we have 'lost' China, in what sense did we

311

ever 'have' it? How can we be sure that we wouldn't have lost it no matter what?"

To Luce the questions were "good questions" but "somewhat infuriating" and he attempted to answer them:

First of all, I dismiss your Question Three by saying I do not know how many Americans agree that the U.S. is "reaping the fruits of a disastrous policy," and this question is of very secondary interest. The right question is: "Is it so?" I say it is. For me, personally, if not as an editor, I and one other man whose judgment I respect are a majority. And the truth will be made plain by wrath if not by reason. . . .

1) "Should we be anti-anti-anti Communist?" Yes. The Ship of Public Opinion, or of Man's Emotion, including Mass-Intellectual opinion, is always lurching to one side or another—and often it lurches violently into the sea of disaster. Of this there are endless examples. In my judgment as a skipper, Public Opinion, especially among the Upper Middle Class (much of our audience), has lurched to anti-McCarthyism. So we need to counter that lurch.

2) How do you "fight" Communism—in the U.S., except as McCarthy "fights it?" You do it in two ways, among others: As Nixon has fought it (or as Judge Medina, or Tom Murphy did).[9] By asking such intelligent editors ás T.S.M. to keep awake when they read such things as Playwright Miller wrote in the New York *Times*.[10]

4) About China. You are right that "lost" is an over-simplification. But I will tell you the sense in which we "had" it. We had it in the sense that never in human history did one great (and racially different) country have such a good name in another country as the U.S.A. had in China. In a sense the "good will" toward the U.S. in China was "too good" to be true—but there it was. The hard pragmatic matter is that (to anticipate the second half of your question) a government "friendly" to the U.S. might now be ruling China which would completely alter the "balance of power" situation in the world,

[9] Harold R. Medina, U.S. district judge, presided in the case of eleven Communist leaders tried and convicted under the Smith Act, 1949. Thomas F. Murphy, assistant U.S. attorney, was chief prosecutor in the Hiss trials.

[10] Arthur Miller had written that the current troubles of the Broadway stage were attributable to McCarthyism.

312

and, with this totally different "balance," there would be some sense in the Acheson-Kennan "containment" policy. . . . But the reason I believe China did not *have* to go Communist was because I was there in 1945, and I trust my judgment as a reporter. (It troubles me that you don't.) . . .

P.S. Your questions are not unloaded—unconsciously. For example, you ask how can we be "sure" that we needn't have "lost" China. How can we ever be *sure* that it wouldn't have been better to let Hitler win World War II in Europe (and Russia)—or at any rate, not to have taken any steps to prevent his victory? Can you answer that one? [11]

A week later Luce wrote again to Matthews; *Time*'s editor had told him that the magazine's coverage of the campaign should be "fair— even dashed fair!" Luce was prepared to acknowledge that "fair play is certainly a great and living ideal which we would want to adhere to" but not at the expense of another ideal, "namely, being true to one's beliefs." *Time* had been reporting corruption in government "with some proper indignation"—it could not be indifferent to it just because it was an election year; it had reported the Hiss-Chambers case "with immense self-conscious concern for 'fairness' but also . . . with some awareness of the depth of the issue" and could not now "take a 'red herring' attitude just because there's an election." The magazine could not suddenly take the view that the "loss" of China was nobody's fault and couldn't be helped.

Matthews did compose a reply on this issue:

It seems to me that the reasons for my quadrennial unhappiness have not changed one iota in . . . twelve years. I may be quite wrong, but it seems to me that *Time* has changed much more than I.

Between campaigns, I think we could say, with some semblance of truth, that *Time* on average and in intent was about 51% agin the government (a very healthy goal, I've always thought, for an admittedly biased but never admittedly partisan magazine). But during Presidential campaigns, and increasingly so (it seems to me) with each successive one, *Time* has tended to take a partisan position that was much closer to 100% than

[11] Matthews did not reply to this memo; a month later Luce wrote him again, "You wrote me a memorandum under date of August 22. . . . I took some trouble to reply. Could I inquire whether the reply served any purpose?"

313

51% agin the government. If this shift from a not-so-partisan to out-and-out partisan position has been less apparent this year, I think it is because the shift, this time, began long before the campaign opened.

*Is Time* a Republican magazine? It has never announced itself as such; perhaps it would be better if it did. Open partisanship would certainly be better than surreptitious. Though best of all, *I* think, would be to be openly non-partisan. To which you will probably retort that, as you have patiently tried to make plain to me, the issues *Time* has consistently stood for also happen to be Republican issues. What possible answer have I got to that?

Only this: that the argument in your letter, although quite clear, *was* unconvincing, because it is quite irrelevant to what makes me unhappy about *Time*. There is a kind of partisanship, I suppose, that is both noble and integritous (my simple word for that is "fair")—though the more partisan, the less fair it's bound to be. All I'm concerned about is "the integrity of our reporting." How can *Time* possibly hope to attain and maintain a real integrity if it's partisanly concerned with getting somebody elected?

When I was NA editor during the 1940 election, you once got so disgusted with *Time* that you exiled yourself from the 29th floor for the duration. Perhaps I should take a leaf from your book.

Unfortunately for Matthews' own peace of mind he did not so so. He continued to preside over the magazine feeling, as he later wrote, "an opposition of one . . . isolated." [12]

When the time approached for *Time*'s cover story on the Democratic candidate in late October, the emotions generated by the election were at a high pitch. The cover story on Stevenson was obviously a critical assignment. Assistant managing editor Otto Fuerbringer volunteered to write it. Matthews, managing editor Alexander, National Affairs editor Max Ways and the writers in Ways's section all welcomed the idea. Fuerbringer was an experienced hand. He had joined *Time* in 1942. The son of a distinguished Lutheran theologian, who was president of Concordia Seminary in

[12] *Name and Address* (Simon and Schuster, 1960), p. 270.

St. Louis, Fuerbringer had been educated in the Lutheran parochial schools and the St. Louis Cleveland High School before going on to Harvard where he became president of the *Crimson* in his senior year. He returned home to work on the St. Louis *Post-Dispatch* where he caught the eye of its assistant city editor, Roy Alexander. Three years after Alexander joined *Time*, Fuerbringer, on Alexander's recommendation, was offered a job as a National Affairs writer; he became senior editor in charge of the section in 1946 and was named assistant managing editor in 1951, a post he had been filling without title since Matthews had gone on his sabbatical.

When Matthews became editor and Alexander managing editor, it had been agreed that Matthews would personally edit most of the cover stories. On finishing his first draft of the Stevenson story, Fuerbringer handed it in to National Affairs editor Ways. After some changes Ways sent the copy on to Matthews, who, on reading it, hit the ceiling. Later Matthews described the article as "a clumsy but malign and murderously meant attack." [13] Fuerbringer's recollection was that in the article as revised by Matthews there were thirteen points with which he disagreed. When he attempted to raise these, Matthews refused to discuss them. "I told him then," said Fuerbringer, "that this was the first time and I hoped the last time that a writer on *Time* would ever be told that he could not discuss an article with his editor." The resulting article was not very good and obviously battle-scarred. While it was generally favorable to the Democratic candidate, it included the statement that Stevenson had "never so much as slapped the wrist of the Cook County Democratic organization, the most corrupt and powerful of existing big-city machines." In the earlier Stevenson cover *Time* had made a point of Stevenson's fight against the corrupt politicians.

As National Affairs editor, Max Ways was the man caught in the middle of an unpleasant situation; he rode it out but after the cover went to press, he told Luce that he did not want to be put into such a position again. Luce promised, "I'll see to it," then wrote to Matthews that he personally would take over the editing of the Eisenhower cover scheduled for the November 3 issue with Henry Grunwald as the writer. "I should be glad to have you read it as soon as it is written and send direct to me your questions and suggestions for changes. I will handle it from there on out." "At that

[13] Ibid., p. 271.

point," Matthews said later, "I decided to resign."

While *Time*'s report of the election campaign of 1952 was biased in favor of Eisenhower, no attempt was made at any point to forecast the outcome; burned by their rash assumption of a Dewey victory in 1948, the editors shied away from appraising the trends. In its last state-by-state survey before the election, *Time*, leaning over backward to be cautious, failed to anticipate the Eisenhower landslide. The article concluded: "All this adds up to a highly doubtful but not necessarily a close election. In state after state, analysts say they expect Stevenson to carry by a narrow margin—or Ike to carry by a substantial margin. Nobody is overconfident. In fact, both sides are genuinely afraid of defeat."

Luce was jubilant over the outcome. The staff working on *Time*'s election extra remembered him coming into the office after midnight and going from desk to desk, shaking hands with his editors. Said one of them, "He sure did sparkle."

Three Time Inc. staff members had been directly involved in the election, not as journalists but as speech writers. Shortly after Stevenson was nominated, Eric Hodgins, who had been on leave from *Fortune* to work on the report of the President's Materials Policy Commission, accepted a bid from Stevenson's Springfield headquarters to join the candidate's staff. He telegraphed Allen Grover that "my status as Time Inc. employee is for larger heads than mine to decide." Grover replied: "Nobody here seems to feel that your misguided activities in Springfield have any effect on your status. . . . Nobody here, including Harry, thinks that this needs to be altered because you are working for Adlai Stevenson." Hodgins remained on leave until after the election when he rejoined the editorial staff of *Fortune*.

In the Eisenhower camp were vice president Jackson and *Life*'s articles editor, Emmet John Hughes; they were recruited by Luce. "When the Republican convention was over," said Luce, "I expected that most any minute I would receive a call from someone in the Eisenhower organization to provide one or more of our most talented people to serve full time as speech writers or otherwise. No such call came. I was relieved." But just before Labor Day, Stanley High, a roving editor for *Reader's Digest* on leave to write for the Republican candidate, asked to see Luce; he was invited to dinner. "I never saw such a beat-up, tired man as my friend," Luce recalled. "He had

316

been doing nearly all the speech writing and he was exhausted in mind and body. Sherman Adams [the governor of New Hampshire who was Eisenhower's chief aide] had sent him to me. I told [High] to go home to bed and that I would get busy."

Luce asked Jackson to take leave and head the speech-writing staff for Eisenhower because "my notion was that C. D. was the world's best crash-organizer." Jackson was known to the general, having worked for him at his World War II headquarters. Luce then asked Hughes to back up Jackson. Hughes, a Princetonian, had begun his writing career by publishing his undergraduate thesis, *The Church and the Liberal Society*.[14] He had served during World War II as press attaché in the U.S. embassy in Madrid before joining *Time* as a Foreign News writer in 1946. Later he headed the Rome and Berlin bureaus before being called home to become articles editor of *Life*.

The Jackson-Hughes team made important contributions to the Eisenhower campaign. It was Hughes who suggested and wrote perhaps the most influential speech of the campaign, in which Eisenhower said, "I shall go to Korea." Eisenhower's grateful acknowledgment of Jackson's services was contained in a longhand letter to Luce: "Grabbing a minute that, through staff oversight, belongs to me, I must tell you what a god-send C. D. Jackson is to me in this turmoil of 'running' for office . . . C. D. J. has saved my sanity—such part as is salvageable—and is giving us all a lift." Later Jackson and Hughes extended their leave to serve Eisenhower in the White House, Jackson as special assistant to the President, Hughes as administrative assistant.

There was at the time some speculation that Luce might be offered the post of ambassador to the Court of St. James's; in an interview in 1967 at Gettysburg, Eisenhower said he never considered Luce for any post in his administration for the "simple reason" that he did not think Luce desired one. The one post which would have tempted Luce, Luce knew would not be offered—that of Secretary of State. After the election he got word to the President-elect urging that he consider Thomas E. Dewey for this position, a surprising gesture in view of his close association and admiration for the man who did become Secretary, John Foster Dulles. Luce, for all his

[14] Princeton University Press, 1944.

317

friendship with Dulles, had some doubts as to his ability as an administrator, and he had long been convinced that a reorganization of the State Department was overdue. He also thought that Dewey would be tougher in "worldwide debate."

Luce did call on Eisenhower personally to ask one favor: he felt that his wife deserved well of her party and merited consideration for a post in which she could serve it and her country. Eisenhower needed no such reminder; he himself had had her under consideration for a Cabinet post and did in fact offer her the job of Secretary of Labor, which she refused. Both she and her husband were delighted when she was appointed ambassador to Italy.

Their subsequent residence in Rome, where Luce spent much of his time for the next four years, was perhaps one of the happiest periods in Luce's life. The role of consort was a subordinate social position that did not bother him in the least. Rome provided a change from the day-to-day demands of publishing, a chance to refresh his editorial enthusiasm and recompense for the leave of absence he had broken off so abruptly in 1950. He had more leisure to pursue new interests—learning Italian, for one thing—and could indulge his love for travel. He established his own office at 19 Corso d'Italia, kept up a continuing dialogue with his associates in New York and commuted back and forth frequently.

Shortly after the election Luce gave a dinner for the *Time* staff at the Union Club in New York. Many of those who had supported Stevenson felt that *Time* had been unfair in its treatment of their candidate. Matthews urged the dinner as a conciliatory gesture—after other presidential election campaigns there had been similar get-togethers of the staff—and Luce readily agreed.

The entire editorial staff was invited: editors, writers, researchers. Luce introduced himself as the man often referred to as the "father of *Time*." He went on: "They keep telling me that practically none of you know me. Evidently yours is not a case of life with father. And since you have gotten along so well without him, it is perhaps as embarrassing for you as it is for me that an absentee parent should suddenly be put on view for your inspection." He thought some embarrassment might also arise from the fact that "it has never been said to you before, and that you don't know, that I'm your boss," suggesting, he felt, that "I have not been a very good boss."

It was an extraordinary speech, delivered from notes, in which

318

he ranged over history. He discussed the prophets of the modern age: the cynics, Marx and Nietzsche; the "shallow humanistic optimists," Wells and Comte. He reiterated his own faith, which he had held for a lifetime, in the bright future of America. He discussed the strengths and weaknesses of *Time*; he was at times scandalizing (*Time* stories, he said, should contain more "corn"), and often eloquent on objectivity in journalism, value judgments, responsibility to facts and the need to search constantly for truth—matters he had worried over many, many times with senior colleagues. As extraordinary as anything in the discourse was its length and its sustained thought.

But some pro-Stevenson diners listened with chagrin. They had hoped for, and thought they were entitled to, some words of contrition from Luce for his overt support of Eisenhower. None were forthcoming. Toward the end of the evening, opening himself to questions from the floor, he gave an ironic and not very graceful answer to the question of whether he would continue to serve as editor-in-chief. "I told you I was your boss," he said. "I guess that means that I can fire any of you. I don't know anybody around here who's got a contract, have they, Roy [Alexander]? So I could fire any of you. I could fire all of you until Roy got hold of me and said, 'this guy is crazy,' and put me in Matteawan or something. But I don't know anybody who can fire me. Sometimes I wish there were. Well, as long as I don't get fired, I propose to serve as *Time*'s editor-in-chief." Luce misread the temper of his audience if he thought such remarks would salve feelings so bruised by the campaign. Matthews and a few of his friends repaired to a bar where Matthews said that so far as he was concerned there was nothing to do but resign.

He did in fact offer his resignation a few days later. But Luce talked him out of it and offered him a new assignment. Matthews was to go to London and survey the possibility of publishing a *Time-in-Britain,* the project which he had begun dreaming of in 1942. If it proved to be a feasible business proposition, he would become its first editor. With spirits somewhat revived he went off to London early in the new year.

He wrote to Luce shortly after his arrival. "At this point I feel impelled . . . to say that I am very glad to be here, that I feel full of hope (well-founded or not) that something useful may come of my trip, and that I am grateful to you—*personally,* not officially— for making this visit possible." By May, Matthews had produced a prospectus for a new magazine very different from the U.S. *Time*, a format which provided for three sections: news, views and reviews. It would draw some material from the U.S. magazine but originate new material for the British audience. The project was at first favorably received by management; Luce wrote to Larsen: "Tom Matthews' editorial formula for a *Time-in-Britain* appealed to me more than I thought it would." Later Luce wrote to Edgar Baker, who had gone to London to survey the business prospects, that on the basis of Baker's report "I feel that $1,000,000 investment is not too much in view of the fundamentally 'optimistic' prospects which you discern. And in general I feel that the project is worthwhile from the intangible point of view—a great experiment." However, in August when further investigation had cast doubt on the viability of a *Time-in-Britain,* Larsen cabled Luce: "My very negative feeling [is] shared by all VP's and so definitely recommend abandonment. If you feel project should have still further consideration suggest we hold everything until your return." But to this Luce replied: "Your conclusions are accepted and therefore believe it is best to make decision immediately. Please consult Linen and inform Matthews"; Larsen did so forthwith.

"I was sorry to report our decision to Harry," he cabled. "But ten times so to report to you in view of the tremendous amount of thought and work you have given to it." Matthews, whose faith and hope in the project had been so high he had signed a three-year lease on a London apartment, cabled back: "Why did you keep me standing on tip-toe so long if you weren't going to kiss me? Ah well." With this, at last, he left Time Inc.

# Growth and Diversification
## 1952–56

T HE KOREAN WAR fed the economic recovery and ushered in a prolonged and buoyant period of prosperity, and Time Inc. prospered accordingly. As the pace of the economy quickened, advertisers increased their appropriations to capture a greater share of a surging market. From 1952 to 1956 the amount spent on advertising in American magazines increased from $615,800,000 to $794,700,000. *Time*'s gross advertising revenues rose from $32,-664,000 to $42,599,000; *Life*'s fairly soared—from $96,898,000 to $137,454,000.

In August 1951, after a study of the current balance sheet, Luce wrote to his associates: "We have $10,000,000 sitting idle . . . money . . . not needed as protection against 'hard times' because we have plenty of protection in our breakeven point plus capital and surplus against the ordinary hazards of the business cycle." At least half of it, he said, was "available for suitable investment in our business." In addition, he "guesstimated" that, with the excess profits tax enacted to pay for the Korean war, Time Inc. might have as much as $11,000,000 in 1952 from which the government would extract 80 percent—or as he put it, "$11,000,000 worth of 20-cent dollars"; this suggested that Time Inc. should make plans to spend some of

321

that money before the government got it. The two situations presented, Luce wrote, "our No. 1 problem of business-judgment-policy"—an investment problem "bigger than you think." But he warned: "One of the characteristics of our business is that there isn't much you can do just with money. Perhaps our resources of Inspiration and Perspiration are already being employed to the limit and are not capable of significant expansion. Unfortunately our Auditing Department is not able to give us an inventory or balance sheet of our I & P, but nevertheless as part of our strategic planning we have to keep in mind some estimate of our I & P capabilities."

Actually, there was no shortage of "I & P," and the stage was set for a new phase of expansion that in the next four years would see the launching of a trade journal, an edition of *Life* in Spanish, the acquisition of television properties, the formation of a pulp and paper company, the decision to build a new headquarters in New York City and the start-up of a major new magazine.

The trade journal (for the homebuilding industry) was a rib plucked from the old and much respected *Architectural Forum*. Its creator, so to speak, was Pierrie Prentice, who was serving at the time as the *Forum*'s editor and publisher. He had concluded that the *Forum* was trying to serve two different industries: heavy construction, working largely in steel and concrete, and the postwar $12-billion housing industry, working largely in wood. He had first sought to cover both fields by subordinating the magazine's title to its subtitle, which was *The Magazine of Building*. Then he proposed that the magazine be published in two separate editions which, after a brief period of transition, would become two different magazines. On a circulation of 72,000 and advertising revenues of $1,800,000 the *Forum* was losing about $30,000. Prentice estimated that, if it were split into two magazines, they might eventually gross together as much as $4,000,000 and produce earnings of $1,000,000 before taxes.

His plan was approved, and in January 1952 the magazine (or magazines) appeared in two editions: *The Magazine of Building – Architectural Forum* and *The Magazine of Building – House & Home*. Subscribers to the original *Architectural Forum* were offered a choice: to receive either edition for a year or both editions for six months. After a brief transition period, the nomenclature "The Magazine of Building" would vanish from both editions. Luce was somewhat con-

322

fused by the procedure and wrote to Larsen: "Will you please kindly tell me, once and for all, the correct names of all the magazines I am theoretically connected with in the building and/or architectural and/ or home field? Have it any way you want. Or let Prentice have it any way he wants. . . . But, please, in the interest of minimum sanity, have it some way. Or, if you prefer, give me full and absolute authority to settle the matter. And, by God, I will." Patiently, Larsen persuaded Luce to give Prentice the months needed to bring about the divorce. In a relatively short time, in September 1952, *House & Home* appeared on its own with a circulation of 100,000—40,000 above its base—enabling its publisher to boast that the new magazine had more specialized circulation than any U.S. trade journal. *Architectural Forum,* resuming its original name, had a circulation of 46,000.

Prentice continued as editor and publisher of both magazines but devoted most of his attention to *House & Home.* He traveled from coast to coast to meet the new house builders, the lumber dealers, suppliers and mortgage bankers who made up *House & Home*'s constituency. His missionary efforts on behalf of the magazine enhanced its reputation, and in time he acquired a personal influence in the industry that in some ways exceeded that of the magazine itself. *House & Home* offered a very special service to the house builder who, in the fifties, was very often a small contractor with a business that had suddenly outgrown his experience. He was dealing with many unfamiliar problems—town planning, interior design, financing and merchandising. The magazine was for him both friend and mentor; at the same time *House & Home* explained the builder's problems to the building supply dealer, the mortgage broker and the banker.

The combined first-year earnings of the two magazines had been projected at $148,000; instead the first year showed losses of $505,-000 due to the fact that advertising in both of them fell below expectations and in the case of *House & Home* circulation grew too fast. The profit and loss account also pointed up a significant factor in the failure of both magazines ever to realize a profit. As part of Time Inc., Prentice's building magazines division found itself saddled with high overhead and high-priced executive talent that were out of proportion to its earning power. By the end of 1953 the losses for the two magazines had accumulated to $1,100,000.

In defending himself Prentice argued, "I think it is only fair to ask the Management and the Directors to remember that after taxes the Company's net investment . . . is not $1,100,000 but $200,000."

He remained confident that *House & Home* would attract advertising revenues sufficient to put it into the black. As to *Architectural Forum* he was not so confident. In mid-1954 his entire editorial and business management joined him in proposing an editorial reorganization of the magazine aimed at increasing its circulation (and its costs), again in the hope of increasing advertising sales.

But by the time top management received Prentice's proposals for the *Forum,* the company was deeply involved in a far more expensive magazine project, and with the repeal of the excess profits tax there were no more "20-cent dollars." The decision was to relieve Prentice as editor and publisher of *Architectural Forum,* and he was directed to concentrate all his energies on *House & Home,* which appeared to have a greater prospect of proving profitable. This was a disappointment to him assuaged only in part by a note from Luce, who wrote to his former Yale classmate and longtime associate: "You are one of the few people in Time Inc. who are capable of being a publisher. . . . And that means a very great deal to me. . . . It is recognized that in the last five years you have done a tremendous job in the tremendous field of building. . . . It now looks as if I and others . . . may have been responsible for urging you to launch *House & Home* too big, too quickly. . . . You say that 'it is not open to argument' that *House & Home* is a success. Unfortunately, it *is* open to argument, at the Board of Directors' table, . . . because of the crude fact that it does not show a profit. . . . The chance for an economically significant magazine is with *House & Home,* which we want you to have the best possible chance to realize."

*House & Home,* an acknowledged leader in its field, continued to be published by Time Inc. for another ten years. Year after year successive budgets forecast a breakthrough that never came. One year the magazine showed a minuscule profit. It retained a solid readership, it carried a substantial volume of advertising, but expenses outran income.

*Architectural Forum* was assigned to the management of Del Paine, who continued as publisher of *Fortune* as well. The company, he was told, would be satisfied if the magazine could break even; a profit would be appreciated but was not immediately expected. "We would be glad to continue *Forum* as a really high-class, break-even—or not-lose-much—distinguished architectural magazine," Luce explained. He had valued the *Forum* from the time it was first acquired by the company in 1932. "To influence architecture is to influence life," he wrote. He later referred to American architecture as "my favorite mid-Century topic—anyway one of my favorites."

Paine promptly named Charley Bear *Forum*'s general manager; in a division of staff between the two building magazines Douglas Haskell, who was brought to the *Forum* by Prentice in 1949, became its editor; Joseph C. Hazen, Jr., remained as its managing editor.

*Architectural Forum* made many distinguished contributions in its field. In the late thirties under the inspiring leadership of editor-publisher Howard Myers it was an early advocate of modular design, of radiant and solar heating, of the low-cost house, and it instigated and led the campaign for the "packaged" mortgage.

After Myers' death, in the late forties and early fifties under Prentice the magazine was engaged in a variety of crusades—from promoting modern houses, to attacking the clichés of existing school planning, to arguing for a wider use of curtain walls, to fighting outmoded codes, to restoring contact between home builders and architects. And the *Forum* became the first architectural publication to be heavily concerned with urban redevelopment, the first editorial voice to ask insistently what was to be done about city patterns and urban renewal. Under editor Haskell the *Forum* evinced a deep and outspoken interest in the architectural and economic future of the cities.

In 1956 Paine proposed embarking on a new editorial program to try to widen *Forum*'s appeal. Both Larsen and Luce enthusiastically approved the project. Luce wrote, "After 24 years, I think we should now make a serious try to do what we aimed to do when we bought the *Architectural Forum.*" Circulation climbed steadily, but the magazine continued to lose money. Though for many years the losses of the *Forum* were easily sustained by an expanding company, the increasing expenses of publication made its continuance less and less justifiable.

(In 1964, after thirty-two years of publication by Time Inc. and coincidental with the sale of *House & Home* to McGraw-Hill, a publishing house with long experience in the field of trade magazines, the company announced the suspension of *Architectural Forum* with a special August-September issue. Management encouraged continuance of its publication under other auspices. The American Planning and Civic Association, later Urban America, Inc., a well-established nonprofit organization which was a pioneer in the city planning movement, took it over and began publication in April 1965 under the *Forum*'s last managing editor, Peter Blake, as editor; its art director,

Paul Grotz; and Lawrence W. Mester, former general manager, as publisher.)

In January 1953 the company published its first foreign-language magazine, *Life en Español*. Such a project had been considered as early as 1940 and had been vetoed until *Time-Life* International's Edgar Baker came forward early in 1952 with the argument: *"Life International* published only in English denies the very essence of *Life.* Only 10 percent of the world's population knows the English language and most of this 10 percent consists of the people who are already 'on our side.' . . . If we are to reach the great majority, the people who are 'not on our side' . . . we must translate."

Like *Life International,* the Spanish edition was to be a fortnightly with most of the material drawn from two issues of the domestic edition but with provision for certain original editorial matter. William Gray, then *Life International's* edition editor, recruited a small staff of experienced Latin American journalists headed by Alberto R. Cellario, who had been news editor of *La Prensa* in Buenos Aires before its takeover by the dictator Juan Perón. In addition to translating, the staff was expected to give the magazine a special character of its own. Baker set a goal of 150,000 circulation for the first year, 250,000 in three years.

The announcement of the new magazine was greeted with a storm of opposition from Latin American publishers. They saw in it not only a form of *Yanqui* imperialism but unfair competition as well, arguing that Time Inc. was trying to siphon advertising dollars from Latin American periodicals. There were threats in Cuba of legislation to restrict *Life en Español's* circulation and in Venezuela and Mexico vigorous protests from press groups. *Time-Life* International had its work cut out for it to overcome prejudice and demonstrate good will. One effort along this line was to sponsor, with the City of New Orleans, an international conference to explore private investment opportunities in Latin America. The conference, held in 1955, was attended by more than 1,000 Latin American, U.S. and Canadian businessmen.

Readers liked the magazine; the first issue sold out and circulation built steadily to a level of more than 400,000. *Life en Español's* staff provided more and more original material. Among the notable Latin American and Spanish writers and artists who contributed to the magazine during its sixteen years of existence were cellist Pablo Ca-

326

sals, who wrote his memoirs in an exclusive series; Chile's Nobel Prize-winning poet Gabriela Mistral; Jorge Mañach, dean of Cuban journalists; and Gregorio Corrochano, Spain's leading authority on the bull ring. When the magazine sponsored a literary contest it drew 3,000 entries.

However, only in three of its years did *Life en Español* show a profit. This was primarily due to its failure to attract sufficient advertising. Though originally aimed at a mass audience, *Life en Español* tended to appeal to the better-educated, higher-purchasing-power groups, but never in sufficient numbers in any one of Latin America's many diverse markets to provide the penetration required by high-volume advertisers.

*Life International* suffered many of the same handicaps. It achieved a worldwide circulation of over 600,000 but only twice in its existence did its income exceed $500,000.

(In 1969 the decision was made to suspend publication of *Life en Español;* in 1970, to end *Life International.* A statement issued at the time said, "Though the international editions of *Life* have served a world audience with distinction, their revenues did not warrant their continuance.")

In June 1952, with Inspiration and Perspiration still in large supply, Time Inc. bought a 50 percent interest in stations KOB and KOB-TV in Albuquerque, New Mexico. Its partner in the venture was Wayne Coy, former chairman of the Federal Communications Commission. This acquisition was a first step leading to a profitable subsidiary, Time-Life Broadcast, Inc.

Though Time Inc.'s sporadic interest in various aspects of television had been intense, the purchase of KOB-TV did not represent a decision to take an operating position in the new medium so much as a tentative move to acquire experience. By the following year the company had acquired a majority interest in the Intermountain Broadcasting and Television Corporation of Salt Lake City, operators of the KDYL stations.

In July 1954 Time Inc. acquired KLZ-AM and KLZ-TV of Denver as wholly owned and operated stations. The decision having been taken to be sole owner and operator of its stations (and in compliance with the FCC's multiple-ownership limitation of five very-high-frequently television stations), it disposed of the Albuquerque stations in 1957 when it acquired the Bitner television and radio properties

(WOOD Grand Rapids, WFBM Indianapolis, WTCN Minneapolis)
for the then record sum of $16,000,000. It then incorporated a sub-
sidiary, TLF Broadcasters, Inc., to run its stations. The subsidiary,
later reorganized as Time-Life Broadcast, Inc., was headed by Weston C. Pullen, Jr. The Salt Lake City radio and TV properties were
sold in 1959, and subsequently Time-Life Broadcast sold the Minneapolis stations and acquired KOGO-TV-FM in San Diego and KERO-
TV in Bakersfield, California.

After the closing of *The March of Time* television operation, the
company made no immediate effort to enter the programming field
on a national basis. Time-Life station managers were encouraged to
undertake innovative local programming, particularly in civic affairs.
In the years under Time-Life auspices the stations (four of which
were NBC affiliates and one CBS) won numerous awards, and their
operations contributed substantially to Time Inc.'s income.

(In October 1970 the company announced plans to sell its television and radio properties and pursue its interest in cable television,
in which it already had considerable holdings. One move was to increase its holdings to become the principal stockholder in Sterling
Communications, Inc., franchised through a subsidiary to render
cable television service to the southern half of Manhattan. In 1972
the radio stations were sold to several purchasers for $10,800,000
and the television stations to McGraw-Hill, Inc., for $57,180,000,
Time Inc. retaining only its television interest in Grand Rapids and
a small FM radio station in San Diego.)

The largest of the Time Inc. projects to be launched in the expansionist year 1952 marked a major departure from corporate policy,
which hitherto had restricted the company to the business of journalism. In December 1952 the East Texas Pulp and Paper Company
was incorporated, an enterprise owned jointly by Time Inc. and the
Houston Oil Company.

As far back as 1937, in his "mad search for paper" to supply the
seemingly insatiable demands of the infant *Life,* Charles Stillman had
visited a new bleached sulphate pulp mill which the Champion Paper
and Fibre Company had built at Houston on the ship channel. "I
saw what a magnificent place Texas was to make paper, which had
been completely neglected by the rest of the industry," said Stillman.
"Champion had sort of walked into a paradise wilderness that nobody else seemed to realize existed. One thing that Champion had and

never used was first refusal on all the pulpwood off the lands of the Southwestern Settlement and Development Corporation . . . and that turned out to be owned by the Houston Oil Company."

On Stillman's recommendation Time Inc. invested in Champion to help finance the construction and installation of a paper machine alongside the bleached-pulp mill to supply *Life* paper. With an eye on Houston Oil's enormous timber holdings—660,000 acres of pine-woods—Stillman also recommended investing in the oil company, and in 1941 he began to buy its stock for the company's portfolio.

After the war, with *Life*'s paper requirements once more outrunning supplies, Stillman's thoughts turned again to Texas. "We gave serious consideration with Champion to the building of a new pulp and paper mill," he said. "Champion had located and purchased a site in just the right place to use the Houston Oil Company's timberlands." This was at Evadale, twenty miles from Beaumont. When Champion decided against the project, Time Inc. acquired the site. Meanwhile, the Houston Oil Company had become very interested in part ownership of any mill that would use its timber, and in 1952 a fifty-fifty partnership with Time Inc. was agreed upon. But neither Houston Oil nor Time Inc. had within their organizations anyone of sufficient experience to direct such a project.

Stillman had a hunch. A man whom he much admired, Richard A. McDonald, was retiring as executive vice president of the Crown Zellerbach Corporation. "If there was ever a man not ready for retirement, it was R. A. McDonald," said Stillman. He and president Harold Decker of Houston Oil offered McDonald the post of chief executive officer of the new enterprise; he refused the post because of his age but he did agree to organize the new company. The East Texas Pulp and Paper Company was thereupon incorporated. It signed a sixty-year stumpage agreement for wood supply from the pinewoods around Evadale owned by the Southwestern Settlement and Development Corporation. While construction on the mill went forward under McDonald, the new company launched a talent hunt for an executive officer and found him in the person of R. M. ("Mike") Buckley, forty-four, a former executive of the Soundview Pulp Company of Everett, Washington, who was made executive vice president and general manager.

Stillman's original purpose was to provide a paper supply for the Time Inc. magazines, but construction of a pulp mill was the first and essential step. Actually, the mill proved to be more profitably

329

employed in the manufacture of pulp and paperboard than magazine stock, and, except for a small quantity of cover stock for *Fortune,* it has never made paper for any of the Time Inc. magazines. The construction of the mill was completed on schedule and it began operating in December 1954.

Meanwhile, through Stillman's purchases of Houston Oil stock in the open market, Time Inc. had become the biggest single shareholder in that company, owning 130,440 shares of the stock outstanding, or 9.9 percent. In May 1953 Stillman reported to the directors that the company was about to cross the line "from a stock position to participation in property" and requested the approval of the Time Inc. board for further purchases, which he recommended. Stillman then became a member of the Houston Oil Company board of directors, and Time Inc.'s holdings climbed to 10.6 percent.

In 1955, on the strength of local rumors, a flurry of speculative buying began pushing up the price of Houston Oil Company shares and brought to its headquarters this interesting query from one would-be plunger: "Have seen [the stock] jumping all over the board out here from 102 to 118 in two or three weeks, on a very modest dividend return but wide-open hotair as to long-term gain potential. . . . Out of plain curiosity I decided to take a ticket on ten shares for the buggy ride, and now that I have my ticket will you kindly advise me where I am going. . . . P.S. Dame Rumor has it that through your timber holdings up there in Piney Woods . . . Henry Luce has his big mouth in the affair, so will my ten tickets get me into the publishing business? . . . If all the ballyhoo I have been hearing . . . is right, I would not have to worry about a 'diversified portfolio' as just 100 tickets with you boys [would] automatically have me spread all over the economic spectrum."

The directors of Houston Oil were in fact considering liquidation of the company, having received offers so advantageous that they could not be refused in the interest of the stockholders. The liquidation would be without gain or loss to the company and the amounts distributed to shareholders taxable only at the capital gains rate. In January 1956 the Houston Oil directors voted to take such action, the Atlantic Refining Company acquiring its oil and gas properties, and Time Inc. acquiring Houston Oil's 50 percent interest in the East Texas Pulp and Paper Company, including the Southwestern Settlement and Development Corporation. Time Inc. financed its acquisition of East Texas from its share of the liquidation ($18,615,000,

330

after paying the capital gains tax; the original investment was $3,508,-000) plus a bank loan of $19,000,000 by East Texas. Thus in one final stroke Stillman acquired for Time Inc. a wholly owned and profitable business which he had been instrumental in creating, plus enormously valuable timberlands.

(Eastex Incorporated—the company's longtime nickname which was made official in 1965—became Time Inc.'s most profitable non-publishing source of income and an important counterweight to the more volatile publishing business. In 1971, a recession year for magazines, Eastex accounted for 15 percent of Time Inc. revenues, 40 percent of income before taxes and extraordinary items.)

Growing business meant a growing number of employees and made urgent again the need to find new company headquarters; the space in the Time & Life Building in Rockefeller Center could not be expanded because of existing leases.

After the outbreak of the Korean war Time Inc., like a number of New York-based companies, had done some "catastrophe planning" against the possibility of nuclear attack. This had led to the purchase for $159,000 in 1951 of a possible headquarters site of fifty-five acres in suburban Westchester County, an hour from midtown Manhattan. Eero Saarinen, the architect, was asked to survey the site to see if it were suitable for a campus-like complex.

When the staff got wind of the plan they rebelled. Billings reported the universal feeling that "New York City does provide some mystical spark to the magazines. . . . The country is no place . . . to do a good high-pressure news job. You vegetate. You end up smoking a pipe." Howard Black announced that, while others might move, his ad salesmen would stay in New York, close to Madison Avenue. Saarinen's report quashed the project; the site was not well chosen for its purpose, he said. (Later some of the land was condemned for highway construction, the condemnation award almost equalling the original investment; the remainder was sold in 1968 for $1,000,000.)

Early in 1954 Luce started another search when he posed the question: "Shall we set out to create the *ideal* headquarters for Time Inc.?" His ideal envisaged horizontal structures rather than a vertical building and included such special facilities as an art gallery, a reading lounge and perhaps even a chapel. If located in the city, he proposed that the building, or buildings, be spread over several blocks, and if in the country they might include a swimming pool, gardens

and tennis courts. Above all, Luce insisted, "The *ideal* headquarters
. . . cannot be in any skyscraper slab. . . . All we may require is
an efficient (air-conditioned) anthill.[1] But we can easily agree, I
hope, that an anthill is *not* the *ideal*." Luce himself had no prejudice
against moving out of New York and suggested that the search for
new quarters should include Philadelphia and Baltimore.

One attractive site on which Time Inc. acquired a short-term option was a parcel of land in New York between First Avenue and the
East River adjacent to the United Nations on which now stand the
twin luxury apartment towers of the United Nations Plaza. Gordon
Bunshaft of Skidmore, Owings & Merrill developed a plan for a
headquarters complex that would have included a hotel. It was finally
abandoned as too costly. Meanwhile another 370-acre site was located between Philadelphia and Wilmington, near the appropriately
named town of Media, Pennsylvania. Saarinen was called in again
and he sketched a plan for a collegiate-like campus that included a
golf course. An effort was made to keep this project secret under the
code name "Phillywil," but it soon leaked and again aroused opposition from the staff. John Billings, reflecting the feelings of many of
them, commented: "It was such a fool idea that I could not believe
it would cause so much bloody commotion. It never concerned me
personally because I had no intention of trekking off into the wilderness with John the Baptist Luce and a few apostles and subsisting
on locusts."

All roads then led back to mid-Manhattan. Having abandoned the
search for the ideal site, management sought a solution that would
simply provide the most space for its money. The New York Coliseum, then under construction by the Triborough Bridge and Tun-
nel Authority, offered such space in its tower office building. But the
building was the center of controversy because the authority chairman, old Yaleman Robert Moses, was using funds for its construction that had been obtained from the federal government for slum
clearance. *Architectural Forum* had attacked this as a gross misuse
of federal subsidies, and the propriety of Time Inc. renting office
space in a project which one of its own magazines had denounced
was open to question. As the pros and cons were being discussed at
a luncheon of Time Inc. executives, a secretary interrupted the
meeting with the news that the main exhibition floor of the Coliseum

---

[1] The Time & Life "anthill" at 9 Rockefeller Plaza was not air-conditioned.

had collapsed. This killed any further consideration of the Coliseum. Meanwhile Rockefeller Center, Inc., anxious to retain Time Inc. as a tenant, had made several proposals, including space in a building which it proposed to construct on a site between Fiftieth and Fifty-first Streets on the Avenue of the Americas. In a counter offer, Time Inc. proposed that it become a partner in the new building. "Our thesis, stated simply, was to end up owning any real estate that we had paid for in rent over the lease term," Stillman explained to the directors. On December 13, 1956, Rockefeller Center, Inc., and Time Inc. announced plans for the construction of a new Time & Life Building to be erected by a newly organized corporation, Rock-Time, Inc., which was 55 percent owned by Rockefeller Center and 45 percent by Time Inc.

Luce abandoned the quest for "ideal" quarters reluctantly. "We *are* buying: working quarters which are agreeable and efficient and in the location preferred by most of our employees," he wrote to Stillman when the deal was completed. "The intangible value which we are *not* buying is the value of having a building of which we can be especially proud and which the public would take note of and identify with Time Inc. . . . So, let's set out to buy 'standard first-class 1960 style' but let's be very tough about not leaking a lot of money here and there on frills that don't add up to anything really 'special'. . . . We might ration out a few hundreds of thousands for a special spot or two. Larsen and I can judge of this when the time comes."

The negotiations leading up to the formation of Rock-Time, Inc. had been handled by Charles Stillman and Weston Pullen. The massive job of planning and coordinating the construction and design details and overseeing the move into the new building fell upon Allen Grover as chief management representative and Henry Luce III as principal operating executive. Hank Luce, like his father and grandfather before him, had graduated from Yale; after his service in the navy during World War II he had been an assistant to Joseph P. Kennedy, member of the Commission on Organization of the Executive Branch of the Government. Following his work as a reporter on the Cleveland *Press,* he joined the Washington bureau of Time Inc. in 1951 as a reporter, later transferring to New York where he wrote for the National Affairs and Foreign News sections of *Time.* He was working a short stint in the circulation department when Larsen assigned him to the new building project.

Notwithstanding his original prejudice against a Manhattan sky-scraper, Luce senior took a great deal of pride in the new building. On laying its cornerstone in June 1959 he said, "It is a workshop, one of the handsomest, we think, that ever was. It rises here in the center of New York City because for much of the important work of the world, this is the best location. . . . This building speaks more eloquently of the future than of the past. It speaks most boldly and most confidently of the immense amount of work *to be done* in years to come. . . . The Time & Life Building will be written about for a moment . . . and then it will stand for decades to be seen. It may no longer be heard about, but it will certainly be heard from."

In 1952 when the American Institute of Management paid Time Inc. the compliment of including the company in its list of the ten best managed corporations, Eric Hodgins recalled that the news "caused even those among management to utter harsh, humorless laughter." [2] Hodgins' memory in this case attests merely to the fact that managers, like prophets, are seldom held in high esteem within their own estab-lishments. The management did not conform to Harvard Business School norms, but then, Time Inc. was no ordinary business.

"The one thing which is unusual about Time Inc. is that we have to combine the practice of journalism with all—*all* the aspects of any other business organization," said Luce in delivering the McKinsey Foundation Lectures on management at the Columbia University Graduate School of Business. "Time Inc. has everything General Motors has—*plus* our main job, the practice of journalism. . . . Furthermore—and this is our proudest boast—Journalism has the top priority. . . . So, then, the most interesting thing about our com-pany is how we set up a management which is required to produce a profit and yet has no control over our essential product, the editorial content of our magazines."

In the fifties the company was, in one sense, managed as a benevo-lent and indulgent monarchy because of the presence of the surviv-ing founder. No important policy decision was made without Luce's concurrence. Sometimes it was essentially his decision; sometimes it was a ratification of somebody else's; occasionally it was an indul-gence of another's against Luce's own hunch or judgment. In an-

[2] The others: American Telephone & Telegraph, National City Bank of New York, Statler Hotels, Du Pont, B. F. Goodrich, Grand Union, Minnesota Min-ing & Manufacturing, National Cash Register, Procter & Gamble.

334

other sense the company was a collegium of old associates long accustomed to working together without a sense of hierarchy, a collegium whose members deferred to Luce but never felt themselves subservient to him. A committee of the vice presidents and publishers met periodically with president Larsen to exchange information and make operating decisions.

The system worked with a sense of intimacy and continuity, a sense that extended as well to the board of directors. Until the death of Robert A. Chambers in 1951, three of the six outside directors were original supporters of Hadden's and Luce's improbable enterprise—Chambers, vice chairman William V. Griffin and Samuel W. Meek; a fourth, Artemus L. Gates, who returned as a director after his wartime service as assistant secretary of the navy, had been on the board since 1931. In 1951 Paul G. Hoffman, an early *Fortune* enthusiast who had first been elected to the board when he was president of the Studebaker Corporation in 1948, was re-elected as a director after two-and-a-half years' service as administrator of the Marshall Plan. He was a longtime close friend and associate of Time Inc.'s chairman, Maurice T. Moore.

As an executive, Luce was always a well-ordered person who scheduled his time with care. As the company expanded he operated with the help of a small staff which was never permitted to isolate him from his principal associates. His chief assistant, Grover, handled his personal business and acted as his informant on corporate matters; Billings, as deputy, dealt with the editors in his absence. Luce's assistant Kip Finch handled many details in relation to Luce's outside associations, as did his executive secretary, Corinne Thrasher.[3] Dur-

---

[3] Miss Thrasher came to Time Inc. as Mr. Luce's secretary in 1932 after considerable business experience. It was a most satisfactory arrangement because Luce couldn't dictate and she couldn't take shorthand. At their first meeting Luce told her, "If you can read my handwriting, we'll get along fine." She could, and was frequently interrupted for translation services by uncomprehending recipients of the Luce scrawl. A prodigious worker who spoke her mind freely, she struck awe in the heart of many a Time Incer. Once when she asked a member of the Washington staff to make an appointment for Mr. Luce to see President Roosevelt, she was told that Luce should be at the White House at eleven A.M. but that is wasn't possible to say just when the President would be free. To which Miss Thrasher replied: "Who do they think they are, having Mr. Luce wait around the White House? You just call and tell them we must have a definite time." Told that this was impossible, Miss Thrasher called the White House herself—and got a definite appointment.

ing the Rome interval Luce kept in touch with the main office by cable, air mail and air express.

Under Larsen as president and chief executive officer responsibility was subdivided officially between the executive vice presidents —Black for publishing, Stillman for manufacturing and finance. Reporting through Black on the corporate level was vice president Bernard Barnes, handling personnel, staff relations, publicity and public relations. Under Stillman was Brumbaugh, deep in paper contracts, postal rates, technological research, production and distribution. With the emergence of the new group of strong publishers—Linen on *Time,* Heiskell on *Life* and Jackson, followed by Paine, on *Fortune*— the magazines as company divisions developed more and more autonomy. A notable example of the new trend was the splitting up in 1951 of the company's circulation department, which had hitherto been headed by circulation director Francis DeWitt Pratt under the supervision of Larsen personally, into individual units for each magazine with circulation managers directly responsible to their publishers.

However, after Stillman had returned from his leave of absence with the Marshall mission in China in 1948, he was less directly involved than formerly in the publishing side of the business. His leave, he said, "cut me off from much of what I had been involved with up to that time and in effect I had to start all over again to decide what I was going to do next. . . . I felt that I had something going with the Houston Oil Company which I, better than anyone, could cause to bear fruit, in an important way, for Time Inc. I also felt that Time Inc. had to find new activities and products [because] we had already created enough magazines for any one company based largely on national advertising revenues."

While the top executives understood their roles and missions, the organization seemed often to bewilder outsiders. A young management consultant who had been helpful in reorganizing the subscription fulfillment departments in Chicago was confused on his first meeting with the ranking executives in New York. He asked comptroller Arnold Carlson, "Who's your boss?" Carlson hesitated and then said, "Stillman." Black interrupted with the comment, "The hell he is—I am." Then Heiskell chimed in, "I am, for my operation." In fact, Carlson worked most closely with Brumbaugh. In his subsequent report the consultant wrote, "Organizational and departmental definitions are indistinct and lack objective standards."

This was true; the company operated with few stated regulations.

336

"Unlike most places, we haven't enough rules," said a report prepared for Black in 1953. "There should be more of a feeling of the necessity for economy than there is. This can emanate only from topside or, a worse alternative, eventually from stockholders. One approach would be to talk not just of profit but of the percent of profit." Such a recommendation challenged a company-wide laxness in respect to budgetary control. Heiskell recalled that at one period any publisher or managing editor could commit up to $500,000 without higher authority; below that level a senior executive could commit $100,000, and three or four rungs down expenditures of $500 to $1,000 seemed to require no consultation whatever. The company's salesmen and correspondents tended to be free spenders, and sporadic "economy drives" were not particularly effective. Luce, strongly aligned with the would-be economizers, once wrote: "We do indeed need to 'cajole, get mad, follow up.' I would add that the 'we' needs to be represented by some one identifiable person—the corporate 's.o.b.'. . . . I can't remember when we ever had him."

But economy drives are seldom effective in prosperous times, and the years under discussion, 1952–56, were extremely profitable for both *Time* and *Life*. Though *Time* in 1954 suffered a mild setback along with the economy, its revenues and circulation steadily increased under publisher Linen. A major *Life* problem during the same period was how to handle the volume of advertising, as reflected in this note from Luce in March 1953 just before he left for Rome: "The most serious problem is that there are too many ads. . . . If there were fewer ads the editorial show would be more impressive. So what? So I don't know; so I don't worry. I *like Life!*" In August 1954 when Luce, Larsen, Black, Jackson and Heiskell met to consider the present and future of *Life,* Luce summed up the feeling of the meeting in these euphoric terms: *"Life* is a tremendous and tremendously successful magazine. . . . Conversations about *Life,* and even set bull sessions, are apt to turn out to be a little frustrating. Sure, everyone comes up with a good point or two, but there is apt to be the feeling that nobody's point is going to make any noticeable difference in *Life*'s immense life."

Nevertheless, there was management agreement that while the profits were high, the ratio of income to revenues could be substantially improved. At the beginning of 1955 Brumbaugh, convinced that the proper approach was not through economy drives but in long-range planning, was given authority by Larsen to set up the company's first profit improvement program, which set profit goals and standards for each of the company's divisions. The program looked beyond the 1955 budget to establishing a real breakthrough in 1956. This plan assigned even more responsibility to the individual publishers for their goals and the attainment of them and required divisional heads to report any deviation from the standards they themselves set. Brumbaugh said of this program: "I wanted them [the publishers] to stick their necks out. While each division could define its goal, the question was always how to do it." The program was coupled with special incentive bonuses based on profits and a stock option plan for senior executives.

The profit improvement plan made some improvement in the year-end 1955 results. Net income was $9,196,000 (vs. $8,057,000 for '54) with the operating profit margin rising to 7.6 percent from 6.3 percent in 1954.[4] The big payoff came in 1956: a net income of $13,850,000 (excluding capital gains from the liquidation of investment in the Houston Oil Company) and an increase in the profit margin to 10.9 percent, the best record in six years. When the annual report for 1956 was issued, *Advertising Age* headlined its account of the company's achievement: "Glittering Report Reveals Time Inc. as Most Diversified U.S. Publishing House."

"Diversification" included a major new magazine enterprise that was launched in those expansionist years: *Sports Illustrated,* a magazine that had taken thirteen months in planning and $3,278,000 of expenditures before the first issue was published and was to lose, over its first ten years, many millions of dollars.

---

[4] When *Fortune's* first "Directory of the 500 Largest U.S. Industrial Corporations" appeared as a supplement to the July 1955 issue, Time Inc. was #176. Suggested by assistant managing editor Edgar P. Smith, the "500" became a major annual feature of the magazine.

# 7,792 Magazines Plus
# Sports Illustrated

A MONG THE PROJECTS that Briton Hadden listed in his notebook
for consideration, once *Time* became successful, was a "spt.
mag." Hadden dreamt of one day owning a major league
baseball club and all his life was an avid reader of the sports pages.
His co-founder, Luce, had little interest in sports although he at one
time played tennis and, in his later years, an indifferent game of golf.
After Hadden's death no more was heard of a "spt. mag."

*Time*'s own coverage of sports figures had long been surrounded
by the legend that a jinx hung over those who appeared as cover
subjects. Among the victims were Elizabeth Arden Graham (May 6,
1946) who lost her Illinois racing stable in a fire on the day *Time*'s
cover hit the newsstands; Leo Durocher (April 14, 1947) who was
suspended as manager of the Dodgers the day before his cover
reached Brooklyn; Ben Hogan (January 10, 1949) who not only lost
a big tournament but also suffered a near-fatal auto accident within
weeks after a cover story about him appeared. There were a number
of other such happenstances—hardly an auspicious omen for Time
Inc.'s next venture in publishing.

In the early fifties Larsen set up a development department to
review the many suggestions for expansion—"with a prejudice against
projects in the magazine field." One suggestion had been put forward

by a young circulation executive, Robert Cowin. Returning from a readership survey in Columbus, Ohio, he reported that he had been "amazed at the number of women who said their husbands constantly have their heads buried in some kind of sports literature. I'm sure that Time Inc. could put out a sports publication so far above and ahead of anything being published today that the demand would be overwhelming." He predicted that it would be welcome "on every cocktail table of the millions of wide-awake people who crowd the public and private golf courses at six A.M., the high school tennis courts as well as Churchill Downs. With the trend toward a shorter work week and more holidays, the number of people and the time they spend engaged in their favorite sporting activity is growing at an enormous rate. Why not cater to this obvious interest?" Cowin's idea had been shot down by the officially stated "prejudice against projects in the magazine field."

Luce, however, did not share the prejudice. "Anybody can make money with money," he said at a staff luncheon. "But we are supposed to be magazine publishers. Wouldn't it be a good test if we found out if we could bring out another successful magazine?" In May 1953, writing Billings from his new office in Rome, he suggested that Daniel Longwell, then chairman of *Life*'s board of editors, "come up with a definite proposal for a new magazine—if and only if—this seems good to you and Larsen."

Meanwhile, he had received a page-and-a-half letter from Howard Black, a man known for his extreme reluctance to commit words to paper, which he read with great interest. Albert Cole, then general business manager of The Reader's Digest Association, Inc., had offered (Black reported) to sell Time Inc. the magazines *Popular Science* and *Outdoor Life,* in which Cole and a group of associates privately owned a controlling interest. Also: "The lawyer for Ogden Reid's sister, Lady Ward, has contacted Di Gates [Artemus L. Gates, a director of Time Inc.]—we can buy the New York *Herald Tribune.*" [1] Then Black offered Luce some ideas of his own. One was to put out a six-page letter giving "your viewpoint (or Time Inc.'s) on what is going on in international politics." Another was a low-priced

---

[1] In his letter Black was oversimplifying a complex family situation in respect to the *Herald Tribune*. From time to time Luce did entertain various proposals to get into the newspaper field, but no sale of the New York *Herald Tribune* could have been completed without the consent of Helen Rogers Reid, then chairman of the board.

magazine for the working man explaining in simple terms the technology of new manufacturing processes. And finally Black raised the possibility of "a Sports Weekly—everything in sports—hunting, fishing, boating—a picture magazine—10¢ a copy. I'm not sure of the price for I feel that we should not have more than 1,500,000 circulation." Luce cabled immediately: "Your letter makes wonderful reading. Don't you wish we were ten years younger?" In thinking over these various projects, Luce said, "The compass needle always came back to sport."

Early in June 1953 Luce called a meeting of Larsen, Black, Stillman and other executives. He suggested that they skip a formal agenda and talk about a sports magazine. "Within 60 seconds everyone present agreed," Luce said later. "During the meeting, which lasted two hours, there was no discussion about *whether* there should be a Time Inc. sport magazine, but *how* it should be." Stillman had been asked to make a marketing survey in preparation for the meeting; it indicated that there was not enough advertising in the sports field to make the magazine viable. His findings were ignored. He recalled, "No one had a chance to disagree. I wasn't asked anything, didn't say anything. They were letting me do my thing, and I wasn't going to step up and tell them they couldn't do their thing. . . . They were just hell bent for election to do [it] and now I'm glad they did." As Luce put it, "I can't imagine a magazine being created under conditions of such spontaneous combustion."

On July 10, 1953, the company house organ, *f.y.i.,* announced that a new experimental department had been established. It was organized by *Life* staff writer Ernest Havemann and Richard Neale, a member of the promotion department.[2] Havemann was picked because, in addition to his talents as a writer, he was a sports fan whose enthusiasm extended to the dubious investment of his own money in racing thoroughbreds. His journalistic career began on the sports desk of the St. Louis *Star-Times.* He next joined the *Post-Dispatch* where he met Roy Alexander who later recruited him for *Time* "because

[2] Other members of the early experimental department were reporters Clay Felker and Donald Schanche of *Life* and Francis ("Hank") Brennan, a former art director of *Fortune* and *Life,* then art advisor to the editor-in-chief. Jim Murray of the Los Angeles bureau was recruited by Havemann. Douglas Kennedy, *Time*'s Sport editor, was so enthusiastic about the proposed magazine that he persuaded Havemann to take him on. From the business side came Eleanor Montville, Neale's assistant, and Charles L. Gleason, Jr., on loan from the comptroller's department.

341

Havemann was the only man who could beat me on rewrite." Havemann had shifted from being a Washington reporter to become a National Affairs writer on *Time,* then moved over to *Life.*

Neale shared Havemann's intense interest in sports; at Yale he had been sports columnist on the *Daily News* and after joining *Life* he had helped organize, on a suggestion from Howard Black, one of that magazine's most successful promotions: *Life* invited its readers to "compete" against the reigning pro, Ben Hogan, on a "National Golf Day." On May 31, 1952, more than 87,000 contestants paid a one-dollar entry fee—the proceeds of which were divided between the United Service Organizations and the Professional Golfers Association—to play an eighteen-hole round on their own courses against Hogan's round on the course of the Dallas Northwood Club; 14,667 contestants, aided by handicaps, turned in a better score than Hogan's medal round of seventy-one and won bronze medallions inscribed "I beat Ben Hogan." After this demonstration of the interest in golf and of *Life*'s influence with the affluent middle class, Neale needed no persuasion to cast his future with a sports magazine.

The rationale rested on an economic assumption: that the fast-growing leisure-time activities of the American people would create the kind of readership that would make the magazine a unique advertising medium. The theory was bolstered by "The Changing American Market" series which *Fortune* began publishing in 1953; the titles of these articles indicated their thrust: "The Rich Middle-Income Class," "The Lush New Suburban Market," "The Sunny Outlook for Clothes," "$30 Billion for Fun."

"When Roy Larsen first talked to me and said we figured on a circulation of perhaps a million and a half," Havemann recalled, "I said I thought the figure was—I remember the words—'ridiculously conservative.' "

An effort was made not to disclose the nature of the project but the whole of Time Inc. soon knew that it was a sports magazine and promptly named it "Muscles."

Three weeks after accepting his assignment, Havemann startled management by resigning in a saturnine letter to Billings. "I feel that we should abandon the project, that any time or money we spend on it will be wasted and that if we should ever actually publish, it would be a costly failure. You may disagree with me—indeed the general enthusiasm for the magazine has been so great that in sending you

342

this memo I feel something like a leper. . . . I was all enthusiastic and having a wonderful time—and then this bad case of logic set in. . . . I'm convinced the idea's all wrong and nothing will ever persuade me otherwise—not even if the magazine comes out and has 10 million circulation, which I certainly hope is what happens if you go ahead with it."

Havemann's "bad case of logic" was set out in an accompanying eleven-page memorandum in which he proved to his own satisfaction —"brilliantly," Luce said later—that sports did not have a common denominator of interest. Attempts to bring out general sports magazines had failed; the only successful periodicals were those with special appeal: *Outdoor Life, Field & Stream, Yachting,* and *Sporting News* (baseball); subscribers to these magazines would have little interest in a new weekly. Havemann also came to the conclusion that there was simply not enough worthwhile sports news to fill a weekly of forty editorial pages the year around and that the current sportswriters were pretty pedestrian and incapable of rising to Time Inc.'s standards.

Havemann was not alone in his misgivings. Billings, although he kept his doubts to himself, had little enthusiasm for the project. A year later, in July 1954, he confessed in a letter to Jackson, "When Harry came up with this experiment my heart sank with personal dismay, because here was a publishing enterprise for which I had no heart, no knowledge, no enthusiasm." Billings' negative reaction to an article on golf, submitted as an example of what the reader might expect to find in the new magazine, had been one factor in Havemann's resignation.

Larsen, Billings and Black reviewed the project, and Billings, despite his skepticism, reported to Luce that what was needed was an experienced editor to translate the ideas into "something tangible in dummy form on which a reasonable judgment could be made. And to hell with theory for the time being!" Larsen found some evidence to support Havemann's opinion: "the word 'sport' is poison to the advertising agencies." But he believed that Havemann and his associates might have been thrown off by the stated objective of 1,500,000 in circulation. Instead of going after a mass circulation and including a whole gamut of leisure-time activities, the magazine might better "appeal to the *Sportsman* (which might be its name)" and cater to "a class market now being neglected by all save *The New Yorker.*"

Havemann was asked to take another crack at the job. He declined, preferring to return to *Life*'s editorial staff, and Billings drafted Sidney L. James, assistant managing editor of *Life*. James was an experienced editor and a man of vast enthusiasm for new ideas. Like Havemann a product of St. Louis journalism (he started as a cub on the St. Louis *Times* later shifting to the *Post-Dispatch*), he first worked for *Time* as a stringer there. In 1936 he was hired as a writer in New York, later was sent to Chicago, then Los Angeles, as bureau chief. His work was outstanding and he was recalled to New York, first as National Affairs editor for *Life,* then as assistant managing editor. He had occasionally edited *Life* in the absence of its managing editor, a valuable experience for what was to come.

Billings reported to Luce that in tackling his new assignment James "refused to get bogged down in the swamp of semantics and theory. He liked the idea of a 100% sports weekly, either mass or class, and he set out to provide as much material for it in stories written and pictures laid out and dummy pages headlined as possible before your return in September."

When Luce returned from Rome, James and his acting art director, Hank Brennan, had ready a series of rough paste-up layouts. They watched anxiously as Luce studied their work. Luce's reaction was that of a man whose eyes had been opened to a whole new world. The layouts projected a magazine far more exciting than he himself had anticipated. The editor-in-chief invented on the spot one of the projected magazine's most effective promotion slogans: "The wonderful world of sport!"

The project now commanded first-priority attention. Luce had become a somewhat remote figure to many junior writers, researchers, salesmen and promotion men. But he became a very familiar figure to the members of the experimental department. Gerald Holland, who joined James's staff in October 1953, recalled: "Sometimes it seemed that we saw more of Luce than we did of our wives. Some of us were assigned to escort him to sporting events and explain the action and identify the players. For others of us there began the era of the lunch." [3] Every aspect of the new magazine was analyzed. Once, Luce fired one of his unexpected questions: what's the purpose of the magazine, what's its justification? He looked around the table, to be met by an embarrassed silence. Dick Neale finally tried an answer: Ortega y Gasset, the Spanish philosopher, characterized the age as

[3] "Lunches with Luce," *Atlantic Monthly,* May 1971.

one of materialism and non-intellectuality; perhaps a sports magazine matched the mood of the times. Luce shook his head. More
silence. Clay Felker tried.[4] Felker, on graduating from Duke University, had worked briefly as a statistician with baseball game broadcasters on radio before joining *Life*'s research staff in 1951. He told
Luce that he had once asked Ernie Harwell, the broadcaster for the
Giants, how he justified devoting his life to "an adolescent game
played by men." He had replied, "Well, this is a pretty terrible world,
and a lot of people need their minds taken off it, and if I can contribute a little happiness I have made a good contribution." Luce nodded.
Socrates, he ruminated, had said that "the unexamined life is not
worth living"; perhaps, therefore, the new magazine's purpose would
be to examine life in sports. Later he expanded the rationalization:

> There would not be a tremendous interest and participation if
> sport did not correspond to some important elements—some-
> thing deeply inherent—in the human spirit. . . .
>
> Sport has aspects, too, of creativity. Man is an animal that
> works, plays and prays. . . . No important aspect of human
> life should be devalued. And if play does correspond to some
> elements in spiritual man, then it is a bad thing for it to be de-
> valued. And sport has been devalued. It has become a low-brow
> proposition. It does not get serious attention.
>
> The new magazine will be a re-evaluation of sport—not an
> over-evaluation—to put it in its proper place as one of the great
> modes of expression.

In December 1953 Larsen reported to Luce that the business forecast was such that "all in all [1954] looks like a good year in which
to start a new magazine project." An analysis indicated that with a
circulation base of 500,000 to 700,000 weekly and a sale of 1,600
advertising pages per year the sports magazine could break even; with
2,600 advertising pages it could make a profit of $2,000,000. Larsen
concluded: "I think we have an able bunch of people covering all
the infield and outfield positions in the company and I think we have
enough depth of material to take on and put over a really successful
new venture in 1954."

Luce, who had done some worrying over the Havemann memorandum, finally resolved his doubts. "We in Time Inc. have become

[4] Editor and publisher of *New York* magazine since 1967.

345

perhaps too biased on the side of 'high powered' journalism," he wrote. "We are apt to neglect (or scorn) the humble tasks of good magazine making. Notable example of what we fail to do: the *Reader's Digest* with all that infinitely painstaking fitting in of jokes, sayings, oddments. *Sport* will succeed if we can get a staff (with the right leadership) willing to do the humble, anonymous tasks of magazine making."

Harry H. S. Phillips, Jr., advertising director of *Time,* was assigned to be the publisher. Phillips' advertising career had begun with the N. W. Ayer & Son, Inc., agency and he had been a salesman for both *Time* and *Life* before becoming a member of *Time's* New York management in 1941. William W. Holman, formerly Eastern advertising manager for *Life,* appointed advertising director in September, now began recruiting his branch office managers from the existing Time Inc. sales staff. In assigning two of its ablest salesmen and in giving Holman the green light to recruit from the existing sales staff, Time Inc.'s management was giving the new project every advantage.

In January 1954 a printed dummy was distributed to prospective advertisers with advertising rates set at $3,150 per black-and-white page based on 450,000 weekly circulation. At the same time test letters went out soliciting charter subscriptions at a special rate of $6 a year against a regular after-publication rate of $7.50 a year. Per-copy price was 25 cents. For sentimental reasons the first test mailing began with the same sentence that was used in the first *Life* mailings ("The enthusiasm now prevailing in the offices of *Time* and *Life* is one which I hope you will share in the very near future") and was directed to the same list that had received the *Life* test mailing: *Time* subscribers in Minnesota.

The dummy—140 pages with four-color covers and color inserts— was entitled simply "The New Sport Magazine" and was introduced by the editors as a "for instance" only. The dummy included advertisements, lifted, with the permission of the advertisers, mostly from *The New Yorker,* to which "The New Sport Magazine" bore a strong physical resemblance. The articles and pictures ran the gamut of participation and spectator sports—from fox hunting to wrestling.

Reaction inside and outside Time Inc. was mixed. Havemann, no disinterested critic, wrote, "I still think it merely proves—by being no better than it is after all the effort that has gone into it—that you just can't lick the problems. I further think that to compose a critique of the dummy would be like trying to pick the deadest fish on a mackerel boat." Writing in *Barron's,* Robert Cantwell, a former Time Inc. writer, said: "Despite every possible advantage in the way of backing, enthusiasm, a fresh subject, a trained staff, a handsome format, superb color pictures, the net result was [a] somewhat disappointing . . . combination of *The New Yorker, Esquire,* fragments of *Town & Country* and a sawed-off version of *Life.*" Shortly afterward he joined the staff of the new magazine. Bert Bell, commissioner of the National Football League, believed it would be "a great thing for sports." Novelist Faith Baldwin wrote: "In the words of my son it is terrific. The older has just asked for a three-year subscription! And the younger announces, 'I'll buy that.' " The magazine of advertising, *Tide,* was somewhat noncommittal: "the new magazine adds up to something quite new."

Larsen, Black and Phillips all assured Luce that the first word-of-mouth reaction they received personally was entirely favorable. It was also misleading for, as they later discovered, the comments did not represent the considered judgment of media buyers as opposed to that of the top agency executives. Even though many media men were avid sports fans, they had a deep-seated prejudice against spending money to advertise high-quality products in sports magazines; sports connoted an atmosphere conducive to moving only such products as athletic equipment, shaving creams and razor blades. Luce's "wonderful world of sport" (except for such pastimes as golf, tennis and polo) was, in their minds, "a mug's world." Particularly, it was of no interest to women. While Time Inc. management was not unaware of this prejudice, it underestimated its depth and force.

Still another factor militated against the magazine as a national advertising medium. The world of sports in 1954 was still largely parochial and seasonal. The big leagues in baseball did not extend from coast to coast; pro football, though building fast, was confined to twelve clubs mainly located east of the Mississippi. In the United States, National League hockey was confined to four cities. Pro basketball was an East Coast phenomenon. In his memo Havemann had argued that, after summer baseball and football in the autumn, there would be the long winter stretch with no compelling news interest.

Beginning in February 1954 James and his staff, undaunted, produced trial runs of various sections of the magazine which were distributed under the imprint of "MNORX." "We felt that this five-letter disguise with the actual O and R in proper place," James explained, "would shield our intentions but preserve the integrity of

347

the logotype design we were working on." In April a second dummy went to press under conditions simulating actual publication. Designed by Leo Lionni, art director of *Fortune,* it was a great improvement visually over the first. But Tom Donnelly, writing in the Washington *News,* for one flatly predicted the new magazine was "doomed to failure." Noting that "sports fans are firmly conditioned to a style of writing at once labyrinthine and rococo," he cited the "gentle clarity" of a lead for a story on bowling in the dummy issue and concluded it was "as out of place in a sports journal as a chaste, crisp radish would be atop a super deluxe banana split." Continuing skepticism in the advertising world was reflected in *Tide,* which polled its "leadership panel," a selected group of advertising executives, and found that three out of five would not subscribe to the magazine, although 43 percent would advertise in it. The advertising manager of Lee Tire & Rubber thought it would have "excellent readership" but his counterpart at Allied Chemical & Dye was "disappointed in the layout and general appearance." Other typical comments: "It's a hybrid. Do baseball and boxing fans mingle with fox hunters in pink coats?" "Too snooty. It should get down to the level of the common man and not be so New Yorkerish." In conclusion *Tide* quoted an unnamed executive: "I'd give it fair attention if I got it free."

Up to the point of the second dummy the final decision to publish had not yet been made. At last, in April 1954, Holman's salesmen were summoned to a convention at Myrtle Beach, South Carolina, to hear Larsen announce that the company had now decided to go ahead. As the salesmen, amid cheers, adjourned to the bar to drink to the success of their new magazine, publisher Phillips and managing editor James received a disquieting telephone call. Luce asked them to return immediately to New York; he had just reviewed the latest editorial budget and it was far too high.

The James estimate for the first year of full-scale editorial operations was $2,768,000—much higher than had been first projected. Earlier budgets had been based on the assumption that a sports magazine, unlike *Time, Life* and *Fortune,* would be able to operate with a small nucleus of editors and depend on outside contributors, presumably newspaper sportswriters and columnists. But their contributions to the dummies had been unsatisfactory; the sportswriters were unused to the heavy editing of Time Inc.-trained editors and they were often offended when asked to revise or rewrite copy. "Little wonder that they became as a group our biggest knockers for a while

348

after the appearance of Vol. 1, No. 1," said James. In preparing his latest budget, James had assumed the new magazine would have to be largely staff written.

This came as a shock and disappointment to Luce; he had never reconciled himself to the ever increasing editorial budgets of his successful magazines. He had told James that he hoped that the new magazine would operate on a lean budget and thus serve as an example to the other managing editors. Luce pointed to the bottom line total of James's budget and said sternly, "This may be the end of the magazine."

James and his business manager, Ray Ammarell, were aghast. They worked over the weekend to revise their figures. On Monday they appeared before Luce, having reduced the budget by more than $1,000,-000. A part of this was accomplished by a Luce ruling that permitted James to eliminate intracompany charges allocated to the new magazine for operation of the news bureaus, the picture collection and the photo lab. James also dropped provisions for twenty people on his prospective staff. "Okay, we've got a magazine," said Luce, "Do you mean that if these figures had not come up right there would not have been a magazine?" asked James. "No better time to kill it," Luce replied.

Off to Rome again, Luce left Grover the job of getting the other managing editors to agree to absorb those operational charges that had been taken off James's back. Grover wrote that obtaining their grudging acceptance required "a real push . . . a lot of explaining, some wheedling and some head-knocking. . . . But gee whiz, these things take time, and editors can be exasperating when they talk like accountants, and vice versa."


On May 17, 1954, *Advertising Age* reported: "Time Inc.'s new sports weekly will make its first appearance Friday, August 13 (issue date: August 16), but only Mr. Luce knows now what people will ask for when they walk up to newsstands, quarters in hand." At this point not even Luce knew what the magazine's name would be. A list of more than a hundred possible titles had been compiled, but only one seemed right to Luce: *Sport.* It was the name of a monthly already being published by MacFadden Publications, Inc., an out-and-out fan magazine in the adulatory style of the movie magazines, with a claimed circulation of 418,000. It was for sale for $250,000; Luce was willing to go to $200,000 but no higher.

With the matter still undecided, Harry Phillips was lunching at the Plaza when a friend, Stuart Scheftel, stopped by his table and said, "Oh, by the way, I own the title of the magazine *Sports Illustrated,* and if you want it I am willing to talk about it." *Sports Illustrated* had been founded as a monthly in 1935 by two former Time Inc. writers, John Escher and Samuel H. McAloney, but folded after two years of publication. After the war the title had been revived by the Dell Publishing Company, again unsuccessfully. Time Inc. offered $5,000 for the name. "I had hoped you would offer $10,000," said Scheftel, "but I'll take the $5,000 provided I get a free subscription."

In June 1954 Luce returned from Rome to take an active hand in putting together the first issue; he wrote to Billings, who was on leave, "*Sports Illustrated* is a lot of fun though, of course, not without its nervousness too." C. D. Jackson also wrote to Billings describing the "feverish" activity and noting that Luce's nervousness derived from the fact that "while he is not flying blind, this is really quite different from any previous endeavor of his. What I mean is that there was a fairly solid line tying *Time, Fortune* and *Life* together [while] the line to *Sports Illustrated,* is, at best, dotted, and when Harry solemnly considers cartoons and finds it difficult to smile as he leafs through several dozen, or when he tilts back in his chair, puts the tips of his fingers together and goes into a deadpan dissertation on 'jokes,' those dots get spaced quite far apart."

James, according to Jackson, was showing "an intellectual and emotional equilibrium which is quite remarkable. I sometimes feel that Harry is secretly worried over the fact that Sid is not visibly showing more strain, and I had to tell him one day not to be upset because for once he had found a managing editor who did not fight him every inch of the way or look like death on a holiday."

As the first issue neared, the mail brought in 350,000 charter subscriptions, which enabled the publisher to firm up the 450,000 circulation base, almost twice that of the pre-publication guarantee of *Life* and the highest ever for a publication with a per-copy price of 25 cents. Holman's salesmen signed up 200 accounts for $1,300,-000 of advertising. One week before publication *Business Week* commented: "The record to date doesn't mean that *Sports Illustrated* will be a success automatically—though it must encourage Henry Luce, who frequently ends his remarks about the magazine, '. . . if, of course, it's a success.' But even in Luce's terms, the new publication has a leg up on success."

*Barron's* stressed the very big gamble that Time Inc. was taking: "Publishing remains as risky a business as ever, which is to say that it is far riskier than most. There are today [1954] some 7,792 magazines in America, but out of some 3,182 launched since the war only a handful have established themselves as institutions in their field. The rate of mortality here—as instanced by the collapse or suspension of *Quick, Park East, Today's Woman, Gentry, World* and *Science Illustrated*—is terrific.[5] . . . Backed by all the gear, tackle and talent of Time Inc., *Sports Illustrated* is obviously no fly-by-night, but it is a plunge into the unknown for all that, competing with some eighty-nine specialized sports publications (*The Blood-Horse,* the *Chess Review,* etc., etc.) and seeking as it does to dramatize on a national scale activities that more often than not have mainly only local interest."

It was with great expectation mingled with some apprehension that Luce and top management awaited the public reaction. To see that Vol. 1, No. 1 was launched with proper fanfare, Time Inc. mustered all of its promotional skills. There were merchandising displays from coast to coast, radio and television interviews with the founding editors and cocktail parties for the charter advertisers. In the planning one hitch developed: Young & Rubicam, the agency for *SI,* as the magazine was now referred to in interoffice memoranda, had trouble in drafting an acceptable advertisement announcing the first issue. After various versions were rejected, Luce wrote the following copy:

There has never been a National Sports Weekly. Furthermore, it has been brilliantly proved that there never can be. People's interests are too varied. The fisherman cares nothing for baseball. The skier couldn't care less about the Kentucky Derby.

Maybe. Maybe that's the way it was. Maybe that's still the way it partly is. But one thing is sure: the world of Sport is a wonderful world and everyone enters it with Joy.

And so we enter it—as journalists, editors, writers, photographers, resolved to put something of the joy and awareness of Sport into the form of a magazine. . . .

Soon, in Vol. 1, No. 1, we'll begin where we are, in the

[5] *Quick,* a pocket-sized super digest of the news, published by Cowles Magazines, fascinated Luce because it carried summary to the nth degree. Contrary to the view held by most of his editors, Luce believed that *Quick* had the makings of a successful publication. It did attain a circulation of 1,300,000 before Cowles ceased publishing it in 1953.

351

middle of things: the unpredictable headline happenings of the week, then the enduring picture of field and stream, then a battery of expert columns wherein the lure of many a famous sport will be expounded with loving care.

You don't have to read it—not any of it. Sport is Liberty Hall. It compels nobody. You don't have to read about it in order to be a better executive or a better housewife or to do your duty as a citizen in the Hydrogen Age.

But you'll surely want to have a look at this new magazine. . . . You may find that it makes more enjoyable what you already enjoy. And *that* could have consequences.

One consequence could be that, at last, America will have a great National Sports Weekly.

The copy was handed to Young & Rubicam's account executive. He in turn submitted the advertisement to George Gribbin, the agency's creative director, without telling him who wrote it. Gribbin's comment was, "Whoever wrote this—we ought to hire him."

Vol. 1, No. 1 of *Sports Illustrated* went to press on Monday night, August 9, 1954, forty minutes ahead of schedule, and first appeared on the newsstands on Thursday morning. It had help from staffmen recruited from the other Time Inc. magazines along with talent from the outside. The assistant managing editor, Richard Johnston, came from *Life;* the news editor, John Tibby, was a former senior editor of *Time.* Paul O'Neil, transferred from *Time,* wrote the lead story—a stirring account of the "mile of the century" in which England's Dr. Roger Bannister and Australia's John Landy became the first two men in history to break the four-minute mark in the same race. Gerald Holland, who wrote the article which set the theme for the issue and justified the publication of a sports magazine—"The Golden Age Is Now"—was a newcomer. So was the art director, Jerome Snyder. The color photographs of the Ezzard Charles–Rocky Marciano fight, which provided a dramatic introduction to what the new magazine would offer by way of a new dimension in action photography, were contributed by former *Life* photographer Mark Kauffman, who also supplied the cover shot of a night baseball game.

The issue consisted of 144 pages and included a vacation guide to trout fishing in the Rockies and a fine portfolio of sporting pictures by the American artist George Bellows. Seventy-four pages were advertisements representing a fair cross-section of blue-ribbon accounts, including a double-page spread from the Ford Motor Company, which had chosen the first issue of *Sports Illustrated* to announce its new sports car, the Thunderbird.

Advance ballyhoo sold out the first issue; 90 percent of the magazines vanished from the newsstands on the first day. Early Thursday morning Luce made his own tour of inspection of the newsstands in Grand Central Station and the nearby hotels, returned and wrote Black: "What I chiefly saw was *Look* in the corner position of Stand No. 1, and *Collier's* next to it—with *Life* somewhere off Southeast by South. Same condition on other stands and in Hotel Roosevelt." He was not exulting over a sellout but complaining about a seeming lack of enterprise in newsstand promotion. By the end of the first day telegrams were pouring in from the circulation representatives saying that they were getting angry calls from newsdealers for additional copies. The promotion department—to remind everyone of the policy on controlled growth—hoisted a sign: OCCUPANCY BY MORE THAN 500,000 PERSONS IS DANGEROUS AND UNLAWFUL. The August 17 minutes of the president's committee concluded with this notation: "All in all, it appears that the Company has launched a successful publication."

Reader response was excellent. Four out of five of the first letters to the editors were favorable; insert cards in the newsstand copies brought a flood of additional subscriptions. Luce personally sent out a number of copies, including one to President Eisenhower, who indicated that he had at least glanced through it for he wrote, "I know I shall find much of interest in it, perhaps too much for my own peace of mind. There is, for instance, a certain article on page 55 ["The Vacation Guide to Trout Fishing"]." Lord Beaverbrook found the magazine "fascinating" but "for 25 cents there is too much value." After noting some specific criticisms and suggestions, he added: "Now I have criticized the magazine as though it were my own paper. I wish that was the case." Gardner Cowles, the founder-publisher of *Look,* called the first issue "a superior job. My guess is the magazine will have some birthpains in the next few months and then, perhaps, a few growing pains in the following year, but I believe eventually it will be a great success."

Perhaps the least enthusiastic reaction was within Time Inc.'s own family. In the beginning, the name "Muscles" fastened on the experimental department reflected simply lofty condescension. There was also some vexation over Time Inc. entering on so undignified an

353

enterprise. In the Time & Life Building's lobby the names of *Time, Life* and *Fortune* in heroic-sized letters dominated one wall. Logically, the new addition should have been blocked in at the bottom but there wasn't room there, so *Sports Illustrated* was put at the top. The addition was made over a weekend. James took a wry view of the result. "No symbolism was intended, but the visual result seemed to beg the question: could *Time, Life* and *Fortune* support *Sports Illustrated* for long?" He was also amused at the reaction of other company employees arriving for work on Monday morning. "Grumblings about this effrontery perpetrated in behalf of an upstart child reached the executive floor without delay."

There was a more substantial cause for grumbling. The costs of launching *Sports Illustrated,* though not disclosed at the time, were all too evident, and word spread among the staff that the new magazine probably would reduce profit sharing. One top executive was heard to refer to the magazine as "Harry's yacht." Such remarks, the disgruntlement and the lack of confidence around Time Inc.'s office swiftly found their way into the grapevine along Madison Avenue, where the advertising agencies warily watched Luce's latest gamble.

The management of Time Inc. anticipated losses in starting up a new magazine, but as Luce said, "Perhaps in the case of *Sports Illustrated* we tended to forget what a very risky thing it is to start a new magazine and how difficult; if so, we have paid for that lapse." The loss in 1954, including the start-up costs, was more than $6,000,000.

This far exceeded pre-publication estimates, which had anticipated a limited circulation that would hold down losses. Also it had been assumed that, with reader enthusiasm demonstrated, advertisers would respond. The budget called for the sale of 500 advertising pages between the first issue in August 1954 and the year end; it was with difficulty that Holman's salesmen sold 319 pages. To fatten thin issues, editorial pages were added, throwing the budget still further out of kilter.

In October Grover wrote to Luce, again in Rome: "The difficulty lies in advertising. There seems no doubt that the small agencies, who have to decide on one splurge for their clients, are skittish. They bring up the example of *Flair,* on which a number of them were badly burned when it was discontinued.[6] Roy Larsen says it is un-

[6] *Flair,* a lushly printed monthly launched by Gardner Cowles, whose wife Fleur was its editor, folded after a year of publication, in 1950.

354

thinkable that we should suddenly decide to discontinue *Sports Illustrated* and that we must convince these small agency people—and some big ones—that we really mean to publish this magazine with all the resources and ingenuity of Time Inc. Meantime the advertising prospects are fairly thin. A big decision that will have to be made before the 1955 budgets is just how much loss Time Inc. is willing to earmark for 1955 for *SI.*"

Later that month, in a show of strength, Time Inc. announced that *Sports Illustrated* would increase its circulation base to 525,000 and raise its advertising rates by 9 percent. But this did not stop rumors that the magazine was in trouble. In a frank memo to all Time Inc. salesmen Howard Black identified the rumors and denied them:

Rumor One: *Sports Illustrated* is going to become a fortnightly. *SI* is a weekly and will continue to be a weekly because sports occur on a weekly basis. . . .

Rumor Two: Harry Luce didn't like the idea of *Sports Illustrated* in the first place, is apathetic about it now. Harry Luce started *Sports Illustrated,* and he loves it.

Rumor Three: Advertisers have turned "thumbs down" on *Sports Illustrated*. This is ridiculous. . . . We have more advertising running in *Sports Illustrated* at this stage of its career than either *The New Yorker* or *Life* had at a similar time after their launching.

Black was not overstating Luce's enthusiasm. From Rome Luce cabled Larsen in December: "This issue . . . looks and reads good to me." And Larsen replied that *SI* was making "really fine progress on the editorial and circulation fronts but with painfully slow but steady progress on the advertising front."

The high revenues enjoyed by the other magazines in 1954 enabled the company to absorb the loss on *Sports Illustrated* with no great impact on the profit and loss statement. The annual report spoke with confidence of the future of Time Inc.'s newest magazine:

Even though it aimed at a total circulation of 450,000, the circulation of every issue in 1954 exceeded 500,000. . . . Excellent newsstand sales have provided a steady source of new subscriptions. Renewals of a group of test short-term subscriptions have been running well ahead of our expectations.

This all adds up to a strong circulation picture for your Company's new national weekly.

Currently, incoming orders for advertising space from a wide variety of advertisers give encouraging indications of recognition by advertisers of *Sports Illustrated* as an important new advertising medium.

The management was doing a little wishful thinking.

Editorially, *Sports Illustrated* in its first year, as was inevitable, displayed a certain unevenness in approach and format. In February 1955 Luce tried his hand at drafting an ideal formula which he said should be "the melding of the *strict functionalism* of the newsmagazine with the *free* play of an editor's enthusiasm and enjoyment." *SI* was trying to combine elements of *Time* and *Life* with touches of *The New Yorker,* and Luce and his editors were seeking to establish a pattern characteristic of the subject matter. Yet uneven as it sometimes seemed, *Sports Illustrated* communicated the enthusiasm of the amateur rather than the cold expertise of the professional. Adventurous from the first, it called to the unfamiliar role of sports reporters some of the most distinguished writers of the time. Nobel Prize winner William Faulkner eagerly accepted assignments to cover hockey and the Kentucky Derby. Dick Johnston remembered Faulkner's response when he was first approached about the Derby: "He looked up sort of shy and said, 'You know, all mah la-afe I've been hopin' someone would pay me to go to a horserace.' " John Steinbeck, an enthusiastic fisherman, jumped at the chance to write about his favorite avocation. Budd Schulberg, novelist and screenwriter, was a boxing buff who relished his assignment to dig into "Boxing's Dirty Business," laying the ground for a follow-up that gained for the new magazine more newspaper space than any article in any Time Inc. magazine since *Life*'s "Birth of a Baby." At first the millionaire president of the International Boxing Club, James Norris, who virtually controlled prize fighting in the United States, blustered and threatened libel suits but thought better of it when the evidence unfolded in *Sports Illustrated*'s pages. Schulberg's article and the series that followed helped bring about the reform of half a dozen state boxing commissions. When *Sports Illustrated* suggested a rerun of the fiercely contested Kentucky Derby of 1955 between the winner Swaps and the place horse Nashua, the fans so overwhelmingly

356

clamored for a match race that it was staged at Washington Park in Chicago. Nashua won. John P. Marquand, the novelist and social historian of the proper Bostonians, an early reader of *Sports Illustrated,* proposed to his fellow New Englander Roy Larsen a satiric series about an American establishment phenomenon—the country club—and the resulting stories about life at fictitious Happy Knoll provided enlightening commentary on the subject.

By June 1955 Luce could tell his editors that he thought the new "pattern" was "pretty good" and that the magazine was reaching an audience that was "literate (even verging on literary)" and one with "broad interests as well as deep interest in sports-in-general as well as in one or two sports, but it is more interested in some sports than in others; an audience which is happy to lift its eyes from the day's baseball scores and observe a fine Alaskan bear shoot or the finest fishing club in the Andes. If all this causes anyone to say that *SI* is too highbrow or whatever, let them say it. We are not writing for bums or illiterates. All suggestions that *SI* is too highbrow are to be ignored by us. What cannot be ignored by an editor is that his magazine is too dull. Our objective is to produce an interesting magazine for literate people of broad interests, interesting and sometimes even 'exciting.' " What was certainly true was that the readers of *Sports Illustrated* who liked it, liked it very much indeed. Roy Larsen publicly announced that the renewal percentage of *SI* charter subscriptions was "rapidly approaching the extremely high figure of 70 percent"—an unusual announcement; publishers don't generally disclose such secrets. Meanwhile a survey of the magazine's subscribers in Grand Rapids, Michigan, confirmed Luce's intuitive sense of the *SI* audience; the readers were predominantly youthful, prosperous, with good jobs, comfortable homes and a rising standard of living.

Advertising sales remained slow, however. On one of Luce's trips home from Rome he and Larsen—as Larsen put it—"put on our salesman's caps" and hit the road. The results were not encouraging; Luce lamented to Arthur Tatham, head of the Tatham-Laird agency in Chicago, "Somehow our readers seem to see what we are doing, but we haven't yet articulated it well enough in a professional or technical or formal sense." In an effort to attract new advertisers *Sports Illustrated* took the innovative step of introducing regional editions for New York, Chicago and the West Coast. New revenues were thus attracted, but the apathy of the advertisers in general was still not overcome and Luce, commenting on the record, wrote: "It

357

does not make me feel good about the job we have done in the last eighteen months and with millions of dollars in the field of communication to advertisers—formerly known as 'selling.' Did anybody ever say we were good salesmen?"

One of the persistent rumors on Madison Avenue was that the magazine would be folded. "The usual story is that there is a split in the management of Time Inc. about *SI,*" Larsen wrote to Luce, "and that you are 'anti' and may at any moment pull the plug." The story fed on the fact, said Larsen, that Luce had never made a public statement on behalf of *SI* as he had once made for *Life* before the American Association of Advertising Agencies. On that memorable occasion he had asked the Four A's, as the "appropriations committee of the American press," for $100,000,000 in advertising to see *Life* through its first ten critical years. One of Time Inc.'s most influential friends in advertising, Leo Burnett, head of the company that bears his name, was among those who urged Luce again to try his hand at such a statement. On Burnett's twentieth anniversary Luce had written him, "Time was when a new publishing phenomenon called *Life* was recognized but not grasped by the advertising fraternity. One of the few who did 'grasp' and was willing to risk quite a pile of chips, was yourself. And this I will never forget." Seeking now to oblige Burnett, Luce attempted to explain "the meaning, the purpose, the raison d'être of *Sports Illustrated.*"

It was in the form of a letter to Burnett, to be distributed to the trade, in which Luce described the paradox of the time—the omnipresent threat of nuclear holocaust and man's pursuit of happiness. Luce pointed out that the average citizen, like President Eisenhower, while acknowledging the threat of nuclear war, had to assume that "peace is possible, even probable; more than that, you live and work as if it is, right now." And peace, Luce wrote, means

enjoyment of life, the pursuit of happiness. It means, in short, *Sports Illustrated. . . .*

What? Is Sport the goal of life? Certainly not. . . . But if you ask most any American what he's going to do with peacetime—leisure—what's he going to do next weekend, what's he going to do next winter, next summer, what's he planning now for his pursuit of happiness—one sure part of the answer (and a large part) will be something to do with Sport. He and she are going to Florida to lounge on the beach—and fish or sail. He

358

and she are going to Alaska to shoot a bear. He and she are going this weekend to the football game. And they're going to Arizona because there they get not only scenery but golf. Meanwhile their son is writing home about being substitute tackle on the Freshman team; their daughter has unaccountably got hold of a bow-and-arrow and Junior is taking tennis lessons. And cousin Fred has, of all things, bought a racing horse. And this is what they talk about when they've finished with the H-Bomb and with how come Mary got engaged to John. *The greatest common denominator of leisure activity and of human conversation among Americans pursuing happiness is—sport.* . . .

And so what we got excited about was creating a magazine for *those* people to make it the finest we know how.

Not chi-chi. Not snobbish. Not phony. But a magazine which loved Sports and would be worthy of this greatest common denominator of pleasurable interest among civilized men. . . .

We have made that magazine . . . we have also made a unique advertising medium. . . . To put your money, now, on *Sports Illustrated* is to put your money on the hopes of the American people in a very simple, human way—in a way universally understood and richly appreciated.

I hope, Sir, that somewhere in this letter you may have found the key to our enthusiasm, the core of our faith in the purpose we serve.

Burnett thought the letter "magnificent." Apart from satisfying Burnett, the Luce letter made clear beyond any doubt his own commitment to the new magazine. Advertising sales did not pick up.

The editorial staff, at Luce's insistence, was smaller than that of *Time* even though *Sports Illustrated* writers were producing about sixty pages of editorial matter to the newsmagazine's forty. "The work was unbelievably exhausting, but it was great for the morale," James recalled. Roger Hewlett, a *Time* writer who switched over to *Sports Illustrated,* remembered that,

more than those of any other mag in the family, the *SI* edit crowd were conscious of a difference between them and other Time Incers, and hence they felt a clannishness absent everywhere else at 9 Rockefeller Plaza. *SI* lived on the wrong side of the Time Inc. tracks, and like all ghetto dwellers, its staffers

359

were made constantly aware of the fact. I was in a position to notice this perhaps more than others, because I came down out of the big paternal mansion on the hill to live and work in the edit slums. . . . I was appalled, as the recent resident of the *Time* edit floors, where you pressed a button at your desk to summon copy boys to cater to your every slightest whim, to find that there were no personal services of any kind. . . . And those marvelous ladies on *Time* who wrote our queries and gleaned our information and held our editorial hand and cleansed our consciences were nowhere to be found. . . . Their places were taken, if at all, by eager young men who knew where the Yankee locker room was in the Bronx but had seemingly never heard of a library. So everybody—editors, writers and layout artists—did their own job virtually unassisted—and took considerable pride in the fact, while old colleagues from other edit staffs sneered quite audibly at lunch—until one really stopped having lunch with them—and made a great point of the fact that they threw this particular magazine into the wastebasket as soon as the copy boy brought it around to them. There was the same attitude toward *SI* . . . in the various news bureaus. . . . It seemed to us *SI* queries were turned over to an apprentice office boy to handle while the real bureau men busied themselves finding out how many sandwiches Elizabeth Taylor ate for *Time*'s People page.

The experience of being in on something new, something that Time Inc. had never done before, and the personal recognition that came in the form of by-lines were also factors in keeping the morale high. As the editorial budget was expanded and young writers were taken on to grow with the magazine, some of the pressure was gradually relieved. By the end of the fifties *SI* was about 70 percent staff written, 30 percent non-staff—a complete reversal of the original expectation—with the larger proportion of non-staff work coming from contract writers.

In looking for another senior editor to fill out the top management staff, Luce made an inspired move in offering the post of assistant managing editor to Andre Laguerre, chief of the *Time-Life* London bureau. At that point in his career he was probably the magazine's most respected foreign correspondent. Early recognized for his political astuteness, Laguerre in 1951 spent a year working on Luce's personal staff, a tour of duty that marked him for promotion. Many in the company were surprised when Luce announced Laguerre's new appointment; very few of them knew of his intense interest in sport. When asked why he had left his prestigious post in London, Laguerre replied, "For the past twenty years . . . I have been covering mostly politics and international affairs, where mediocrity is unfortunately and too often the best way for a man to get ahead. There is no place for mediocrity in sports. I'm looking forward to working in a field where a striving for excellence and a dedication to performance count so much." John Tibby, *SI*'s news editor, was also promoted to that rank; with Dick Johnston, the magazine thus had three assistant managing editors.

Midway through 1956 Luce thought he saw a marked improvement in *SI*'s editorial performance. "Reports that come to me are typically in terms of contrast between how 'people' feel about *Sports Illustrated* now compared to a year ago," he wrote. "A year ago 'they' didn't think much of it, now 'they' think it's just fine. Probably the most important aspect of improvement has been in knowledge-able or 'authoritative' reporting on major sports."

By the end of its second year of publication *Sports Illustrated* had raised its circulation base to 600,000 and advertising sales reached 1,137 pages. But the magazine was still in the red. In January 1957 Luce wrote to Larsen: "First, to make a real success of *Sports Illustrated* is Time Inc.'s No. 1 publishing job for 1957. Real success may be briefly defined as putting *SI* in a position to come close to breaking even in 1958. Close to breaking even in 1958 may be defined as having a deficit in 1958 of not more than 10% of the gross." Luce's goal was not achieved in 1957 or 1958—or, in fact, for several more years. Less determined men than Luce and Larsen would have given up on the magazine long before, but the pride and reputation of Time Inc. were too much involved; more important, the prospect and the promise of the magazine were always such that the break-even point seemed tantalizingly close.

The struggle took its toll: in 1959 H. H. S. Phillips, Jr., the first publisher, was relieved and reassigned to the corporate staff; Bill Holman, the advertising director, resigned to fulfill a long-deferred desire to study for the Methodist ministry; Richard Neale, who had been a member of the original task force, also left the company. Arthur Murphy, Jr., general manager of *Life* and former manager

361

of *The March of Time,* took over from Phillips. To fill Holman's job Luce drafted Llewellyn L. ("Pete") Callaway, the advertising director of *Fortune.* When Callaway was asked to go to the rescue of *SI,* he demurred; he told Luce that he "could go out blindfolded on Fifty-first Street and tap anyone with the absolute assurance that they would know more about sports than I." Luce replied, "That's not what we want you for—we've got too many golfers around here anyway."

These changes had barely been made when a new personality interjected himself into the situation and brought about further shifts. Hedley Donovan, who by then was editorial director of Time Inc., assigned himself to a tour of duty on *Sports Illustrated.* Luce was surprised and not entirely pleased. His view at the time was that *SI* was a first-rate magazine editorially and that its troubles were all on the publishing side, i.e., some failure of salesmanship and promotion in overcoming Madison Avenue's timidity about the new magazine. Donovan (who had played varsity hockey at Oxford) differed: "My own view was that the magazine was not as good editorially as Luce thought and that I was a more natural reader of *SI* than he was and probably a better judge of ways it might be improved."

Out of Donovan's tour came a set of quite detailed recommendations, some about personnel and some about format. In arriving at these Donovan had drawn on the ideas of many *SI* people, particularly Art Murphy, the publisher, Andre Laguerre and Dick Johnston. It was Murphy's suggestion that he give up the publisher's role, which Donovan felt would be the ideal position for James. From this change it followed that a new managing editor had to be selected and the choice was Laguerre.

In its first five years of existence *Sports Illustrated* editors and publishers had endless debates on the contents "mix"—the acceptable balance between sport per se and leisure-time topics (fashions, food and special columns such as Charles Goren's on bridge) that were deemed necessary to broaden the readership base. To Laguerre this argument had been carried to extremes, "as if it were somehow desirable to conceal the fact that we are a magazine about sport in the first place." On taking over, Laguerre asked for a charter to curtail expansion of the so-called general departments at the expense of sports, arguing:

There have been times when our general material has not been general enough, yes, but to increase the quota would be to out-

362

general ourselves; the result might or might not be a successful magazine, but it would not be a sport magazine. Should there, on the contrary, be more "hard sport" and less of the other? Many readers and many of our staff would say yes. They resent it when they think we are overloaded with fashion or the recreations of the wealthy. They share in the sport mystique; some of them regard sport as an art form, and most of them as more than recreation; there may be some immaturity in their attitude, but these people have the flame which makes any journalistic enterprise interesting, and with which we tamper at our peril.

Luce agreed up to a point; Laguerre's statement was "okay or almost okay" with him. His reservation was that it was not necessary "to resent a look at the recreations of the wealthy. . . . Today the 'recreations of the wealthy' rapidly become the shared interests of hundreds of thousands and millions."

One of the first problems to which Laguerre addressed himself was improving the physical appearance of the magazine. With the help of a new art director, Richard Gangel, *SI* made remarkable strides in its visual presentation; its sports photography had always been outstanding, but Gangel added another dimension by assigning artists to provide imaginative interpretations of sporting events. The magazine moved steadily toward a more sophisticated and expert interpretation. The full story of the development of the magazine under Laguerre is that of another decade, outside the scope of this volume. James's enthusiasm had brought the magazine into being; Laguerre's editing helped it to fulfill the expectations of its founders.

(While editorial quality improved steadily and advertising sales rose from 1,693 pages in 1959 to 1,901 pages in 1962, *SI* remained in the red. In 1963, when Callaway resigned as advertising director of *Sports Illustrated* to become publisher of *Newsweek,* Andrew Heiskell, by then chairman of the board, undertook a review of sales strategy. He concluded that in the past *Sports Illustrated* had been selling *against* other media in situations where its specific case was weak; i.e., against *Esquire* in apparel, against *Holiday* in travel and against *House Beautiful* in the home field. He concluded that *Sports Illustrated* should sell itself not against the specialty magazines but as a newsweekly of general interest competing with its elder brother *Time* and with *Newsweek* and *U.S. News & World Report.* He pointed out that the circulation of the sports magazine had the same demographic profile as the newsweeklies and merely reached its

363

readers through a different readership appeal. It would be an over-simplification to suggest that the adoption of a new sales strategy turned loss into profit. But the fact is that in 1964, after ten years of losses, the magazine made its first profit, and it has remained profitable ever since. In mid-1972 with a circulation of 2,208,000 *Sports Illustrated* was the most important magazine profit center in Time Inc. next to *Time* itself.)

Luce often referred to this, the last of the magazines he founded, as "a baby born late in life" and one for which he had a special feeling. James commented: "He certainly was a mature parent. Indulgent at times, at times hypercritical, and always fiercely protective. He enjoyed enormously the conflict with his colleagues over the offspring and its chances in life. The new baby certainly added zest to its father's last chapter."

# Having Your Own Man in the White House

URING TWENTY YEARS of Democratic administrations Time Inc. had easily exercised its critical assessments of the man in the White House. After the inauguration of Dwight Eisenhower in January 1953 (which *Time* saw as bringing to the office "Ike's own qualities for leadership and an impressive Cabinet"), the editors found themselves in a novel position: a favorable attitude toward the President's performance was certainly imposed upon them in order to validate their judgment that Eisenhower had been the proper choice; having their own man in the White House was an uncomfortable journalistic experience in more ways than one.

Shortly after the inauguration the Washington office reported that fellow correspondents in the capital were asserting that the Time Inc. magazines "are incapable of criticizing the Eisenhower Administration." The appointments of Mrs. Luce as ambassador to Italy and Emmet Hughes and C. D. Jackson to the President's staff lent color to the charge made by one New York columnist that *Time* was a "house organ of the Republican Administration." The charge worried Luce only slightly. "The problem will take care of itself," he said, "and mainly we have just to go about our business of good reporting." He felt impelled then to make a statement on journalism—

one of his rare speeches on the subject.[1] His platform was the University of Oregon School of Journalism.

He recalled how in *Time*'s early days a friend, on returning from a trip around the country, had told him that the magazine was gaining respect and that its readers would now expect it to be "a public utility." He had retorted, "I'll be damned if I'll be a public utility," and went on to say:

> The main concern of journalism—and the *only* justification for freedom of the press—is *res publicae*—the reporting and discussion of those matters which bear clearly and directly on the business of the Republic . . . essentially political affairs . . . to be dealt with by the political organs of a free society. The primary function of journalism is to tell as many of the citizens as possible, as effectively as possible, what the *res publicae* are, and what the *rational* debate on those subjects is.

At the same time he believed that the press was called upon to be a "vessel of Truth":

> The owner-editor cannot honorably evade his personal confrontation with every aspect of truth in every aspect of his paper. This sense of personal responsibility should be and can be shared with every member of the staff. Every reporter and sub-editor should know that he is expected to be a man of intellectual integrity and that his honest coping with truth, in every department of the paper, will be respected. There is plenty of room for wide differences of opinion and taste—under a roof supported by a few pillars of conviction. But these differences should never be evaded. When basic differences of conviction are made clear, then men who wish to be both honorable and free will part company. We are called to be the servants of Truth: let us serve it together when we can, and separately when we must.

At about the same time, Luce suggested to *Time*'s editors that the forthcoming thirtieth anniversary issue—March 9, 1953—would be a suitable occasion on which "to 'explain' ourselves—having in mind Jefferson's phrase about 'a decent respect to the opinions of man-

---

[1] Rare because, as he said, "a pretty good definition of a journalist is someone who knows a little about everything and not very much about anything. Thus for a journalist to talk about journalism is in some strange way unjournalistic."

366

kind.' . . . I suggest that *Time* should take the occasion of its 30th birthday to come out *for* Intellectuality, *for* Progress, *for* the democratic proposition that men *can* know enough (about everything) for reasonably good self-government." What made these propositions pertinent, he said, was the current rampant McCarthyism and the fear, among intellectuals, of a new wave of anti-intellectualism; the ever-present threat of nuclear war; and more particularly the frustrating situation in Korea. All were contributing to an underlying pessimism about the future and about the possibility of progress. And on top of all this was a widespread skepticism about the press.

National Affairs editor Max Ways undertook the translation of Luce's memorandum into *Time's* birthday manifesto under the title "Journalism and Joachim's Children." The article, which filled five full pages, began by stating *Time's* birthday theses to be:

*That despite the "complexities" of the day, democratic public opinion can know enough to make the right decisions—provided that the press and the intellectuals do their job.*

*That public opinion is now hampered by a crisis among the intellectuals over the possibility and meaning of progress.*

*That if this crisis is solved—and there are signs that it will be— an opportunity for great progress lies ahead, especially in the fields of law, government, economics and international relations.*

Taking inspiration from a recently published book, *The New Science of Politics,*[2] by Professor Eric Voegelin of Louisiana State University, Ways sought to explain the current confusion in intellectual circles— the "pattern of chaos"—as a survival of the Gnostic heresy in modern political thought. Joachim of Flora (circa 1132–1202), a Christian Gnostic, held out the possibility of perfection on earth, which men could achieve through "hidden knowledge." Gnosticism survives in present politics, ran Ways's argument, in the tendency of modern intellectuals to substitute "magic operations in the dream world" (as Voegelin put it) for a politics of reality. For example:

*It is hard for a Gnostic to believe that a successful cold war can avoid a total hot war, or that a successful limited war can avoid a larger war. . . . That is why Gnostics denounce as steps to total war all efforts to win the Korean war. The only war Utopians can think about is Armageddon.*

[2] University of Chicago Press, 1952.

The Soviet Union was described as internally "a primitive absolutism" where at the highest levels

*Gnostic ideas may still dominate. . . . The world revolution has not yet been made reality, and Communists are therefore still free to dream about it. . . . This accounts for a seeming contradiction: tactically, Russian policy is realist and therefore more effective than Gnostic Western policy; strategically and long-range, Russian policy is Gnostic and still seeks the Marxist millenium of world revolution.*

McCarthyism, too, was ascribed to Gnosticism in that "an opportunist politician [was] capitalizing on the public frustration that inevitably followed the failures of Gnostic politics." In conclusion the birthday manifesto recalled that *Time,* in its original prospectus, had stated some "prejudices." On its thirtieth birthday *Time* stated some "convictions, some compass bearings" by which it considered the news:

*That God's order in man's world includes a moral code, based upon man's unchanging nature and not subject to man's repeal, suspension or amendment.*

*That, as Supreme Court Justice [William O.] Douglas said, "we are a religious people whose institutions presuppose a Supreme Being," and that American history cannot be understood or correct policy formed except with recognition of that fact. It follows that equality before the law is based on each man's dignity in God's sight; that political liberty is based on the soul's freedom to accept or reject the good; that legal equality and political freedom must be applied without discrimination of race or creed.*

*That those rights should be enforced, even in favor of those who oppose U.S. institutions, subject only to the state's duty to protect its authority. As Justice [Robert H.] Jackson said, the Bill of Rights is not "a suicide pact."*

*That the opportunity for great progress, especially moral progress, lies before society.*

*That all attempts, revolutionary or reformist, of progress based on the idea that man is perfectible will lead to stagnation at best and calamity, at worst.*

*That political progress means a politics based upon reality (without the cynical connotation of Realpolitik); that such a policy, skillfully pursued, may well lead to removing the Communist threat without total war.*

*That the American Proposition is still valid and wants restating in its deepest connection with the truths of spiritual freedom.*

*That the intellectual, whom society needs, must be 1) free to think, and 2) encouraged to press his conclusions on public opinion. That if the public acts on his views and they turn out to be wrong he should not be held accountable criminally. That he should, however, expect the public to hold him accountable and criticize him, perhaps bitterly, for his error. That an intellectual without enough nerve to accept this penalty should get out of the intellectual business.*

*That the same goes for a journalist.*

Surprisingly, this philosophical essay drew the largest reader response of any single article in 1953, except for the cover story on Dr. Alfred C. Kinsey, the sex researcher. A number of readers were inspired to offer their own, and some equally long, philosophical commentaries.

The news late in the winter of 1952–53 was, as Luce expressed it in a memo to the editors, "qui-vivish . . . in the sense of 'good' things that might happen." And at this point the editor-in-chief saw nothing about his man in the White House to criticize: "Nearly everyone seems to agree that he [Eisenhower] has made a good start."

At the end of the President's first month in office *Time* summed up: "All in all—for better or worse, Ike Eisenhower had boldly taken the wheel and steered the U.S. back toward the promised middle of the road, like a man who knows exactly where he is going, and why." But shortly thereafter *Time* made the discovery that "the Administration was getting nowhere," and advised: "It was high time for Ike to get moving."

Eisenhower's performance on the world stage, where he was expected to shine, had so far been less than dynamic. In March 1953 Stalin died and, as *Time* said, "history had reached a crossroad, and . . . it was imperative for the U.S. Government to restate its direction in foreign policy." When no restatement was forthcoming, *Time* did manage its apologist's role: "The President would not be hurried; he wanted Stalin's successors to show their hand first." But *Life* was frankly impatient. Here was "a unique chance for effective action," an opportunity to exploit weaknesses that might appear in the transfer of power.

In April *Life* began publication of a four-part series, "The Ghastly

369

Secrets of Stalin's Power," by a Communist defector, NKVD General Alexander Orlov, and in an editor's introduction pointed out that "the Russian system, which cannot exist without the concentration of absolute power in one man, is again being put to the test as it was when Stalin wrested control of the Soviets from Trotsky." [3] The implication again was that the President, by being overly cautious, was letting opportunities slide. When shortly thereafter Eisenhower responded to peace feelers put out by the new Soviet regime, challenging it to demonstrate its sincerity by positive action, *Life* muted its criticism. The President, *Life* said, had "seized the initiative from Moscow and given the sacred word 'peace' an American definition.

But this applause from Time Inc. was cut short. In July the President ended the Korean war, as he had promised in his campaign he would, but with an armistice that was not at all to the liking of *Time*'s managing editor Alexander and his assistant, Fuerbringer. They wanted a conclusive end to that imbroglio that would give some promise of future peace in Asia. That had also once been Luce's idea. On an excursion to the Far East after the election he had met General James A. Van Fleet, the U.N. commander, who had convinced him that if the administration would give him additional troops he could take the offensive and "destroy" the Communists.[4] Such an offensive would involve casualties—40,000 was Van Fleet's private estimate—but better 40,000 casualties, he argued, than a long war of attrition such as then seemed inevitable because of the stalled truce negotiations. Van Fleet's basic argument was summed up in the unanswered question of a frustrated field commander: "Why, when we can annihilate [the enemy] if we want to—why, when Korea is so much more favorable a battleground for us than for them, are so many of us [Americans] for peace at any price?" Unlike MacArthur, Van Fleet did not envisage re-establishing Korea's historic border,

---

[3] As a member of the Soviet secret police, Orlov had been an inside witness to Stalin's destruction of his opponents and his articles were mainly concerned with the purges of the thirties. Orlov had also been an NKVD operative in the Spanish Civil War and was blamed by some veterans of the American volunteer Abraham Lincoln Brigade for the execution of some of their comrades. Because of this, Orlov lived in fear of both Russian and American Communists. He and his wife hid away in a Bronx apartment, avoiding all contact with their neighbors. Even after selling his memoirs to *Life*, Orlov was so fearful of revealing his identity that the only man on the staff he would deal with was managing editor Thompson.

[4] Wryly, Luce noted after his return from Korea that the word "destroy" sounded "much more startling in a New York restaurant than in Seoul."

the Yalu River, but rather establishing a new border about twenty miles north of Pyongyang, territory which would embrace about 90 percent of all Koreans and which Van Fleet felt could be defended by the U.S.-trained ROK forces.

In its issue of January 26, 1953, *Time,* in an article entitled "A Will & a Way," had proposed Van Fleet's course of action (without attribution to the general); when Van Fleet retired, *Life* invited him to write a series of articles on the Korean war. These appeared in May 1953 just before the conclusion of the armistice, by which time the Van Fleet proposals had apparently been weighed and rejected by the Eisenhower Administration.

*Time* called the July armistice "neither victory nor defeat . . . stalemate without killing [which] could be accepted but not celebrated . . . stalemate produced by a paralysis of wills at political levels." The article ended with a warning: "If the U.S. and its allies develop no more will and purpose than they showed in the Korean war, then further costly stalemate is the best that can result."

Luce, writing from Rome, did not agree. "The Korean Truce has been settled on as good terms as the situation which prevailed when [Eisenhower] took over permitted," he told his editors. He continued to defend Eisenhower. When he proposed substantial reductions in the defense budget, and Billings sent him a note that "Eisenhower's cuts . . . have us worried," he replied: "I cannot help but feel that [for] $40 or $50 billions . . . you should get quite a lot of defense. . . . I, for one, have lost faith in the Defense Department. I do sincerely feel that for various reasons which have developed over the years, *Time-Life* editors are too much biased in favor of The Services. . . . I think the Pentagon . . . has not only been guilty of bad policy decisions, but I have no doubt they have wasted more billions of the taxpayers' money than all the departments of the U.S. government put together since George Washington. . . . A little economic austerity wouldn't hurt The Services—and especially the Air Force. Repeat to our air-minded colleagues: especially the Air Force."

*Time* let Eisenhower make his own evaluation of his first six months in office. Replying to reporters, the President had called his approach to problems "gradualism." With the Republican Party divided in its thinking, his job, he said, was "not to create friction, not to accentuate differences, but to bring people together." But neither Eisenhower nor Luce could persuade the editors that he deserved very high marks. *Fortune's* managing editor Donovan told Luce, "We gave him approximately B-minus." In an August editorial *Fortune* commented that the administration "looked less effective in those areas where Ike was supposed to be best qualified—military preparedness and foreign relations. . . . Sensible in principle was Secretary [of Defense Charles E.] Wilson's determination to find economies in the defense budget. Whether he had found the right economies was something else again: Wilson had not succeeded in convincing the country that he knew exactly what he was doing, particularly with respect to the Air Force."

Luce's thoughts by now were reaching out in another direction. He became convinced that the strong military bias of American foreign policy needed to be balanced by an economic policy that would stimulate world trade, particularly by a drastic reduction in the American tariff. Soon after he took office, Eisenhower had appointed a commission to review American trade policies under the chairmanship of Clarence Randall, former head of Inland Steel Company. The Randall Commission had now come up with a report that *Life,* in an editorial, called "fuzzy and undramatic."

Disappointed, Luce prodded his editors to take up the cause, writing to Billings: "In Eisenhower's comprehensive and impressive 1954 program, one big thing is missing—just as if he had dressed up in white tie and tails and top hat but one of his trouser-legs was missing. The missing trouser-leg is World Economic Policy." Billings replied: "The brethren, as you call them, are all interested in the problem and, by and large . . . agree with your general premise—yes, it 'makes sense.' But they are by no means agreed among themselves as to ways and means. . . . Jack [Jessup] is for total world trade whereas Max [Ways] sees regional free trade areas as the desirable first step—to get Europe trading freely among itself before you try to integrate it with the U.S. economy."

Luce found all this rather frustrating; he commented to Grover that beside the new magazine on sports, the one thing on his mind was world economic policy, but

since I seem to be almost, not quite, the only person I know who is heated up on this subject, the presumption is I am somehow crazy. It is not like China—because in that case my feeling was . . . nobody knew or cared a bloody thing about China except the Communists and a few old China hands. . . .

BUT—a hell of a lot of people know about Economics and practically all of them know more than I do. So I have that odd feeling that everybody is being a damn fool except me!

As Vice President in charge of me (and other problems) you must give this matter a Top Priority. Object: to quiet me down on this subject. Or join the crusade yourself. I hope the former— because God knows I don't want any more crusades. I should like to devote myself to the golfing aspects of the Eisenhower Administration.

When Luce in April 1954 attempted personally to do some lobbying for tariff reform in Washington, he found he could rouse little enthusiasm, and he was particularly disappointed in the negative attitude of his friend, the Secretary of State. He told Dulles that while he agreed that "there is little intensity of feeling on this subject . . . there cannot be until you and the President show that *you* consider it of the very greatest importance." When in June, bowing to an adamant protectionist faction, the administration withdrew even the half-hearted measures proposed by the Randall Commission, *Time* called the action "one of the worst failures of the Eisenhower Administration."

Dien Bien Phu fell to the Communists in May 1954, and with the subsequent Geneva Agreement in July, temporarily bringing to an end seven and a half years of fighting in Indochina, Time Inc.'s editors came to what was probably the lowest point in their dejection over the Eisenhower Administration. For four years, under Truman and Eisenhower, the United States had been giving economic aid and military supplies to the anti-Communist forces in Indochina. Like many others, Time Inc.'s editors had considered it essential that southeast Asia be kept out of the hands of the Communists—even though this meant supporting the French power there. ("Almost the last example," as *Time* had put it, "of white man's armed imperialism in Asia.") *Time*, in other words, accepted the situation as one of *Realpolitik,* while deploring France's presence there and meanwhile finding little to applaud in France's military performance.

*Life,* in 1953, made a troubling contribution to the bitter story of the war. The magazine had sent David Douglas Duncan to Viet Nam in April, and after three weeks at the front he cabled managing editor Thompson that the war was "a hopeless quagmire, sucking men and money out of sight, and may prove fatal unless we face the issue squarely. . . . All Hanoi bets are against us sounding off since apparently they cannot get [the truth] printed . . . because it seems anyone who sounds off gets tagged as a Commie." Thompson responded, "I think you have a hell of a nerve sounding off at this point about betting what we wouldn't print."

After eight weeks in Viet Nam Duncan arrived back in New York with his pictures and his story, the point of which was that the French were fighting badly and the war was all but lost. Thompson was away on vacation; assistants felt that Duncan was too hard on the French, but he had been in Viet Nam and they had not. The story ran, along with an editorial pointing out that since Duncan had left Viet Nam the French had changed command and all was not yet lost; the editorial in no wise lessened the impact that Duncan's story had in France. Diplomatic protests were made in Washington. From the White House Jackson wrote to Billings that the French were "in a tizzier tizzy than I have seen them in for a long time. I have also been shown confidentially some communications from the Foreign Office in Paris which reveal an abnormally great degree of hurt and rage." Billings was prepared to accept the French reaction philosophically. "I suppose all our dealings with the touchy French are subject to such uproars," he wrote to Luce, "and we must get accustomed to them." Not so the editor-in-chief. To him Duncan's story was "a monstrous piece of mistiming" (the French had begun offensive action with some success), and he cabled Billings to put Duncan "on the inactive list until such time as Thompson and I can come to a full understanding as to his future activities"—a rare kind of order from Luce.

Thompson, back in the office, immediately protested. "The managing editor should be held completely responsible," he said. He added that Duncan was "quite contrite" and now understood "that it is no out for *Life* to say 'it's under Duncan's by-line so anything he reports goes.'" At that time Duncan's home was Rome, where he kept an apartment, and he was headed there for a brief vacation. Luce invited him to the embassy residence where they held two long conversations. Duncan reported afterward to Thompson: "He wanted to make two points clear. The first was that my story was untimely. I added, 'True, but untimely?' and, I believe, his was an affirmative nod. The second was that I must get along with you. [I replied] that

374

my prime responsibility was to report each story as I saw it. . . . He mentioned that it was, of course, the editors' problem to establish and maintain top policy. . . . The second meeting ended . . . I believe, with fuller understanding having been reached between the two of us." Luce cabled Thompson tersely: "Encounter with Duncan ended satisfactorily—he has not—repeat not—fired me yet."

Subsequently *Life* made an effort to assuage French opinion by publishing an article by Donald R. Heath, U.S. ambassador in Saigon. It could be summed up by its headline: "France Is Fighting the Good Fight."

As the war continued on its inconclusive way, becoming more and more unpopular with the French at home, the Time Inc. editors applauded an Eisenhower statement early in 1954 in which the President reaffirmed his belief in the importance of the Indochinese front, the statement in which he first put forward "the domino theory." ("You have a row of dominoes set up, you knock over the first one, and what will happen to the last one is the certainty that it will go over very quickly. So you could have a beginning of disintegration [in Southeast Asia] and that would have the most profound influences.") But in mid-summer came the Geneva Agreement partitioning Viet Nam along the seventeenth parallel and scheduling reunification elections in two years, to which the United States acquiesced although it did not sign the treaty. *Time* saw this outcome as appeasement and a "Republican failure to free foreign policy from the paralyzing, defensive spirit in which the Democratic Administration was caught," and *Life* said bluntly: "The Eisenhower foreign policy has proved virtually as ill-starred as Roosevelt's and Truman's."

Photographer Robert Capa had flown off to Viet Nam in April 1954 on a temporary assignment from *Life*. He had lived a charmed life through the Spanish Civil War and World War II, then had left the *Life* staff to set up the cooperative picture agency, Magnum Photos Inc. He stayed clear of the Korean war. "I am very happy to be an unemployed war photographer," he said, "and I hope to stay unemployed as a war photographer till the end of my life." He was in Tokyo for Magnum when Thompson appealed to him to fill in for a month in Viet Nam in the unexpected absence of staff photographer Howard Sochurek. War, which Capa once likened to an aging actress ("more and more dangerous and less and less photogenic"), seduced him again. He went off in high spirits. When he found his fellow journalists in Hanoi griping about the censorship, he chided them: "You guys . . . don't appreciate that this is a reporter's war. Nobody knows anything and nobody tells you anything, and that means a good reporter can go out and get a beat every day." With *Time* correspondent John Mecklin, Capa set out one morning with a French mechanized task force. "This is going to be a beautiful story," he told Mecklin. "I shall be on my good behavior today. I shall not insult people and I shall not even mention the excellence of my work." When the column came to a halt at the report of a Viet Minh ambush ahead, he decided to go forward on his own, telling his companion to "look for me when you get started." A few minutes later there was an explosion, and a French soldier returned to the column to report, *"Le photographe est mort."* They found Capa's body beside a hole blasted out by a land mine. The French awarded him the Croix de Guerre with palm and shipped his body home with full military honors.[5] He was forty years old, the first U.S. newsman killed in Indochina.

The Geneva Agreement called for "a reappraisal" of foreign policy, said Luce. A group of the senior editors were assigned to examine various aspects of American policy. Billings found the exercise futile: "I have been through the labyrinth a number of times," he wrote. "By the time you finish threading your way backward and forward, you often come out on a world scene which has materially changed since you began your study, and your conclusions have less relevance than you had hoped." But what the reappraisal did reveal was that many of the Time Inc. editors were even more disappointed with the Eisenhower-Dulles conduct of foreign affairs than was indicated by the criticisms in the magazines. There were exceptions. Hedley Donovan felt that the editors of *Time* and *Life* had gone too far in blaming France and Britain for the outcome at Geneva. *Time*'s Max Ways felt that the public had an inordinate appetite for crises to which the magazines, as did all the other media, catered. "Repugnant as the task may be from the viewpoint of 'normal' journalism, I think we have got to make more of an effort to build the framework of discussion as distinguished from reporting the news," he wrote.

[5] As a memorial to Capa *Life* created the Robert Capa Medal, which is awarded by the Overseas Press Club for journalistic photography of excellence involving extreme personal danger.

"Let us not delude ourselves that we are, under present circumstances, contributing much merely by tossing our weekly pitchfork of high-grade hay into the variant winds."

Luce, for his part, suggested a moratorium on editorial criticism of the administration's foreign policy until Eisenhower and Dulles had had time to formulate a new program that would "make the U.S. feel less frustrated"; if this was not forthcoming by, say, January 1955, then the editors would have to speak out. Meanwhile there was "plenty of extremely difficult plain reporting to do." The moratorium did not extend to domestic affairs.

Luce and his editors had been confident that Eisenhower would cut Senator Joe McCarthy down to size. Early in the new administration, when McCarthy sent his aides, Roy Cohn and Gerard David Schine, scurrying through Europe sniffing out subversive books in the U.S. Information Service libraries, *Time* was inclined to treat the whole thing as a farce under the derisive headline, "Schnuffles & Flourishes." [6] But in June *Time* devoted the equivalent of four columns to a striking phenomenon:

> Abroad, among its strongest allies, public discussion of the U.S. is almost monopolized by McCarthyism. . . .
> [But] the European myth of McCarthyism . . . itself was first pumped up in the U.S., and in the U.S. today McCarthyism is more myth than man—but not the less dangerous for that.

The myth—in *Time*'s view—"was not created by parthenogenesis. It was busily fertilized not only by McCarthy, but by one notable group of McCarthy's enemies: the apologists for the New and Fair Deals," who, by trying to divert attention from past Communist infiltration of the government, "began to construct the myth of McCarthy's great power and his menace to liberty. . . . President Eisenhower will have to deal again and again with McCarthyism, which is a major liability to [his] foreign policy, his domestic policy and his party."

The President, however, continued to ignore McCarthy and McCarthyism, and the senator had waxed in insolence and arrogance; his popularity rose to a new high in the opinion polls. In November 1953 the administration paid a price for its silence when McCarthy

[6] A German paper called the pair *Schnüffler* (snoopers).

turned on the White House itself. He accused the administration of being soft on Communism and boasted that he, McCarthy, would be the issue in next year's congressional elections.

Time Incer C. D. Jackson tried to persuade his associates on the President's staff and Eisenhower himself to strike back, going so far as to draft a militant statement slapping the senator down. "The President read my text with great irritation," Jackson noted, "slammed it back at me and said he would not refer to McCarthy personally—'I will not get in the gutter with that guy.' " Instead the President issued a mildly reproving statement which McCarthy shrugged off contemptuously.

From January to June 1954 McCarthy all but monopolized the headlines with his "investigation" of the U.S. Army; the index for *Time* during the first six months of 1954 shows a third as many entries for Senator McCarthy as for the President, including three cover stories—on McCarthy, on his aides Cohn and Schine, and on Ray Jenkins, the counsel to the Senate investigating committee. The cover story on McCarthy, written by Henry Luce III, concluded:

> McCarthy will be around for a while. Opportunity keeps knocking, and McCarthy, the opportunist, will be there to fling wide the door.
>
> On his office wall, a framed anonymous quotation says: "Oh, God, don't let me weaken. Help me to continue on. And when I go down, let me go down like an oak tree felled by a woodsman's ax."
>
> The ax that will cut down McCarthy's power will have to be a lot sharper than those in the hands of Stevens & Co. [Secretary of the Army Robert T. Stevens, who was then bearing the brunt of McCarthy's attack] last week. That mighty oak must be approached with caution; it is covered with *Toxicodendron radicans,* i.e., poison ivy.

In Rome, meanwhile, Hank Luce's father recorded an encounter which bears witness to the passions McCarthy aroused. He reported the incident in a letter to Billings, "because it has a bearing on Topic A—McCarthy":

> Arrived here a few days ago Mr. and Mrs. T. S. Lamont and Mr. and Mrs. Paul Cabot. Between them, as you know, they are practically Mr. and Mrs. Harvard. . . . We had them to lunch

at the Villa Taverna [7]—an extremely pleasant occasion.

Then last night I went to a small dinner for them at a restaurant and Cabot and I found each other at the end of a table. We got into a hell of an argumentative fight. Without giving a blow-by-blow account, some of the items were: Cabot thinks Dean Acheson one of the greatest of all U.S. Secretaries; he also thinks Hiss is probably innocent and, of course like other Harvard characters, he is hysterical about McCarthy—"the end of U.S. liberty."

I was very rude—said that what annoyed me most in the U.S. was not Commies but these Park Avenue and Cambridge muddleheads. I guess I got pretty offensive. You can imagine the argument.

After an hour of hammer-and-tongs, we came to sort of a gentlemanly agreement. But—what the hell—it's when I run into a Paul Cabot that I almost become pro-McCarthy. You know—it takes a Capitalist to make one feel like a Communist and one is never so Capitalist as after an encounter with a Socialist!

You better show this to Roy [Larsen].[8] Oh!—Cabot at one point accused me of being a worse menace than McCarthy and thanked God that he was sure Roy Larsen was okay. He credits Larsen with maintaining a true Crimson liberalism in Time Inc. My compliments to Roy!

Why do I bother you except as a means of upchucking my nausea? Because—and I guess all our serious brethren will agree—we still have a two-front war on our hands: one against McCarthy, one against that complacent upper-class Achesonianism. Our task: to walk the middle ground with an equanimity *not* displayed by me. . . .

Years later, looking back on the Eisenhower years, *Time's* editor-in-chief likened the McCarthy episode to a "bad dream" and wrote: "Ike presented himself to his critics as a sitting duck. Should not the President have denounced with righteous anger this vulgar and uncouth disturber of the peace? Certainly he should have. *But* Ike, I think, had a way of thinking that irrational nightmares go away. And this one did." In December 1954 the Senate formally condemned

---

[7] The embassy residence.
[8] Harvard '21, like Paul Cabot and T. S. Lamont.

McCarthy for his defiance of that body's rules of conduct, which had "tended to bring the Senate into dishonor and disrepute." The senator was never the same man afterward. In reporting his death in May 1957 *Time* commented on his last years: "A new kind of quietude shrouded his life. He was lonely and plainly beaten."

The trauma of McCarthyism in 1954 was compounded by the case of J. Robert Oppenheimer which, like McCarthyism, left scars on the American body politic not yet fully healed. In May 1953 a *Fortune* article had raised some disquieting, and controversial, questions about Oppenheimer. The article, by Charles J. V. Murphy, was entitled "The Hidden Struggle for the H-Bomb: The Story of Dr. Oppenheimer's Persistent Campaign to Reverse U.S. Military Strategy." Murphy had just returned from active duty with the Air Force chief of staff. He charged that Oppenheimer, known as "the father of the atomic bomb," an advisor to the Atomic Energy Commission, was attempting to use his influence to the detriment of military policy and the nation's security through his opposition to the development of thermonuclear weapons. After President Truman's decision to go ahead with the H-bomb, and before the first thermonuclear device had been exploded, Oppenheimer had organized the ZORC group (so named for the initials of the scientists who comprised it),[9] whose purpose was to push for the conclusions of the Lincoln Summer Study and thus lessen American dependence on the Strategic Air Force and on nuclear weapons. The study, which researched the problems of coping with an atomic attack, recommended a vast early-warning network and other accoutrements of a defensive nature. The National Security Council rejected the Lincoln Study, and as a result, said Murphy, "the development of thermonuclear and fission weapons continues apace. And SAC . . . retains its mighty mission."

Oppenheimer and many scientists, particularly those in the ZORC group, were furious with *Fortune*. But the squall over Oppenheimer subsided until, in April 1954, the New York *Times* broke the news that the scientist had been suspended in December from his position with the AEC as a security risk and that he was under investigation by a special panel headed by Gordon Gray, president of the University of North Carolina. After eight weeks of closed-door hearings,

[9] Jerrold Zacharias, Robert Oppenheimer, I. I. Rabi, Charles Lauritsen.

which established Oppenheimer's onetime association with a number of Communist sympathizers, the panel, by a vote of two to one, absolved him of any charges of disloyalty but denied him access to classified material as a security risk. By a vote of four to one the AEC, under the chairmanship of Rear Admiral Lewis Strauss, confirmed the judgment of the panel.

The arguments that ensued were exceedingly bitter. In a *Harper's* magazine article the Washington columnists Joseph and Stewart Alsop proclaimed Oppenheimer "an American Dreyfus," the victim of personal spite on the part of Admiral Strauss. Coincidentally, two Time Inc. reporters, James R. Shepley, chief of the Washington bureau, and Clay Blair, Jr., who covered the Pentagon, published *The Hydrogen Bomb*, a book on the origin and development of thermonuclear weapons.[10] The book could be criticized as an oversimplified narrative of complex events, which gave it a color of partisanship. It included a detailed account of Oppenheimer's opposition to the hydrogen bomb and focused public attention on Dr. Edward Teller, the brilliant Hungarian-born scientist whose "flash of genius" in 1951 had made thermonuclear fusion possible. It recounted how Teller and Oppenheimer in 1945 had co-authored a scientific paper that confirmed the feasibility of a hydrogen bomb and how Teller, after the explosion of the first Soviet atomic bomb, had tried to mobilize his fellow scientists for immediate development of the H-bomb. Teller's recommendation, however, had been turned down by the Atomic Energy Commission Advisory Committee under chairman Oppenheimer. After Truman decided to go ahead, Teller was named to head a new atomic laboratory at Livermore, California. The competition from Livermore was—according to the authors—responsible for spurring the scientists at the original Los Alamos laboratory into work that finally produced a "droppable H-bomb." *Time* reviewed the book and the controversy in an article that the editors felt was a calm reappraisal of the whole affair:

> Certain journalists have said that the book . . . is part of an anti-intellectual wave that is making it impossible for scientists to work for the Government of the U.S.
>
> Such a conflict would be even more serious than the H-bomb delay. For if the U.S. cannot continue to enlist the support of

[10] David McKay Company, 1954.

science, if it cannot solve the critical problems of the relationship between the national interest and the pursuit of knowledge, then the U.S. will not survive—and will not deserve to survive. . . .

By far the most violent and sustained attack on the book comes from the brothers Alsop, Joseph and Stewart. Their columns in papers throughout the land have carried this sensational piece of news: "Before very long, the Eisenhower Administration is likely to have to answer a short, highly practical question: 'Do we really need scientists, or can we just make do with Lewis Strauss?' " They think that Strauss must go because he confirmed the verdict of the Gordon Gray board which withdrew Oppenheimer's security clearance—although neither the board nor Strauss reflected on Oppenheimer's loyalty. . . .

They said [that the case against Oppenheimer] was a plot, and they showed no reticence about describing the motives of the anti-Oppenheimer plotters. Air Force "zealots" knew—or rather "smelled"—Oppenheimer's opposition to the doctrine of defense centering on strategic air-atomic striking power. These men knew that he was "vulnerable" because of his past Communist associations, so they decreed his demise. . . .

But this theory of anti-Oppenheimer motive will not account for Admiral Strauss, no Air Force "zealot." The Alsops supply Strauss with a far baser motive than zealotry. It seems—and this will surprise hundreds of his business, official and intellectual acquaintances—that Strauss is an incredibly vain, arrogant and vengeful man. Years ago, Oppenheimer had the misfortune to humiliate Strauss in an argument about isotopes, say the Alsops, and Strauss never forgot.

The Alsops also compare the Oppenheimer hearings with the Dreyfus case. There are differences. Oppenheimer's chief "judge" was Gordon Gray of North Carolina, one of the five or ten university presidents in the U.S. most respected by the academic community of the nation. The procedure of the Gray board was scrupulous, and most of the weighty testimony against Oppenheimer came out of his own mouth.

Dreyfus was legally lynched by perjured and forged testimony sustained by a group of reactionary pinheads. There is no dirtier thing that could be said of Lewis Strauss than that he set up a Dreyfus case. . . .

The struggles related in *The Hydrogen Bomb* took place in

382

a Government (and in a nation) that was confused about its own strategic situation and unclear about its aims. A determined pressure group can play havoc in such a situation. To relate the story of how one such pressure group almost did, is not to set up a conflict of science *v.* the state. It is to warn that feeble top leadership can lead even the mo؛ powerful nations into moral danger.

Not the least of the editors' disappointment with the Eisenhower Administration so far was what it felt was the President's failure to assert the power of the White House against the party's conservative old guard. *Life* had carried a major article on the disarray of the party's ranks under the headline: "Is the Republican Party Trying to Commit Suicide?" *Time* had told virtually the same story under the well-worn head, "The Mess in Washington." In Luce's judgment Eisenhower's best opportunity to redeem the party's position was to focus attention on the world scene and in August 1954 he respectfully told him so: "At this moment only ,a very small fraction of the energy of the American people is directed to overcoming the world crisis. It is my belief that the people will follow your leadership in putting much more of their energies into this job. They are waiting for a signal. So are we here at Time Inc." Eisenhower's reply was cordial: "Probably because I live in an atmosphere of daily—if not hourly—crisis, I tend to forget the obvious fact that the nation as a whole does not share the sense of urgency that so many of us feel. For all you do to keep the people informed I am grateful."

The off-year elections that November caused little surprise. While Eisenhower continued to enjoy personal popularity, he could not transfer it to Republican congressional candidates. He said he was campaigning hard but the effect was not palpable. Republicans were reduced to a minority party in both houses. *Life* was resigned and philosophic: "Eisenhower . . . must now attempt to run a coalition government. . . . Yet that is exactly what Eisenhower's whole experience has fitted him to do."

At Christmastime, however, Luce and his editors took a considered view of world affairs. There appeared to be a substantial improvement in the free world's position following the Geneva Conference on Indochina; the NATO alliance was strengthened by the admission of West Germany; the crumbling defenses of Southeast Asia were shored up by SEATO; and there was a new hopeful climate in the Middle East. In the light of all this *Time* even felt justified in making

Dulles Man of the Year for 1954. On the horizon was a forthcoming top-level meeting on disarmament—the Geneva summit conference of 1955—and while the editors were not too sanguine about the chances for any important agreements with Soviet Russia, the article said that the chances "are less dark than they were before a practical missionary of Christian politics [i.e., Dulles] began his extraordinary year."

With the end of December 1954 editorial director John Shaw Billings' name disappeared from the masthead of the magazines. He had been physically absent from the office since May, when by arrangement with Luce, he took a long leave with what Luce called "a blank check" to return to his post or to any other post of his choosing "to do as much or as little as [he] liked—or *niente*." Primarily, Billings' retirement was due to the fact that his wife's health was such that she could no longer stand the stress of New York living—which Billings himself detested—and his desire to spend the rest of his days on his plantation in South Carolina. But he also told Luce in a farewell letter that he felt himself becoming "a silly old figurehead" (at fifty-eight) whose views were ignored and whose advice went unsought by a younger generation of editors. Billings' feelings would certainly have come as a shock to his younger editorial colleagues; they held him in undiminished respect, second only to Luce himself. In the later years, if they bypassed him, it was because Billings in his role of editorial director seemed more and more to withdraw from active participation in the day-to-day issues, content to be Luce's deputy and leave the initiative to others. Billings was at his best when he was on the bridge—as managing editor of *Time*, as the man who succeeded in translating a journalistic idea into a magazine as managing editor of *Life*. On his retirement Luce wrote to the staff:

> That Billings is a master of the art of journalism is acknowledged by every fellow professional who ever worked with him. That his craftsmanship was matched and guided by an unwavering sense of principle will be remembered by the senior personnel of Time Inc. who went to him so often for guidance on so many matters, big and small. And all who worked with him will understand that it is impossible to speak of John Shaw Billings . . . except in terms of friendship and personal respect. . . . Billings was a touchstone of good journalism and sound principle.

384

# *Brinkmanship*

I N JANUARY 1955 fresh winds of crisis began blowing out of Asia. Since September 1954 the Chinese Communists has been sporadically shelling the offshore islands of Quemoy and Matsu; now they began to make threatening moves that seemed to portend an invasion of these islands and of Formosa itself. As the headlines got bigger, Eisenhower, in response to press conference questions, appeared to imply that he would welcome a move by the U.N. to sponsor a cease-fire. From Hong Kong John Osborne, who had returned to the Far East as the *Time-Life* senior correspondent in 1953, cabled that the President's remarks had had a devastating effect on Nationalist morale. Luce sent Osborne's cable to Eisenhower, who was preparing to ask the Congress to pass a resolution authorizing him to take such steps as he deemed necessary to defend Formosa. The President wrote Luce:

Thank you for your note and for the dispatch that accompanied it. Foster tells me that he has already talked to you on this matter and you know our general attitude.

The documents that I am today sending to the Congress establish beyond a doubt the seriousness of the view we take toward continued Communist attacks and our readiness to meet the issue head-on.

385

At the moment there seems to be a great deal of misunderstanding about the effect of a "cease-fire." The Communists
with their continental bases and power of concentrating when
and where they choose have a tremendous advantage over any
small island-based air force. Moreover, as long as actual fighting
persists anywhere, there is always the danger that some hot
bullet will hit a powder keg.

In the meantime, we are acting in cooperation with the Chinese Nationalists; we are not trying to dominate them. We are
certainly not trying to force upon them any action of any kind
that they would deem of serious damage to their political or
military position.

Luce replied that he felt reassured and in passing offered an explanation of why he had forwarded Osborne's cable:

You have told me how, in your proper theory of democratic
government, you counted on editors among others to perform
an educational task. We try to do that—although of course
never as well as we should. But in foreign affairs, as distinct from
domestic affairs, I have often noted that whereas the press, or
any given journal, can effectively *support* a strong position taken
by the President, it is usually not effective in advocating a
stronger position than the President takes. Thus, for example,
there was almost 100 percent support for Truman's police action in Korea, but if Truman had not taken that action, few
would have urged him to. He would have been heavily attacked
for "loss of Korea" but there would have been little advocacy
of positive action. Such perhaps is the "irresponsibility" or
"buck-passing" or timidity of the profession to which I am devoted.[1]

[1] In August 1955 Luce had his own idea for a peaceful settlement of
"the China question," which he tried out in a letter to C. D. Jackson. He
proposed that the United States send to China "the strongest Economic Mission
ever assembled," that would have in mind the expenditure by the United
States in China of $20 billion over a period of ten years to improve living
standards. In its first year the mission would study how the objective could
best be achieved; in its second it would seek to work out a compromise
compatible with Chinese Communist ideas. Coincidentally the Chinese would
be invited to convoke a political convention, one-half of the delegates to
be selected by the Communists, one-quarter by the Kuomintang, and the other
quarter selected or elected under U.N. auspices, representing the Chinese
overseas and at home who declared themselves independent of both parties.

As spring gave way to summer, most of the world outside of Asia enjoyed an unusual respite from crises, and a mood of relaxation took over, capped by the summit meeting of the Big Four (Bulganin, Eden, Faure and Eisenhower) at Geneva. The mood was reflected in the news columns. The files in the Time Inc. archives show an unusual dearth of problem papers. The summit, held in July, was viewed by both *Time* and *Life* as a triumph for Eisenhower; his "open skies" proposal and his general demeanor as the leader of the free world meant, said a *Life* editorial, that "the championship of peace has changed hands," a judgment that at the same time was tempered by the warning that the meeting was "a beginning, not an end, [and that] the far-famed 'relaxation of tensions,' achieved without a single meaningful agreement, means simply this: that the West can now proceed more confidently to make the world freer and safer, by means old and new."

The euphoric mood in the United States was punctured in September by the flash from Denver telling of Eisenhower's heart attack. The story in *Time,* even as his first term was drawing to a close, read like his political obituary: "Last week, before his heart attack, the weight of informed opinion was heavily estimating that he would run [again.] This week, even if his recovery is as rapid and thorough as possible, the balance swung toward the strong probability that he would not." With uncertainty about Eisenhower's candidacy, interest in the Democratic nomination perked up; Adlai Stevenson declared himself in November and was challenged by New York Governor Averell Harriman and the ever hopeful Senator Estes Kefauver.

"I do not see what the Democrats have got—or can get," Luce wrote from Rome, "that faintly compares with what the Republicans had in 1952. But then the Republicans talk as if they didn't have anything except Eisenhower. That being the case, even Eisenhower might be beaten unless he remembers and understands why he got elected in the first place. It wasn't just his smile."

The good will of the Geneva summit had since evaporated, the cold war was colder than ever, and even as Luce wrote, the Democrats were making an issue of foreign policy. Stevenson was making

---

Luce's concern was that Communist efforts to industrialize China overnight would so over-strain food resources that terrible famine might result. He wanted to avert "a great human disaster."

speeches saying that the world situation was "more perilous than it has been since Korea." It was a promising line of attack because, with Eisenhower out of action, the administration seemed to be drifting on the tide of events. When Dulles tried to silence his critics by arguing that foreign policy should not be the subject of political debate, he was roundly rebuked by the pundits, including the editors of *Time*. They quoted the New York *Times*'s Arthur Krock, who had pointed out that if foreign policy were eliminated from the campaign debate it would deprive the Republicans of their best asset: that Eisenhower had kept the country out of war.

In its January 16, 1956, issue, with the intention of giving the administration a helping hand in this debate, *Life* inadvertently laid Dulles wide open to his enemies; it did it in the article which was announced on the cover with the blurb: "Three Times at Brink of War: How Dulles Gambled and Won." The author was Jim Shepley, who had first suggested shortly after the Geneva Conference an article to show how "international lawyer Dulles guides his able client Ike through the intricacies of grand diplomacy." The editors were not interested at that time, but when Shepley suggested the article again in November he was told to go ahead.

Dulles' direction of U.S. foreign affairs [Shepley wrote] is under attack these days as the presidential election year gets under way. The new information made available to this writer, however, bulwarks the substantial case to be made for Dulles, a case that until now has not been made as strongly as it could because important sections of the record could not be made public.

The article was based on a tape-recorded interview that Dulles had given to three members of the Time Inc. staff: Charles J. V. Murphy, who was then at work on a series of *Fortune* articles reviewing the record of the Eisenhower Administration and who had arranged for the interview; John R. Beal, who covered the State Department and who was writing a biography of Dulles; and Shepley, who had asked to be included. The Secretary of State received them at home and talked freely because it was his understanding that whatever he said was for background only; if any quotations were used, they must first be checked with his office, a requirement that *Life* complied with.

The article began by describing how Dulles had been awakened at two in the morning of June 18, 1953, by a message from Korea that Syngman Rhee had unaccountably freed the North Korean prisoners of war, thus removing a prime reason for the Communists to discuss an armistice:

> And at that moment, as his fully aroused mind shook off the fog of sleep, Dulles saw himself and the nation standing on the brink of a new war. It was the first of three times during the Eisenhower Administration when the U.S. was brought perilously close to war—and when the new policy of deterrence instituted by Dulles preserved peace.

The other occasions were in April 1954 just before the fall of Dien Bien Phu and in 1954–55 when "menacing Communist maneuvers" were made against Quemoy and Matsu. Shepley quoted the Secretary of State as saying:

> "You have to take chances for peace, just as you must take chances in war. Some say that we were brought to the verge of war. The ability to get to the verge without getting into the war is the necessary art. If you cannot master it, you inevitably get into war. If you try to run away from it, if you are scared to go to the brink, you are lost. We've had to look it square in the face—on the question of enlarging the Korean war, on the question of getting in the Indo-China war, on the question of Formosa. We walked to the brink and we looked it in the face." [2]

In advance of publication *Life*'s publicity department distributed copies of the article to Washington correspondents, to be released when the magazine appeared on the newsstands two days later. When Dulles was first questioned about the story at his press conference and was reminded that the release was still under embargo, he cut off further comment. With *Life*'s appearance the story hit the morning newspaper front pages. That afternoon Senator Hubert Humphrey, brandishing a copy of the magazine, rose in the Senate to accuse Dulles of distorting history, breaching bipartisanship in an election year and damaging the reputation of the United States before the world. Not yet fully aware of the intensity of the opposition fire, Dulles issued a statement: "The Secretary has now read the *Life*

[2] A year before Shepley's article appeared in *Life, Look,* in February 1955, published an article by Fletcher Knebel of its Washington bureau entitled 'We Nearly Went to War Three Times Last Year—but Ike Said No." The lead sentence read: "Three times within the past ten months, the United States stood on the brink of war with the Communists in the Far East." The article, which did not quote Dulles, passed virtually unnoticed.

article. He feels the statements specifically attributed to him do not require correction from the standpoint of their substance." He also said that he had not reviewed or censored the article. This all but direct confirmation of what *Life* printed spurred on the opposition pack; Stevenson, Harriman, Senators Kefauver, Symington, Sparkman, Fulbright and Mansfield all joined the attack. Eisenhower should repudiate Dulles, said Stevenson, for "play[ing] Russian roulette with the life of our nation." The repercussions were world-wide, said *Time*: "From London to New Delhi, diplomats and editorial writers pounced on Dulles."

The Secretary did little to quiet the clamor by pointing out that a policy of seeking "to prevent war by preventing miscalculation by a potential aggressor" was a national policy expressed explicitly in mutual security treaties ratified by the Senate. James Reston of the New York *Times* wrote: "Mr. Dulles has added something new to the art of diplomatic blundering. This is the planned mistake. He doesn't stumble into booby traps; he digs them to size, studies them carefully, and then jumps."

Luce was much distressed. He wrote to Ed Thompson:

It may be that we have added to the "confusion" we deplore. . . .

The key word in the whole discussion is Peace. The key word of the Shepley-Dulles article was War. War and Peace are two sides of the same coin and if there is one thing which we of Time Inc. have tried consistently to do it is to keep always before our readers the fact that War and Peace are two sides of the same coin. For the most part this is not popular. Peace is, except at brief moments, the vote-getting word. . . . War-mongering is about as bad an epithet as there is. Peace-mongering, which has probably caused much more evil and misery than War-mongering, does not sting as an epithet.

One of the aspects of Dulles' greatness is that over the years . . . he has kept to the fore the relatedness of War and Peace. And this again was the moral of the Shepley-Dulles article.

The editor-in-chief then attempted to take Dulles off the hook in a public statement. The Secretary had not, he said, cleared the article; while Dulles saw an early draft and checked the quotations, the Secretary had not seen the article in its final version: "Responsibility for the published article, both as to substance and phraseology, be-

longs to the Editors of *Life* and to no others." The use of the word
"brink" in the headlines was unfortunate because it did not reflect
the main emphasis of the article, which was on the administration's
"vigorous pursuit of peace," said Luce. "If anything in our account
of the Secretary's position caused any misunderstanding among our
readers or the public, we heartily regret it. At the same time, we are
bound to say that any fault of ours was furiously compounded by
those who, for the moment, put prejudice or personal advantage
above the best interests of the United States." [3]

The Luce statement had at least the effect of deflecting Democratic fire from Dulles to Time Inc. Paul Butler, chairman of the
Democratic Party, made a familiar charge: "Mr. Luce's attempt to
explain away the shocking remarks of Secretary of State Dulles is
nothing more than a continuation . . . of an editorial policy blindly
dedicated to support of the Eisenhower Administration. . . . The
Luce magazines consistently prove themselves to be house organs
for the Eisenhower Administration and the Republican Party."

From the row a new word was born: brinkmanship, attributed by
some dictionaries to Adlai Stevenson, who himself said that he could
never be sure whether "I read it, or heard it or dreamed it up." [4] On
December 2, 1955, two days before Dulles met with his Time Inc.
interviewers, Stevenson had said in a Miami interview that he did not
like "intemperate statements" such as "massive retaliation," which
"frightened our allies more than our enemies and brought us to the
brink of war in Indo-China and the Formosa Strait." At one point
in the first draft of the Shepley interview, Dulles was quoted as saying, "Some Democrats say that we were brought to the verge of war."
In the course of clearing the draft Dulles suggested deleting the
reference to Democrats. If the passage is read with "Democrats"
reinserted, it appears that Dulles was replying directly to the Stevenson interview and unconsciously echoing Stevenson's own phrase
when he told Shepley, "We walked to the brink."

*   *   *

[3] In 1964 Luce told an interviewer from Princeton University who was
questioning him in connection with the Dulles archives: "They were coming
down on [Dulles] like a ton of bricks . . . and he was pretty upset about
it. . . . I just felt that here was a situation in which he was under very heavy
attack for which he really oughtn't particularly to take the blame."

[4] Quoted in Alfred H. Holt, *Phrase and Word Origins*, rev. ed. (Dover Publications, Inc., 1961), p. 37. The editors of the scholarly *Oxford English Dictionary* in Volume I of *A Supplement* (1972) unequivocally credit Stevenson
with originating *brinkmanship*.

With nerve ends both in Washington and Time Inc.'s offices still vibrating from the Dulles affair, in February 1956 *Fortune* found itself in a row with the President's White House aides. In one of his articles on the Eisenhower Administration, Charles J. V. Murphy described how the President had utilized the National Security Council to develop a so-called new look for the defense establishment in his first year in office. Murphy sent proofs of the article to the White House as a courtesy. Because the article dealt with events in 1953 and was wholly laudatory, he was astonished when Sherman Adams, the President's chief aide, telephoned to say that it violated security and must be changed. For details Murphy turned to the President's special assistant on national security, Dillon Anderson, who asked Murphy if he had been cleared for security. Murphy said he had not been. In that case, said Anderson, he could not discuss the serious and sensitive matters involved in the article.

C. D. Jackson, who by now had returned from his service on the White House staff and was working as Luce's deputy with the managing editors and publishers, talked with James Hagerty, the President's press secretary, who promised to resolve this absurd impasse. At Hagerty's instructions Anderson—flanked by Colonel Andrew Goodpaster, the President's military staff secretary, and Allen Dulles, director of the Central Intelligence Agency and a good friend of Murphy—received Murphy in solemn session. All three of them were agreed, they told him, that the article in its present form would give aid and comfort to the Russians. Murphy asked for specifics. He had written at one point that "the course decided upon by the President in the National Security Council was . . ." This, said the three, would be acceptable if it were changed to "it presently became evident that the course decided upon was . . ." At another point Murphy, in referring to the task forces appointed by the President to explore various alternative strategies, wrote, "their inquiry became known as Operation Solarium—a sunny context for an ice-cold judgment." The three suggested that this read, "for several intense weeks they each developed their case for the competitive strategies." When an exasperated Murphy returned with these and similar changes to New York, he, managing editor Donovan and Jackson agreed that they did not justify calling back an article already off the presses.

But when Jackson called Hagerty to tell him of *Fortune*'s decision, the press secretary said that "the old man" was upset and that if the article appeared without changes the White House would have to say that the magazine had been warned it was violating security and that the head of the CIA agreed it would give aid and comfort to the enemy. By this time Luce had been apprised of the situation. Eisenhower was then at the Georgia estate of Treasury Secretary George Humphrey. Luce tried to reach him there but could not and talked instead to Humphrey, who agreed to take *Fortune*'s case to Eisenhower. When Humphrey called back to say that the President objected to the article in its present form on the grounds that it contained information on the intimate decision-making processes of the President and asked that the changes be made, Luce decided that *Fortune* would have to comply.

After supervising the revisions, Donovan sat down and wrote a protest to Luce and to Jackson:

> As to why I think [your decision] was wrong, I would be glad to hold forth at your convenience. I will only say here that the decision struck me as particularly wrong on a day when we had devoted the M.E. lunch to discussing ways for Time Inc. to do a more searching job on the state of U.S. policy. I am thoroughly confused as to how we do more searching reporting of the national interest if we can also be obliged to change "The President decided" (something everybody knows he decided—three years ago) to "It was decided."

To which Luce wrote an apologetic explanation acknowledging that the article was "excellent and useful" but

> as many a good journalist knows, the "national security" in these recent years is often invoked by bureaucrats, both high and low, for what we may politely call highly subjective reasons. Nevertheless, as an Editor under the crisis regimes of Roosevelt and Truman as well as of Eisenhower, I have always felt that if a Presidential authority insisted that something was contrary to security interests, I was bound, in the last analysis, to yield to his dictum, however arbitrary. I was not able to evade the application of this perhaps mistaken principle in this case.

It was an expensive yielding because not only was the entire run of the issue (some 300,000 copies) off the presses, but 100,000 copies were already in trucks bound for the post office. Washington columnist Drew Pearson got hold of the story and printed an item that did much to further the impression that the Time Inc. magazines, Luce and the Eisenhower Administration were all in the same bed.

Luce was an uneasy bedmate, however; he grew impatient with the Eisenhower Administration and with his old friend the Secretary of State again in early 1956 at their failure to make some effective response to a dramatic development in Moscow.

At the Soviet Union's Twentieth Party Congress in February, Khrushchev had overturned the sacred image of Stalin, revealed him as the murderous dictator he had been and made official the new foreign policy of "peaceful coexistence" with the West. Dulles' first public reaction, in testimony before the Senate Foreign Relations Committee, was that the new Soviet policies were evidence of past failure; but a *Life* editorial pointed out that "the Administration has yet to figure out a response to this new Communist line."

Luce, who was in Rome, wrote a note to Jackson: "I do think that the longer-range interests of the U.S. and of humanity are being jeopardized by the current do-nothingism of the Eisenhower-Dulles Administration. And unless things begin to change I foresee for myself and you a somewhat painful and embarrassing summer." That same night he had dinner with C. Douglas Dillion, U.S. ambassador to France, who was very critical of his boss, the Secretary of State, and he wrote again to Jackson: "Last night, Dillon, in his very mild-mannered way, ticked off the series of boners which J.F.D. has made in the last few months. . . . If we were American patriots *and* Democrats, we could make such a case against J.F.D. as would really raise the roof. But what is our position? Perhaps more than any other editors we combine two things: 1) commitment to Ike-Dulles and 2) responsible concern for foreign policy. . . . We may have to blow the whistle. Before I do that *I* will have to have a heart-to-heart [talk] with our two friends. Meanwhile you must have your big talk with Foster. I need all the help I can get but it is my job."

Jackson's subsequent talk with Dulles, he cabled Luce, was a "sobering and saddening meeting." The interview had begun by Jackson telling Dulles that he had the impression that the foreign affairs of the United States were in a bad phase. Dulles acknowledged this to be so: "We find ourselves in very difficult times," Jackson quoted the Secretary of State as saying. "So long as the Soviets under Stalin continued to behave so badly in public, it was relatively easy for our side to maintain a certain social ostracism toward them. . . .

Now . . . frowns have given way to smiles. Guns have given way to offers of economic aid. . . . It is very difficult for the United States to say to its allies that all of this means nothing, that it is a trick, that the ostracism must be maintained." Jackson's overall conclusion was that "we would be making a grave mistake, and committing a real unfairness, by unlimbering on J.F.D. editorially."

*Time* had already "unlimbered" on Dulles in a small way. In March he had made a trip to the Far East, and in reporting it *Time* in the lead article of its National Affairs section had printed an unflattering picture of him lying on the beach in Ceylon. The caption read, "Traveler Dulles Resting on Ceylon Beach. Across the world the breakers roared." The story that went with the picture concluded, "It was high time for the traveling salesman to get back to the factory, there to produce some foreign policy to sell."

But some of *Time*'s editors thought that the magazine under Alexander and Fuerbringer was still letting its Republican bias show. Foreign News editor Thomas Griffith wrote to Luce "reluctantly" that the magazine was in danger of "losing the esteem that you and I (and so many others on the staff whose opinions I cannot believe you are indifferent to) want *Time* to deserve and to have." Once the magazine used to "cheat a little" in the final month of the campaign but now, he said, "it is a four year proposition." He argued that *Time* did not have the power to win elections and that "our efforts (particularly our clumsy ones) hurt only us." He told Luce the many good things about the Eisenhower Administration "would be better celebrated if the reader could trust *Time* not to omit the bad."

Griffith was not a disinterested witness; he had himself been National Affairs editor from 1949 to 1951, after which he swapped jobs with the Foreign News editor, Max Ways. A close friend of Matthews, Griffith had an intellectual approach to politics with a distaste "for the gamier side" which left him "neither Republican nor Democrat though perhaps with a lingering indulgence of Democrats." [5] His views were openly declared and respected by his associates. Ways no more liked Griffith's slant on foreign affairs than Griffith liked Ways's on national affairs but there was no personal animosity between them.

Luce sent for the Foreign News editor on receiving his note—"with some formality," Griffith recalled. "My memory fails me on what he

[5] *The Waist-High Culture* (Harper & Brothers, 1959), p. 102.

actually said though I remembered my interpretation of it; that he acknowledged and made no attempt to excuse the biased *Time*; that he had heard from others besides me; that he valued my honesty in writing him. It was Harry at his best, as if trying to convince me I should stay around and my protests were getting a hearing."

The Griffith protest preceded but probably played no part in the changes that were presently to take place in *Time*'s editorial lineup. It was not Luce's habit to intervene directly in the internal organization of a magazine. It was Ways himself who precipitated the change. Ways, whose political education had begun at the knee of his father, a Baltimore newspaperman turned politician, had a perceptive and realistic view of the interrelationships of the bureaucracy, Congress and the administration, and his imprint on the National Affairs section was positive and personal. But he had become bored with his job, and was seeking an opening on either *Life* or *Fortune* that would offer greater opportunities in writing as opposed to editing. The office of chief of the London bureau had opened up with the drafting of Laguerre for *Sports Illustrated,* and Ways volunteered for that post. He went off to London where he served from 1956 to 1958; a year later he joined *Fortune*'s board of editors.

He was succeeded as editor of the National Affairs section of *Time* by Louis Banks. Banks, a graduate of the University of California in Los Angeles (class of '37), had been a reporter and rewrite man on the Los Angeles *Examiner* before serving in World War II as a naval flight officer. He joined Time Inc. as a Los Angeles correspondent in 1945, transferred to Washington in 1948 and became a *Time* writer in 1949; in 1955 he was appointed a senior editor.

It fell to Banks to supervise *Time* coverage of the election of 1956, which was, however, a colorless rerun of the 1952 race between Eisenhower and Stevenson. The polls showed from the first that Eisenhower was almost a certain winner; his campaign ran smoothly under the slogan, "Peace, Progress and Prosperity."

Although the Time Inc. magazines were clearly for Eisenhower, they continued to ‎have mixed feelings about his conduct of foreign affairs. When *Life* came out for him in an October editorial, it did so on domestic grounds and warned against complacency in the international arena.

In October Luce gave a number of interviews to Alvin Davis of the New York *Post*, who was doing a series on "The Father of *Time*," which gives a contemporary picture of the editor-in-chief's attitude before the election. Some excerpts from one of the interviews, which began with Davis asking:

> Suppose Stevenson were President. What effect would that have on you, on *Time* and on the country?
>
> [Luce] leans back, says he's troubled by the question, wishes he could talk to us after the election. *Grins.* . . .
>
> Well, he suggests, he certainly wouldn't despair for the Republic. Wouldn't despair for the Republic? Now *we* sit up. . . .
>
> Golly, we say, you seem awfully relaxed about it. Your magazine certainly doesn't show it. *Time* is more partisan than ever this campaign.
>
> "Looking backward some 20 years," he says, relaxed as you please, "*Time* has been more partisan at some times than at others. This period would be one time when we are not very partisan."
>
> Sir, how can you say that? We can't put a calculus to partisanship, but the feeling this year is unmistakable.
>
> "I still say the present would be one of those periods in which we are not very partisan. . . ."
>
> It seems to us, we say, that *Time* is more and more involved each election year. In '52, except for the second Stevenson cover story,[6] *Time* showed overwhelming partisanship.
>
> "This is how I felt in '52. For a long while I thought it was important for this country that the Republican Party come to power so the country could have the experience of living under it. . . . Of course, I do want Ike elected again."
>
> Ah, we say, but not with the same desperation. You mean the big issue of '52 is gone?
>
> "Yes."

Davis notwithstanding, *Time* and *Life* treated Stevenson during the 1956 campaign with a great deal more sympathy and respect than in 1952. Early in the campaign *Life* spoke of the high-level tone of the campaign: "All in all, Ike sounds like a man the Wilsonian idealist Adlai could cheerfully vote for, while Adlai himself expounds the American Proposition in a manner worthy of Wilson, and with equal ardor. No one can answer the question whether the American people still possess ardor, or whether the candidates can arouse it.

---

[6] Davis probably meant the first one: "Sir Galahad & the Pols."

But we earnestly urge the candidates to go on trying, staying on the high ground they have taken."

There was a determination in some quarters to ensure a fair coverage. In June 1956 Bill Furth, who had been executive editor of *Fortune* since 1942, joined Luce's personal staff as his assistant and in that position functioned at times as a monitor of the editorial conscience.[7] When *Time* had a cover article on vice presidential candidate Richard Nixon which, as one reader put it, "sounded as if his mother wrote [it]," [8] Furth complained to Luce: "The Nixon cover unfolded as a defense of Nixon against vilification from other quarters. To that end it redressed the balance of bias in the public press. But, read in its own context, *Time*'s story presented a man practically without a flaw—and thus sacrificed credibility."

Eisenhower's re-election was overshadowed by stunning and dramatic events overseas; never, short of world war, did news break so fast and so confusingly as in the last weeks of October and early November 1956. On October 21 the Polish Communists, defying Khrushchev and the Soviet army, elected Wladyslaw Gomulka, who had been purged by Stalin, as head of their party. The Polish defiance had repercussions in Hungary. There a rebellion of such force erupted that the Soviet leadership vacillated and temporarily withdrew its forces from Budapest.[9]

Once again *Time* and *Life* reporters and photographers converged

[7] In January 1959 Furth was named executive assistant to the editor-in-chief and his name appeared on the mastheads of all the magazines.

[8] The article was written by James Keogh, who also wrote a book on the vice president, *This Is Nixon* (G. P. Putnam's Sons, 1956). In 1972 he published *President Nixon and the Press* (Funk and Wagnalls).

[9] During the lull the Hungarian team left for the 1956 Olympic Games in Australia. The team was still en route to Melbourne when news came of the Soviet invasion that restored the hard-line Communist government. As thousands of Hungarians fled their country, the Olympic team was cruelly torn between allegiance to their birthplace and revulsion at the regime. Word came to *Sports Illustrated*'s editors in New York that some members of the team and their coaches were seeking asylum in the United States; Sid James cabled assistant managing editor Andre Laguerre, who was in Melbourne supervising the Olympic coverage, that if the Hungarians approached him, the magazine was prepared to help. Thirty-eight members of the team were flown to the United States; on their arrival Dick Neale and the promotion department arranged for a nationwide tour, which raised $10,000 for the Hungarian Relief Fund. When the tour was over, *SI* helped all but five of the team, who wished to return to Europe, to find homes and schools or jobs in this country.

on a scene of conflict—from Vienna *Time* correspondent Edgar Clark; from Bonn *Life* correspondent John Mulliken and photographer Mike Rougier; from Paris *Life* correspondent Timothy Foote and photographer John Sadovy, a Paris free-lancer enlisted by Foote; Erich Lessing, a Magnum photographer working for *Life*, was also on hand. All were at one time or another caught up in the violence in Budapest. Foote and Sadovy were captured by the Russians and stood against a wall. They expected to be shot, but, after first stripping the film from Sadovy's cameras, their captors set them free. Sadovy later produced the most dramatic pictures of the revolt: the execution of a squad of hated security police by the enraged freedom fighters. When the Russian troops returned to crush the revolt, Clark and Rougier, the last of the Time Inc. staff to leave, were stopped at the border. Clark reported: "We found two Soviet tanks, one pointed toward Austria, the other at us. Out popped several little black Mongolians fresh from the steppes. Stupid, mean little men waved guns at us, and said 'Go back or we'll shoot.'" The Russians held the two for forty-six hours before allowing them to cross into Austria. The Iron Curtain closed down on Hungary again.[10]

On October 29, as the revolution raged in Budapest, the Middle East erupted with an Israeli invasion of Egypt. Two days later Anglo-French forces, on the pretext of protecting the Suez Canal which Nasser had seized in July, joined the attack on Egypt—a stupefying climax to a situation that had been festering for years.

From the time of the officers' revolt against King Farouk in 1952, the editors of *Time* and *Life* had followed events in Egypt closely. In May 1956 Luce had gone to Cairo to interview Premier Gamal Abdel Nasser and had come away very much impressed with the Egyptian leader, and while he recognized the vital dependence of Britain and Europe on the oil of the Middle East, he was sympathetic with Nasser's aspirations and believed that a settlement giving the Arabs an equitable share in the oil revenues was essential. Eisenhower invited Luce to report in person on his interview. Luce was disappointed with the meeting, and he left Washington with the feeling that the administration's policy in the Middle East was "the typical D.O.S. policy of sophisticated drift."

[10] The *Life* photographs of the Hungarian revolt, together with the correspondents' dispatches, were reprinted as a paperback book, *Hungary's Fight for Freedom* (Time Inc., 1956), and the profits from the publication were turned over to the International Rescue Committee.

399

However, when Dulles withdrew the U.S. offer to help in financing the Aswan High Dam, the Secretary of State convinced Luce when they lunched the next day that this was the right move. Jackson, who was also present, quoted Dulles: "If [Nasser] turns to the Russians now, and they say no, this will undermine the whole fabric of recent Soviet economic carpetbagging all over the world, but particularly in the Arab world. If the Soviets agree to give Nasser his dam, then the U.S. is working up plans to lay it on thick in the satellite countries as to why their living conditions are so miserable with the Soviets dishing out hundreds of millions to Egypt." *Time* lauded Dulles' action in a lead story: "On the broad chessboard of international diplomacy, the U.S. moved decisively . . . in a gambit that took the breath of professionals for its daring and won the assent of kibitzers for its instinctive rightness. . . . It was highly possible that Chessmaster Dulles already had his opponents in check." This rhetoric provoked Manfred Gottfried, chief of foreign correspondents, to explode to *Time*'s Alexander: "This is the kind of ill-chosen limb that *Time* gains nothing by going out on. . . . 'Instinctive rightness'—my ass." But even when Nasser in his stunning riposte seized the canal, Luce continued to string along with Dulles' decision on Aswan. ("It was quite a move. When one speaks of a particular move in chess, one usually means a move that precipitates decisive action. The question then is whether the precipitator can move on to victory.") Luce's hope was that the canal crisis would result in an overall settlement within the framework of world law. Suez, as he said in a speech to the Connecticut Bar Association, pointed to the "imminent necessity for more and more international agreements clearly made and clearly enforceable." When, despite Dulles' strenuous efforts to restrain them, Britain and France attacked, Luce found the situation "sick making." He told his editors, "I haven't been able to believe it's really happening—I keep thinking it's just some bad story somebody told me. Perhaps the most immoral aspect of the Eden action is that, instead of using the Hungarian event for Freedom's sake itself, he seizes on it as an occasion for his own retrograde adventure." [11]

"War in the Middle East gave Russia the chance to muffle the sounds of its own savage conduct in Hungary," *Time* said. "Russia

[11] Sir Anthony Eden was prime minister of Great Britain at the time of the Suez crisis.

400

abruptly abandoned its promises of reforms and retreat, and ruthlessly turned to crush Hungary's gallant patriots. . . . The aggression in Egypt provided the Russians with what, if it was not a sanction, was at least a cover to allow their brutalities full rein. It was a measure of the betrayal of mankind's best hopes by Britain and France that the embarrassed West could not even cry shame with one voice." *Life* was equally condemnatory of the action that Britain and France had taken.

There were those within Time Inc. who felt that the editors of *Time* had ignored the complicity of the United States. When Luce, in a cable to the London office, complimented it on its coverage of the crisis, Ways replied: "For once my tail won't wag to pat on head. I am deeply ashamed of *Time*'s coverage . . . *Time* wants to narrow blame to Eden. My disgust at him is unbounded, but point of story is that whole West drifted into this mess and there is still no sign from Washington that anybody is making a real effort to get out of it. Again and again *Time* shows how good Ike and Dulles look compared to Eden. What a case for complacency that is."

As Eisenhower through direct pressure on the British and through the United Nations brought about a cease-fire and U.N. forces moved into Egypt to keep the peace, Luce clung to the thought that the whole affair might have a constructive influence in the direction of world law. He persuaded Nasser to issue a statement promising "strict observance of all the international law which now exists. More than that, I desire the expansion of international law to meet the needs of the complex modern world." *Life* pointed out that "Nasser's words, strikingly in contrast to his deeds, are a challenge to the U.N. If the U.N. can test their sincerity with a legal settlement that is just to Nasser and his adversaries, the next phase of U.N. history will be off to a good start indeed. . . . The Egyptian crisis . . . can be a turning point in U.N. history, if the U.S. leads the way."

It was a turning point but not quite in the way that *Life* envisaged; as the crisis subsided, Washington commentators, notably James Reston and the Alsop brothers, argued that the end result was a victory for the Soviet Union in that it gave the Russians a foothold in the Middle East. Not yet prepared to accept this view, *Time,* in a quite intemperate story, attributed these opinions to the influence which British and French diplomats exerted at "receptions and cocktail parties and all kinds of informal gatherings." The Reston report was dismissed as "nonsensical" while the Alsops were said to have "swung even more wildly." Reston wrote to Luce: "Honestly, Harry, is it 'nonsense' to report that the Russians and the Egyptians have scored a tremendous victory? . . . And if I report it, should I be ridiculed as a character who picks up his information at cocktail parties?" The Alsops called the article "grossly offensive," even "libelous."

Luce, in replying to Reston, conceded that the tone of his letter, in contrast to the *Time* article, was "admirable and altogether worthy of a scholar and a gentleman. . . . I think that *Time* would have been right in dissenting from your evaluation but was in fact unjustified in the terms in which it did so." To Joe Alsop, Luce expressed regret if *Time* had given the impression that he and his brother had been improperly influenced, because "anyone who has followed your writings . . . will surely agree that your conclusions reflect strong personal convictions." A year later, when challenged on the program "Meet the Press" to defend *Time*'s judgment of 1956 calling Dulles' action in connection with the Aswan High Dam the move of a "chessmaster," Luce freely conceded that on that occasion the magazine had been wrong.

In November 1956 Mrs. Luce resigned as ambassador to Italy, explaining that her health would not permit her to continue in that post. During her four years in Rome she had carried out an exacting schedule in spite of ever more frequent attacks of a debilitating and inexplicable illness. Only after extensive tests made at the laboratories of the U.S. Naval Hospital in Bethesda, Maryland, was it finally discovered that the ambassador was suffering from arsenic poisoning. The source of it was a fine dust falling from rosettes on her bedroom ceiling that were covered with a paint having a high content of arsenate of lead. Mrs. Luce had been breathing the fumes and drinking coffee powdered with the dust. The room was redone with a nontoxic paint, and there was no recurrence of Mrs. Luce's illness, but she wanted relief from her post in Rome. She retired in triumph. At first the ambassador had been received by the Italians with mixed feelings ranging from unconcealed skepticism about the ability of a woman to fulfill the duties of the office to outright derision. When she departed, Italian and U.S. newspapers saluted her for a job well done.

Though Luce had enjoyed his stays in Italy he was more than eager to return home; some new problems in publishing, in particular on *Life,* urgently claimed his attention.

402

# The War of the Multimillion Magazines

THE WHOLE MAGAZINE BUSINESS suffered a severe shock in December 1956 when the Crowell-Collier Publishing Company announced that it was discontinuing publication of the sixty-eight-year-old *Collier's* and the eighty-three-year-old *Woman's Home Companion*. A loss of $7,500,000 which the two magazines accounted for that year threatened the existence of the parent company and its profitable record, book publishing and encyclopedia operations. Some 400 staff members lost their jobs. *Collier's*, with a fortnightly circulation at the time of 4,180,000, and *Woman's Home Companion*, with a monthly 4,229,000, were casualties in the deadly numbers game then going on.

The unfulfilled subscriptions of *Collier's* and the *Companion* were up for sale: Time Inc. management considered whether *Life* should take over all or part of the *Collier's* list. With *Life's* circulation base at 5,600,000 and delivered circulation at 5,800,000, adding a million or so subscribers would strengthen it against television and widen its substantial lead over the *Saturday Evening Post* and *Look*. The temptation was strong. But there was, for one thing, the spectre of antitrust—*Life* was already getting twenty cents out of every advertising dollar spent on magazines. Advertising director Clay Buckhout was not sure that increased circulation derived from *Collier's* could be sold to Madison Avenue, since one reason for the demise of *Collier's* was that it failed to convince advertisers that it held a strong position in any segment of the American market. Also, circulation director John Hallenbeck was doubtful about the added value of such an investment because *Life* already had a healthy circulation. A finally compelling argument against the investment was that the cost of fulfilling any new circulation acquired would put a big dent in *Life's* profits; while *Life* in December 1956 was completing a record year in which the division would ring up a new high net income of $17,400,000, it was the first time in several years that *Life* had returned what management considered to be a satisfactory rate of profit in relation to its volume of business. Time Inc. said no to *Collier's*.

But to *Look's* Gardner Cowles the *Collier's* list seemed to be a golden opportunity. There had been five mass magazines of general interest competing for the advertising dollar, now there were four: *Reader's Digest* (which had been taking advertising since 1955) with a 10,700,000 circulation base; *Life* with 5,600,000; the *Saturday Evening Post* with 4,850,000; and *Look* with 4,200,000. Cowles snapped up the *Collier's* list and *Look* promptly announced a 15 percent increase in its base, which was dangled before advertisers with no increase in the cost per thousand. In 1957, in a single year, *Look* increased its advertising revenues by $9,000,000.

The managers of *Life* did not regard their situation in early 1957 with any complacency. Besides the suddenly swollen biweekly *Look,* there was the competition from the increasingly aggressive advertising sales staff of the *Reader's Digest*. And there was the growing, ponderous fact of television. In the four fat years 1952–56, advertising expenditures in television rose from $453,900,000 to $1,206,700,000.

Nevertheless *Life* was fairly confident of its position. In 1956 it had carried a record 4,655 pages of advertising; in November of that year, as the magazine approached its twentieth anniversary, the advertising news column of the New York *Herald Tribune* noted that American advertisers in those twenty years had invested in *Life* an estimated $1,250,000,000. In peak advertising periods *Life* was often forced to ask advertisers to postpone or transfer advertisements from certain issues because the demand for space had outrun the capacity of the bindery. Because the rate of subscription renewals was high, Hallenbeck was having no difficulty in maintaining the circulation base. If there was any weakness it was in newsstand sales, but this was attributed to the increased subscription sales effort; the population shift from the city centers to the white, middle-class, expanding suburbs in which so much of the subscription circulation was concentrated; and the growing interest in sports, which competed with all the media for leisure-time attention.

In presentation *Life* had acquired a high professional sheen. Its influence was nationwide and demonstrable—not so much politically, perhaps, as its editor-in-chief would have desired, but as a trendsetter, a taste-maker, and, in a very special way, as an educator exploring art, nuclear fission, the world of nature.

When the news came of the end of *Collier's, Life* had been considering raising its prices. In November 1956 publisher Heiskell and Hallenbeck had recommended an increase in the subscription rate plus a rise in the per-copy price from 20 to 25 cents. Luce objected, resting his "case *contra*" not on publishing economics but on another and broader base: since *"the purpose of* Life *is to be a magazine for all the people . . .* no needless barrier should be placed upon the ubiquitous availability of *Life."* The challenge to management and to the publisher, he said, was "to run a tight ship, to be good business-men, efficient publishers, *without* [having] for our common guide and touchstone the simple principle of maximizing of profits." But he proposed a reluctant compromise: holding the per-copy price to 20 cents and increasing only the price of subscriptions. Heiskell suggested that action be postponed until he reconsidered *Life's* strategy in the light of the new competitive challenge.

Meanwhile, the *Saturday Evening Post* made its move; it raised its circulation base from 4,850,000 to 5,200,000 effective October 1957 with no increase in the advertising rate per thousand. In March Heiskell recommended that *Life* increase its base from 5,600,000 to 6,000,000 in September 1957, and that it increase the advertising rate and the cost per thousand in two steps, the first to be effective in September. This strategy was adopted. In order to reassure the advertiser that he wasn't being asked to pay the whole freight, announcement of the second step-up was accompanied by news that the per-copy price would be increased from 20 to 25 cents effective in October, and that subscription price adjustments would follow in 1958. Luce went along reluctantly with the hike in the per-copy price. Later he regretted having done so.

Obviously the publisher would not have recommended these increases if he had not been confident of *Life's* ability to deliver a

highly readable editorial package. Yet at the same time he had certain reservations about editorial direction; in April he wrote managing editor Thompson that he felt the magazine was becoming "an
institution. It is in fact more than an impression as the word itself
is used over and over again by persons from all levels." He quoted
some reader reactions: "*Life* has matured . . . is not prejudiced
. . . is not controversial . . . is for everyone . . . lacks urgency
or vitality . . . is cultural (or too cultural)." Most of this was good,
Heiskell agreed, "yet at the same time it frightens me. Because we
have been in business twenty years and because of our promotion,
our readers know what to expect. . . . How can one be an institution
and yet be new and different and surprising each week? . . . Now
that we have created and promoted this 'institution' what should we
be doing about it? Should we continue to promote the big stories, or
should we lean more heavily toward news and human interest?"

Heiskell did not intend this so much as criticism as a starting point
for discussion. But the managing editor was annoyed. He conceded
that *Life* had become an institution but disputed the allegations of
blandness and neutrality. "Many think we *are* prejudiced, including
me (although I think on the side of the angels)," he wrote. "We are
controversial; we are urgent and vital; we may be too cultural but
again this is on the side of the angels unless overdone. . . . In reading your comments it seems . . . as if you were describing the
*Atlantic Monthly* and not *Life*. . . . There are a lot of things in the
last six months (which start with the Hungarian uprising) which
have excited me and I think our readers. . . . Incidentally, as to
promotion, isn't human interest what you are stressing in the present
series of Monday ads? They seem to indicate we're loaded with intimate human interest and I believe them."

The publisher did not pursue the subject. The problem of *Life*'s
future was suddenly less pressing than the problems of *Life*'s present.
A recession of unexpected severity in 1957 soon began cutting into
*Life*'s advertising orders; there was the increasing pressure from *Life*'s
competitors and, with the downturn of business, efforts centered on
strengthening the sales promotion and marketing operations.

In the deepening recession Time Inc. and the rest of the publishing
world were diverted from their business problems by two severe
shocks to the nation. The first came when President Eisenhower dispatched units of the 101st Airborne Division to Little Rock, Arkan-

sas, to enforce the Supreme Court decision on desegregation of public schools. On the issue of October 7, 1957, *Life* carried one of its grimmest covers: a color photograph of stern-faced, helmeted paratroopers standing guard before Little Rock's Central High School.

On the issue of civil rights for black citizens the sympathies of the Time Inc. publications had been made self-evident from the earliest years. *Time*'s editors had repeatedly courted the displeasure of Southern subscribers by their treatment of news involving blacks. In 1956 *Life* had undertaken a history of the Negro in America from slavery to the present; there was a storm of protests from Southern readers, many cancellations of subscriptions and even the threat of a few advertisers' withdrawals.

One of the articles in the series was a poignant story on the life of Willie Causey, a woodcutter, and his wife Allie Lee, a teacher in a segregated school in Shady Grove, Alabama, who was quoted as saying: "Integration is the only way through which Negroes will receive justice." The story infuriated the white townspeople. Causey was put out of business and his truck was seized by creditors, his wife was fired, and the family was on the verge of destitution when *Life*'s editors learned of their plight. When efforts to restore them to their former employment failed, *Life* relocated them and continued to concern itself with the welfare of the family.

Covering the Little Rock trouble, *Life* photographers Francis Miller and Grey Villet and reporter Paul Welch were victims of mob violence; the Little Rock police jailed Villet and Welch on open charges, while Miller was arrested for "inciting a disturbance"—as he put it, "for hitting a guy in the fist with my face."

While *Life* wholeheartedly supported the President's action in sending the paratroopers, it found fault with him for using his authority in a way which "left room for doubt as to whether he himself believes in the law he is enforcing." His attitude, said the editorial

left room for inference that the President equates the 14th Amendment with the 18th (Prohibition), a disagreeable thing which has to be enforced even though it may be unwise.

It would have been the better part of leadership for the President to reflect the true situation, which is this: *since the time of the 14th Amendment in 1868, the American Negro has so far advanced in economic status and in his expectations as a citizen that a living and progressive law, adjusting itself to changed*

407

*realities, must now include desegregation as a part of this citizenship.* People might violate the 18th Amendment without feeling guilty, but grown people who curse and spit upon children have a cause to feel guilty, violating, as they do, not only the 14th Amendment but Christ's commandment, "Love thy neighbor." [1]

The second shock was the launching by the Soviet Union of *Sputnik I* on October 4 followed by *Sputnik II* on November 3, 1957. "A new era in history had begun, opening a bright new chapter in mankind's conquest of the natural environment and a grim new chapter in the cold war," said *Time*. Neither *Time* nor *Life* discerned in the Sputniks the grim implications, bordering on the hysterical, that were seen by some politicians and pundits, who equated Russian technological advance with the imminent decline and fall of the United States. *Life* did urge a speedup of the American space program to ensure that "Sputnik's monopoly of outer space will be brief."

The attitude of *Time* and *Life* provoked an indignant letter to Luce from Eric Hodgins, who was on leave from *Fortune*. He complained that "in reading *Time*'s National Affairs section . . . I can detect . . . no more change of heart or tone than the 'oops' of a man who has spilled a very ordinary plate of beans. . . . I am writing out of a suspicion . . . that Time Inc. will not, on its present course, find even the adequate things to think or say henceforth in the face of overwhelming new world circumstances. . . . [My] feeling is that the era of the domination of our national policies, culture and all society by what let's call Businessmentality has somehow or other got to come in for such heavy modifications that its own mother wouldn't know it."

Luce replied: "Any accusation that Time Inc. has not done its fair share in alerting to the urgency of the crisis will not stand up.

---

[1] Commenting on the black revolution and Eisenhower's role, Luce, writing in 1966, said: "Ike did not lead it, did not identify with it. Ike sympathized with the Negro cause. He himself was proud of the fact that there was no segregation in the military services—his own professional bailiwick. But Ike was, by temperament, a gradualist, a moderate and a willing moderator. He was not a revolutionary, although he presided over an age of multi-revolutions. Later on, he regretted having appointed [Chief Justice Earl] Warren. Some like to imagine a scene where, instead of sending [troops], he, Ike, had gone there himself and taken Negro children by the hand and led them into school. I like to imagine it myself." Luce personally made his own commitment. He chaired the 1947 fund-raising campaign for the Urban League and served on its various committees for many years.

We have not indulged (much) in the . . . racket of doom-calling. But sometimes, if anything, we have overbilled the crisis. . . . You, not engaged here every day, cannot realize the amount of daily concern about whether we are 'getting things straight.' "

Hodgins' letter prodded Luce into a memorandum reviewing what his magazines had been saying over the years. On Communism, for example, Luce wrote:

> Some may say we have given the impression that the Soviet Union is collapsing; obviously that is not so, but we have pointed to its economic failure and political unreliability. And, of course, to its wickedness.

On constitutional principles he was confident that his editors had always recognized that

> there should be room and opportunity for disagreement on the application of basic principles. So, we have held stoutly for the Warren desegregation decision while others have disagreed. But no publications have done more to restore to visibility The Founding Fathers and their life-giving principles and to relate U.S. Constitutional Principles to current facts of life.

If there had been a failure, Luce thought,

> it might be that we have not scolded enough—have not scolded what's wrong with American Business and Americans generally. Perhaps. We have not been a common scold. Our main aim has been to be constructive and progressive.

When Luce asked his assistant, Bill Furth, if a version of his memorandum should be distributed to the staff, Furth told him no, writing:

> To be sure, the statement does reassert sound principles which guided Time Inc. in the past, and which we consider to be as sound as ever. . . . And yet our country is in trouble; maybe bad trouble; certainly new trouble. . . . Should the employee-reader infer that if only those principles had been followed by our leaders and lawmakers, we would not be in this trouble? . . . As a "point of view" [your résumé] sounds defensive and self-justifying.
>
> Two or three citations may illustrate my argument. . . . We early identified the threat of Soviet imperialism, consistently

409

sounded the "on guard" at the frequent price of great unpopularity. But I do not think we were clear as to the full scope of the Soviet threat. . . . [The] *caveats* were offset in our pages by a countervailing *credo*—viz., that a gang-ridden, imprisoned society such as the Soviet Union could not generate a dynamic capable of any threat more complex than a) external subversion or intimidation; or b) if finally challenged, pushing of the button of suicidal war. Now we are confronted with disconcerting evidence of Soviet potency in science, education, and . . . potential economic competition. . . .

My remaining points might be related to Domestic Politics. . . . Certainly we have been "disappointed" over the Administration's lack of vigorous leadership. . . . But it can be argued that we have been too forbearing . . . a little too solicitous of the President's peace of mind, a good bit too reassuring. . . .

I believe that the articulation of a Time Inc. point of view . . . is obliged to employ constructive hindsight. . . . We must recognize that if we had been singing national popular songs as we sang "Over There!" in 1917—our ditty of recent years would be drawn from none other than Irving Berlin himself. Title: "Anything You Can Do I Can Do Better." A good many people now think they hear a nick in the record. Permit me one more metaphor. I believe that our current point of view must take stock of what the sports broadcaster, at the moment of a tying run, calls "a brand new ball game."

The Furth memorandum was dated December 4, the same day on which the much publicized U.S. satellite *Vanguard* exploded a few seconds after its launch. Luce scrapped his memorandum; in a terse comment on the current news he informed his editors that "it's a brand new ball game" might henceforth be an appropriate slogan for the magazines' editorial attitude. The new perspective was reflected in *Time*'s Man of the Year story:

With the *Vanguard*'s witlessly ballyhooed crash at Cape Canaveral went the U.S.'s long-held tenet that anything Communism's driven men could do, free men could do better. Whatever the future might bring, in 1957 the U.S. had been challenged and bested in the very area of technological achievement that had made it the world's greatest power. . . .

Unquestionably, in the deadly give and take of the cold war,

410

the high score for the year belongs to Russia. And unquestionably, the Man of the Year was Russia's stubby and bald, gar-
rulous and brilliant ruler: Nikita Khrushchev.

One upbeat interlude in Time Inc.'s introspections occurred that fall.
This was the convening in San Francisco in October 1957, under the
sponsorship of *Time-Life* International and the Stanford Research
Institute, of the first International Industrial Development Conference. The idea for this meeting grew out of the Inter-American
Investment Conference which had been held in New Orleans two
years before. The success of this regional meeting prompted ideas
for a similar conference global in scope, and tentative plans were
being formulated when Dr. Weldon B. Gibson of the Stanford organization approached TLI's Edgar Baker with the idea of joint
sponsorship of such a meeting.

Baker had no difficulty in selling this ambitious project to top
management. The basic idea was to bring together representatives
of the highly industrial nations with those of the underdeveloped
countries for a meeting of minds on mutual problems. It was conceived as presenting a forum, free from official pressure, for an
exchange of ideas for future development. The response to the invita-
tions was even greater than anticipated; when the conference assembled there were 600 bankers, government officials and business
leaders representing fifty-six nations of the free world—as *Time* put
it, "an international Who's Who of high finance and high office." [2]
The host city lavishly entertained its guests with a reception at the
Palace of the Legion of Honor, and *Time-Life* International invited
all the conference guests to a special gala performance of the San
Francisco Opera.

The keynote address was delivered by the president of the World
Bank, Eugene Black. The principal speech at the conference banquet,
by Vice President Richard Nixon, was a statement on economic policy
in strong support of increased private investment abroad. As *Time*

[2] They included such men as Vittorio Valletta, president of Fiat in Italy;
Marcus Wallenberg of Enskilda Banken in Stockholm; H. V. R. Iengar,
friend and advisor to India's prime minister and governor of the Reserve
Bank of India; G. D. Birla, chairman of the United Commercial Bank of
Calcutta; Hermann Abs of the Deutsche Bank of Frankfurt. From the United
States: Nelson Rockefeller; RCA's chairman General David Sarnoff; the
head of Lehman Brothers foreign department, Marcel Palmaro; and George
Meany, president of the AFL-CIO.

reported, "To world-minded businessmen, apprehensive over a U.S. drift to protectionism, Nixon's proposals were a heartening reaffirmation of official intent to work for freer trade, a vital contribution to economic betterment of underdeveloped nations." [3]

As it turned out, 1957 was the second best year in the company's history, second only to 1956—although its net income was well below the management's very high expectations. The year also marked the culmination of a long-range program for improving the position of the company; various projects and transactions completed in the two-year period ending December 1957 increased working capital by $22,430,000—to $72,804,000.

It was also a year in which there had occurred a significant discussion of Time Inc.'s future growth. This was triggered by a request from the new East Texas subsidiary for approval of a program to expand its operations.

The acquisition of the East Texas Pulp and Paper Company had been predicated on an understanding that "the primary business of Time Inc. is journalism" and that future claims by Eastex on the company's purse were to be subordinated to those of the magazines. However, to Stillman this did not mean exclusive emphasis on magazine publishing because, as he reminded the board in late 1956, while "we all want Time Inc. to continue to be a 'growth company,' [this] cannot continue to be if we think only in terms of the growth of our magazines as they stand today, plus new 'magazine' products. . . . We already constitute almost one third of the 'magazine field.'" Therefore the company "must *allocate* despite this priority [for magazines] what can reasonably be allocated to support its profitable and promising excursions into other fields."

At the time of the East Texas acquisition there had remained a possibility that it might one day produce paper for *Life* and/or *Time*. However, discussions had been held with other companies as well, the most promising of which were with Crown Zellerbach Corporation, which had located a mill site at St. Francisville, Louisiana; availability of raw material and transportation facilities made this site a more advantageous place from which to turn out quality coated paper. In

[3] So successful was the International Industrial Development Conference that it has continued to meet every four years, no longer sponsored by Time Inc. but under the co-sponsorship of the Stanford Research Institute and the Conference Board.

412

January 1957 Time Inc. and Crown Zellerbach joined in forming the St. Francisville Paper Company to construct a mill for this purpose. This meant that Eastex's future would remain in products other than magazine paper. When Stillman, on behalf of Eastex, asked approval of a $5,000,000 program to acquire converting companies, Luce questioned the investment:

> I suppose everyone agrees that the starting of a magazine is just about the riskiest undertaking there is. . . . We may tend to think that other businesses can be calculated without a serious element of risk. . . .
>
> What I am driving at . . . is to get a clear statement on *why* we are expanding. Are we forced to it in order to save our investment [in the mill]? Or is it because the profits of expansion are enormously attractive? . . .
>
> *In general* I am against further investment at this time. And for the simple reason that . . . we have a number of sizable investments which have not as yet paid off. . . . We have the TV stations which we are just getting acquainted with. We have the Rock-Time building . . . And we have *Sports Illustrated.* . . .
>
> I should like to see more maturity in these investments before embarking on further investments.

Stillman pointed out that the Eastex investment had been debated and approved by the board and that the non-publishing ventures of the company had "been cautiously and deliberately designed to provide centers of growth which will *minimize* the burdens on the Management . . . by building up centers of management and money or credit which will stand on their own bottom and grow from within . . . without involving top management of the magazine businesses." The policy gave the stockholders the benefit of growth through the use of the company's capital and know-how outside of the range of its central business. But he concluded: "This requires confidence and the delegation of authority and responsibility. We should continue, in my opinion, to encourage and support management in areas where we are or can be well organized, well managed and soundly financed —in or out of the magazine business." Chairman Tex Moore supported Stillman, telling Luce that if he felt that the expansion of Eastex should not be undertaken he should consider the alternatives, of which "one is to realize upon your investment and get out. . . .

Unless you are going to go forward . . . we should sell [the mill] right now."

Luce was not then prepared to accept Stillman's philosophy that future "growth must be considerably or even mainly in non-publishing fields" because, he wrote, that "would be a profoundly radical departure and therefore to operate on that philosophy or even to tend to operate on that philosophy would be improper until said philosophy is formally adopted." The question, however, was eminently proper, said Luce, and deserved a "clear and meaningful answer."

The objections to the Eastex expansion were withdrawn, but in recording the approval Stillman noted that "for longer range planning . . . the Time Inc. Board reserves judgment." The question raised by Stillman's definition of policy was not immediately resolved, at least in Luce's mind. It was difficult for him to accept the idea that the future growth of the company could be in areas outside magazine publishing.

# No Reason To Become "America's Weekly Pain-in-the-Neck"

TO THE QUESTION, which is your favorite magazine, Luce invariably answered, "The one that is in trouble." As 1958 began, that magazine was *Life*. Despite the newly announced circulation base of 6,000,000 its quantitative advantage over the competition had tended to diminish; newsstand sales continued to decline and advertising sales were slow. Some months earlier Luce had asked *Life*'s publisher: "Are there not ways whereby *Life* can hold its audience without performing ever greater feats?" The question referred to the pressure on the editors to produce new and better series to maintain circulation. In January 1958 Heiskell returned a kind of answer:

> *Life* has proved it can deal with the world of crisis and super science. In fact, one might ask, as one reviews the 150–200 pages devoted to these subjects since October 4 [the launching of *Sputnik I*], whether we have not gone too far. In the sense of our responsibility to the country the answer is of course "No." However, with regard to the interest of the people I simply note that this is the first great news crisis in our times accompanied by continuously *lower* newsstand sales. If the reader is interested

in the world situation he is not reaching for *Life* (or *Time*) to tell him about it.

Heiskell, who had suggested to managing editor Thompson the year before that *Life* was becoming too much of an "institution," then went on to say to Luce that he had recently told Thompson that it might be a good moment to take some time off to think about the question: How do we gain the attention of our readers in 1958?

With Heiskell's memorandum Luce's attention became riveted on *Life*. If there was any "re-thinking" of the magazine to be done, he wanted to do it. Thompson was told to stay on the job; the editor-in-chief would do the thinking. Thompson accepted this development stoically, for he wrote: "If I cluck-clucked a bit at your suggestion . . . that I not bother my purty little ole head about thinking—you were about to come up with something—you shouldn't have paid much attention, as I guess you didn't."

The fourth managing editor since *Life*'s launching, Thompson had a genial cornball approach that masked a formidable intelligence, a passion for excellence and personal ambition. On taking over the job in 1949 he had told Luce:

It comes natural to me to regard the managing editor (in this case myself) as "the old man," a newspaper term applied to m.e.'s from 21 to 71. "The old man" to me is a guy who brings a strong personal flavor to editing. He has some crotchets which are the subject of wry office jokes, but all in all he is considered fairly Jovian. He rides his subordinates hard but is inclined to say nice things behind their backs. They feel that he will not pass the buck to them when he gets into trouble with the owner or other higher authority. Being "the old man" doesn't mean that one is a fatuous old do-gooder. While a certain amount of rough-diamond kindliness is involved, it means that "the old man" drives with a pretty tight rein, that he blows his top promptly when some stupidity is perpetrated, that he plunges zestfully into editorial projects which interest him (which should be almost all the time).

Thompson came close to projecting this romantic image to a temperamental staff. If his senior associates sometimes fretted at the concentration of personal authority that he insisted upon, they were forced to admit that the *Life* editorial operation was free of inhibiting bu-

416

reaucracy. Thompson maintained a person-to-person, shirt-sleeve, open-door policy; any *Life* photographer, reporter, writer was free to sound off.

Presiding over a predominantly young staff, he showed a willingness and skill in developing talent; he trained the two *Life* managing editors who would succeed him. George P. Hunt had moved from *Fortune* to *Life* in 1948 and, as an aspiring artist himself, had written about art before Thompson assigned him to the Military section, then sent him to Chicago and Washington for field experience. Thompson brought him back to New York and in June 1955 Hunt became an assistant managing editor. Ralph Graves was one of *Life's* new breed of journalists. He had been a sergeant-cryptographer in the Army Air Forces before enrolling at Harvard. He joined *Life* in 1948 as a researcher in Modern Living and shortly went to San Francisco as a reporter, where in his off hours he wrote a novel, *Thanks for the Ride*.[1] He returned to New York as a writer and then became chief of the Chicago bureau. He was recalled to New York to be assistant articles editor in 1955 and in the same year published his second novel, *The Lost Eagles*.[2] He moved steadily upward through the editorial ranks.

*Life* in the fifties was once described by John Shaw Billings as "the largest and most complex editorial operation in magazine history." The managing editor had to juggle the contents of as many as six issues at a time: color forms closed six to eight weeks in advance, other forms from three weeks to forty-eight hours before press time; some form or other closed every day in the week except Sunday. Photographers would often shoot literally hundreds of photographs for a single story. From the contact sheets the film editor, Margaret ("Peggy") Sargent, would select thirty to forty to be enlarged. Her job was one of such selectivity that Thompson once called her "the most important member" of the staff. The editor, researcher, writer (and often the photographer if he were available and not out on a story) would cull the best of these and make a rough layout to be submitted to the managing editor. In late-breaking stories the enlargements went right to the managing editor's desk.

Layout sessions might be attended by everyone involved in producing the story and any other editors or writers who happened to be passing by—Thompson liked an audience. At his elbow on the im-

[1] J. B. Lippincott Company, 1949.
[2] Alfred A. Knopf, 1955.

portant stories stood Charles Tudor, art director from 1945 until he left *Life* in 1961 to join the corporate production department. A graduate of the Cleveland Art School, Tudor had worked as a newspaper artist for the Cleveland *Press* and the New York *Telegram* and then for the Rural Resettlement Administration. He had also been a contributing artist to *The New Yorker* and *Town & Country*. He not only made an imprint on the magazine but on the *Life* books, some of which he designed.

Communication between Thompson and Tudor over layouts was almost telepathic. Thompson would select a picture, draw a squiggly line on a layout sheet, and look at Tudor, who would nod, shake his head or shrug his shoulders. Thompson would mutter. The squiggly lines would take a certain shape, and then, with the pictures selected, Tudor would sweep down, pick up the pictures and disappear. In an hour or two the layout would appear on the managing editor's desk for revision or final approval.

*Life*'s men and women saw themselves as serious and dedicated journalists who believed no subject was beyond them. Luce had inspired the first of what were called "the big acts," *Life*'s "History of Western Culture," which was turned into the second of the *Life* books under the title, *Life's Picture History of Western Man*.[3] Under Thompson the big acts got bigger and more ambitious; most successful was "The World We Live In," a thirteen-part series that ran from December 1952 to December 1954—a project that involved some of *Life*'s best photographers,[4] ten specially commissioned artists, 255 consultants. It was edited by *Life* Science editor Kenneth MacLeish, and the text was written by Lincoln Barnett. The circulation department, rather cool to the series when it was first announced, was astounded to find that whenever an illustration from "The World We Live In" appeared on the cover, newsstand sales rose, disproving the notion that only pretty girls sell magazines.

The instructor of several generations of *Life* writers, arbiter of its style under three managing editors, the man responsible for approving every headline and every word of text before it went to the managing editor for final approval was Joseph Kastner, copy editor for

[3] The first was *Life's Picture History of World War II*, published in October 1950; it became a runaway best seller, with a net profit of close to $1,500,000 by the end of the year.

[4] Major contributors were *Life* staff members Fritz Goro, Alfred Eisenstaedt, Andreas Feininger, Loomis Dean, J. R. Eyerman and contract photographers Gjon Mili and Roman Vishniak. In book form the series sold 650,000 copies and made a profit of more than $2,500,000.

twenty years. A onetime office boy, subsequently a junior writer on *Fortune,* he had been moved onto *Life* before publication of its first issue and had risen through the ranks to become one of its top editors. He also played an extracurricular role in company affairs as a onetime chairman of the Time Inc. unit of the New York Newspaper Guild and was influential in averting a threatened strike in 1946. His job required all-around knowledge, stamina and infinite patience in fitting copy to the exacting requirements of layout. He could have been the most hated editor on the staff; he was actually one of the best liked— a good uncle to young writers, a goad to jaded older hands, and regarded by the women on the staff as "the brotherly wolf" who could be counted on to support them against unreasonable male editors and writers. He was a confidant, a wailing wall to whom all could pour out their frustrations.

Editorial week on *Life* reached a climax on Saturday night when the last sixteen pages of the magazine went to press. Thompson would brighten perceptibly whenever there was any prospect of a late-breaking story turning a long day's work into a longer night's. Though *Life*'s competitors could not handle news on any comparably fast schedule, its editors spared no expense or trouble to get a major news story in the current issue. This often involved complicated logistics, such as moving a large section of the National Affairs or Foreign News staff bodily to Chicago in order to close the time gap between layout, the writing of the story and the press start. Late closings meant an inhuman work shift that could begin at ten on Saturday morning and continue right through until eight on Sunday morning. Production staffs performed miracles to get the magazine out on time.

The men and women on *Life* were convinced, nevertheless, that they had more fun than their associates on any of the other magazines. Part of the feeling sprang from a strong sense of collective effort generated by the easy informality with which they worked. The *Life* offices were always overcrowded; there wasn't a clean desk on the floor. One pair of writers equipped themselves with a hi-fi rig and wrote to music. One copyreader regularly brought her dog to the office on Saturdays. The magazine was famous for its parties; any excuse would do for "a pouring." One Foreign News editor regularly flew the cocktail flag on the national day of members of the United Nations. On the late nights the production chief was authorized to produce a bottle to ease the tedium of long hours but a spoilsport deputy managing editor insisted that the whiskey must not appear until ten P.M.

419

In 1955 the publisher proposed and the managing editor enthusiastically seconded the idea of combining the issues that usually appeared in the weeks of Christmas and New Year's Day into a special double issue devoted to a single subject. The subject decided upon was Christianity, completing the series on "The World's Great Religions" that had run earlier in the year. Sensing correctly that the idea might seem revolutionary to the advertising trade, half a dozen heads of the biggest agencies were invited by Luce to a luncheon to hear the editors and Clay Buckhout explain the plan. The idealism was applauded, but the juxtaposition of the Gospel and crass advertising worried some agency men more, apparently, than it did the editors. Leo Burnett, an old friend of *Life,* made the radical suggestion that *Life* carry no advertising at all in the special issue. A somewhat embarrassed silence followed this suggestion; Luce and his associates were not prepared to go that far. Many advertisers did shift their advertisements to other issues; the liquor industry, which normally ran its heaviest advertising at the end of the year, stayed out of the issue altogether.

The editor of the double issue was Sam Welles, son of an Episcopal canon. In addition to having been *Time*'s Religion writer at one time, he had been a roving correspondent in Europe and the Middle and Far East as well as Ottawa bureau chief. Welles was called from his post as chief of the Chicago búreau to undertake this job. Later the entire religion series was reprinted in a greatly expanded book, another of the *Life* books that sold hundreds of thousands of copies.

To no field, perhaps, did *Life* address itself with greater seriousness than to art. The original prospectus promised that *Life* would bring the reader "the best contemporary art." The editorial interest of Time Inc. in art went back to the early days of *Fortune* when its art editor, Eleanor Treacy, sought to avoid commercial artwork and commissioned Charles Burchfield, Paul Sample, Reginald Marsh and other recognized artists to illustrate articles. Before the launching of *Life,* *Time* had added color pages that it devoted to the American-scene school of painting. *Life* followed in the *Time* tradition. Eighty-nine color reproductions of American paintings that first appeared in *Life,* with accompanying biographies of the artists written by *Life*'s Art editor, Margit Varga, were used to illustrate a book, *Modern American Painting,* written by Peyton Boswell, Jr.[5]

But "modern" was a word not wholly appreciated by Luce or his

[5] Dodd, Mead and Company, 1939.

editors, who were far more partial to the conventional American-scene painters. In 1943, speaking at the Dayton Art Institute, Luce had expressed the hope that after the war American art would take a more positive turn than was indicated by the radical and iconoclastic schools: "There is a reason to hope . . . that Art may fulfill itself in the re-creation of a more believing society."

As it turned out, the postwar trend in modern art did not take the turn that Luce had hoped for. For a time, resisting the trend, *Life* devoted much of its attention to Renaissance masterpieces, which had never before been shown in color in the pages of a mass magazine.[6] However, mindful of the promise in the *Life* prospectus, and somewhat influenced by his own art advisor, Hank Brennan, Luce proposed that at least six times a year *Life* should reproduce the best examples of contemporary art "whether or not we as editors like it." At the same time he advanced "the tentative point of view that almost no painting of any great importance—or lasting interest—is currently being produced."

He asked his friend Nelson Rockefeller what he thought. Rockefeller was president of the board of trustees of the Museum of Modern Art in New York, on which Luce also served. Rockefeller remembered that Luce said he and his editors were wondering whether they should attack modern art as a destructive force. There was a meeting with other trustees and museum officials. The upshot, according to Rockefeller, was a complete turnabout on the part of Luce. "We ended the evening with Henry Luce being convinced that modern forms of artistic expression were the only area left in democracy where there was true fredom . . . and there were 'no holds barred.' He changed from a deep concern that modern art was a destructive force to the conclusion that it was one of the great bastions of freedom and strength in our lives."[7]

---

[6] Access to such art had been shut off during the war. Capping its postwar foray into the European treasures, *Life* sent Frank Lerner to Rome in 1949 to photograph the entire series of frescoes painted by Michelangelo on the Sistine Chapel ceiling. These ran in *Life*'s Christmas issue that year. Several years later these photographs, together with others from *Life*'s files, were enlarged, mounted and illuminated and displayed in museums and art galleries in the United States and abroad and on several occasions in Time Inc.'s Reception Center, where they drew capacity crowds. The Sistine Chapel reproductions were also a part of the Vatican Pavilion in the New York World's Fair of 1964–65.

[7] Nelson Rockefeller, "The Arts and Quality of Life," *Saturday Evening Post*, Summer 1971, p. 73.

Controversy raged over the subject in those days—as it always rages over radicalism in the arts. *Life* sponsored a Round Table at the Museum of Modern Art to which a dozen dedicated leaders in the field were invited. Out of this meeting, a report of which was published in *Life* October 11, 1948, came a reaffirmation of the artist's inalienable right to be free—but not irresponsible. *Life* continued to reproduce modern American painting in all its forms; it was, in fact, the first magazine of general circulation to devote color pages to Jackson Pollock.[8]

Dorothy Seiberling, who became Art editor in the mid-fifties, could say that in her own experience *Life* had emerged from a period of indecision to look at developments in modern art with seriousness, with objectivity, yet not without humor or independence of viewpoint. Luce supported this attitude to a degree. He congratulated *Life* for the enthusiasm it conveyed for art. But he added: "To overcome my skepticism and perhaps the skepticism of quite a few truck drivers, you will have to be sure that each page has beauty or fascination and *Life* thinks it is just about the most wonderful thing it ever did." On abstract expressionism he was never convinced. When it was under discussion in 1959, he made clear his distaste, insisting that while it should be shown in the pages of *Life,* the editors had an obligation to express their "attitude" toward it. "We presented it without any particular attitude," said Miss Seiberling, "and he gnashed his teeth but let us go our way."

The seriousness with which *Life* approached art, science and religion was matched by an increasing professionalism in the Fashion, Modern Living and Entertainment departments. There had been a time when the "male chauvinist" editors of *Life* took what can best be described as a derisive view of fashion. They were swiftly re-educated when Sally Kirkland, a former editor of *Vogue,* became *Life*'s Fashion editor; the magazine's coverage of world fashion and the designers earned it a standing and respect in the industry. What Mrs. Kirkland did for fashion, Mary Hamman, a former managing editor of *Mademoiselle's Living* and an alumna of *Good Housekeeping,* managed to do for the household arts and interior decorating. Out of her articles on gourmet cooking, published in *Life* from 1951

---

[8] The three-page spread on Pollock, in the August 8, 1949, issue, kicked up the biggest reader furor of any *Life* story that year. Of the 532 readers who wrote to the editors about it, only 20 were favorably inclined toward the artist or toward *Life* for publishing his paintings.

422

to 1958, came *Life's Picture Cook Book,* which in two years sold 284,000 copies. From the first, *Life* had devoted much space to the movies and to the theater, and under Entertainment editor Tom Prideaux gained distinction in the field. In 1958 associate editor Mary Leatherbee produced a memorable double issue on entertainment which was a gay and colorful celebration of the lively arts.

In the beginning *Life* was a picture magazine; words took second place. But as the magazine matured it was ably served by a growing staff of gifted writers. None was more versatile or productive than Robert Coughlan. He had joined *Fortune* in 1937 as an apprentice writer shortly after graduating from Northwestern University; he transferred to *Life* in 1943 and became its text editor, but after six years of editing chose to go back to writing and until his retirement produced more than seventy articles for *Life* on almost as many subjects. John Thorne brought a poetic touch to picture essays. Robert Wallace could write with deep sentiment and outrageous humor. One young writer, Maitland Edey, made his mark with a piece on "The White-footed Mouse," subsequently showed himself to be a man with superior editing skills and became an assistant managing editor; later he became the editor of Time-Life Books. Ernest Havemann, who had retreated from the *Sports Illustrated* project, was nevertheless a talented and highly valued contributor to *Life* as a staff writer, later as a free lance. The first black writer to join *Life's* staff was Earl Brown, a former editor of the *Amsterdam News* in New York. Brown had been a stringer for *Time* and *Life* and joined *Life* full time after that magazine published his profile on Joe Louis. While at Time Inc. he served three terms as a New York City councilman; he later joined Mayor Robert F. Wagner's administration. *Life* also published, in the late forties and fifties, the work of some of the most celebrated and popular writers in the English language— among them Evelyn Waugh, Graham Greene, Alan Moorehead, Robert Penn Warren, Carl Sandburg and James Michener. A major *Life* first occurred in 1952 with the publication, complete in one issue and before its appearance in book form, of Ernest Hemingway's *The Old Man and the Sea.*

But above all *Life* remained a picture magazine, and words always yielded priority to pictures. Earlier chapters have told of the risks that *Life* photographers took in covering the news; as a matter of fact, the magazine devoted the greater part of its space to non-news photography. Here the achievement of the photographer was in expand-

423

ing the boundaries of the art. In the *Life Library of Photography,* published in 1970–71 by Time-Life Books, its photographers have produced a definitive series of books on their craft. The record of their work, much of it of enduring value, is in the bound copies of the magazine. The memorable photo essays by W. Eugene Smith on a country doctor, on life and death in a Spanish village and on the work of a black midwife demonstrate how the camera can make a deeply moving statement about the human condition. Gjon Mili, a Massachusetts Institute of Technology graduate in electrical engineering who forsook his profession to become a photographer, pioneered the use in commercial photography of stroboscopic light that enabled the camera to freeze in the fraction of a second the poetry of motion. Dmitri Kessel's camera caught in color the awe and grandeur of the famous European cathedrals. Nina Leen's fondness for animals provided *Life* with many memorable stories, perhaps the best known being the continuing story of Lucky, a stray pup she adopted after his rescue from a Texas roadside. Another nature photographer of distinction was Wallace Kirkland, while Fritz Goro's extraordinary capacity to capture and illustrate advances in the world of science brought the nuclear age to *Life*'s pages. Two other photographers with a capacity for combining news sense and human interest were Lisa Larsen and Cornell Capa. Miss Larsen was particularly skilled in "bringing out the endearing in people," and her picture story of the courtly vice president, Alben Barkley, barnstorming on behalf of Democratic candidates in 1950, contributed much warmth to his image as the "Veep." Capa, brother of the celebrated Robert, produced moving essays on such diverse subjects as the treatment of retarded children and the story of five missionaries who were murdered by native Indians in the jungles of Ecuador. In 1949 Gordon Parks brought to the editors an unforgettable essay on the life of a Harlem gang leader: a year later he joined the staff, to work for *Life* in the Paris bureau, going on to a career of distinction as writer, poet, composer and motion picture director.

This was the magazine that was in trouble and that Luce began rethinking in 1958. The editor-in-chief was concerned about certain criticisms of *Life* from outside. One attack in particular, by the journalist Lucius Beebe in his widely quoted weekly newspaper, the *Territorial Enterprise* of Virginia City, Nevada, came to Luce's attention. Beebe had written:

For a quarter of a century now, take or leave a little, the most powerful single influence on American taste and its social destinies has probably been *Life* Magazine. . . .

In recent months, however, *Life* has suddenly become aware . . . that . . . the American Dream and, indeed, the American Epic are drawing to a close. It admits in a hair-raising signed article by George Price [9] that the Russians are so far ahead of us in everything that the days of the American Republic are numbered, and very correctly attributes this state of things to the fact that Americans vastly prefer TV comedians, Cadillacs and pro football to the dreary precautions of staying alive.

Yet it is difficult to remember when . . . *Life* has not devoted its most mature and effective enthusiasm to promoting what it now deplores. It has lavished billions of dollars worth of space on rutting Texas cowboys . . . on creating television comedians, on the mammary glands of Italian actresses, on Detroit motor car designers, on Hollywood starlets . . . and on basketball monsters, all the things it now, in the shadow of Judgment Day, is busy renouncing. . . .

Yet even while it interprets the handwriting on the wall and admits that the American eagle is a gone goose, *Life* has no least or slightest intention of itself renouncing the things that have accomplished the end of its own world. . . .

It has been by indirection and complacency a powerful agency in the undoing of the United States. . . . The American people, however, in this final contingency, will have the satisfaction of knowing that they have been washed up once and for all in the very best dynaflow, rotary motion, jet propelled, low fuel consumption, no laundress-red hands washing machine. As advertised in *Life.*

This challenged Luce's own concept of *Life*'s past and present role. He felt that *Life,* founded during the decade of the Depression, had had "both a natural and an assumed mission—to restore to Americans some delight and confidence in America." He put down in his

[9] George R. Price, fellow of the American Association for the Advancement of Science, in an article published in *Life* in the issue of November 18, 1957, entitled "Arguing the Case for Being Panicky," contended that the United States had frittered away twelve years since World War II while the Communists had gained on it and that the time had come to put a higher value on liberty than on luxury living.

notes: "By 'natural mission' I mean it is the nature of good photographs to give pleasure. Even if the subject is one of poverty or violence, there is a kind of pleasure . . . in sympathetic understanding. But the special magic of pictures is that they can make the normal, or the 'good,' interesting. Our *assumed* mission took the form of asserting American historic, moral and other values in preparation for meeting 'The Gathering Storm.' "

Comparing 1958 with the days of *Life's* founding, Luce wrote: "Instead of being a sick nation, America is now self-accused of being 'complacent.' We put too much store by our (shoddy?) riches. We are too proud of the American Way of Life. At least they say we were before Sputnik—and Little Rock. . . . Yet I think one need remains much the same . . . to validate America for its own sake and for its mission in the world. The basic characteristic of The New Age is that it combines great 'material' (and other?) progress with great danger. Is *Life* therefore caught in a bad jam between its duty to point out danger and its nature to provide enjoyment? My answer is an emphatic NO. . . . This next stage is the stage of really getting used to Abundance. We discover that the Age of Abundance is *not* the age of soporific tranquility; it is not static. It is dynamic. So maybe you don't like it. Too bad. Example: cities have to be torn up and rebuilt. . . . *Life* does *not have to* put on a solemn sour face about the 'horrible problem of cities.' *Life* can show *accomplishments* in this realm—the new auto-less center of town in Fort Worth —thus inviting to more accomplishments. . . . There is a time even in *Life* for the grim stating of a grim problem. [But] just because the Age of Abundance contains plenty of problems is no reason why *Life* has to become America's weekly headache and pain-in-the-neck. Leave it to someone else to achieve sanctity via the hair-shirt."

But *Look,* meanwhile, was embarked on a promotion campaign that worried Luce. It was built around the theme that *"Look* likes people." *Look* was advertising its concern for "the exciting story of people . . . what they do, what they feel, what they want, what they think . . . an ever changing story told with warmth, understanding and wonder." Luce was shown a *Look* memorandum sent to an advertising agency: "Standing above and apart from man, *Life*—in spite of all efforts at informality—remains the lofty pundit, superior, condescending, jesting, ponderous with moral instruction for the lesser masses. Standing shoulder to shoulder with man, *Look* remains the perennial wide-eyed tourist, making new discoveries about the world and sharing them with its friends. *Life* sets forth answers; *Look* asks questions. *Life* is impersonal; *Look* is personal. *Life* likes theories, causes, paradoxes, heroes and vast movements in time and space; *Look* likes people."

Luce's reaction to the *Look* memo was that it was "taking a sure-fire American line." But, he added, "There's another personal reason why, I think, *Look* feels its charge of 'impersonality' will be effective. That personal reason is me. I have been widely regarded as 'aloof,' 'cold,' 'inhuman,' etc. This has been the despair of our public relations department. I'm sorry, for *Life*'s sake, I have this reputation but . . . it won't amount to much *if Life* itself demonstrates a capacity for 'humanness.' "

There was a tendency at *Life* to attribute its troubles mainly to television. Luce discounted the argument: "I think the *opportunities* are mostly the same in 1958 as in 1938. The truth in the theory of decline-of-opportunity may lie in the fact that it's harder now to make a big story out of the normal. . . . Take pigs. Pigs are still a big product. And pigs are still mighty interesting to look at. An essay on a biggish modern Pig Farm would be a good essay—on account of the *pigs*. It would be too bad to dull it all up with an attempt to solve the farm problem. And miss the fun of pigs is pigs. . . . Too many [photographers] seem to want to outdo themselves and each other—by snapping the atom in its flight through a bumble-bee's stomach, etc. This produces some remarkable results and I'm all for it. But we may lose a lot more than we gain—because the photographers don't concentrate so lovingly on the simple, striking, wonderful human things that are right under their noses. This tendency of photographers is compounded by editors who want to prove something intellectual or something. Except for a few Grade A Intellectuals, *Life* editors should be known for the quickness and sureness of their *picture-eye*. . . . As between a technically interesting picture and a humanly interesting picture, *Life* should infallibly and without exception print the humanly interesting picture."

What was to be done? "Where do we go from here? [How do] the middle-aged managers of a middle-aged magazine . . . renew their youth and mount up, again, like eagles?" Luce's answer to his own questions was to turn back again to *Life*'s past:

> There *was* magic in *Life* (I say "was" because past seems a little more certain than present). . . . What magic? By definition, *magic* is undefinable. . . .
> The magic of *Life* is obviously connected with the magic of

pictures. . . . There are many aspects to this magic. One of them is that a picture will invite my attention to a subject which otherwise, at any given moment, I would ignore. Today I may not be in a mood nor feel the need to read the finest article about the Prime Minister of Britain but I will stop to watch him take off his shoe—and to look a little more closely at his face and to wonder what manner of man he, and the British, are. . . .

I think if we are to mount up again, it has to be on the wings of picture-magic. I don't say we've lost it—by no means. . . . What has been lost is a kind of simple faith in pictures as such. In any case, there has grown up a sort of intellectualist analysis which concludes that on account of one thing and another, including 21 years of *Life* itself, picture-magic has burned itself out and is no more available. I reject this view and I oppose to it a faith in *both* the sophisticated and the simple.

If I am wrong, if we can no longer rely on the old basic picture-magic, then someone must come up with a whole new rationale for . . . *Life*. I have not felt that necessity.

His re-thinking of *Life* had begun in January; at the end of the month an edited version of his notes was distributed to Heiskell, Thompson and selected senior executives. Early in February 1958, two months before his sixtieth birthday, the exercise was abruptly suspended. At his vacation home on the Biltmore Estates in Phoenix, Arizona, Luce came down with a severe chest cold; although he consulted his doctor, he characteristically minimized the illness, demanding only to be left alone to sleep. Sometime past noon on February 5 Mrs. Luce took him a cup of soup and found him sitting up in bed and staring at her. "I'm dying," he said. She summoned the doctor and an ambulance and Luce was put on a respirator; he peered out from behind the mask and said enigmatically, "How embarrassing this ought to be for the editors of *Life* when *Life* really goes to a party!" At the hospital he perked up and announced to his wife: "Don't pay any attention to what I said. This is not *it*." It wasn't "it," but he had been stricken by a pulmonary embolism followed by a coronary occlusion, which put him on a regimen of anticoagulants for the rest of his life. The attack was relatively mild, however, and it was not thought necessary to disclose the nature of his illness even to his colleagues; Phoenix newspapers reported it as pneumonia.

\* \* \*

428

Concern about Luce's condition was soon dispelled by evidence of a vigorous and rapid recovery. Though the editor-in-chief did not return to his New York office until April, a stream of memoranda, suggestions and notes flowed from Phoenix. Even before he left the hospital he was needling *Time* editors to look into the farm scandal. For light reading he had been dipping into Max Lerner's thousand-page *America as a Civilization* [10] and was shocked to learn—as he wrote to Furth—that "70 percent of Americans, urban, pay 90 percent of taxes and elect only 20 percent of legislatures. *Time* would be more exciting if it would get more *excited* about such things." To Roy Larsen he apologized for "being benched when we are faced with tough problems."

His illness made one difference. The Luces had bought the Phoenix house after their return from Italy because Mrs. Luce, who had stayed at Elizabeth Arden's Maine Chance, was greatly taken with the climate. Luce was even more enthusiastic than she was; the Phoenix house became much more "home" than their Ridgefield, Connecticut, estate or their New York apartment. Though this meant that he was absent from New York for considerable periods during the winter months, he had learned from his stay in Rome how to keep in touch with headquarters.

*Life* remained his first order of business. Some of the news he received from New York did not encourage a leisurely convalescence. C. D. Jackson predicted that the company's second quarter could be "a stinker" because the recession continued to slow down advertising sales in all the magazines except *Sports Illustrated,* which was countering the trend. The real headache continued to be *Life* because "the bloom is off *Life* on Madison Avenue. . . . Mass editorial appeal has been spotty. . . . Newsstand sales are very bad. . . . Pollyanna might report differently but that is the way I see it." Another communication came from Larsen; he and Black were considering how *Life* could take the lead in a collective effort by all magazines to counterattack the common enemy, television. Incidental to this proposal Larsen mentioned that *Look* had once more raised the stakes in the numbers game by announcing a delivered circulation of 5,800,000, which put *Look* and the *Saturday Evening Post* in an almost neck-and-neck position and only about 300,000 below the delivered circulation of *Life*.

[10] Simon and Schuster, 1957.

Luce took Larsen to mean that *Life*'s position was such that it could no longer go it alone, or recover a decisive lead over the others. This he could not accept because

> I guess I still have in mind that *Life* can be and must be *the outstanding* magazine. . . . If a goal like that is still relevant and realistic . . . 1) we would have our direct competition well licked and 2) we would get plenty of advertising $$$, no matter how many $$$ went to TV or skywriting or whatever. If [this] is the proper goal, then it seems to me that what we have first of all on our hands is a Circulation Battle—with *Post* and *Look* and maybe *Digest*. This battle—and maybe it should be called a war—should be fought vigorously by every means. By all the editorial exertion and brains we can muster. And by Promotion. And by dollars. . . . Maybe we should cut back on newsstand price and subscription price. We would make things very expensive for *Post* and *Look*—and sacrifice our own profit position in the process.

Larsen was in full agreement: *Life* must reposition itself as the leader; but he did not think it necessary to reduce newsstand and subscription prices. An ideal goal for *Life,* he felt, would be a circulation of 6,750,000 by the summer of 1959, but in the present state of business the cost of attaining that goal would be too high, and so he opted instead for 6,300,000 and increased subscription rates. It was executive vice president Howard Black who came up with a prescient and radical suggestion: *Life* should quit the numbers game, settle for 4,000,000 Grade A subscribers and sell the quality instead of the quantity of its audience to advertisers. "What is so holy about a guarantee of 6,000,000 circulation?" he asked. While he admitted that such a move might be premature, "If I am right, our problem is not just for now. It is a permanent one so I am all for facing it now for now and for the future." He added that prices should be lowered. With advertising psychology what it was at the time, Black's proposal was hard to accept. A unilateral reduction in circulation would have been trumpeted by *Life*'s competitors as surrender and defeat; circulation wars—like other wars—generate their own momentum. In any case, no move was made then to increase *Life*'s circulation; efforts were concentrated on solidifying its 6,000,000 base.

In line with Larsen's and Black's feeling that *Life* should take the lead in inspiring a joint advertising sales effort by magazines against television, *Life*'s publisher undertook a demonstration of faith in magazines. The year before, *Life* had begun to publish the results of its pioneering Study of Consumer Expenditures, the most comprehensive of its kind to be undertaken by a private company. One hundred ten thousand interviews with over 15,000 families had been conducted by Alfred Politz Research, Inc., over fifteen months at a cost of $1,500,000, and follow-up interviews would continue for two more years. The study classified consumer expenditures by goods and services, by region, by education and by income category. It also related these expenditures to the media; a most impressive finding was that five major magazines (*Life, Saturday Evening Post, Look, Reader's Digest* and *Ladies' Home Journal*) reached 64.8 percent of U.S. households, accounting for 72.9 percent of total household expenditures. Now, acting on this finding, *Life* canceled its TV advertising and shifted a large part of its TV allocation to the pages of its competitors.

Luce meanwhile continued to ride herd on the editors. When one of his story suggestions was not acted on quickly enough, he complained that the staff was too big and the machinery too cumbersome. "Months pass, we get in and out of hospitals, or jails, while we wait for a *Life* story to get done." When the *Time* editors reported that the chemise in dress fashions ("the sack") was dead, Luce took their word against that of *Life*'s Fashion editor, Sally Kirkland, and told Thompson, "*Life* would have been much smarter if it had said that it's a lousy style and won't last." Thompson usually tried to insulate his staff from top management complaints and in passing this on to Mrs. Kirkland he wrote to her, "I have already bawled him out. He said, 'I apologize but can't I sink a needle in once in a while, isn't that what I'm here for?' " The Fashion editor replied tartly, "Mr. Luce is perfectly at liberty to call me a lousy *Life* editor, but I don't think he, any more than that shaky fount of fashion knowledge, *Time* magazine, can call me a lousy fashion editor. It occurs to me that if we were to announce that the chemise was 'dead' in the face of the percentage of ladies we see on the streets [wearing it], we would be as much in danger of subordinating our independent judgment to *Time* [and] H.R.L. as if we slavishly followed *Vogue-Harper's*-Paris dictates, which we don't."

Another recurring complaint was that *Life* didn't try hard enough to win women readers. Luce wanted a woman staff writer on the magazine—nine men were so listed on the masthead at the time: "Can't we resolve that the next star-writer shall be a woman? Plenty of women can write rings around plenty of men." Luce told Thompson, "The trouble with *Life*'s editors is that they hate women."

"Caught with my ripostes down," Thompson replied when he recovered his composure, "I will simply say, 'tain't so.' Compared to other Time Inc. publications . . . we are a veritable hotbed of feminism." In addition to the women department heads—Sally Kirkland, Dorothy Seiberling, Mary Leatherbee and Mary Hamman—*Life*'s only correspondent in Rome was Dora Hamblin. Thompson could also point to an assistant picture editor, Lee Eitingon, an assistant science editor, Nancy Genet, and an assistant international editor, Irene Saint. This was not to mention Marion MacPhail, chief of research, and the more than fifty formidable women reporters and researchers under her whose influence on the contents of the magazine was very great. When the editor-in-chief proposed that *Life* appoint a woman as assistant managing editor, Thompson was agreeable: "There's nothing wrong with the idea. . . . It's a question of finding the woman."

As 1958 drew to a close, Luce appeared to feel that *Life*'s editorial achievement was such that he could tell top management that now "the key to the recovery of success for *Life* lies in General Promotion." He wrote to Larsen:

> The principal thing that *Life* suffers from is that it is not regarded as in a class by itself. . . . It isn't only TV that diminished the apparent unique greatness of *Life*. There was the fact that the *Post* and *Look* were catching us in circulation—and the *Digest* entered the competition. And one more thing needs to be said here and that is that *Look* became a "good" magazine. And the *Post* is a good magazine. And *Reader's Digest* . . . if you like that sort of thing. So, here's a bunch of "good" magazines and while a particular person may have his preferences—in general, no one has to agree that any one magazine is way out in front.

Luce felt nevertheless that there persisted in many quarters a feeling that *Life* had "special qualities of greatness," and that this claim should be articulated. As to TV, "this is for us a time of opportunity," he wrote. "TV may continue to hold its huge audiences—but what

TV is, is now understood, i.e., mostly junk and old movies and westerns. It's not much of a 'window on the world.' "

But publisher Heiskell did not share his optimism about promotion being the key to success. In March 1959, when it was evident that the nation's business recovery was coming much more slowly than in either of the two preceding postwar recessions, he complained: "*Life* is not in a natural state of equilibrium." Circulation costs had greatly increased because of a decreased response to the direct-mail solicitations; newsstand sales had fallen off still further; in the past two years *Life* had suffered a decline of 1,200 pages in advertising, and orders in early 1959 were sluggish. Heiskell wrote:

> In effect, your publisher is saying: "with the means at my disposal I can maintain a barely adequate level of performance. If we want real improvement, the editorial product will have to supply it. It is of course quite possible that your publisher may be wrong. If so, he is willing to take direction or bow out."

He coupled this with a criticism of the magazine: the editors had "smoothed and polished the product to perfection. But [they have] also removed all traces of breathlessness, enthusiasm and point of view. We are very rational, very factual and not very human. . . . To do its job and be successful *Life* must not only have a soul, but this soul must be recognized by the reader."

Thompson, who had been under fire and had made adjustments in emphasis and direction to meet the criticism, felt that the condemnation was too sweeping, that it was unfair and inaccurate. "Can the Managing Editor do less than match the Publisher and offer to bow out if he is judged wrong and unreformable?" he wrote Luce and Heiskell. The publisher denied that he had intended a blanket condemnation, and after a conversation with Luce, Thompson was somewhat mollified. He was ready to accept Luce's interpretation of what Heiskell had meant: "What Andy is saying (he reported back to Heiskell, quoting Luce) is that he's helpless and telling you and me to go off and be geniuses every week. . . . He said he didn't think he and I should be required to be geniuses *all* the time. . . . Conceivably I can be a full-time genius to my own satisfaction but I may not be able to convince him and you."

This translation of who meant what evidently satisfied everyone; in any case it was agreed that the editors must re-examine *Life*'s future editorial policy.

433

One of the ironies of the situation was that as the *Saturday Evening Post, Look* and *Life* had drawn closer to each other in circulation, their editorial contents had tended to take on certain similarities. In founding *Look,* Cowles had not intended to enter into competition with *Life* but to leave to *Life* the coverage of the news (in which as a fortnightly *Look* could not compete) while exploiting the human interest story in pictures—also a strong point of *Life.* In the early fifties the *Post* had appealed to a new audience by exploiting the popular interest in such figures of the entertainment world as Bing Crosby and Arthur Godfrey (which *Life* had also done with great success); the *Post* series on Godfrey had been responsible for 800,000 additional newsstand sales. Now, in the late fifties, the *Post* editors, fearing that they were drifting too far to the light side, shifted in the direction of *Life*'s serious side with a series entitled "Adventures of the Mind." Meanwhile the thrust of the Luce and Thompson discussions of *Life*'s editorial future was toward lightening the intellectual load by seeking more spontaneity—more pictures for their own sake, less news for the sake of news.

Thompson, however willing he was to re-examine *Life*'s editorial agenda, could not help but feel that the criticism of his policies derived at least as much from the competitive situation as from the readers' dissatisfaction with the product. He was not willing to concede that *Life*'s competitors had improved editorially and pointed out to Luce that much of the gap-closing in the past two years had been "brought about by expenditure of circulation monies." And he ventured to add that some of *Life*'s Time Inc. stablemates were not exactly big profit makers. To this Luce replied:

I don't think they [*Life*'s competitors] can keep up "profitless prosperity." Maybe they can. Maybe we're in a bum business. . . . We (Larsen, Heiskell, me, etc.) are seeking a publishing policy which will enable *Life* to perform at proper profit levels, while dealing with competition. But if we can't find any way to fight except with dollars, then that's the way we'll fight. As to Time Inc. stablemates, I don't think your point is so good. A crucial point is *rate* of profit. From this point of view *Time Canada* was (and may still be) our best baby. *Time* is better than *Life.* And so is *Fortune.* . . . What *Life* has done is to make Time Inc. *very big* instead of just big. (Without *Life* we would never have built that huge skyscraper.) But *Life*'s rate of profit has, at best, been only fair, and currently is poor.

It was against this background that management was formulating a new publishing strategy. "The Big Decision," as Heiskell entitled the proposal, called for increasing *Life*'s circulation base by stages from 6,000,000 to 7,000,000 in the early 1960s and announcing immediate reductions in both newsstand and subscription prices. It was a decision of such magnitude that a special meeting of the directors was called on April 27, 1959 to ratify it. At 6,000,000 *Life* was keeping one step ahead of the competition. In announcing a proposed one million increase at lower prices, *Life* was laying down a new gauge of battle to its competition.[11] The news was broken first to *Life*'s sales staff at its annual convention, to which Luce telegraphed: "Our announcement about *Life* means that we believe in a competitive economy and that we propose to compete the hell out of everybody on every front. The top editors of *Life* are enthusiastic about our declaration of faith and purpose."

It was felt that *Life* had no choice but to take this step. *Life* was in direct competition with television, radio, newspapers and newspaper supplements and the other large-circulation magazines; all other considerations aside, the feeling was that "advertisers always buy growth." *Life*'s circulation growth in the late fifties, furthermore, had involved commitments for the company predicated on long-range projections of the magazine's growth. In announcing its 7,000,-000 circulation goal the company cited the details of these commitments. The new mill at St. Francisville, Louisiana, was just about completed. An agreement had been entered into with R. R. Donnelley & Sons Company to extend its operations in a new printing plant being built at Old Saybrook, Connecticut. Contracts had been let for electronic, computer and tape recording installations to speed circulation fulfillment in Chicago. All in all, this expansion and quality improvement program involved an investment by Time Inc. and its suppliers of more than $60,000,000.

The consequences of the *Life* decision were far-reaching and portentous, not only for *Life* but for its principal competitors. The story extends beyond the scope of this volume, through the sixties and into the seventies, in the course of which the *Post,* then *Look* and finally *Life* ceased publication, leaving the *Reader's Digest* as the sole survivor in the field of general interest multimillion magazines.

[11] The newsstand price of *Life* went from 25 cents to 19 cents, a price that had been extensively pretested. Luce, who had repeatedly urged a reduction, had held out for 20 cents as more attractive. "I would *like* to be for 19 cents," he said, "but just can't bring myself to it."

# Time *Under Attack*

OF ALL THE MAGAZINES, *Time* seemed most nearly to be operating in an ideal situation as the fifties drew to a close. In
contrast to the erosion of *Life*'s earnings and the frustrating
losses that dogged *Sports Illustrated, Time* remained consistently
profitable and was maintaining 2,350,000 circulation with relatively
little promotion. Morale was high.

Publisher James Linen had a closely knit team on the business side.
He was an ebullient, sympathetic and congenial administrator who
knew how to delegate responsibility. Two of his associates were fellow
alumni of Williams College: Frederick S. ("Fritz") Gilbert, his general manager, had been a classmate and had sold advertising for *Life*
and *Time;* Bernhard M. Auer, his circulation director, had been a
campus subscription agent and had joined Time Inc. in 1939 as an
office boy. The business manager, James A. ("Gus") Thomason, had
served with Linen in the OWI; a bluff, easygoing man, he could
tighten the purse strings without conveying a sense of stringency. The
advertising director, John McLatchie, selected for that job by Linen,
had had long sales experience with *Time.* The promotion director was
Nicholas Samstag, an ingenious, somewhat sardonic idea man.[1]

---

[1] Author of *Persuasion For Profit* (University of Oklahoma Press, 1957);
*Come and See My Shining Palace* (Doubleday & Company, Inc., 1966).

Coming from sales himself, Linen was able to give a strong lead to his corps of salesmen. They were not involved in the competition of numbers as were *Life*'s salesmen; *Time* led its two nearest competitors, *Newsweek* and *U.S. News & World Report,* by a wide margin of circulation. But advertising competition was intense and *Time*'s volume had fallen slightly; the advertisers needed to be reassured that the magazine, as it grew in circulation, retained a quality readership; and they needed to have their feelings assuaged when the editors, as they often did, gored some cherished ox. Perhaps more than any of *Time*'s previous publishers, Linen enlarged the magazine's contacts in the world of business. He did this to some extent by carrying a very large burden of public service.[2]

Fortunately, all the analyses of *Time*'s circulation, which was climbing at the rate of about 100,000 a year, supported the magazine's claim to a very special audience of the higher educated, higher income segments of the American community. Auer had set a new circulation strategy that reduced its dependence on indiscriminate mass mailings, substituting newspaper advertising, insert cards and careful promotion among small, highly productive groups. This strategy was particularly successful in winning new readers in schools and colleges, thus raising a next generation of *Time* readers (Auer hoped). The effect was a steady improvement in revenues from circulation.

There was a good working relationship between the publisher's office and the editorial management, which continued as a well-organized group. Managing editor Alexander, thirteen years older than Linen, was happy to leave the public representation to the publisher while he concentrated on editing. Alexander was a reassuring, veteran figure to his younger staff. He seldom lost countenance under the most extreme provocation. His day began with mass and communion, which brought him to his office well ahead of his staff, even if, as after some convivial occasions, he had had only a few hours of sleep or none at all. He had an appreciation for lively copy and ran things with a

[2] In the late fifties he was active in the United Community Funds and Councils of America (of which he was president from 1956 to 1958), the American National Red Cross, the Connecticut Community Chest and the hospital in Greenwich, Connecticut, where he lived; he was also chairman of the board of trustees of Adelphi College and on the boards of the Hotchkiss School, the Cordell Hull Foundation for International Education, Athens College in Greece, the Boys' Clubs of America and the United States Council of the International Chamber of Commerce.

relatively light hand. Senior editor Banks said of him, "He gave his editors enough rope to hang themselves, if such was their inclination." With their common background on the St. Louis *Post-Dispatch,* Alexander and his assistant managing editor, Otto Fuerbringer, had a workable relationship such as had not always existed between the two jobs. Theirs was a highly professional and businesslike administration.

Among Alexander's senior editors were men who would fill in future years the top editorial executive posts in the company, among them Louis Banks, Tom Griffith, Henry Anatole Grunwald. Others in the editing ranks were James Keogh, who, after President Nixon's election, joined the White House staff; Robert J. Manning, who became editor of the *Atlantic Monthly;* Osborn Elliott, who became editor and board chairman of *Newsweek;* Robert Shnayerson, who became editor-in-chief of *Harper's.*

In the early days of *Time* Hadden and his uninhibited associates wrote the magazine with little more help than that afforded by newspaper clippings, a few well-thumbed reference books and their vivid imaginations. By the middle fifties the editorial operation had become complicated and costly. In addition to the corps of researchers in New York and the full services of the Associated Press, the writer had also at his command one of the world's largest private news services. Such a service had been no part of the original scheme of the newsmagazine; in fact, Luce for years resisted the whole idea of correspondents until eventually convinced that the news as presented in the press often raised more questions than it answered.

When the news service, greatly expanded during World War II, was divided in 1945, a chief of correspondents was made responsible for the United States and Canada and another for countries abroad. David Hulburd continued to administer the domestic side until 1948 when he resigned; Manfred Gottfried, the former *Time* managing editor who had succeeded Wertenbaker as chief of foreign correspondents, held the post until 1957. In adding to the staff he had taken over, Gottfried made a special effort to find men who spoke the language of the country to which he assigned them. He also made it a policy to shift correspondents from country to country before they became stale. At home men like James McConaughy, who covered Congress and was later Washington bureau chief; John Beal, who covered the State Department; William S. Howland, who for seventeen years as bureau chief in Atlanta covered the South; Barron Beshoar, an experienced reporter who covered the Rocky Mountain states—all brought to their work intimate knowledge and access to important sources. Abroad, in addition to people already mentioned in these pages, the company was expertly served by such able correspondents as Honor Balfour, an Oxford graduate and twice a candidate for the House of Commons, who in twenty-eight years with Time Inc. covered British politics under eight governments; Frank White who covered first Bonn and then Paris, and Eric Gibbs, a journalist of Canadian birth who as London, Bonn and then Paris bureau chief covered the postwar reconstruction of Europe with perception. Luce came to value and appreciate their contribution; it has been said he expected them to achieve the stature of ambassadors in their respective countries.

The corps tended, at times, to become a group apart. In the postwar years the correspondents continued to write primarily for the information of the editors, not for publication. This resulted often in frustration for the correspondents and exasperation on the part of the editors, who felt that their men in the field had little appreciation of the limitations imposed by space in a magazine devoted to "effective summary." (After he took over the managing editorship in 1968, Henry Grunwald invited the correspondents to file more directly for publication.)

The routine demands on the editors and writers in the New York office were heavy. Not only did the writer have to digest the reports of his correspondents but an immense amount of other material bearing on an assigned story. Whereas in the early days *Time* writers might dash off eight or ten columns a week, by the 1950s a forty-line story could require four or five hours of concentrated work. As the deadline neared, a writer's working day could stretch to twelve or fourteen hours. Particularly heavy were the demands made on writers of the cover stories. In the case of late-breaking news a cover article might have to be written in a matter of hours, but many a cover story required weeks of preparation.

Such covers dealt with leaders in science, medicine, religion, arts and letters. They were the work of writers and researchers who remained anonymous except for occasional mention in the Publisher's Letter. But they could match their expertise with journalists anywhere. Jonathan Leonard's covers in Science spanned the opening of the nuclear age to the space age during his twenty years as editor. Gilbert Cant wrote *Time*'s Medicine section from 1949 until his retirement in 1970. He had been hired in 1944 as a naval expert to write for World

Battlefronts.[3] Put into the Medicine section "cold," he made himself an expert in the medical field, winning two Lasker awards for his coverage. For a story on the effects of weightlessness, he made some forty power dives in one morning in an air force jet fighter. For many years *Time*'s Art writer and critic, later an historian of American art,[4] was Alexander Eliot, who did covers on Diego Rivera, Augustus John, Picasso. One of *Time*'s memorable covers was that on the theologian Paul Tillich, written by Douglas Auchincloss. After reading it Mrs. Tillich wrote in: "Thank you very much for telling me things I didn't know about my very difficult husband." Alistair Cooke, the radio-TV commentator and longtime correspondent in the United States for the *Manchester Guardian,* once wrote that *Time*'s Books section was "the most influential book page in the country." It was headed for more than a decade by Max Gissen. Among the most admired and certainly one of the most polished writers in the back of the book was *Time*'s drama critic from 1938 to 1961, Louis Kronenberger. In addition to his reviews he managed to write graceful and literate books of essays [5] and to edit the Best Plays series from 1953 to 1961 and half a dozen anthologies.

A cover assignment represented a very special challenge, requiring the writer to immerse himself in his subject while also reading hundreds of thousands of words of peripheral matter. The writing involved great compression and was often excruciating work. Inevitably the senior editor and the managing editor would have suggestions for inserts and other additions while insisting that the final version remain within the assigned length. The *Time* cover was held to high standards of journalism and style. If it fell short, it was not for a lack of effort.

Editing, it is sometimes said, is easier than writing; the editor does not experience the false starts, the hesitations that attend the composition of a first draft. But the demands on *Time* senior editors were no less exacting than those they made on their writers. A senior editor was expected to keep abreast of a hundred different trends in the subjects under his special supervision and to read attentively a great deal of the material for all the stories he was expected to edit. If

[3] While he was war editor of the New York *Post,* Cant wrote *The War at Sea* (1942) and *America's Navy in World War II* (1943); later he wrote *The Great Pacific Victory* (1946)—all published by The John Day Company.

[4] *Three Hundred Years of American Painting* (Time Incorporated, 1957).

[5] Among them: *The Thread of Laughter* (1952) and *The Republic of Letters* (1955), published by Alfred A. Knopf.

the cover fell in his section, he edited that as well as the other articles routinely assigned to him. If a story failed to measure up, he was expected to rewrite it. Onetime senior editor Max Ways warned the author of this history: "Don't make us all sound like a bunch of God damned Senators defining our 'positions.' That we did—but what kept us up all night was not the reconstruction of the world but the search for relevant, interesting and true facts." Much of the hard work on the magazine was related to style, manner, tone of voice, presentation. The over-riding concern was to present a coherent account of the week's news that made sense to the ordinary reader.

Money alone could not have compensated for the mental and physical toll that *Time* exacted from its staff. None were more dedicated than the researchers, women drawn to *Time* by their own deep interest in the current news and the fascination of being personally involved in it. They came from colleges, newspapers, government offices, industry; many of them had worked abroad. For a woman with a specialized background, academic or professional, there was the opportunity to continue to explore developments in her field.

With "researcher," a term adopted by Hadden and Luce originally to confer status, *Time* in fact created a new career for women. Most accepted the fact that they would not become writers; those who wanted to be correspondents had to be satisfied to be sent out from time to time to a domestic or foreign bureau to fill in for people away on vacations. Their own long vacations (one month) gave them a chance to travel; as a group they were probably the liveliest trippers at *Time*.

Their job (a two-fold one) was critical to *Time*'s operation. At the outset they had to produce original and supporting material for the writer's assigned story; they searched for facts through interviews, news bureau files, news clips, encyclopedias, esoteric material exhumed from libraries. Smart writers accepted them (and leaned on them) as trusted partners in the story process.

As "checkers" they then adopted a sterner mien. Before any article went to press they had to certify to its accuracy, anointing with a red dot facts that had been checked against an authoritative source, with a black dot sources that were reasonably acceptable but not necessarily infallible. The undotted stood out like a stark, unanswered question, to be fought over and (usually) amended or discarded. In *Time*'s past a handful of valiant women journalists—Mary Fraser,

441

Patricia Divver, Content Peckham, to mention a few of *Time*'s head researchers—set their colleagues an example of standing firm against a generation of impatient and overconfident males.

Their position was celebrated in verse by Roger Hewlett, before he went off to *Sports Illustrated*. He wrote it, Hewlett said, "with no apologies whatever to Irving Berlin, the father of a onetime *Time* researcher, who wrote the music and called it 'You're Not Sick, You're Just in Love.' " [6] Hewlett called his verse "Checking *Time*":

> *A writer, looking arrogant:*
> I write stories that are fine and true
> I give every man his proper due
> Though my facts are set in vivid hue
> I never lie, I never lie.
>
> I can clarify the most obscure
> With a style that's lean and clean and pure
> Though my sentences are never dense
> In all my evidence
> I never lie . . .
>
> *A researcher, looking doubtful:*
> I don't think we can say this
> I don't like how we play this
> I'm not sure that's the way this was.
>
> They did not sign the pact here
> I don't think this is fact here
> We can't know what this act here does.
>
> I don't like window dressing
> We don't know, we're just guessing
> We may be over-stressing too.
>
> There is nothing that you say
> That occurred in quite that way
>
> They're not lies, they're just not true.

[6] From 1950 to 1952 Irving Berlin's daughter, Mary Ellin, was a researcher in the back of the book.

Hewlett leaves the issue unresolved; of course, clashing viewpoints had to be resolved, sometimes by the change of a word, a phrase modified; sometimes, when differences were irreconcilable, an editor might initial an article and send it to press over the researcher's objection. He did so at his peril, for, as most men on *Time* had learned, the researchers were right most of the time.

But *Time,* for all its professional competence, did not please a lot of people in this period, as it had never pleased a lot of people in any period. The infant *Time* had been cocky and impertinent; a middle-aged *Time* found itself accused of arrogance and dogmatism. A report prepared for publisher Linen in February 1958 on letters to the editor noted a rise in the complaints that the magazine was conveying the feeling "that it can do no wrong, that its own standards of good taste, morality and intelligence are universal and absolute." Many of the complainants were "the kind of reader *Time* has always proudly claimed: educated, professional people—lawyers, engineers, college graduates, lifetime subscribers—many of whom give the impression that they write more in sadness than in anger." While interpretative reporting was now more acceptable to those readers than it had been some years before, and *Time* could take some credit for the changing public attitude, readers "do not approve of *Time*'s giving only one side of a debatable issue. . . . They seem to think: *Time* may be right about Suez, Dulles, Kennan, et al., but these are debatable questions on which intelligent, loyal Americans may disagree without being either soft in the head or inclined toward Communism."

While the report could not be called conclusive, based as it was on a small minority of readers who made the effort to write in, it merited and got serious consideration. Recognition of a need to modify the attitude of *Time* in the direction of stricter objectivity was indicated in a note Fuerbringer wrote to Luce: "I think we have solved the matter of our tone toward the Eisenhower Administration. It wasn't so much a matter of being pro-Eisenhower—it was those adjectives. At a time, for instance, when Ike was demonstrably weakened physically, we seemed to apply the adjective 'vigorous' to him with more persistence. We seemingly couldn't just describe what was done, we had to keep alerting the reader to how good it was. I think that is all well in hand now, as is our once somewhat too defensive attitude toward Ike and his Administration, which sometimes verged on arrogance."

443

*Time* even bore down on the administration to the point where the White House evidenced some sensitivity. When Eisenhower went off on a late winter vacation, *Time* complained about "a badly needed feeling of presence—specifically the presence of the President of the U.S. at his desk, giving attention to the daily details that make long-range plans and policies work." Another time it said the President had cut his work load by as much as 25 percent because he no longer had the stamina for a full day's work, a statement that provoked the President's chief aide, Sherman Adams, to call his old White House colleague C. D. Jackson to protest that the magazine was "a little rough." Jackson soothed him by replying that the editors were "overcompensating for all the accusations they face about being 'Eisenhower captives.' "

This was not the way National Affairs editor Banks saw it. Far from "overcompensating" he thought *Time* was still sidestepping an important fact. He had written Luce: "Our Washington boys have pretty well convinced us that the biggest unreported story in the U.S. today is the way [Eisenhower] has let things go."

At a time when the editors were avowedly making a conscious effort to overcome criticism, *Time* made an unsupported, sweeping charge of journalistic dereliction on the part of the nation's newspapers. In a story in its Press section headlined "Silver Lining the Slump" it reported that "newspapers from Seattle to Savannah were doing their unlevel best to bull their way through one of the nation's biggest—and most botched—running stories: the recession." A number of editors wrote in citing the stories they had run on the recession; there was plenty of evidence of how seriously they regarded it. *Time* printed their letters with the comment: "Holding to the proposition that the recession was downplayed by much of the U.S. press, *Time* nonetheless concedes that some of its documentation was off the beam of sound reporting. *Time* erred." How *Time* so "erred" in the face of all its safeguards cannot easily be explained; embarrassment may explain the curtness with which the error was acknowledged. Luce considered the Press section in *Time* of particular importance and he was always upset when it appeared unknowing or inept. In a memo to Furth he noted: "*Time* has been very grudging about its admission of errors—in Editkomment or elsewhere. If I knew how to make an order stick, I would order this mulish grudginess to stop."

The article in the Press section turned up as an exhibit in a critique of *Time* which appeared in October 1958 in the Providence *Journal-Bulletin,* to be widely reprinted in other publications. It was written by a *Journal* reporter, Ben H. Bagdikian, who had once been a *Time* stringer.

> When it has a mind to, *Time* can develop the possibilities of a news event more imaginatively than almost any other news organization in the world; its writing and editing is bright, sometimes brilliant. But is it the Truth?
>
> The elusiveness of Truth must have worried the editors of *Time* occasionally. But if so, they have spared the reader this human doubt. Each week the world is created absolute and dogmatic, the good guys on one side, the bad guys on the other, with *Time* holding the only scorecard. Only when the reader checks back does he discover that the good guy of October may be the bad guy of January, that Truth and *Time* change.

Bagdikian went on to cite some changing *Time* judgments on public figures and events. He then quoted *Time* against itself. In a Press story the magazine had once said: "Thoughtful newspapermen know that the facts alone seldom can [speak for themselves], that they speak clearly only when they are told in proper order and perspective —and thus interpreted by an honest journalist." Bagdikian continued:

> Does the reporter collect all the facts he can and then draw a picture based on the facts? Or does he have a preconceived idea and collect only the facts that bear it out?
>
> In American politics and foreign news, *Time*'s reporting appears to be governed by an iron rule: when the facts fit the mold of *Time*'s wishes, the reporting can be superb; when they do not fit the mold, *Time*'s reporting can be so distorted as to raise serious questions about responsibility in mass communications.

When the Bagdikian critique appeared, the publisher's department was having an outside survey made of student reading habits in the universities. It was finding a disturbing undercurrent of annoyance with *Time* among both students and faculty. Mention of *Time,* the survey noted, was often accompanied by derogatory remarks: "slanted," "cloaking bias," "sly getting point across," even omitting facts when they did not agree with *Time*'s point of view.

*Time* was also drawing more than its usual quota of attacks from abroad, not through "omitting facts" but by a candid reporting of them that offended sensibilities. One case involved Fidel Castro. From 1953, when he unleashed his first attack against the Batista dictatorship, *Time* had given him extensive coverage, and when he took over the government, *Life* ran his picture on the cover. The picture was made by Andrew St. George, a *Life* contract photographer who had known and become friendly with Castro when he was still in the hills. Jerry Hannifin, a correspondent from the Washington bureau who was in Havana at the time, reported: "I gave Fidel Castro a copy of the current issue of *Life*. He grabbed it, looked at the cover and said, 'Ah, St. George did this.' He quickly turned to the spread and remarked, 'Now, at last, we get the truth.' " A week later, however, when the new revolutionary government began its blood bath, *Time* reported:

> The executioner's rifle cracked across Cuba last week, and around the world voices hopefully cheering for a new democracy fell still. The men who had just won a popular revolution for old ideals—for democracy, justice and honest government— themselves picked up the arrogant tools of dictatorship. . . . The Cuban rebel army shot more than 200 men, summarily convicted in drumhead courts, as torturers and mass murderers for the fallen Batista dictatorship. The constitution, a humanitarian document forbidding capital punishment, was overridden.

At the time, the Latin American edition was being printed in Havana, and Castro had not yet extinguished the free press. While the issue containing the *Time* story was in the bindery, the stitchers struck because of the "derogatory statements against Castro." A police official called in by the plant owners persuaded them to continue working, telling them, "*Time* was good to us when we were in the hills, when it meant the most. If they want to sell themselves to someone else now, it's their business." But from that point on the Castro regime was increasingly hostile, and *Time* soon closed its Cuban operation.

The Time Inc. reporting was subjected to a wholly unwarranted and unfair attack in this country by Herbert Matthews, of the New York *Times*. Matthews, who had interviewed Castro in his mountain fastness, had developed a proprietary and defensive attitude about the Cuban dictator to the point where he had become a propagandist for him. In a speech before the Overseas Press Club in New York he charged the Time Inc. editors with extreme partisanship. In his indictment he cited the Andrew St. George portrait of Castro, which,

446

Matthews said, had been chosen "deliberately to make Castro look like a beast."

In January 1959 James Bell, chief of the Hong Kong bureau, was refused a visa to the Philippines and his effigy was burned in the streets of Manila because he had filed reports on the widespread corruption, high living and general ineptitude of the Philippine government. At the beginning of March a report in *Time*'s Latin American edition provoked rioting in La Paz, Bolivia, in which two people were killed and the American embassy stoned. This was a 100-line article on the economic chaos in Bolivia, which had received more U.S. aid per capita during a period of six years than any other country in the world. *Time* reported:

> Last week a U.S. embassy official added up the results and made a wry face. "We don't have a damn thing to show for it," he said. "We're wasting money. The only solution to Bolivia's problems," he went on to wisecrack, "is to abolish Bolivia. Let her neighbors divide up the country and the problems." [7] Up in the clouds of La Paz (alt. 11,900 ft.), inside the drab, grey palace where he is guarded by a constantly manned machine gun, Hernán Siles Zuazo, 44, Bolivia's President, admitted: "The situation is critical and explosive."

Resentments mounted. The Philippine ambassador to the United States, Carlos Romulo, denounced *Time* at a dinner given by the Women's National Press Club in the capital: "One of your magazines of comment should print in bold type on its cover—'All the news as we angle it.' . . . Isolated facts, true in themselves, are not necessarily the truth. . . . Truth can be said without adjectives that hurt the sensibilities of an entire people, for truth is truth and needs neither decoration nor derogation to make it appear as truth."

The criticisms, the letters report, the Bagdikian essay and the survey of campus readers had prompted Luce to ask Furth to draw up a "proposition" that all the editors could ponder and discuss. Furth delivered in March 1959, a month before the Romulo attack:

> The proposition is as follows: the editorial tone of *Time* is unacceptable, or even repellent, to a substantial number of readers

---

[7] The "wisecrack" appeared only in the Latin American edition, which then carried longer stories on Hemisphere news than the domestic edition.

or ex-readers. For discussion purposes, these persons may conveniently be labeled "intellectuals," including "eggheads.". . .

There is nothing new in the fact that *Time* has plenty of critics. That has been true for 36 years and will be true—and ought to be—to the end of *Time*. That is not part of the proposition. The proposition is that in spite of the highest circulation ever, there are worrisome signs that *Time* suffers a lack of respect among people who may have a significant effect on *Time's* future. . . . And, finally, there are the individual reactions and word-of-mouth reports of individuals in the Time & Life Building. It is fatuous to repeat at this point that the majority opinion from all these latter sources is heavily pro-*Time*. We are concerned today with the minority "anti." And so I report that an appreciable number of senior Time Incers, in various functions, editorial and managerial, are troubled by certain tendencies of *Time*.

Our outside critics charge *Time* with unconscionable bias at best; with dishonesty at worst. Our inside critics know better than that. They are troubled by *Time*'s manners and mannerisms; by the lapses of taste or judgment that make *Time* vulnerable to the meaner charges from the outsiders. It is not argued that the editors are necessarily wrong; it is argued that they tend to dismiss or denigrate the opposing view. As one colleague put it, "the winds of controversy do not blow freely through the pages of *Time*."

No one wants to see *Time* become an "on-the-one-hand-on-the-other" journal. In an earlier conversation, HRL summed up quite differently. He said, *"Time,* like a good lawyer, should demonstrate its grasp of the opposing side of a case. *How* the writer conveys the essence of the opposition is a problem in artistry."

Another troubled thought, voiced by a colleague, is a seeming effort by *Time* to "close the books on history" each week. This leads *Time* into the assertion of final-sounding judgments which may prove to be less than valid.

"Inside" critics are unanimous in these wishes: to see *Time* not necessarily loved, but respected—even by those who disagree with it. To see *Time* establish firmly a reputation for fairness. And finally—to see *Time* win the credit it deserves for its incomparable feat of gathering and organizing the news in depth.

Furth's proposition was the beginning of another anxious re-examination of *Time*'s editorial attitudes.

Ironically it was Luce's wife who suffered most from the stir *Time* kicked up in Bolivia. The article, with its contemptuous crack, had appeared in the same issue of *Time* that reported that Mrs. Luce had been nominated to be ambassador to Brazil.

It was a nomination that appeared certain of confirmation. The Senate Foreign Relations Committee, on the motion of Senator Wayne Morse, had informally voted to confirm her and waive the usual hearings because of her previous confirmation as ambassador to Italy. In order to allow any objections to be filed, however, no action could be taken officially for six days. Luce, even more eager than his wife for her to resume her diplomatic career, had already completed arrangements to set up an office in Rio de Janeiro such as he had established in Rome. Quarters had been rented, and a manager assigned.

On the news of the riots in Bolivia, Mrs. Luce, who was then in Phoenix, telephoned Acting Secretary of State Christian Herter offering to withdraw her name. Herter, who had expressed official concern at the *Time* story and, according to a New York *Times* report, had told the Bolivian ambassador that he "found it impossible to believe a member of the embassy staff would have made such a statement as that cited in the magazine article," [8] assured Mrs. Luce that this was not necessary. In Rio Brazilian officials advised the press that Mrs. Luce was still welcome as an ambassador.

The incident, however, gave an opportunity to some victims of *Time* barbs to pay off a few old scores. Former President Harry Truman, speaking to the World Press Congress at the University of Missouri, cracked: "What a nice thing it is to have Mr. Clare Boothe Luce in the grease in Bolivia. He spent a lot of time trying to put me in the grease but never succeeded." John T. O'Rourke, editor of the Washington *Daily News,* who claimed to have been a victim of *Time*'s "false reporting," proposed that the congress adopt the motion of a Central American newspaper editor condemning the magazine for "deteriorating the understanding between the United States and Latin America." Washington columnist Drew Pearson wrote in his nationally syndicated column:

[8] George de Carvalho, chief of Time Inc.'s Rio bureau, who had gone to Bolivia to cover the economic crisis, said the statement had been made to him facetiously by the director of the Point IV program in that country.

449

Bolivian riots against Americans, inspired by *Time* magazine, will make it extremely difficult for Mrs. Clare Boothe Luce, wife of the publisher of *Time,* to serve effectively in her new post as U.S. Ambassador to Brazil.

The reason is that the Luce family has been so closely tied up to the Eisenhower Administration that when *Time* magazine suggests Bolivia be carved up among its neighbors, the idea is interpreted as having Eisenhower support. . . .

If Mrs. Luce takes her post as Ambassador to Brazil it would be a source of continued resentment to Bolivians. For Brazil has a long border adjacent to Bolivia.

The Senate Foreign Relations Committee changed its mind and held open hearings on Mrs. Luce's nomination. Senators Fulbright and Morse devoted their questioning to certain partisan political speeches which Mrs. Luce had made long before her appointment as ambassador to Italy, and intimated that her partisanship proved her unfitness as a diplomat. In the end the committee voted to recommend for confirmation, with Senator Morse, chairman of the Latin American Affairs Subcommittee, casting a lone dissenting vote. On the Senate floor he delayed action on the recommendation with a three-and-a-half-hour tirade against Mrs. Luce. "Is she honest? Is she reliable?" he cried. "I am satisfied that Mrs. Luce does not meet either criterion." He asserted that Mrs. Luce's confirmation would "confirm in the minds of many Latin Americans—certainly Bolivians—the already present deep suspicion that *Time* magazine was speaking for more than itself when it suggested . . . that Bolivia be partitioned" because the Luce policy was "woven through the fabric" of the Eisenhower foreign policy. Nevertheless the Senate voted seventy-nine to eleven to confirm her. Half an hour later the Associated Press carried a statement from Mrs. Luce: "I am grateful for the overwhelming vote of confirmation in the Senate. We must now wait until the dust settles. My difficulties, of course, go some years back when Senator Wayne Morse was kicked in the head by a horse."

Mrs. Luce's remark offended many senators, who took the floor to say so. Mrs. Luce decided that she no longer wanted the post and she told her husband, in effect: "You got me into this, now help me get out of it"; he did, issuing a statement that he had asked her to offer her resignation because her "mission has now been profoundly compromised . . . deliberately, cleverly and irresponsibly . . . by

450

a few angry men who intend at her expense and at the expense of our Latin American relations to settle their little grievances with *Time.*"

The *Christian Science Monitor* called the whole affair "a tragedy of errors and low-grade comedy." While President Eisenhower called Mrs. Luce's remark about Senator Morse "ill advised," although "perfectly human," he saw "no major impairment of her usefulness for the post we intended." But Mrs. Luce was adamant; when she resigned she said that the climate of good will necessary to her assignment was "poisoned by thousands of words of extraordinarily ugly charges against my person, and of distrust of the mission I was to undertake." The New York *Times* commented: "In offering her resignation, Mrs. Luce has shown a greater degree of good judgment and personal responsibility than was displayed by her chief antagonist in this controversy. The tactics pursued by Senator Morse of Oregon in this whole affair seem to us to have been beneath contempt."

---

# The New Management

WHEN HE CAME BACK to his office after his recovery from the 1958 heart attack, Luce told Corinne Thrasher, "I'll never retire, I'll die at my desk." As a matter of fact, his brush with mortality must have started Luce thinking about the person to whom he might transfer his power—before he died at his desk. He approached a decision in widely spaced steps; it would be 1964 before he would finally surrender the title he had held for so long—that of editor-in-chief. The first step, in early 1959, was to summon Hedley Donovan to his apartment. As Donovan recalled the conversation:

> After [he] had been talking with me about the bad state of the modern novel, and the politics of America, Asia and Europe, and a couple of good movies he had seen lately, and the theories of a certain theologian he was distressed I hadn't heard of, and also a dozen or more projects and people and problems at *Fortune* . . . he said in a somewhat apologetic way that he had to bring up something "rather personal." He wondered if I would be interested, "not right away, in a few years or so," in being the next Editor-in-Chief of Time Incorporated. At the end of the evening, with a touch of the ceremoniousness that could be both

warm and ironic, he summed up, "Well, it is left, then, that you are complimented by my suggestion, and will at least think about it, and I am complimented by your suggestion that the present Editor-in-Chief is good at his job."

Nothing happened immediately. Donovan was then still managing editor of *Fortune*. An announcement that he would become editorial director of Time Inc. was made in July 1959 shortly after he returned from a trip to Europe. Just before his departure he had learned that Luce had not yet discussed the impending appointment with either of his two senior managing editors, Alexander of *Time* and Thompson of *Life*. Luce was mildly vexed when Donovan suggested that he do so—"Can't I ever just *do* something?" he complained—but he wrote to Donovan, who was by then in Germany:

> Your nomination is confirmed by the exclusive Senate of two. Actually we should include in this confirmation process Messrs. Larsen, Moore, Furth and Paine. Roy [Alexander] was decidedly for having an Editorial Director and for you. I had the feeling that Ed [Thompson] didn't think the appointment was entirely necessary though he was all for you.
>
> And now speaking for myself, it is a most happy milestone for me. I look forward to at least several years of personal partnership with you during which we will, I hope, help to make a number of desirable things happen in and for Time Inc. and for its readers.

Luce's announcement came as a surprise to the staff. Hitherto the title of editorial director, as personified by John Shaw Billings, connoted the elder statesman; Donovan was forty-five. Why should a younger man prefer it to the daily challenges that faced a managing editor? Moreover, Donovan had never worked on *Time* or *Life*.

Luce for his part had made no secret of his long admiration for Donovan. In 1956, writing to Emmet Hughes trying to persuade him to join *Fortune*'s board of editors, Luce had said, "Donovan ranks with the best Managing Editors it has been my good fortune to have." Donovan had made *Fortune* the kind of magazine that Luce had always wanted but which former managing editors had been unable to deliver to Luce's complete satisfaction. Donovan had a mind of his own. Arriving late for a lunch, Luce explained that he had been delayed by an argument with *Fortune*'s managing editor over tax reform and he added with obvious satisfaction, "I couldn't budge him an inch." Luce discerned in his new editorial director the judicious and measured temperament that would be needed to moderate and yet to lead an editorial establishment of such complexity.

Donovan set out to learn what he did not know about editing the other magazines, choosing *Sports Illustrated* for the first of his apprenticeships. Subsequently he temporarily took over the managing editorship of *Time* and then *Life*. "Luce was enthusiastic about my making the *Time* visit," he said, "but I think he felt that I was a little foolhardy to try *Life,* and was relieved when I got through it without major damage."

Donovan's successor on *Fortune* was his executive editor, Duncan Norton-Taylor, whom Luce once called "one of the most thoroughly professional pros in our business." It was one of the few occasions at Time Inc. when an older man succeeded a younger one as managing editor; Norton-Taylor was fifty-five. He was a graduate of Brown University, worked as a cub reporter on the Newark *Star-Eagle* and the Brooklyn *Daily Times* and was an editor for some years of a detective magazine in the Frank A. Munsey group until his magazine, like the other Munsey pulps, began to slide into the past. Then he free-lanced as a fiction writer. In 1939 he applied for a writing job on *Time* and was hired by Gottfried, who later admitted that he was impressed by the applicant because he himself had once aspired to be a detective story writer. In twelve years on *Time* Norton-Taylor wrote a record sixty cover stories for National Affairs and during the war for the Army and Navy and World Battlefronts departments. He served briefly and, by his own admission, apprehensively, in the South Pacific as a war correspondent, recording his experiences in a book, *With My Heart in My Mouth.*[1] In 1951 he transferred to *Fortune* as a member of its board of editors; five years later he was made an assistant managing editor and, two years after that, executive editor. In the editorial ranks where so many of his colleagues were professed liberals, Norton-Taylor felt no embarrassment at labeling himself a Taft Republican.

Over on the business side of Time Inc. Larsen had also been casting his mind forward to the sixties. In May 1959, two months before the announcement about Donovan, the company recognized the heavy responsibilities then being carried by two of its younger executives

---

[1] Coward-McCann, Inc., 1944.

and signaled increasing responsibilities for them in the future by electing James Linen, publisher of *Time,* and Andrew Heiskell, publisher of *Life,* to the board of directors.

As part of his long-range planning Larsen had initiated, at David Brumbaugh's suggestion, a study of Time Inc.'s executive compensation and incentive plans. The committee study, which was delivered to Larsen shortly before the election of Linen and Heiskell as directors, contained some surprises for both Luce and Larsen and was a major factor leading to a sweeping reorganization of executive management. The report found that 1) while Time Inc. compensation was good and its special benefits outstanding,[2] these conditions in some cases had an undesirable "locking-in" effect; 2) many in the higher echelons felt that there was a tinge of "socialism" in that salaries did not differentiate sufficiently between the "really able" and the "merely good"; and 3) the relatively low-level salaries which Luce and Larsen paid themselves tended to impose a psychological and financial ceiling on their associates.[3] It also found a good deal of restlessness throughout the executive ranks. Many of the senior executives were talking vaguely about early retirement while at the middle level younger men were grumbling about the lack of opportunities for advancement. In evaluating the committee's report, which also confessed that the incentive bonus and stock plans had not paid off as handsomely as anticipated, Brumbaugh pointed out that the only way in which the company could improve that situation was by improving the profit margin. Though gross revenues had doubled in eight years, he pointed out, the profit level had remained—except for 1956— about the same. After Luce read the report, he wrote to Larsen,

the old wheels of capitalism began to turn. . . . Everything depends on men—on having the right man in the right job at the right time. Therefore, if Time Inc. has not been as successful in the last few years as it should have been—the essential trouble must be, as per the platitude, men. . . .

I hope you and I will be able to say that 1959 was the year in which we got the Time Inc. Team properly organized . . . the year in which it became clear to all of us in the Top Man-

[2] Trust, profit-sharing and medical plans had existed since 1938. The employees' profit-sharing-savings fund, reorganized in 1951, had tripled in value by 1959.

[3] In 1959 Luce's salary was $80,000, Larsen's $75,000. They did not participate in the profit-sharing funds.

agement, editorial and publishing, that we are really determined to have the best damned organization we can. This is really the basic thing to do about Brumbaugh's challenge. The only way you can get higher profit, outside of bull luck, is to have profit-making men.

What lies heavy on the stomach is all that stuff about everybody planning to quit in a few years! I spoke about this with some heat when last I saw you. And I think this attitude will disappear . . . the minute we make clear that we are out for Success in deadly earnest. You and I have already, I think and hope, made a considerable beginning on reorganization. . . . It is a reorganization not only of men but, as per your 1960 castup, a reorganization of Expectations.

The letter ended by suggesting that the two have dinner and talk it over. After the dinner Luce wrote Larsen:

I don't want to let this day pass without putting something on the record. In our many years together, yesterday evening was, for me, just about the most completely satisfying and gratifying ever!

I was, and am, especially impressed by the way you have thought out the "T.O." problem. "Wid a bit of luck" the next couple of years should be very constructive.

I should just like to add—in what is surely a permissible sentimental vein—that I think it's quite wonderful that after 37 years we can think and work together as well as or better than ever—and for my part most agreeably.

Luce and Larsen met for dinner in July 1959. The reorganization was announced in April 1960.

In the interim Luce worked out, with the agreement of *Time*'s managing editor Alexander, a shift in the editorial management of *Time*. As Alexander recalled it:

Luce called me up to his apartment and asked me if I didn't think it was time for me to give the job up. I said I certainly did. I was ready. He said fine, he'd make me editor and that I should take four or five months to look around for a successor. I said, "Look, we both know there is only one man to be my successor and that's Otto [Fuerbringer]." He grinned and said sure, he knew that. I told him I wanted to be relieved next week and not

456

stay around as a lame duck. He grinned again and said, "Then can I call Otto and tell him?" I said sure, and we were both happy.

Alexander had been eleven years on the job (the first year as acting managing editor). Fuerbringer had been his assistant managing editor the entire time. To fill that post now Luce and Alexander agreed on the Foreign News editor, Tom Griffith, and the changes—"the most important announcement about *Time* in ten years" Luce called it—took place in March 1960.

Unlike certain shifts in managing editors in *Time*'s past, the change-over was smooth and harmonious. Fuerbringer was accustomed to command and thoroughly schooled in his job since he had edited the magazine in Alexander's absence on vacation and trips. Griffith's seniority and acknowledged competence made him the logical deputy. Alexander, as editor, did not choose to play an active role in the magazine's management but conceived his function to be that of critic and advisor, an attitude that greatly eased the way for his successor.

The problem of corporate reorganization to which Luce and Larsen addressed themselves in 1959 involved a re-thinking of the role of every senior executive. Luce, although he had made the first move toward appointing a new editor-in-chief, was not yet ready to surrender the title. Larsen felt strongly that any meaningful change must take the form of a grant of real authority to younger men and was prepared to step down from his own position as president. He pressed the point that if the company did not open opportunities to younger men, it might well lose the two men best qualified by age and experience to carry on the business—Linen and Heiskell.

Both men were restless. By 1960 Linen had held the position of publisher for fifteen years; Heiskell had been publisher for fourteen years in title, but he had been closely related to the job since 1942 when he became general manager of *Life*. Larsen believed that both men were vulnerable to outside offers. Linen was evidencing a strong interest in Connecticut politics. His personality, as well as his connections in the Republican Party (his wife, the former Sara Scranton, was the daughter of Pennsylvania's longtime National Committeewoman, Mrs. Worthington Scranton, who had been a power in the GOP; Mrs. Linen's brother William was later to become that state's governor), marked him as a potential candidate for state or national office. A group in Connecticut was urging Linen to run for governor.

Heiskell had already asked for a change of scene. He was married then to the actress Madeleine Carroll, who wanted to live in Paris— an idea that strongly appealed to her husband. He proposed to Larsen that he become Time Inc.'s senior executive abroad, a job for which he was eminently qualified by a European education and a gift for languages. Larsen stalled on this request because he felt that Heiskell was needed in the head office.

Apart from the danger of losing two valuable executives, a company once too centralized had now become too decentralized and needed to be brought together. There was little communication between the two executive vice presidents, Stillman and Black. As has already been noted, Stillman of his own volition had surrendered most of his operating responsibilities in publishing to concentrate on investments and in particular his special baby, the burgeoning and successful subsidiary, Eastex. Supervision of the publishing operations by Black was increasingly difficult because of the diverse problems of each magazine. Moreover, as Heiskell recalled, "Each division had become a separate duchy. There was too much competition between the magazines." In December 1959 an interim step had been taken by Larsen to redefine responsibilities by making David Brumbaugh and C. D. Jackson administrative vice presidents, staff officers to absorb some of the increasing pressures on the president's office.

This was only a prelude to the more sweeping and extensive reorganization of April 1960, which came as a complete surprise to the staff and the publishing world. In a joint statement, Luce and Larsen announced "with an expression of pride and confidence, that we have been able to form a Management which will match the great opportunities of the future." Andrew Heiskell became chairman of the board, replacing Maurice T. Moore, who remained as a director and chief counsel; James Linen became president, with Roy Larsen taking the position of chairman of a new executive committee; David Brumbaugh became executive vice president, treasurer and a director; Charles Stillman became chairman of a new finance committee and Howard Black was made senior vice president, both remaining members of the board.

Three new publishers were appointed at the same time. *Fortune* was not affected, but on *Life* C. D. Jackson moved in as publisher, returning to the magazine of which he had at one time been general manager. On *Time* Linen was succeeded by Bernhard Auer, the former circulation director. It was also at this time that *Sports Illustrated* publisher Arthur Murphy returned to the corporate staff as vice president in charge of production; Sidney James, as Donovan and Murphy had recommended, became that magazine's publisher and Andre Laguerre its managing editor.

The reorganization of 1960 was, as Luce had put it, "a reorganization of Expectations." While the new management inherited some problems, notably those of *Life,* it also was in a position of great strength. Time Inc. revenues were once again at an all-time high even though net income of $9,303,000 was well below the then corporate record of 1956. At the point where this book opened, in 1941, the total assets of the corporation were $25,175,000; in 1960 they had risen to $230,585,000.

# "No Curves, No Sliders, No Sinkers"

T HE EDITORS OF *Time* chose President Eisenhower as Man of the Year for 1959.[1] In December he had returned from a journey to Europe, Asia and Africa which had been a triumph of personal diplomacy. He had been hailed by millions and had become, said *Time,* "the nation's image in one of the grand plebiscites of history. . . . Eisenhower towered as the world's best-known, best-liked citizen." The President wrote to Luce that he wished he could find some way to acknowledge the tribute but that he was embarrassed even to mention it: "At any rate I shall do my best to avoid causing you any regret for your action." Luce replied:

> The story [was] written from the heart as well as from the head of all concerned. Let me add personally that one of the deep satisfactions of my life is that I once went all out in the advocacy of a certain man for the Presidency of the United States and after seven years can say that I never for a moment regretted it. . . . Not that I have not disagreed with you or your administration on some occasions, and not that I don't often ask for more, like Oliver Twist. As sometimes you see in print. But my unqualified statement stands.

[1] General Eisenhower had been Man of the Year for 1944.

Luce felt no similar compulsion to go all out for a presidential candidate in 1960. His longtime friend Nelson Rockefeller could not make up his mind whether to run for the Republican nomination. He had been seeking support for his candidacy for six months but had to face the realization that the party organization was solidly for Vice President Nixon. Luce stood apart this time from intraparty politicking, not personally committed to Rockefeller in any way and regarding Nixon as a progressive Republican well qualified to carry on the Eisenhower tradition.

In December 1959 Rockefeller suddenly appeared to be throwing in the sponge with a statement which explained why "I am not, and shall not be, a candidate." The announcement was in part written by Emmet Hughes, then Time Inc.'s chief of foreign correspondents and a volunteer advisor to the New York governor. Though he had been closely associated with Eisenhower, Hughes had become extremely critical of the administration's foreign policy and, on his own time, had written a book on the subject [2] which *Time* in its review had deemed somewhat overdrawn: "Author Hughes seems to find Soviet diplomatic maneuvers venturesome, flexible and imaginative, however brutal, and American diplomacy uninventive, bumbling and myopic, however decent."

*Time* reacted waspishly to the Rockefeller statement:

The tone of his statement was as eyebrow raising as his decision to back down. He skirted any pledge of support for his only rival, Vice President Richard Nixon. . . .

Although sources close to Rockefeller swore that he was friendly to Nixon, Rocky's statement indicated that he was ready to serve as a witness for the prosecution of the Eisenhower Administration. . . . As far as the Democrats were concerned, nothing became Rocky's candidacy like his leaving of it. . . .

Loyal Rockefeller partisans refused to see the withdrawal as a retreat. They dreamed headily that somewhere along the line Dick Nixon might stub his toe . . . and that delegates would call for a Rockefeller draft at the Chicago convention. Beyond that they had another dream: that somehow Nixon might get defeated in 1960. Presumably that would finish Nixon and open up to Rockefeller the vista of 1964.

But such dreams ignored a jarring fact that was plain to all.

[2] *America the Vincible* (Doubleday & Company, Inc., 1959).

461

In the here and now of the 1960 campaign, Rockefeller had left the field before a shot had been fired.

Before the story went to press there had been a major row on the editorial floor. When the statement was issued, Hughes told his fellow Time Incer, Jack Olsen, the reporter assigned to the Rockefeller camp, that it was intended to gain leverage against the conservative elements of the party and that actually Rockefeller was keeping his options open. Olsen and Richard Clurman, deputy chief of *Time*'s domestic correspondents,[3] were furious that the editors would not accept this inside interpretation. There is no question but that the editors had come to look askance at Hughes (partly because of his turning on the Eisenhower Administration).

After *Time* went to press, Clurman told Luce, who had not been consulted, that "the argument with the editors was the most unprofessional, close-minded, and irrelevant I have ever had at Time Inc." Luce did not like the story either and rebuked the editors:

The tone of this week's Rockefeller story does not reflect my views. To conclude, for example, that he "left the field before a shot had been fired" is to sign off with a very down beat—and I think one that is also not the truth. Not only do I think that Nelson is a big national asset; more precisely, I think his statement kept him in as an influential person in the Republican party, and this is the point I would have stressed. His statement said he "expected" to support the nominee of the party. I see no possible reason why he should have come out for Nixon. For many months now it seems to me N.A. has been a) good to very good, b) "fair"—in the sense of being fair-minded. Some sort of factional emotion got into this story. Please consider what it was and extirpate it.

The *Life* editorial of the following week reflected Luce's views; it said that the Rockefeller withdrawal was "timed to do the least harm to the Republican party and to his own power to influence it. It may even strengthen his hand." It continued:

[3] Clurman, a graduate of the University of Chicago, joined *Time* in 1949 as a writer after working on *Commentary*. As the writer of the Press section, he wrote a cover story on Alicia Patterson Guggenheim, the founder of *Newsday*. A year after this appeared, she invited Clurman to join her staff as Newsday's editorial director. After three years there he resigned and returned to *Time* as deputy chief of correspondents.

If the candidates should be Nixon and Kennedy, the irrational antipathies which both men arouse (Jack for being Catholic, Dick for being "divisive") could make this election more heated than enlightening. In any case, the issues will need all the clarification the voters can get. Rocky has promised to speak out "with full freedom and vigor on these issues." . . . So whether he needs it or not, Nixon now has a forensic pacesetter in his own party. This gives him good reason and opportunity, not to follow Rocky's lead on any particular issue but to continue to carve out clear positions of his own. . . .

The Democrats need a similar spokesman. . . . And the voters need clear spokesmen on both sides, for the issues of 1960 are more important than party loyalties or personalities.

In the aftermath of the Rockefeller row Hughes accepted the governor's standing invitation to join the Rockefeller brothers' personal staff as their senior advisor on public policy. He resigned from Time Inc. in March 1960.

The following month James Shepley, who had become a friend of Nixon during his service as Washington bureau chief, took a leave of absence as chief of the domestic news service to join the vice president's staff as campaign assistant, and Hedley Donovan, who had been disturbed by Hughes's close involvement with Rockefeller while still a member of the editorial staff, took the occasion to nail down a company policy. He drew a distinction between participation of staff members in local politics and their identification with a national candidate: "Anyone who is exercising an appreciable individual influence in the campaign of a candidate for national office has become a part of Time Inc.'s reportorial subject matter. A Time Incer who wishes to work with the national staff of a candidate for national office may not do so on a 'spare time' basis; he must apply for a leave of absence, and the leave must be for a minimum of three months."

On a higher level, well above partisan politics, *Life* launched a series of articles to search out, in that election year, the "American purpose in the world," which Luce had asked his editors to explore. It was an old theme with him, going back at least to "The American Century" written in 1941. In 1958 he had called Max Ways back from the London bureau to make a survey of what the Time Inc. magazines had been advocating by way of foreign policy. Ways subsequently developed his own ideas in a book, *Beyond Survival,* published in September 1959.[4] In a foreword Luce said that the object of the book was "to spur the government and people of the United States to arrive at some convictions—intellectual convictions about what they are doing in the world. . . . Recently I have found . . . their most commonly shared opinion is that the United States lacks a clear sense of purpose in its world activities."

Ways's book argued that U.S. policy makers were not to blame; that the fault lay in the American people, who lacked a sense of purpose; to recover it the United States should turn back to the philosophy of the Founding Fathers; the American purpose should be to extend and protect institutions of order and freedom in the world, but no such policy could be mandated by a government but must grow out of the convictions of the people themselves.

*Life* enlisted eight distinguished Americans to respond to what Luce called "a summons, of some urgency" to a debate on the national purpose. They were Adlai Stevenson, Archibald MacLeish, David Sarnoff, Walter Lippmann, Clinton Rossiter, John W. Gardner, Billy Graham and Albert Wohlstetter. The series, which began in May, did not seek to arrive at a consensus but aimed at stimulating nationwide debate. In order to get the widest possible circulation for the articles, and forswearing any self-interest, *Life*'s editors persuaded the New York *Times* to publish them simultaneously and to offer them, without charge, to newspapers which were clients of that paper's news service. Thirty of the nation's largest newspapers carried the series, and subsequently republication rights were offered without charge to newspaper, radio and TV stations throughout the country.[5] Some thirty national organizations, ranging from the National Education Association to The Brookings Institution, agreed to put the national purpose on their agenda. After the political conventions Nixon and John F. Kennedy both contributed articles on the subject to *Life*.

The series appeared at a troubled moment. In May 1960 Francis Gary Powers and his U-2 were shot down over the Soviet Union. The administration first claimed that Powers was engaged in high-altitude

[4] Harper & Brothers.
[5] The articles, together with a contribution by James Reston of the *Times,* were published as a book entitled *The National Purpose* (Holt, Rinehart and Winston, 1960).

weather reconnaissance, but then reversed itself to admit that he was on an intelligence mission. Khrushchev used the incident to torpedo the summit meeting which had assembled in Paris. Adlai Stevenson and Senator Kennedy promptly attacked the administration's handling of the U-2 affair, and *Life* was inclined to agree with them, editorializing: "It is one thing for everybody to give our unhappy President a warm welcome home; it is another to pretend that his trip was a success. On the contrary, his diplomacy was caught in a confusion of lies and blunders and there is some truth in Adlai Stevenson's partisan charge, which will doubtless haunt the campaign, that Eisenhower handed Khrushchev the crowbar with which he wrecked the summit."

In June Nelson Rockefeller, who had been mulling over the implications of the U-2 affair, decided to speak out. "I am deeply convinced, and deeply concerned, that those now assuming control of the Republican Party have failed to make clear where this party is heading and where it proposes to lead the nation." He then issued a nine-point program of his own. *Time* reported Eisenhower's reaction this way:

> After reading Nelson Rockefeller's blast . . . President Eisenhower remarked with a trace of bitterness in his voice: "I see the fine hand of Emmet in this." By Emmet he meant Emmet John Hughes, his own speech-writer during the 1952 and 1956 campaigns.
>
> The President's recognition of a familiar style and tone was accurate. Emmet Hughes, 39, wrote most of Rockefeller's manifesto. . . . And if it is remarkable that a man who wrote Eisenhower campaign speeches should write a Rockefeller statement sharply criticizing the Eisenhower Administration's record, it is even more remarkable that he is a Democrat (a "dissident" or "wandering" Democrat, he specifies), who, under the President's auspices, delivered a major address to the 1956 Republican convention.

*Time* dismissed the Rockefeller statement—a little too hastily in view of the subsequent fight it stirred up in the Republican platform committee—as a "firecracker [which], having made everybody jump, had left not a tremor behind." *Life* thought that "the fact that [Rockefeller] ended his earlier candidacy just before the primaries began and reversed it—in all but name—the day after they ended, makes his

465

performance seem a bit shoddy"; *Life* nevertheless described his statement as "a bombshell" which served "the best interests of his party, as well as the nation, by demanding a sharp debate on the great issues confronting the U.S."

Luce felt personally involved. He had originally recommended Hughes to Eisenhower, and even though Rockefeller's ghostwriter no longer worked for Time Inc., he felt that he must explain his own position to the President. He did not disagree with much that Rockefeller said but he disliked his tactics. His letter to the President reverted to "the very involved subject of Emmet Hughes, his book, his Rockefelleritis, etc." He had not, Luce wrote,

> liked any of it—and I hope you understood that all along. Which is no excuse for my not having written you. . . . The book [*America the Vincible*] was written without my approval. [Hughes] asked for my criticism of the manuscript and I sent him quite a bagful. But to no effect. Last fall I thought things might right themselves. . . . Then came this Rockefeller business. Nelson never asked my advice about Emmet—not even one sentence worth. In April I had lunch with Nelson alone in Albany. We talked about Nixon and I thought all was well. Enough . . . the whole matter must be unpleasant to you. But maybe these few words of mine will cast a little light onto a murky business.

Eisenhower's reply was gracious. Luce had cleared up some misgivings; Rockefeller was being too much influenced by a man who had no capacity for giving sensible advice, the President said.

Subsequently, in June, as a result of the national purpose series, Luce was invited to testify before the Senate Subcommittee on National Policy Machinery. Victory in the cold war, Luce said to the committee, did not necessarily mean total war or a demand for unconditional surrender of the enemy; a limited definition of victory would be "to sever the state power of Russia and Red China from the mission of their present Communist rulers to Communize the world." But even this limited objective meant that the United States must be prepared for total war. In his judgment the nation was not so prepared "in the physical defense and protection of the people . . . civil defense and, specifically, shelters. We believe we will not strike the first blow in nuclear warfare. Therefore we must be prepared to receive it. We are not so prepared. No one knows how many millions

466

of dead and wounded we can afford and still have a nation." Then, referring to a decision taken by the President in 1958 to reject the Civil Defense Administration's recommendation for a great nation-wide shelter construction program, Luce declared: "It is shocking that the federal government announces to the people that it will be able to do nothing to protect their lives for several weeks after the opening of hostilities. The determination to build shelters and thus lessen the real danger of the annihilation of the American people will be the clearest sign that the leaders and government of the United States have determined to win the cold war."

Lest his statement be construed at the White House as a general indictment, Luce again wrote to Eisenhower to spell out the matters in which he disagreed with the President but to say that his "overall position is basically in agreement with yours." The letter concluded by telling the President that the editorial page of *Life* in the week before the convention would be devoted to an appreciation of Eisenhower in the White House. The editorial was written by Jessup.

> Eisenhower's record is well worth inspection. Of the many flaws the Democrats will find in it, historians will probably agree at least on one. There is some substance to the charge that Ike has rather reigned than ruled. He has tended to assume, as you can in the Army but not in the White House, that an order once given is self-executing; a certain lack of follow-through has marred some of his best intentions, notably the rejuvenation of the Republican party. He has been an easy boss. But that is not to echo the commoner (and mistaken) charge that he does not make decisions. Ike has made plenty of decisions. And most of them were right. . . .
>
> He has been the least "divisive" of modern presidents—and the most widely beloved. . . .
>
> His luck has run out lately at Sverdlovsk, Paris and Tokyo.[6] But let not these setbacks be confused with flaws in the solid structure of allied political, military and economic strength built in the Eisenhower era. . . .
>
> At home the case is open and shut. The Eisenhower economic policy has been virtually a textbook model of how to befriend and stimulate a free-market system. . . .

[6] Powers' U-2 was shot down over Sverdlovsk; Paris was the scene of the wrecked summit meeting; Eisenhower's journey to Tokyo had been canceled in June because of fierce anti-American demonstrations by students there.

467

The Kennedy-or-Nixon era will be different. It may be grim or it may be great. It can scarcely be more sunny or fruitful than these Eisenhower years, in which so many age-old visions of the good life first became real.

The editorial brought from Eisenhower a letter which, Luce told the President, was "surely one of the most interesting that any President ever wrote."

PERSONAL AND CONFIDENTIAL

August 8, 1960

Dear Harry: . . .

I plead guilty to the general charge that many people have felt I have been too easy a boss. Respecting this there are one or two things that you might like to think over. (I do not mean to defend, merely to explain.)

Except for my first two years as President, during which I enjoyed the benefit of a very skimpy majority in the Congress, I have had to deal with a Congress controlled by the opposition and whose partisan antagonism to the Executive Branch has often been blatantly displayed. The hope of doing something constructive for the nation, in spite of this kind of opposition, has required the use of methods calculated to attract coopera-tion, even though a natural impulse would have been to lash out at partisan charges and publicity-seeking demagogues.

Another point—the government of the United States has be-come too big, too complex, and too pervasive in its influence on all our lives for one individual to pretend to direct the details of its important and critical programming. Competent assistants are mandatory; without them the Executive Branch would bog down. To command the loyalties and dedication and best efforts of capable and outstanding individuals requires patience, under-standing, a readiness to delegate, and an acceptance of re-sponsibility for any honest errors—real or apparent—those associates and subordinates might make. Such loyalty from such people cannot be won by shifting responsibility, whining, scolding or demagoguery. Principal subordinates must have confidence that they and their positions are widely respected, and the chief must do his part in assuring that this is so.

Of course I could have been more assertive in making and announcing decisions and initiating programs. I can only say that I adopted and used those methods and manners that seemed to me most effective. (I should add that one of my problems has been to control my temper—a temper that I have had to battle all my life!)

Finally, there is the matter of maintaining a respectable image of American life before the world! Among the qualities that the American government must exhibit is dignity. In turn the principal governmental spokesman must strive to display it. In war and in peace I've had no respect for the desk-pounder, and have despised the loud and slick talker. If my own ideas and practices in this matter have sprung from weakness, I do not know. But they were and are deliberate or, rather, natural to me. They are not accidental.

As ever,

Ike

The Time Inc. magazines had followed Senator John F. Kennedy's career for a long time and with great interest. Luce was an old friend of Kennedy's father; Jacqueline Kennedy's stepfather, Hugh D. Auchincloss, had been a classmate and friend of Luce at Yale. In 1940 Joe Kennedy had persuaded Luce to write an introduction to his son's book, *Why England Slept,*[7] in which Luce said of the author, "If John Kennedy is characteristic of the younger generation—and I believe he is—many of us would be happy to have the destinies of this Republic handed over to his generation at once."

In 1956, when the senator was making his unsuccessful bid for the vice presidential nomination at the Democratic convention, the Luces were guests of the senior Kennedys at their Riviera villa, following the proceedings in Chicago from there. Luce cabled his editors that Kennedy had emerged as "a considerable national figure" and they would do well to devote more space to him. Late in 1957 *Time* did its first cover story on Kennedy because he appeared to be the front runner for the 1960 Democratic nomination. The story contained a quote from Jackie about her father-in-law—"actually, he's a nice old gentleman we see at Thanksgiving and Christmas." Joe Kennedy telegraphed Luce: *"Time* did a great job for Jack but that nice old gentleman quote has resulted in Jackie being cut out of my

[7] Wilfred Funk, 1940.

will and I am having a talk with my lawyers about suing you for libel. . . . Happy Thanksgiving." To which Luce replied: "Thanks for the Thanksgiving message. Considering how wrong you are about practically everything it is truly remarkable how much good you have done including to me. Regarding the article all I can say is that if we had as good a story as that every week we could afford all the libel suits you could bring."

Despite Luce's friendship with the Kennedys, *Time* reported the pre-convention maneuverings of the Democrats so evenhandedly that Hubert Humphrey's campaign manager, James Rowe, wrote to Washington correspondent Hugh Sidey after a Humphrey cover story: "I was charmed and delighted. . . . Some people . . . keep asking me why I am for Hubert Humphrey. . . . I have tried many times to articulate my reasons but without much success. I found that articulation in your story. . . . You have said it far better than anyone else so far." After the magazine's cover story on Lyndon Johnson, John Steele, chief of the Washington bureau, reported, "Sam Rayburn [Speaker of the House and one of Johnson's principal supporters] has been extremely friendly ever since the [Johnson] cover." In its July 11, 1960, issue *Time* ran a cover story on the Kennedy family with measured reference to its most outstanding member. The following week *Time* carried the story of how John Kennedy had won the nomination in Los Angeles.

During the convention Luce had a telephone call in New York from Joe Kennedy. As he recalled it:

He said he was going to be in New York Friday on his way to Europe and could I see him? We made a date for five o'clock at my apartment at the Waldorf. It did not occur to me that that meant that Joe would be leaving Los Angeles before the convention was over.

Five o'clock came but no Joe. Seven o'clock and still no Joe. My son Henry was with me, having come to dinner. Soon after seven, the phone rang and, with a typical burst of expletives, Joe told me his plane had been delayed. I asked him whether he would like to come to dinner. He would. Half an hour later he was there—ruddily hale, hearty and happy. He consumed a couple of lobsters while we exchanged small talk about the convention and the nomination of his 43-year-old son for the Presidency of the United States.

Jack Kennedy was scheduled to make his acceptance speech

470

at ten o'clock our time. How come Joe had not stayed in Los Angeles to hear the bands play? Anyway, there he was with me and Henry.

When we adjourned to the living room after dinner, Joe still showed no signs of getting down to business. So I opened up. I said my attitude (as editor-in-chief of Time Inc. publications) toward Jack could be very simply stated. Let us divide the question into two parts: domestic policy, foreign policy.

As for domestic policy, naturally it was to be assumed that Jack would adopt a "liberal" policy. Old Joe broke in with blazing blue eyes and many a goddamn. He said: "Harry, you know goddamn well no son of mine could ever be a goddamn liberal."

I told Joe to hush. It was the nature of American politics that in order to win, a Democratic candidate for the Presidency had to take a liberal position (while, of course, retaining the automatic support of the solid South) and that we would not hold that against him.

"But," I said, "if Jack shows any signs of going soft on Communism (in foreign policy)—then we would clobber him."

Joe said, "Well, you don't have to worry about that."

There wasn't much more to say as we waited. . . . Then the TV came on and there was John Fitzgerald Kennedy with voice and gesture and face and figure that would soon become imperishable in the world's vision.

What must have been the emotions of that father watching and listening to that son? Mission accomplished—almost, for there was still the election. Life fulfilled beyond all the hazards of chance. It would take a very great dramatist-novelist to portray Joseph Patrick Kennedy's emotions—to mix the rhythm of earthy selfishness and higher loyalties.

When the speech was done, we chatted for a while, and then Joe got up to leave. At the doorway, he turned to me, took my hand again and said: "I want you to know that we are truly grateful for all that you have done for Jack."

It was a moment after the door had closed before my inner ear took in these words. I was touched, of course, but what had I done? Had I ever done too much?

While the Republicans waited to meet in their convention, the Time Inc. magazines appraised the Democrats' performance. *Life* congratulated the party on its candidate and on its platform, saying that the Democrats had done the country

> at least one great political service. They urge us all to look forward again—instead of backward, upward or around. . . .
>
> As the performance was impressive, so the invitation is exciting—as exciting as anything in our politics since 1940. The analogy is not with the issues or emotions of that year, but with the aura of unexpected renovation around the challenger. Senator Kennedy has many points of difference from Wendell Willkie. He is a pro, not an amateur; he is fully in charge of the majority party, not a convert to the minority party; and he is not up against the other party's all-time champ. So Kennedy may win and what could be more different than that?

Of the platform the editorial said: "It is the most utopian platform ever presented by either majority party. Let that fact be weighed in the scales of the 'soaring '60s' before one also calls it (as one can) the most cynical platform in history. It is a literate and cohesive summary of every conceivable political promise."

*Time* thought that the platform was "a well-made document: straight-forward, clear, brief and—as platforms go—probably the most coherent blueprint for utopia ever to come out of a convention."

Praise such as this, even with its reservations, plus the very full coverage given the candidate, revived rumors that had floated around before the convention that the Luce publications might come out for Kennedy. The *Wall Street Journal* reported: *"Time* toys with the surprising notion of backing Kennedy. . . . Editors expect a pro-Kennedy approach starting in August." Luce addressed himself to this gossip on *Life's* editorial page of the August 15 issue:

> *Life,* on its editorial page, will come out either for Nixon or for Kennedy. Ever since last January *Life* has made it very clear as to *how* it would arrive at its choice. We began by listing the major issues, indicating our general attitude toward each. . . .
>
> We have applauded both candidates for saying that world policy—and U.S. purpose—makes up the paramount issue. We have said that on "domestic" issues the Republicans start off with the best of the argument—and that Kennedy must prove that his pursuit of the Democratic utopia will not run us toward

472

economic disaster. . . . We will listen hard to both candidates and hope all citizens will, too. . . .

In discharge of editorial duty, and for whatever interest it may be, *Life* will express its views not later than October.

There was a feeling in some Time Inc. offices, however, that the editors of *Time* had already made their decision. *Time*'s coverage of the Republican convention and its treatment of Nixon had been so effusive as to cause Luce's executive assistant Furth to protest to Donovan: *"Time*'s current issue . . . strikingly illustrated something you have often said: 'If about a dozen sentences were omitted or phrased differently, what a whale of a difference it would make.' After a number of months of encouraging improvement in political posture, I feel that the current *Time* slumps badly. The tone . . . is clearly the tone of *celebration,* with accents of 'onward to victory.' I fear the effect is strong enough to discourage the uncommitted reader from looking to *Time* for detached coverage of the coming campaign."

Shortly after the Republican convention *Time*'s managing editor Fuerbringer, working late on a Sunday night, was suddenly clapped by a spectacularly painful headache. He was rushed to New York Hospital and subjected to a prolonged series of debilitating and painful tests that never did produce a diagnosis of the problem. His convalescence was to keep him out of the office until after the election. In the emergency the editor-in-chief's first impulse was to turn back to Alexander; but Alexander assured Luce that assistant managing editor Griffith was fully qualified to edit the magazine in Fuerbringer's absence.

Griffith and the National Affairs editor Banks were agreed on one thing: *Time*'s election coverage would be as fair to both sides as possible without sacrificing any of the magazine's vivid reporting. *Time* would follow the news where it led. But beyond that it would make every effort every week to say the best that could be said about each candidate—and the worst. Banks had already laid out the schedule for *Time*'s covers in advance and Griffith approved it.

The coverage of the campaign went smoothly, without intraoffice controversy. Banks recalled only one moment of irritation; Griffith protested the Republican tone of a particular story and Banks flared back; Griffith let it pass but later came to see Banks in his office and said, "Let's you and me have one basic understanding. We may not

473

always see the facts the same way but let's neither one doubt the other's motives." Griffith recalled that throughout the campaign Luce often came down to his office to talk things over and ask what stories were planned. But never once did he ask to see a story in advance or complain about the coverage.

Which candidate would *Life* endorse? In an oral history interview for the Kennedy Library in 1965 Luce said: "I think that in the long run we were always going to be for Nixon." However, he found himself mightily attracted by Kennedy. In August the Democratic candidate accepted an invitation to lunch with the Time Inc. editors in Rockefeller Center. He came (John Steele wrote to Luce) because he "hoped for sympathetic coverage from *Time* and eventually your editorial endorsement through *Life.*" The luncheon was pleasant, and the candidate made a deep impression. Afterward Luce had a personal experience of Kennedy's extraordinary popular appeal. Escorting his guest to his waiting limousine, the host found that, purely on the rumor that Kennedy was in the Time & Life Building, a large crowd had filled the lobby and three policemen had to clear the way to the car. After the luncheon Kennedy wrote Luce, "While I have a faint feeling that your 1960 endorsement of the book may be the last one I shall get [8]—nevertheless you were very generous at the luncheon, and made it a happy two hours."

In October Luce called a meeting of his senior editors and opened it with the question: whom are we going to support for President? The discussion was frank and free, with *Time*'s Griffith arguing the case for Kennedy. *Life* announced the outcome of the discussion in two editorials: it supported Nixon on account of his and his party's stand on domestic issues. On foreign policy issues, *Life* felt, there was very little to choose between the candidates. Luce himself was disappointed that Nixon had not articulated a more imaginative foreign policy, one closer to his own, but "having endorsed him on domestic grounds we couldn't very well go against him."

The coverage of the campaign by the magazines, particularly *Time,* won the approval of many readers. The Charlotte, North Carolina, *Observer* commented: "*Time* is playing it cool and straight and fair. . . . This week's issue describes the two men as they race about the hustings, and it describes them with an impartiality that not even Democratic National Headquarters could protest. . . . In other

[8] Kennedy was referring to Luce's agreement to write a new foreword to the new edition of *Why England Slept,* which was to be published in 1961.

words, no curves, no sliders, no sinkers." Arthur M. Schlesinger, Jr., the Harvard historian then working for Kennedy, was quoted as saying, "This is the best *Time* political coverage since 1936, the best and the fairest."

In the aftermath of the Republican downfall Luce wrote to Nixon: "I am deeply disappointed that you will not be President the next four years." But he had anticipated Nixon's defeat; several weeks before the election he had written a memorandum for his private files:

> As a sold-out Eisenhower bull and as a Yankee (pre potato famine) I am of course unhappy about this total prospect [a Democratic victory]. But a lot of good can be seen in it, as follows:
>
> 1) Journalistically, it will be exciting.
>
> 2) It will shake up the country and perhaps bring on a great new burst of the old American dynamism—which cannot function continually and may have got a little tired in the last couple of years.
>
> 3) It will be good for Free Enterprise in the following sense: Free Enterprise, like Freedom itself, has to be forever struggled for and is itself a struggle. With the party of the enemies of Free Enterprise in power, businessmen and others will have to fight like hell for their cause. They are already fighting to be more efficient—they will have to be even more efficient.
>
> 4) The idle rich and the Texas rich and the wheeler-dealers —Eisenhower should have socked all these with a real tough Tax Reform. The Democrats ought, in their avowed nature, to go after these malefactors. And probably will. Only trouble is that the Democrats, who believe less than Republicans in regular honest Free Enterprise, have a softness for deals of all kinds. However, on the whole, the shock to Free Enterprise (and to the rich) may be a good thing.
>
> 5) It will be a pleasure to have the majority intellectuals riding high politically.

Luce also wrote to Kennedy:

> On August 15th you wrote me a very gracious letter in which you expressed a "faint feeling" that my endorsement of your book might be the last one you would ever get from this quarter.

Well, one never knows and it's hard to tell! But I hope you will have a look at *Life*'s editorial in the current issue (dated November 21). It doesn't constitute an endorsement but it shows that we didn't find it difficult to find respectful and complimentary things to say about the President-elect. . . .

To liken you, potentially, to T. R. is about as far as praise can go in this editorial corner.

In any case, I value your letter—your great courtesy in writing it—and I figure that in that piece of paper I have had a good capital gain since November 8!

When next I see you, you will be "Mr. President." So let me now pay a nostalgic salute to my friend, Jack, and to his remarkable performance to date.

A few weeks before his inauguration on January 20, 1961, Kennedy replied from Palm Beach:

Many thanks for your kind letter, and for the generous editorial in *Life*.

It is agreeable here—very quiet—but I can hear the roar of the distant storm that is about to break on us all on the 20th. . . .

# Epilogue

In May 1963 *Time,* The Weekly Newsmagazine, celebrated its fortieth anniversary with a spectacular event: a dinner to which were invited over six hundred of the people who had appeared on its cover. The invitation in itself was an audacious gesture, for the articles had often been more critical than complimentary. Nevertheless 284 accepted—most of them paying their own fare to New York. It was a truly glittering occasion, not likely to be repeated, bringing together at one board such disparate celebrities as Gina Lollobrigida, Walter Reuther, Casey Stengel, Dr. Jonas Salk, Common Market pioneer Jean Monnet, Senator Edward Kennedy, General of the Army Douglas MacArthur, Francis Cardinal Spellman, who brought a personal message from Pope John, Vice President Lyndon Johnson and theologian Paul Tillich, who was the principal speaker. A succession of toastmasters beginning with Luce and ending with Bob Hope introduced the guests, a roll call that went on past midnight.

President John F. Kennedy declined an invitation but sent a personal message that reflected his family's long relationship with Luce personally and Kennedy's own ambivalent feelings about *Time:*

Every great magazine is the lengthened shadow of its editor. . . . Henry R. Luce has shown himself one of the creative editors of our age.

477

*Time,* in its effort to embrace the totality of human experience, has instructed, entertained, confused and infuriated its readers for nearly half a century. Like most Americans, I do not always agree with *Time,* but I nearly always read it. And, though I am bound to think that *Time* sometimes seems to do its best to contract the political horizons of its audience, I am especially glad that it has worked so steadfastly to enlarge their intellectual and cultural horizons. This has contributed materially, I think, to the raising of standards in our nation in recent years.

I hope I am not wrong in occasionally detecting these days in *Time* those more mature qualities appropriate to an institution entering its forties—a certain mellowing of tone, a greater tolerance of human frailty, and most astonishing of all, an occasional hint of fallibility. For *Time*—congratulations.

To this Luce replied: "I hope that *Time*'s Number 1 subscriber will always be the President of the United States, especially one who reads us with such very fine-toned, judicious, judicial sensibility. About one of the greatest personal privileges of the editor-in-chief of *Time* is to have at least some degree of dialogue with the President. . . . I assure him, as far as I am concerned, the dialogue will continue to be as interesting as possible for us both." Then, as an afterthought, Luce remembered an admonition he had just received from "one of the great editors of America," Roy Roberts of the Kansas City *Star:* "Don't get too mellow with age!"

A year after the anniversary dinner, in April 1964, Luce retired as editor-in-chief, recommending that the directors appoint Hedley Donovan as his successor. Luce took the title of editorial chairman. This completed the reorganization of management begun in 1960 and committed the future of the company to a triumvirate—chairman Andrew Heiskell, president James Linen and Donovan. The timing of the announcement was something of a surprise. Luce had seemed in no hurry to give up his responsibility, and there was still a good deal of skepticism that he would surrender all authority with the title. As a matter of fact, Luce continued to exert an influence so long as he lived. But he was serious about investing the new editor-in-chief with the same responsibility he had held. Introducing Donovan at the company dinner marking the occasion, he said: "[His office] is no longer a personal prerogative derived from a legendary and/or murky past. Today it becomes a very constitutional office by order of the Board of Directors. . . . Freedom of the press is responsible only to conscience, and conscience can only be found in a man. Here in Time Incorporated we strive to achieve a consensus . . . formed and informed and reformed by the conscience of the individual. . . . But we cannot evade the demand for a general coherence and for a clear sense of direction. . . . And this must come from the Editor-in-Chief." Luce then invited his associates to listen "with the inner ear" to what Donovan had to say.

Luce and Donovan had not shown each other their speeches. When Donovan warned Luce that his own speech was "pretty long," Luce replied, "They'll listen." No one listened more attentively than Luce himself. The new editor-in-chief posed some new challenges to his colleagues. The editors had reason to be proud of some enemies they had made and intended to keep them. But he reminded them that there were some others "acquired rather carelessly." Some of their competitors were "better publications than they used to be" and magazine audiences were more demanding. "There is no question of talking down to them. The problem, the opportunity, is to talk far enough up. . . . We, Time Inc., have had something to do with creating this state of affairs in America. If it puts some pressure on us today, that is only fair." Donovan ended with an affirmation of journalistic independence:

> The vote of Time Inc. should never be considered to be in the pocket of any particular political leader or party. The vote of Time Inc. is an independent vote. Not an independent vote in the sense of some snooty or finicky disdain for political parties. And certainly not independent in the sense of any wishy-washy confusion as to what we believe. But independent in the sense that we are in no way beholden to any party, have no vested interest in any party.

Luce led the applause. In October while Luce was traveling in the Far East, *Life,* for the first time in its history, endorsed a Democratic candidate for President: Lyndon Johnson against Barry Goldwater. Luce told his associates he was happy that Donovan and not he had had to make the decision, and he also let it be known that he thought the new editor-in-chief was doing a good job.

* * *

Why did Luce retire? All Luce himself ever said was "it just seemed like a good moment." There were, of course, other reasons. He had had the job for a very long time. His sojourn in Rome had proved that his physical presence in the Time & Life Building was not essential to the smooth functioning of the organization. His stays in Phoenix grew longer and longer, and he was glad to shift more and more of the burden to Donovan. His absences, however, seemed to weigh on his conscience, for he recognized that while he could—if he wanted to—operate by remote control, an expanding organization properly had to be run in New York. Also, by installing a successor while he was still around, he was in a position to give him whatever backing and authority might be needed.

Finally, the company was prospering as never before. In four years, from 1960 through 1964, the new publishing management of Heiskell and Linen increased net revenues from $287,121,000 to $412,507,000 and net income from $9,303,000 to $26,526,000. This reflected expanded sales and continued control over costs by all major divisions of the company. To its established publishing ventures there had been added an exciting new one: Time-Life Books. Since 1950 Time Inc., through the *Life* division, had published a number of very profitable books. Each of these was sold as a single volume promoted by mass mailing to *Time* and *Life* subscribers. In the later fifties the company began to consider entry into book publishing, and late in 1959 Jerome S. Hardy, a vice president of Doubleday & Company, joined the *Life* publisher's staff to take charge of book projects. Norman Ross, a member of the *Life* editorial staff, was made books editor. In 1961 a separate division, subsequently called Time-Life Books, was formed under Hardy as publisher and Ross as editor. By 1964 the division was selling some nine million volumes in the United States and Canada and two million abroad in eleven languages.

Also, in 1964 the revenues of Time-Life Broadcast were at a new high level, and at the Eastex mill a $23,000,000 expansion had been completed which had increased its production capacity by 50 percent.

Luce in retirement continued to have a journalist's intense interest in public affairs. He also persevered in his speech-making, doggedly pursuing his philosophic inquiry into the law and its potential for world peace. This interest derived from his desire to redefine the aims of "The American Century" in terms more acceptable to his critics and free of the "egoistic corruption" of which theologian Reinhold Niebuhr had once complained. As early as 1943 Luce had suggested to his editors that the main job of any future world organization should be "to search out, to extemporize, to test, to articulate the *common law* of mankind." He thought the acceptable foundation for a world order could be found in the concept of natural law. And America, whose philosophy of government was rooted in moral law, in his belief, now had both the opportunity and the duty to initiate the next step forward for the world community.

In October 1956 he had made one of his most significant speeches before the Connecticut Bar Association: "Our Great Hope: Peace Is the Work of Justice." This speech, reprinted in *Fortune* and the *Journal of the American Bar Association,* was, according to Charles Rhyne, later president of that association, influential in helping to found the World Peace Through Law movement which is still very much alive today. In that speech Luce noted that much of Khrushchev's famous exposition to the Twentieth Soviet Congress had been devoted to Stalin's violation of Soviet law. From this he concluded: "If rulers feel they must *appear* lawful then to an extent they must be lawful . . . the challenge to be lawful is the most effective challenge at the bar of world opinion." As a followup, he plugged for repeal of the Connally Amendment, which limits U.S. participation in the World Court. "World law can grow only . . . through the accretion of precedent and example," he said. "To the extent that we set the example we shall have added to the precedents which help extend world order under the rule of law." In an eloquent speech after his retirement, to the World Peace Through Law conference in Washington in September 1965, he prophesied that world government might become a fact—"by, say, the year 2000. . . . The world we are determined to have is a world characterized by the rule of law . . . which binds the pride of nations to the common good and which protects the individual from the arrogance of governments. . . . For we are concerned not only for law and order; we are concerned equally for human liberty." To the end of his life Luce was steadfast in this vision of the future.

Luce also in his retirement years devoted much time to two projects on behalf of the Presbyterian Church; one was the United Presbyterian Church's $50 Million Fund, for a broad program of the

481

church's development; the other was the Washington, D.C., National Presbyterian Church and Center, from its inception to money raising to finance it. A soaring bell tower there, dedicated in 1972, commemorates his devotion to his lifelong faith.

Another project, and one that was left unfinished, was the manuscript, part memoir, part commentary, about events during his lifetime and the people who shaped them, in which Luce argued that American policy succeeded best when it was true to American moral principles.

If there were moments of misgiving in Luce's busy retirement—John Davenport once asked him how he liked it and Luce responded "it ain't good"—there were many more signs that he had come to enjoy the role of elder statesman. His close friend of his later years, the Reverend John Courtney Murray, S.J., believed him to be "a contented, happy man."

Death came suddenly to Luce in the early morning of February 28, 1967. A week earlier he had been in New York, exuberant, questioning, criticizing, suggesting; as one editor recalled, "just like old times." On his return to Phoenix he accompanied Mrs. Luce to San Francisco where she made a speech to the Commonwealth Club—to which Luce had contributed a final uplifting paragraph. While in San Francisco he resumed his role of inquiring reporter and insisted that bureau chief Judson Gooding take him on a tour of the Haight-Ashbury district, then the capital of hippiedom.

On a Sunday morning after his return to Phoenix he sent for and then asked the cook to remove his breakfast; he apologized, assuring her that it was only because he was not feeling well. When he stayed abed all morning, Mrs. Luce sent for his doctor. He was running a slight temperature and coughing, but blood pressure and pulse were normal. On Monday Mrs. Luce and the doctor insisted that he go to the hospital for tests. That night when Mrs. Luce called—he had persuaded her to leave his bedside to attend a dinner to which they had both been invited—he said he was feeling better, would watch Perry Mason on television (a favorite program they often watched together) and would go to sleep. At three o'clock he got out of bed and went into the bathroom; his nurse heard him call out and rushed to find him on the floor, dying of a coronary occlusion.

The obituaries hailed Luce as the most influential and innovative editor of his time, recounting in many columns his fabulous success story. Luce died with his faith in God, a moral order in the universe and the providential mission of the United States unshaken. He had had great satisfactions from the influence which he felt his magazines had exerted in the public interest.

This was reflected in his will, in which he stated that "Time Incorporated is now, and is expected to continue to be, principally a journalistic enterprise, and, as such, an enterprise operated in the public interest as well as in the interest of its stockholders. I desire that my executors and my trustees shall be enabled to hold my stock . . . and to vote such stock in the best interests of said corporation . . . as a journalistic enterprise." Upon his death, pursuant to his will and an earlier trust, the greater part of his Time stock was vested in The Henry Luce Foundation, Inc., bringing its holdings to 880,494 shares, or 12.7 percent of the common stock of Time Incorporated. The foundation had been set up in honor of his father, Henry Winters Luce. His son, Henry Luce III, is its president. The other members of the foundation are Luce's younger son, Peter Paul Luce; Mrs. Elisabeth Luce Moore, his sister; her husband, Maurice T. Moore; and Luce's two longtime associates, Roy Larsen and Charles Stillman.

In December 1972 millions of *Life*'s readers and the whole of the publishing world learned with a sense of shock that the magazine would cease publication with the last issue of the year. The management decision was taken only after the magazine had sustained some $30,000,000 in losses (pre-tax) starting in 1969. Ever since the late 1950s *Life,* like the other multimillion circulation magazines of general interest, had faced the severe and constantly encroaching competition for the advertising dollar from television. In the fall of 1972 *Life* was faced with soaring physical costs, declining advertising sales and circulation and almost punitive postal rate increases (170 percent over five years). In taking the difficult and personally traumatic step of suspending *Life,* chairman Heiskell and editor-in-chief Donovan wrote, "We persevered as long as we could see any realistic prospects, within a reasonable time span, of a turnaround in *Life*'s economy. We can no longer see such a prospect."

From coast to coast and from many countries overseas came expressions of regret and tributes to the magazine's influence. Earlier chapters in this history told of *Life*'s role in the 1940s and 1950s. The later years were also journalistically spectacular. Under its two last managing editors, first George Hunt (1961–69) and then Ralph Graves, the magazine maintained the tradition of the earlier years: to cite only a few examples, an investigative series on Associate Justice Abe Fortas led to his withdrawal from the Supreme Court; Lennart Nilsson's incredible pictures of life before birth (in 1965) broke new barriers in photography; the magazine's coverage of the Viet Nam war, notably in the compassionate photography of Larry Burrows, who was reported missing in 1971, had a profound impact. The poet James Dickey, a sometime contributor to *Life,* summed up the feeling of so many readers: "I can't begin to calculate all the things I have learned from *Life.* I'm not quite the same person I was because of what I saw and read in its pages." Perhaps better than anyone else, an editor summed up the judgment of other journalists. William Shawn, managing editor of *The New Yorker,* said, *"Life* invented a great new form of journalism. It contributed much to the American community that was valuable, often reaching moments of brilliance and beauty. It's extremely sad to see it go; *Life* was a triumph from beginning to end." Hedley Donovan said, *"Life* will go on in many ways and places, not least in its influence on the other magazines and books of Time Inc."

Notwithstanding the suspension of *Life,* the company remains primarily, as Luce had hoped, a journalistic enterprise, though it has expanded into other diversified fields. The company has greatly increased its book publishing operations with the acquisition of the old and respected Little, Brown and Company, Inc., of the New York Graphic Society Ltd., several book clubs and minority interests in book publishing companies in England, France, Spain, Germany and Mexico. It entered the field of education first by acquiring the textbook publisher, Silver Burdett Company, then joining with the General Electric Company in the creation of the General Learning Corporation. In the wholly owned subsidiary, Selling Areas-Marketing, Inc., it provides a data service for food manufacturers and marketers. Eastex Incorporated continues to expand. New operations have been undertaken in the record, film, weekly newspaper and video cassette fields. In the spring of 1971 the company set up a small task force to study new magazine ventures. The group devoted itself to the exploration of publications of specific subject matter, magazines for which the reader would pay a higher share of the cost and thus make them less dependent on advertising revenues for profitability. The first of this new genre to be published was *Money,* a monthly magazine of personal finance, which made its appearance in October 1972, with William Simon Rukeyser as managing editor and Peter Hanson as publisher.

The management for these expanded and diversified enterprises underwent an important change in 1969 when president James Linen became chairman of the executive committee and the directors named chairman Andrew Heiskell chief executive officer and James R. Shepley as president to succeed Linen. Roy Larsen became vice chairman of the board. Donovan continued as editor-in-chief, the partner and peer of chairman Heiskell in Time Inc.'s tradition of separate and equal "church and state."

Shepley, after his editorial career, had become assistant publisher of *Life,* then publisher of *Fortune,* and then of *Time.* Henry Luce III, who was a vice president of the corporation and chief of the London bureau at the time of his father's death, was elected a director and returned from the London post, first to become publisher of *Fortune,* then succeeding Shepley as publisher of *Time;* in 1972 Luce returned to the corporate executive ranks as vice president for corporate planning.

Three group vice presidents were appointed in September 1972 to serve under Heiskell and Shepley. Arthur Keylor, a member of the board, was made a group vice president for magazine publishing and, in addition, remained in charge of domestic and international production of all Time Inc. publications and the subscription service division; he had been previously general manager, then associate publisher of *Life,* then publisher of *Fortune.* Charles Bear became group vice president in charge of Selling Areas-Marketing, Inc., Printing Developments, Inc., the company's newspaper interests and real estate. He also retained his duties as vice president for administration, secretary of the company and vice president-international. The third group vice president, Rhett Austell, continued to be responsible for Time Inc.'s interests in books, records, education, films, cable television, broadcast and video cassettes. In Austell's group the company had established a significant precedent when Joan D. Manley, who joined the book division in 1960 and handled its direct mail, was made publisher of Time-Life Books, the first woman to head a major Time Inc. division; in 1971 she was elected a vice president. Under the realignment of responsibility Bernhard Auer, publisher of

485

*Time* for seven years and then executive vice president in charge of publishing, remained a vice president and became assistant to the chairman of the board.

In the sixties the editorial control of the Time Inc. magazines, under Hedley Donovan, was shifted to new and younger men. On *Fortune,* Duncan Norton-Taylor stepped down in 1965 to make way for Louis Banks; then in 1970 Banks moved on to become the editorial director of all corporate publications and Robert Lubar stepped into the managing editor's post. On *Time* when Otto Fuerbringer, who had been managing editor since 1960, relinquished his command in 1968, Henry Anatole Grunwald, who first joined *Time* as a copy boy in 1944, took over. Fuerbringer, a corporate vice president, subsequently became editor of the company's magazine development group.

Fifty years ago, in March 1923, the first issue of *Time,* The Weekly Newsmagazine, appeared with this simply stated purpose: "To keep men well-informed." This was an ambitious goal for two untried, fledgling journalists. Today's "era of radical change," as *Fortune* has characterized the times, will continue to challenge all journalists; to keep people well informed remains the ultimate goal of Time Incorporated.

# Index

487

491

# Index

505

ROBERT T. ELSON worked for Time Inc. for twenty-five years, serving in varying capacities from writer to deputy managing editor and then general manager of *Life*. His last post before undertaking the writing of this two-volume history was that of chief correspondent in London for the Time-Life News Service.

DUNCAN NORTON-TAYLOR had a distinguished career at Time Inc. extending over nearly thirty years. As a writer and then senior editor of *Time* he wrote some sixty cover stories. After transfer to *Fortune,* where he served on the board of editors, he became successively executive editor and managing editor.

MARGARET QUIMBY has been a senior editorial researcher of *Time;* ELSA WARDELL was previously a member of the editorial research staff of *Fortune;* MARIE MCCRUM previously was a member of the corporate staff.